10
for Parents

FIONA CASTLE
AND
JOYCE GLEDHILL

KINGSWAY PUBLICATIONS
EASTBOURNE

Published by
KINGSWAY PUBLICATIONS
Lottbridge Drove, Eastbourne, BN23 6NT, England.
E-mail: books@kingsway.co.uk

Designed and produced for the publishers by
Bookprint Creative Services, P.O. Box 827, BN21 3YJ, England.
Printed in Great Britain.

Contents

Marriage

The Many Roles of Mum

A Time for Everything

Topical Subjects for Women

What on Earth Are We Doing About . . . ?

Introduction

Joyce and I have been involved for many years with running a Parents and Toddlers group with a difference. It is called 'Pop In' and we invite parents from the neighbourhood to do just that. With the help of caring and dedicated volunteers, we provide crèches for babies (0–1), for toddlers (1–3) and for pre-schoolers (3–5).

While the children are being looked after, the parents can relax and chat over a cup of coffee, and then listen to a talk that we hope is relevant to their lives and situations. We aim to provide an atmosphere of love and security, where people can build up trust and share their pains, joys and problems. Counselling and 'listening ears', as well as ongoing support, are available where necessary.

In these surroundings we have found that parents are comfortable about hearing talks that will explain life from a Christian perspective. We know that the Bible is relevant today and that when we put its advice into practice it works. We pray that parents will start to see the 'big picture', and realize that what has worked for us could work for them too.

We generally use speakers who have personal and practical experience of the topics covered, because to tell a personal story of triumph through disaster is much more attractive than a finger-wagging 'this is how it should be done' lesson. So you don't need 'high-powered' speakers! Remember, 'triumph' does not necessarily mean that a person is over their crisis or problem, but it does mean they are able to deal with it in a godly way.

I know from my own experience how lonely it can be for first-time mothers who have perhaps given up interesting, lucrative jobs and who may be far away from any supporting relatives and family. They know no one and have at that stage little time or opportunity to make friends. This is one of the reasons that a group such as 'Pop In' is such a success. The coffee is free, the crèche and the talks are free, and people can meet like-minded friends. Doctors, health visitors and clinics are glad to recommend these opportunities to their patients.

Because many of the helpers have school children, we confine our activities to term times. It is for this reason that we have planned the talks in sections with a theme for each term. These are merely guidelines for the topics we have found most successful, and they are easily adapted to suit your own style and ideas.

One word of warning! Through our own experience we have always prayed our programmes into existence. We have found that when we have based our programmes on 'good ideas' they have fallen apart halfway through the planning, so we know we have to spend time praying and offering the term and the programme to God, and asking him for a word from the Bible. This then becomes the central verse for the theme for the whole term and is the heading for the printed programme. We have found the programme starts to take shape when we know that God is right at the heart of all that we are doing.

So this book is not to enable you to cut corners, but to equip you to serve the mothers who will be coming through your doors and to love them with Christ's love. We have described the opportunities we have had through 'Pop In' only as a guideline and to inspire your imagination to begin an event that would be appropriate for your area and for the women you are aiming to reach.

Fiona Castle

How Not to Misuse This Book

Many of the talk outlines contain more points than you or your chosen speaker will want to make. If you try to cover all the ground, or study all the biblical references, you could have a lot of tired or confused listeners on your hands!

So please remember to *be selective* when you read through the outlines. If something sets you thinking, work with it, developing the point in your own way. Perhaps you can illustrate from your own life, or give examples from a local situation. But where a point doesn't gel with you, please discard it. Simplicity and brevity win every time.

Fiona and Joyce

Parenting (Part 1)

'Children are a gift from the Lord; they are a reward from him.'

(Psalm 127:3 NLT)

1. The Importance of Parenting

BIBLE REFERENCES

Psalm 127:3
Proverbs 1:8–9
Proverbs 4:1–4

TALK OUTLINE

Why is parenting important?

- It provides stability/security as a base for life.

- It establishes values/attitudes in children.

- It fosters a sense of purpose in life.

- It protects from danger/harm.

- The results last a lifetime.

Why is it such a challenge?

- Children come without instructions.

- Parents come without any training.

- Many skills are needed to parent – we are mainly able to learn these in the process of parenting.

- Each child is different and has different needs and a unique personality.

- There are no guaranteed formulas.

- The specific challenges change at each stage.

- In our society there is pressure on parents to be perfect.

- The childhood years pass quickly.

- Parents only have one attempt – there is no rewind facility.

What are the basic ingredients for parenting?

- Time.

- Unconditional love.

- Hard work/persistence.

- Varied skills.

- Realism: parents are not perfect – they do make mistakes, but need to (a) acknowledge them and (b) learn from them.

Conclusion

- Parenting is not supposed to be a burden, but a blessing.

- Parents need to accept responsibilities, work hard at parenting and enjoy the benefits!

TEACHING POINTS/DISCUSSION STARTERS

- Help parents to appreciate the significance of the job they are doing, and to value their time spent in this capacity.

- Discuss with parents in the group the degree of impact their own parents have had on them. Which aspects of their childhood have affected them the most, and which have had the least long-term impact?

- How is parenthood portrayed in the media? Is this realistic and helpful or the reverse?

ADDITIONAL IDEAS/RESOURCES

Reading

- *Parenting Isn't for Cowards* by Dr James Dobson (Galahad Books, 1997).

(See also Talk 32: The Competent Teacher.)

2. Loving Your Child

BIBLE REFERENCES

John 13:34
John 15:12
1 Corinthians 13:4
Colossians 3:12

TALK OUTLINE

Why is it important to love your child(ren)?

- To meet a basic need in all humans – a baby is born with the need to be loved and never loses that need.

- To foster self-assurance – to make them feel good about themselves.

- To instil security – help them feel confident in their own and other environments.

- To prevent fear and guilt developing within them.

- To further their complete development – psychological, emotional and spiritual.

- To encourage general health and well-being.

- To encourage them to have a loving attitude towards others.

- They are constantly demanding reassurance of that love, sometimes with a direct question ('Do you really love

18

me?'), or a gesture (arms held open inviting a hug) or by seeking attention/affirmation through good/bad behaviour.

● Without love, parenting is a daunting and burdensome task!

What is love?

● Real love is unconditional – loving the child no matter what their appearance/gifts/behaviour/speech/attitude, and expecting nothing in return.

● Acceptance: no child is perfect, so appreciate their good points!

● Showing patience, kindness, loyalty – not jealousy, pride, selfishness, touchiness or holding grudges. Believing in the child, expecting the best and defending them. (See 1 Corinthians 13:4–7.)

How do we convey that love?

● We demonstrate love in parental/adult relationships.

● It is vital to be clear and consistent in communicating our love. It is easy for a child to misunderstand what a parent thinks and believes.

● Eye contact is vital to convey love (refusing eye contact implies rejection).

● Physical contact – a hug, a kiss, a touch on the shoulder, a stroke on the face/hair – is a natural part of everyday life.

● We should show focused attention, spending time alone with the child with no other distractions.

● We can speak to the child, saying that we love them, voicing praise and admiration.

● We should discipline in a fair and consistent manner.

Conclusion

- It is important for a parent's behaviour to be consistent with their words of love to a child.

- The love we know in childhood shapes the love we know and are able to give in later life.

TEACHING POINTS/DISCUSSION STARTERS

- Stress the centrality of love in all a parent's dealings with their children.

- Discuss the way in which parents experienced love in their own childhood (expressed verbally or by certain actions).

- Ask parents to think about and discuss new ways in which they could demonstrate their love for their children.

ADDITIONAL IDEAS/RESOURCES

Reading

- *How to Really Love Your Child* by Dr Ross Campbell (Alpha, 1998).

3. Building Self-Esteem in Your Child

BIBLE REFERENCES

Psalm 139:13–16
Romans 12:3
Philippians 2:3–9
1 Peter 4:10

TALK OUTLINE

What is self-esteem?

- Feeling confident about yourself: dignity, self-worth, self-respect, feeling accepted and special.

Why is it important to build self-worth in children?

- To meet a basic emotional need for acceptance and self-value.

- The effects are long-lasting: many adults have a low self-image, formed primarily in childhood.

- To provide protection from peer pressure: a confident child can say no more easily to things that may be harmful or dangerous.

- To enable children to form closer/better friendships and relationships. They are more likely to form positive friendships and relate more easily with high self-worth.

- It helps maintain physical and mental health: e.g.

depression and eating disorders occur more frequently among children with low self-esteem.

How can we promote self-esteem in children?

- Effective affirmation involves our time, speech, attitude and actions.

- Loving, clear and firm discipline forms the basis of security – a secure child knows the boundaries and expectations for them.

- Spending time with our children is a precious gift to them. It assures them that they are worthy of being number one priority (important).

- Spending time with children can involve talking with them, doing things together or just being together.

- Our speech can affirm or destroy a child's confidence. Be wary of destructive comments ('If only you were like...', 'Don't be stupid', 'If only you weren't around I could ...').

- Discussing a situation with a child when they feel shy or low in confidence makes them feel less isolated and gives the opportunity to point out positives to replace the negatives.

- Asking children their opinion or sharing with them something of our joys and frustrations gives them dignity.

- Assure a child that many people who appear confident are really lacking in confidence themselves.

- Praise a child whenever they're thoughtful or have really done their best (avoid all comments being critical!).

- Have a positive attitude: show willingness to speak to/be with the child.

- Smile at them to show the pleasure we derive from their company.

- Ensure our actions affirm the child.

- Positive physical contact (a hug, a pat on the back) boosts confidence.

- Give children responsibility (tasks appropriate to their age): this confirms our confidence and trust in them.

- Include children in our activities.

Conclusion

- Children need to know they're accepted for who they are and not what we want them to be.

- Praise and affirmation is unlikely to make children big-headed, and it is vital to their self-esteem.

TEACHING POINTS/DISCUSSION STARTERS

- Encourage parents to have a positive mindset towards their children. Ask them to think of all the negative messages they may give to their children, and then think of positive messages they could give in their place.

- Think back to your own childhood and share one positive encouragement and one discouraging message given to you by your parents.

- Discuss whether it is easier to be positive and encouraging towards children or negative and discouraging.

ADDITIONAL IDEAS/RESOURCES

Talk illustration

The Ten Worst and Best Things to Say to Children

The Worst
'You're so stupid'
'You could do so well, if only...'
'Why can't you be more like...?'
'I wish I didn't have kids'
'You must always obey grown-ups'
'Wait until your father gets home'
'Look at all I've given up for you'
'You're a liar, a thief and a lazy good for nothing'
'Don't be silly, there's nothing to be frightened of'
'I'm going to leave you'

The Best
'You've always been a plus in my life'
'Telling is OK'
'I am proud of you – you did that so well'
'I said NO'
'It's all right to cry, or feel sad or scared'
'It's OK to make mistakes'
'You're so clever to have worked that out'
'You don't have to do anything'
'I like you because you're you'
'I love you'

Permission to republish from
Michele Elliot
KIDSCAPE
152 Buckingham Palace Road
London
SW1W 9TR

4. Disciplining Your Child

BIBLE REFERENCES

Proverbs 3:11–12
Proverbs 23:13
Proverbs 29:15
Ephesians 6:1–4
Hebrews 12:5–11

TALK OUTLINE

What is discipline?

- It's a topic that provokes strong feeling among parents.

- It is often misunderstood as being merely punishment.

- Discipline has a much wider definition and includes all aspects of loving training and correction.

- It aims to 'shape the will without breaking the spirit'.

- It does not deny children freedom, but rather enables them to live in the freedom of greater security in knowing where the boundaries of acceptable behaviour lie.

Why should we discipline our children?

- To help them develop acceptable behaviour patterns and thus make social integration and interaction easier.

- To develop their awareness of other people's needs and concerns.

- To teach them a moral code so that they are able to distinguish right from wrong.

- To help them develop self-discipline and self-control.

Tips for effective disciplining

- Start early: a baby can learn that the world does not revolve entirely around its own needs.

- Be prepared to spend time and be persistent in confirming standards and correcting a child's behaviour.

- Make sure you assess the situation correctly: is the child's behaviour a mistake, an accident, born of tiredness or frustration, an attempt to get your attention, or a deliberate challenge to your boundaries?

- Choose the appropriate action/response for each situation, and be sure to carry out your promised reaction.

- Administer punishment calmly. A parent's anger destroys a child's self-worth and their respect for the parent.

- Be consistent in your response.

- Praise a child for correct behaviour. Children like to please, and when they find that certain behaviour gets a positive response they are more likely to repeat it.

- Set a good example. Children are greatly influenced by the behaviour of their parents!

Conclusion

- Discipline and love go hand in hand. Be sure to reassure children that you continue to love them, even though you may dislike their behaviour.

TEACHING POINTS/DISCUSSION STARTERS

- Aim to convince parents of the importance of disciplining children: to create a happy home, to help children make sense of life, and for the wider benefits of promoting a more ordered society.

- Ask one or two parents to share some experiences: for instance, a solution to a common challenge (how to handle a toddler tantrum) or a request for advice on an unresolved situation.

- Discuss in small groups the way in which parents' own experiences of being disciplined as children shaped the way they approach the discipline of their own children.

ADDITIONAL IDEAS/RESOURCES

Reading

- *The New Dare to Discipline* by Dr James Dobson (Kingsway, 1993).

- *The Strong-Willed Child* by Dr James Dobson (Kingsway, 1978).

- *How to Really Love Your Child* by Dr Ross Campbell (Alpha, 1998).

Talk illustrations

Read out the following quotes, then ask parents to guess when they were written:

'The children now love luxury; they show disrespect for elders and love chatter in the place of exercise. Children are tyrants, not the servants of their households. They no longer rise when their elders enter the room. They contradict their parents, chatter before company, gobble up dainties at the table, cross their legs and tyrannise their teachers.'

Socrates, 469–399 BC

'I see no hope for the future of our people if they are dependent on the frivolous youth of today, for certainly all youth are reckless beyond words . . . When I was young we were taught to be discreet and respectful of elders, but the present youth are exceedingly impatient of restraint.'

Hesiod, Greek poet, eighth century BC

12 Easy Rules: How to Make a Delinquent Child

1. Begin at infancy to give the child everything he wants. In this way, he will grow up to believe that the world owes him a living.
2. When he picks up bad language, laugh at him. This will make him think he is clever.
3. Avoid the use of the word 'wrong'. It may cause a guilt complex. This will condition him to believe later, when he is arrested for stealing a car, that society is against him and he is being persecuted.
4. Pick up everything he leaves lying around: books, shoes, clothes. Do everything for him so that he will be experienced in throwing all responsibility on others.
5. Let him read any printed matter he can get his hands on. Be careful that the cutlery and drinking glasses are sterilized, but let his mind feast on rubbish.
6. Quarrel frequently in the presence of your children. In this way they will not be too shocked when the home is broken up later.
7. Give a child all the spending money he wants. Never let him earn his own. Why should he have things as tough as you had them?
8. Satisfy his every craving for food, drink and comfort. See that every sensual desire is gratified. Denial may

lead to harmful frustration.

9. Never give him any spiritual training. Wait until he is 21, and then let him decide for himself.

10. Take his part against neighbours, teachers, the police. They are all prejudiced against your child.

11. When he gets into real trouble, apologize for yourself saying, 'I never could do anything with him.'

12. Prepare for a life of grief. You will be likely to have it.

Article made available by Portsmouth Area Family Concern.

5. Building Happy Childhood Memories

BIBLE REFERENCES

Luke 6:37
1 Timothy 5:8

TALK OUTLINE

Why is it important to build happy childhood memories?

- It helps provide a stable and secure base for children's future lives.

- It demonstrates parents' love for children – establishes a solid emotional foundation.

- It establishes a close bond between family members – important for the survival of the individual family and of the family unit as a blueprint for society at large.

- It maintains the level of trust, respect and openness between parents and children: ensures the relationship is positive.

- It boosts self-esteem in children. It shows we value them sufficiently to want to spend time with them and do something special with them.

- It helps secure long-term relationships with our children. If we ensure they have a proper place in our busy timetables, they are more likely to fit us into theirs in the future!

What prevents us from building such memories?

- Time: our busy schedules with work, home, the wider family and community commitments.

- Tiredness from other activities.

- Our own attitude – unwillingness to sacrifice time and effort to share special times with our children.

- Lack of experience/appreciation of the pleasure such times bring for both parent and child alike.

- Finance: a misconception that memorable means money!

- Lack of ideas for things to do together.

Some suggestions for memory-building

- Pencil time into your diary regularly to spend time together as a family or with individual children: 'spare time' doesn't create itself!

- Cut out unnecessary activities to leave yourself energy to enjoy time with the children.

- The childhood years pass quickly. Remember that it's all too easy to miss the opportunity to build memories with your children and you'll be more willing to be flexible and give up other plans.

- Switch off the television: passive activity is not as memorable, nor as effective for building good relations with our children.

- Talk to other parents and enquire at the local public library for ideas for simple, inexpensive and appropriate things to do with your children.

- Remember that it's not what you do that really counts, but the fact that you do it together.

Specific ideas for regular or spontaneous activities

- Make and toss pancakes together for Shrove Tuesday.

- Hide small Easter eggs around the home and garden for an egg hunt.

- Try different local play areas and beauty spots for summer picnics.

- Collect leaflets, labels and pictures from your summer holiday and make a book or holiday collage for the wall together.

- Pick blackberries together on a country walk.

- Collect conkers.

- Eat jacket potatoes around a bonfire on Bonfire night.

- Send children on an Advent hunt, with clues left around the home for a small treat or privilege each day of Advent.

- Label Christmas presents with a clue to keep them guessing about the contents.

- Establish your own family Christmas traditions.

- Organize (or let older children organize) a Christmas quiz for all the family, with different rounds on music, TV adverts, the contents of the local newspaper, nursery rhymes, etc.

- Bake and eat something together: pizza with different toppings, small cakes, ice cream sundaes, etc.

- Go out for breakfast, or cook breakfast on a barbecue in the garden.

- Camp out in the garden overnight and prepare a midnight feast.

- Have a bite to eat at a local café.

- Turn your lounge into a cinema with a video and popcorn at half time!

- Walk together: follow a planned circular route and help each other understand the directions, or just kick up the autumn leaves in the park.

- Take early wakers outside for a walk to discover the sleepy world around them.

- Play ball together.

- Laugh together – see the funny side of situations and they'll become family anecdotes/jokes.

Conclusion

- Building happy childhood memories requires thought and time, but brings the reward of a happy and secure child and makes parenting loads more fun!

TEACHING POINTS/DISCUSSION STARTERS

- Help parents to appreciate the importance of doing special things with children to strengthen the family unit and build security and confidence into children.

- Encourage them to see that activities don't need to be elaborate or expensive to be memorable. It's usually the cheap and simple events that stand out in a child's mind into adulthood!

- Ask parents to share with each other in small groups the memories they have of regular activities or special occasions from their own childhoods.

- Suggest that parents share one idea of something different or special they have tried with their children.

ADDITIONAL IDEAS/RESOURCES

- *Let's Go with the Children*: a booklet of ideas for places to visit and things to do with the children published for different counties. Contact your local tourist office.

- Public libraries typically hold information on events and places in the locality that would be suitable for children, and even organize events themselves.

6. Giving Your Child Time and Attention

BIBLE REFERENCES

Genesis 33:5
Psalm 127:3
Proverbs 22:6
Ecclesiastes 3:1
Mark 10:13–16

TALK OUTLINE

Why is it crucial to give time and attention to our children?

- Children know they are loved when parents choose to spend time with them rather than with other people – when love is more than words.

- Parents choose to have children – it's then their responsibility to make sure they thrive with love, care and security.

- Our years as parents with children are short and irreplaceable.

- If we want to be friends with our children as adults, we need to start when they're babies.

Why do parents spend so little time with their children?

- Parents commonly fail to realize the deep need of children for time and attention: brief time and other activities only *seem* to satisfy them.

- A recent emphasis on 'quality' time with children has prevented parents from understanding that such quality time usually results from quantity input.

- Urgent matters in our lives crowd out the important things, such as spending time with the children.

- Parents often feel ill-equipped to spend meaningful time with children.

- Parents who themselves did not receive time and attention as children find it more difficult to provide this for their own children.

What do we mean by time and attention?

- Time can be spent in short bursts or long sessions, can be planned or spontaneous, but quality time typically only results after quantity time has been invested.

- Children can be given time together or individually.

- Focused or full individual attention is vital to the self-esteem and security of children, and involves time with a single child alone.

- We need to listen to, look at and touch our children in addition to speaking to them to show them they have our attention.

- Putting aside time and giving children our undivided attention promotes good communication.

When can we find this time?

- Some opportunities will present themselves spontaneously.

- In the main we need to consciously plan for times of focused attention.

- We need to evaluate the way we spend our time, and re-prioritize if necessary.

- We need to be realistic.

- Mealtimes provide a natural daily opportunity to spend time together and share about the events of the day and opportunities or concerns about the next day.

- Bedtime can be a daily opportunity for focused attention – for a story, chat or prayer together – and can be maintained well into the teenage years.

- Reading or doing homework together can provide a useful opportunity.

- Play-time together is important – from the early years with playdough, models or swings, to teenage years with sports activities and creative crafts.

- Working together can achieve the double aim of completing a task more quickly and spending time as a team together: for instance, cooking, gardening or fixing the bike.

- Shopping can be turned into a 'together time' at all ages, from allowing a toddler to help select purchases, to discussing with the teenager a whole range of issues while shopping.

Conclusion

- Children need time and attention, and it should be a parent's goal to give the child the dignity and security of time 'given up' for them.

TEACHING POINTS/DISCUSSION STARTERS

- Aim to convince parents that time sacrificed to spend with their children is worthwhile, both in the short term and throughout the children's lives.

- Ask parents to try to identify one time in the week when they could regularly spend more time with their children.

- Ask parents to suggest a range of different activities they could each undertake with their children on a one-off basis.

ADDITIONAL IDEAS/RESOURCES

Reading

- *How to Really Love Your Child* by Dr Ross Campbell (Alpha, 1998).

Talk illustration

My dishes went unwashed today,
I didn't make the bed,
I took his hand and followed
Where his eager footsteps led.

Oh yes, we went adventuring,
My little son and I . . .
Exploring all the great outdoors
Beneath the summer sky.

We waded in a crystal stream,
We wandered through a wood . . .
My kitchen wasn't swept today
But life was gay and good.

We found a cool, sun-dappled glade
And now my small son knows
How mother bunny hides her nest,
Where jack-in-the pulpit grows.

We watched a robin feed her young,
We climbed a sunlit hill . . .
Saw cloud-sheep scamper through the sky,
We plucked a daffodil.

That my house was neglected,
That I didn't brush the stairs,
In twenty years, no one on earth
Will know, or even care.

But that I've helped my little boy
To noble manhood grow,
In twenty years, the whole wide world
May look and see and know.

                                    Author unknown

7. Fathers Are Parents Too!

BIBLE REFERENCES

Luke 15:17–24
Colossians 3:21

TALK OUTLINE

The importance of fathers

- The role of a father is crucial and lasts a lifetime.

- A father is a role model as a male, father and husband: children may not always listen to their parents, but they never fail to imitate them!

- Children who have not experienced the love of a father find it more difficult to establish good relationships themselves in life.

- Demonstrating a secure husband/wife relationship helps produce secure children.

- Fathers help maintain authority and take responsibility.

- Fathers teach boundaries and help enforce discipline.

- Without a dad, homes don't work as well as they should.

- Boys suffer from the absence of a loving, disciplined and reliable dad, and seek other 'heroes'.

- For girls, the quality of relationship with their father

affects how they relate to other men.

- Fathers are important to support and encourage Mum in her role.

- Fathers have far more influence on their children than they realize.

Why is it difficult to be a good father?

- Men may not have had a good father role model themselves.

- Work pressures leave fathers with little time or energy to invest in their children.

- Fatherhood is demanding over the long term compared with fathering the child.

- Men often find it difficult to adapt to home life because of the huge contrast between their home and work environment.

- Fathers often find themselves excluded or the secondary parent as the child naturally gravitates to the person they spend most time with (Mum).

- Men often feel inadequate in their role as Father. They don't have the intensive training in childhood for parenting, nor the natural support or advice of friends and family that is often available to women.

- Fathers are often trapped in the vicious circle of not appreciating how much their time is needed until they have spent time with their children, and not spending the time until its importance is appreciated.

- There is rising media pressure to be a 'superdad'.

How can we help fathers fulfil their potential?

- Fathers need to know what children appreciate in a dad (kindness, instruction, fairness, gentleness, love shown to

Mum, promises kept, being around when needed, sharing in their interests, encouragement, love in spite of failures, time).

- Encourage fathers to be available to be with their children in sports, school and home activities.

- Suggest that fathers take their children to their place of work and help them understand what they do there.

- Mothers need to be sensitive to a father's possible sense of inadequacy: encourage dads to play their role and affirm their contributions.

- Persuade fathers that the only place where they're indispensable is at home!

TEACHING POINTS/DISCUSSION STARTERS

- Demonstrate to parents the vital role that fathers play in their children's upbringing. Help them to recognize why it is often more difficult for men to feel comfortable in their role, and suggest ways to encourage them to feel fulfilled as parents.

- Discuss the main thing each person has learned from their father.

- Ask parents to talk about one thing they really appreciated about their own fathers.

- Discuss one thing parents would have liked to change about their fathers.

ADDITIONAL IDEAS/RESOURCES

Reading

- *How to Be a Hero to Your Kids* by Josh McDowell (Word, 1993).

Further suggestion

- Invite a father and son/daughter team to talk about the way in which the father has tried to be a good father, and the things the son/daughter has particularly appreciated and remembered.

8. Letting Children Go

BIBLE REFERENCES

Proverbs 22:6
Luke 2:48–49
1 Corinthians 13:11

TALK OUTLINE

The importance of letting go

- Parents don't own their children: it's their responsibility to prepare children for independent living and decision-making.

- It's inevitable that children will become independent: preparation for this time makes it easier for parents to trust their children and let go, and easier for children to make that transition.

- It is natural for parents to want to protect children from danger, but being overprotective is counterproductive and prevents children from vital learning experiences that equip them for freedom.

- Preparation to help children become 'streetwise' is better than coping with mistakes made in freedom.

- Clinging on 'sours' the parent/young adult relationship: the top complaint from young adults is the unwillingness of parents to let them go and allow them adult status and a freedom to live their own lives.

Principles for letting go

- Move the perimeter fence gradually from an early age to give safe limits.

- Allow rules to give way to freedom and trust.

- Recognize signs in children wanting independence and work out how to respond.

- Trust children to carry out tasks: this helps them to become trustworthy.

- Regulate the speed and guidelines given for independence according to the individual child's ability to handle freedom: you need to know your child!

- Delegate responsibility to children: allow them to work out the detail, but be on hand to take overall responsibility.

- Allow children to make mistakes: praise what they have achieved and then encourage them to try again.

- Talk to children about issues that are important to them: don't let friends, TV or magazines be the main source of information and influence in shaping their ideas and values.

- Help children to develop social skills, encouraging good interaction with others: this will help their integration into the wider world.

- Boost children's self-esteem whenever possible: this will be of particular help in making wise sexual choices later on.

- Help your children to make choices at all stages: talk through the various options and consequences.

- Keep talking to your children at all ages: it's easier to let go if you have good lines of communication open.

Some practical suggestions for 'lengthening the lead'!

- Allow toddlers to feed and dress themselves and brush their own teeth.

- Allow young children to carry out simple, safe household/garden tasks.

- Teach children to swim or ride a bike safely.

- Allow children to cross a road on their own after training.

- Allow a child to catch a bus to see a friend.

- Use TV/radio programmes, magazines and newspapers shared together to discuss, inform and advise.

- Move from strict bedtimes to more flexible times and then gradually to freedom in choice of time.

- Give children pocket money, and gradually increase this to cover more areas of expenditure (for instance, include a clothing allowance).

- Make sure children have experience of household jobs of increasing difficulty to make them independent.

- Encourage sleepovers at their own and friends' homes.

Conclusion

- Whether we like it or not, our children will leave home and be independent in their choices in all aspects of life. The wisest thing parents can do is to give their children the best possible preparation for this.

TEACHING POINTS/DISCUSSION STARTERS

- Aim to stress the inevitability of children's growing independence, and the wisdom of not counteracting this but rather being actively involved in encouraging it.

- Ask parents to consider how they have already started to encourage independent thought and action in their children.

- Ask parents how much or little freedom they were granted as children, and how they reacted to this.

ADDITIONAL IDEAS/RESOURCES

Talk illustrations
'You are the bows from which your children as living arrows are sent forth.' (Kahlil Gibran, *The Prophet*)

'She's Leaving Home': song by John Lennon and Paul McCartney, 1967.

9. Helping Children Make Wise Choices

BIBLE REFERENCES

Proverbs 4:3–9
Proverbs 22:6
Proverbs 29:15
Luke 2:52

TALK OUTLINE

Why do we need to help our children choose wisely?

- In Western society adults are faced with a bewildering array of choices every day, so being able to make good decisions needs to be a well-developed skill beginning in childhood.

- A child's initial ability to choose is limited by their experience and focus on self.

- Children need to learn that choices result in consequences for themselves and others, and a choice of one thing invariably means the sacrifice of another.

- Children need to be able to distinguish between important information and less important or irrelevant information in the process of making choices.

- While at home, children have an opportunity to make choices in a safe/sheltered environment, when choices made may not have long-term consequences, or where the consequences of a poor choice may be lessened. They can thus use their experiences in younger days to help avoid mistakes in adult life, where consequences are likely to be more serious.

How can we help our children to choose?

- Start as early as possible, helping them, for example, to choose between one toy or another.

- Gradually move from the position of making all their choices for them to accepting their choices and helping them to live with the results of their choices.

- Increasingly give them space to work out things for themselves, but be available to help them assess various possibilities.

- Reassure them of your continued love and support whatever choice is made.

- Allow them to experience the results of their choices: do not be overprotective.

- Give positive guidance and support rather than negative criticism: tell children what they can do, rather than focusing on the things they can't do.

- Let your children see how you make choices: talk about decisions with your partner and allow children to observe the process and know the outcome.

- Praise children when they have approached a problem in a wise manner or made a good choice: this gives them confidence in approaching future decisions.

- When discussing children's ideas, first stress all the good or wise aspects of their decision, then make suggestions about other aspects they could consider.

- Help children to see the wider context of their decisions, such as the impact on others in the family and the effect on lifestyle.

How can we help develop decision-making skills in children?

- Suggest some choices for a birthday party: for instance, taking four close friends to the cinema or having games in the garden with a dozen friends.

- Ask a toddler to choose between visiting the library straight after breakfast and returning to paint afterwards, or painting first with a visit to the library afterwards.

- Involve children in choices for household shopping.

- Offer the choice of purchasing either a magazine or sweets, for instance.

- Allow an older child to choose whether they want pocket money on a weekly or monthly basis.

- Help children to choose which weekly activities they would like to be involved in, considering cost, dates, time and location.

- Choose together how to spend an hour out or a day off, or where to spend your holiday.

- Involve children in the choice of secondary school.

- Talk through the implications of choices of GCSE subjects.

TEACHING POINTS/DISCUSSION STARTERS

- Help parents to understand that making choices is a natural part of everyday life, and that practice throughout childhood with parental guidance will help children to make wiser choices in adulthood.

- Ask parents to get into pairs and tell each other about a

decision their child has made or is about to make, offering suggestions to each other about the things that need to be taken into account.

- Read out a case study of a family situation where a decision has to be reached by a child, or involving a child. Form small groups and ask each group to consider what decision they would make and why, and how they would help the child to understand all the choices open to them. Compare and contrast the results from each group.

- Discuss how parents present were encouraged in, or discouraged from, making decisions while at home. How has this affected their method of decision-making now and their ability to reach good decisions?

10. Adolescence

BIBLE REFERENCES

Exodus 20:12
Mark 13:12

TALK OUTLINE

What do we mean by adolescence?

- The period of gradual transition from childhood to adulthood.

- A period of physical and emotional change prompted by biochemical (hormonal) changes.

- A period of growing independence.

- A potentially turbulent stage of development.

What are the characteristics of adolescence?

- Physical changes are the most obvious – a child's body prepares itself for parenthood (growth spurt, development of sex organs, voice breaking, change of basic body shape).

- Emotional changes – everything is felt more intensely in adolescence (small matters seem important, parents seem irritating, there is confusion over beliefs, a search for own identity independent of parents/family).

- Conformity – the desire to be like everyone else (fear of being different or abnormal).

- A happy and co-operative pre-adolescent can become sullen and depressed (there may be anxiety and sudden changes of mood).

- They may be easily embarrassed.

- Low self-esteem – there may be feelings of inferiority and low self-worth in terms of beauty, intelligence or finance.

- Tastes in music, clothes, food, friends and leisure go though a period of experimentation.

- There is a lack of communication with parents.

- Friends become more important than parents (parents are no longer heroes).

- An adolescent will seek more independence in thought and action.

How can parents handle adolescence?

- It is helpful to catch children before adolescence begins and explain the changes. This takes away some of the anxiety and loneliness of adolescence and makes them better able to cope with changes.

- The parent's role is to be an anchor: there is a need to be loving, patient and understanding.

- Don't take adolescent rejection of a parent's values, lifestyle or beliefs personally – these all need to be tested in the adolescent years.

- Give the adolescent respect and dignity wherever possible.

- Keep the lines of communication open.

- Allow the adolescent increasing independence.

- Choose your battles! Try not to be idealistic or perfection-ist as parents, as fighting every battle can destroy the base of friendship you've established over the previous ten or twelve years. Play down minor issues while standing firm on major ones.

- Keep on encouraging and praising the adolescent to boost confidence.

- Don't exhaust yourself during the day – keep time and energy to spend with the adolescent child and to handle issues arising!

- Encourage dads to be involved – male authority and leadership is vital.

- Be firm in enforcing the main boundaries (curfew time, use of the phone/car, attitude to drink/drugs).

- Treat the adolescent like an adult, but don't be surprised at childish behaviour!

TEACHING POINTS/DISCUSSION STARTERS

- Stress that adolescence is a turbulent time, but with some preparation and understanding it is more easily handled.

- Ask parents to discuss the major traumas of their own teenage years.

- Discuss the ways in which teenagers show their need to belong or conform during this period, and why it should be so important at this stage of life.

ADDITIONAL IDEAS/RESOURCES

Reading

- *Preparing for Adolescence* by Dr James Dobson (Kingsway, 1982).

- *The Parentalk Guide to the Teenage Years* by Steve Chalke (Hodder & Stoughton, 1999).

Parenting (Part 2)

'Teach your children to choose the right path, and when
they are older, they will remain upon it.'

(Proverbs 22:6 NLT)

11. Communicating with Your Child

BIBLE REFERENCES

Proverbs 13:17
Ecclesiastes 3:7
Ezekiel 40:4
Matthew 13:16
James 1:19
James 3:9–12

TALK OUTLINE

What do we mean by communication?

- It is defined as an exchange of information, and involves giving and receiving.

- It involves listening and observing as well as talking.

- Our children can communicate with us through words, silence, behaviour and body language.

Why is communication vital between parent and child?

- It is the key to building a good relationship of mutual openness and trust.

- It is the key to understanding our children, and thus to being able to guide and correct them appropriately.

- It is an important means by which we convey love to our children as a basis for discipline.

- It is vital to enable children to consult/confide in parents about their worries or problems.

Why is communication so difficult?

- Time pressure (from work, other children and TV) is probably the main enemy of communication.

- Parents don't always understand a child's *need* to talk: children don't often ask for time to talk, although they request transport and material things.

- Parents often fail to recognize the ways in which a child is communicating fears, often betrayed in throw-away comments, tantrums, solitariness or bed-wetting.

How can we develop good communication with our children?

- There is no absolutely right or wrong way of communicating – it depends on the parent and child. So it is important to find a style and timing that suits both in order to develop trust, understanding and openness.

- Start early: try to understand your child's language as a baby (the cry of hunger/pain; a pained or content expression; a playful or angry kick!).

- Communicate with your baby: it needs to learn through touch, sight and smell. Remember to convey your love in a hug.

- Get into the habit of making time to initiate communication with your children, as well as responding to requests for attention.

- Listen to your children (what is and is not being said) and observe their body language and behaviour (stamping, slamming the door, biting).

- Allow children to talk about their own tastes and preferences and reasons for choices.

- Try not to cut children short in their conversation – you may miss the real topic of concern!

- Find a good time to talk regularly: bedtime, working together, a long walk, mealtimes.

- Respond to young children straight away while the issue is fresh: older ones are more able to wait and recall the matter.

- Try to answer a child's questions: preventing their queries will lead them to seek information elsewhere.

- Talk from an early age about the human body to help a child feel at ease in discussing it. They will then find it more natural to talk about sex and relationships at a later date.

- Encourage children to own up to mistakes or accidents at an early age. They are then more likely to trust you enough to confide in you at a later stage.

- Keep children informed about family difficulties: concealing issues from children breaks their trust in you.

- Talk regularly about day-to-day issues: it will then be more natural to communicate about more serious matters.

Conclusion

- Good communication needs working at regularly.

- Occasionally we all say things or react in ways that we regret. As long as there is usually a positive line of communication with your children, this will do little to damage their confidence and trust in you.

- Be aware of the power of communication for good or bad: it's a myth that 'sticks and stones may hurt my bones but words will never harm me'.

- Work hard to reduce the negative messages you send to

your children and try to make a habit of conveying positive messages.

TEACHING POINTS/DISCUSSION STARTERS

- Stress the centrality of regular two-way communication in a healthy relationship between parent and child.

- How open do parents feel communication was with their own parents? How could this have been improved?

- Discuss in twos or threes the main difficulties parents find at present in communicating with their children.

12. Peer Pressure

BIBLE REFERENCES

Romans 12:12
2 Corinthians 11:3
1 Timothy 4:12
1 Peter 1:14

TALK OUTLINE

What do we understand by peer pressure?

- It is the pressure to be socially acceptable – to be just like everyone else in appearance, action, thought or possessions.

- Peer pressure can be positive in helping individuals achieve a goal or adhere to standards, but it can also be negative in persuading people to adopt goals or standards that would not naturally be their own.

Why is peer pressure such a strong influence?

- Human beings have an inborn desire to belong and to be acceptable to others.

- Equally, they have a fear of being different or being rejected.

- Such desires and fears stem from feelings of insecurity or lack of confidence.

- Such feelings occur in all age groups, for both genders, across all cultures, but are probably most keenly felt during the adolescent years when young people are trying to establish their own identity.

- Pressure to conform has been intensified greatly in Western society by the growth of the media: we are constantly bombarded with direct or indirect statements about 'the ideal' or 'the norm' in terms of behaviour, appearance and thought.

How is peer pressure likely to affect our children and ourselves as parents?

- Peer pressure is felt by parents before the child is even born, in the choice of the right place for birth, the right method of birth, the appropriate baby equipment and clothes, and whether to breastfeed or not.

- There is pressure on parents for their child to develop and pass certain milestones at a 'normal' age (sitting up, crawling, walking, talking, being toilet-trained, etc.).

- Pre-school children become aware of other children's toys and home routine, and begin to copy these and pressure parents to do the same.

- Once at school, children begin to compare their life experiences and attitudes and possessions with those of others, and try to persuade each other to adopt whatever is the norm.

- Throughout the junior/middle school years, peer pressure becomes more apparent in the areas of holiday activities, birthday parties, clothing, pocket money, possessions, bedtimes, and the amount of independence allowed to children by different parents.

- Pressure becomes acute in adolescence, when young adults are unsure of their own identity and are easily persuaded to adopt the general norms.

- The main danger in peer pressure is that it can cause a child or young person to do things they know are wrong and either get into trouble by lying or stealing, or damage their own health through alcohol, cigarettes or drugs.

How can parents help their children to cope effectively with peer pressure?

- A child with high self-esteem is most likely to be able to distinguish between helpful and harmful pressure and resist the latter. It is our responsibility as parents to boost self-confidence throughout childhood/adolescence and show them that it's OK to be different.

- Parents need to discuss pressure situations that arise in their own lives, and show by example the process of standing back from the pressure and evaluating the merits and drawbacks of conforming.

- It can be helpful to get to know your child's friends (invite them over for tea, include them in family events) in order to be able to detect possible sources of pressure and help your child resist these where necessary.

- Encourage positive friendships for your children.

- Talk through pressures your child is likely to encounter at an appropriate stage, and discuss the consequences of going along with the crowd or taking a different line. They are more likely to be able to resist harmful temptations if they have already thought them through in the cool light of day.

TEACHING POINTS/DISCUSSION STARTERS

- Parents need to appreciate that the art of coping with pressure to conform, and discerning helpful from harmful conformity, can be learned very early on in childhood and throughout the growing years.

- Take a flip chart or whiteboard and draw one circle in the middle to represent a child. Around this circle draw ten additional circles, and in each one write one of the following: parents; school and education; watching TV and video; reading books, magazines and comics; friends of their own age; family; others; church, youth and children's groups; doing nothing; clubs. Look at the circles and try to decide which have the most influence on your children. Parents could then assess whether they are happy about the strength of this influence and whether they would like to change or add anything.

ADDITIONAL IDEAS/RESOURCES

Reading

- *Preparing for Adolescence* by Dr James Dobson (Kingsway, 1982).

13. Single-Parenting

BIBLE REFERENCES

Psalm 68:3–6
Psalm 146:9

TALK OUTLINE

What are the special challenges for a lone parent?

- Lone parenting is a 24-hour-a-day job, with no one to offer relief or delegate to.

- The reasons for single-parenting are varied (death of a spouse; partner an invalid; divorced or separated from partner; sexual encounter outside a long-standing relationship), but each carries its own emotional difficulties and burdens into the task of parenting.

- Although over 12 per cent of families in the UK are now lone parents with dependent children, a single parent faces greater isolation and loneliness by virtue of being alone and as a result of social attitudes towards lone parents.

- Children demand of a lone parent different types of physical and emotional support that would traditionally be provided by a mother and a father.

- Financial pressures tend to be more acute than in a two-parent family: a lone parent may find it difficult to finance everyday life, and so holidays, birthdays, Christmas and leisure become a burden rather than a pleasure.

- Research now shows that contact with the other parent is helpful in the long-term development of the child. However, such contact may be non-existent, erratic, and even distressing for the child or first parent or both.

- Lone parents may place the impossible burden on themselves of providing for their children in the best possible way and protecting their children from as much as possible.

- Lone parents often have low self-esteem because of the reasons for their situation and impose unrealistic standards of parenting on themselves.

- Fearfulness for children is greater for a lone parent: parent and child may cling to each other because of their close day-to-day relationship. The lack of immediate back-up in the form of a partner in case of illness or accident causes anxiety.

- There may be difficulty in disciplining children effectively because there is no back-up.

- It can be difficult to make space for fun together in the midst of the practical chores and responsibilities. Children should be encouraged to help. This will make them feel more involved and it will also free up time for leisure.

Some tips for lone parents

- Single parents need to remember how important they are to their children: no one else loves them like they do, and by committing time and effort to children in the difficult days they will see the reward in the long term as their children grow into stable and secure adults.

- They need to accept offers of help from family, friends and neighbours, and not feel they are being a burden or try to be independent.

- They should look for support from schools, churches and other local organizations, recognizing that it's impossible for a lone parent to supply all a child's needs.

- They should try to organize opportunities for children to relate to a person of the same sex as the missing parent – through family, friends, church or youth group – as this will minimize difficulty for the child in adult relationships.

- Single parents should try to have as much contact as possible with parents of children of a similar age: this helps identify which challenges are common to all parents and enables them to benefit from each other's experiences and wisdom.

- They should try to make contact with other single parents in their area: they may be able to team up and spend some leisure time together, look after each other's children, or help each other with practical tasks.

- Single parents need to be positive with their children – talking to them, hugging them, listening to them and being available to them.

- Parents who are separated or divorced may need to explain to the children that this is because of a problem between the adults and not because of the children (who often believe they're responsible for the break-up).

- They should try to talk regularly with the children, as it is the unknown or unsaid that children often find most hurtful and puzzling.

- They should try not to criticize or talk negatively about the other parent, as this forces the child to choose between the two.

How can other people support and encourage lone parents?

● They can offer company (invite lone parents and their children to join in a family mealtime) or practical assistance (help with gardening and DIY).

● They can offer to babysit during the day or evening to allow the parent some time off.

● They can be encouraging: positive words for parent and child cost little but provide an invaluable boost to each.

● They can make a cake or meal for the family.

● They can look out for low-cost household items and extras (cheap holiday breaks, factory-outlet shoes, supermarket bargains) and pass on the information.

● They can offer special help if parent or child is ill.

● It is important to be aware of the loneliness of single fathers and try to arrange some male support.

TEACHING POINTS/DISCUSSION STARTERS

● Aim to raise awareness of the special pressures on lone parents and the advice and practical help that can be offered in support.

● Think of a single-parent family in your community or locality. How could you or your partner best help that parent and child?

ADDITIONAL IDEAS/RESOURCES

Reading

● *Single Moments* by Lynda Hunter (Focus on the Family, 1998).

14. Street-Proofing Your Children

BIBLE REFERENCES

Psalm 111:10
Proverbs 18:10
Matthew 10:16
Colossians 2:3–4

TALK OUTLINE

What is involved in street-proofing children?

- Protecting children from danger is instinctive in parents.

- While children are younger we can provide protection for them, but as they become more independent, they need to have adequate self-protection.

- Parents need to teach their children to be aware of danger without creating unnecessary fear and anxiety in them.

- Most accidents occur at home, but it's the out-of-home dangers that tend to worry parents.

- Supervision and preventive measures can protect children from many home dangers. This develops an awareness of danger in parents and children alike.

The following are potential dangers in the home

- *Baby walkers* – never leave a child alone in a walker.

- *Baths* – always test the temperature before the child gets in.

- *Changing* – don't leave a baby on a high surface; look to see what's in your baby's reach.

- *Cots* – lie the baby on its back or side; ventilate the room well; don't overheat (use light bed covers).

- *Fires* – keep a guard around fires and heaters; keep matches out of reach; install smoke detectors.

- *Garden* – be aware of poisonous plants (e.g. ivy, privet); teach children not to eat berries or seeds.

- *Liquids/medicines* – keep out of reach or in a locked cupboard.

- *Stairs* – install gates top and bottom; teach toddlers to come down backwards.

- *Pets* – supervise younger children; wash hands after touching pets; ensure tetanus immunization in case of bites or scratches.

- *Ponds/water* – put protective screens around or cover up water.

- *Sun* – avoid long exposure; use high factor sun cream; cover delicate or sore skin.

- *Toys* – ensure no small pieces detach; beware strings/cords.

- *Windows* – install locks; ensure small openings; beware windows that open outwards.

The following are potential dangers outside the home

- *Roads* – develop road awareness gradually (it is not safe to let children cross alone until at least eight years old); gradually allow children to cross alone (supervise, then spot check occasionally).

- *Sex* – ensure children pick up correct facts from an early age.

- *Smoking, drinking and taking drugs* – inform children of potential attractions versus dangers; practise saying no (less likely to be caught off guard); be vigilant (observe if a child changes friends); make sure life isn't boring (boredom is the main reason for experimentation); supervise children (lack of supervision is a significant factor in drug abuse).

- *Stranger danger* – teach a set of rules regarding strangers, having first defined what we mean by a stranger.

Rules for children

1. Never talk to a stranger.

2. Never go with a stranger.

3. Never accept anything from a stranger.

4. Practise saying 'No, I have to go', and running.

5. If touched by a stranger, scream.

Rules for parents

1. Don't leave a child waiting alone.

2. Arrange for children to walk in pairs.

3. Know where children are and who they are with.

4. Don't allow young children to go into public toilets alone.

5. Check babysitters or other adults who will spend some time with your children.

Some general tips on street-proofing

- Make children aware of danger early on in life, and

prepare them to avoid or cope with it.

- Train/practise what to do in different situations.

- Build self-esteem and self-control in children – the ultimate protection.

- Strike a balance between making children aware of danger and creating fear or anxiety in them.

- Listen carefully to your children and observe their behaviour.

- Provide a solid family base. This is more important than sound knowledge about dangers.

TEACHING POINTS/DISCUSSION STARTERS

- Aim to put across the importance of careful preparation and guidance in helping children to face different types of danger.

- Ask parents what they find most difficult about preparing their children to face potential dangers.

15. Bullying

BIBLE REFERENCES

Romans 12:17–21
Ephesians 4:31–32
Colossians 3:12–13
2 Peter 1:7

TALK OUTLINE

What do we mean by bullying?

- Bullying involves repeated/persistent teasing and often either threats of aggression or actual physical aggression by one child towards another.

- Between half and two-thirds of all bullying occurs either at school or on the way to or from school.

- Such behaviour causes distress and damage to a child's self-esteem.

- Bullying can make a child's life a misery, and the effects can last well into adulthood.

- Bullying has been called 'the silent nightmare'. Children being bullied are often ashamed to admit to it; bullies try to make sure they're not caught in the act.

Why do children bully?

- They may have learned such behaviour from their parents.

- They may have been over-indulged and be used to getting their own way.

- They may feel insecure and need attention (the most usual reason).

- They may be a secure, loved child, but need to find success.

What type of child is likely to attract bullying?

- A very over-protected child is more vulnerable.

- A child who has been bullied by his parents.

- An insecure child.

How can I tell if my child is being bullied?

- There may be deteriorating performance at school.

- There is a reluctance to go to school.

- They may keep being late going to or returning from school.

- They may start taking a different route to or from school.

- Certain days or lessons may be avoided.

- There may be mystery illnesses such as stomach pains and headaches.

- There may be cuts, bruises, damaged clothes or possessions.

- There may be loss of clothing or other belongings.

- They may keep avoiding other children.

- There is a decline in confidence.

- There may be unusual night behaviour (nightmares, sleepwalking, bed-wetting).

- There may be changes in daytime behaviour (loss of appetite, crying, forgetfulness, lethargy).

- They may develop an unusually bad temper.

What can we do in advance to prevent bullying?

- Explain to children that bullying is wrong and that an adult needs to know about it.

- Help children to avoid being in a situation where they would be vulnerable: tell them to stay with friends, away from places where bullying takes place, and not to carry expensive possessions or money.

- Warn children that certain behaviour can attract a bully.

What should we do if our child is being bullied?

- Bullying shouldn't be swept under the carpet, but dealt with as swiftly as possible before it gets worse.

- Children need help in tackling bullying, but not necessarily direct intervention in the bullying situation.

- Gently ask children if anyone is being unkind, and listen carefully to the answers: remember, it's not easy for a child to talk about bullying.

- Try to find out as many facts as possible.

- Try to help the child understand that the bully has a problem that explains their behaviour.

- Reassure the child that something can be done about it.

- Keep a record of incidents.

- Sometimes, inviting the bully to tea or to play will help prevent further occurrences.

- If bullying is taking place at school, approach an understanding member of staff: the bully can often be stopped by giving them responsibility.

- Try to help children avoid the bullying situation or stand up for themselves more confidently.

- If the bullying occurs outside school, make the bully's parents aware of the situation via the school or another third party.

What if your child is the bully?

- Lovingly tell your child that you know what is happening.

- Explain that the way he is behaving is not kind.

- Try to understand what may have caused the behaviour.

- Usually extra encouragement or responsibility will prevent further occurrences by boosting the bully's self-esteem.

- It may be appropriate to talk to the mother of the bullied child, apologize and arrange for both mothers and children to have tea or do something else together.

TEACHING POINTS/DISCUSSION STARTERS

- Help parents to realize the seriousness of bullying, and to raise their awareness of the telltale signs of the problem.

- Ask parents whether they were bullied as a child, how they felt, and how it was dealt with.

- Present a case-study scenario of a child with various possible symptoms of bullying, and ask the parents to suggest how they would tackle the problem.

ADDITIONAL IDEAS/RESOURCES

- Include in the talk a brief interview with someone who experienced serious bullying as a child, or someone who was a bully themselves.

- Ask them to explain how they felt, whether it was easy to seek help, and how it was resolved.

- Ask the bully to try to explain why they think they behaved in this manner.

Reading

- *The Parentalk Guide to the Childhood Years* by Steve Chalke (Hodder & Stoughton, 1999).

16. Garbage in, Garbage out

BIBLE REFERENCES

Proverbs 13:20
Proverbs 22:6
Philippians 4:8–9
Colossians 3:2

TALK OUTLINE

What is the problem?

- Just as output from a computer depends on the quality and accuracy of input, so too the material we feed into our children determines much about the sort of people they become.

- Many studies have highlighted the dangers associated with time spent watching TV/videos, playing computer games, or accessing the Internet.

- Young children now have easy access to a wealth of inappropriate material, particularly involving violence and sexual violence.

- Messages contained in reading material, TV and radio programmes, films, videos, computer games and pop music are increasingly negative and destructive.

- Interactive games encourage imitation of negative behaviour.

- Research has frequently linked exposure to negative media messages with subsequent negative behaviour (for example, the James Bulger case or primary school children copying Power Ranger body kicks).

- Frequent absorption in electronic games adversely affects academic ability as well as social skills in children.

- Constant exposure to 'shocking' material is desensitizing our children.

- A decline in physical health of children is associated with frequent TV and computer usage.

- Messages of attack, destruction and combat aren't necessarily the values we want to pass on to our children.

- Much material attempts to rob childhood of its innocence and force children into early adulthood.

What can we do about it?

- Parents can act decisively to limit damage to their own children but can also help combat the spread of unhelpful material nationally by complaining to the relevant source of material and public authority (for example, the National Viewers and Listeners Association and Broadcasting Standards Commission).

- Start in the early years to be aware of the content of reading and audio-visual material encountered by your child – it will then be more natural for both you and the child in later years to continue this vigilance.

- Start early to enforce standards about the type of material allowed and appropriate length of time spent with the TV or computer. It is much easier to relax standards subsequently, if appropriate, than it is to tighten control.

- Install the TV, video, computer and video games in a central area rather than a child's bedroom. This prevents children isolating themselves and makes adult supervision and control easier.

- Be creative in suggesting and providing alternative occupations to TV and computer games.

- Check magazines, school and library books for suitability of material and withdraw where appropriate.

- Discuss with children why certain material is inappropriate, and help them to become independently critical.

- Watch TV or videos with children if possible, and certainly if doubtful about content. This provides the opportunity to discuss the content.

- Be aware of material used in friends' homes, and encourage children to have a strategy if something inappropriate is suggested.

- Encourage children to be selective in their viewing and reading by parental example.

TEACHING POINTS/DISCUSSION STARTERS

- Aim to raise awareness among parents of the power of the modern media to shape young minds, and the level of negative messages included in both written and audio-visual material.

- Ask parents to think of a TV programme, book or magazine they have shared with their children and evaluate its positive and negative messages.

- Ask parents what they would do if their child had visited a friend and watched a video intended only for an older age category.

- Ask what messages children are receiving through the music they listen to. How helpful are these messages, and how could you help them to be discriminating in their tastes?

● Use the circles of influence diagram as a discussion starter (see Talk 12: Peer Pressure).

ADDITIONAL IDEAS/RESOURCES

Reading

● *Children at Risk* by David Porter (Kingsway, 1998).

● 'The Television Song' by Roald Dahl (from *Charlie and the Chocolate Factory*).

17. Gadgets and Guilt

BIBLE REFERENCES

Haggai 1:6
Matthew 6:33
Matthew 7:9–11
Philippians 4:12–13
James 2:2–5

TALK OUTLINE

The issue

- Parents today are under acute pressure to supply their children's every need ('to do the best for their children').

- Pressure comes from other parents, children and the media.

- Parents and children are materially focused to a degree never experienced before.

- Advertising encourages parents to meet their children's material demands in order to make them happy.

- Children now have more pocket money to spend than ever before, which has encouraged advertisers to focus their attention on the young.

- A vicious circle develops: meeting a child's every request makes the child even more demanding.

- Material benefits don't meet children's emotional needs.

- Pocket money is no substitute for love for a child. Love means time spent with the child.

- Looking back to childhood, few gifts are remembered or seen as important, while time together with parents is more frequently recalled and provides an important base of security.

- Giving in to our children's material requests is also fuelling early discontent: possessions do not bring lasting satisfaction.

- Parents often find themselves in the difficult situation of not providing what is requested and feeling guilty at depriving their children, or else giving their children all they request and feeling guilty at not giving them time and attention instead.

Why does the issue arise?

- Stress is the most usual reason behind the giving of gifts in lieu of time with children: our diaries are so crowded that it is easier to give something to keep the children quiet than give ourselves.

- Tiredness from the business of life results in the same as above: it takes less effort to give/buy something than input time and attention.

- The increase in households with both parents working is partly prompted by the desire to give children more in terms of material possessions, and the need to give children more is partly prompted by the fact that parents have so little time at home.

- The persuasiveness of the media, other parents and our children is powerful.

When does this pressure occur?

- From the moment of birth or before: we are encouraged to provide all the necessary equipment of the latest style and colour, and a well-equipped nursery.

- There is pressure to provide educationally stimulating toys in the first few years.

- Provision of adequate pre-school activity of all types is promoted as vital (toddler groups and playgroups, gym, swimming and other activities).

- At school, requests for fashionable clothing, toys and outings continue and intensify.

- Families strive to provide the ideal holiday, extra-curricular activities and family outings.

How can we address the issue?

- We need to appreciate that as parents we enjoy giving good things to our children and we shouldn't feel guilty about that desire, but . . .

- We need to recognize that material things do not meet the basic need in children to be loved.

- We should try to give more time and attention to children: once they have greater self-esteem the intensity of their demands often reduces.

- We should check our motivation for giving money or gifts and try to avoid giving 'hush-money'.

- We should learn to enjoy the simple/low-cost things in life together, which will take away some of the pressure to earn.

- We can accept that as parents we will continually have the tension of wanting to give our children the best possible start in life, but at the same time ensuring we do not substitute goods for time and love.

TEACHING POINTS/DISCUSSION STARTERS

- Aim to challenge parents to assess the balance they have in giving to their children, and to identify any need to redress the balance.

- What do you remember from your childhood and gain most pleasure/security from in retrospect?

- Have you ever been given something material when what you really wanted was just to talk to someone? How did it feel?

- Have you struggled with low self-confidence since childhood? What could have been done to raise your self-esteem?

18. Problems with Eating

BIBLE REFERENCES

1 Corinthians 3:16
1 Corinthians 6:19–20

TALK OUTLINE

The importance of eating

- Most parents are acutely aware of the importance of children obtaining nourishment of sufficient quantity and quality for healthy growth and general fitness.

- Family mealtimes form a secure framework in which everyone can participate and receive love, comfort and attention.

- Mothers often see the provision of food as the gift of love to family members.

- There is much media emphasis today on healthy eating from an early age to increase longevity and reduce potential major illnesses and physical conditions.

What are the problems associated with eating?

- Babies and children may begin at a very early age to refuse food offered to them.

- Some children may be extremely fussy or particular in their preferences.

- Anorexia and bulimia are extreme problems that usually occur among adolescent girls, but may begin or continue in later years.

Why do problems develop?

- Babies and young children often refuse food because their parents have unrealistic expectations of the amount they need to eat when they are simply not hungry.

- Children may have been offered or obtained between-meal snacks and thus reduced their mealtime appetite.

- Children are individuals and thus inevitably have food preferences. If these preferences are over-indulged, it can reinforce fussiness and lead to refusal of all but the preferred foods.

- Anorexia and bulimia tend to occur in girls when they are at an extremely body-conscious age and the fashion to be thin reinforces a girl's natural desire to be slim and attractive. Girls suffering from these conditions frequently have low self-esteem, or are subjected to extreme or unrealistic expectations in terms of achievement, behaviour and success.

How can we try to handle such problems?

- It is vital that food has positive, pleasant and not unhappy or stressful associations: research shows that mealtime stress is often linked to children developing eating disorders in later life.

- Family mealtimes are not only helpful to the healthy function of the family as a social unit, but also provide the opportunity to spot any problems or disorders at an early stage.

- Try not to make food a battleground: calmly encourage children to eat what is given to them, and if they refuse, remove the dish and make them wait until the next meal to eat. Hunger will certainly encourage them!

- Try not to force a child to eat what is offered to them: a mother may find this difficult because she regards the offer of food as the expression of her love for a child, and its rejection as a rejection of herself.

- Try to maintain family mealtimes as happy oases through the teenage years – perhaps at the weekends and evenings. This, combined with continued encouragement of the emerging adolescent, will go a long way in preventing (and enabling detection of) any eating disorder.

- If you do observe extreme thinness or unusual behaviour after mealtimes, keep a close eye on the situation for a few weeks, and if there is no change talk to the child and consult your doctor.

- If your child does struggle with food and mealtimes, be assured that the majority do grow up to enjoy a wide variety of foods.

TEACHING POINTS/DISCUSSION STARTERS

- In *Pole to Pole* Michael Palin observed: 'In almost every country I visited, sharing of food was an important social activity, which is how it should be. A shared meal is the best forum for airing of grievances and celebration of pleasures yet devised.'

- Encourage parents to value and preserve family mealtimes amid all the busyness and stress of family life, and to maintain a calm communicative atmosphere at the table.

- Ask parents to discuss how they regarded mealtimes as children. How does this colour their approach to food now?

ADDITIONAL IDEAS/RESOURCES

- Act out two family scenarios and then discuss the effects of each one. The first is a family kitchen, where each member enters in turn, pops their own plate in the microwave, eats and leaves, with the final two members fighting for the microwave at the same time and the mother complaining loudly that the others have not cleared away properly. The second scenario is in a family kitchen where the mother places all plates on the table together, calls the family and a brief but happy mealtime is shared.

19. Stress

BIBLE REFERENCES

Psalm 55:22
Psalm 62:5–8
Psalm 86:7
Isaiah 41:10
John 14:27
Philippians 4:6–7
1 Peter 5:7

TALK OUTLINE

What do we mean by stress?

- Strain, tension, effort, and demands on physical or mental energy.

- Stress is nothing out of the ordinary: life is full of unavoidably stressful situations.

- A certain amount of stress is healthy and stimulating – tackling challenges can be enjoyable and boosts morale when completed successfully.

- Each person is different: a source of stress for one may be a source of pleasure for another, and each has a different tolerance level.

- It becomes of concern when the demands on physical or mental energy exceed ability, with negative symptoms such as changes in behaviour or physical health.

Physical symptoms of too much stress include

- A change in eating patterns, with associated poor digestion.

- A change in sleeping patterns.

- Fidgeting, nervous habits.

- Headaches and muscle aches.

- Tearfulness.

- Poor complexion and pallor.

- Fatigue, sluggishness and loss of energy.

- Sickness and low resistance to infection.

- Loss of weight.

Mental symptoms of too much stress include

- Loss of self-confidence.

- Disinterest.

- Poor memory.

- Poor concentration and not finishing tasks.

- Irritability, anger and moodiness.

- Resorting to alcohol, smoking, crime, and possibly suicide.

- Physical hyperactivity.

- Indecisiveness.

- Unhappiness and a negative outlook.

- Withdrawal.

ADDITIONAL IDEAS/RESOURCES

Talk illustrations

20 Active Ways to Cope with Stress
Get up 15 minutes earlier
Prepare for the morning the night before
Set appointments ahead
Make duplicate keys
Always make copies of important papers
Repair anything that doesn't work properly
Ask for help with jobs you dislike
Have goals for yourself
Stop the bad habit
Ask someone to be your 'vent partner'
Do it today
Plant a tree
Feed the birds
Stand up and stretch
Memorize a joke
Exercise every day
Learn the words to a new song
Get to work early
Clean out one cupboard
Write a note to a faraway friend

20 Relaxing Ways to Deal with Stress
Tickle a baby
Pet a friendly dog or cat
Don't know all the answers
Look for the silver lining
Say something nice to someone
Teach a kid to fly a kite
Walk in the rain
Schedule play time into every day
Take a bubble bath

Read a poem
Listen to a symphony
Play patty cake with a toddler
Take a different route to work
Remember that stress is an attitude
Remember that you always have options
Have a support network of people, places and things
Quit trying to 'fix' other people
Get enough sleep
Talk less and listen more
Relax, take each day at a time – you have the rest of your life
to live

Author unknown

A Hug
Feels good
Dispels loneliness
Overcomes fears
Builds self-esteem (wow! they actually want to hug me!)
Slows down ageing (huggers stay younger longer)
Eases tension
Fights insomnia
Keeps arms and shoulder muscles in condition
Is ecologically sound, does not upset the environment
Is democratic – anyone is eligible for a hug
Is portable
Affirms physical being
Is energy-efficient, saves heat
Makes impossible days possible
Makes happy days happier

Author unknown

(See also Talk 64: Stress in Children.)

20. Children with Special Needs

BIBLE REFERENCES

Psalm 18:6
Psalm 32:7
Jeremiah 30:17
1 Corinthians 15:51–53

TALK OUTLINE

For this talk to be effective it needs to be given by someone with personal experience of parenting a child with special needs. This could be one speaker, or alternatively two speakers who have experience of different special needs and can thus compare and contrast their experiences.

They should aim to present their own personal story of family life with a special child, and cover the difficulties and joys of parenting this member of their family. This could include difficulties of a physical, emotional, financial, relational and other nature.

Marriage

'Give honour to marriage, and remain faithful to one another ...'

(Hebrews 13:4 NLT)

21. Is Marriage a Dying Institution?

BIBLE REFERENCES

Genesis 2:24
Proverbs 5:18–20
Proverbs 18:22
Mark 10:5–8

TALK OUTLINE

Is marriage dying?

- Recently the media have focused on soaring divorce rates, the dive in the number of marriages and the sharp increase in cohabitation.

- Four out of ten marriages now end in divorce, and it is more rife in the UK than elsewhere in western Europe.

- One in four households is now inhabited by a single parent (widowed, divorced or unmarried).

- There is an increase in singleness as an alternative to marriage.

- However, over 80 per cent of those aged 10 to 17 still expect to marry when they're older.

- Most people aged 30 to 60 are married (80 per cent).

- Most people who have broken marriages enter a new one (90 per cent).

The following list represents typical pressures on most marriages

- Different expectations.

- Different backgrounds.

- Different personalities.

- Differences between men and women.

- Lack of communication.

- Romance stifled by everyday routine.

- Not making time for each other.

- Sexual difficulties.

- Financial pressures.

- Influence of parents/in-laws.

- Stubbornness of both partners in not making an effort to deal with problems.

- Failure to ask for help before it's too late.

Some pressures are more acute in modern society

- Time pressure is more acute, with men working longer hours and an increasing proportion of women with full-time jobs.

- As women are more financially independent, it is more feasible for them to live alone, either without marrying, or when separated or divorced.

- Divorce is easier to obtain than it was for previous generations.

- There are more alternatives to marriage, and thus the attraction of marriage has diminished.

- In a culture promoting choice, marriage is seen as optional.

- In a culture promoting individuality, 'creeping separateness' of partners is increasing.

- The media have encouraged unrealistically high expectations of partners in marriage.

- Marriages are expected to succeed easily, while marriage in reality requires hard work and commitment.

- There is a continuing trend towards nuclear families combined with job mobility, which means that wider family support for married couples is less immediate and natural.

- There is a lack of marriage preparation – either organized or natural within the family.

- There is a growing number of couples marrying as teenagers – the younger the age at marriage, the greater the likelihood of divorce.

- There is growing infidelity – possibly the major trigger for marital breakdown.

Why is marriage so important?

- It is God's idea: life works best when we follow the Maker's instructions.

- It offers times of unique joy.

- It creates the most secure environment for raising children.

- It is intended to be a means of lifelong mutual support.

- It is a living symbol of Christ and the church.

- Stable marriages have historically been characteristic of stable societies.

- Divorce is costly, not only in financial terms, but in terms of emotional damage.

- It has proved to be good for health: married people live

longer and enjoy better health than single or divorced people.

- There is a basic human need to experience love and faithfulness.

- It is important to the achievement of full potential in each partner.

- It provides a place for openness, honesty and unconditional love.

TEACHING POINTS/DISCUSSION STARTERS

- Aim to stress the importance of marriage in the Bible, and the continuity of marriage despite adverse trends.

- However, be realistic: marriage doesn't just happen on its own – it requires hard work and commitment. The following talks look at some of the main stumbling-blocks to healthy marriages, and suggest how we can overcome these or avoid them.

ADDITIONAL IDEAS/RESOURCES

Reading

- *The Sixty-Minute Marriage* by Rob Parsons (Hodder & Stoughton, 1997).

- *Loving Against the Odds* by Rob Parsons (Hodder & Stoughton, 1998).

- *The Secret of Loving* by Josh McDowell (Here's Life Publishers, 1985).

Talk illustration

The Promise of Marriage

By my own free choice I am now committed to your happiness, security and well-being. I will do all in my power to draw out the full potential in you and to make our marriage work. I will love you with a tender love. If you have tried and failed and just need a hand in yours in the darkness of disappointment, you can count on mine. I am dedicated to your growth and fulfilment as a person.

I am committed to love you with an unconditional love. You do not have to be fearful that love will be taken away. You will not be punished for your openness or honesty. There is no admission price to my love, no rental fees or instalment payments to be made. There may be days when disagreements and disturbing emotions may come between us. There may be times when psychological or physical miles may lie between us. But I have given you the word of my commitment. I have set my life on a course. I will not go back on my word to you ... I will not reject you! I am committed to your growth and happiness. I will always love you.

From *Unconditional Love*
by John Powell
(Thomas More Association, 1989)

22. Communication

BIBLE REFERENCES

Job 19:2
Proverbs 18:21
Proverbs 25:11
James 3:8–10
1 Peter 3:10

TALK OUTLINE

What do we understand by communication?

- The dictionary definition is: 'The act of imparting or giving information', but true communication involves both speaking and listening.

- Communication involves not only the spoken word, but also silence, facial expression, the eyes, and body language.

- Communication in a personal relationship involves sharing not just information, but also feelings.

Why is good communication fundamental to a healthy marriage?

- A lack of it is cited as the primary reason for marriage breakdown.

- It is a powerful tool to strengthen a marriage relationship.

- Hasty communication can be destructive.

- It aids mutual understanding.

- It prevents difficulties and problems developing undetected.

- It gives each partner the dignity of knowing they matter to the other.

- It meets a basic human need to share, be listened to and be understood.

Why is good communication so difficult to achieve?

- Busyness is the number one enemy of effective communication: our packed schedules allow little natural opportunity to talk to each other.

- We are often quick to talk, but less willing to listen and understand.

- Lack of communication can occur when couples *are* talking, but not talking about anything that really matters.

- Men typically find it more difficult than women to communicate on a one-to-one basis.

- Men and women have different conversational styles: men typically speak to convey information; women more usually speak to show involvement and caring and to build up relationships. (For instance, a woman often shares a problem with a man, simply seeking understanding and support, but the man offers her a solution instead!)

- Partners may have a lack of common interests or goals, and may talk about things the other partner is not really interested in.

- One partner may seek to be fulfilled solely by conversation with their marriage partner, while the other confides in friends and family.

- General tiredness militates against effective communication.

- Lack of time to be alone and the opportunity to talk 'to ourselves' makes it more difficult to talk to others.

- Parents often spend too much time with the children at the expense of time together as a couple.

- Timing conversation is an art: late evening is the time when most couples really talk, but it is the time when they are most likely to be exhausted.

- Couples who have been married for some time often take each other for granted and no longer make the effort to talk.

- We often communicate with a hidden agenda instead of entering into a conversation with openness and flexibility.

- Sometimes it can be difficult to find the right words.

How can we improve communication in our marriage?

- Develop the habit of talking to each other early in married life.

- Plan regular times to talk to each other, and don't let meetings, the telephone, the children or other distractions interrupt.

- Reorganize the home schedule to make more natural time for each other.

- Switch off the television!

- Find a time of day that is conducive for both to talk: over a meal, during a walk, in bed.

- Communicate with your eyes, facial expressions, touch and body language as well as with words.

- Try to understand the differences in style of conversation between men and women, and make allowances for this to minimize misunderstanding and resentment.

- Be a good listener, and try not to answer before the other person has finished speaking. Give some response to show you're listening.

- Take a real interest in your partner's work, leisure pursuits and opinions.

- Try not to speak hastily in anger – think carefully first!

- Make suggestions in a positive, not hurtful, way.

- Remember to spend time encouraging one another, and voicing your appreciation of your partner.

- Be quick to admit when you're wrong, and ask forgiveness. Tell your partner you forgive them when they've made a mistake.

- Maintain stimuli outside the marriage: each partner can then offer more for the other to respond to.

- Beware your tone of voice: does it send a positive or negative signal to your partner?

- Build up trust in your partner by preserving confidences.

- Try not to mind-read!

TEACHING POINTS/DISCUSSION STARTERS

- Reinforce the fact that lack of communication is the main reason cited for marital breakdown, and thus emphasize that it's worth starting early and putting real effort into developing open and valued communication.

- Discuss in small groups how much time each person typically spends talking to their partner per day. How could they create space for more time in the regular routine? How can they arrange to spend a longer time together?

- Ask parents to work out the ideal circumstances in which to hold a conversation with their partner.

ADDITIONAL IDEAS/RESOURCES

Reading

- *Loving Against the Odds* by Rob Parsons (Hodder & Stoughton, 1998).

- *The Secret of Loving* by Josh McDowell (Here's Life Publishers, 1985).

Talk illustration

> To keep your marriage brimming
> With love in the loving cup
> If ever you're wrong, admit it,
> If ever you're right, shut up.

Ogden Nash

23. Making Time for Each Other

BIBLE REFERENCES

Ecclesiastes 3:5
Mark 6:31

TALK OUTLINE

Why is it important to spend time with each other?

- We need time for love to grow.

- We sometimes need to spend quantity time together in order to have quality time.

- We need time together to build upon our understanding of each other.

- Time to laugh, talk, be friends, make love, share work together is a rich investment and reaps mutual respect, love, understanding and commitment.

- We have a basic human need to be with those we love.

- There is a biblical principle that the most important relationship after the one we have with God is the one we have with our partner.

What prevents us from spending time together?

- Despite all the time-saving devices of modern living, we have less time available to spend with our partner and family than our predecessors did.

- Pressures of work, community involvement, leisure activities and children all limit the time left to spend as a couple.

- We often put the children's needs before our own as a couple, and thus erode the stable foundation of a close, loving relationship upon which they rely.

- We often do not appreciate the importance of spending time together until it is too late and a 'creeping separateness' has developed between us.

- Couples tend to take each other for granted as married life proceeds.

- We believe that life will slow down after the next hurdle, and postpone any effort to make time.

- We may actually be unwilling to make space and time for each other rather than being merely forced apart by circumstances.

How can we make time for each other?

- Arrange to undertake some of the home duties together (shopping, gardening, cooking), and thus work to create more free time to spend together as a couple.

- Readjust the everyday schedule so there are regular times to spend briefly together.

- Plan to spend more time at home in the same room as each other, even if you are doing different things.

- Plan in the diary regular times to walk, have a meal or share a leisure activity (for example, meet up for lunch once a week), and determine to defend this time fiercely from all distractions (telephone, children, neighbours, meetings).

- Plan an occasional day/night/weekend away together.

- Learn to say 'no' when asked to take on extra responsibilities – you can't please everyone.

- Appreciate the importance of your partner: together you are both crucial to the stability of your household.

- Your closeness should continue after the children have grown and left home.

TEACHING POINTS/DISCUSSION STARTERS

- Convince parents that time together is absolutely fundamental to the healthy growth of a relationship. Prompt them to think creatively as to how they could make space in their diaries for each other, and how they could make that space attractive to each other.

- Ask parents to consider the main thing they should change to make more time for their partners. How can they make that change?

ADDITIONAL IDEAS/RESOURCES

- Suggest parents make a list of the top ten things they enjoy doing with their partners, and then draw up a realistic schedule to do each of those within a specified time period.

24. Romance

BIBLE REFERENCES

Genesis 29:20
Deuteronomy 24:5
The Song of Songs

TALK OUTLINE

What do we understand by romance?

- Romantic love has been called 'the thrill factor' or 'the spark in a relationship'.

- It includes joy, intimacy, excitement and anticipation of time together.

- It is not to be confused with infatuation, which is more superficial and involves fantasy. Infatuation fades, while romantic love is more realistic, has more depth and grows.

- Romantic love involves a thrill at your partner's appearance, words and actions and shared experiences.

- Romance has often been ridiculed: laughed at by cynics or considered unnecessary, or as a lower form of love, by purists. However, there is much biblical, literary and historical evidence for its existence and value.

Why is romance important?

- The relationship between husband and wife was intended

by God to be joyful and exciting.

- Research confirms that most people have a deep longing for romance.

- Physicians and psychologists confirm that romance is beneficial to the human body and mind: it boosts self-image, gives a sense of well-being and brings out the best in us.

- Romance encourages us to work at a relationship further.

What stifles romantic love?

- Busyness and lack of time for each other.

- Taking each other for granted – laziness.

- Individualism.

- Nagging.

- Lack of opportunity to express our feelings, particularly with children around!

- Lack of imagination.

How can we rekindle the flame of romance?

- Remember the things that first attracted you to your partner (which you may now take for granted).

- Stop being critical of your partner and start being appreciative.

- Give your partner time and attention (write letters or cards, telephone them, buy small gifts, give lots of affection, build them up in public).

- Take more interest in your partner's work and activities.

- Pay attention to your appearance in preparation for your partner arriving home (comb hair, change clothes . . .), and make them look forward to coming home.

- Tell your partner you love them.

- Make special times when you are alone together.

- Create the right climate for romance: dim the lights; make a cosy area near an open fire; sit outside in the moonlight; walk through a beautiful garden or woods; visit an intimate restaurant or have a candlelit meal at home; take a picnic lunch to a quiet park.

- Touch each other tenderly.

- Give each other plenty of eye contact.

- Give some thought to your nightwear.

- Work hard for your partner's happiness, regardless of effort, paying special attention to small things you can do to please them.

- Produce a certificate for your partner to spend an entire evening or weekend alone with you.

- Plan a surprise outing together (theatre visit, weekend away, walk to a local beauty spot).

- Hold hands.

- Pore over old photographs together and remember things you did when you first met.

TEACHING POINTS/DISCUSSION STARTERS

- Encourage parents to pay more attention to their partner, to use their imagination and to create the right environment for romance.

- Invite parents to talk in twos and threes about the things they first did with their partners which gave them a thrill (walk in the park; cosy chats around the fire).

- Suggest times and ways in which partners can create special time together, and resolve to implement one of these within the coming week (perhaps a candlelit dinner at home for two, with all children barred after 8 pm).

ADDITIONAL IDEAS/RESOURCES

Reading

- *Love Life for Every Married Couple* by Ed Wheat (Marshall Pickering, 1984).

25. Understanding the Male Perspective

BIBLE REFERENCES

Genesis 1:27
Genesis 2:18
Genesis 2:24
Ephesians 5:25–28

TALK OUTLINE

Introduction to the gender differences

- Be careful of generalizations: they may not apply to all men, or men may not want to admit to them for fear of being exposed.

- The Bible makes it very clear that men and women were created separately and are very different.

- God intended men and women to be complementary (designed to make up for each other's differences and weaknesses).

Main areas of difference: the male perspective

- The purpose and style of communication varies between men and women.

- Men speak to convey facts or information, while women speak to make connections and build relationships.

- Men prefer a brief résumé, whereas women like to know

all the details.

- Men pick up direct questions or commands; women hope men will be sensitive enough to 'read between the lines'. This leads to confusion and frustration.

- For men, facts are crucial to their understanding, while for women ambience is key.

- Men feel closer to women when speaking about facts; women feel closer to men when speaking about feelings.

- Men try to find a solution to a problem, while for women half of the solution is in the sharing.

- Difference in perspective/focus occurs between men and women: women see household jobs that need to be done, while men need to have their attention drawn to these jobs; there is sometimes a different appreciation of beauty and recall of detail.

- A man needs a lover and a mother. Men are contented with food, comfort and sexual engagement. A woman's needs are more complex, and include intimacy, friendship and affirmation.

The involvement in the home often differs

- Men often run their lives and do little to help in the home; women tend to juggle external activities with running the home.

- Men are often insensitive to women's needs in the home.

- Men don't tend to undertake small tasks in the home spontaneously; women tend to find help with small things supportive.

- Men tend to use the television to help them unwind; women tend to view watching television together as a sharing activity.

Sexuality is an area of fundamental difference

- It is an area of greater expectation (and disappointment) for men because of natural appetite, media portrayal, etc.

- Men are more interested in sexual expression than women, although a woman's sex drive increases in her late 40s and 50s – just when a man's sexual urge is declining!

- An exhausted man still finds energy for sex; an exhausted woman is exhausted!

- Men are less prudish and more visually stimulated than women: they enjoy glamorous nightwear/underwear, while women can be self-conscious.

- Men are more focused on sex than intimacy; women more on intimacy than sex. Each pretends to be interested in the other area to gain what they desire.

- Men worry that wives only partake in sexual activity as part of the 'marriage deal'.

Implications for wives

- Gaining an understanding of the needs and perspectives of men in their differences helps wives to understand and meet those needs more often, and reduce the level of misunderstanding.

- Wives can then attempt to communicate more succinctly and directly when appropriate.

- In appreciating the importance of sexual activity, wives can try to meet this need more closely.

- Wives can try to make more effort with their appearance.

- Wives can try to make helpful suggestions for husbands to integrate or help in the home more.

TEACHING POINTS/DISCUSSION STARTERS

- This topic ideally requires a male speaker who is able to illustrate many of the outline points with personal, anecdotal illustrations. This brings the relatively dry framework above to life, in particular when the stories are amusing.

- Aim to help parents understand the major contrasts between men and women, and encourage efforts to meet each other's needs and avoid misunderstandings.

- Ask parents to think of examples in their relationships of differences in understanding between partners. How could they have handled this difference of perspective in another (more helpful) way?

- Ask parents to share the main areas in their relationships where their priorities differ markedly from those of their partners. How can partners accommodate those differences in each other and move towards a united approach?

ADDITIONAL IDEAS/RESOURCES

Reading

- *Man to Man About Women* by Dr James Dobson (Kingsway, 1976).

26. Understanding the Female Perspective

BIBLE REFERENCES

Genesis 1:27
Genesis 2:18
Genesis 2:21–24
Genesis 3:12
Proverbs 31:10–31
John 8:1–11
Colossians 3:18–19

TALK OUTLINE

Introduction to gender differences

- Women and men seek different things from a relationship. It is important to understand each other in order to be able to live in harmony (as with two instruments in an orchestra).

Main areas of difference: the female perspective

- Women seek affirmation in marriage.

- A woman's self-esteem comes largely from other people's opinion of her; men gain confidence primarily through success in the workplace.

- Women are more prone than men to a negative self-image, and this is often compounded by spending time alone at home without other adult contact or conversation. So praise and affirmation are important to the woman, because they demonstrate that she's valued by the man.

- Affection is important to women: a woman's need for hugs, cuddles and affectionate gestures is significantly greater than a man's.

- In time spent together, the ambience/environment is crucial for a woman to respond to a man.

- Women understand gestures such as flowers or other gifts, notes and cards to demonstrate affection (unless these are obviously given with an ulterior motive).

- Conversation is crucial to women: on average a woman uses 25,000 words per day, men only 2,000!

- Women talk in a personal way, men in a more practical and factual manner.

- Women like to talk things through at the end of the day, while men prefer peace and quiet. (Counsellors recommend 15 hours per week of conversation or similar attention to maintain a healthy marriage.)

- Women don't need a reason to talk; men don't need a reason to make love!

- Women seek security in marriage because they find security in people and places. Men find security in their success at work.

- Honest and open communication provides some of women's security; men, however, like privacy of thought. They often hide the truth to prevent worry or conflict with wives, but this breeds insecurity instead.

- Understanding is vital: women seek understanding of their experiences (pregnancy, childbirth, motherhood, PMT). They benefit from comprehension of how their time in the home is spent, often with no apparent visible achievement.

- Women need appreciation of their need to do several things at the same time; men prefer to focus on one thing at a time.

- Practical support and assistance with household tasks is appreciated, but women typically need to ask men directly for this as subtle hints don't work. Practical help with the children is appreciated – not just with the fun things, but also with the routine care and discipline of children.

- Women need 'space': it is vital for a woman to have the opportunity to pursue a hobby, go for a walk, have a relaxing bath ('time out' from duties).

- It is typically more difficult for women to make space for themselves because of the consequences for the rest of the family (mums feel guilty at having created the opportunity). Men appear to be able to 'opt out' with little regard for the family or guilt.

TEACHING POINTS/DISCUSSION STARTERS

- Aim to underline the distinctions between men's and women's needs and expectations in a relationship.

- Ask women in what area they feel they are most misunderstood by their partner. How could they lessen that misunderstanding?

ADDITIONAL IDEAS/RESOURCES

Reading

- *Man to Man About Women* by Dr James Dobson (Kingsway, 1976).

- *Opposites Attract* by Tim LaHaye (Kingsway, 1992).

27. Parents and In-laws

BIBLE REFERENCES

Genesis 2:24
Exodus 20:12
Deuteronomy 5:16
Ruth 1:14–16
Ephesians 6:1–4

TALK OUTLINE

Ideal relations with parents/in-laws

- The Bible outlines a relationship of independence between a married couple and their parents ('one flesh'), yet one that retains respect for the older generation. This presents a challenge to every married couple to appreciate and involve both sets of parents, yet establish well-defined boundaries to their involvement.

- Mutual independence must be established, parents letting their children go and children not being too dependent on parental support.

- A husband or wife should not be over-dependent on parents or seek their advice and support instead of their partner's.

Over-dependence may result from the following

- Habit (living at home until marriage).

- Need (spouse not providing necessary help and support).

- Lack of maturity (unable to make decisions independently).

Over-involvement by parents may result from

- Lack of alternative skills and interests (especially mothers).

- Unrealistic desire to perpetuate family life.

- Jealousy of child's partner in marriage.

An unhealthy balance between the two generations can become evident in the following areas

- Arranging wedding plans (*whose* wedding is it?).

- Setting up home (choice of location, type of home, furnishing).

- Structure of couple's relationship (degree of independence, leisure interests, friends).

- Raising children (discipline, clothing, equipment, eating habits, schooling).

- Financial affairs (establishing financial priorities, financial management).

How can we promote a healthy balance?

- Partners should be open with each other, discussing any over-reliance on parents or parents' intrusion in their relationship early on, and agree a strategy!

- Keep communication lines open: inform parents about activities, work, concerns, children's development, etc.

- Arrange family reunions.

- Ask advice on some matters where parents have relevant experience.

- Allow parents to provide practical help if offered (e.g. with the home, garden, children).

- Praise parents whenever they have been particularly supportive or, equally, tactfully uninvolved.

- Be polite but firm if parents attempt to be over-involved.

- Arrange celebrations, holidays and leisure activities without always involving parents as well. This says, 'We love to share time with you, but we also need to spend time on our own.'

TEACHING POINTS/DISCUSSION STARTERS

- Help parents to be aware of the tremendous support and encouragement available through the older generation, while being mindful of the dangers to any married relationship of over-involvement or over-dependence on parents.

- Ask parents to write down confidentially any area of involvement with parents/in-laws that has caused resentment or frustration, then quietly think about how this could have been avoided or dealt with. Suggest forgiving the offending party and making any appropriate gestures to establish the correct balance at the earliest opportunity.

- Invite parents to outline any challenging situations with parents/in-laws and pool advice on how to deal with the situations.

- Ask parents to think of ten things they really appreciate about each of their parents/in-laws, and think about how these things could add to their family life in a non-intrusive way.

28. The Three As: Acceptance, Appreciation, Affirmation

BIBLE REFERENCES

Proverbs 12:4
Proverbs 25:24
Matthew 22:39

TALK OUTLINE

Introduction

- Positive input can motivate both you and your partner to greater commitment to each other, and encourages partners to be all they could and should be in the relationship.

- It is easy to fall into the trap of negativism, but continually highlighting the gaps and mistakes in your partner's thinking, speech and actions erodes their value and commitment to the relationship.

- There are three basic steps to being able to relax with your partner and enable them to fulfil their potential: accept your partner, warts and all; appreciate all their finer points; affirm their words, actions and qualities.

Acceptance

- It is dangerous to enter marriage thinking we can change each other: partners need to accept one another as they are.

- Acceptance means being tolerant of a partner and

accepting their differences in gifts, opinions, background and personality.

- Just as we seek to be accepted with all our failings, inadequacies and quirks of temperament, so we need to provide similar acceptance for our partner.

- There is a basic longing in human beings to be accepted: the evidence is seen throughout school years (toys and games, social activities), young adulthood (clothes, music) and into maturity (homes, jobs, children).

- Acceptance doesn't mean we agree with all that is said, but we realize our partner believes what they're saying.

- We need to learn to compromise and be willing to see our partner's view, and admit when we are wrong.

- We need to learn to listen to our partner and understand their point of view.

- Acceptance involves giving a partner the freedom they need to grow and mature.

- Acceptance means preserving individuality within a close relationship.

- Acceptance means saying, 'You're OK and I admire the way you are!'

Appreciation

- To appreciate your partner is to be sensible of and grateful for all the good qualities they possess.

- It is helpful to think of all the qualities in your partner that attracted you to them initially.

- Consider how you'd cope without your partner, and what in particular you would miss.

- Focus on what you have in your partner and your

relationship, rather than on what you don't have – it is easy to fall into the trap of negativism.

- Write down the positive things your partner contributes to your relationship (work, income, actions, appearance, manners, DIY, gardening, paperwork, childcare, sense of humour).

- A positive mindset will alter the way you relate to your partner, and it will elicit a more positive response from them.

Affirmation

- Affirmation means practising the power of praise, complimenting your partner and voicing your acceptance and appreciation. Don't wait until it's too late – your partner can't guess your feelings for them.

- When we show our gratitude for even small things, this boosts our partner's self-esteem, and encourages them to do even greater things!

- We also need to learn not to mind if our partner doesn't voice their appreciation of our contribution: wives are missed when the dinner *isn't* on the table, or the button is *not* on the shirt!

- We should be willing to stop what we're doing to welcome a partner home, or to listen to what they have to say. This gives them the dignity of knowing that their words have value.

- We need to work at our communication: men are bad listeners, but women take ages to get to the point.

- We can choose to allow a partner to do things they really like: watch their favourite TV programme, play a round of golf, go out in the evening with their male/female friends.

- We can try to reserve our teaching and correction

(criticism!) for private moments, and not tear our partner down in public.

- We can be sensitive and available when a partner has 'failed' at work, sport or socially – this is when we're most needed.

- We can tell a partner they're the best mum/dad or wife/husband in all the world.

- Praise and affection will motivate your partner to fulfil their potential in your relationship.

TEACHING POINTS/DISCUSSION STARTERS

- Encourage parents to adopt a positive mindset towards their partners, actively seeking to identify good attributes rather than focusing on the negative.

- Suggest parents jot down ten things they really appreciate about their partners, then determine to share some or all of these with their partner later in the day.

- Ask parents to think of one thing that really irritates them about their partner. How could they alter their reaction to this? Maybe they could encourage a change in the source of irritation? (For example, a wife irritated by her husband dropping dirty laundry on the bedroom floor might solve the problem by moving the laundry basket into the bedroom.)

- What could you do or say this week to make your partner feel really special?

ADDITIONAL IDEAS/RESOURCES

Reading

- *The Secret of Loving* by Josh McDowell (Here's Life Publishers, 1985).

Talk illustrations

'To love you as I love myself is to seek to hear you as I hope to be heard, and to understand you as I long to be understood.' (David Augsburger)

The ideal wife
What every man expects

- Always beautiful and cheerful. Hair that never needs curlers or beauty shops. Beauty that won't run in a rainstorm.

- Could have married a film star, but wanted only you.

- Never ill – just allergic to jewellery and fur coats.

- Insists that moving furniture by herself is good for her figure.

- Expert in cooking, cleaning house, fixing the car or TV, painting the house, and keeping quiet.

- Favourite hobbies: mowing the lawn and shovelling snow.

- Hates credit cards.

- Her favourite expression: 'What can I do for you, dear?'

- Thinks you have Einstein's brain but look like Mr Universe.

- Wishes you would go out with the boys so she could get some sewing done.

- Loves you because you're so sexy.

What he gets

- She speaks 140 words a minute with gusts up to 180.

- She once was a model for a totem pole.

- A light eater – as soon as it gets light, she starts eating.

- Where there's smoke, there she is – cooking.

- She lets you know you only have two faults: everything you say and everything you do.

- No matter what she does with it, her hair looks like an explosion in a steel wool factory.

- If you get lost, open your wallet – she'll find you.

The ideal husband
What every woman expects

- He will be a brilliant conversationalist.

- A very sensitive man – kind and understanding, truly loving.

- A very hard-working man.

- A man who helps around the house by washing dishes, vacuuming floors, and taking care of the garden.

- Someone who helps his wife raise his children.

- A man of emotional and physical strength.

- A man who is as smart as Einstein, but looks like Robert Redford.

What she gets

- He always takes her to the best restaurants. Some day he may even take her inside.

- He doesn't have any ulcers; he gives them.

- Any time he has an idea in his head, he has the whole thing in a nutshell.

- He's well-known as a miracle worker – it's a miracle when he works.

- He supports his wife in the manner to which she was accustomed – he's letting her keep her job.

- He's such a bore that he even bores her to death when he gives her a compliment.

- He has occasional flashes of silence that makes his conversation brilliant.

From *The Secret of Loving*
by Josh McDowell
(Here's Life Publishers, 1985)
Used by permission of
Tyndale House. All rights reserved.

29. Stress in Marriage

BIBLE REFERENCES

Psalm 62:5
Matthew 6:25–34
Luke 12:22–23

TALK OUTLINE

What do we mean by stress?

- Strain, tension and excessive demands on the marriage relationship.

- Some stress can be healthy and stimulating: it can spur a couple to resolve a situation or achieve something additional.

- Stress becomes a problem when it is essentially destructive in nature, and when demands on a couple's mental and physical energy exceed their ability to cope. This may bring about changes in behaviour, ill health or breakdown in marriage.

What are the signs of stress in marriage?

- Deteriorating communication or lack of conversation.

- Withdrawal or isolation of one partner.

- Increased irritability or anger.

- Loss of appetite (for food and sex).
- A man working increasingly long hours.

What are the potential sources of stress in marriage?

- Natural gender differences.
- Different backgrounds/expectations of each partner.
- Different personalities.
- Different priorities.
- Work/unemployment/both partners working.
- Financial pressures.
- Children.
- Parents/in-laws.
- Time pressure and fatigue.
- Lack of communication/conversation.
- Shortage of time alone for the couple – absence of romantic love.
- Ageing.
- Sexual pressures/problems.
- Unfaithfulness (this can happen quickly and wreak havoc).

How can we help prevent/alleviate damaging stress?

- Spend time together regularly.
- Keep open lines of communication.
- Appreciate/accept differences between each other due to gender and different backgrounds.
- Discuss finance regularly and adopt an agreed strategy.

- Suggest ways in which we can enjoy the children more and alleviate some of the stress.

- Be open but firm with parents and in-laws.

- Try to clear time in the busyness of our schedules.

- Start to appreciate and affirm our partner.

- Try to make sure our partner looks forward to coming home.

TEACHING POINTS/DISCUSSION STARTERS

- Aim to demonstrate the wide variety of sources of stress in any marriage, and emphasize the importance of regular and honest communication between partners to maintain awareness of the issues and offer an opportunity to resolve these jointly.

- Ask parents to think of the one thing that currently causes the most stress in their marriage. How could they start to tackle this?

ADDITIONAL IDEAS/RESOURCES

- Conduct a mini-survey of parents present, and establish the top ten sources of stress. If numbers permit, divide into ten small groups and each make practical suggestions for tackling one area/problem.

30. Married Again

BIBLE REFERENCES

Matthew 5:32
Matthew 19:6–9
Romans 7:2–3

TALK OUTLINE

Introduction

- Most people who divorce also remarry.

- Recent statistics show that the chances of success for a second marriage are higher than for a first marriage: only one-sixth of second marriages also result in divorce.

- Those who have been widowed and remarry are most likely to succeed in their marriage.

- Those who remarry a bachelor/spinster are statistically least likely to succeed.

- If both parties are divorced, they are generally more likely to succeed.

What are the special difficulties in a second marriage?

- Complications arise from the problems of the first marriage being taken into the second: broken hearts and homes, children, financial difficulties, guilt.

- There may be a reluctance to form another relationship because of the effects of the break-up of the first.

- A bachelor/spinster may have higher expectations and greater demands, and not realize the effort required to make a marriage work.

- There may be difficulty in keeping the memory of a first husband/wife from intruding in a second marriage.

- There may be problems in accommodating children from the first marriage.

- It may be difficult deciding whether to have children in the second marriage – usually a higher priority for women than for men.

- There may be difficulties in visiting arrangements for the other parent from the first marriage.

- There may be resentment from children or anger towards a step-parent.

- There may be an absence of married life '*à deux*' before children.

- There may be financial pressures/constraints – especially concerning alimony.

Some special ingredients for the success of a second marriage

- Take time over the decision for a second marriage: the first marriage may have taken place in haste, or because of home/financial pressures.

- Recognize faults in yourself that may have contributed to the breakdown of the first marriage in order to avoid repeating past mistakes.

- Deal with the past: find forgiveness for past mistakes.

- Someone from a happy marriage which ended with the

death of their partner is more likely to succeed in a second marriage because they have the experience of living harmoniously with another person, and are used to thinking of another person and being prepared to compromise.

- Find a balance between not forgetting the first partner and making the second feel unique.

- Make a new start to the way things are done – forget how they used to be done.

- Understand the tension between children of one parent and their step-parent, and exercise self-restraint.

- Accept financial constraints rather than fight against them.

TEACHING POINTS/DISCUSSION STARTERS

- Aim to make parents aware of the added complications within a second marriage so that they may be more sensitive towards friends in a similar situation, and better equipped to provide practical help and support for them.

- Ask parents to consider what would be the greatest challenge to them in a second marriage. How would they best tackle this?

ADDITIONAL IDEAS/RESOURCES

- This topic is best spoken about by a Christian who is experiencing a second marriage. They can use the above outline as a prompt for sharing their own experiences of the challenges they are facing. It would be unwise and unrealistic to expect someone who has not gone through this experience to talk on the topic. At the very least, the speaker should interview another person in this position about key points, or ask them to relate their experience in their own words.

The Many Roles of Mum

'Her children arise and call her blessed;
her husband also, and he praises her.'

(Proverbs 31:28)

31. The Contented Wife

BIBLE REFERENCES

Proverbs 31:10–31
Philippians 4:12
Ephesians 5:22–33
1 Timothy 3:12

TALK OUTLINE

What is a contented wife?

- We feel contented or fulfilled in a role when we understand the requirements of that role, appreciate its value and feel we have done a good job in meeting the requirements.

- The Bible tells us that a wife of noble character is of great value – worth more than rubies or jewels.

- A man who is cared for and treated with respect and dignity in his own home enters the working world from a positive/firm foundation, with high self-esteem.

What prevents us from doing a good job or valuing our work?

- Society and the media rarely acknowledge or attribute value in being a housewife. This may result in low self-esteem in women who dedicate themselves to the roles of wife and mother.

- Husbands often do not voice their appreciation or praise

139

of a wife's work or achievements, so wives can feel taken for granted.

● Husbands may not behave in a way that commands respect from their wives (drunkenness, abuse, unfaithfulness).

How can you become more like the wife your husband needs you to be?

● Appreciate the high value of the role of wife – to your husband, for your children and for society. This will motivate you to do the job well.

● Proverbs 31 provides us with the (perhaps daunting) picture of a wife busily caring for and providing for her family. Providing food, clean clothing, love and understanding goes a long way to meeting a husband's basic needs in a wife.

● Use a little imagination in planning, preparing and presenting nourishing, economical and appealing meals.

● Provide a listening ear and understanding of his day/problems.

● Take time together to maintain joint interests/activities.

● Keep communication lines open, use your tongue wisely to show respect and appreciation for your husband's qualities, and choose your time to speak wisely.

● Try not to nag, ridicule or humiliate your husband.

● Pay attention to your appearance (fitness and general attractiveness) to ensure your husband really looks forward to coming home to you.

● Encourage openness and honesty in your relationship, and share matters without hesitation. This demonstrates your respect for your husband and nurtures friendship between you both.

- Discuss what you really expect of each other as wife/husband, and how you can both best meet those expectations.

- Accept differences in attitude, opinion and personality – give your husband space and dignity to be true to himself.

- Encourage your husband to take time out for his own leisure pursuits and friendships.

- Respect his wishes – try to carry out tasks he has requested.

- Think of special things you could do to please him: arrange a special trip; cook his favourite meal; invite a special friend.

- Behave as if you were the esteemed wife of a respected leader: such behaviour tends to be self-fulfilling.

TEACHING POINTS/DISCUSSION STARTERS

- Aim to encourage wives to believe in the crucial importance of their role to their husbands, their children and society generally.

- Ask wives to consider how well they have adapted to their role. Which aspects do they find particularly fulfilling, and which especially frustrating or difficult?

- Which of the suggestions made could they put into practice this week to make a difference to their husbands and help them to feel more fulfilled?

ADDITIONAL IDEAS/RESOURCES

Reading

- *The Power of a Praying Wife* by Stormie Omartian (Kingsway, 1997).

32. The Competent Teacher

BIBLE REFERENCES

Deuteronomy 6:7
Judges 2:10
Proverbs 22:6
2 Timothy 3:16
Titus 2:1–15

TALK OUTLINE

The importance of teaching our children

- When we teach our children, we not only affect their generation, but generations beyond. 'A teacher affects eternity; he can never tell where his influence stops' (Henry Brook Adams).

- The Bible tells us that teaching in early years will be carried forward into the rest of life (Proverbs 22:6).

- Parents have the awesome responsibility and power to make or break lives.

- The Bible clearly states that it is the parents' responsibility to communicate God's way of living to their children – otherwise they are left to absorb the ways of thinking prevalent in society.

- A mother is the child's first and most influential teacher.

What should we teach our children?

A basic outlook on life:

- Our faith.

- The difference between right and wrong (important contrast to the concept of tolerance in today's society).

- Priorities (God, family, work, community).

- Ambitions/goals: finding God's plans for work, marriage, family.

- Character training: behaviour, speech and attitudes.

- Love, commitment, persistence, industry.

- Encouragement, kindness, generosity, truthfulness.

Acceptable behaviour:

- Potty training, brushing teeth, general cleanliness.

- Eating nutritious food, using cutlery, table manners.

- Fastening shoelaces, ties and buttons.

- General courtesy – mastering the basic skills.

- Self-control.

- How to tackle problems.

How to relate to other people:

- Valuing other people in all their differences.

- Respect and obedience for parents, teachers, leaders.

- Living with other people/sharing.

- Working together as a team.

- Responsibility – carrying out tasks, saving for purchases.

- Compassion and helpfulness towards others.

Information/knowledge:

- Numeracy and literacy skills.

- Artistic/creative skills.

- Practical home skills (cooking, ironing, gardening).

- Ways to find out answers to questions (academic, practical everyday).

The way in which we teach our children

- It is important to have a good relationship with our children. Biblical training is always done in the context of a deep, loving relationship.

- A teacher needs to be respected in order for teaching to have weight.

- We can teach by example or verbal instruction, passing on wisdom about behaviour, attitudes and values, as well as imparting information. Like this we instil good or bad ways of thinking and acting in our children.

- What we don't do or say can be as significant as what we do.

- We need to pray for wisdom and guidance. Teaching our children is a daunting prospect, and we need to accept that we won't be perfect examples.

TEACHING POINTS/DISCUSSION STARTERS

- Emphasize the wide scope and continuous nature of the teaching that is undertaken in the home.

- Ask parents to consider where they need to be better examples to their children, and how exactly they could achieve this.

- What things did their own parents do or say that have

particularly shaped their own attitudes to money/work/
friends/life/relationships?

● What sort of things should we desire for our children?
What seems to motivate us in our children's eyes?

ADDITIONAL IDEAS/RESOURCES

Talk illustration

Children learn what they live

If a child lives with criticism
   He learns to condemn.
If a child lives with hostility
   He learns to fight.
If a child lives with ridicule
   He learns to be shy.
If a child lives with shame
   He learns to feel guilty.

If a child lives with tolerance
   He learns to be patient.
If a child lives with encouragement
   He learns confidence.
If a child lives with praise
   He learns to appreciate.
If a child lives with fairness
   He learns justice.
If a child lives with security
   He learns to have faith.
If a child lives with approval
   He learns to like himself.
If a child lives with acceptance and friendship
   He learns to find love in the world.

Author unknown

33. The Capable Nurse

BIBLE REFERENCES

Matthew 4:23–24
Matthew 8:7
1 Corinthians 12:9, 28
James 5:14–15
3 John 1:2

TALK OUTLINE

Introduction

- A time of illness or injury is significant in the parent–child relationship.

- A parent is the main source of comfort and encouragement.

- A parent is a source of wisdom and knowledge, and builds up a child's security and trust in them.

- It is important to recognize symptoms for correct diagnosis.

- It is important to know the appropriate treatment: when to seek professional help; when/how to administer home treatment.

It is important to recognize symptoms and know when to seek help

- Childhood accidents: falls, burns, etc.

- Childhood illnesses: chicken pox, mumps, measles, tonsilitis.

- Eczema/asthma.

- Hearing/sight problems.

- Learning disorders (dyslexia, dyspraxia).

The essential tools for a home nurse

- Basic first aid kit and training.

- Basic family medicines.

- Useful extras such as a spray antiseptic, sting relief cream.

- Home health reference book: for example, *The Good Housekeeping Family Health Encyclopaedia.*

What being a home nurse means

- Taking time to listen to the problem/observe the symptoms.

- Deciding on a course of action.

- An opportunity to provide security and love for the child.

- An opportunity to encourage an open trusting parent–child relationship.

TEACHING POINTS/DISCUSSION STARTERS

- It may be preferable to invite a speaker with medical qualifications of some kind (a health visitor or a parent who is qualified in first aid).

- Aim to encourage parents to take an informed approach to their children's health, and to appreciate the importance of their healthcare to the security of the child and close parent–child relationship.

- Ask parents how well equipped they are at home to cope

with the most frequent childhood accidents and illnesses, then make a list of the vital extras they may need to acquire.

● Discuss how you could decide whether to call for professional medical help in different situations (severity of symptoms, etc.).

ADDITIONAL IDEAS/RESOURCES

Reading

● *The Good Housekeeping Family Health Encyclopaedia*

● *St John's Ambulance First Aid Manual*

Further suggestion

● The speaker could compile a list of basic first aid items and family medicines to meet the majority of home treatment needs.

34. The Caring Mother

BIBLE REFERENCES

Isaiah 49:15
John 21:15
1 Corinthians 13:4–7
Galatians 5:22

TALK OUTLINE

How can a mother show she cares?

- By being concerned about the well-being of her children.

- By providing for her children's needs.

- By looking after/watching over her children.

- By supervising, exercising caution and avoiding harm.

- By being affectionate and loving.

- By meeting physical, emotional and spiritual needs of children.

- By caring through actions, attitudes and words. This can be proactive (initiated by mums) or reactive (response to a situation).

Proactive caring:

- Planning, thinking and doing ahead.

- Preparing meals, clothing.

- Making home a welcoming place.

- Being prepared for potential needs (store of useful items).

- Providing discipline, training and teaching.

- Communication: sharing ideas, listening and speaking.

- Checking on details of activity, inviting friends, organizing birthday celebrations.

Reactive caring:

- Compassion in case of injury or illness.

- Taking time to listen, help or make suggestions.

- Being approachable and flexible to respond to children's needs.

Provision for physical needs

- Food and clothing.

- Nursing.

- Playing games.

Caring for a child's emotional needs

- Being sensitive to a child's fears, hopes, disappointment, joys.

- Boosting self-esteem/confidence (with acts and words of encouragement).

Meeting a child's spiritual needs

- Praying for children (James 5:16).

- Praying with children.

- Demonstrating own spiritual commitment in actions and words.

Caring involves both actions and words

- Both combine to demonstrate our love and concern for our children.

- Sometimes actions speak louder than words.

- Sometimes 'a word in season' speaks volumes.

Conclusion

- Caring involves humility, unselfishness, kindness, gentleness, patience, generosity, thoughtfulness, friendliness, forgiveness.

- We shouldn't be overawed by pursuing perfection as parents, but aim for excellence in the above qualities.

TEACHING POINTS/DISCUSSION STARTERS

- Caring is an attitude or mindset that should invade every aspect of parenting, and is grounded in love.

- Ask parents to think of the special ways their own parents demonstrated their particular care for them.

- How could parents show their care more openly to their children this week?

ADDITIONAL IDEAS/RESOURCES

Reading

- *The Power of a Praying Parent* by Stormie Omartian (Kingsway, 1996).

35. The Child Psychologist

BIBLE REFERENCES

1 Chronicles 28:9
Psalm 147:5
Proverbs 3:5
Proverbs 20:5
Jeremiah 33:3

TALK OUTLINE

What does it mean to be a psychologist?

- Psychology is the study of the mind and how it works, and associated behaviour, attitudes and characteristics.

- A psychologist needs an understanding of children's behaviour and our responses as parents.

- To have an understanding that difficulties arise because mental processes are invisible, thus difficult to detect.

- To recognize that a child's mental life affects his thinking, remembering, recognition, understanding and dreaming. It also includes the emotions/feelings (pleasure, anxiety, frustration and boredom).

- To have an understanding that the mental life is expressed in behaviour (speech, actions, attitudes).

Why do we need to be a child psychologist?

- Children don't come with an instruction manual – we have to work out their needs.

- Children lack the experience and maturity to be able to understand their own feelings and behaviour.

- If a child's expected and real behaviour don't match, we need to understand why.

- To help children gain an understanding of why they behave as they do and to take appropriate action.

- To diagnose underlying causes of disturbed/unusual behaviour or illness.

- To understand how experiences are shaping a child, and how a child reacts to circumstances (e.g. tension between parents, a grandparent's death, school situation, father's absence).

- To understand how our own behaviour/reactions as parents can influence children (parental tension, unhappiness, depression, lack of sleep all threaten a child's security).

- To understand why certain behaviours occur, in order to take the right course of action (tough/tender; encouraging/discouraging).

We need to understand a variety of behavioural patterns

- A baby's crying.
- Toddler tantrums.
- Silence or constant chatter in a child.
- Rebellion or submission.
- Illness (tummy ache, headache, nausea, eczema/asthma, general pallor).

How to improve your psychology skills

- Remember that it takes time and practice: we often feel good at guessing other people's feelings, but we are not always correct!

- Spend time with your children to come to know their strengths and weaknesses and typical behavioural patterns.

- Observe your children both alone and when interacting with other children and adults.

- Listen to the things your children say and don't say.

- Watch your child's body language.

- Have regular communication with your children, involving both listening and speaking.

- Read about typical child behaviour and changes in behaviour.

- Talk with other parents to determine whether behaviour is usual, and to exchange tips for tackling difficulties.

- Talk to childcare experts/behavioural psychologists to gain understanding, reassurance and advice.

- Above all, seek God's wisdom and understanding through reading the Bible and through prayer.

TEACHING POINTS/DISCUSSION STARTERS

- Underline the importance of parents getting to know their children in order to be able to diagnose behavioural causes correctly. Emphasize the need to understand 'why' in order to select the correct course of action.

- Ask why a child might be silent and withdrawn. What things are most likely to upset a child?

- Ask parents if they recognize any of their own

behavioural patterns in their children.

- Ask how they usually know if their child is upset or worried about something (quiet or loud behaviour; longing for solitude or company; body language; facial expression; hunger or loss of appetite).

- Ask how children usually react to specific circumstances, and what type of behaviour in their children they find most difficult to understand and consequently deal with effectively.

ADDITIONAL IDEAS/RESOURCES

- Devise a short questionnaire for parents. Distribute this a few weeks before the talk, in time to collect in and analyse the answers to use as a basis for the talk.

36. The Constructive Listener

BIBLE REFERENCES

Proverbs 1:5
Proverbs 8:33
Proverbs 18:15
Matthew 7:26–27
Mark 4:9
Luke 8:18
James 1:19, 23

TALK OUTLINE

What do we mean by constructive listening?

- 'Listening' is hearing what someone is saying; making an effort to hear something; paying attention.

- 'Constructive' is putting to good use; putting into practice through interpretation; being useful.

- Listening is more than hearing. Listening is a vital part of two-way communication.

- We can listen not only with our ears, but with eyes, mind and heart.

- Listening to the prompting of the Holy Spirit regarding our children is vital.

Why is it important to be a constructive listener to our children?

- To help in understanding our children.

- Children are often unable to explain clearly what they feel or mean – they need our help in understanding themselves.

- To help make wise decisions for or with our children.

- To strengthen the parent–child relationship.

- To build up trust and openness in our children to enable them to share their joys and concerns. Not listening encourages their withdrawal.

- Listening to someone shows love and care for them.

- When a parent wants to listen and is trying to understand, it boosts self-esteem.

- The most frequent complaint by teenagers of their parents is: 'They don't listen to me!'

How to become a more effective listener

- Concentrate on listening, both to what is and what is not said.

- Don't be too busy thinking about your own answer to listen properly.

- Observe accompanying body language and behaviour.

- Make eye contact with your child as they speak.

- Try to really hear the other person, regardless of differing opinions and convictions.

- Ask God for Holy Spirit sensitivity to your child's communication.

- Listen to other sounds apart from words: the cries of a

baby, sighs or screams of a toddler, grunts or silence of a teenager.

- Set aside special times to listen (bedtime, home-from-school time).

- Be spontaneous and flexible, willing to stop and listen when a child is wanting to communicate.

- Give the child some response to show you're listening (nod, give a word of confirmation, smile, ask for more information, reflect on what's said, express encouragement and appreciation for what's shared).

- Don't interrupt. Take time to understand the full communication.

TEACHING POINTS/DISCUSSION STARTERS

- Encourage parents to give their children dignity by listening carefully to what they are trying to say.

- Why do we find it so difficult to listen to our children?

- How can we help our children to express their ideas, feelings and intentions more clearly?

ADDITIONAL IDEAS/RESOURCES

Talk illustrations

'It is the province of knowledge to speak and it is the privilege of wisdom to listen.' (Oliver Wendell Holmes)

'I know you believe you understand what you think I said. But I am not sure you realize that what you heard is not what I meant!' (Author unknown)

'Sensitive listening is reaching out to the other person,

actively caring about what he says and what he wants to say.'
(H. Norman Wright)

His thoughts were slow,
His words were few and never formed to glisten.
But he was a joy to all his friends,
You should have heard him listen!

Author unknown

37. The Christian Comforter

BIBLE REFERENCES

Isaiah 49:15
Isaiah 66:13
Matthew 11:28
Matthew 25:35–36
1 Corinthians 13:4–7
2 Corinthians 1:3–7
1 Peter 3:8

TALK OUTLINE

What do we mean by being a comforter?

- It is bringing the love and comfort of Jesus' presence into the home.

- It is bringing relief, ease and contentment to others.

- It involves listening, understanding and being compassionate in relieving the symptoms or dealing with the source of 'discomfort'.

- It involves kindness, gentleness, forgiveness and providing refuge and security, shelter and protection.

- It is putting an attitude of heart into action.

When do our children need comfort?

- In cases of illness/injury.

- After the demands of a school day.

- When something is broken or lost.

- When someone has let them down.

- When they are disappointed.

- When they are lonely.

- When they are tired, hungry or thirsty.

- When they are struggling to learn something new.

- When they've done something wrong, or been wronged.

- When they are left out by other children.

- When they are nervous about a new experience.

- When they are experiencing stress.

How can we be more comforting?

- By being there.

- By being prepared to spend time with our children.

- By being flexible/willing to put aside our own activities.

- By being gentle and understanding.

- By listening carefully and showing we're listening and trying to understand.

- By being tough yet tender – to provide security and love.

- By being humble and unselfish.

- By being approachable (Jesus welcomed children, tax collectors, Pharisees, soldiers, prostitutes).

- By being open and honest.

- By being generous with time and possessions.

- By being patient and forgiving.

- By allowing ourselves time and space in the day for refreshment to build up reserves and thus be better equipped to comfort others.

- By praying for Holy Spirit sensitivity to our children's needs and the compassion of Jesus to handle each individual situation.

TEACHING POINTS/DISCUSSION STARTERS

- Help parents to understand their importance in acting as a buffer for children against the stresses and strains of the outside world.

- What prevents you from being the comforter you'd like to be (tiredness, impatience, ignorance of children's needs)?

- In which situations, or at which times of day, do your children most need your comfort? How can you adapt to be available/equipped to meet those needs?

38. The Conscientious Housekeeper

BIBLE REFERENCES

2 Chronicles 15:7
Proverbs 12:24
Proverbs 31:10–31
Ecclesiastes 9:10

TALK OUTLINE

Introduction

- A housekeeper is defined as 'a woman employed to look after a household' or 'a manager of domestic affairs'.

- Housework is defined as 'stopping the filth becoming apparent'!

- The media have downgraded and devalued the role of housekeeper.

- We need to think positively about the role of housekeeper and use the title 'homemaker' more, as it is potentially a very creative role.

- The role requires a vast range of skills and capabilities: cook, cleaner, accountant, buyer, secretary, decorator, florist, gardener, chauffeur, nurse, launderer, seamstress, repairer, tidyer, manager.

- The nature of the role has changed with the invention of many labour/time-saving devices.

- Being a conscientious/effective housekeeper is still hard work, and it is often not acknowledged by the family. They notice only when something *isn't* done!

- We have often absorbed our own mothers' methods/standards of housekeeping: these may be either restricting or motivating!

Why is the role of housekeeper so important?

- It provides an opportunity to show love and care to the family in a very real and tangible way.

- The housekeeper has the power to make or break a home.

- It is the central linchpin of the home, providing a stable and organized framework for family life, and being vital to the smooth running and success of all that happens within and outside the home.

- It involves meeting many practical and emotional needs: providing comfort, sustenance, refuge, motivation, security, pleasure.

How can we find more fulfilment in our role?

- When we are more effective we find more satisfaction in running the home.

- Fulfilment depends on our attitude. We need to be realistic, as over-ambition breeds resentment and dissatisfaction.

- We need to view homemaking as a challenge: the demands are always changing.

- We need to appreciate the rewards: a table cleared of food; the smell of home cooking; the sheen of newly polished furniture; the beauty/order of gardening; the smell of fresh laundry.

- We need to be prepared for hard work!

- Being creative brings extra fulfilment: it creates an atmosphere of thoughtfulness, and creative touches make a home.

Some ways to be more creative:

- Experiment with simple painting and decorating techniques.

- Make a special photograph arrangement.

- Make a 'Welcome Home' sign when partner/children have been away.

- Produce seasonal specialities: pancakes, Easter eggs, Advent candles.

- Make your money go further by looking in local charity shops for bargain gifts, and watching out for bargains in local shops or supermarkets.

Some ways to be more disciplined:

- Get up early.

- Think/plan ahead.

- Keep fit and healthy to respond to the physical demands of the job.

- Be organized: establish a weekly schedule of jobs for each day.

- Make lists of errands/phone calls/letters, and tick off each item once completed for real proof of achievement.

- Keep a sense of humour! Try to see the funny side of things.

TEACHING POINTS/DISCUSSION STARTERS

- Aim to convey the centrality and impact of the homemaker, and give practical tips for greater fulfilment in the role.

- Ask parents to think about how to reorganize the week to ensure that all the basic jobs are done, allowing more free time for themselves.

- How can mums (subtly!) help their families to be more appreciative of their efforts?

- How can parents begin to consciously recognize the value of their role? (For example, think of the consequences of *not* doing the job! Think of how many pages of instructions are needed to enable someone else to take over for a day!)

ADDITIONAL IDEAS/RESOURCES

Reading

- *How to Live with a Working Wife* by Jim Douglas (Pan, 1983).

Talk illustrations

'Marriage is a bribe to make a housekeeper think she's a householder.' (Thornton Wilder)

'Real housewives know that housework is a combination of what you have time for and what you have to do so things don't look absolutely awful.' (Jim Douglas)

39. The Cherished Lover

BIBLE REFERENCES

Genesis 29:20
Deuteronomy 24:5
The Song of Songs

TALK OUTLINE

Introduction – why romance involves effort

- Security in a relationship often brings routine and boredom. There is a need to work at keeping romance alive.

- After a time, partners tend to make less effort to look attractive to each other and to make themselves interesting.

- Leading busy lives often means couples have little time together or are tired, and as a result their relationship suffers.

- Worries about work/money/health can affect desire.

- There may be a tendency to relax and take each other for granted.

Tips to maintain/revive the flame

- Recognize signs of boredom early on. Ignoring them may lead to greater dissatisfaction.

- Talk openly and regularly about your relationship: aims, dreams, dissatisfaction.

- Discuss how to improve/maintain/revive interest in each other.

- Plan a project jointly – working together brings closeness.

- If spending too much time together, plan separate activities.

- Break the routine: if you are usually at home, go out or away; if you are often out, stay at home.

- Take a short break or holiday where you can be more objective and relaxed, away from everyday pressures.

- Plan time together without the children. It is wise to ensure that a partnership exists independently of children – there is a danger of relating to each other only through the children.

- Remember that there is a need to combine the comfort of security and the adventure of change in a relationship.

- Be encouraged that surviving a difficult patch together can bring greater confidence in the relationship.

The three As of romance

- Appearance: take pride in your appearance. This tells your partner they matter.

- Atmosphere: create a relaxing, gentle, welcoming, quiet and peaceful atmosphere – an ambience of care and openness.

- Attitude: appreciate your partner's presence, acknowledge things about them which attract you, encourage them to express their feelings.

(See also Talk 24: Romance.)

TEACHING POINTS/DISCUSSION STARTERS

- To maintain romance in a relationship requires effort: take a break in routine; create an environment conducive to romance; ensure continued personal attractiveness to your partner.

- Ask parents to consider what is mainly responsible for stifling romance in their relationships. What can they begin to change in this area this week?

- What are the main factors encouraging romance in their relationships: time of day, location, particular activity, partner's appearance?

ADDITIONAL IDEAS/RESOURCES

- Put together a display board to feed the imagination with pictures of ideas for spending time together: couple on a country walk; sitting by an open fire; a candlelit dinner.

40. Christ's Ambassador

BIBLE REFERENCES

Matthew 5:13–14
Luke 17:21
John 14:23
2 Corinthians 2:15
2 Corinthians 5:20
Ephesians 5:33

TALK OUTLINE

Note: You may wish to adapt this outline in accordance with the number of Christians/non-Christians attending.

What does it mean to be Christ's ambassador in your home?

- An ambassador represents his country in another, and is a messenger or agent.

- To bring the fragrance of Christ into your home.

- To be Christ-like in your thoughts, words and actions.

- To be salt and light in your home: to encourage a longing for God among your family members.

- To take a stand for God's values where these are being eroded or challenged.

Qualities of Jesus and the fruits of the Spirit (Galatians 5)

- To show love of an unconditional nature.

- To experience joy (contrast with happiness, which depends on circumstances).

- To have peace (resulting from personal security).

- To have patience (in the midst of all frustrations!).

- To show kindness (of thought, word and deed).

- To have goodness (purity, good disposition).

- To have faithfulness (to God, family and friends).

- To have gentleness (of manner and speech).

- To have self-control (amid the many demands).

Behaviour to avoid

- Sexual immorality/impurity.

- Debauchery (intemperance/lewdness).

- Idolatry (money, material things, other gods).

- Witchcraft (involvement with occult practices).

- Hatred.

- Discord (disagreement or strife).

- Jealousy.

- Fits of rage.

- Selfish ambition.

What are the obstacles to our successful ambassadorship?

- Human nature! We need to grow more and more like Christ and ask forgiveness for our failings, but not sink under guilt when we miss the target.

- Tiredness. Fatigue tends to reveal the worst side of our nature.

- Non-Christian members of the family resisting or rejecting our faith and any attempts we make to live it out in the home.

How can you best fulfil this role in your home?

- Set aside time daily to focus on God's priorities for your home.

- Allow God's Spirit to lead you in every aspect of your role: homemaking, parenting, being a good wife.

- Be loving, caring, respectful and dignified to enable God's name to be honoured through your presence in the home.

- Show respect for your husband: don't criticize him publicly, think of his needs, do things especially for him.

- Demonstrate your commitment to God's priorities by setting aside time for prayer and reading the Bible, and taking part regularly in your church.

- Put God first, your husband second, the children third, the church fourth and then community activity.

- 'Walk the walk', don't just 'talk the talk'!

TEACHING POINTS/DISCUSSION STARTERS

- Aim to encourage parents in the potential of their Christian witness in the home, in helping non-believers to find faith in Christ themselves and encourage/strengthen Christian members in their own walk.

- Ask parents in which situations in the home they find it most difficult to be Christ-like. How could they change their attitude/reactions?

- Which of Christ's attributes (fruits of the Spirit) do they most need to acquire? Pray for that specific provision.

ADDITIONAL IDEAS/RESOURCES

Reading

- *How to Be the Happy Wife of an Unsaved Husband* by Linda Davis (Whitaker, 1986).

A Time for Everything

'There is a time for everything, and a season for every activity under heaven.'

(Ecclesiastes 3:1)

41. A Time to Be Born and a Time to Die (Ecclesiastes 3:2)

BIBLE REFERENCES

Life
John 3:1–8, 16
Acts 16:31
Romans 8:10
1 John 5:12

Death
Psalm 23:4
John 12:24
John 14:2
1 Corinthians 15:42, 52
2 Corinthians 5:10
Colossians 3:1–3
1 Thessalonians 4:13, 18
Hebrews 9:27

TALK OUTLINE

A variety of topics can be used with these Bible references.

- Preparing for a new baby.

- The spiritual issues of birth and death.

- New birth through Jesus.

- Coping with bereavement.

● The wonders of creation.

TEACHING POINTS/DISCUSSION STARTERS

● The secret of peace is to accept God's perfect timing.

● Do you get angry when God's timing does not match your timing and expectation of life's plans? Is despair or rebellion the result?

42. A Time to Plant and a Time to Harvest (Ecclesiastes 3:2 NLT)

BIBLE REFERENCES

Plant
Genesis 2:8
Psalm 1:3
Jeremiah 17:8
Matthew 15:13
Matthew 21:33
Luke 13:6

Harvest
Genesis 8:22
Deuteronomy 16:15
Joel 3:13
Matthew 9:37
John 4:35
Hebrews 12:11
Revelation 14:15

TALK OUTLINE

- Building strong families: we reap what we sow, therefore a sacrificial investment has to be made in our children – of time, love and teaching by example and discipline.

TEACHING POINTS/DISCUSSION STARTERS

- What sort of investment are you making in the lives of

your family right now?

- Do you enjoy spending time with your children, or are you tempted to entertain them with material things?

- 'We are what we sow.' What does this mean in your life?

ADDITIONAL IDEAS/RESOURCES

- A simple lesson in gardening or caring for house plants.

43. A Time to Tear Down and a Time to Build (Ecclesiastes 1:3)

BIBLE REFERENCES

Psalm 127:1
Proverbs 14:1
Matthew 16:18
1 Corinthians 14:12
Ephesians 4:29
1 Thessalonians 5:11
Hebrews 3:4
Hebrews 11:10

The stone the builders rejected
Psalm 118:22
Matthew 21:42
Mark 12:10
Luke 20:17
Ephesians 2:20–21
1 Peter 2:7

TALK OUTLINE

- We tend to be creatures of habit. Do you feel insecure when you have a new situation to face?

- Where does your security lie?

TEACHING POINTS/DISCUSSION STARTERS

- Discuss a new start: moving house; coping with a new school; starting a new job; making new friendships.

- Discuss the parable of houses built on sand or rock (Matthew 7:24).

ADDITIONAL IDEAS/RESOURCES

- A demonstration of simple, inexpensive changes a woman can make in the home.

44. A Time to Laugh (Ecclesiastes 3:4)

BIBLE REFERENCES

Psalm 126:2
Proverbs 31:25
Proverbs 14:13
Proverbs 15:13
Proverbs 17:22

TALK OUTLINE

- Laughter is the best medicine. Do we take ourselves too seriously? How can we make more laughter in the home? How can we lighten up our relationships?

TEACHING POINTS/DISCUSSION STARTERS

- A smile is the only facial expression that does not cause tension in the muscles.

- Do people feel better for being with you?

- When people ask how you are, do you respond cheerfully, with a smile, or do you always respond, 'Not bad'?

- How can you become a person who looks on the bright side of life rather than the negative?

ADDITIONAL IDEAS/RESOURCES

- Have a time watching favourite classic comedy video clips together. Just enjoy them and show that Christians can have a good time without a 'crunch' at the end!

45. A Time to Mourn (Ecclesiastes 3:4)

BIBLE REFERENCES

Psalm 30:11
Psalm 34:18
Psalm 147:3
Isaiah 61:2–3
Isaiah 66:13
Jeremiah 31:13
Matthew 5:4
Revelation 21:4

TALK OUTLINE

When is loss experienced?

- When a child goes to school for the first time.

- When a child leaves home.

- When something is stolen.

- When things go wrong financially.

- When independence is taken away because of illness, imprisonment or the birth of a child with a debilitating illness.

- When old age/retirement arrives.

- When redundancy strikes.

TEACHING POINTS/DISCUSSION STARTERS

- What are the emotions we experience with loss? (Anger, bitterness, depression, misery, shock, despair?)

- How do we work our way through these emotions?

- Is what we are experiencing a loss of expectation – of what could have been had this disaster not happened?

- How do we resolve this?

46. A Time to Dance (Ecclesiastes 3:4)

BIBLE REFERENCES

2 Samuel 6:14
Psalm 149:3
Psalm 150:4
Jeremiah 31:4, 13

TALK OUTLINE

- Have a celebration.

- Run a keep-fit class.

- Organize a tap dancing class!

47. A Time to Embrace and a Time to Refrain (Ecclesiastes 3:5)

BIBLE REFERENCES

Genesis 2:18–25
Proverbs 5:15
Proverbs 31:12
Ecclesiastes 9:9
Jeremiah 3:20
Matthew 19:4–6
Mark 10:6–9
1 Corinthians 7:3
Ephesians 5:21–33
Hebrews 13:4

TALK OUTLINE

How can you keep your relationship strong and so resist the temptation of an affair?

● Communicate – learn to be a good listener.

● Make time for each other. Keep romance alive.

● Face up to difficulties together.

● Don't sweep problems and grievances under the carpet. They won't disappear.

● Look for the good things in your relationship and focus on them.

● Encourage your partner. People thrive on praise.

TEACHING POINTS/DISCUSSION STARTERS

- What ideas can you share that will keep your marriage alive and healthy?

- How can you build better understanding into your relationship?

- What one thing can you do for your partner today that will make them really happy?

48. A Time to Keep and a Time to Throw Away (Ecclesiastes 3:6)

BIBLE REFERENCES

Psalm 51:1–15
Psalm 139:23–24
1 Corinthians 13:11

TALK OUTLINE

- A practical talk on time management: make a list of achievable goals; be realistic about what can be accomplished; we can always find time to do what we really want to do.

- Dealing with the past: we can either feel that we are 'victims', or we can face our problems, deal with them and move on!

- Building memories through spending time with our children: children love continuity of special family traditions for birthdays, Easter, Christmas. It gives security.

TEACHING POINTS/DISCUSSION STARTERS

- If you go on living your life the way you are at the moment, will you be proud, at the end of your life, about the way you've lived it?

- What changes could you make to help you get rid of the 'rubbish' and make your life more effective?

- Life is short, so don't waste it!

ADDITIONAL IDEAS/RESOURCES

- Discuss things we sometimes hoard, such as souvenirs, mementoes, letters, etc.

49. A Time to Love and a Time to Hate (Ecclesiastes 3:8)

BIBLE REFERENCES

Proverbs 17:5
Proverbs 22:9
Proverbs 29:7
Proverbs 31:20
Matthew 25:31–46
Luke 10:25–37
Luke 15:11–32
1 Corinthians 12:26

TALK OUTLINE

- Loving at all times (Luke 15:11–32 – parable of the prodigal son): unconditional love for your children and a willingness to forgive.

- Hating injustice (Luke 10:25–37 – parable of the good Samaritan; or Matthew 25:31–46 – the story of the King).

- Whatever you tolerate, you will never change. Sometimes we feel so inadequate and small, and the problems of world suffering seem so enormous. What can we do? God knows we can't change the world, but we can make a world of difference to some.

TEACHING POINTS/DISCUSSION STARTERS

- What sort of injustice and inequality do we see in our own community?

- What can we do about it?

- What can we do to make a difference to the lives of those in the developing countries?

- Mother Teresa was once asked how she could feed all the hungry children who came to her in Calcutta. She replied, 'One at a time.'

- Are you able to sponsor a child? It would be a good opportunity to involve the whole family and educate your own children about the needs of others.

50. A Time for War and a Time for Peace (Ecclesiastes 3:8)

BIBLE REFERENCES

Genesis 13:7–9
Proverbs 17:27
Proverbs 26:17–22
Matthew 5:23–26, 43–48
Matthew 12:25
Matthew 18:15–17
Romans 16:17

TALK OUTLINE

- Resolving conflicts in families, with in-laws, with neighbours, in the workplace.

- Forgiving someone who has wronged us is very hard, but it is the only antidote to anger, bitterness and resentment, all of which are very corrosive.

- Jesus calls us not only to forgive our enemies, but to love them and pray for them.

- Whether between individuals or nations, war is fought at tremendous cost with tragic consequences.

TEACHING POINTS/DISCUSSION STARTERS

- How can we make a start in resolving conflict in our own circumstances?

- What part does pride play in our unwillingness to forgive?

The Fruit of the Spirit

'The fruit of the Spirit is love, joy, peace, patience,
kindness, goodness, faithfulness, gentleness
and self-control.
Against such there is no law.'

(Galatians 5:22–23)

51. Introduction to the Theme

BIBLE REFERENCE

Galatians 5:16–23

TALK OUTLINE

- Explain the conflict between the 'old' and 'new' life.

- The Holy Spirit living in us, when we have given our lives to Christ, enables us to grow and then exhibit the fruit.

- God gives us the choice.

- When he lives in us he helps and enables us to make the right choice.

- It's choosing to allow the Holy Spirit access in our lives, so that he is firmly planted in us to produce the good fruit through us.

TEACHING POINTS/DISCUSSION STARTERS

- Ask the group to make a list comparing wrong desires with right desires:

Evil	Good
destructive	productive
easy to ignite	slow to anger
self-centred	self-giving
oppressive and possessive	liberating and generous

decadent	uplifting
sinful	holy
deadly	eternal life

- Measure these up against 1 Corinthians 13:1–7.

- Which of these qualities would you want the Holy Spirit to produce in you?

ADDITIONAL IDEAS/RESOURCES

- A short testimony from, or interview with, someone who has become a Christian, highlighting the evidence of change in their lives.

- A flipchart or whiteboard could be used to describe the fruit of the Spirit in people's lives.

52. Love

BIBLE REFERENCES

Matthew 5:41
Matthew 6:2
Luke 6:35
John 13:34
Galatians 5:22

TALK OUTLINE

Why is love so important? What is real love?

- Love is not a feeling but a commitment.

- Jesus was the perfect demonstration, when he laid down his life for us.

- Jesus said, 'Love one another as I have loved you' (John 13:34).

- Love is a decision of the will – I can choose to love.

- Love is not selective – anyone qualifies.

- Love does not simply refrain from harming enemies; it does good things for them (Luke 6:35).

- Love does the unexpected – lovely surprises, things to make another person's face light up because of your thoughtfulness.

- Love is a desire for the best for another (selfless, not

jealous of another's success).

- Love means making your wildest dreams come true for someone else.

- Love is not satisfied with everyone else's standard – it goes the second mile (Matthew 5:41).

- Love does not look for recognition, so don't do your good deeds in public (Matthew 6:2).

TEACHING POINTS/DISCUSSION STARTERS

- The most important fruit that Jesus calls us to exhibit is love. If this isn't present, the others won't be either!

- What is love? Explain and discuss the different kinds of love.

Brotherly love: Psalm 133; Romans 13:8–10; 1 Thessalonians 4:9; 1 John 2:10

Romantic/marital love: The Song of Songs; Titus 2:4

Love for enemies: Luke 6:27–36

Agape/God's love: Matthew 22:37–40; John 3:16; 1 Corinthians 13:1–4, 14:1; 1 John 4:16–19

53. Joy

BIBLE REFERENCES

Nehemiah 8:10
Psalm 16:8–9
Habakkuk 3:17–18
Matthew 6:19–21
Philippians 4:4, 12–13
Hebrews 12:2
James 1:2
1 Peter 4:12–13
Revelation 21:4

TALK OUTLINE

- Explain the difference between happiness and joy: happiness is because of something that happens to make you happy; joy is present even when life is a disaster, because it is not dependent on circumstances.

- Joy is a state of heart, mind and soul, dependent on our relationship with Jesus.

TEACHING POINTS/DISCUSSION STARTERS

- We can be rich when we have very little materially, if we have Jesus.

- We can know joy even in the midst of appalling circumstances.

ADDITIONAL IDEAS/RESOURCES

Talk illustrations

~~'A joyless Christian is a contradiction of terms.'~~ (Lloyd Ogilvie)

'Joy is peace dancing.' (Jim Graham)

54. Peace

BIBLE REFERENCES

Psalm 4:8
Psalm 29:11
Psalm 32:7
Psalm 34:14
Psalm 119:165
Isaiah 26:3
Isaiah 43:2
Matthew 5:9

TALK OUTLINE

- Peace, like joy, is not dependent on circumstances.

- It is not the absence of conflict, but the assurance that we belong to God through Jesus, and he knows the end from the beginning.

- When we are going God's way, we have peace, even when life isn't working out the way we expect.

- Peace is the selfless, self-giving, self-losing, self-forgetting, self-sacrificing love of God, standing serene, strong and stable in spite of every insult and trial.

TEACHING POINTS/DISCUSSION STARTERS

- Are you a peacemaker or a fault-finder? Do you lose your

peace when faced with opposition or a tough situation?

- What would you need to change in yourself to restore that peace?

ADDITIONAL IDEAS/RESOURCES

Talk illustration

'Peace is joy resting.' (Jim Graham)

55. Patience

BIBLE REFERENCES

Psalm 40:1
Ecclesiastes 7:8
Isaiah 30:15
Lamentations 3:26
Habakkuk 2:3
Luke 21:19
Romans 2:7
Romans 5:3–5
Romans 8:24–25
1 Corinthians 13:4
James 1:2–3
James 5:7–8
Revelation 3:10

TALK OUTLINE

- We *learn* patience by going through trials.

- Impatience has its roots in our personal agenda: traffic jams; contracts not fulfilled on time, etc.

- God uses life's difficulties to build our character, and problems to develop perseverance.

- We are not obeying God if we want things to go only our way.

- The beginning of patience is surrendering our agenda to

God's will and developing an eternal perspective.

TEACHING POINTS/DISCUSSION STARTERS

- What makes you impatient? What about your partner?

- What qualities do you need in order to develop patience in your life?

- Use some of the Bible verses pertaining to patience to spark off personal anecdotes.

ADDITIONAL IDEAS/RESOURCES

Talk illustration

There is a story of a lady who asked her vicar to pray for patience for her. He prayed, 'Lord, send my sister tribulation.'

'No, no, Vicar,' she exclaimed. 'I didn't say that!'

'But, my dear, tribulation produces patience!' he replied.

56. Kindness

BIBLE REFERENCES

Ruth 2:10–12, 20
Proverbs 11:17
Matthew 7:12
Luke 6:35
Romans 11:22
1 Corinthians 13:4
Ephesians 4:32
Titus 3:4–5
Hebrews 12:5–6
2 Peter 1:7

TALK OUTLINE

- Kindness is the sign of a loving heart.

- Kindness is also having the courage to put wrong things right. For example, it is not kind to overlook wrong behaviour in a child, because of the long-term consequences.

- Kindness is dealing with wrong in the right way (see Hebrews 12:5–6).

TEACHING POINTS/DISCUSSION STARTERS

- Think of a situation in your own life that needs dealing with. Are you afraid to confront it because of the

209

consequences? How can you tackle it with kindness?

- What act of kindness would you like someone to do for you today? Are you prepared to do that for someone else?

57. Goodness

BIBLE REFERENCES

Proverbs 17:13
Lamentations 3:25
Matthew 12:35
Romans 8:28
1 Timothy 5:10

TALK OUTLINE

- Goodness is not merely being good at something.

- Goodness is godliness. It is doing something positive that would exhibit our likeness to God.

- Goodness is often misinterpreted and derided with statements like 'She's a do-gooder' or 'He's a goody-goody', implying that someone is spineless, insipid and weak, or trying to get into someone else's 'good books'.

- Our words advertise our character. Often what we say shows people what is inside us.

TEACHING POINTS/DISCUSSION STARTERS

- The late David Watson said, 'If you are holding a cup and someone nudges it, what spills out? Whatever is in the cup...' So it is with us. We may look fine on the outside until someone nudges us (i.e. irritates us or causes us

211

pain), then whatever we are carrying inside comes tumbling out.

- What would spill out if you were nudged today?

- Are you tolerating something that needs changing?

- What we tolerate, we cannot change. Mother Teresa didn't just love Calcutta's outcasts, she hated the conditions that enslaved them and set out to do something about them. That's goodness!

58. Faithfulness

BIBLE REFERENCES

Psalm 57:10
Proverbs 3:3–4
Proverbs 14:22
Isaiah 38:19
Isaiah 61:8
2 Thessalonians 3:3
Hebrews 3:14
Revelation 2:10

TALK OUTLINE

- Faithfulness is a foundational quality that God expects from his people.

- We feel secure with a friend/partner or family member who is faithful to us.

- Our relationship with God is based on his faithfulness to us, not vice versa.

- Jesus prayed for us 2,000 years ago (John 17:9–23) that we would remain faithful and obedient.

- God has not called us to be successful, but faithful.

TEACHING POINTS/DISCUSSION STARTERS

- 'You can count on me.' 'I will never let you down.' When

have people made a statement like that to you? Did they keep their promise?

- What is your promise to your partner? To stick by them? To build them up? To encourage them and believe in them all your days?

- What were your marriage vows? Have you managed to keep all of them?

- Sometimes faithfulness means sticking by people even when they let us down.

59. Gentleness

BIBLE REFERENCES

1 Kings 19:12
Proverbs 15:1
Proverbs 25:15
Zechariah 9:9
Matthew 21:5
1 Corinthians 4:21
2 Corinthians 10:1
Philippians 4:5
Colossians 3:12–13
1 Thessalonians 2:7
1 Timothy 6:11
James 3:17
1 Peter 3:15

TALK OUTLINE

- Violence is the way of the world and gentleness is the antithesis of violence.

- There is peace in the heart of a gentle person and a calmness that has a knock-on effect for those around.

- Jesus was gentle but not weak. Meekness is not weakness.

TEACHING POINTS/DISCUSSION STARTERS

- As a mother, do you exhibit gentleness?

- Discuss types of discipline and when it is right to use it.

60. Self-control

BIBLE REFERENCES

Proverbs 16:32
Proverbs 25:28
Romans 12:1
1 Corinthians 10:13
James 1:13–14
2 Peter 1:6

TALK OUTLINE

- Self-control means disciplining ourselves to become godly people – not by other people's standards but by God's!

- Lack of self-control affects us personally.

- Our bodies are temples of the Holy Spirit (1 Corinthians 6:19). We owe it to him to take care of them.

In what ways can lack of self-control affect us individually?

- Eating too much or too little.

- Drinking too much alcohol.

- Smoking.

- Drug abuse.

- Laziness (lack of exercise).

- Gratuitous sex.

In what ways can lack of self-control affect others?

- Anger.
- Slander.
- Gossip.
- Criticism.
- Tearing down the fragile self-esteem of a child.
- Untidiness.
- Laziness (leaving responsibility to others).
- Abusing other people's belongings.

TEACHING POINTS/DISCUSSION STARTERS

- Self-control is almost impossible to achieve on our own, and it demands an incredible amount of will power. But when our lives are under the control of the Holy Spirit, we begin to know the amazing power of God to become what he wants us to be.

- 'We take captive every thought to make it obedient to Christ' (2 Corinthians 10:5). Is that true in your life?

- Do you see areas of weakness that, with the help of the Holy Spirit, you could change?

ADDITIONAL IDEAS/RESOURCES

- 'WWJD?' ('What would Jesus do?') is a saying that has become popular with young people, appearing on jewellery, T-shirts and many other products. Discuss situations where you would ask yourself this question.

Stress

'Give all your worries and cares to God, for he cares
about what happens to you.'

(1 Peter 5:7 NLT)

61. The Stress of Modern Living

BIBLE REFERENCES

Psalm 55:22
Psalm 86:7
Isaiah 41:10
1 Peter 5:7

TALK OUTLINE

What makes life stressful today?

- Its frantic pace.

- Travel (we expect to travel further, faster).

- Standards and expectations: we compare ourselves with others.

- Pressure to acquire what others have: keeping up with the Joneses.

- Pressure of the media through advertising: fashion, food, style, size.

- Time pressure: so many things to do and so little time.

- So many choices: shopping; extra-curricular opportunities for children; leisure activities.

TEACHING POINTS/DISCUSSION STARTERS

- We need goals that are achievable and realistic. Many mothers are perfectionists. They work constantly to keep up with all their goals, and tiredness adds to the stress, which can then become depression.

- Make a list of all the pressure on your time each week. Next to each item, estimate the hours per week each task takes.

- Set priorities in terms of importance. Discover through this what you should be doing and what could be left out in order to make life more tolerable for you and those around you.

- If you're too busy to do everything you've planned to do, you're busier than God wants you to be!

62. The Stress of Marriage

BIBLE REFERENCES

Genesis 2:18–25
Proverbs 5:18
Matthew 19:4–6
Mark 10:6–9
Hebrews 13:4

TALK OUTLINE

- It has been said that it is only the fact that couples are so in love that enables them to survive all the changes and adjustments that take place in the first year of marriage. It takes patience and tolerance to allow the dust to settle.

- Stress can be caused through pressure of work, long hours and therefore exhaustion. There is little time for communication and conversation. A series of small issues not dealt with can be a cause of stress/strain in the relationship.

- If a row eventually ensues, all the other issues that have not previously been dealt with will come pouring out. They may have little to do with the reasons for the row. Therefore we need to keep short accounts, i.e. settle each problem as it happens.

- Sexual problems not dealt with can cause tension, stress and misunderstandings. There may be different expectations of each other and unmet needs.

TEACHING POINTS/DISCUSSION STARTERS

- Discuss the main causes of stress in your marriage. What ways can you think of to alleviate the stress?

- How can you learn to focus on and appreciate things about your partner that will build up and strengthen your relationship?

(See also Talk 29: Stress in Marriage.)

63. Stress as a Parent

BIBLE REFERENCES

Proverbs 3:11–12
Luke 15:17–24
Ephesians 6:1–3
2 Timothy 3:14–15
Hebrews 12:5–11

TALK OUTLINE

- Many mothers are perfectionists. They want to be perfect wives, mothers and hostesses, and have perfect children!

- They end up feeling like failures because they never match up to their own expectations of what they ought to be or what they think other people expect them to be. This causes endless stress and tension in a family.

- A mother is the pivotal point of the home. If a mother is stressed, it's not long before the family catches the stress.

- Mothers who work outside the home also have the stress of holding the two in balance and being successful in both areas.

The following disruptions of routine can cause stress

- A child getting sick.
- An unexpected guest arriving.

- A family member dying.

- The car breaking down.

- The telephone ringing endlessly.

- Mother-in-law moving in.

TEACHING POINTS/DISCUSSION STARTERS

- As a mother it is easy to look at all that needs to be done in the week and feel completely overwhelmed. It's important to make attainable daily/weekly goals. Making lists for daily chores, and weekly, monthly and annual events/appointments, can help to unravel the problems of stress. Remember that you can only do one thing at a time!

- Ask for suggestions that will help to reduce stress, such as ways to organize your life and not take on too much, as well as how to say 'no' without feeling guilty.

- How can we learn to be grateful for what we have, rather than complain about what we don't have?

- In the same way, how can we learn to be pleased and proud of what we have achieved, rather than being stressed out and guilty about what still needs doing?

64. Stress in Children

BIBLE REFERENCES

Ephesians 6:4
Colossians 3:21

TALK OUTLINE

Is stress a problem in children?

- Stress today is adversely affecting children as much as adults: the innocent, relaxed days of childhood are being eroded.

- More people than ever are being employed to help stressed children.

Symptoms of too much stress include

- Loss of self-confidence.

- Disinterest.

- Poor memory, poor concentration and not finishing tasks.

- Irritability, anger and moodiness.

- Physical hyperactivity.

- Indecisiveness.

- Unhappiness and a negative outlook.

- Withdrawal.

- Poor academic performance.

- Reversion to earlier habits (bed-wetting, thumb-sucking, tantrums).

What are the main sources of stress for children?

- Death of a parent or close family member.

- Problems at school.

- Difficulties in making friends.

- Fear of the unfamiliar.

- Parents who are overprotective, too critical, demanding, unfaithful to their promises, not available for their children.

Other challenges are more prevalent in modern society

- Family breakdown or marital strain is a huge source of emotional stress that robs children of stability.

- Unemployment in parents results in extra stress at home.

- Poor nutrition: a diet high in sugar, salt, caffeine, fats and additives attacks healthy development of body and brain.

- Child abuse and violence destroy children's trust in adults: children are more aware of this through the media.

- Increase in freedom: children are given more responsibility and are left alone at home while parents work, which increases isolation.

- Economic pressures: facing the prospect of parents' inability to meet material expectations produces stress.

- Our children face a world of greater uncertainty.

How can you help your children to limit or cope with stress?

- First realize that you can't remove or protect children from all stress, nor would it be helpful or realistic to do so.

- Help children to develop an effective strategy to cope with stress, by teaching them to respond to or cope with stressful situations.

- Take your children's concerns seriously (fear of the dark, maths test, etc.) and don't trivialize them. Teaching them to respond in small situations will help them to face larger challenges.

- Communication is vital: talking about concerns and being a good listener; praising positive reactions. Talking through problems itself relieves stress, and understanding the source of stress goes a long way towards controlling the symptoms.

- Boost children's self-image by giving them time, love and attention: a child who likes himself and knows he's valued handles stress more effectively.

- Take care of the health of the child (diet, exercise, sleep), as many stressful situations unique to children are most effectively relieved by physical activity.

- Give children realistic expectations: help to motivate them, but also teach them to accept their limitations and know what can and can't be changed.

- Help children cope with failure by accepting it and not thinking of it as the end.

- Help children develop self-discipline by providing structure and the stability of a disciplined environment.

- Strengthen family bonds to provide a base of security; ensure children are surrounded by adults they can rely on.

- Try to resolve your own problems – a child's problems will often disappear as a result!

- Keep children's commitments and activities within limits,

and review them regularly.

- The pursuit of a hobby/pastime often provides pleasure which diminishes stress (music, chess, reading, walking, sports).

- Be watchful for early signs of stress building up.

TEACHING POINTS/DISCUSSION STARTERS

- Encourage parents to know their child well enough to be able to spot the signs of stress early on, and to provide a loving and supportive home and thus the necessary stability to face potentially stressful situations.

- Ask parents which situations have caused their children the greatest stress, and exchange ideas as to how to help children in those circumstances.

- Divide into small discussion groups and share sources of stress for parents and how these can be dealt with effectively.

(See also Talk 19: Stress.)

65. Stress in the Wider Family

BIBLE REFERENCES

Deuteronomy 12:7
Joshua 24:15
Proverbs 31:27
1 Timothy 5:8
1 Peter 3:8

TALK OUTLINE

- The larger the household, the more the stress level rises because of power struggles within the family, often over who is right, who should be obeyed, and who lays the ground rules.

- Children play one adult off against another. It takes great skill and patience to manage a large household successfully.

- It is a well-known fact that Christmas is a very stressful event in terms of coping with the wider family.

- This can be true of many family events. Going on holiday with a large group can also be stressful. The more people there are, the more difficult it becomes to satisfy all needs and expectations.

What are the main reasons for stress across the generations?

- Jealousy.

- Strife.

- Low self-esteem.

- Trying to please everyone.

- Different goals and expectations.

- Unresolved anger.

- Pressure to conform.

- Over-dependence.

TEACHING POINTS/DISCUSSION STARTERS

- We need to recognize that we are all imperfect and we come into relationships with agendas and baggage from the past.

- We can give thanks to God for the people we find difficult, believing he is in control of all our circumstances.

- How can we, in practice, allow God's love to flow through us to the people in our families who make life difficult for us?

- How can we cultivate a desire for the best for those around us?

66. Stress in the Workplace

BIBLE REFERENCES

Psalm 39:6–7
Psalm 145:14
Proverbs 12:24
Proverbs 16:3
Jeremiah 29:11–14
Mark 4:19
Mark 6:31
2 Thessalonians 3:10–11

TALK OUTLINE

- A survey has found that two-thirds of the workforce are under stress. Work is good and important. It is the way we approach work that determines our stress level.

Pressure at work can be caused by a variety of situations

- Being forced to work long hours by the threat of other people ready to take your place if you don't comply.

- Being responsible for unrealistic goals.

- The fear of redundancy.

- Performance-related pay.

- An increased feeling of anonymity (a number rather than a valued person).

- A feeling of being disposable.

- Instability in the workplace (no job is secure or for life these days).

- The stress of getting to work (overcrowded and unreliable trains or buses, traffic jams).

- Aggravation and tension build-up, without the opportunity of releasing tension.

- The need to get things done faster and better than our competitors.

- Constant choices and instant decisions.

- Constant upgrading of technology.

- Confusion of direction, causing insecurity and undercurrents of discontent.

- Moral frameworks being undermined.

- Family frameworks being undermined.

- The boss and bad management, or bullying.

TEACHING POINTS/DISCUSSION STARTERS

- Brains need to rest just as bodies need rest.

- Suggest some ways in which stress can be released.

- Three questions are the basis of most stress: Who am I? Where am I going? Am I loved and loveable?

67. Financial Stress

BIBLE REFERENCES

Proverbs 11:28
Isaiah 55:2
Matthew 6:24
Matthew 22:17–22
Luke 8:3
1 Timothy 6:6–10

TALK OUTLINE

- Many of our life goals require money: travel; education; marriage; family; retirement; even helping others. How do we define the difference between what we need and what we want?

- It is a fact that many homes are empty five days a week, and weekends are spent cleaning, painting, repairing, washing and gardening. We rarely have time to enjoy the home we are working so hard to keep.

- Sometimes we spend because we are depressed, and having a credit card gives us a false sense of purchasing power.

- If we overspend, we pile up debts that consume our energy, health and even our sanity.

- Demands are put on us by society and the media to have the latest TVs, video recorders, computer games, cameras, designer clothes, new cars. These all add to the stress of modern living. How do we resist such pressures and still retain our 'street cred'?

TEACHING POINTS/DISCUSSION STARTERS

- Christians are taught to put their trust in God not money to provide security. Explain the benefits of this in regard to Philippians 4:11–13.

- Discuss how we can take control of our lives through taking control of our finances.

- How much of our financial stress is caused through our children demanding to have what the neighbours' children have?

- How can we use our income to enhance our lives and reduce stress?

- If your husband is the only 'earner' in the household, how can you support him and reduce his stress level by being more careful how you spend the money he earns?

68. The Stress of Loneliness

BIBLE REFERENCES

2 Samuel 22:7
Psalm 27:10
Psalm 62:2
Psalm 68:4–6
Isaiah 41:10
Matthew 28:20
John 16:32

TALK OUTLINE

- Loneliness is a common sickness in today's world.

- You do not have to be alone to be lonely.

- Many people living in urban areas are acutely lonely.

- The results of loneliness can be a turning inwards and dwelling on problems in an unhealthy way.

- Isolation can turn to self-pity and depression.

- A person with a social conscience who stands up against injustice can feel very lonely when they stand alone.

- Change of job or home and getting divorced or separated can trigger a breakdown of the immune system, psychiatric problems, alcoholism and depression.

TEACHING POINTS/DISCUSSION STARTERS

- How can we combat loneliness or help those who are lonely?

- A lonely young woman asked a counsellor how she could find a friend. The counsellor asked her to name the qualities she would like in a friend. When she had made her list, the counsellor told her to go and be that person to someone else. Consider this story and discuss how it can be implemented in your own life and circumstances.

- How do we recognize the symptoms of loneliness? What can we do to help?

(See also Talk 93: The Lonely.)

69. Stress Through Fears and Phobias

BIBLE REFERENCES

Psalm 4:8
Psalm 32:7
Psalm 46:1–2
Psalm 91:11
John 14:27

TALK OUTLINE

What do we mean by phobias?

- Terror of apparently harmless situations; fear, aversion or hatred that is irrational.

- Phobias are related to events and experiences that would not normally provoke such reactions. They produce symptoms such as sweating, a dry mouth, weak legs and palpitations, and they seem to have no logic or reason. Sufferers' reactions are out of control – they can't just 'snap out of it'!

What sort of phobias exist?

- Mild phobias, where the sufferer overreacts when they encounter the cause (for example, spiders, birds, small animals, snakes). Avoidance is the easy answer.

- Disabling phobias, such as fear of cancer. Sometimes these are a symptom of some underlying emotional illness, in which case a GP would normally make a referral to a psychiatrist. Phobias with underlying emotional illness include claustrophobia and agoraphobia.

What can the sufferer do about phobias?

- It is important for the sufferer to know they are not alone.

- It is vital to know when to seek help: that is, if the problem is too difficult to manage; if life is being disrupted by the symptoms; if others are encouraging them to seek help.

- It is helpful to openly admit to the fear and then face it.

How can you help yourself or others to deal with a phobia?

- Talk about it and laugh about it!

- Face it with a friend alongside you.

- Read about the cause.

- Increase exposure and keep a record of progress.

- Eventually tackle the situation alone.

- Help someone else in a similar situation.

TEACHING POINTS/DISCUSSION STARTERS

- Ask parents to talk about their fears and phobias and suggest possible ways to overcome them.

- Ask parents about their children's phobias. Where did the children learn these fears? How can they 'unlearn' them?

70. Stress Through Grief

BIBLE REFERENCES

Deuteronomy 33:27
Psalm 34:18
Psalm 147:3
John 11:30–36
2 Corinthians 1:3–7

TALK OUTLINE

- Grieving is an exhausting process.

- The death of a spouse causes greater stress than all other domestic issues. The death of a close family member is also high on the list.

- One of the reasons for such stress is that there are so many things to organize immediately after a death: funeral arrangements; sorting out the will; financial arrangements.

- All of these things have to be done by the partner who is left after possibly many years of shared responsibility.

- The fear of being alone in the house as an elderly widow also causes stress and anxiety.

TEACHING POINTS/DISCUSSION STARTERS

- People going through stages of grief need affirmation, not advice.

- Those who are grieving need hope. Discuss ways in which you could share hope with a person who has never heard about Jesus.

- ~~Discuss your own experiences of grief and ways in which~~ stress can be relieved.

- What was most helpful and unhelpful to you?

Looking Back

'What has been will be again, what has been done will
be done again; there is nothing new under the sun.'

(Ecclesiastes 1:9)

Looking Back

The following talks should really be based on personal testimonies. Choose people who have the wisdom of experience and a sense of humour and can tell amusing anecdotes about past memories.

BIBLE REFERENCE

Titus 2:3–5

'[The older women] can train the younger women to love their husbands and children, to be self-controlled and pure, to be busy at home, to be kind, and to be subject to their husbands, so that no-one will malign the word of God.' (Titus 2:4)

71. Becoming a Mother-in-law

BIBLE REFERENCES

Ruth
James 1:5

TALK OUTLINE

How to let go and allow the new couple to become 'one'

- Be sensitive – accept that your child has as many faults as your son or daughter-in-law.

- Be positive about the addition to your family: e.g. experiences, lifestyles and personality.

- Be helpful – striking the balance between being supportive and interfering.

- Learn to bite your tongue sometimes and say nothing!

- Learn to cope with the pain of watching when relationships struggle or collapse.

- Learn to remain impartial when accusations are made against your son or daughter.

- Learn to shift your own time from parenting to developing your own interests.

ADDITIONAL IDEAS/RESOURCES

Talk illustration

● 'A son's a son till he takes a wife. But a daughter's a daughter for all of her life.'

72. Becoming a Grandparent

BIBLE REFERENCES

Psalm 37:25
Proverbs 17:6

TALK OUTLINE

- Grandparents are in a special position to have freedom to enjoy their grandchildren with the benefit of experience and without ultimate responsibility.

- Grandparents can give love, time, encouragement and confidentiality, to build up a unique relationship they didn't have time to build with their own children.

- Grandparents should be careful about giving advice! Life is very different now from when they were parents.

- Grandparents should be careful not to think their way was the best and should not be offended when their valuable insights are disregarded!

- Grandparents are allowed to do some of the things parents would not approve of!

ADDITIONAL IDEAS/RESOURCES

Talk illustration

- 'If I'd known how wonderful grandchildren would be, I'd have had them first!'

73. The Wisdom of Experience

BIBLE REFERENCES

Proverbs 3:13
Proverbs 4:7

TALK OUTLINE

- Invite an older woman to talk about her marriage – its ups and downs and the reasons for its success.

- Thirty years ago young couples did without what they couldn't have – credit was not readily available. They consolidated their relationships through the hardships and the pride and achievement of gradually building up their creature comforts.

- Today, expectations of young people are possibly too high. Before getting married they want everything in place.

TEACHING POINTS/DISCUSSION STARTERS

- Outline/discuss positive input to marriage that has worked: time, love, attention, romance.

- Outline/discuss negative input that has caused damage: criticism, lack of time together, excessive focus on the children.

- Describe testing times for relationships: children all pre-school age, teenagers, children leaving home.

74. A Mother Looks Back

BIBLE REFERENCES

Proverbs 31:28–31
Proverbs 29:15

TALK OUTLINE

- Invite a mother who has raised her children to adulthood and is still standing! She will be equipped to give sound and godly advice to young mothers.

Outline the main changes between previous generations and our modern culture, highlighting the following points

- Motherhood is often downgraded now instead of valued.

- The rise in the number of working mothers.

- The changing emphasis on education.

- The growth and change in children's leisure activities.

- The rise in materialism.

- The increase in labour-saving devices, and the lack of time available now!

- Changes in practicalities (feeding, nappies, etc).

Look back at the highs and lows of different stages of motherhood including

- Babies.

- Toddlers.
- Early years at school.
- Teenage years and exams.
- Leaving home, but remaining 'friends'.

TEACHING POINTS/DISCUSSION STARTERS

- Read Titus 2:4–7
- In many cultures the Matriarchs of the family are revered as having the wisdom of years and experience. However, in Western culture the older women are often sidelined as old-fashioned and irrelevant.
- Explain the dilemma and ask older mothers to share from their own experiences (both good and bad!).

ADDITIONAL IDEAS/RESOURCES

Reading

- *The Sixty-Minute Mother* by Rob Parsons (Hodder, 2000).

75. A Father Looks Back

BIBLE REFERENCES

Proverbs 10:1
Proverbs 13:1
Proverbs 15:20
Proverbs 23:22–24

TALK OUTLINE

- Invite along a father who has seen and grasped the importance of spending time with his children and has reaped the rewards.

- A man's perspective as being the breadwinner has changed with the ensuing feminist society.

- Many hard lessons are learned through being an absent father, working away from home or with long hours.

TEACHING POINTS/DISCUSSION STARTERS

- What lessons for eternity can be learned through successful parenting?

- What changes in attitude have occurred between children to fathers and fathers to children compared with Victorian times.

- How was a father able to be a good role model a hundred years ago, compared with that of today?

76. Childhood Memories

BIBLE REFERENCES

Matthew 18:2–6
Mark 10:16
1 Corinthians 13:11

TALK OUTLINE

- Invite someone to talk (in a positive and helpful way!) about the differences between their own childhood and the way children experience life today.

- Compared material possessions (toys, games, etc.), family relationships, school life, leisure time, holidays and travel.

TEACHING POINTS/DISCUSSION STARTERS

- A week ahead get the parents to prepare to share one childhood memory each that has had a profound effect on the rest of their lives, for good or bad.

- Discuss what lessons can be learned from the way parents coped with each situation shared.

77. Seize the Moment

BIBLE REFERENCES

Psalm 31:15
Psalm 90:10–12
Psalm 139:16
Proverbs 27:1
James 4:13–17

TALK OUTLINE

- Ask someone to speak about an opportunity taken, and 'having no regrets'.

- If you knew you had only a week to live, what would you do with your time?

- Measure that up with your normal life and busyness at the moment and see what you would or could change.

- What is on your 'to do' list next week?

- What will have lasting significance?

- What can you remove from it to make life better for you, your children and your husband?

- What can you put on it that will be an investment for their future?

78. There's Nothing New Under the Sun

BIBLE REFERENCE

Ecclesiastes 1:9

TALK OUTLINE

- Invite someone to talk about history repeating itself.

- Modern technology is advancing at an unprecedented rate, but the basics of life itself continue from generation to generation: for example, physical needs, emotional needs, the need to work.

- People often fail to learn the lessons of history, but need to learn from personal experience: for example, materialism versus contentment, war versus peace.

TEACHING POINTS/DISCUSSION STARTERS

Highlight and discuss continuity in various aspects of life

- Family structure, joys and concerns.

- Children and family pressures.

- Violence and the growth in media coverage.

- The role of work and pressures involved.

- World events and world resources: inequality of distribution, limited resources.

79. When I Was at School

BIBLE REFERENCES

Deuteronomy 4:9
Psalm 78:5–8
Proverbs 23:23
Titus 2:1–3

TALK OUTLINE

- Ask a teacher to talk about the education system today compared with past decades.

Compare the past with the present in the following areas

- The structure of the school day.

- Changes in pupil/teacher relationships.

- School building and facilities.

- School lunches versus packed lunches.

- Changes in methods of teaching.

- Lesson content (the 3 R's versus the National Curriculum).

- Testing, examinations and league tables.

- The school age and development of higher education.

- Journey to and from school for children.

- Extra-curricular activities (sport, art and music).

80. Lest We Forget

BIBLE REFERENCES

Psalm 27:3
Psalm 46:9

TALK OUTLINE

- Ask a grandfather or grandmother to talk about their wartime experiences, and how they coped.

- There will always be war while there is one new generation growing up without experiencing its horrors.

- Imagine the emotions of a young man going off to war – someone's father, son or husband: the sacrifice, the fears, the futility, the loss, the hope.

TEACHING POINTS/DISCUSSION STARTERS

- Discuss why it is so important to remind young people of the sacrifices that were made: valuing life and peace; abundance as opposed to rationing, loss and deprivation.

Topical Subjects for Women

'A woman who fears the Lord is to be praised.'

(Proverbs 31:30)

81. Self-Esteem

BIBLE REFERENCES

Psalm 139
Psalm 8:3–8
Jeremiah 1:5
Matthew 10:29–31
Romans 12:3
1 Corinthians 6:19–20

TALK OUTLINE

- To think of ourselves more highly than we ought is pride and arrogance.

- To think too little of ourselves is false humility.

- In between arrogance and false humility is an honest appraisal of our own worth. That is self-esteem.

- God values us highly because he loves us deeply.

Lack of self-esteem in young mothers

- Young mothers often find that their self-esteem is at rock bottom.

- They may have given up a lucrative career when they married and started a family.

- They may have moved from their home environment to where their husband's job is.

- They may have no friends and little time to cultivate friendships.

- The worst part is that if they sacrifice their career to be a full-time mother, society demeans and degrades them.

- Young mothers need to be encouraged that motherhood is the most important job they will ever do.

- They should stand firm when people say, 'Are you just a housewife?', or, 'Don't you have a job?'

- Encourage mothers to know how much God loves and values them.

TEACHING POINTS/DISCUSSION STARTERS

- Low self-esteem is one of the psychological diseases of our modern culture. The media flaunt youth, beauty and material success so we are constantly bombarded with images of people we see as better than ourselves. We compare ourselves with the perfect body, job or intelligence of another and feel inadequate.

- How can you build up your self-esteem? Count the number of different jobs you do in one day and think about how versatile and multi-skilled you are.

ADDITIONAL IDEAS/RESOURCES

Talk illustration
You are very special
'In all the world there is nobody, nobody like you. Since the beginning of time there has never been another person like you. Nobody has your smile, your eyes, your hands, your hair. Nobody owns your handwriting, your voice. You're special. Nobody can paint your brushstrokes....

'You're special. You're different from any other person who has ever lived in the history of the universe. You are the only one in the whole creation who has your particular set of abilities. There is always someone who is better at one thing or another. Every person is your superior in at least one way... Like a room full of musical instruments some might excel in one way or another but nobody can match the symphonic sound when all are played together. Your symphony.

'...You're special and it is no accident you are. Please realize that God made you for a special purpose. He has a job for you to do that nobody else can do as well as you can. Out of the billions of applicants only one is qualified. Only one has the unique and right combination of what it takes, and that one is you.'

Author unknown

82. Juggling Family and Work

BIBLE REFERENCES

Joshua 24:15
Psalm 127
Mark 10:31
Luke 10:40–42

TALK OUTLINE

- Mothers who work can never have it all. To have a career and a family means that each will suffer at the expense of the other. There cannot be a perfect situation.

- A mother may have a high-powered job, but within a week of her leaving she will have been forgotten, whereas parenting has its influence long after the parents are gone.

TEACHING POINTS/DISCUSSION STARTERS

- What would make you want to go back to work while your children are still young?

- What are the good/bad points of this dual role?

ADDITIONAL IDEAS/RESOURCES

- Interview a working mother or single father to talk about the difficulties as well as the perks of their dual role.

83. The Role of a Wife

BIBLE REFERENCES

Genesis 2:24
Proverbs 31:10–31
Ephesians 5:21–22

TALK OUTLINE

- The Bible has a lot of down-to-earth, common-sense things to say about marriage which, when put into practice, work.

- Proverbs 31:10 credits the good wife with great intelligence and a capacity for excellence, not with a retiring and subservient manner. Her attractiveness comes from her character, not her looks.

- Like most situations in life, a successful marriage is based on praise, encouragement, affirmation, trust and communication.

- The opposite is true when partners constantly criticize one another, always focusing on the negative rather than the positive.

- In the turmoil of raising children, it is difficult to keep communication lines open.

- Marriage has to be worked at daily. Spend time working at it together.

(See section The Many Roles of Mum.)

84. The Role of a Mother

BIBLE REFERENCES

Psalm 113:9
Proverbs 1:8–9
Proverbs 29:15
Proverbs 30:17
Isaiah 49:15
Isaiah 66:13
1 Thessalonians 2:7

TALK OUTLINE

- For better or worse our mothers and fathers influence our lives more than any other factor. It is much easier to become a parent than to *be* one!

- Children are all different and therefore need different applications of discipline, love and time.

- The role of a mother is varied – nurse, psychologist, academic genius, peacemaker, disciplinarian, taxi driver, cook and most of all role model.

- We remember the way our own mothers disciplined, encouraged and criticized us, and very often we find ourselves repeating the process. This proves the influence our mothers have on our lives.

- The way we discipline our children gives them a moral reference point for the future.

- Praise and encouragement are essential tools for healthy discipline.

- We will never be perfect mothers, so we have to be willing to say 'sorry'.

TEACHING POINTS/DISCUSSION STARTERS

- How do we balance all the roles and still maintain our sanity?

- Do we have unrealistic expectations of what we can achieve in a day?

- Does anyone have any tips for remaining stress free in the midst of chaos?

85. Making Time for Yourself

BIBLE REFERENCES

Genesis 2:1–3
Psalm 23:1–3
Psalm 55:6
Psalm 116:7
Psalm 127:2
Matthew 11:28–30

TALK OUTLINE

- Being a mother is a 24-hour-a-day commitment. You are never off duty while there is a child in the house.

- Because we live in an age of speed and busyness, we often take pride in the amount we achieve each day and neglect to make time for ourselves.

- A mother tends to feel guilty if she relaxes.

- God did not intend us to live in a perpetual state of hurry. He encourages us to draw aside and rest (Psalm 127:2).

- We can always make time for something we really want to do.

- It is good for children to know when it is Mother's time for a break. They can play, but mustn't bother her. She can then relax with a book or magazine with her child. Sounds far-fetched? It is a discipline that a child can learn!

TEACHING POINTS/DISCUSSION STARTERS

- How can a busy mother give herself time off? Pool suggestions.

- Suggest that about four mothers who know and trust each other get together one morning a week, with one mum looking after all the children while the others get their hair done or do the shopping undistracted.

- Perhaps one of the dads could cope with the children for a couple of hours on a Saturday morning for a similar escape.

- Are there keep-fit classes in the area where a crèche is provided?

86. Divorce

BIBLE REFERENCES

2 Samuel 12:1–23
Matthew 5:32
Matthew 19:3–9
Mark 10:2
1 Corinthians 7:11–13, 27

TALK OUTLINE

- At the heart of divorce is the deterioration of something that we expected would fulfil our hopes, dreams and desires.

- If a marriage is beyond repair and divorce has taken place, putting the past behind and making a new start is of paramount importance.

- Going into a new relationship and dragging baggage from the past with us is starting from a position of weakness. Getting rid of the baggage can be achieved most effectively by dumping it at the foot of the cross. Jesus died for all the sin, the mistakes and the mess in our lives, forgives us and gives us a new start.

- If your marriage is in a mess but not irretrievable, then think about seeking counselling and trying to start afresh.

- Children are always affected in an adverse way by arguments, fights, separation and divorce. It causes great insecurity.

What are the ten most common reasons for divorce?

- Growing apart.
- Not feeling loved and appreciated.
- Sexual intimacy problems.
- Serious differences in values and lifestyle.
- Unwillingness to meet each other's needs.
- Feeling put down or belittled by spouse.
- Emotional problems.
- Conflict over handling money.
- Frequent fighting and an unwillingness to forgive.
- Conflict of roles (who does what).

TEACHING POINTS/DISCUSSION STARTERS

- Being single again after divorce often results in acute loneliness and isolation. Discuss this and see how it can be resolved.
- Mothers need to show their children they are strong enough to care for them alone in order to bring back a semblance of security. How can they do this?

ADDITIONAL IDEAS/RESOURCES

Reading

- *The Secret of Loving* by Josh McDowell (Here's Life Publishers, 1985).
- *The Better Marriage Guide* by Michael Lawson (Hodder & Stoughton, 1998).
- *Love Must Be Tough* by Dr James Dobson (Kingsway, 1984).

Further suggestions

- A talk from someone who has been able to make a new start in their life would be particularly effective.

- This is such an enormous topic it cannot be explored in depth in one talk. Books and videos from Care for the Family (phone 02920 811733) are very helpful.

87. Widowhood

BIBLE REFERENCES

Psalm 68:5
Psalm 146:9
Isaiah 1:17
Isaiah 66:13
James 1:27
Revelation 21:4

TALK OUTLINE

- Statistically, the death of a spouse is the most stressful experience we will ever go through, with divorce close behind.

- The shock and trauma of this kind of bereavement cause exhaustion.

- People experiencing bereavement are often unaware that it is natural to feel exhausted, and need to be reassured that it is normal.

- Suddenly a woman is on her own, to cope perhaps with young children and all the pressures of the family, the bills, and things that go wrong in the house.

- A woman may be facing situations never discussed during the marriage, such as finances and the will, and there is anger and exasperation that the husband is no longer there to give advice and support.

- Facing the end of the day and closing the front door with no one to share events of the day with can be very bleak.

- Loss of expectation is an enormous factor in this situation: seeing the children grow up together, retirement and shared activities you may have been looking forward to – these will all now be unrealized expectations.

- Practical support is vital for the first two years.

- It is not just anniversaries that are difficult to cope with but unexpected things that trip a person up, such as a song on the radio, or talk of a place which evokes happy memories of times before the death.

- At some point people are able to move on, but it's different for each person. There is no blueprint. Moving on could simply mean being able to turn out the cupboards and drawers of things belonging to the partner who has died.

Practical ways to help

- Regular visits or phone calls; interest in the children, especially from a male figure; affirm it's all right to cry!

- Be there for them. Never mind words – hugs and a listening ear are far more important.

- Encourage the bereaved person to get out into the world as soon as possible. The longer they leave it, the more difficult it becomes. A person might never get over their sorrow, but they can get through it with help from caring friends.

TEACHING POINTS/DISCUSSION STARTERS

- How can we be made aware of the needs of a bereaved person and be sensitive?

(See also Talk 70: Stress Through Grief.)

88. Pressures of Society

BIBLE REFERENCES

Psalm 119:32
Psalm 146:7
John 8:32–36
Romans 12:2–6
Galatians 5:1
Philippians 3:12

TALK OUTLINE

- Society sets standards and we often fail to match up to them.

- We push our children to achieve in order to be approved by society, and if they don't match up they feel like failures. What a start to life!

- When we get married we think we will become a perfect wife, perfect homemaker and perfect mother. Problems arise when we realize we cannot manage it! There never was a perfect mother, wife or homemaker. So we live with a sense of failure and guilt.

- It is more important to be a happy, loving wife than to have the perfect figure you see on the front of glossy magazines. It is better to create a happy atmosphere in the home where your children's friends will love to play than to have an immaculate house.

- Your husband struggles for success in the workplace, for affirmation and approval from the boss, knowing that there are others ready to take over if he fails. This pressure can cause stress, depression, breakdown and ulcers. The long hours he has to work have a detrimental effect on the family.

- When our lives belong to Jesus, he sets us free to be what he wants us to be, not what society says we should be. The peace that brings is amazing.

TEACHING POINTS/DISCUSSION STARTERS

- What are your life's goals?

- What would you do differently if you knew this day was your last on earth?

- What, in the light of the last question, is most important to you?

89. Creating a Welcoming Home

BIBLE REFERENCES

Isaiah 58:7
Matthew 25:35–36
Hebrews 13:2
1 Peter 4:9
3 John 1:5
Revelation 3:20

TALK OUTLINE

- Hospitality is keeping a loving welcome in your home at all times and a generous heart towards the needy.

- It is far more than having your husband's boss to dinner. It is an attitude of heart.

- Many of us feel that we're not very good at entertaining, that our cooking is not 'cordon bleu' and that people want to be impressed! But it is not elaborate food that is at the core of hospitality. It is the warmth of the welcome and the relaxed, comfortable environment.

TEACHING POINTS/DISCUSSION STARTERS

- It is important that you make your home welcoming for children/teenagers, so that your children always feel confident that their friends will be warmly accepted. Always be willing to provide cakes, biscuits and coffee at any time they might drop in! The mess they make is nothing compared with knowing where your children are and who their friends are!

• Discuss ideas on entertaining children/teenagers and how to always be prepared for the unexpected guest.

ADDITIONAL IDEAS/RESOURCES

• This session could be a practical demonstration of easy ways to entertain; a few fail-safe recipes and tips and hints on how to put guests at their ease and give them a good time.

• Warn people ahead of time that ideas and recipes will be shared, in order that everyone can contribute something.

90. Time Pressure

BIBLE REFERENCES

Psalm 55:22
Ecclesiastes 3:1
Matthew 11:28–30
John 14:27
John 16:33
Galatians 6:9

TALK OUTLINE

- Mothers who are involved with small children often feel they are like elastic bands pulled in all directions and ready to snap. There are so many jobs to do and roles to fulfil, and only 24 hours in the day. They are on a treadmill, constantly running and getting nowhere.

- There are so many expectations to conform to: the ironing needs to be done; the gym kit has to be washed; meals should be on the table on time. When these expectations are met there is little praise, only complaints when they are not met.

- A mother starts the week with an enormous list of jobs to be done, and if by the end of the week they're not all done, she feels depressed and a failure.

Learning to cope with time pressure

- It is important to set realistic goals. Tackle one project at a

time and be pleased when it's done rather than thinking of
them all and feeling overwhelmed.

- Plan ahead. Use your diary to remind you of events and
  put in your husband's appointments as well as your own,
  and the children's too so that they can be co-ordinated.

- Write down family birthdays and prepare all cards and
  presents at the beginning of the month to avoid last-
  minute dashes.

- Check and prepare school clothes before holidays.

- Write down the date when your car next needs servicing.

- Make time for yourself! Learn to say 'no'. Remember that
  every time you say 'yes' to other people, you are saying
  'no' to your children – however worthy the request may
  be.

- Children spell love T.I.M.E., so make time for your
  children and for your husband.

Questions to ask if you are feeling stressed

- Who are you doing it for?

- What are you trying to prove?

- Is it making you a better person?

- Does it help your self-esteem?

- Are you seeking approval?

(See also Talk 19: Stress.)

What on Earth Are We Doing About . . . ?

'You are the salt of the earth...You are the light of the world.'

(Matthew 5:13–14)

91. Our Community

BIBLE REFERENCES

Matthew 4:23
Matthew 5:13–14
Matthew 7:12
Matthew 21:13
Mark 3:2
Luke 4:18

TALK OUTLINE

- Jesus was intimately concerned with social issues.

- He confronted hypocrisy (healing on the Sabbath).

- He hated greed and injustice.

- He did whatever he could, wherever he was, to heal the sick and broken-hearted.

- If we follow Jesus' example, we will have concern for local issues as well as national issues.

- Most of us do not need to repent of great evils we have done in this world, but we do need to repent of the apathy that has prevented us from doing anything at all.

TEACHING POINTS/DISCUSSION STARTERS

- Read some quotes from local papers about issues affecting the area.

- Discuss how to support local projects.

- What are the local problems that your community has to face? How could you make a difference in your community? (For example, start a Neighbourhood Watch programme, offer support groups, etc.)

92. The Elderly

BIBLE REFERENCES

Job 12:12
Job 32:7
Psalm 90:10
Proverbs 17:6
Ecclesiastes 12
Joel 2:28
Titus 2:1–5

TALK OUTLINE

- In society today there is an emphasis on youth. If a man is made redundant at the age of 40 his chances of re-employment are diminished. The benefit of experience and wisdom seems to be of no account.

- Similarly, those who have reached retirement age are sidelined and often derided by society. Yet it is a time when they could be most useful to a community. Their child-rearing responsibilities are over and they have the benefit of life experience to impart (Job 12:12).

- In many Eastern countries grandparents are revered as patriarchs and matriarchs of the family, and their wisdom is applied to the young.

TEACHING POINTS/DISCUSSION STARTERS

- If possible, interview a lively elderly person who can explain the hopes and needs of the elderly.

- What can we do for the elderly in our street/neighbour-hood?

- What can we do to support carers of the elderly? (For example, a husband looking after a wife with Alzheimer's disease.)

- How can we involve the elderly in our lives or church fellowship, and help them to feel valued and useful?

93. The Lonely

BIBLE REFERENCES

Deuteronomy 31:6
Deuteronomy 33:27
1 Kings 19:3–10
Psalm 68:4–6
Psalm 139:7–12
Proverbs 18:24
Isaiah 41:10
Luke 5:16
John 14:1–3
Romans 12:5

TALK OUTLINE

- In this over-populated world there is more loneliness than ever.

- Fifty years ago, families would live in the same street or the same village for several generations. Now they are more fragmented, causing loneliness and loss of friendship.

- Even within families, mealtimes are rarely shared together, with children disappearing into their own rooms to watch television or play on a computer.

- Loneliness can cause depression.

TEACHING POINTS/DISCUSSION STARTERS

- Do we know people around us who are lonely?

- How can we sensitively include lonely people in our lives, without being patronizing?

- What can we do in our own family situations in order to share more time together and have fun?

(See also Talk 68: The Stress of Loneliness.)

94. The Bereaved

BIBLE REFERENCES

Psalm 16:10
Psalm 23:4
Psalm 89:48
Isaiah 25:8
Romans 8:36
1 Corinthians 15:26, 55
1 Thessalonians 4:13
Hebrews 2:14
Revelation 21:4

TALK OUTLINE

- We go through all the emotions of bereavement to a greater or lesser degree whether we lose a loved one through death or we are made redundant, or even if we lose a precious possession.

- We need to identify these feelings of grief and loss, and come to terms with them.

- If parents lose a child through death, they are experiencing loss of expectation of what that child would have become. These thoughts may last a lifetime, and the worst thing we can say is that they will get over them. They might come to a point of acceptance, but they have to face the fact that life will never be the same.

- Similarly, if a mother gives birth to a child with physical/mental disabilities, she and her partner have to come to terms with being responsible for caring for that child for the rest of their lives. The loss of freedom in that case is enormous.

- People are often at a loss as to what to say or do for the bereaved, so they either say nothing or avoid them. Both of these reactions can be seen as rejection. If you don't know what to say, own up. A hug can be much more precious than words.

TEACHING POINTS/DISCUSSION STARTERS

- How can we help those who are grieving?

- Look for opportunities to do washing, ironing, baking, shopping, either for them or with them, particularly if they are feeling too vulnerable to venture out.

- How can we become better listeners?

(See also Talk 70: Stress Through Grief.)

95. The Rich/Poor Divide

BIBLE REFERENCES

Leviticus 23:22
Proverbs 10:15
Proverbs 30:8
Matthew 25:35–40
Luke 4:18
Luke 21:4
Acts 2:45
Acts 10:4
Philippians 2:1–8
Revelation 2:9
Revelation 3:15–20

TALK OUTLINE

- The poverty we experience in the West is nothing compared to that experienced in the developing world due to wars, famine, droughts, earthquakes and floods, as well as the results of man's greed, exploitation and persecution.

- We are rich/poor according to our spiritual status (Revelation 3:15–20).

TEACHING POINTS/DISCUSSION STARTERS

- What can we do that will make a difference?

- How do we make use of the resources we have been given?

- Are we acquisitive or generous with what we have?

- When could we make sacrifices to help those in need?

- What organizations functioning locally could use our time/money/resources?

ADDITIONAL IDEAS/RESOURCES

Reading

- *God's Heart for the Poor* by Philippa Stroud (Kingsway, 1999).

Further suggestions

- Many charitable organizations have videos on these subjects, which are quite explicit.

- If you know of an aid worker or missionary who could talk on this topic, the personal anecdotes would bring the subject to life in a powerful way.

- A testimony of someone who has recognized their own poverty before inviting Jesus into their lives would be another way of dealing with the topic.

96. Racial and Cultural Differences

BIBLE REFERENCES

Genesis 23:4–7
Exodus 23:9
Leviticus 19:33
Micah 6:8
Acts 8:26–40
Acts 9:21–25
Colossians 3:11
1 John 3:15

TALK OUTLINE

- Many of the problems we have with racism are based on fear. We don't understand a different culture or approach to life.

- Colossians 3 tells us that cultural differences mean nothing when we have Jesus.

- Many wars are fought in the name of religion.

- You can't continue to hate someone you pray for.

- God created and loves people of every race and culture.

TEACHING POINTS/DISCUSSION STARTERS

- How many different ethnic groups are there in our neighbourhood?

- What are we doing to make them feel at home and accepted?

- What sorts of prejudices are lurking in us? How can we deal with them in order not to be judgemental?

- How can we be sure that our standards are good standards?

- Do we have love in our hearts for those of a different race?

- Are we prejudiced against someone because of where they grew up or where they now live?

- Do we judge people by the size of their houses, the cars they drive or where they go on holiday?

- Do we jump to conclusions about people without knowing all the facts?

ADDITIONAL IDEAS/RESOURCES

Reading

- *Lord, Make Us One But Not All The Same* by Joel Edwards (Hodder & Stoughton, 1999).

97. The Homeless

BIBLE REFERENCES

Isaiah 58:7
Matthew 25:35–36
Romans 12:13
1 Peter 4:9

TALK OUTLINE

- If we've never experienced homelessness it is difficult to imagine how it must feel to sleep in a park or curl up in a shop doorway, with nowhere to wash, no lavatory and no money for food.

- There is no 'typical' homeless person. People become homeless for a variety of reasons.

- Many homeless people are mentally ill or have opted out of so-called normal society. Some are in total despair, having lost their job/home through accumulated debt. Many are substance abusers, including alcoholics.

- Some who are homeless are aggressive and abusive and make a living out of begging, but others are too ashamed even to ask for money.

TEACHING POINTS/DISCUSSION STARTERS

- How can we help? It is better to give money or clothes to

the charities that work with the homeless than to give money directly, as this could be misused.

- What can be done in society or parliament to bring about change?

- What are we prepared to do individually?

ADDITIONAL IDEAS/RESOURCES

Reading

- *God's Heart for the Poor* by Philippa Stroud (Kingsway, 1999).

Further suggestion

- If possible, invite someone who works with the homeless to come and give this talk.

98. The Media

BIBLE REFERENCES

Matthew 5:13
Matthew 28:18–20
John 15:19
John 17:18
2 Corinthians 10:4–5

TALK OUTLINE

- God is looking for excellence from his people, as well as for us to be salt and light in the world.

- We need to encourage excellence in the media, as well as confronting evil.

- We should not just ignore what we hear on the radio, see on TV and read in the newspapers. We should take the time to comment – to praise as well as condemn. One letter or phone call really does make a difference.

TEACHING POINTS/DISCUSSION STARTERS

- Do you monitor what your children watch on TV?

- Do you limit the time they spend in front of it?

- Do you encourage alternative activities?

ADDITIONAL IDEAS/RESOURCES

Reading

● *Children at Risk* by David Porter (Kingsway, 1998).

Further suggestion

● If possible, invite a speaker who is involved with the media or journalism, or someone with an articulate social conscience.

99. Supporting the Family Unit

BIBLE REFERENCES

Genesis 2:24
Exodus 10:2
Joshua 24:15
Psalm 68:6
Psalm 102:28
Ephesians 2:19
Titus 2:4–5

TALK OUTLINE

- Families are God's idea.

- There is no better place to learn the essential principles of life than in the family.

Successful families 'parent with purpose'

- They have clear lasting values, providing stability.

- They express love and appreciation, encouragement and support.

- They are prepared to serve one another.

- They enjoy laughter and fun, and are open with one another.

- They have an ability to cope with crises and difficulties.

● They have good communication and spend time together.

TEACHING POINTS/DISCUSSION STARTERS

● Discuss personal tips that help to build a strong family.

ADDITIONAL IDEAS/RESOURCES

Reading

● *The Spirit-Filled Family* by Tim and Beverly LaHaye (Kingsway, 1996).

100. Teenagers

BIBLE REFERENCES

Deuteronomy 6:7
Psalm 119:9
Proverbs 6:20–23
Proverbs 29:15
Ephesians 6:1–4

TALK OUTLINE

How to cope with teenagers

- Have as few rules as possible.

- 'Choose the mountain you want to die on!' (Don't major on minor problems.)

- Say as little as possible.

- Build bridges, not barriers.

- Keep communication lines open.

- Spend time sitting and talking about trivial things in order for them to be open to talking about important issues.

- Be willing to apologize when you make a mistake.

TEACHING POINTS/DISCUSSION STARTERS

- How do we make the transition from discipline to trust?

- How do we prepare for letting go of our children?

- How do we build self-esteem in our teenagers?

- How do we believe in our teenagers and love them unconditionally when their behaviour is intolerable?

ADDITIONAL IDEAS/RESOURCES

Reading

- *How to Really Love Your Teenager* by Dr Ross Campbell (Alpha, 1995).

Fun Ideas

1. Christmas brunch

We have found a Christmas brunch to be very successful. Instead of coffee and a talk, we set up tables for eight to ten people, and provide fresh orange juice, hot rolls or croissants, fruit and mince pies, with lashings of coffee and tea.

We provide a cabaret with a singer or a keyboard player for sing-along carols, and perhaps the minister of the church will give a short Christmas message or a reading. We then get all the children from the crèche to come and sing a carol to their mothers (which they have rehearsed all term) and there's not a dry eye in the house!

2. Easter celebration lunch

This we serve after the morning group meeting. We invite all the mothers to contribute, if they wish, by putting their name to one item on a list (for example, hot cross buns). We supply whatever is not accounted for and set up lunch for mothers and their children in the church hall.

Lunch consists of soup, crusty bread and soft rolls, cheese, crudités (chopped celery/cucumber/carrots/courgettes, etc.) and cooked, chopped sausages. Hot cross buns, fruit and coffee and tea finish off the meal.

We supply chocolate Easter eggs for all the older children

and chocolate buttons for the babies. Older children present their mothers with a home-made Easter card or gift (made in the crèche during previous weeks).

3. Social evenings

Summer barbecues; supper or fondue parties (cheese or chocolate) with a Christian video, for the winter.

4. Clothing, toy and equipment exchanges

Mothers can bring good quality outgrown children's clothes with a safety-pinned name and price tag, and can buy their next season's wardrobe for their children. They can also sell maternity dresses and cots/prams for very reasonable prices, but they must be in good condition. This is a popular event for the mothers. Unsold goods are either taken home or left for distribution to needy families or charities.

5. Photo shoot

Mothers can have photos taken with their children for Christmas presents for relatives and friends (contact a local schools photographer). The mothers pay the going rate, which you tell them about beforehand. They pay only if they want the photos (to be arranged with the photographer).

6. Charity stands

These are where mothers can buy 'fair trade or Traidcraft' gifts and Christmas cards. Details can be found in Christian magazines or by contacting the charities concerned (such as TEAR Fund).

7. Sharing skills

Encourage the women to demonstrate curtain-making, stencilling, murals, home decorating, DIY for women, flower arranging, etc. Many of these skills are easy when you know how, and with a little encouragement from the experts.

8. The Alpha Course

We have on several occasions adapted this course to suit the morning meetings, substituting the evening meals with as many calorie-loaded cakes and gateaux as we could make! The videos are very easy to watch and non-threatening for those who know nothing about the Christian faith. Contact the Alpha Office on 0207 581278 or visit the website at www.alpha.org.uk

9. Other fun events can include

- Make-up demonstration.

- Facial massage.

- Colour Me Beautiful.

- Recipe swap.

- Cookery demonstrations.

- Riverboat or canal trips.

- A coffee 'picnic' at a local beauty spot or local park area for children to play.

- Baby-sitting circle (if you can get your own fellowship motivated, offer baby-sitters for evening events).

- Musical events with musicians/singers.

- Prom Praise coach trip to Albert Hall, or similar event.

Recommended Reading

Dr Ross Campbell, *How to Really Love Your Teenager* (Alpha, 1995).

Dr Ross Campbell, *How to Really Love Your Child* (Alpha, 1998).

Steve Chalke, *The Parenttalk Guide to the Childhood Years* (Hodder, 1999).

Steve Chalke, *The Parenttalk Guide to the Teenage Years* (Hodder, 1999).

Linda Davis, *How to Be the Happy Wife of an Unsaved Husband* (Whitaker, 1986).

Dr James Dobson, *Man to Man About Women* (Kingsway, 1976).

Dr James Dobson, *The Strong-Willed Child* (Kingsway, 1978).

Dr James Dobson, *Preparing for Adolescence* (Kingsway, 1982).

Dr James Dobson, *Love Must Be Tough* (Kingsway, 1984).

Dr James Dobson, *The New Dare to Discipline* (Kingsway, 1993).

Dr James Dobson, *Parenting Isn't for Cowards* (Galahad Books, 1997).

Jim Douglas, *How to Live with a Working Wife* (Pan, 1983).

Joel Edwards, *Lord Make Us One But Not All The Same* (Hodder, 1999).

Lynda Hunter, *Single Moments* (Focus on the Family, 1998).

Tim LaHaye, *Opposites Attract* (Kingsway, 1992).

Tim and Beverly LaHaye, *The Spirit-Filled Family* (Kingsway, 1996).

Michael Lawson, *The Better Marriage Guide* (Hodder, 1998).

Josh McDowell, *The Secret of Loving* (Here's Life, 1985).

Josh McDowell, *How to Be a Hero to Your Kids* (Word, 1993).

Stormie Omartian, *The Power of a Praying Parent* (Kingsway, 1996).

Stormie Omartian, *The Power of a Praying Wife* (Kingsway, 1997).

Rob Parsons, *The Sixty-Minute Marriage* (Hodder, 1997).

Rob Parsons, *Loving Against the Odds* (Hodder, 1998).

David Porter, *Children at Risk* (Kingsway, 1998).

Philippa Stroud, *God's Heart for the Poor* (Kingsway, 1999).

Ed Wheat, *Love Life for Every Married Couple* (Marshall Pickering, 1984).

Index of Themes

Locators refer to theme numbers, not page numbers

Index of Bible References

Locators refer to theme numbers, not page numbers

100 Instant Discussion Starters

by John Buckeridge

100 'strange but true' stories will get any group
thinking, laughing, possibly outraged – but definitely
talking!

- Fully indexed by themes and Bible references
  for ease of use.
- Questions and 'application' sections, follow
  each anecdote, plus an extensive list of Bible
  references to lead into a group study.
- Includes guidance on how to run discussion
  groups.
- Excellent resource for cells or 'after Alpha'
  groups.
- Useful source of material for talks and sermons
  as well!

THE BUILDINGS OF ENGLAND

BEDFORDSHIRE AND THE
COUNTY OF HUNTINGDON AND
PETERBOROUGH

NIKOLAUS PEVSNER

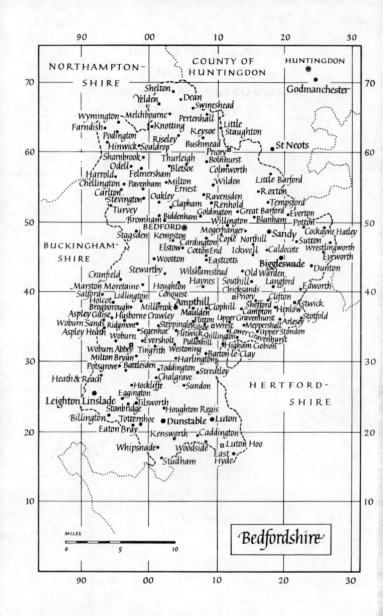

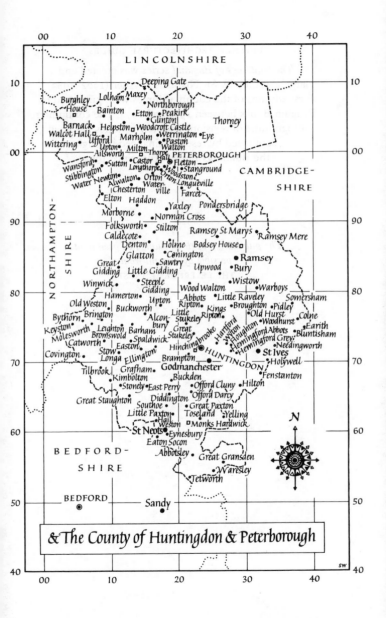

&The County of Huntingdon & Peterborough

*The publication of this volume has been made
possible by a grant from*
THE LEVERHULME TRUST

THE BUILDINGS OF ENGLAND

Bedfordshire and the County of Huntingdon and Peterborough

BY

NIKOLAUS PEVSNER

★

YALE UNIVERSITY PRESS
NEW HAVEN AND LONDON

YALE UNIVERSITY PRESS
NEW HAVEN AND LONDON
302 Temple Street, New Haven CT 06511
47 Bedford Square, London WC1B 3DP
www.pevsner.co.uk
www.lookingatbuildings.org
www.yalebooks.co.uk
www.yalebooks.com
for
THE BUILDINGS BOOKS TRUST

Published by Penguin Books 1968
First published by Yale University Press 2002
2 4 6 8 10 9 7 5 3

—

ISBN 0 300 09581 3

—

—

Printed in China
through World Print
Set in Monotype Plantin

—

To the
Inventor
of the
ICED LOLLY

CONTENTS

Map References

★

The numbers printed in italic type in the margin against the place names in the gazetteer of the book indicate the position of the place in question on the index map (pages 2–3), which is divided into sections by the 10–kilometre reference lines of the National Grid. The reference given here omits the two initial letters (formerly numbers) which in a full grid reference refer to the 100-kilometre squares into which the country is divided. The first two numbers indicate the *western* boundary, and the last two the *southern* boundary, of the 10-kilometre square in which the place in question is situated. For example Ampthill (reference 0030) will be found in the 10-kilometre square bounded by grid lines 00 (on the *west*) and 10, and 30 (on the *south*) and 40; Abbotsley (reference 2050) in the square bounded by grid lines 20 (on the *west*) and 30, and 50 (on the *south*) and 60.

The map contains all those places, whether towns, villages, or isolated buildings, which are the subject of separate entries in the text.

FOREWORD

*The title of this volume, Bedfordshire and the County of Huntingdon
and Peterborough, is unwieldy but correct. The Soke of Peterborough, however, had already been published in* The Buildings
of England *as part of Northamptonshire.* That was in 1961.
What I have done now is to reprint it here, trying to correct what
mistakes it may have contained and to eliminate what has since
disappeared and add what has since been built.*

*Bedfordshire and Huntingdonshire information was extracted
admirably and very fully indeed by Mrs M. Metcalfe (then Beryl
Barnett). Mistakes which may appear in the following pages are
more likely to be mine than hers. The intensive journey through the
two counties was done in companionship with Hamish Halls. He did
a first-class job of driving and took over all the travelling chores,
steady, quiet, unruffled, and always dependable. The correspondence
before and after the journey and much else were in good hands with
Mrs M. Cryer (then Wendy Martin). Miss Dorn once again typed my
illegible manuscript as if she had been given print. It always seems a
miracle to me.*

*And there are many more whom I ought to thank here; first of
all George McHardy for visiting nearly all the churches with my
typescript and correcting and adding to it; then all those incum-
bents who have answered my questions and read proofs of the
entries in the gazetteer which concerned them, all those owners of
houses who allowed me entrance (and to whom I owe it to state
firmly here that inclusion of a house in the gazetteer does not mean
that it is open to the public), and all those who have helped in other
ways, especially Mr William Collier, who placed at my disposal
the text of a projected but then abandoned guide to Bedfordshire,
and the librarians of the principal libraries of the two counties and
in particular Mr Cyril Hargreaves of the Bedford Public Library,
Mr R. V. Keyworth of the Huntingdon County Library, Mr F.
Gardener of the Luton Public Library, Mr Barry Hall of the*

---

* The following are the places in the Soke of Peterborough: Bainton,
Barnack, Burghley House, Castor, Deeping Gate, Etton, Eye, Glinton,
Helpston, Lolham, Longthorpe, Marholm, Maxey, Milton, Northborough,
Paston, Peakirk, Peterborough, Sutton, Thorney, Ufford, Upton, Walcot
Hall, Walton, Wansford, Werrington, Wittering, Woodcroft Castle.

Northampton Central Library, and Mr A.V.Mountfort of the St Neots Library. In addition I am greatly indebted to Mr F.W. Kuhlicke, Director of the Bedford Museum, and Mr P.G.M. Dickinson, the County Archivist of Huntingdonshire, and moreover the Duke of Bedford, Mr Burman, Vicar of Flitton, my friend Alec Clifton-Taylor, Mr T. A. Edwards, headmaster of Ramsey Abbey School. Mr F. A. Fowler of Dunstable, Squadron Leader Hathaway at Chicksands, Canon John J. F. Scammell, vicar of Leighton Linslade, Marshall Sisson, architect and expert on Kimbolton, Mr M. Urwick Smith at Luton Hoo, and Mr F. White at Wrest Park.

Furthermore, I have to thank in this as in all preceding volumes the Ministry of Housing and Local Government (here abbreviated MHLG) *for allowing the full use of their lists of buildings of architectural and historic interest, the National Monuments Record* (NMR) *for help with their magnificent collection of architectural photographs, Mr Peter Ferriday* (PF) *for having deposited on permanent loan his great card index of Victorian church restorations, and Mr Geoffrey Spain* (GS) *for lists of Victorian buildings which he sent me.* GR *refers to the late H.S. Goodhart-Rendel's index of Victorian churches,* TK *to Sir Thomas Kendrick's lists of Victorian stained glass.*

The introductions to, and gazetteer of, prehistoric antiquities were contributed by Mr Derek Simpson, the introduction and gazetteer of Roman remains by Professor Barry Cunliffe, the introduction to the geology of Bedfordshire and Huntingdonshire by Professor Terence Miller.

The principles on which the following gazetteer is founded are the same as in the thirty-three volumes of The Buildings of England *which precede it. I have myself seen everything that I describe. Where this is not the case the information obtained by other means is placed in brackets. Information ought to be as complete as the space of the volume permits for churches prior to c.1830 and all town houses, manor houses, and country houses of more than purely local interest. Movable furnishings are not included in secular buildings, though they are in churches. Exceptions to the latter rule are hatchments, chests, chairs, plain fonts, and altar tables. Royal arms, poor boxes, bells, coffin lids with foliate crosses, and brasses of post-Reformation date are mentioned occasionally, church plate of after 1830 only rarely. Village crosses are omitted where only a plain base or a stump of the shaft survives. As for churches and chapels of after 1830, I had to make a selection, and this is dictated by architectural value or by significance otherwise in the light of*

architectural history. The same applies to secular buildings of the
C19 and C20.

*I am only too well aware of the inadequacies of my gazetteer.
Anyone who studies the volume on Huntingdonshire of the Royal
Commission on Historic Monuments can see for himself how many
timber-framed houses, how many staircases, how many domestic
fitments are left out, and can guess from that how much more is
missing for the C18 which the Royal Commission at the time of the
Huntingdonshire volume did not include and for Bedfordshire
altogether. I therefore wish to end by entreating users of my book
to advise me of serious omissions and to draw my attention to errors.*

BEDFORDSHIRE

★

INTRODUCTION

BEDFORDSHIRE is a county of pleasant, not of exciting land-scape. Variety is greater in architecture than in scenery indeed – partly thanks to the variety of building materials, surprisingly great for so small a county. In size Bedfordshire comes thirty-ninth in England, in population thirty-second. Materials range from the flint and stone and flint chequer at the s end around Luton to the oolitic limestone at the N end bordering on North-amptonshire, and from ironstone to the brown carstone cobbles of the middlemost area (Harrold, Wymington, Swineshead etc.). Totternhoe stone, used much in that neighbourhood, is a clunch of poor quality for external use but satisfactory for internal carving (Eaton Bray etc.). Sandstone is used between Bedford and Luton (Clophill, Silsoe, etc.), and about the greenest of all green sandstones at Husborne Crawley. Brick appeared only slowly, but became predominant in the parts where no first-class building stone existed.

The geology explaining these building materials is presented separately on p. 29. On p. 31 prehistoric remains are summed up, on p. 34 Roman remains. So we can start here with ANGLO-SAXON ARCHITECTURE and leave it for the Norman after one sentence or two. There is nothing Anglo-Saxon in Bedfordshire to compare with Huntingdon and Peterborough. Stevington and Thurleigh have towers with openings into former *porticus*, i.e. side chambers, St Peter at Bedford a w tower which is now the crossing tower, Clapham a w tower – both these with Norman tops – and Turvey-some windows, and that is all.

NORMAN ARCHITECTURE is not abundant either, but there is one major building: Dunstable, of which most of the nave sur- 15 vives, below *c.*1150–60, on the gallery level *c.*1180–90, in the façade from *c.*1180 to the dedication in 1213 and after, i.e. into the full-blown E.E. The façade is confused, the nave interior 27 unified and powerful.

Dunstable was the most important MONASTIC FOUNDATION

in the county. It was Augustinian and had been established in
1131. Other Augustinian priories were Bushmead with part of
the refectory range in existence, and Caldwell (Bedford), and
Newnham (Bedford), both gone entirely. Benedictine were
Millbrook (later at Beadlow) and Grovebury (Leighton Linslade), a cell of Fontevrault, both again no longer surviving even
in parts. Warden and Woburn were Cistercian, and there was
also a cell of Woburn at Leighton Linslade. At Chicksands, one
of the much rarer Gilbertine houses, vaulted undercrofts of the
W range and part of the C15 cloister are preserved. Of Friars'
establishments there were only two: Blackfriars at Dunstable
and Greyfriars at Bedford. Harrold had a house of Augustinian
canonesses, Elstow a house of Benedictine nuns. At Elstow there
is the vaulted C13 Outer Parlour, a detached C15 campanile,
and five bays of the church, of which three are early C12.

p. 86

So we are back with Norman architecture. At Elstow also is a
small sculptured panel of about 1140 with Christ seated and two
saints, very French. There is very little other sculpture. At
Cranfield is another seated figure, very defaced, and Thurleigh
has a primitive tympanum with Adam and Eve, the tree and the
serpent. The tympanum at Ravensden has just chequerboard
decoration. Flitwick has a fragment with the beakhead motif.

19 Fonts are quite frequent, but only Dunstable needs mention
here. Of MONUMENTS the Milton Bryan coffin lid with a strange

p. 126 cross and interlace must be C12. There are of course arcades where
aisles were added to older churches. They mostly have round
piers with square capitals and abaci. The development into E.E.
can be followed by steps in various directions: round arch to
pointed, unmoulded arch to slight chamfers and full chamfers,
square to round abaci, and so on. In Bedfordshire the square
abacus seems to have been used right to the end of the century
(see e.g. Shelton).

Bedfordshire has not a single castle, except for the early
MOTTE AND BAILEY CASTLES, i.e. Norman earthworks. Of
these Bedford and Totternhoe were the most important. So we
move to EARLY ENGLISH ARCHITECTURE, only to find that
here also major monuments are rare, and only one is of the
26 highest beauty: Felmersham of c.1220–40, with its reposeful W
front, its grand crossing, and the fine balance achieved in the
nave by arcade piers alternating between round and octagonal
not only along the arcade but also across the nave. What is of
unusual wealth in the county is stiff-leaf capitals, from the early
ones of before 1200, with small leaves keeping closely to a bell

left exposed for most of its height, to the bigger leaves still close
to the bell, and in the end to the rich, mature 'wind-swept'
leaves. Of special interest are the approximately datable specimens at Studham and Chalgrave consecrated in 1219, the w bays 23
of Elstow also of about 1220, and the Eaton Bray capitals where 24
c.1220 can be compared with superb c.1240. Eaton Bray also has 29
a font with stiff-leaf of c.1240. Architecturally as against decora- 20
tively one more building must be referred to: the proud crossing
tower of Leighton Linslade.

  Thomas of Leighton, i.e. of what is now called Leighton Linslade, made the iron railings round Queen Eleanor's monument
in Westminster Abbey. That was in 1293, and as the county has
some beautiful IRONWORK of the C13, this has been ascribed to
him. But the wonderful door scrolls of Eaton Bray and those of
Turvey and Leighton Linslade may well be earlier C13 work and 36
rather indicate a workshop tradition from which Thomas emerged
(cf. e.g. the door in St George's Chapel at Windsor of c.1250).
At Leighton Linslade, also of the C13, is a stone SEAT – and that
is a rare thing (but cf. Farcet in Huntingdon). Of other stone fitments the DOUBLE PISCINA at Toddington deserves notice. It
is of the type with two pointed arches under one round arch.
This is the time when in Bedfordshire effigies begin to appear on
FUNERARY MONUMENTS. The oldest is probably the abbot of
Pipewell buried at Chicksands. Then there are, of about the
same time or a little later, i.e. from the late C13 into the C14, a
Knight at Salford, Ladies at Goldington and Oakley, a Civilian
holding his heart at Yelden, and so on to the late C14 Knight at
Houghton Regis. Typical of the C13 are coffin lids with foliated
crosses. Most of these are not listed in this book, but there are
two specially interesting ones at Pavenham and Oakley, where
the cross grows out of a beast (cf. St Neots, Huntingdon). The
motif occurs in others as well. By then new materials had come
into use, brass and alabaster, but Bedfordshire has no early
examples. The earliest brass is in fact with a date of death only
of 1391 (Wymington), i.e. it corresponds in date not even with
the Dec but only with the Perp style.

  DECORATED ARCHITECTURE, if one wishes to see fairly
complete examples, will be found at Dean, at Langford, and at
Swineshead (where the tower has a curious shallow w porch).
Marston Moretaine has a detached tower. It also has a vaulted
vestry, as has St Mary at Luton. Dates are rare but not wholly
absent. At Shillington in 1333 the Bishop of Lincoln admonished
the parishioners to repair their nave. So the nave will be after

that, and the chancel was probably done just before. At Lower Gravenhurst the man 'qe fiet faire' the new church died about 1360, and at Wymington John Curteys who, according to the inscription on his brass, also built the church, died as late as 1391, and yet it is still Dec in style. There is no record of when Perp first appeared. Of individual Dec motifs some good tomb recesses must be quoted, especially Dean, Milton Ernest, Swineshead, and Yelden,* and a word must be said about piers and their shapes. The octagonal pier carrying a double-chamfered arch was common already in the C13 and remained common to the end of the Middle Ages. The two together in the following gazetteer are simply referred to as 'standard elements'. The C13 25 had also known quatrefoil piers, true ones and those which are really a square with four semicircular projections. What the Dec seems to have introduced and liked is the quatrefoil enriched by 45 four slim shafts in the diagonals. DECORATED CHURCH FURNISHINGS are naturally more plentiful than Norman or 42 E.E. The most spectacular piece is the stone font canopy of Luton. There is an exquisite early C14 wall painting of the Crucifixion at Turvey, and Chalgrave has extensive wall paintings of about the same date. Also early C14 is the stained glass at Cockayne Hatley. Dec screens survive at Campton and Potsgrove but are of no special merit, and traceried C14 doors survive at Luton and Swineshead. The details are as characteristically different from the C15 tracery of the door at Biggleswade as are the details of the Campton and Potsgrove screens from the many Perp screens all over the county. The best of these are at Felmersham, Oakley, and Stagsden.‡ After the screens the stalls, and especially the misericords. Those of Leighton Linslade come from St Albans Abbey; more are in St Paul at Bedford. After the stalls the benches. The majority of the ends are just straight-topped with thin buttresses, but there are poppyheads at Northill and in a number of other places (Houghton Conquest, 53 Stevington). Four Perp pulpits remain – at Dean, Elstow, Tempsford, and Yelden – and some stone reredoses. By far the best must have been the one of which parts now make up the pulpit of St Paul at Bedford. The Nottingham alabaster panels at Sandy 44 and (in fragments) at Blunham also belonged originally to reredoses. That leaves the former pall at Dunstable of c.1530§ em-

---

* And Abbotsley in Huntingdonshire.

‡ Some screens have paintings on the dado, but none of these are of much value.

§ Rather than c.1516.

broidered with figures in Henry VIII costume on the border,
and the survey of Perp church furnishings is complete.

But we have not so far examined PERPENDICULAR ARCHI-
TECTURE. A few words first on towers and steeples, because they
refer not only to Perp but also to earlier evidence. The earliest
spire is at Souldrop (C13). In the s of the county there are no
spires, and the towers have often higher stair-turrets, in the N
spires are quite frequent. C14 examples are Dean, Swineshead,
and Yelden. St Paul at Bedford has a recessed spire, and five
others exist plus two whose spires are connected by delicate
flying buttresses with the pinnacles on the corners of the tower.
Broach spires are about equally represented: five, and one which
is recessed as well. At Wymington the lucarnes at the foot of the
spire are so high and so broad that they form an octagon as the
preparatory stage of the spire. As for whole Perp churches, five
deserve to be singled out: St Paul at Bedford, a hall church with
wide aisles; Toddington, large and good; Totternhoe with some 57
fine features; Flitton probably of c.1440–89 with piers of the
most typical section (four shafts and four diagonal hollows –
in the gazetteer to be called standard moulded section), and 46
Willington built by Sir John Gostwick, Master of the Horse of 51
Cardinal Wolsey and Treasurer of the First Fruits of Henry
VIII. He began the church about 1530, and it is characteristic of
the late date that the porch is placed symmetrically between two
large transomed windows. There is a Renaissance feeling in this.

Sir John Gostwick also built himself a house at Willington.
Of this only a smallish range and the dovecote survive. Both have
stepped gables and nothing of the Renaissance. Sir John died in
1545, and his monument in the church is completely plain. It is
high time to catch up with MONUMENTS; for there are fine ones
in Bedfordshire. John Curteys at Wymington to whom we have
already had to refer died in 1391. He has a monument with
brasses and a big ogee arch. Of almost exactly the same date is
the much more lavish Wenlock Monument in Luton parish 56
church between chancel and N chapel with its splendidly high
arch. The date of death here is 1392. Opposite is the charming
little chantry chapel of Richard Barnard, † 1492, with its miniature vault. At Clifton is the only alabaster monument of the 52
complete type with tomb-chest with angels holding shields and
two recumbent effigies. It is early C16. Cardington has two tombs
between chancel and chapels, again with very elaborate architectural surrounds: one has the tomb-chest of Sir William
Gascoigne † 1540. The effigy is a brass. But the best BRASSES in

pp. the county are earlier, one at Elstow who died in 1427,
85, Thomas Wideville and his two wives at Bromham, † 1435, and
60,
102 Isabel Conquest at Houghton Conquest † 1493 with husband
and son.

The way is now clear for starting on the exploration of the
C16 – except for one postscript on SECULAR BUILDINGS not yet
mentioned. Only two are houses. The first of them is rather the
minor remains of a house – the derelict fragment of Someries
Castle outside Luton which dates from the second half of the C15
and represents the first use of brick in the county. Warden
Abbey, Old Warden, another brick fragment, of after 1537
follows. The others are a number of fine bridges and causeways,
especially Bromham, Turvey, Harrold, and Great Barford, the
58 handsome Market Cross of Leighton Linslade, and the Moot
Hall of Elstow of c.1500, which is timber-framed with brick infilling and has instead of the usual open ground floor partition
walls creating six individual shops each with its own entrance.
This is the only timber-framed building in the county which a
summary has to include. The climax of timber-framing which
the Elizabethan and Jacobean decades brought in some counties
has no parallel in Bedford.

The major ELIZABETHAN AND JACOBEAN MANSIONS are
of brick or stone, and only one of them, in ruins for well over a
70 hundred and fifty years, is really major: Houghton House,
Ampthill of c.1615, with additions of about 1640 to which
reference must be made later. The Jacobean building is on an
H-plan with four angle turrets, and pedimented cross-windows.
In two ways it was very progressive for its date. The centre of
the house is two rooms deep, and the hall was entered not close
to one end, as was the custom, but in its middle, as John Thorpe
just at that time proposed in some of his drawings and as was
indeed done at Aston Hall near Birmingham in 1618 etc. The
other houses are Hillersdon Hall built in 1616 on the E-plan into
the ruins of Elstow Nunnery; Turvey Abbey, interesting
chiefly for the balustrading and two large mullioned and transomed windows from Easton Maudit in Northamptonshire; and
Bletsoe Castle, one range of a house built round a quadrangle.
It has a flat front with mullioned and transomed windows.

Bletsoe Castle was the house of the St Johns, and in Bletsoe
church among the St John MONUMENTS there is that to Sir
John who died in 1559, and this starts the series of Elizabethan
and Jacobean monuments which is considerable in Bedfordshire.
The St John Monument already has the figures kneeling towards

one another across a prayer-desk, one of the favourite compositional schemes of the age. It repeats shortly after at Elstow († 1566) and still at Cockayne Hatley († 1627) and Willington († 1630). There is nothing Gothic left in any of these. The transition from Gothic to Elizabethan can best be seen at Eaton Bray, where Lady Bray's monument has motifs of both styles mixed. She died in 1558. Pure Early Elizabethan at its national best is the alabaster monument at Turvey to the first Lord Mordaunt. 62 He died in 1560. The monument, whose sculptor, *T. Kirby*, is known, has a recumbent effigy, pairs of Roman Doric columns, caryatids above, and a solemn top pediment all across. The second Lord's, who died in 1571, is an eight-poster with three recumbent effigies. That is the most ambitious Elizabethan type. A completely different type, specially characteristic of the early Elizabethan decades and specially well represented in Northamptonshire, has no effigies and indeed no figures at all. In Bedfordshire this is represented very well at Tilsworth († 1582). 63 The turn of the century brings no changes. Between 1600 and 1625 the main Elizabethan types continue. John Burgoyne † 1604 at Sutton has the recumbent effigy, the two columns and strapwork, Sir Edmund Anderson † 1605 at Eyeworth the same elements. The monument of 1603 at Bromham is a five-poster. The fifth Earl of Kent † 1614 at Flitton has just a tomb-chest with effigy and a back panel, and there is not much difference when we move on to the early forties with a monument at Marston Moretaine and one at Colmworth. The latter has below particu- 73 larly noble caryatids.*

But new types are coming on. The frontal demi-figure, used chiefly for divines and academics, appears at Everton († 1624), at Houghton Conquest in 1629, at St Paul in Bedford († 1633), and still for a vicar of Meppershall who died in 1672. A great exception and as inventive as anything of those years at court and in Westminster Abbey is the monument at Turvey to the third Lord Mordaunt who died in 1601. This is a tomb-chest with a black-marble cloth draped over it and a white inscription plate on the black. With this we move out of the world of Queen Elizabeth I, and so a temporary stop is necessary; for the monuments ought not to be taken out of the context of the churches and their other furnishings.

* It should here be noted in passing that Turvey with the Mordaunt tombs and even more Flitton with the de Grey–Earls of Kent tombs belong to those collections of funerary sculpture in village churches which are a distinguishing feature of England.

ELIZABETHAN AND JACOBEAN CHURCHES are of course rare. The Middle Ages had left enough. At Elstow work of 1580 on the former nunnery church is entirely in the Perp tradition. The W tower of Blunham is largely of 1583. At Holcot about 1590 the general tenor remains Perp, but the windows have mullion-and-transom crosses. The W tower of Knotting is of 1615, and that is all one can say about it, and at Campton as late as 1649 the N arcade and the N chapel are again Perp in intention.

It is different with the CHURCH FURNISHINGS. Here the Elizabethan style was quite different from the Perp, and there was no question which to use. In quantity the leading item of equipment was plate. The Elizabethan Settlement insisted on cup and cover paten, and they had to be replaced after the ravages of the radical Reformation. So in the years 1569–70 eighteen Cups and Patens or single Cups or single Patens were provided. The pair at Pavenham is silver-gilt. In addition one is of 1568, one of 1571, and one of 1577. Of other dated items there are the pulpits at Sutton (1628) and Leighton Linslade (given 1638), the screens at Odell (1637) and Campton (c.1649) with two tiers of closely set balusters, and the chancel gates at Knotting (1637), installed after cock-fighting had been staged in the chancel.

The first reflection of the revolution in English architecture brought about by Inigo Jones is the additions made to Houghton House, Ampthill about 1640 or thereabouts. They establish STUART ARCHITECTURE in Bedfordshire; for the Stuart Style is the post-James I style, whether that is dynastically accurate 70 or not. Two ambitious frontispieces were added to the house. The one with two arched loggias one on top of the other, attached columns in three orders, and a top pediment is reminiscent of that part of Castle Ashby in Northamptonshire which has been attributed to Inigo himself, the other with loggias screened by three orders of columns with straight entablatures and again a top pediment has no parallel but also presupposes a frame of mind which, at that early moment, few other than Inigo can have been in. In Bedfordshire anyway nothing can be compared with these two frontispieces, and indeed no architectural events can be reported for a whole generation after. The interesting provincial developments of the fifties to seventies e.g. which we get in Huntingdon and Peterborough are absent, and we can move straight away into the nineties, i.e. the time of mature Wren. *Wren* in fact was himself at least in touch with Lord Ashburnham, for whom Ampthill Park was begun in 1694,

though Captain *Wynne* also was a few years later, i.e. in 1706.
Here we find the top pediment, the hipped roof, the doorway
with columns set against rustication, and the open curly pediment. Of 1688 is the staircase from Houghton House now in the
Swan Hotel at Bedford, and this has the characteristic twisted
balusters. Again just outside Ampthill is the Oxford Hospital
(for former college servants) built in 1697 which, though otherwise entirely in the so-called Wren style – cf. e.g. Morden College
in London of 1695 – still has wooden mullion-and-transom
cross windows. In this respect Eggington House of 1696 is up to
the minute; for here are the segment-headed windows and the
panelled parapet which were favourite motifs under Queen
Anne and indeed George I.

As there are no church buildings to report between Campton
in 1649 and the later C18, and no CHURCH FURNISHINGS
except the gorgeous heraldic glass of 1664 at Northill, the brass 77
chandelier of 1728 at Milton Ernest, and the charming and very
exceptional bread cupboard of 1729 in the same church (three
tiers of four arched pigeon-holes and a steep pediment), we can
only look for parallels with the Houghton to Eggington development amongst MONUMENTS, and in that field much was in fact
done. The search for new types had been initiated early, as we
have seen. It is continued in the Anderson Monument of † 1638
at Eyeworth, where we get two demi-figures holding together a
heart and the bust of their little girl in a circular recess below,
and in the Wentworth Monument of † 1632 at Toddington 72
with a frontal seated figure under a baldacchino. This may be of
the mid C17. In the 1650s and 1660s, as it happened, particularly
much was done, from so rare a type as that of the Countess of
Elgin at Maulden in 1656 showing her rising in her shroud out of
a kind of oblong basin – a conceit favoured by the age of Donne –
to cartouches without effigy but with characteristic gristly or
fleshy ornament. Two other monuments at Maulden († 1663)
have good portrait busts. A bust in an oval recess is at Pulloxhill
(† 1653), and there appears here already the open scrolly pediment.* It also crowns a monument at Tilsworth († 1666).
Specially rich in work of these years is Flitton. The monument
to the ninth Earl of Kent of 1658 still has the traditional tomb-
chest with effigies, but also two typically Mannerist allegorical
figures in the Nicholas Stone tradition. By Nicholas' son *John
Stone* is a monument of 1655 at Campton. This has the gristly 74
ornament, but otherwise the composition is already quite classical.

* Earlier still in Huntingdon.

At Flitton a monument of the same year 1653 has a reredos, as it were, and no figures, and this again is unhesitatingly classical. A monument, again at Flitton, of 1673 on the other hand shows Lady Jane Hart semi-reclining. Two other monuments of the seventies must be added to finish the series, one at Higham Gobion († 1674) because the man recorded was professor of Arabic at Cambridge and hence the end of the inscription is in Arabic, the other, at Sutton, because it is by *Grinling Gibbons* himself, better known for his wood-carved leaf, flower, and fruit – such as it has come to Luton Hoo from Cassiobury in Hertfordshire – than for work in stone. The monument at Sutton has an urn and cherubs. After that there is a gap, at least among specially notable pieces. Minor tablets abound and are, with their garlands and putto heads, often very good indeed.

The gap begins to close only about 1740. As the monument by *Green* of Camberwell at Dunstable († 1712) is still stylistically pre-Georgian, the Earl of Harrold at Flitton of 1726 is the first of truly GEORGIAN MONUMENTS. It has the Earl semi-reclining in the way it had been done for fifty years (*see* above), but he is now in Roman dress, white on a black sarcophagus. The sculptor is one *Dowyer*, otherwise totally unknown. Also semi-reclining and also in Roman dress is the Duke of Kent † 1740, attributed to *Rysbrack*, the finest funerary monument in the county. The architectural parts were designed by *E. Shepherd*. Again in Roman dress and standing assertively like a Roman Emperor is Sir Samuel Ongley † 1726 at Old Warden by *Peter Scheemakers* and *Laurent Delvaux*. By Scheemakers is one more monument, the first of the Whitbread monuments at Cardington. It probably dates from after 1766 and has two busts not of special merit. That leaves only two more of before 1770, and then there is another gap. They are by *Benjamin Palmer*, but only one of them is a monument (St Paul Bedford † 1768). The other is the statue of
89 Sir William Harpur on Harpur's little school building of 1756 just w of St Paul's.

It is the only Georgian public building of interest in the county. Other GEORGIAN ARCHITECTURE on the other hand is more fully represented than anything we have had to summarize so far. But this does not apply to churches. Whipsnade and Melchbourne (1779) are a meagre harvest.* But it applies fully to HOUSES, and here the coverage is even, from the years just before George I to the end of the dynasty. At the start are one exceptional and a few typical buildings. The exceptional one is

---

* Melchbourne has arcades of Tuscan columns.

Thomas Archer's Pavilion at Wrest, an essay in the Borrominesque 86 in its plan with interlocking triangles, one expressed in apsidal ends the other in oblong ends, like chapels round a perfectly circular domed room. The details, especially the doorway, have all Archer's interesting mannerisms. Typical Queen Anne on the other hand are Hinwick House of 1709–14 and Hinwick Hall 88 of about the same years. There are the giant pilasters, the window with moulded surrounds, the doorways with open curly pediment. The Hall is a little more naïve than the House. Hawnes, Haynes, with a thirteen-window front is of the same type, but about ten years later. Palladianism appeared first probably – not early – in the Bowling Green House in the park of Wrest about 1740, but at its grandest in *Flitcroft*'s w front of Woburn 90 Abbey of 1747 etc. Flitcroft also built the enormous stables, two large quadrangles. His interiors at Woburn are splendid too. 91 He was followed first by *Chambers* and then by *Henry Holland*, who from 1787 onwards worked on the s range and furnished it 93 in his exquisitely restrained taste. Holland also built the majestic Sculpture Gallery (as a conservatory). While this was done for the fifth Duke of Bedford, Southill, his most perfect *ensemble*, was done for Samuel Whitbread, the brewer. Here is a sociologically eminently telling fact, and just as telling in its own way is that the Duke of Bedford commissioned Holland to design a hotel, i.e. an inn, for Bedford. The Swan Hotel is indeed the 92 noblest English hotel of the age, very severe and classical with its ashlar masonry and pediment. Holland enlarged Avenue House at Ampthill in the same years for another brewer. In the surprisingly large gardens behind the house is a wooden garden temple which came from Houghton House. Ornamental garden buildings are altogether plentiful in Bedfordshire. At Woburn Abbey are *Holland*'s Chinese Dairy by the lake, several temples, and the thatched Thornery with tree-trunk veranda; at Southill, by another lake, a Fishing Temple with portico was put up, at Wrest a Bath House and Grotto as early as c.1758–60. They are by *Capability Brown*, whom a column in the park at Wrest commemorates and who did the superb grounds of Luton Hoo from 1764 onwards. The house at Luton Hoo was by *Robert Adam*, but little of that can be recognized now, and his most ambitious plans were not even considered for execution. The large bow-window on the E side survives, but it was originally surrounded by a giant portico.*

---

* As a postscript to the Adam style the *Wedgwood* black-basalt font at Cardington must not be forgotten. It was given in 1783.

Soane worked at Mogerhanger Park in 1809 etc. The chief
interest lies in the façade and the rooms with apsidal ends on the
first floor. The façade of Turvey House is a puzzle. The house
dates from 1794, yet the façade must be some time later, on the
strength of its freely used Grecian motifs. *Sir Robert Smirke*'s
sweeping remodelling *c*.1827 etc. of Robert Adam's Luton Hoo
is in a more correct and competent Grecian. The hexastyle
portico is excellent, even if not moving. More ponderously
Grecian is the Doric façade of the Public Library (former
Literary and Scientific Institution) at Bedford of 1834 (by
T. G. Elger), but the large Bedford Modern School opposite,
begun *c*.1825 by *John Wing*, continued by *Blore* in 1829, is Tudor.*
Altogether the anti-classical revivals were thriving by then. Their
chief representatives in Bedfordshire are *James Wyatt*'s not at
all inspired neo-Gothic of Chicksands Priory (1813) and the
whole-hog Picturesque and *orné* of *Humphry & J. Adey Repton*'s
Henry VII's Lodge at Woburn Sands. This dates from 1810–11
and displays timber-framing with closely set vertical studs,
brick-nogging, and highly ornamented terracotta chimneys.

This overcrowding with motifs of the past has a parallel in
three Bedfordshire churches which magpie-squires filled with
woodwork picked up on the Continent, mostly in the Netherlands, and supplemented by English Tudor and Stuart and indeed Late Georgian and Early Victorian bits. The churches in
82 question are Cockayne Hatley, where the collecting was done in
the twenties, and Old Warden and Pavenham, where it was done
in the forties.

VICTORIAN ARCHITECTURE is heralded by the fanfare of
98 Wrest Park. This, considering its date, 1834–6, is a building
& unique in England in its consistency of style. It is done in a French
99 *Dixhuitième* throughout, externally and internally, and the interiors are very lavish indeed. The French Baroque and Rococo
had in fact been revived in England by Benjamin Wyatt already
occasionally in the 1820s, but never with so much conviction

* The only other PUBLIC BUILDINGS of these years are the former
Workhouse at Bedford of 1794–6 (by *John Wing*), the Gaol at Bedford of
1801 (by *John Wing*) and 1840 (by *John Brown* of Norwich), several more
Workhouses of *c*.1835, all still classical, and the fine classical front of the
former Biggleswade Town Hall (by *J. T. Wing*) of 1844. The Wings, architects, went through several generations. Edward Wing of Aynho worked
there in the 1720s and on to 1730 or later. A Wing of Leicester (the same ?
built the remarkable church of Galby in 1741, very different from Aynho.
His son moved to Bedford and died there in 1794. The son of the latter, i.e.,
John, did the buildings here mentioned and died in 1826, and finally there
is James Tacy Wing, whom we can follow into the 1840s.

and panache. The architect is not known for certain, but seems to have been a Frenchman called *Cléphane*. After that, the door was wide open to historicism in all its stylistic aspects. In Bedfordshire it is less secular than ecclesiastical architecture which allows one to survey these aspects. The neo-Norman fashion characterizes the forties, as in all other counties. Examples are East Hyde by *Ferrey* of 1840–1 and St Cuthbert at Bedford by *Woodroffe* of 1844–7. But Gothic of course was the standard. However, Gothic can mean many things. The somewhat lean Commissioners' type with long lancet windows is represented in Holy Trinity Bedford by *Brown* of Norwich (1839–40). An amazingly early case of archaeologically knowledgeable imitation of Perp is Silsoe of 1829–31 by *T. Smith* of Hertford. *Scott*'s Ridgmont of 1854–5 on the Bedford estate is High Victorian 'Middle Pointed', i.e. late C13 to early C14 in style, and handled both competently and confidently. *Slater* at Mogerhanger in 1860–1 is just as competent, but more personal and of an austerity inherited by him from his erstwhile partner Carpenter. *Clutton* is quite a different case. His churches in Bedfordshire are amazingly original and of a breadth and unfussy, unostentatious boldness entirely his own. This applies to the large parish church of Woburn (1865–8) with its wide hall-church space and its French Early Gothic arcade columns set two-deep, and to Aspley Heath (1868) with its straight-headed windows, its German 'stump' tracery, and its totally original rose window. Rose windows with unexpected tracery patterns also occur in *Woodyer*'s Haynes in 1850 and Northill in 1862. The only other famous church architects represented in Bedfordshire are *Butterfield*, chiefly with one of his rare houses, Milton Ernest of 1856, and *Street*, whose chapel at Luton Hoo is or rather was Byzantine and not Gothic. It was built into the house in 1875. After that there is not a single church to the day of writing which would have to be included in this survey.

It is different with CHURCH FURNISHINGS, where at least in stained glass *Morris* (i.e. *Burne-Jones*) takes us to 1893 or shortly after (Marston Moretaine) and *Kempe*, admittedly not of Morris calibre, into the new century. By then his style (and even more that of his successor *Tower*) was getting out of date. Only one piece of church furnishing, the lectern at Cardington, reminds us of the emergence of a true C20 style in art. It dates from 1955, admittedly a very late date, and was designed by *Sir Albert Richardson* and carved by *Frank Dobson*.

For MONUMENTS we must go back to the Late Georgian

decades to catch up. Nothing after 1770 has yet been dealt with.
But there is a white mourning woman seated on the ground in
Thomas Banks's monument at Flitton († 1790), the *Bacon* monu-
94 ment of 1799 at Cardington to Samuel Whitbread, more moving
than Bacon usually is, two *Bacon Juniors* at Blunham († 1805)
and Odell († 1807), a *Flaxman* († 1815) at Sharnbrook, and a
Chantrey of 1832 at Milton Bryan with a white recumbent
96 effigy. *H. Weekes* in his Whitbread monument at Cardington of
1849 is still Grecian. Classical also still are *Westmacott* c.1845
at Millbrook and the little known *Terence Farrell* in his monu-
97 ment at Flitton of 1853 with the compassionately carved mourning family. It is a mad jump from there to the only other
memorable church monument in the county: Caroline Jane
Shuttleworth † 1899 at Old Warden, signed by *C. H. Mabey*.
This is in an unbridled Baroque – like a Magdalen in a Belgian
church.

There is nothing like that in SECULAR ARCHITECTURE, in
fact there is hardly anything of note prior to 1900 – a *Norman
Shaw* house at Leighton Linslade of 1880 and much more rewarding public buildings by *Basil Champneys* at Bedford, the
102 County Offices designed in 1886 and the Girls' High School designed in 1878 – but immediately after 1900 Luton Hoo received
its almost total internal remodelling for Sir Julius Wernher, the
South African captain of industry, at the hands of the Paris-
trained and Paris-based *Mewès & Davis*. They are known as the
architects of the Ritz, the Carlton, and the Waldorf, and that
shows at once to anybody who knows or knew these hotels with
what panache they could handle the materials of the French C18.
103 Luton Hoo is their *chef d'œuvre*, especially the palatial white
staircase hall, but also the other large apartments with their
marble-faced walls or *boiseries* and their large mirrors.

No more after that than a postscript as a reminder that the
International Modern of the 1930s is not quite missing (*Christopher Nicholson*'s Gliding Club at Dunstable is of 1935–6, *B.
Lubetkin*'s Whipsnade work of 1934 etc.) and that the Space Age
also has left a mark – nearly a quarter mile in circumference –
105 in Bedfordshire, the modestly termed Antenna at Chicksands.

FURTHER READING

The Victoria County Histories (VCH) have done Bedfordshire completely, though a long time ago (1904–14). For the Georgian century,
so far as houses are concerned, the best source, as always, is *Country
Life*. In addition over the last years the *Bedfordshire Magazine* has

proved useful. For individual places, one can consult F. A. Fowler:
Dunstable Priory, 1962; for Leighton Linslade R. Richmond: *Leighton
Buzzard and its Hamlets*, 1928; J. Dyer, F. Stygall, and J. Dony: *The
Story of Luton*, 1964; and for the region round Woburn, the Aspley
Heath Historical Society's *A History of our District* (revised ed. by
W. F. Cooper), 1962.

GEOLOGY OF BEDFORDSHIRE AND HUNTINGDON

BY TERENCE MILLER

These two counties occupy a roughly oblong fifty-by-twenty-
mile strip slightly across the geological grain of the East Mid-
lands, which in South Bedfordshire has a SW–NE orientation
swinging to N–S through Huntingdonshire, where it is almost
entirely concealed under the fens.

   Three main features dominate the physiography: the escarp-
ments of the Cretaceous Lower Greensand and Chalk in South-
East Bedfordshire; the wide, flat valley of the Great Ouse
running through both counties like a recumbent reversed S; and
the fenland of East Huntingdonshire. The first of these is the only
considerable tract of relatively high and well-drained ground.
For the rest Bedfordshire and Huntingdonshire spread over a
variety of Upper Jurassic clays – Oxford Clay, Ampthill Clay,
and Kimmeridge Clay – together with a narrow strip of Lower
Cretaceous Gault Clay in the SE. Unless one is a palaeontologist,
or an amateur of the minutiae of Jurassic and Cretaceous strati-
graphy, the geology is rather a dull affair.

   In the Great Ouse valley above Bedford and in the extreme N
of Huntingdonshire older, harder limestones emerge from beneath the dominant clays. These, the Lincolnshire and Great
Oolite Limestones, were formerly quarried about Water Newton
and Alwalton, and near Bedford, principally for lime. The Alwalton 'marble' can be seen in a few small pillars in Peterborough Cathedral. It is not of course a true marble but a hard,
compact limestone which will take a polish.

   No 'solid' rocks are seen in the deep fenland, except where a
temporary clay-pit is opened to provide material for the dyke
walls, or an 'island' like that of Ramsey sticks up above the silt
and peat. Along the fen margin, however, particularly round
Peterborough and Fletton, huge pits have been excavated in the
Oxford Clay, to provide the raw material for the major British
brick-making industry. On a smaller scale such pits, opened in

clays of various ages, can be seen through the two counties as far
south as the Lower Greensand scarp, and even beyond this in
the Gault vale which runs from Billington (s of Leighton Linslade) to the upper tributaries of the Cam E of Biggleswade.

The clay country is without distinctive form. Low, rounded
elevations – hardly worthy to be called hills – separate the stream
courses. Only between the Ouse and the Nene valley (in Northamptonshire) does the land rise slightly towards the margin of a
limestone ridge. Most of the countryside is in addition plastered
with a blanket of glacial clay, silt, or sand, with an abundant
scatter of stones and boulders of all sorts and sizes. One 'boulder'
of flinty chalk, near Catworth, is said to be ½ m. long and 12 ft
thick.

In South Bedfordshire, however, a more positive scenery is
found. Here, from Woburn NE to Potton and (appropriately)
Sandy, the Lower Greensand produces a strong, well-wooded
ridge overlooking Bedford and the Great Ouse valley. The ridge
is continuous except for the wide cross-valley of the Ivel around
Biggleswade, where the bedrock is again covered by thick sheets
of glacial and river-spread sands, gravels, and clays. The Greensand – somewhat misnamed, as it is usually a fine golden-brown
with sweeping lines of oblique stratification – is well seen where
the M1 motorway cuts through the ridge. There are interesting
varieties in the Greensand. Near Leighton Linslade it is an extremely pure 'silver sand', in the sense of having a very high
silica content, and is extracted for glass-making. Farther E along
the outcrop, near Silsoe, it has an abnormal proportion of iron
oxide and appears in certain churches as 'carstone', a hard, dark
brown gritty rock like coarse gingerbread which turns up again
in North Norfolk. Isolated masses of a similar kind, some thin
and tabular, others rounder and more bouldery, are scattered
throughout the main Greensand mass. Again, at Shenley Hill,
isolated compact masses of a pinkish-yellow pebbly or sandy
limestone occur. These, if one is lucky enough to find one, are
crammed with a fascinating collection of small fossils – sea shells,
fish teeth, crab claws, sea urchins, barnacles, and many others.

SE of the Greensand ridge the next higher formation, the
Gault Clay, forms a wide vale – its nature suggested by place-
names like Barton-le-Clay – and SE of it again there follows
the main scarp of the Chalk. This high ground – reaching 600 ft
around Whipsnade, Dunstable (where the steep scarp front
makes conditions ideal for sail-planing), and Luton – is an extension of the Chiltern ridge-line. Its basal Chalk layers were once

quite extensively mined for the phosphatic nodules contained in them and formerly used for fertilizer. The main mass of the Chalk is too soft for building. Here and there harder layers occur, and one of these, the Totternhoe Stone, a darker grey than most Chalk, slightly gritty, and with a distinctive 'curly grain', was formerly worked as a freestone. It can be seen in Dunstable Priory and Woburn Abbey.

Neither Bedfordshire nor Huntingdonshire can claim any natural sources of good building stone. Within fifty miles, and along convenient waterways lie (or once lay) plentiful supplies of famous English freestones in the Cotswolds and Lincolnshire. Only of clay for the making of bricks is there an abundance, and in former times no doubt good stands of oak for timbering must have grown on the heavy soils of the district.

PREHISTORY OF BEDFORDSHIRE

BY DEREK SIMPSON

Some of the earliest English discoveries of Palaeolithic tools were made in the county. Large numbers of hand axes of Acheulean type have come from gravel deposits at Caddington and Bedford together with numerous cores and waste flakes produced in the manufacture of finished tools.

However, the earliest surviving field monuments belong to the period of the first farming communities, who must have settled in the area from c.3000 B.C. The most numerous monuments of these immigrants are the long barrows beneath which they buried their dead (e.g. Knocking Knoll, Pegsdon; Leagrave, Luton; Galley Hill). Six examples have been recorded in Bedfordshire. A monument on Dunstable Down may be a long mortuary enclosure intimately associated with long barrows elsewhere in Britain intended as structures in which corpses might accumulate until their numbers warranted the construction of a long barrow. At Kempston is a possible cursus, a third category of ritual or ceremonial monument again associated with long barrows and long mortuary enclosures elsewhere. A mixed farming economy appears to have been practised, grain-growing being indicated among other evidence by cereal impressions on pottery, and stock-raising by animal bones found in the ditches of causewayed camps. Maiden Bower, Dunstable has long been known as an example of this category of hill-top enclosure, one of whose functions appears to have been the temporary corralling of cattle for purposes of identification, barter, and slaughter. Other possible camps exist at Maulden Firs, Barton-le-Clay and at Cardington. From the ditch at Maiden Bower came sherds of typical, well-fired, round-based Western Neolithic wares, sherds of which have also been found on Barton Hill and Galley Hill, Barton-le-Clay and in a barrow in the Five Knolls cemetery, Dunstable. Even light forests must have presented a formidable obstacle to these primitive agriculturists, and to clear tracts of land for cultivation and grazing both flint and stone axes were employed. There is a considerable body of evidence for the working of suitable stone outcrops in Britain and for the distribution of the products of these axe factories. Stray finds of flint and stone axes are known from the county, but only one of the stone axes, from Great Barford, has been examined petrologically. It was shown to be a product of one of the Cornish axe factories. Among the other finds of this period one may mention leaf-shaped flint arrowheads from various localities and an antler comb, used in skin dressing, from Maiden Bower.

For the later Neolithic (from c.2000 B.C.) there is as yet insufficient material from the county to build up a detailed picture. Two main elements appear to be represented: on the one hand, the continuing and evolving material traditions of the descendants of the first Neolithic colonists, best expressed in pottery, such as that represented at Eaton Socon, Kempston, and Barton Hill, Streatley, which is less well fired and more profusely ornamented than the wares of the preceding period but whose decoration and form betrays its ancestry in earlier ceramic traditions; on the other, new immigrants representing a series of folk movements from the Low Countries to eastern Britain characterized by drinking cups or Beakers which they placed in graves with their dead. Finds of Beaker material in Berkshire are concentrated along the banks of the Ouse and in the Chilterns. The former group of finds probably represents riverine penetration from the east coast. The Chilterns settlement can most reasonably be explained in terms of a landward movement along the Icknield Way. The evidence for settlement by Beaker groups is represented entirely by graves – either flat graves, as at Clifton, or covered by a round barrow (Dunstable Down, Five Knolls Group) – or by stray finds such as the archer's wrist-guard from Sandy and the fine flint daggers from Kempston and Jackdaw Hill, Leighton Linslade.

These disparate elements at the end of the Neolithic were knit together at the beginning of the Bronze Age (*c.*1650 B.C.) into a distinctive society and culture. The evidence is again largely provided by burial monuments. The ubiquitous bowl barrow continued to be constructed, but new and exotic forms appear at this time – notably the bell barrow. The barrow cemetery at Five Knolls, Dunstable belongs to this period and includes three large bell barrows surrounded by a common ditch. One of the barrows in this group produced a cremation burial in a collared urn, a form of pottery which develops from Neolithic ceramic traditions. Other urn burials have been found at Barton Hill, Streatley, Foulkes Pit, Kempston and Elstow. Few of the barrows of this period have been excavated, and those that have are generally poorly furnished with grave goods other than pottery. A small bronze knife dagger was found in a barrow (since destroyed) at Marina Drive, Dunstable and stray finds of barb and tang arrowheads of Early Bronze Age type have been found at Maiden Bower, Dunstable and Leagrave, Luton. Sherds of collared urns have also come out in association with a boundary ditch system at Dray's Ditches, Luton and with a hut and furnace pit at Totternhoe.

For the Middle and Late Bronze Age the evidence is even more scanty. Sherds of coarse, badly fired bucket urns have been found at Toddington and Dray's Ditches. The greater quantity of metalwork in circulation at this period is reflected in the increasing number of stray bronzes. The majority of these finds are of isolated socketed axes, but one large metalsmith's hoard of sixty socketed axes was found at Wymington, and further hoards of scrap bronze and ingots at Park Close and Fancott, Toddington and Ickwell Bury.

The introduction of the knowledge of iron-working by settlers from the continent in the c6 does not in fact appear to have markedly changed the economic pattern as established in the Middle and Late Bronze Age. The normal economic unit appears to have been the small isolated farmstead with its associated group of Celtic fields. The finds from Totternhoe indicate just such a settlement, marked by an enclosure ditch and storage pits; the adjacent group of Celtic fields are probably to be related to it. Growing unrest and possible land hunger are however attested by the appearance of the first hillforts (e.g. Maiden Bower, Dunstable; Caesar's Camp, Sandy). Such forts indicate the corporate activity of large numbers of individuals and the existence of larger political and social units, while the multiple banks and ditches of Dray's Ditches (Luton), the western-most of a series of such dykes, is probably to be related to a tribal territorial area.

By the beginning of the first century A.D. the whole of Bedfordshire, together with neighbouring counties to the N and E, was united into a single kingdom. The kingdom was that of the most powerful of the Belgic tribes of Britain, the Catuvellauni, who, under their great king Cunobelin, established suzerainty over the whole of South-East England. The greater political complexity of this last hundred years of prehistory in the area is matched by increasing technological sophistication, the most marked developments being the introduction of wheel-turned pottery produced on an industrial scale and by an established coinage, the later forms bearing the names of Catuvellaunian kings or of their war god Camulos. In Bedfordshire there is a marked concentration of these coins at Limbury, many bearing the name of Cunobelin or of his father Tasciovanus. A feature of the archaeology of Catuvellaunian territory is the series of princely vault burials richly furnished with fine metalwork, amphorae containing wine, and other imported luxury goods from the classical world. No undoubted example of such a chieftain's grave has yet been found in the county, although an ill-recorded C19 find at Old Warden included a finely ornamented bronze mirror, shale vessels, and (possibly) amphorae and may belong to this class. The pair of bronze bowls, ceremonial bucket, and fish-head spout from Felmersham could certainly all have graced the table of a Belgic prince.

ROMAN BEDFORDSHIRE AND HUNTINGDON

BY BARRY CUNLIFFE

THE area with which we are concerned has so far yielded few Roman sites of particular note. The reason is not difficult to see, for much of the region consists of a vast expanse of Oxford clay which was presumably thickly wooded at the time and difficult to cultivate. The clay-land is, however, cut by the valleys of the Ouse and its many tributaries, and it is along their gravel terraces that Roman peasant settlements densely cluster. It is in these regions, too, that the few known villas are situated.

The region was essentially rural. No large urban centres are known, but small settlements grew up along the main roads at

places such as Water Newton, Godmanchester, Sandy, and probably Dunstable, serving no doubt as posting stations as well as
local markets. Water Newton (Durobrivae), 44 acres in extent,
was the most important of these. It was sited at a major river-
crossing at the point where Ermine Street – the Roman version of
the Great North Road – bridged the Nene. Furthermore, it lay
at the centre of one of the most highly developed pottery indus-
tries in the country, and would have served as the main base
whence kiln products would have been distributed by river,
canal, and road, to all parts of the country.

The significance of the Nene crossing is further emphasized
by the fact that several military sites have been found in the area.
On the outskirts of Durobrivae a fort is known, and a mile or so
along the road to the N a marching camp has been recognized.
More recently, a camp capable of taking half a legion has been
discovered down-river at Longthorpe, and the suggestion has
been made that the site might have housed half the IX Legion
before permanent quarters were built for it at Lincoln. At any
event, military occupation is unlikely to have lasted much into
the Flavian period, after which the peasant farmers would have
peacefully and unpretentiously continued their activities.

BEDFORDSHIRE

*

AMPTHILL

ST ANDREW. The church, of ironstone, like all the churches in
this part of Bedfordshire, stands close to the E end of the
little town and still enjoys an almost unimpeded view into the
rolling country around. The church consists of W tower with
higher stair-turret, nave and aisles, a two-storeyed S porch,
and a chancel. It is all Perp outside – though over-restored –
but inside the four-bay arcades are of tall early C14 piers of
the quatrefoil type with four thin shafts in the diagonals. The
arch mouldings are typically early C14 too. So is the chancel
arch. The Perp nave roof has angels and a ceilure above the
former rood. In the N aisle NE corner an image niche. – SCULP-
TURE. Head of a lantern cross (S aisle E). – Wooden angel from
the roof (W tower). – STAINED GLASS. In one N aisle window
a panel of old bits. – (EMBROIDERY. Frontal S aisle altar.
Spanish C18.) – MONUMENTS. Brasses to William Hicche-
cok, a 'wolman', † 1450 and his wife ($35\frac{1}{2}$ in. figures), to the wife
of John Lodyngton † 1485 (15 in.), and to John Bernard † 1506
and his wife ($17\frac{1}{2}$ in.). All these are on the W wall of the nave.
In the N aisle E wall brass to Sir Nicholas Hervey † 1532
(24 in.). – Very fine standing monument without any figures
to Richard Nicolls † 1672 at Sole Bay. The cannon ball which
killed him is in the steep pediment. This crowns a centre
piece between the two sides of a broken pediment. – Second
Earl of Upper Ossory † 1818. A slender column with an elegant pitcher – that is all.

Two CHAPELS in Dunstable Street tell a story of Noncon-
formity. The BAPTISTS in 1870 still did the traditional, anti-
churchy Italianate job, and did it poorly – yellow brick, three
bays, big pediment, arched windows – but the METHODISTS
in 1884, using blue brick with red dressings, built in the E.E.
style, to a much larger scale. Even they, however, still re-
frained from a steeple.

Ampthill is essentially a cross of streets. At the meeting point is the MOOT HALL of 1852, brick, with shaped gables and the cupola of its predecessor. Also at the meeting point the OBELISK PUMP, 1784 to *Sir William Chambers*'s design. Engraved directions and distances to four places as well. At the start of DUNSTABLE STREET at once the WHITE HART, early C18, of seven bays and three storeys. Doorway with open pediment. Further down a number of good late C17 and C18 houses. Among them No. 103 has a doorway with hood on scrolly brackets (and No. 98 in the garden an Early Georgian brick GAZEBO with pyramid roof). Further out on the l. the former WORKHOUSE, 1835, red brick, large, of the standard cross plan with octagonal centre. The windows are still arches. No Victorian signs yet. Opposite the new RURAL DISTRICT OFFICES, 1964–5 by *Sir Albert Richardson, Houfe & Partners*, completed in 1965 and quite unbelievable for their date – still symmetrical simplified neo-Georgian, with cupola.

Back to the Moot Hall and out w along WOBURN STREET and WOBURN ROAD. On the N side a group of pairs of picturesque *cottages ornés*, thickly thatched. They are dated 1812, 1815, and 1816. Then on the s side the new COURT HOUSE, pleasant and unmonumental, 1963–4 by *J. C. Barker*, the county architect. Yet further out, up behind the parking space, KATHERINE'S CROSS, to commemorate Ampthill Castle and Katherine of Aragon who lived there during the divorce proceedings. It was erected in 1773 by the Earl of Upper Ossory and designed by *James Essex*. The foot has close and dainty tracery, the cross itself arms whose ends are little transversely-set crosses. Again a little further out turn l. to Littlepark Farm and go a little beyond to the OXFORD HOSPITAL for College Servants. This is an exceptionally stately almshouse, founded by John Cross of Oxford University in 1697. Chequer brick, five-bay centre with one-bay wooden pediment and lantern and three-bay wings. Two storeys plus dormers, hipped roof, wooden cross windows. From the sides the group is simply a three-bay doll's house. Small chapel in the middle below the pediment.

Back again to the Moot Hall, and now E towards the church. CHURCH STREET is the best street at Ampthill and AVENUE HOUSE is the finest house. It was built about 1780 for John Morris, the Ampthill brewer, and enlarged for him on the r. by *Holland* in 1792–5. It was before then quite a modest red terrace house of five bays, and only the very elegant doorway is a Holland addition. The rooms are small, except for the

one large room in the extension. Inside are good fireplaces.*
The great surprise however is the garden, which is as large as
though the house were in the country. Below to the w is the
former brewery. On the N is a wooden temple, which was
bought by Morris when Houghton House (*see* below) was dismantled in 1794. It is of wood and rather heavy, with the
pilasters and triglyph frieze of the doorway. A few houses
further on in Church Street are the iron GATES from
Houghton, a very fine C18 piece. Behind, lying back, an C18
three-bay house with a good doorway. More good doorways to
come. On the other side No. 37, early C18, five bays and three
storeys with stone quoins and a square middle projection,
making the open porch on the ground floor. Nice staircase.
At the corner of the approach to the church is DYNEVOR
HOUSE, dated 1725. To this house Morris's gardens originally belonged. This is a seven-bay chequer-brick house of two
and a half storeys with parapet. Doorway with fluted pilasters
and a triglyph frieze. The first-floor windows have frilly
lintel bricks. Opposite BRANDRETH HOUSE has the most
curious corbels to its door-hood, a motif occurring in other
doorways in this part of Bedfordshire as well. The flanking
columns bend forward without any capital to be brackets for
the hood. On the l. of this the FEOFFEE ALMSHOUSES with
a timber-framed front and a one-storeyed C18 wing at the
back.

In Bedford Street there is nothing to report, but that it is the
approach to the three most important buildings outside the
centre. Up Park Street and Park Hill and along a footpath one
reaches RUSSETT'S LODGE, a very curious pavilion added to
a C17 cottage. It is of three bays, one storey, blue brick
headers, and has heavily (but smoothly) rusticated window
surrounds. Doorway with bulgy Doric pilasters and a frieze.
Top pediment (of brick slag?). Stone quoins.

From the road to Bedford a turn to the l. takes one to Ampthill
Park, a turn to the r. to the ruins of Houghton House.

AMPTHILL PARK (Cheshire Home). The manorial history of
Ampthill is complicated, and as it comprises Houghton House
(*see* below) as well, it may be summarized here. Ampthill belonged to the Kings, and *c.*1615 James I gave the land on
which Houghton House and Ampthill Park stand to Mary
Countess of Pembroke. Then, in 1661, Charles II handed a
portion over to John Ashburnham. This was the portion on

And *Sir Albert Richardson*'s miscellaneous collections; for he lived here.

which the first Lord Ashburnham built Ampthill Park in 1694. The rest of the estate went with Houghton House. It is not known who designed Ampthill Park, but *Wren* was consulted by the Lord for the family pew in the parish church and in the end designed it, and Captain *William Wynne*, the architect of Buckingham House, certainly advised in 1706 on interior matters. The house is eleven bays wide and of basement and two storeys. It is of blue brick with red dressings and has a three-bay pediment with coat of arms and a hipped roof and a spacious doorway with unfluted Ionic columns in front of rustication and a wide open curly pediment. A wide curving open staircase with wrought-iron handrail leads up to it. The garden side is similar but has a doorway with Doric pilasters and a big open segmental pediment. In the top pediment is later c18 decoration, and indeed the house was enlarged and redecorated under *Chambers* in 1769–71. He added the pilastered links and the plain wings. The l. one has a broad canted bay and contained the library, one large room throughout. In only one room are richly carved door surrounds of c.1700; the rest of the decoration is of the Chambers period. Good stucco in Saloon and Library. Pretty early c18 Powder Cabinet on the first floor. At that time the house belonged to the second Earl of Upper Ossory – *see* below.

(THE CEDARS (former workhouse). 1835–6 by *James Cléphane*. It has 'an unusually distinctive architectural character'. *Industrial Archaeology in Bedfordshire*, 1967, p. 31.)

70 HOUGHTON HOUSE. Houghton House is a mysterious building, and the last word has certainly not yet been said about its date or dates and its architectural history. It is said that it was begun about 1615. The owner then was Mary Countess of Pembroke, sister of Sir Philip Sidney. After she died, about 1630, the house went to Thomas Bruce, first Earl of Elgin (*see* Maulden). His son was the first Earl of Ailesbury. In 1738 the Duke of Bedford bought the house, and his son, the Marquis of Tavistock, lived there from 1764 till he was killed in an accident in 1767. It was then occupied by the Earl of Upper Ossory, and was finally dismantled by the Duke of Bedford in 1794.

Houghton House is of brick with stone dressings. Basically it belongs to a normal Jacobean type. The plan is H-shaped with two square projections in the two re-entrant angles of the s façade. The windows are upright, mullioned-and-transomed and pedimented. There are two storeys, but owing to

the fall of the land to the E there is here a high basement under.
This may be left from an older house on the site (buttresses).
The N front has two canted bay windows in the projecting
wings. The W side also has a recessed centre. A little less normal, but far from unique, are the four square angle turrets.
They had, at least in the early C19, concave-sided pyramid
roofs. There were then also plenty of shaped gables. So far there
is nothing worth special architectural comment. But the house
is two rooms deep, and has its hall in the middle of the S front,
entered in its middle and left towards the room behind also
by its middle, and this abandoning of the traditional hall
position and arrangement, i.e. of the screens passage etc., would
be very early indeed for 1615 (but cf. Aston Hall, Birmingham,
1618 and several of John Thorpe's designs). Nor is this all:
for the S, N, and W fronts all have in their middle prominent
decorative features which are impossible for 1615 and point
unmistakably to a date about 1635–45 or so. On the S side
the porch has very odd details in the doorway and the window
above it. The big keystones cannot be overlooked. Those of
the doorway carry a segmental pediment. Also, above the
inner doorway is a horizontally placed oval. Much more
spectacular are the centre pieces or frontispieces of the N and
W sides. To the N it is a three-bay arcaded element with
Tuscan columns. There were two storeys of this plus a third
with an arched window and two arched niches plus a one-bay
attic with volutes l. and r. and a pediment. A comparison for
some of these motifs is the N front of Kirby Hall of 1638–40.
But the W frontispiece of Houghton House has no comparison.
It was in its original, complete form of three loggias one on
top of the other with columns carrying not arches but straight
entablatures. The ground-floor columns are Tuscan with a
frieze of decorated metopes. The doorway again has a horizontally placed oval. The two lower loggias are of five bays,
the top one has three and is crowned by a pediment. In the
hall are two chimneypieces. The work here assigned to c.1635–
45 has been attributed to *Inigo Jones*, but there is no evidence
at all.

To the E of Houghton House is a C17 six-bay HOUSE with a
hipped roof. Doorway with big corbels.*

* Ampthill House was demolished about 1953–4.

ST PETER. A complicated history. It starts with the chancel added to the preceding church. This has lancet windows, mostly renewed, but a Dec E window with reticulated tracery. At about the same time the nave received a one-bay NE chapel which, very soon afterwards (see the bases of the piers), was lengthened W by a further bay. A length of wall and a wider span to the W arch mark this second stage. A still longer length of wall further W marks where the original W wall of the nave was. Only a little later the S arcade was built. It was of five bays, the Perp tower encroaching on the W bay. So by then a considerable W extension had been decided on, and another two bays were added to the N aisle in the early C14. The arcade elements are standard throughout. Externally there is less of interest. The W tower is of 1877. The N aisle has a Dec W and a good Perp E window with crenellation in the head. The S aisle windows are Perp too. So is the chancel arch. So are two niches in the N aisle, one of these very pretty. The S doorway with continuous mouldings corresponds to the S arcade. – FONT. An elaborate Perp piece, unfortunately much mutilated. Statuettes against the shaft, in the East Anglian way. Bowl with scenes from Genesis and the Crucifixion, also in the East Anglian way. – FAMILY PEW. Mid Elizabethan, with thin columns and a broad, bold dolphin frieze. – ROOD SCREEN. Tall, Perp, with two-light divisions. – PLATE. Cup of 1730, Paten probably of 1730. – MONUMENTS. In the N aisle W bay a C14 tomb recess. – In the N aisle E bay another, very plain Perp recess. – Anne Edwards † 1733 and her son † 1760. A good standing monument with a grey obelisk and on it two well-done oval portrait medallions.

FAIRFIELD HOSPITAL (Three Counties Hospital). A vast group of buildings, mostly of yellow brick, starting with those by *George Fowler Jones* of York, 1857 etc. They cost in the first four years £114,831. In 1868 came a £22,000 extension, in 1877 a £72,000 extension (GS). By then there were 1000 beds. The oldest part is the main building. The chapel dates from 1878–9. It has a square and bare SW tower with steep pyramid roof, a wide nave with a big roof, and a polygonal apse.

ASPLEY GUISE

ST BOTOLPH. Of ironstone, externally almost entirely Victorian.
The w tower e.g. is Perp, but the w window is Victorian.
There is in fact a date 1855, when the s aisle was built. How
much else was done then? The arch from tower into nave is
very fanciful – not a bit archaeologically faithful. Can this be of
1855? The N arcade again is genuine, i.e., like the tower, Perp.
– FONT. Drum-shaped, with four shafts. Is it late C13? –
SCREEN (N aisle). Perp. Of one-light divisions. – PULPIT. A
made-up piece with Netherlandish C17 panels and English
late C17 decoration. – STAINED GLASS. The s aisle w window
by *E. Baillie* and *G. Mayer*, 1854. Completely pictorial. –
Earlier still looks the s chapel E window, in spite of a date of
death 1852. The MEMORIALS which flank it also seem *c*.1840:
the Rev. John Vaux Moore † 1864 l., Mrs Moore † 1820 r. –
The s chapel s window is by *Kempe, c.* 1900. – PLATE. Cup
and Paten on foot, 1754. – MONUMENTS. Defaced late C14
Knight on a tomb-chest with quatrefoils as well as gabled
niches. – Brass to a Priest, *c*.1410 (18 in. figure). He kneels,
and to his r. is St John Baptist. Mr McHardy suggests that they
once belonged to a foliated cross. – Brass to a Knight, *c*.1500
(23 in. figure). Both in the N aisle floor.

ASPLEY HOUSE. The front is a perfect specimen of its date:
1695. Seven bays, two storeys, chequer-brick, with a three-
bay pediment. Doorway with open pediment on corbels with
cherubs' heads. The l. extension by *Sir Reginald Blomfield*
has been pulled down. The garden side is of *c*.1750, also
seven-bay but with two doorways, with Doric pilasters and
triglyph frieze. Blue headers and red dressings including the
motif of lacing. The middle bay has Venetian windows and a
steep broken pediment cut into by a chimney. Good staircase
with two twisted balusters to the tread. The arches between
it and the entrance hall have been moved to another room.
In this room also a fine late C18 chimneypiece. – At the back
a substantial garden wall sweeping up to a gateway.

s of the garden is GUISE HOUSE, early C18, with a five-bay
front to the garden. Doorway with hood on carved brackets.
Middle window arched. The other main windows with aprons.

OLD HOUSE, N of Aspley House. Timber-framed, with brick
infilling. Of *c*.1575. In one upper room a canted ceiling with
bold early C17 strapwork, bands as broad as metal bands and
with studs. In the middle a panel with Cupid. C18 staircase.

9030

ASPLEY HEATH

St Michael. 1868 by *Clutton* (cf. Woburn), with alterations and additions by *Sir Arthur Blomfield*, 1889, and with a N war memorial chapel. Clutton's work is amazing, the strange and bold single columns to separate nave from aisles, even more the four-light, straight-headed windows with their odd, exclusively German, 'stump' tracery, and yet more the completely free N rose window with a cross of two mullions and two transoms. These things are obviously not Blomfield's, though the chapel is no doubt largely his.

Silverbirches, at the end of Silverbirches Lane. By *Brewill & Bailey*, 1898. Typical of its date. Brick, gabled, with mullioned windows and a pretty, square, domed turret above the entrance.

2030

ASTWICK

St Guthlac. Not in a good state at the time of writing. The church has a short W tower literally surrounded by mystery; for off it to the S is a tall blocked triple-chamfered arch much too big to belong to a porch. Was the tower then a crossing tower before the present nave and chancel were built? Hardly; for there is no indication of an arch to a nave W of the tower, and instead of a N transept arch is just a small arch as of a doorway but with remarkably big stones. The tower now has a Perp doorway to the W. Perp nave windows of three lights, Perp chancel arch. In the chancel E wall two brackets, one with a head. – Benches. The plain buttressed type of the county. – Box pews and a two-decker pulpit. – Plate. Chalice of 1794.

Rectory House, N of the church. Dated 1720. Five bays, red brick, pitched roof, still wooden cross-windows.

0030

BARTON-LE-CLAY

St Nicholas. The church has E.E. arcades, more elaborate on the S side, standard on the N side. The SW and SE responds are of three detached shafts with shaft-rings and have capitals with close stiff-leaf. The piers are circular, as are those of the N arcade. Plain, bold moulded capitals. Double-chamfered arches. The W bay followed soon. Good low-pitched roof with angels and carved bosses, the stone corbels supporting the

beams with C14 faces. Over the former rood a ceilure. Chancel
late C13, see particularly the SEDILIA, PISCINA, and EASTER
SEPULCHRE. Impressive Perp W tower with higher stair-
turret. Tierceron-star vault inside.* Externally a nice variety
of materials. – FONT. Originally Norman, see the rope moulding, but re-carved Perp, octagonal with quatrefoils. – BENCHES.
With linenfold panelling. – PAINTING. St Nicholas, 4 ft 8 in.,
early C16 and very good. Is it South German ? – STAINED
GLASS. Small bits in N aisle windows. – PLATE. Cup 1635. –
BRASSES. Richard Brey † 1396, priest; demi-figure 12 in.
long. – Bearded Civilian, 13 in., c.1400.

HILLFORT AND ENCLOSURE, on Galley Hill, close to the
plantation known as Maulden Firs. Both sites were located
from the air. The fort is a roughly oval, univallate structure
covering 2 acres. The adjacent enclosure is again oval, with
maximum internal measurements of 71 ft by 45 ft. There is no
indication of an entrance gap in the line of the ditch. Sherds
of Iron Age pottery were recovered from the latter site.

BATTLESDEN

9020

ST PETER. In the grounds of Battlesden Park, a house of c.1862,
long demolished but with surviving grounds laid out by
Paxton. Paxton had been employed as a garden boy at
Battlesden, and in the end rebuilt the house and remodelled
the grounds for the son of his erstwhile employer. The church
is small and much repaired. But how can it be maintained
now, with so small a congregation? W tower, aisleless nave. In
the tower S wall late C13 window with bar tracery, proving
that the tower was put into the existing nave later. In the N
wall a big three-light early C16 window. Dec chancel arch.‡ –
FONT. Norman, drum-shaped, with a few sparse decorative
motifs. – PLATE. Two Patens on feet, 1674; two Cups, 1676;
Paten, given in 1696. – MONUMENTS. William Duncombe
† 1603. The monument is evidently not in its original shape;
the open scrolly pediment e.g. must be of the late C17. – Lady
Elizabeth Duncombe and her husband, undated, but probably
mid C17, though inspired at several removes from Italian
later C16 Mannerism. Big cartouche with fleshy, gristly surround.

* Upstairs in the tower a fireplace (*Beds. Mag.* I). This suggests a dwelling,
and there is indeed an outer doorway up there. It must have been accessible
by a wooden stair or ladder.

‡ Mr McHardy points out two image brackets l. and r. of the E window
and suggests that the putti on them are re-cut Perp angels.

0040

BEDFORD

INTRODUCTION

Bedford was a trading place already in the C10. Shortly after the Conquest a CASTLE was built of which nothing now remains but the lower part of the motte or mound, 160 ft in diameter. The castle lay E of the Market Place and extended as far as Newnham Road. The motte is just W of the latter and N of Castle Walls, the continuation of Embankment. The inner bailey was to its N, the outer bailey to its W, i.e. N of the Swan Hotel. The N boundary of the site is Ram Yard. The castle was still defended in the Civil War. In the Middle Ages Bedford had two Augustinian priories, NEWNHAM, founded c.1165 and originally the collegiate establishment of St Paul, the principal parish church, and CALDWELL, in Kempston Road (founded c.1154).* There also was a GREYFRIARS house in Bromham Road (founded by 1238). Of none are there any telling remains. In the C18, largely thanks to the Ouse being navigable then, Bedford was prosperous in a moderate way. Defoe about 1725 called it a 'large, populous, well-built and thriving town', Torrington in 1793 'vile, unimproved and without trade' – but that may tell more of the characters of the writers than of the condition of Bedford. Industry began to expand in the mid C19, but the rate of growth accelerated much after the Second World War.

MEDIEVAL CHURCHES

ST PAUL, St Paul's Square. The major church of Bedford. It is a large town church, and over-restored. The total length is 167 ft. Externally there is little of genuine untampered-with detail. The church has a crossing tower with a recessed spire. Three sets of lucarnes in alternating directions. The earliest feature of the exterior is the E.E. doorway. The rest all appears C14 and C15. Aisles and clerestory are embattled. Two-storey S porch with quatrefoil base-frieze. Statue niches on the upper floor. One-storey N porch. Four-bay S chapel.‡ Two-storey NE vestry. The interior is almost as totally re-done as the exterior. Of the transepts the N one is of 1865–8, of the five-bay aisles the N one of 1884. The chancel chapel arcades are entirely of 1878–9, though the S chapel existed (see e.g.

---

* A long wall, N of the Ouse opposite Fenlake, is said to have belonged to Newnham Priory.

‡ Mr Kuhlicke points out that this chapel was called newly built in 1416.

the ANGLE PISCINA). Only the s aisle arcade is partly original. Its date must be the early C14. Quatrefoil piers, double-chamfered arches. The crossing arches belong to about the same years, but are again a rebuilding of 1868.* The most interesting feature of the interior is that it is a 'hall', i.e. that the aisles are of the same height as the nave. For that reason they have clerestory windows. The aisles are about as wide as the nave, adding to the sense of spaciousness created by the hall motif. Good C15 roofs in nave and s aisle. – FONT. Dec. Base with a little ballflower and fleuron decoration. – PULPIT. This is really part of the stone canopy of a former reredos, very ornately done, with the miniature rib-vault inside the top part of a niche. The date must be the early C16. It is a very intelligent adaptation. – SCREENS. The rood screen is by *Bodley*. – s chapel screen Perp with one-light division. – STALLS. In the chancel. Carved arms and MISERICORDS. One shows a barbican-like abbreviation of a castle. – STAINED GLASS. In the N aisle one window by *Kempe*, 1892, another, it seems, by *Holiday* and *Powell's*, i.e. with typical Walter-Cranish foliage and figures influenced by the Pre-Raphaelites. Date recorded: 1885. – PLATE. Chalice and Paten 1570; Plate 1698; Chalice 1718; Portuguese Thurible 1744; Plate 1824. – Also an inlaid Spanish Cross. – MONUMENTS. s of the altar is the indent of a brass to Simon de Beauchamp † 1208. If the brass were preserved, it would be by far the earliest in England.‡ – In the s chapel brass to Sir William Harpur, Lord Mayor of London, † 1573 and wife. He is in armour, but also wears his alderman's gown. 20 in. figures. – In the chancel Andrew Dennys † 1633, rector of St John. The usual frontal demi-figure with a cushion in front of him. – Thomas Christie † 1697. Tablet with black columns and a scrolly open pediment with an urn. – Again in the s chapel Sir William Harpur † 1768 and Dame Alice. By *Benjamin Palmer*. Obelisk with an oval medallion with the two profiles. – Many more good tablets. – The church has fine C18 iron RAILINGS and GATES.

In ST PAUL'S SQUARE is a STATUE of John Howard. This is by *Alfred Gilbert*, 1894.

ST JOHN BAPTIST, St John's Street. The church was probably the chapel of the Hospital of St John (on which *see* p. 53. The chancel is Dec, see the chancel arch, the SEDILIA and

* This was done by *R. Palgrave* on lines laid down by *Street* (F. W. Kuhlicke).

‡ Information from Mr F. W. Kuhlicke.

PISCINA,priest's and the doorway. The E lancets date from 1869–70, when also the side arches were made and the typically High Victorian hammerbeam roof on naturalistic leaf corbels was put on. The aisleless nave has C19 lancet windows. Perp W tower with quatrefoil base frieze and a doorway with big leaf in the spandrels. – PLATE. Chalice and Cover Paten inscribed 1570; Paten 1724; Chalice, Cover Paten, and Paten inscribed 1726.

ST MARY, St Mary's Square. The church has a Norman crossing tower with big twin bell-openings. The top is Perp. Inside, the four tower arches are all re-done. The W arch has a Victorian hood-mould of dogtooth. Norman also are the transepts. In the S transept a problem arises: the E wall has a large blocked Norman window, but this cuts into a smaller round-arched window higher up, to which corresponds a W window. Both have deep single splays without any rebate. In the S wall of the transept is much herringbone masonry. So the most likely date is the second half of the C11. The chancel is Dec, see the reticulated tracery and the cusped intersected tracery, both drastically renewed. The E window is of c.1875–80. The nave has Perp arcades, the N one original, the S one of 1853. The N aisle windows have uncusped, i.e. C16, lights and straight tops. The piers are thin and of the standard moulded section. Thin arches too. – BENCHES. Plain, Georgian. – SCULPTURE. One good Norman head from a corbel-table. – PLATE. Chalice 1569; Cover Paten 1583; Paten on foot 1684; Cover Paten 1721; Flagon 1761; two Almsdishes 1762. – Also a C16 German Processional Cross. – MONUMENT. Major William Mills † 1838. By J. Loft of 92 Dean Street, Soho. Mourning young people by a pedestal. A palm-tree behind. Quite good.

ST PETER DE MERTON. The archaeological thrill of the church is the Anglo-Saxon evidence. The church appears now to have a Norman central tower. In fact it originally had an Anglo-Saxon W tower, and the present chancel was the nave belonging to it. This is evident from the fact that the chancel is just that little wider than the tower. The tower has long-and-short quoins, visible on the W face inside. On the N as on the S one exceptionally huge upright stone. Also in the tower are traces, visible outside, of blocked upper windows, and there is, visible again inside, one of those fairly frequent doorways in the E face which may have led on to a wooden balcony. Of the present chancel the long-and-short W quoins are equally plain to see,

s outside, N inside the vestry. The twin bell-openings of the
tower are Norman, the very top is of course not genuine.
Norman also, but moved from St Peter Dunstable, the s doorway. It is a fine piece with two orders of shafts, carrying
decorated scallop capitals, with saltire crosses in the abacus,
and roll mouldings, one of them with a spiral beaded band.
The C13 is represented by the E arch of the tower (triple-
chamfered) and two N lancets, one being blocked. The arcades
of six bays look convincingly C14, but are Victorian. – FONT.
Big, octagonal, Perp, with quatrefoils, tracery motifs, and
other motifs. – STAINED GLASS. In the chancel medieval
fragments not originally in the church; partly foreign. –
PLATE. Cup of 1683 and Cover Paten; Paten 1807. – s of the
church C18 iron RAILINGS.

On ST PETER'S GREEN is a STATUE of Bunyan by *Sir J. E.
Boehm*, 1874.

POST-MEDIEVAL CHURCHES

(ALL SAINTS, Iddesleigh Road. 1914 by *G. P. Allen*. Red brick
and stone. Goodhart-Rendel writes: 'Good taste, after
Bodley'.)

HOLY CHILD JESUS (R.C.), Midland Road. 1872–4 by *Gilbert
R. Blount*. Rock-faced, with an incomplete SW tower. Polygonal apse. Geometrical tracery. There is nothing to recommend in the interior.

CHRIST CHURCH, Goldington Road. By *N. F. Cachemaille-Day*,
1956–8. Yellow brick, with tall, oblong windows and a square
tower.

ST CUTHBERT, Mill Street. 1844–7 by *Woodroffe*, the aisles by
F. C. Penrose, 1865. Neo-Norman with a crossing tower. The
details round the crossing quite ornate. – FONT. Returned
from Great Woolston. With four shafts in the corners of the
rounded bowl. Probably early C14. – STAINED GLASS. The E
window with medallions by *Baillie* (TK). – PLATE. Small
Elizabethan Chalice; Cover Paten 1569; Chalice 1774(?).

ST LEONARD, Victoria Road. 1911–13 by *G. P. Allen*. Red
brick without a tower. Lancet windows. It is a standard
product of the early C20, when nothing eventful was demanded
or tolerated.

ST MARTIN, Clapham Road. 1888–9 by *J. A. Chatwin* of
Birmingham. Unattractive externally, much more convincing
inside. Buff stone with thin red-brick bands. E.E. style. No
tower. Double transepts with double gables to N and s,

corresponding to two bays of the arcades inside. Polygonal apse. Inside exposed yellow and red brick.

HOLY TRINITY, Bromham Road. 1839–40 by *John Brown* of Norwich. The Commissioners' type. Pairs of lancets along the sides. Lancets also in the w tower. Three galleries inside. The chancel was rebuilt by *Penrose* in 1866 with two impressively plain arches across.

Of the NONCONFORMIST CHAPELS of Bedford quite a number are of the vaguely Italianate mid C19 type with a big pediment across the front and round arches. The HOWARD CONGREGATIONAL CHAPEL in Mill Street of 1849 is stuccoed, the BUNYAN MEETING of 1850 (by *Wing & Jackson*), also in Mill Street, is red brick,* the ST PAUL'S METHODIST CHURCH in Harpur Street is ashlar-faced. This dates from 1831.‡

PUBLIC BUILDINGS

The principal administrative buildings are in St Paul's Square.

SHIRE HALL. By *Waterhouse*, 1879–81, and unmistakably by the hand that designed the Prudential in London. Red brick and red terracotta. The façade to the river is longer than the symmetrical entrance side. Gothic porch, Elizabethan windows, pavilion roofs.

COUNTY OFFICES, attached on the w to the Shire Hall. By *Basil Champneys*, 1886. A very handsome ashlar-faced building, not large. The façade is quite narrow (two plus two bays) with cross-windows crowned by a steep pediment, a free interpretation of, say, 1660. On the top a cupola.

TOWN HALL. The building consists of two parts, the l. being
89 Sir William Harpur's school-house of 1756. Ashlar-faced, of four bays with two-light windows (very old-fashioned for 1756) and his statue (by *Benjamin Palmer*) in the middle. Doorway with pediment and top pediment over the two middle bays. The r. part is of 1859–61, low and irregular, with a turret, and quite picturesque. The architect was *James Horsford* of Bedford. – The MAYOR'S STALL was formerly in St Paul's. It has fluted Corinthian pilasters and a high pedimented canopy. – INSIGNIA. Great Mace, 1665–6; two smaller Maces, pre-1665; Seal, early C14. – New MUNICIPAL OFFICES lie behind, by *F. W. Dawkes*, the Borough Engineer.

---

* BRONZE DOORS by *Frederick Thrupp* with subjects from The Pilgrim's Progress.
‡ And cost £1,676 14s. 5d.

Seven floors, the top one recessed with a projecting flat roof.

PUBLIC LIBRARY, Harpur Street, facing the Bedford Modern School. A noble, though only rendered, Greek Doric temple front with low one-bay wings. 1834 by *Thomas Gwyn Elger*. Built as the Literary and Scientific Institution.

COUNTY LIBRARY, Embankment. 1885 by *Henry A. Cheers*. Tall with two half-timbered gables, the rest brick, with a very Gothic centre. Built as the Town and Country Club.

MANDER COLLEGE OF FURTHER EDUCATION, Cauldwell Street. 1957–65. By *S. Vincent Goodman*.

COLLEGE OF PHYSICAL EDUCATION, Warwick Avenue. The new GYMNASIUM by *S. Vincent Goodman*, 1955–6, is a very pleasant job.

BEDFORD MODERN SCHOOL, Harpur Street. When the school of Newnham Priory had been dissolved, a secular school was started by letters patent of 1552. Sir William Harpur, Merchant Taylor and Lord Mayor of London in 1561, endowed the school liberally. Its small premises of 1756 have already been mentioned (*see* Town Hall). Between 1769 and 1810 the school grew from 10 to 216 boys.* So in 1834 a new, remarkably large building was occupied. The designer was *Wing*, who, however, died in 1826. The work was then taken over by *Blore*, who built the N part in 1829–30. The rest followed quickly. The building is symmetrical, ashlar-faced, in the Tudor style. High projecting open entrance hall with tierceron-vault.

BEDFORD SCHOOL, De Parys Avenue. 1889–92 by *E. C. Robins* Brick. Symmetrical Gothic main building with a turret. Mullioned and transomed windows. The separate CHAPEL is of c.1908–9 and was designed by *Bodley*. The SCIENCE BLOCK is by *Oswald P. Milne*, 1933, absolutely plain, of brick, with a big hipped roof.

BEDFORD HIGH SCHOOL FOR GIRLS, Bromham Road. 1878–82 by *Basil Champneys*. The best of the Bedford school buildings. In a free Tudor. Symmetrical front, the centre with giant pilasters, very large two-transomed windows, and a cupola. Round the corners some extremely pretty half-domed bow-windows. Undeniably a feminine job, compared with the Bedford School and the Bedford Modern School. In fact

* Mr Kuhlicke clarifies this by saying that the grammar school stayed in the old building till 1889, but that the new large premises were needed for the Lower or Writing School, later called English School.

Champneys was commissioned on the strength of his Newnham College.

BEDFORD GENERAL HOSPITAL, North Wing, Kimbolton Road. This incorporates (central block of the N wing) the former WORKHOUSE of 1794–6, by *Wing*, with an eleven-bay brick front, the seven middle bays being recessed. Two and a half storeys; hipped roof.

H.M. PRISON, Dame Alice Street. 1801 by *John Wing*, cross-shaped. An extension to the N of this, 1819 by *James Elmes*, stands no longer. The present front probably 1840 by *John Brown*. Red brick. Three pavilions, the middle one with the archway in. This pavilion has some chippy rustication. The side pavilions of three bays and two storeys were built as living houses for the governor and the chief warders.

BEDFORD PARK. The SOUTH GATES are ornate work of 1888.

SUSPENSION BRIDGE. Built in 1888 by *John D. Webster*. For pedestrians only.

PERAMBULATION

The best thing visually about Bedford is the way the town has treated its river. Few English towns can be compared. The Embankment is a handsome street, and otherwise there are public gardens on both sides. As for individual streets or private houses on the other hand, there is little of great value, and indeed not much that has to be picked out at all. It hardly makes a perambulation, even in the centre. The centre of the centre is ST PAUL'S SQUARE. Here, besides the public buildings, No. 1 is a rendered five-bay house with a nice early C19 doorway. On the N side the former CORN EXCHANGE, by *Ladds & Powell*, 1871–4, tries to dominate the scene. Stone, of three bays with very big segment-arched first-floor windows and an attic with four big chimneys like pinnacles. Lower one-bay entrance wings. The HIGH STREET runs N and just has the LION HOTEL, probably of *c.*1830, seven bays, stuccoed, with giant pilasters all along and first-floor balconies. The rear part is earlier.

s of the High Street and St Paul's Square one reaches the river, and here in the bridgehead position is that remarkable monument, the SWAN HOTEL, built by *Holland* for the Duke of Bedford in 1794. It is an ashlar-faced, uncompromisingly oblong block of three wide bays by five with a pediment across the front. Porch of two pairs of unfluted Ionic columns, a tripartite window l., another r. The three first-floor windows are under blank segmental arches. In the pediment is a lunette. On the low-pitched temple roof four unrelieved oblong chimney blocks. Tactful extension at the back along the Embankment. Inside, the staircase of Houghton House, Ampthill was re-erected, after that house had been pulled down in 1794. The staircase has twisted balusters and still a string. It dates from 1688.

The BRIDGE is of 1811–13, with its five segmental arches and stone balustrades still entirely in the Georgian tradition.* In ST MARY'S STREET at the very bridgehead opposite the Swan *Ronald Salmon & Partners* are building (at the time of writing) a tower-block on a low podium. It is too early to comment on the design, but the scale is certainly a blow to the immediate surroundings. In ST MARY'S SQUARE, at the S end of St Mary's Street, a late C17 brick house of five bays with a mansard roof. The windows have the characteristic brick frills in the lintels. Altered doorway. On S, to the end of ST JOHN'S STREET, and here, N of the church, the range which was the rectory but much earlier the HOSPITAL OF ST JOHN. Its appearance is 1840-Tudor, pebble-dashed, gabled, with two-light windows under hood-moulds. But the core is said to be of *c.*1216, with Tudor features, especially the roof-timbers of the former hall, now hidden above a ceiling.

Returning N from the hospital turn into CARDINGTON ROAD to see ST MARY'S HOUSE, Queen Anne, of six bays and two and a half storeys, red brick, with a steep two-bay pediment. Later C18 doorway. Opposite, No. 26 has a door-hood on curious forward-curving brackets developed direct out of the framing shafts (cf. Brandreth House, Ampthill) and No. 46, early C19, a fine three-bay ashlar front with a porch on Roman Doric columns and wreaths in the frieze.‡ More Doric porches along here. After that no more in this direction, and much less in others. To the E, e.g., just CROFTON HOUSE in ST CUTHBERT STREET, low, of five bays, red brick, with a pedimented one-bay projection. To the W start in DAME ALICE STREET, i.e. at the N end of the High Street. Two long ranges of ALMSHOUSES, 1801–6, low, of dark red brick, with paired steep dormers. On into BROMHAM ROAD. Genteel Bedford moved here early in the C19. Nos 30–32 has one combined Greek Doric porch with pediment, Nos 38–48 one

* It was designed by *Wing* (*Industrial Archaeology of Bedfordshire*, 1967, p. 16).

‡ Built by *Wing* for himself (F. W. Kuhlicke).

long first-floor cast-iron balcony, and opposite is a ten-bay pair of ashlar-faced houses, again with Greek Doric porches. Turn s along ROISE STREET for just a glance at two ungainly recent tower blocks, turn N along THE CRESCENT for three pairs of red brick houses dated 1825. The centre one has a pediment.

Further w down ASHBURNHAM ROAD is ASHBURNHAM COURT by *Max Lock & Partners*, 1954–5, the best of the new flats at Bedford. Near the s end of Ashburnham Road is, a little to the E, Prebend Street, which skirts the BRITANNIA IRONWORKS, started on this site in 1857. The original buildings, including the fanciful 'mixed Renaissance' gateway, are by *R. Palgrave* of London. *The Illustrated London News* called his building 'a handsome pile' done with 'taste and skill in appropriate embellishment'. Another journal speaks of the gateway as of 'some Sybaritic Castle of Indolence or some luxurious palace of learning'. Finally all the way back to Bromham Road, across the railway, for No. 95, a very nice neo-William-and-Mary job with projecting wings and a hipped roof. It is by *James Cooper* of Bishops Stortford and dates from 1893. Shallow bows on the ground floor in the fronts of the wings. Turn N, up Shakespeare Road, across Clapham Road and up MANTON LANE, for the good factory premises of TEXAS INSTRUMENTS, by *O'Neil, Ford & Colley*, with a series of hyperbolic paraboloid concrete shell roofs.

BIDDENHAM

ST JAMES. Norman the unmoulded chancel arch and one blocked s window, E.E. the tower with one blocked s lancet (but the top and the recessed lead spirelet are of course later), Dec the tower arch, Perp the wide opening into the one-bay s chapel and the two-bay N arcade with a pier of standard moulded section and moulded arches. Dragon-stops for the w and E imposts. Specially nicely detailed Late Perp N aisle windows. – FONT. Octagonal, Perp, with tracery patterns. – (LECTERN. 1901. Brass, copper, and iron. The support is an Arts and Crafts tree.) – SCREEN (s chapel). The dado Early Renaissance, the thin varying tracery still Gothic. – TAPESTRY. Signed by *Rolof Vos*, Flemish, 1549, with a trellis grid and small ornamental motifs. – STAINED GLASS. The E window by *Kempe*, 1897. – PLATE. Cup and Cover Paten of 1569; Flagon of 1689. – MONUMENTS. Brasses in the N aisle: a husband, wife, and son (18 and 13 in.) and two women in shrouds (18–19 in.), late C15 and early C16. – William Boteler † 1601. Kneeling couple in the usual position between two columns, but the kneeling children slightly below in the round, not in relief. Strapwork and arms on the top. – Alice Osborne † 1615. Small tablet with pretty surround.

In the village are several houses by *C. E. Mallows* of *c.*1900 and the following years. They are in the Voysey style and very handsome: THREE GABLES, 17 Biddenham Turn, and further w KINGS CORNER; also WHITE COTTAGE, 34 Days Lane. (w of King's Corner is a house by *Baillie Scott*, and Baillie Scott also did another on the s side of the lane to Church Farm.)

The WAR MEMORIAL CROSS on the Green is by *F. L. Griggs*.

BIGGLESWADE
1040

ST ANDREW. A large church and, like so many, nearly all Perp, but all external detail new. The 'nearly all Perp' excepts most prominently the w tower, which, except for the stair-turret, is of 1720: grey ashlar, with round-arched bell-openings. The rest is ironstone. Long chancel, the seven-light E window of the restoration of 1884. The N aisle and the clerestory have large windows. But the s doorway with two continuous chamfers is early C14. Late Perp two-storeyed s porch with a tierceron-star vault and a bold ogee-arched entrance. The cusping is blank, each cusp with two little blank quatrefoils. The arcades inside are of four bays with standard Perp pier mouldings. High early C14 tower arch towards the nave. Good Perp s aisle roof with bosses. – FONT. Perp shaft with simple tracery motifs. – REREDOS. 1877 by *Withers*, with *Salviati* mosaic. – SOUTH DOOR. C15, with fully traceried head.* – STAINED GLASS. One chancel s window by *Kempe*, 1895. – PLATE. Cup of 1781. – BRASS. William Halsted † 1449 and his wife, labelled Alicia. 18 in. figures. – (John Rudying, who built the chancel. Brass fragments found in 1955. Later C15.)

ST JOHN, St John's Street. 1883 by *Sir Arthur Blomfield*. Yellow brick with red brick decoration. Big bellcote on the nave E gable. Lancets and groups of three stepped lancets. It is ecclesiologically laudable that there are two long w lancets but three stepped E lancets (Trinity!).

* The Rev. J. H. Dominey tells me that it formerly had an *Orate* inscription.

THE LIMES, London Road. The former WORKHOUSE. The typical plan with octagonal centre and wings. Yellow brick. The façade still with pediment. The date is 1835–6. The architect was *Thomas Gwyn Elger* of Bedford.

BRIDGES, over the Ivel. Three pointed arches; C14.

The centre of Biggleswade is the Market Place, a disappointing centre in a visually disappointing little town. The former TOWN HALL is the only building of note. Five-bay stuccoed front with two giant Roman Doric columns in antis. 1844 by *J. T. Wing*. Otherwise in or near the Market Place the former MARKET HOUSE, timber-framed and externally not ancient at all, but with a genuine C16(?) timber roof. Next to the town hall another timber-framed building, the WHITE HART, of hall-house type, but also largely re-done. In the HIGH STREET, visible from the Market Place, the CROWN HOTEL, late C18, with enjoyable Art Nouveau lettering.

Out of the town to the N SHORTHEAD HOUSE, yellow brick, five bays, with a big Tuscan porch and a tripartite window over. Late C18.

Out to the S in the HITCHIN ROAD the tower of a WINDMILL.

Out to the SE along London Road and turn E past a caravan site to STRATTON PARK. The house has been pulled down. It contained a marvellous late C17 staircase with openwork acanthus panels. One panel is preserved in the small successor house.

BILLINGTON

9020

ST MICHAEL, and indeed, like many St Michaels, overlooking a valley from a steep escarpment. A small church with a Victorian polygonal stone bell-turret of 1869 on two big buttresses. But the C13 blank window inside the W wall is real C13 work, probably re-set. – PLATE. Cup and Paten of 1624.

BISCOT *see* LUTON, pp. 116, 118

BLETSOE

0050

ST MARY. Mostly Dec, but the S doorway C13, and perhaps the crossing tower in its bones too. There is a lancet giving on to the present chancel. The arches for the tower on the other hand are Dec, W and E higher than N and S. The nave has reticulated tracery in the W window and flowing tracery in N and s windows. Flowing tracery also in the N transept. The chancel has Dec tomb recesses: with crocketed gable in the N wall, with rather bleak cusping in the s wall. The High Victorian treatment of the nave E wall belongs no doubt to the restoration of 1858 etc. by *Edward Browning* of Stamford (GS). – FONT. Perp, octagonal, with arched panels. – MONUMENTS. In the N transept Sir John St John † 1559 and family. Large standing alabaster monument. He and the sons kneeling to the E, she and the daughters to the W. Two columns and a straight top. Latin inscription in hexameters. It is not an over-elaborate piece. – Frances Countess Bolingbrooke † 1678. Large tablet with two urns and an open pediment. Fine workmanship. It is no doubt by the same hand as the Alston Monument at Odell.

BLETSOE CASTLE. John de Patishull received his licence to crenellate in 1327. But nothing medieval is visible. What remains is one range of a former quadrangle. Long, flat Elizabethan front. Eight bays, two storeys, no gables. Three- and four-light transomed windows. Jacobean staircase. The Lady Margaret, Henry VII's mother, was born here, and Queen Elizabeth I visited. Near by are the remains of a substantial moat, 55 ft wide and about 15 ft deep.

BLUNHAM

1050

ST JAMES AND ST EDMUND. The most interesting feature of the church, speaking from an architectural point of view, is the W tower. It is of ironstone and has several strange motifs, such as clasping buttresses with shallow set-offs, and eight pinnacles, four of them on decidedly post-medieval-looking gablets. There is indeed a date 1583 inscribed, and with this date the Latest-Perp-looking W windows harmonize. Yet the tower is structurally much older; for it has a Norman arch towards the nave, with a strong roll and the outer voussoirs of alternating limestone and ironstone. The W doorway also has a Norman, or rather a Transitional, arch with several rolls and also the alternation of colour of the voussoirs. Visible only inside the tower are two Norman windows. The chancel is structurally C13 – see the SEDILIA and PISCINA and the sill course with its leaf stops. But the windows (not those of course of the Perp clerestory) are Dec. In the s aisle two Dec windows and one Perp. The three-bay arcades are Perp (standard moulded section of the thin piers) but have arches still with the Dec sunk quadrants. The responds are of ironstone. The N and S chapels are both Perp. So is the chancel arch. The chancel roof has interesting bosses – angels, heads, an animal, griffins(?), and also a kneeling cleric. – PULPIT. Elizabethan, with two tiers of the frequent blank arches. – SCULPTURE. Four fragments of Nottingham alabaster, three C15, but the exquisite though headless Virgin undoubtedly still C14. – PLATE. Chalice given by John Donne, 1626; two Patens of 1681; Chalice of 1812. – MONUMENTS. Brasses to Richard Maulaye, mercer, † 1506, and wife, 18 in. figures. – The impressive Late Perp stone SCREEN between chancel and S chapel with a doorway and a straight top with panel tracery under must have belonged to a monument or a chantry chapel. – Dec cusped and sub-cusped tomb recess, chancel N, with a spreading ogee arch and crockets on it. Leaf spandrels. – Susanna Countess of Kent † 1620. This is a very good standing alabaster monument. Tomb-chest with two floral wreaths, shallow coffered arch. Small kneeling figures on the back wall. – Thomas Bromsal † 1705 and Randolph Bromsal † 1711, both by *Edward Stanton* (both behind the font). – Godfrey Thornton † 1805, by *Bacon Jun.* Shallow relief tablet with urn before obelisk. – Mrs Thornton † 1862 by *Samuel Manning Jun.* Elegant group of a kneeling woman by a pedestal with an urn.

RECTORY. 1874. A huge and grim building of yellow brick with half-hipped roofs and plenty of chimneystacks.

BOLNHURST

ST DUNSTAN. A substantial church, quite on its own. Big Perp W tower with pairs of two-light bell-openings. In the nave on the N side two large, transomed Late Perp windows, on the S side mixed windows, one being late C16 or C17. – PULPIT. Jacobean, with plain panels. – SCREEN. Of two-light divisions; not much of it old. – RAILING of the former Francklin pew; marble flooring. – BENCHES. C16, of the usual buttressed design. – ORGAN CASE. By *Pugin.** The decoration outside has sadly deteriorated, but the bold pattern inside is quite fresh. – PAINTING. Large St Christopher over the N doorway. – STAINED GLASS. In a nave N window demi-figure of the Virgin; C15. – The E window is initialled by *W. Holland* of Warwick. It is of 1853. – PLATE. Cup and Paten 1570. –

* *The Organ,* July 1949.

MONUMENT. John Francklin † 1707. White marble, with two columns, an open segmental pediment, two putti on it, and between them an urn. – Dame Dorothy Francklin † 1727. Cartouche with putto heads; very pretty. – Also a funeral HELMET.

BROGBOROUGH

9030

Brogborough has no church, but the brick-works with their more than twenty chimneys make it a prominent object in the landscape. On the N fringe of the brick-works is BROG-BOROUGH PARK FARM, a small square brick house of the mid C17 doll's house type, with big hipped roof and a central chimneystack.

104

BROMHAM

0050

ST OWEN. The church stands on the lawn in the grounds of the Hall, all on its own. The earliest part is the three-bay N arcade, with quatrefoil piers and arches of one step and one chamfer. This work is probably of c.1300. The dainty minor S doorway would go with it. The chancel looks Dec, and the ANGLE PISCINA is, but otherwise it was rebuilt by *Butterfield* in 1868. Of 1868 also the Dyve Chapel. The rest of the church is Perp. W tower with higher stair-turret, S aisle with two windows l. and r. of the two-storeyed S porch.* The N porch has some old timber. – FONT. Octagonal, Perp, with pointed quatrefoils etc. and tracery. – LECTERN. With two bearded heads as poppy-heads. – HOURGLASS STAND. Plain. – BENCHES and other woodwork evidently by *Butterfield*. – STAINED GLASS. Old bits in a chancel S window. – PLATE. Paten of 1737. – MONUMENTS. Brass to Thomas Wideville and two wives, † 1435, excellent figures 4 ft long under ogee gables. The monument was appropriated by Sir John Dyve † 1535. – Sir Lewis Dyve, 1603. Alabaster five-poster with recumbent effigy on a half-rolled-up mat. He wears a long beard. Strapwork on the top. – Lord Trevor, 1732. Standing wall-monument with two putti l. and r. of a black sarcophagus and obelisk. – Lord Trevor † 1764. By *Prince Hoare*. Tablet in several marbles. Woman seated on a black sarcophagus by a black urn. – Eva Trevor † 1842, twelve years old. She is seen floating to heaven. Gothic surround.

* The upper floor contains a LIBRARY given by Lord Trevor in 1740.

Bromham church, brass to Thomas Wideville and two wives † 1435

BROMHAM HALL. The large C14 doorway is probably not *in situ*. (There is also a kingpost roof inside.)

BRIDGE and CAUSEWAY with many cutwaters. There are altogether twenty-six arches. The oldest go back to the late C13. Extensive repairs in the late C15 and much rebuilding in 1813 by *M. R. Salmon*, surveyor to the Duke of Bedford.

BROOM HALL *see* SOUTHILL

BUSHMEAD PRIORY

1060

The priory was founded about 1195 for Augustinian Canons. All that remains of it, attached to an C18 brick house, is the RE-FECTORY range originally S of the cloister. It has angle buttresses and a large entry with a resourcefully trefoiled arch, windows shafted inside and with depressed arches starting with a short vertical piece, and, behind the range, the KITCHEN fireplace. The range was apparently divided into two floors at the time of the Reformation, and new, straight-headed, typically Late Perp windows were put in on the upper floor. – SCREEN on the first floor, and fragments of STAINED GLASS in one window.

About 350 yds S a SUMMER HOUSE, C18 probably, square, of brick and tower-like, with a pyramid roof and at the back the back wall of a former grotto.

CADDINGTON

0010

ALL SAINTS. The story of the church begins with the W quoins of an aisleless nave. They look Anglo-Saxon and may be of the C11. Then follows the (re-set) Norman S doorway. Its arch has zigzag, including that type which operates at r. angles to the wall face, but the colonnettes have early stiff-leaf capitals, i.e. keeping close to the bell. So this must be *c*.1190–1200. The chancel arch is a little later. The responds include keeled shafts, and the capitals also have close stiff-leaf. The arch itself must have been renewed in the early C14 (see the mouldings). A short shaft in the chancel N wall carrying an early C14 stone table-top is contemporary with the chancel arch. Later in the C13 the chancel SEDILIA and PISCINA were made (cusped pointed arches). The early C14 extension is the feature of the highest quality. It is a N chapel or short N aisle added to the then existing nave. The piers have fleurons in the capitals.* And the E window, now opening into the vestry, is a delightful oculus with an inset concave-sided lozenge, all nicely cusped. The aisles are Perp. They have standard elements, but differ in proportion. The finest part of the exterior is the W tower, much repaired, but with picturesque results: flint, stone, and brick, quite irregular. Higher stair-turret. Stately W doorway. Much restoration all round in 1875 (*Ewan Christian*), when e.g. the chancel was rebuilt. – FONT. Big, octagonal, Perp. – PULPIT. About 1650, with typical panels and the exclamation-mark-like vertical motifs. – BENCHES (nave, W end). Early C16, with linenfold on the ends. – HELM. On the chancel S wall. – PLATE. Set presented in 1740. – MONUMENT. John Pedley † 1838. Well-done; without figures. By *Sanders* of New Road, Marylebone. – (CURIOSUM. A CONSTABLE'S TRUNCHEON of 1832.)

CAINHOE CASTLE *see* CLOPHILL

1040
CALDECOTE
1½ m. SE of Northill

ALL SAINTS. 1867–8 by *Sir A. Blomfield*. Yellow brick with red bands and trim. Bellcote on the chancel W gable. Round-arched windows, but Early Gothic roses in the E, W, and S transept S walls. Straight chancel end, low apsed W baptistery. The principal capitals are of the French Early Gothic foliage type, and the chancel chapels have pointed arches. What style then is intended?

1030
CAMPTON

ALL SAINTS. Of the late C13 or c.1300 the S doorway and the S arcade of four bays, though the W bay is interfered with by the Perp tower (rebuilt in 1898). The taller N arcade Perp: yet in actual fact it is of 1649, when the Osborn Chapel with its Late-Perp-looking E window was also built. Unfortunately the outer wall is all of 1898. The chancel, though over-restored too, is early C14, see the PISCINA and the niches l. and r. of the E window. Attached to the N side is an C18 mausoleum of blue and red brick. – FONT. C18. Small oval bowl on square baluster. – SCREENS. Under the tower, a very interesting screen with unusual Dec(?) motifs in two-light divisions. –

* The N aisle W respond must be the re-set W respond of this N extension.

Fragments of another screen used in the PULPIT. They are specially good and certainly C14 Dec. – A third screen between chancel and Osborn Chapel. Two tiers of closely set balusters. The date is no doubt *c.*1649. – COMMUNION RAIL. C18. – BENCHES. Some with buttressed ends. – ARCHITECTURAL FRAGMENTS of the C13 and C14. On the window-sills, perhaps from Chicksands. – PLATE. Set of Sheffield plate given in 1793. – MONUMENTS. Brasses to Richard Carlyll † 1489 and wife, 12 in. figures. – Sir Peter and Sir John Osborn, erected in 1655 and highly memorable. By *John* 74 *Stone*. Two big white altars and two big white reredoses with volutes l. and r. and segmental tops. The fleshy, gristly forms are typical of 1650, but the general tenor is far more classical than one would expect.

MANOR HOUSE. Built *c.* 1591. Timber-framed, with a long symmetrical front with five gables and a central porch.

OLD RECTORY, opposite the manor house. C18, five bays, red brick, with recessed hipped roof. Very plain.

CARDINGTON 0040

ST MARY. Large, and mostly of 1900 (by *George Highton*). Only the tower arch has some re-tooled Norman voussoir stones, the chancel is Late Perp, and the s doorways of nave and s chapel are Perp too. The N chapel windows, though over-restored, are also basically Late Perp. They have panel tracery. Inside, the two-bay arcades to this chapel and the s chapel are Late Perp. Slender piers with standard moulded section, and four-centred arches. The arcades of quatrefoil piers are all of 1900, except for the capitals of the s w respond and the first s pier from the w, which are genuine work of *c.*1300. – FONT. Given by Harriet Whitbread in 1783, who also gave the font to Essendon in Hertfordshire. They are the only ones in England of *Wedgwood* black basalt. Like the Essendon one, that at Cardington stands on a tapering square fluted pillar.* – LECTERN. Designed by *Sir Albert Richardson* and carved by *Frank Dobson*. 1955. An impressively stylized eagle. – MONUMENTS. One of the richest assemblies in the county. The s chapel tomb enclosure has plain C18 RAILINGS. So has the small ledger-stone for Henry Whitbread † 1727. – The earliest memorials are a series of coffin lids in the s chapel from the C12 (cross and interlace; cf. Milton Bryan) to the

* Mr Humphrey Whitbread tells me that a third such font was made for Melchbourne.

c13. – Then follow the two splendid monuments between chancel and N and S chapels. They both have a small doorway with four-centred head on the W and then the tomb-chest with a large canopy over the whole. Elaborate cresting. The tomb-chests have equally elaborately cusped quatrefoils. On the N tomb-chest brasses of Sir William Gascoigne † 1540 and two wives, 3 ft 1 in. figures.* On the other tomb-chest brasses to Sir Jarrate Harvye † 1638 and wife (26 in.). The monument was appropriated for him and altered. To the c17 belong the

HEERE LYES Sᴿ IARRATE HARVYE KNIGHT
SECOND SONNE TO IOHN HARVYE OF
THVRLY ESQ: AND DAME DORATHE HIS
WIFE ON OF THE COHEIARES OF IOHN GAS
COINGE OF CARDINGTON MANNER ESQ
WHO DECESED IN THE YEARE OF HIS AGE
69 IN THE YEARE OF THE LORD 1638

Cardington church, brass to Sir Jarrate Harvye † 1638

* Mr McHardy comments that he was Comptroller of the Household of Cardinal Wolsey, and that the figures are in heraldic attire.

Doric pilasters and the coffered ceiling. His effigy in armour on the other hand is a piece of delicate archaism. – In the N transept Ive Whitbread and his ancestors, by *Peter Schee-makers*, and probably done after 1766. Large, with a high inscription base and on it two well-done busts in front of a grey obelisk. – Samuel Whitbread † 1796. By *John Bacon*,[94] 1799. Large white relief with a pointed top. He lies half-draped on a Grecian couch. Faith by his head points to Heaven, a mourning woman kneels by his feet. This is a work more moving than Bacon usually tries to be. – Samuel Whitbread. By *H. Weekes*, 1849. Grecian background. Hus-[96] band and wife kneel to the r. One of Weekes's best works. – In the s chapel William Charles Whitbread † 1791 as a small child. Simple tablet with a very pretty wreath. – (In the churchyard extension, to the NW, monument to those killed in the R 101 airship disaster of 1930. By *Sir Albert Richardson*.)

The GREEN at Cardington is made specially attractive by extending not only s of the church but also round it. JOHN HOWARD's HOUSE, a three-bay C18 house, is N of the church.* John Howard, the philanthropist, lived at Cardington most of his life. The best house is W of the church: early C18 red brick, five bays, the three middle ones recessed. Asymmetrically set doorway with hood on carved brackets. To the N a big bow. Also along the green several estate cottages built by John Howard. Dates 1763, 1764.

CARDINGTON BRIDGE. By *John Smeaton* for Samuel Whitbread, 1778. Five simple brick arches.

R.A.F. CARDINGTON. The R.A.F. came only in 1936. The site was Short Brothers', who in 1917 built the big classical administration building and the two huge black steel hangars for the two airships, R 100 and R 101. One of the two had been built in 1917 and was lengthened for the R 100 to 157 ft in 1927. The other was built to the same length afresh in 1927. Short Brothers also built the garden village, called SHORTS-TOWN.

CARLTON

9050

ST MARY. On its own amid pine-trees planted to surround it. In the chancel on the N side herringbone masonry and a blocked Norman window. Lengthening took place in the early C14, see the ogee-headed PISCINA, the reticulated tracery

* In the garden VASE on pedestal: 1812.

of the E window, and the tracery of the other windows. C13 W tower with Perp top. S aisle of *c.*1300. One window has three stepped lancet lights, cusped. The three-bay arcade has octagonal piers and arches with one chamfer and two fine hollow chamfers on broaches. The N arcade has quatrefoil piers, and the two hollow chamfers are replaced by one wider one. The date is probably a little later. The windows are Dec too. At the E end of the N aisle is a Perp half-arch. Was it a squint? A one-bay S chapel was at some time demolished.* – FONT. Norman, round, but *c.*1300 made sexfoil at the bottom. Loose scrolls and a top rope moulding. – PULPIT. With Jacobean panels. – SCREEN. Perp, with two-light divisions. The coving has gone. – BENCHES. With the usual buttressed ends.

CHALGRAVE

ALL SAINTS. The church looks curious because in 1889 the upper part of the tower collapsed and has never been rebuilt. It was finished off short. The importance of the church is the E.E. work, which corresponds to a consecration in 1219. Five-bay N arcade with octagonal piers and double-hollow-chamfered arches. Fine stiff-leaf capitals, the leaves big but only high up the bell. The S arcade is Dec and also impressive. Piers of four main and four thin diagonal shafts, typical moulded capitals, typical arches with two sunk quadrant mouldings. The S doorway is earlier than this but later than the N arcade, say of *c.*1250. It is pointed-trefoiled with an odd continuous moulding and in addition one order of columns. Of *c.*1300 the chancel – see the priest's doorway and the chancel arch. The very pretty PISCINA is Dec again (ballflower; ogee arch). Inside, the church is gratifyingly unrestored. – PAINTING. An exceptional wealth of wall-paintings. They are of *c.*1310. In the aisles on the W wall Apostles in pointed niches. On the S wall a large figure of an Archbishop in a niche. On the N wall traces of an angel and other figures and, near the N doorway, a much more sumptuous niche with a large figure and to its E a similar figure. On the N aisle E wall the Annunciation. Also on the nave walls and the inner aisle walls above the arcades shields suspended by painted loops. They are heraldically interesting. Over the N door is a large St Christopher of about 1400. – BENCH ENDS.

* The Rev. P. E. Blagdon-Gamlen tells me that there are traces of a priest's house with living room on the first floor. It was W of the S aisle.

Two with tracery. – MONUMENTS. In the S aisle Knight of
c.1360–70, his feet against a lion. Tomb-chest with shields. –
In the N aisle Knight of c.1380–90 on a tomb-chest with
quatrefoils.

CASTLE, near the church. C12. Low oval motte, and S of it a
small bailey.

CHAPEL FARM see MEPPERSHALL

CHELLINGTON 9050

ST NICHOLAS. To be reached across a field. Dec w tower with
spire. Low broaches and two tiers of lucarnes. Niche below
the W window. E.E. N aisle with W and E lancets and a doorway with a little dogtooth. Dec S aisle with flowing tracery
in the windows. Perp clerestory. Dec chancel, but the E window tracery shows by its two mullions reaching right into the
arch, and in spite of the use of reticulation, that the Perp style
is on the doorstep. Inside, the tower arch dies into the imposts, the N arcade has quatrefoil piers with one chamfer and
one hollow chamfer, and the S arcade has standard elements.
The details of all of them go with the dates assumed from the
exterior. – PULPIT. With Jacobean panels. – STAINED
GLASS. Fragments in the E window, mostly C17. – MONU-
MENT. In the churchyard, to Sir Robert Darling † 1770.
Large structure with a big urn on top.

CHICKSANDS PRIORY 1030

Chicksands Priory was founded for Gilbertines in 1154. The
Gilbertines are the only monastic order created in Britain and
confined to Britain. It was an order whose houses were for both
nuns and brothers. Chicksands was for 120 nuns and 55 brothers.
After the Dissolution, c.1560–70, the premises went to Sir
Peter Osborn.

As one approaches the house now, one is faced with a rendered
block evidently of the early C19, a Victorian brick range to its
r., and older brickwork further r. The early C19 is what gives
the whole building its character. The work was done by
James Wyatt in 1813 for Sir George Osborn, who had however
already about 1760 redecorated the existing building, and of
that work some traces remain in some rooms. But Wyatt made
the symmetrical E front of seven bays with a one-storey porch.

The windows are Gothic, of two lights, and there is a pretty quatrefoil frieze below the eaves which also continues along the s front. This also is Wyatt's, with its canted middle bay. Wyatt of course is responsible for the bold pinnacles too. The other sides are less regular. In the two principal façades there is one small feature only which makes one suspect a more ancient history: the canted oriel l. of the l. bay in the E front. This is indeed of the C15.* What can it have belonged to? It is said that round the corner the E part of the s front contains C12 masonry; but nothing is visible.

As one enters by the E porch one is in Wyatt's Entrance Hall low and impressively vaulted. Above it is the big Drawing Room, mid C19 apparently (c.1835?) and with painted decoration à la Götzenberger. Behind the Entrance Hall and the Drawing Room is the Grand Staircase, also vaulted. It projects into the square courtyard, and this was the original CLOISTER, in its present form Perp, as the two surviving broad four-light windows of the s range prove. Otherwise what remains of the priory is one fine C13 doorway which led from the cloister N into the church, and the whole undercroft of the W range, i.e. the storerooms, of the familiar type with piers along the middle. Seven bays, octagonal piers, single-chamfered arches. There is also a big Perp doorway.

Projecting into the site of the church in the C18 a brick octagon was built, and Wyatt gave the upper floor its thin vault and its four-light W window with very ornate tracery.

In front of the E range on the lawn is the MONUMENT to Thomas of Cotgrave, abbot of Pipewell, a Cistercian abbey in Northamptonshire. Flatly carved effigy and border of foliage scroll. Lombardic inscription. The date is † 1279 or † 1320 or † c.1335 (all these dates refer to abbots called Thomas).

(ORANGERY. Five bays with slim Gothick columns and glazing between. Latin inscription in the entablature. Probably of c.1800. In the grounds four splendid ORIENTAL PLANE-TREES.)‡

½ m. NW of the house is an OBELISK erected in 1815 to commemorate peace after the Napoleonic Wars. (Another OBELISK, c.500 yds SW of Appley Corner, was put up to commemorate the second Duke of Halifax, who died in 1771. He was a brother-in-law of the then Osborn.)

But visually infinitely more impressive than these, and

---

* In it STAINED GLASS fragments, C15 and later.
‡ I owe this information to Mr Allen Hodgson.

even than the priory, is the ANTENNA of the U.S. Air Force,[105] who now have the priory and the land around. It is a vast circle of steel uprights, 120 ft high and nearly a quarter of a mile in circumference, with an inner, more complicated circle in the middle. It looks like a C20 super-Stonehenge, or like the elegant steel skeleton for the biggest bull-fighting arena ever. It is also technically a piece of great importance.

CHILTERN GREEN FARM *see* LUTON, p. 119

CLAPHAM

0050

ST THOMAS OF CANTERBURY. The W tower is not easily forgotten. It is an Anglo-Danish tower, strong and high, even before it received its Norman top piece with the twin bell-openings. Norman also is the simple single-chamfered tower arch, but the windows are Anglo-Danish and double-splayed, and there is a triangle-headed doorway into the first floor. Norman chancel arch, unmoulded. The S and N arcades of two bays – the third is of 1861–2 – are E.E., S just a little later than N. The elements are standard. The chancel dates from 1862–3 and is by *Sir G. G. Scott*. – BENCHES. Three old ends in the N aisle, the details as usual. – LADDER. With Jacobean balusters, to the ringing floor of the tower. – PLATE. Chalice and Flagon, 1687. – MONUMENT. Thomas Taylor † 1689. Standing monument. On the base two mourning putti. Inscription with drapery. Urn at the top. The inscription makes good reading. – CURIOSUM. COLLECTING SHOVEL, dated 1627.

CLAPHAM PARK (Society of the Daughters of the Holy Ghost). The house was built in 1872 for James Howard, founder of the Britannia Ironworks at Bedford. It is not of architectural merit. Red brick, gabled, in a dour Tudor Gothic. – A new CHAPEL was built in 1965–6. It is designed by *Desmond Williams* of Manchester. Circular, with a low-pitched octagonal roof and a lantern focusing the light on the central altar in the blunt, direct way of Le Corbusier's La Tourette. Narrow arched ambulatory, the arches set, as it were, in inner fins, arranged in alternating groups of three and two. – Abstract STAINED GLASS by the *Abbey Studio* of Dublin.

CLIFTON

1030

ALL SAINTS. Dec nave and chancel and an impressive N aisle of 1862 by *Edward Haycock* of Shrewsbury. In the nave a large S

window with reticulated tracery and a small blocked C15 one
to give light to a nave altar. In the chancel one unrestored Dec
N window and the ill-treated SEDILIA and DOUBLE PISCINA.
All the display of lily is of course Victorian. The chancel arch
is very puzzling. The responds are clearly of the early C14
and of a frequent type (half-quatrefoil, with fillets), but they
start high up, and below them are recesses for small altars.
Moreover, behind the responds vertical mouldings run
straight up, and the arch to the chancel itself grows out of
them and the responds together. It is most irregular. Fine
three-bay Perp N arcade, the tall piers of four shafts and four
thin filleted shafts in the diagonals. Instead of a lean-to roof,
Haycock gave his aisle a high-pitched roof, and thus raised
the aisle in prominence. The windows have bar tracery,
except for the W window, which has plate tracery. A mid-
buttress runs up to that window. The arch to the organ
chamber has naturalistic brackets. The W tower is Perp. –
FONT. C13, of the octagonal Purbeck type with two flat
arches each side. – SCREEN. Under the tower dado of the
former screen with painted figures. Not good. – MONUMENTS.
52   Large alabaster monument with recumbent effigies; early C16.
The tomb-chest with frontal angels under arches. They hold
shields. It is a familiar type. – Brass to John Fisher † 1528 and
wife; 28 in. figures.
WELL. 1881. Of timber and coloured tiles Picturesque and debased.

0030
CLOPHILL

ST MARY. 1848–9 by *T. Smith* of Hertford, and, like his earlier
Silsoe, an archaeologically convincing job, i.e. a church which
the casual visitor might regard as genuine. Only the chancel is
short, still in the pre-ecclesiological tradition.* Ironstone, W
tower with higher stair-turret. S aisle. Mostly two-light windows. The fenestration on the N side – 3–2–2–3 lights – also
betrays a still Georgian wish for symmetry. – SCREEN.
Elizabethan, with plain muntins and a length of leaf frieze.
OLD ST MARY, ½ m. NE. Perp. A strange building, very un-
conventional in that it has in the nave just one large five-light
S and one large five-light N window and no others. W tower
with higher stair-turret. Was the chancel arch very narrow?
It is recorded that the chancel was rebuilt in 1819.

* The E window is probably of the restoration of 1879.

In the main street CLOPHILL HOUSE, a five-bay brick house with handsome wrought-iron railings and piers with urns, and, on the opposite side, IVY HOUSE with the same very odd brackets to support the door-hood as at Brandreth House, Ampthill.

CAINHOE CASTLE, $\frac{1}{4}$ m. SE. Motte and bailey castle. The W bailey is the earliest; the other two are later.

COCKAYNE HATLEY

2040

ST JOHN BAPTIST. Of brown cobbles. Good E.E. four-bay N arcade with round piers, strong and simple capitals, and arches of two hollow chamfers. The S arcade is Dec. It is of four bays too and has octagonal piers and arches with two sunk waves. Very tall Perp tower arch. The tower itself is of four stages, the bell-openings a pair of very long two-light windows on each side. The aisle windows are Dec, straight-headed, with reticulation units. The S doorway is Dec too. Finely detailed Perp N aisle E window.

What makes the church unique in the county is its Baroque WOODWORK, brought, mostly from Belgium, in the 1820s by the lord of the manor, Henry Cust, son of Lord Brownlow of Hatley Park across the Cambridgeshire border. Under the tower large SCREEN from Louvain. – The RAILS above are from Malines (cf. communion rail). They display musical instruments and trophies. – The splendid STALLS and STALL BACKS are from Aulne Abbey near Charleroi and dated 1689. [82] The stalls have inlay, and putto heads between them. The backs abound with Catholic saints, looking very Catholic indeed. Thirty years later no one would have dared to introduce such a display into an Anglican church. The saints are in oval foliage surrounds. The front of the stalls to the W has splendid acanthus foliage. – The COMMUNION RAIL again comes from Malines and has lively scenes of putti: Corn Harvest, Vine Harvest, Drinking Water, Gathering Manna. – The READING DESKS have all sorts of collected bits. – More in the N chapel. – The N aisle SCREEN comes from St Bavon at Ghent and is a mixture of parts from c.1540 into the C17.

Other FURNISHINGS. The STAINED GLASS in the N aisle E window is among the finest in Bedfordshire. It comes from Yorkshire. Four Saints under canopies, early C14, the characteristic yellow and green, but also still the deep red and blue of the C13. – In the head also C15 figures. – The E

window is by *Willement*, 1829, still entirely pictorial, but not
in the C18 way. The inspiration is Netherlandish early C16
glass. – Much more staid and conventional *Willement*'s armorial S and N windows of 1839. – PLATE. Set of 1773. –
MONUMENTS. Brasses to a knight of 1430 (38 in.) and on the
same slab a Lady of *c.*1490 (25 in.), to Edward Cokayn
† 1525 and wife (28 in.), and to William Cokyn † 1527 and
two wives (28 in.). – Sir Patrick Hume † 1627. Alabaster. The
usual type with two kneelers facing one another across a
prayer-desk.

COLMWORTH

1050

ST DENIS. All Perp. W tower with recessed spire and three tiers
of lucarnes in the same direction. Pairs of two-light bell-
openings. Very large N and S windows, and buttresses
between them. Cobbled chancel walls. The large windows
create a beautifully airy interior. High, embattled porch, with
springers for a vault. – FONT. Perp; on the underside small
motifs. – STAINED GLASS. Fragments, including a whole
C15 angel, in the N windows. – PLATE. Cup of 1731. – MONU-
73   MENT. Excellent large alabaster monument to Sir William
Dyer and family, erected in 1641. Two semi-reclining effigies
propped up on their elbows, he behind and above her. Three
front columns and a strange cresting of two bald volutes and
a central square with a rounded top to hold the coat of arms.
Against the base three noble caryatids – Faith, Hope, and
Charity – and the kneeling children. A baby grandson stands
at her feet.

COLWORTH HOUSE *see* SHARNBROOK

1040

COPLE

ALL SAINTS. Of buff and brown stone. A Perp church, except
for the W tower (with higher stair-turret), which is probably
earlier – see the arch towards the nave. High C15 S doorway
with big leaf spandrels. Tall three-bay C15 arcades, the piers
with four polygonal projections and four thin diagonal shafts.
Moulded, two-centred arches. The chancel arch is of the same
type. The chapels of two bays, however, have the standard
moulded section and four-centred arches. They probably date
from the C16. All responds here are angel-brackets, those on
the S side re-carved. In the S chapel SE corner yet another,

very good, angel-bracket. – SCREEN. With one-light divisions and delicate detail. – STALLS. With Perp poppy-heads. – BENCHES. Some ends of frame and panel construction, i.e. probably later C16. – PLATE. Cup of 1623. – MONUMENTS. Brass to Walter Rolond, c.1400. He is in armour, the figure 36 in. long (N aisle N). – Brasses to Nicholas Rolond, also c.1400, and wife, 36 in. figures, and John Launceleyn † 1435 and wife, 25 in. figures (both chancel floor). – Tomb-chest of the early C16 with the brasses of Thomas Grey, wife and children (18 in. figures; chancel S). – Tomb-chest with back panel with the kneeling brass figures of Sir Walter Luke † 1544 and wife (chancel N). – A tomb-chest back panel with the kneeling figures of Nicholas Luke † 1563 and wife (N chapel N). – Brass plate with big coat of arms and the kneeling figures of Robert Bulkeley † 1556 and family (S chapel).

COTTON END   *0040*

3 m. SE of Bedford

BAPTIST CHURCH. 1836. Yellow brick, three bays, two-storey fenestration. Arched windows. Big pediment.

In Exeter Wood is a motte and bailey CASTLE, badly overgrown. The low motte is recognizable, however.

CRANFIELD   *9040*

ST PETER AND ST PAUL. Norman N doorway in a bad state. Scalloped capitals. Late C13 four-bay arcades. Quatrefoil piers, double-chamfered arches with broaches.* The chancel arch belongs to the same build. Occasional bits of nailhead in the abaci. Also C13 or early C14 the tower arch, dying into the imposts. The formidable NE vestry seems to be contemporary. The lower E window is Victorian, the upper slit windows are genuine. Perp upper parts of the tower with interesting blank four-centred arches high up. Pairs of two-light bell-openings above these arches. Recessed lead spire. Perp battlements on both sides of the church. Good Perp nave and aisle roofs with carved bosses. – FONT. Early C14, a chamfered square with eight shafts, but the panels carved in the C15 with blank Perp windows. – SCULPTURE. W of the S doorway a Norman figure in relief, seated, alas defaced. – TILES. In the nave at the E end. – STAINED GLASS. By *Kempe*, in the N aisle, 1884. – PLATE. Cup and Paten on foot 1710.

* On the S side only (G MC H).

COLLEGE OF AERONAUTICS. The original buildings are of
c.1936–7 and 1939–40. They are neo-Georgian, the housing of
the Welwyn–Wythenshawe kind.

9060 DEAN

ALL SAINTS. The chancel arch with a little nailhead in the
responds and the N doorway prove the existence of a church
before 1300. Then most of the present building was done, in
the first half of the C14. Dec the W tower with very fine two-
light bell-openings, a pretty top frieze with heads etc., impressive and entertaining gargoyles, and a short recessed spire
(with two tiers of lucarnes). The arch towards the nave dies
into the imposts. Dec also the unusual S doorway with four
orders of very thin shafts and a fourfold roll-moulded four-
centred arch almost like a basket arch. The S arcade of four
bays and indeed the N arcade are Dec too. They have standard
elements, but the piers have clearly been heightened. But
when was that done? Not as late as the erection of the Perp
three-light clerestory; for the roof-line of the roof preceding
that which includes the clerestory is still clearly visible against
the tower and takes the present height of the piers well in.
The nave roof with angels carrying the Instruments of the
Passion and musical instruments, and with an openwork
frieze below the wall-plate, is specially fine. Perp one-bay N
chapel. – FONT. Octagonal, Perp, with the usual quatrefoils,
but unusual big single flowers on the base. – PULPIT. Of
wood, Perp, with simple arched panels.* – By the pulpit front
of a bench with tracery-bits of a SCREEN. – The SCREENS altogether are remarkable. The present rood screen and the
chapel W screens were originally probably all one – with one-
bay divisions, but specially elaborate details, e.g. panel-
tracery along the top of each light. – The gate of the rood
screen is Jacobean. – BENCHES. The usual buttressed type of
ends. – COMMUNION RAIL. C18. – POOR BOX. On a heavy
square baluster. – PAINTING. In the N chapel a small panel
on wood with Christ as the Good Shepherd, kneeling to pick up
a chalice. The inscription is in Latin. – STAINED GLASS. In
the chapel E window and the S aisle W window original fragments including a kneeling donor‡ in blue (W) and two whole
little figures (NE). – PLATE. Cup and Cover Paten 1569;

* Mr McHardy compares it with that at Yelden.
‡ Labelled Johnes Lysset.

Flagon and Salver 1723. – MONUMENTS. Dec tomb recess in
the N aisle. The tomb-chest has six quatrefoils. The recess is
high, and cusped and sub-cusped. On the tomb-chest a C13
slab with inscription in Lombardic lettering. – Brass to Thomas
Parker † 1501, a priest, with a scroll. 20½ in. figure. The brass
belongs to a plain tomb-chest in the S chapel.

WINDMILL, ½ m. NW. A sad sight, with its two sails.

DRAY'S DITCHES see LUTON

DUNSTABLE   0020

ST PETER. Dunstable Priory was founded in 1131 by Henry I
for Augustinian Canons. Of the buildings for the canons
little is preserved (see below), of the church a substantial part.
The E parts, probably the first to be built, are all gone, and so
are the crossing and the very E end of the nave. But the rest
of the nave remains, with the W front. The interior tells the
story of the original building more clearly than the exterior.
We have seven bays of arcade and gallery, but nothing of the
clerestory. The nave is very wide. The bays are separated by
giant wall-shafts of oddly imprecise section: a demi-shaft and
two broader quarter-shafts. The latter at the gallery level
merge with the gallery arches to form a kind of giant arching
as it was more clearly done at Romsey, Jedburgh, and Oxford
Cathedral. These giant wall-shafts are cut horizontally only
by the sill-course of the gallery, a billet-course. The arcades
on the other hand have zigzag hood-moulds, bold in the two
E bays, slighter in the others. To the arch openings there are
triple shafts with scallop capitals, and the arches themselves
have thick half-rolls. The date of all this may be c.1150–60,
but when the gallery was built the late C12 must have been
reached. The arches have finer mouldings, and some capitals
crockets, and the shafts towards the (undivided) openings l.
and r. of the middle one are elegantly detached. In fact three
have detached, the other attached shafts. The core is a Greek
cross with quadrants to connect the arms. The shafts are
set into these – a Lincoln motif. Several other features bear
out this chronology. The S aisle, it must at once be admitted,
is doubtful evidence; for it was completely rebuilt in 1852 (by
Somers Clarke Sen.). It has Norman windows, set high enough
for the cloister to have been beneath, and it has Norman rib-
vaults. The two easternmost ones are in fact original.

The W front of Dunstable is both confusing and confused.
The principal portal is evidently Norman, and very sumptuous,

though it is badly preserved. It has four orders of shafts with lively capitals and arches, including foliage medallions of the Malmesbury–Glastonbury kind, i.e. of *c*.1170–90. The doorway and the tympanum of course were put in in the C15. To the l. of the portal is a piece of Late Norman intersecting arcading with the familiar bobbin motif. It is surmounted by a pointed arch with a Late Norman chain of lozenges. So this may be *c*.1190 too, i.e. later than the arcades but not later than the gallery. The church was indeed dedicated (by Hugh of Wells, bishop of Lincoln) in 1213. But then, in 1222, the two w towers collapsed. This information comes as a surprise; for the arcades make no visible provision for towers. What happened after that was a rebuilding which suggests anxiety and no consistent plan. Immediately s of the portal is a buttress erected in the C15 and connected by a piece of brickwork with a square sw angle-turret which is Victorian. To the N of the piece of Norman intersecting arcading is a C13 N portal, as sumptuous as the older, though smaller. It has five orders and five subsidiary orders, all capitals moulded and finely moulded arches, three of their orders with stiff-leaf, one as a normal trail, one in nailhead-like units, one in square leaves. The nearest parallel is the s transept portal of Lichfield. Above the portal is diapering of the kind known in Westminster Abbey, and also at Higham Ferrers, and above that a small frieze of pointed arches with brackets for statues, and at the N corner is a broad buttress with a canted N side and pointed niches in one of which the lower part of a statue is preserved. Higher up is a more sumptuous frieze of blank arches, with thickly decorated capitals and cusps. This leads straight to the two main w lancet windows. Between them is another, not so high, but also thickly decorated blank arch. The arcading is not and never was repeated s of the s lancet. This tier cannot be earlier than, say, 1250–60. More blank arcading above and Perp battlements. In the C15 a NW tower was put on the NW bay, and it was for that purpose strengthened inside. The tower has a higher stair-turret. Inside, the w wall has a C13 gallery of seven stepped arches. The shafts again have the Lincoln section (cf. above).

The N side of the church has an over-restored Norman doorway with little that is original, except the two charming capitals, one with a rabbit, the other with a negro (cf. Toulouse) and a stag and hounds.* The Perp aisle windows are entirely

* There is also one figured capital in a s wall-shaft of the s aisle.

the restorer's. The E side contains the stone ROOD SCREEN with its two doorways and niches, visible only inside, and, outside, just recent brickwork.* There is also the E part of the Norman pier between the seventh and the lost eighth S bay, and on the N side a big strengthening of the C14, when the transept and crossing tower were rebuilt or remodelled.

The fact that the nave was not destroyed after the Suppression is due to the town having obtained in 1392 the use of the whole nave for parochial purposes.

FURNISHINGS. FONT. Large, circular, Norman. The [19] decoration is partly original and partly re-cut, or entirely C19. – SCREENS. The rood screen is of five wide bays, with cusped and subcusped arches and thickly crocketed ogee-gables. Perp panelling in the spandrels. – In the last bay of the N arcade parts of a mysterious screen with long, decorated balusters, some with imitation Norman motifs. They are typical of certain English work of the mid C17. But the screen also has the arms of Castile, a double-headed eagle, the emblem of the Virgin, and the Five Wounds. Must it then not be Marian? The fragments were found in a pew in the S aisle in 1852.‡ – PULPIT. 1852. Square, of red marble, with two E.E. stiff-leaf bands. – PULPIT CLOTH (S aisle). Given in 1732. – GATES. Wrought iron, C18, in the S aisle. – PALL. The Fayrey Pall, red brocade, with all along the borders embroidered figures. Henry Fayrey, who is supposed to have given the pall, died in 1516. But can the figures be so early? They look 1530. – PLATE. Presented in 1721.

MONUMENTS. Brasses in the S aisle floor. Richard Pynfold † 1516 and wife (19½ in. figures), and Richard Fynche and his father and mother. He died in 1640. Also on a panel in the N aisle husband and wife (19 in.), Civilian (14½ in.), and large husband and wife (40½ in.). – Incised slab to Richard Duraunt, late C13. Good, and with Lombardic inscription (N aisle). – Also a remarkable number of quite ambitious monuments of the first half of the C18. They are to members of the related Marshe, Chew, Aynscombe, Cart, and Dickinson families. Mrs Elizabeth Aynscombe † 1711 (S aisle). Columns l. and r., still-life of death in the 'predella'. – William Chew † 1712 (N aisle). By *Green* of Camberwell. Large hanging monument of reredos type with two standing

* The Rood was by *Bodley* and is now in Bodley's church of St John, Tue Brook, Liverpool.

‡ I want to thank Mr F. A. Fowler for these details.

putti and a death's head between. The centre of the monument is an arch with drapes. At the top an achievement with garlands. No effigy. – Thomas Chew Cart † 1722 (N aisle). Grey obelisk with detached bust under a broken curly pediment. – Frances Ashton † 1727 (S aisle E). Reredos-type. In the tympanum four putto heads. – Mrs Jane Cart † 1736 (N aisle). Classical reredos with pilasters and finely detailed pediment.* – Marshe family, shortly after 1741. Urn before obelisk. – Francis Dickinson † 1747. Urn against back panel with garland and arms. By *Robert Taylor*. – Marshe Dickinson † 1765. With good oval portrait medallion.

Of the PRIORY BUILDINGS hardly anything has escaped destruction. The remains of a GATEHOUSE into the outer court are SW of the church. Carriage and pedestrian entrance. C15. Much further W, i.e. actually in the High Street (*see* below), is the house called THE PRIORY, and the ground floor of this has a long rib-vaulted room, supposed to have been the HOSPITIUM. The ribs are single-chamfered.

OUR LADY IMMACULATE (R.C.), West Street. 1961–4 by *Desmond Williams & Associates* of Manchester. Large, of brick, circular, with lamella roof and spire.

BAPTIST CHAPEL, West Street. 1847–8 by *J. Clarke*. Red brick with yellow brick quoins. Three bays wide, with one-bay pediment. Arched windows.

METHODIST CHAPEL, High Street. 1909 by *Withers & Meredith*. With a NW steeple. Brick, in a free Gothic.

CEMETERY. 1863. Double chapel with a middle gateway. The two façade windows both have geometrical tracery, but the tracery differs – a characteristic High Victorian touch.

TOWN HALL. 1879. Three bays, with a turret, thoroughly debased.

MUNICIPAL OFFICES, High Street, near its N end. White, early C19, probably before 1813, with a porch of two pairs of sturdy Tuscan columns. To its r. a former private house, Late Georgian Gothick, with ogee-headed windows.

QUEENSWAY HALL. 1962–4 by *Desmond Williams & Associates*. The centre of a future Civic Centre (*see* below). The hall itself is oval and has wood-slat walls; wrapped round are the restaurant and other ancillary rooms. Symmetrical front with a rather mannered middle window.

DUNSTABLE SCHOOL. 1887–94 by *E. R. Robson*. Free Tudor.

* The monument to the Cart family in St Mary-le-Bow in London was by *Samuel Tufnell*.

Of plum brick with a flèche. Quite ingeniously composed of two parts, each in itself symmetrical. The entrance with a square tower, set totally asymmetrically, is the link. The hall part is Late Perp, the rest Jacobean. Nice touches of freedom from historicism, e.g. in the hall parapet.

FIRE STATION, at the N end of Dunstable, near the station. By the county architect, *J. C. Barker*, 1962–5. Good.

PERAMBULATION. All the older buildings of interest are in the cross of streets in the centre. The streets represent the ancient Icknield Way and the Roman Watling Street. In WEST STREET the character of pre-C20 Dunstable is best preserved. No individual buildings of note, except perhaps the WINDMILL, W of the Catholic church. In HIGH STREET NORTH next to the town hall a good early C17 gateway. Round arch, columns l. and r., and, above, a gabled upper floor of brick with mullioned windows. On the opposite side the SUGAR LOAF HOTEL, dated 1717. Nine bays, two and a half storeys, blue brick with red-brick dressings. The area E of High Street North and N of Church Street is all in transformation. A modern centre is growing up here which is quite promising. *See p. 413* The Queensway Hall is its focal point. There is also a pedestrian shopping street running N from Church Street.

HIGH STREET SOUTH has the best buildings. THE PRIORY, apart from its medieval vault inside (*see* p. 78), has handsome Early Georgian façades with arched windows. To High Street there are a pedimented doorway and quoins of even size. Inside a fine staircase with three twisted balusters to the tread. A little further S the CART ALMSHOUSES of *c.*1723, a plain two-storeyed row of blue and red brick, and then the CHEW GRAMMAR SCHOOL, of 1719, a fine, steeply pedimented front with a curious turret cupola. Five bays, two storeys. On the doorway two charity children. Jane Cart who founded the almshouses was the daughter of Thomas Chew who founded the school.

In Outer Dunstable industry is growing apace; there are new factories and factory extensions to E, N, and S. To the E there is already no boundary any longer between Dunstable and Luton, and if things go on at this rate with central and peripheral development, Dunstable will soon be a C20 town with one major ancient monument.

In OAKLEY ROAD is a good new building of WHITBREAD'S BREWERY. The architects are *Peter Falconer & Partners*.

GLIDING CLUB, off the Tring Road to the S, *c.*1 m. W of

Dunstable. By *Christopher Nicholson*, 1935–6. Badly kept at the
time of writing, but, with its window band, its semicircular
bow and its rounded corner, the convinced statement of a
young architect under the influence of Mendelsohn's English
work. The club and the hangar are combined in one building.

Dunstable is the site of Roman DUROCOBRIVAE, of which
practically nothing is known. It is situated on an important
road junction, where the Icknield Way crosses Watling Street
(*see* above).

FIVE KNOLLS BARROW CEMETERY. This is the finest barrow
group in the county. It consists of eight sites, comprising
three bowl, three bell, and two pond barrows. The largest
of the bowl barrows is 20 ft in diameter and 5 ft high. It
covered a Late Neolithic inhumation burial accompanied by
a polished flint knife. An Early Bronze Age collared urn containing a cremation burial was inserted into the existing
mound, and during the Pagan Saxon period ninety-eight in-
trusive burials were deposited in it. The three bell barrows
are enclosed within a single ditch. The largest mound, 80 ft
in diameter, and the smallest, 52 ft in diameter, were both
opened in the C19. The former produced sherds of Western
Neolithic and Beaker pottery. Both the pond barrows are
slight structures with diameters of 35 ft and 18 ft and depths
of 2 ft and 1½ ft respectively. Neither has been excavated.

CAUSEWAYED CAMP AND IRON AGE HILLFORT, 1¼ m. NW.
The camp has been partially destroyed by quarrying, but its
flat-bottomed ditch, overlain by the rampart of the later hill-
fort, can still be seen in the quarry section. Sherds of Western
Neolithic pottery were recovered from this ditch.

The hillfort overlying it is of univallate construction with
a V-sectioned ditch 10 ft deep and 25 ft wide. The 11 acres
enclosed by the rampart are provided with entrances on the
SW and N. The former has been proved by excavation to be
original and was revetted with timber uprights.

2040   DUNTON

ST MARY MAGDALENE. W tower 1861 (by *E. Browning*), but
the arch to the nave and the stair-turret both medieval.
Of the time of the restoration also the chancel roof with
heavy hammerbeams and big angels. The stone corbels have
naturalistic flower representations. The old church is of brown
cobble. Much of it is Dec, namely the four-bay S arcade (piers
quatrefoil with four thin shafts in the diagonals), the S aisle

E window with wilfully composed flowing tracery, one S window (reticulated tracery), the chancel with its arch to the nave the plain SEDILIA and PISCINA, and the grand E window. In this, however, in the head, the advent of the Perp is noticeable. Late Dec also the S doorway. The porch was heightened in the Perp style, and Perp also is the N arcade (piers with four polygonal projections and thin shafts in the diagonals). In the S aisle two brackets. One, a big bust, is Dec, the other Perp. – FONT. Octagonal, Perp, with simple tracery patterns. – ORGAN. A pretty Late Georgian instrument. – STAINED GLASS. Some bits in the top of the S aisle E window. – PLATE. Cup and Paten 1569.

DUROCOBRIVAE see DUNSTABLE

EASTCOTTS

(THE BARNS. 1630, altered 1760. With a mid-C18 staircase and on the first floor a tunnel-vaulted passage and three C17 ceilings with coved cornices. MHLG)

COTTON END. See p. 73.

EAST HYDE

HOLY TRINITY. 1840–1 by *Benjamin Ferrey*. Ferrey was one of the first to take archaeological accuracy seriously. He began to do this just about 1841. Yet here he is still entirely in the Commissioners' vein. Neo-Norman with lancet-like side windows. The façade, inspired by the Norman guest house of Canterbury Cathedral, has two large round Norman piers flanking the entrance and open staircases with Norman colonnettes turning l. and r. The l. one leads to the W gallery, the r. one is blind. In addition, there is one asymmetrically placed W turret. It is a distressing display.

(HYDE HOUSE. C18, brick, of five bays, the windows with segmental arches. Doorway with Roman Doric columns. A Venetian window on the S side. Stables with cupola. MHLG)

EATON BRAY

ST MARY. Externally the church is not specially memorable – Totternhoe stone, short W tower with spike, mostly Perp windows, and one (S transept) of four lights with a transom which is dated 1608 – but its interior one will hardly forget. It is surprisingly splendid, thanks to the two arcades of *c.*1220 and *c.*1235–40. Both arcades are of five bays. The S arcade

comes first. Octagonal piers and stiff-leaf capitals with big, full leaves, but only at the top of the bell. The arches have two
24 hollow chamfers, and the responds are large, conical brackets with very flat decoration of large summarized leaves. The N
29 arcade is yet richer. Here the piers have eight shafts and as an additional refinement two of them and the E respond have some of the shafts just slightly detached. The capitals are of the most dramatic stiff-leaf variety. The arches consist of eleven rolls each. Moreover across the aisles was some transverse bracing, and this must have consisted or been meant to consist of a bold single-chamfered arch rising from the outer wall (and in two cases stiff-leaf corbels) to the wall above the arcade. But from the springer of the arcade arches a triple-roll arch starts to rise much more gently towards these big arches and would, if completed, have met them. It is a strange, unnecessarily complicated arrangement, but would have been visually effective in so ornate an aisle. The chancel is basically also E.E., see the ANGLE PISCINA. The interior of the E win-
20 dow looks c.1300. – FONT. The bowl and the splendid stiff-leaf capitals are original and look exactly contemporary with the N arcade. – REREDOS. A handsome Late Perp stone reredos in the S transept. – SCREEN. Perp, tall, of one-light divisions. – SOUTH DOOR. With wonderful ironwork, mostly scrolls; mid C13. Very similar to the doors in St George's Chapel at Windsor, and less similar to the work of Thomas Leighton. – PLATE. Paten on foot, 1730. – MONUMENTS. Tomb-chest with an interesting mixture of Gothic and Elizabethan motifs. The brass plate behind is indeed to Lady Bray and children, and she died in 1558. – Brass inscription to Lord Bray † 1539, but palimpsest of a bishop or abbot of c.1450. – (Also a brass plate with kneeling figures and a long inscription in black letter. The inscription refers to Jane, daughter of Lord Bray † 1539 and Lady Bray † 1558.)

(CASTLE. A castle was built at Eaton Bray in 1221 by William de Cantlowe. Traces of the moat and foundations remain. VCH)

2040   EDWORTH

ST GEORGE. Of brown pebble, gratifyingly not over-attended-to. Dec two-bay aisles, the piers quatrefoil with thin shafts in the diagonals, the arches with two sunk quadrants. Dec also the two doorways, the S probably earlier than the N, and Dec the two aisle E windows. Dec finally the W tower (see the W window). But the crenellation, the clerestory, and the two porches, leaning against the aisles, are all Perp. – PILLAR PISCINA (N aisle E). Square, early C13. – FONT. Octagonal, Perp. With big flowers and shields against the underside and tracery, quatrefoils etc. against the bowl. – BENCHES. Two ogee-topped ends with poppyheads, one normal, one a lion, one a monkey, and one a dressed-up monster. – PAINTING. In the N aisle S wall two kings from the story of the Three Quick and the Three Dead. C14. – STAINED GLASS. In the chancel S many fragments, rather restored. – PLATE. Cup and Paten 1772.

EGGINGTON

ST MICHAEL. Nave of ironstone, chancel of Totternhoe. The chancel arch responds are Dec. Victorian shingled bell-turret. – FONT. Cauldron-like, or rather quatrefoiled with corner shafts, oddly undecided in shape. E.E. – PLATE. Cup and Cover Paten inscribed 1635.

EGGINGTON HOUSE. An uncommonly fine example of latest C17 domestic architecture, completely up to the moment in features. The house was built in 1696 for a Huguenot who became Sheriff of Bedfordshire. Seven bays, three storeys, brick. Segment-headed windows, panelled parapet with urns, door-hood on carved brackets. Staircase with twisted balusters.

ELSTOW

ST MARY AND ST HELEN. Elstow was a Benedictine nunnery. It was founded c.1075 and of its buildings only part of the church and part of the W range along the cloister remain. But the E end is known from excavations. It had a crossing and transepts, a chancel with apse and a later, probably square-ended Lady Chapel. Even the nave is not preserved complete. The first bays from the E are missing. The present E end of the church with the lower windows, so far as they are not of *Sir T. G. Jackson*'s restoration of 1881, is of 1580, when the rest was demolished. It is interesting to see that the details of the windows of 1580 are still entirely in the Perp tradition. Jackson rebuilt the S aisle and over-restored the N aisle. But the clerestory windows, though also over-restored, are basically right and prepare for the interior. The three E bays each side are Norman, the two wide W bays E.E. The interior indeed, impressively high and austere, falls into two parts. The Norman work consists of high arcades, no gallery or triforium whatever, and the clerestory windows. The piers are plainly oblong cruciform, the arches plainly single-stepped. The capitals are mere imposts; only two have the smallest bit of decoration. All this looks early C12. Above the N doorway on the other hand, which is very poor imitation-Norman, is an arched panel of genuine Norman workmanship, and that looks rather 1140 than earlier. It shows, very small, Christ in an almond-shaped glory with St Peter on the l., St John on the r. The style is most decidedly French, and derived from the stage of Moissac, i.e. *c*.1120. The panel has an arched frame with short single-scallop columns and a roll-moulding and a moulding of pellets. The E.E. w extension must be of *c*.1220. It has exceedingly heavy octagonal piers with characteristic stiff-leaf capitals and moulded arches, just one of them decorated with dogtooth. The clerestory lancets are shafted. The present w window is Late Perp (1580?) and not large. It replaces an enormous window. The w front dates in its start from *c*.1220 as well. Central doorway with two orders of stiff-leaf colonnettes. The big buttress to the l. with its nook-shafts is of the same date. The doorway beyond it is in a half-finished state. The lancet above it is original. To the r. of the central doorway all is in disorder (much as at Dunstable) and much is of the restoration.

The church has a broad and solid, fully detached CAMPANILE, N of the E.E. part, i.e. in the same position as e.g. at Chichester (cf. also Marston Moretaine). It is of the C15 and has to each side a pair of transomed two-light bell-openings and on the top a spike.

FURNISHINGS. The FONT is large, Perp, and octagonal. It has quatrefoils on the bowl and on the foot an animal, two heads, and a human figure(?). – PULPIT (s aisle w). Perp. A fine, complete wooden piece with tracery panels. – COMMUNION RAIL (s aisle E). Jacobean. – SCULPTURE. An excellent bracket of intricate foliage on a human bust. Perp. – MONUMENTS. Brasses: Margery Argentine † 1427 (41 in.) and Elizabeth Herwy, abbess of Elstow, † 1527 (36 in.), the former very good. – Sir Humphrey Radclif † 1566 and wife. Kneeling figures with three slim columns, l., r., and between them. – Tablet to Thomas Hillersdon † 1656 and tablet to John Hillersdon † 1684. Both are of high quality, the second in style still rather 1660 than 1680.

The so-called chapter house to the s of the w front must have been the outer parlour. It is a square room with a central

Elstow church, brass to Margery Argentine † 1427

c13 pier of Purbeck marble with eight concave sides. It carries a very curious rib-vault of four bays, but with some ribs transgressing from one bay into the next. The division is in fact rather one oblong E and one oblong W bay. Of wall-shafts there are four in the corners, plus one N and one S, but two W and two E. That makes it possible for diagonal ribs to run from mid-shaft S direct to the NW and NE shafts and from mid-shaft N direct to SW and SE. The rib which should divide the NW square from the SW square, and the NE square from the NW square is carried on only till it meets the joining point of the two diagonal ribs, and there are in addition fragmentary diagonal ribs as well. As a pattern it is unique, and moreover each rib starts not from an abacus but from a bracket set on the abacus. Is that c13 as well?

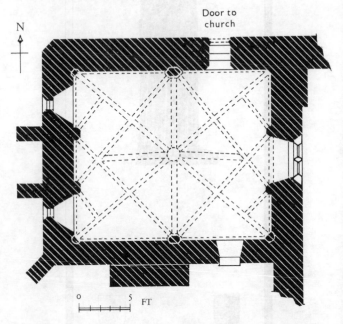

Door to church

N

0 5 FT

Elstow church, 'chapter house', thirteenth century (?), rib-vault

The rest of the W range must be pieced out of the remains of HILLERSDON HALL, built of the stone from the abbey by Thomas Hillersdon, who bought the property in 1616. What survives is on a fragmentary E-plan, with the N bar of the E being the church. The s bar is three bays long and one wide. The middle bar, as usual, is the porch. It has paired pilasters on two floors and a round arch. The windows are mullioned and transomed, in the s bar of two and three lights, in the hall part l. of the porch of three and four.

Recent excavations have exposed the footings of the cloister buttresses. The finds include two mid-C13 arcade spandrels, deeply moulded and one of them with fine foliage. N of the church in a field stands the MOOT HALL, built *c.*1500, of timber with brick infillings. The upper floor overhangs and contains the main room with its original tiebeam roof. Below, the W part was divided into six shops, each with its doorway and small window. The E part contained the staircase. In the village street E of the church a long row of timber-framed COTTAGES with overhanging upper floor.

EVERSHOLT
9030

ST JOHN BAPTIST. An unusually regular Late Perp ironstone exterior, embattled, with straight-headed three-light windows in the aisles, the clerestory, and even the porch. Dec chancel windows, all very restored (by *Scott*, 1863–4). Perp w tower, earlier than the Late Perp work. The interior, as so often, is much earlier. Three-bay N arcade with octagonal piers and double-hollow-chamfered arches, plus a w bay of *c.*1300. What is the date of the three bays? The E respond has a capital of the very latest Norman scallop type and the w respond capital has two tiers of stylized leaves. But the rest must be a Perp replacement. The chancel N chapel is early C14. Pier with four main and four diagonal shafts. Perp s arcade of four bays. In the chancel medieval heads re-set. The PISCINA is original work too – of *c.*1330. – PAINTED DECORATION. By *Edward Aveling Green* (1842–1930), early C20 – the fag-end of Walter Crane's style, far, far away from anything still alive after 1900. – STAINED GLASS. A s window by *Kempe*, 1899. – PLATE. Chalice of 1688–9. – BRASS. Part of a mid C15 brass, just the tablet with six sons.

S of the church CHURCH END FARMHOUSE, early C18, of blue and red brick with a projecting one-bay centre and segment-headed windows.

EVERTON
2050

ST MARY. Dec w tower of ironstone, the rest of the church brown cobbles. The church is essentially Late Norman and unusually complete, see the s doorway with one order of colonnettes with scallop capitals and a round arch already with E.E. mouldings, and see also the aisle w windows and the chancel N and s windows, but above all the three-bay arcades of round piers with multi-scalloped capitals and square abaci and of unmoulded arches. The s capitals are somewhat heavier, i.e. earlier than the N capitals, and both arcades are older than the s doorway arch. Perp clerestory, on the N side with quatrefoil windows. Perp s porch with pretty base-frieze of lozenges with quatrefoils. – STAINED GLASS. Some by *Charles Gibbs* (TK), probably E and s aisle. – PLATE. Elizabethan Cup with Cover Paten; Elizabethan Paten on foot; Flagon of 1694–5. – MONUMENTS. Sir Humphrey Winche † 1624. Very high, but flat, hanging monument with frontal demi-figure. He is holding a book. – Richard Astell † 1777. Urn before obelisk; light-coloured marbles. – William Astell † 1841. Grecian tablet.

HASELLS. The façades of *c*.1720–40. The entrance side is of seven bays, red brick and rubbed brick with a stone balustrade. Porch of four wooden Tuscan columns. Round the corner an earlier-looking eleven-bay front with a three-bay pediment. Fine coat of arms and fine detailing of the middle windows.

²⁰⁴⁰ # EYEWORTH

ALL SAINTS. Brown cobble. w tower with recessed spire. Two tiers of lucarnes in different directions. The w window Dec, the bell-openings Perp. s arcade of standard elements, small quatrefoil Dec s aisle w window, three-light (reticulated) s aisle E window. Dec tower arch and Dec chancel arch. – PULPIT. The stair with twisted balusters, *c*.1700. – STAINED GLASS. Fragments in several windows. – PLATE. Paten of 1623; Cup and Paten of 1625; Flagon of 1638. – MONUMENTS. Sir Edmund Anderson † 1605, Lord Chief Justice of the Court of Common Pleas (chancel s). An ambitious piece. Alabaster. Two recumbent effigies. Kneeling children in relief against the base. Columns l. and r. and a flat back arch. – Sir Francis Anderson † 1616. Also alabaster. Very fragmentary. The three principal figures now kneel frontally. Children also against the base. – Sir Richard Gadburye † 1624, with wife and daughter. Brasses, the parents 3 ft 3 in. long. He wears a hat. – Sir Edmond Anderson † 1638, with wife and daughter. A very good piece. The composition is complicated. The parents are demi-figures. They hold a heart. Top with open segmental pediment with allegorical figures on it. Then, perhaps added, when the moment came, below, the child is seen in a round recess. Hers is a bust with arms, and she holds a little book. L. and r. of her another, rather incongruous open segmental pediment with allegorical figures.

N of the church is an early C17 brick ENCLOSURE. It is oblong and must mark the site of some important building (the manor house of the Andersons?).

FAIRFIELD HOSPITAL *see* ARLESEY

FARNDISH

St MICHAEL. A small church with a short w tower. The only remarkable feature is the s doorway, which must date from *c.*1210. It has three orders of shafts of which two are detached and only the middle one is attached. The capitals are early stiff-leaf. Three orders of plain arches alternatingly brown and beige in colour. Dec s nave windows. The w window is Dec too, and was the nave w window before the tower was built into the nave. The N doorway is blocked and very plain, but could be of the same date as the s doorway. – BOX PEWS with High Victorian Gothic panelling. – PLATE. An unmarked Chalice.

SCOTTS (or GRANGE FARM). Late C17, of three widely spaced bays with three-light mullioned windows and straight hoodmoulds over. The composition is symmetrical, which suggests the proposed date.

FELMERSHAM

St MARY. What can the reason have been for Felmersham receiving the noblest parish church in the county during the noblest age of medieval churches, and moreover a church in spiritual scale, even if not in size, vying with any abbey or priory church? The church came under Lenton Priory in the second half of the C12, but that alone explains nothing. It was built at one go between about 1220 and 1230 or 1240, and it has a classicity and harmony which – rare indeed in the English C13 – includes even the w front. So often E.E. w$_{26}$ fronts, even Salisbury, even Peterborough, have elements and motifs which jar. Here there is nothing to disturb one's quiet admiration. The nave is represented by a doorway of many orders of slim shafts and fine mouldings, and this is flanked by one blank arch l. and one r. with trefoil-headed sub-arches and a plate tracery quatrefoil. Above that is an arcade of seven arches with dogtooth, the supports being composite, of four detached shafts each, three in a row and a fourth in front. Above that a high tripartite composition of richly shafted windows, with pointed arches l. and r. and a segmental arch in the centre. Among all the capitals there is not one displaying stiff-leaf. All are moulded. The aisles have simply one shafted W lancet each. So the church is aisled, but it is a cruciform church, and the crossing tower is nobly E.E. too, below its Perp top stage. Each face has two lancets and a blank arch on either side. Then there are the transepts. That to the N has three widely spaced lancets, that to the S two high lancets and an almond shape over. Moreover there is a shallow E chapel or recess. It is internally separated from the transept by a half-arch. The corresponding arrangement in the S aisle is a full arch. But to these we shall come later. First the chancel, also perfect E.E., with three very far-separated lancets along its sides, their hood-moulds decorated with dogtooth, as is that of the small priest's doorway. On the N side there is no dogtooth. The E window is original only in its jambs. There were probably three lancets here. The doorway to the S aisle is of the same kind as the W portal, but the windows are Dec and straight-headed, and those of N aisle and clerestory are Perp.

The climax inside is the crossing, of cathedral seriousness. To each arch grouped shafts. The mouldings have fine rolls with fillets. But the innermost order is left as a big plain chamfer. In the chancel the lancets have a continuous thin roll. There is a DOUBLE PISCINA with a round arch and two almost straight-sided sub-arches. Now the nave and the aisles. Even here, instead of the usual unevenness, there is perfect poise. Arcades of four bays with alternating round and octagonal piers, alternating also across. It is a beautiful and perfectly logical scheme. The arches have one chamfer and two thin filleted rolls. The S doorway to the inside has a very depressed two-centred arch starting on short vertical pieces. – SCREEN. High and exceptionally beautiful too. Four-light divisions, rich tracery above the doorway, coving, and a cresting frieze. The crockets of the doorway gable develop into little angels. The screen was given by Richard Kyng and his wife (see the *orate* inscription). – PLATE. Cup and Cover Paten 1594.

BARN, s of the church. Stone, eight bays long, late medieval, with tie-beams and more closely set collar-beams.

IRON AGE SETTLEMENT. Gravel digging on the N bank of the Ouse just to the N E of Felmersham bridge revealed a hut floor from which came sherds of pottery datable to the first half of the C I A.D. Associated with the pottery was an important series of bronzes including two bowls, the handle and cows'-head mounts of a wooden bucket, and a magnificent spout shaped like a fish-head. The hut was probably the dwelling of a Belgic craftsman or merchant, the group of finds representing his stock-in-trade.

FIVE KNOLLS see DUNSTABLE

FLITTON

0030

ST JOHN BAPTIST. Of ironstone. All probably of between 1440 and 1489 and already by a de Grey, Earl of Kent. W tower with higher stair-turret. Embattled nave and aisles. Rood stair-turret. Big Perp S doorway. Perp arcades of three bays. The slender piers have standard mouldings. The chancel arch corresponds. The whole E end is taken up by the de Grey Mausoleum or Mausolea, a whole series of rooms, oddly unreligious in character. The earliest is of 1614, the others are supposed to have been complete by 1705, although the latest room to be filled is all C19. – BENCHES. Perp, the ends buttressed. – GATES to the de Grey Mausoleum. Large, wrought iron, C18. – BRASSES (N wall). Alianora Conquest † 1434, a good 29 in. figure, headless. – Mrs Waren † 1544, a 17 in. figure.

The DE GREY MAUSOLEUM is one of the greatest storehouses of monuments in England. A pity that it somehow has the storehouse feeling. Few of the many tombs are of the very best quality. The earliest is the brass to Henry Gray † 1545, a 27 in. figure. – Then follows the monument for which the first room was built: Henry Grey, fifth Earl of Kent, † 1614 and wife. Alabaster. Two recumbent effigies. Tomb-chest and back panel. – Next to this, and far more noteworthy, Henry, ninth Earl, erected 1658. Two recumbent white marble effigies. White and grey back wall with two allegorical female figures still entirely in the Nicholas Stone Mannerism. – Of about the same date (W wall) Lady Elizabeth Talbot, erected 1653. Large, very fine reredos-type monument without figures. Open segmental pediment. Ionic columns, and garlands

hanging parallel with them. – Lady Jane Hart, dated 1673.
White semi-reclining figure. Black and white monument with
garlands l. and r. Inscription with drapes. Open pediment
with shield and garlands. The rest of the mausoleum has a
centre, a N, an E, and a S room. In the centre two similar
memorials: Lady Amabell de Grey † 1727 and Lady Anne de
Grey † 1730. Both without figures. – In the N room Anthony
de Grey, Earl of Harrold. 1726 by *Dowyer*. Semi-reclining
white figure in Roman dress on a big black sarcophagus. –
Also Henrietta de Grey † 1716 and Henry de Grey † 1717.
Identical monuments with steep pyramid background and
semi-reclining effigies. Both white, both very young. – Lady
Mary Gregory. Simple. With urn on pedestal. – In the E
room the masterpiece: Henry de Grey, Duke of Kent, and
two wives, 1740. Designed (and signed) by *Edward Shepherd*
and the effigy of the duke attributed to *Rysbrack*. To his r. a
little lower the first wife. No effigy of the second. Very fine
back wall with inscription panels. – Opposite Philip, Earl of
Hardwicke, † 1790. By *Banks*. Mourning woman seated
on the ground by an urn. – In the S room Henrietta Frances,
Countess de Grey, † 1848. By *Terence Farrell*, 1853. Very
large, with an obelisk back. Relief of the covered coffin and the
mourning family. The upright husband weeps. In the background in the shallowest relief tragic, fate-like figures. Up
against the obelisk an angel carrying her soul to heaven. –
Thomas Philip de Grey, Lord Lucas, † 1859. By *Matthew
Noble*. Effigy, white and asleep. – The de Greys' mansion was
Wrest Park.

FLITWICK

ST PETER AND ST PAUL. A mighty moulding from a Norman
doorway is re-set in the N wall. Fat roll with beakheads and
beakhead-like faces. The S doorway with its continuous mouldings must be E.E. Low three-bay S arcade of quatrefoil piers
with thin shafts in the diagonals. Double-chamfered arches.
The N arcade is a copy of 1858, when the N aisle was added.
All features more or less date from then or *Butterfield*'s
restoration of 1867. Original the chancel arch, half a quatrefoil, and the transomed low-side window of the chancel. Perp
W tower. Nave and S aisle embattled. All ironstone. – FONT.
Fluted trough, probably late C12. – PULPIT. With linenfold
panels and Jacobean framing. – BENCH with linenfold

panelling. – Most of the woodwork is *Butterfield*'s. – PLATE.
Cup of 1569.

THE MOUNT, NW of the church, is the remains of a small motte
and bailey CASTLE.

MANOR HOUSE. Partly later C17, partly 1736, partly mid-
Georgian, but much modernized by *Sir A. Richardson*. The
oldest part is the plain two-storey E front. Brick with
panelled parapet. The Drawing Room is of 1872. (In the garden a GROTTO-cum-BRIDGE. One façade is classical, the
other Gothic.*)

GALLEY HILL see BARTON-LE-CLAY

GOLDINGTON   *oojo*

ST MARY. Perp w tower. Perp chancel with ANGLE PISCINA.
Earlier is the entry arch to a former S chapel. This must be
late C13 (semicircular responds). A new N aisle, or rather N
nave, was built in 1955–6 to the extremely conventional, pre-
modern, design of *Felix J. Lander*. – FONT. Early C14, round,
with ballflower on the underside. – PLATE. Cup inscribed
1695; Paten 1823. – MONUMENTS. Early C14 effigy of a Lady,
placed upright in the porch. – Benjamin Haselden † 1676.
Tablet with extremely pretty detailing, black and white
marble. The top is an open scrolly pediment with an urn set
in.

GOLDINGTON BURY, an C18 house, has been pulled down and
replaced by a tower block of flats, twelve-storeyed, by *F. W.
Dawkes*, the Borough Engineer of Bedford.

On Goldington Green also there is a new block of flats, called
HERON HEIGHTS, and this one to a design raised out of the
run-of-the-mill. By *Max Lock & Partners*, 1963–4. These
flats tell of the proximity to Bedford.

POWER STATION. Designed by *W. N. C. Clinch*, an engineer,
and built in 1951–*c*.60. The cooling towers of the familiar
and always again thrilling shape are 165 ft high.

(RISINGHOE CASTLE, 2 m. E. Of the motte and bailey type. The
motte is *c*.20 ft high and looks much like a barrow.)

GRAVENHURST see UPPER and LOWER
GRAVENHURST

* Information kindly given me by Mr Collier.

1050

GREAT BARFORD

ALL SAINTS. By the river. Perp W tower of limestone, the rest of the church of brown cobbles. The nave E quoins have long-and-short work, i.e. must be Anglo-Danish. The tower has bell-openings which look early C19 and big pinnacles and a spike. The church received its N aisle in 1848, its S aisle in 1860. – SCREEN. The glazed tower-screen with large geometrical tracery must be early C19 too, and is the most effective feature of the church. – PLATE. Cup and Paten inscribed 1697. – MONUMENTS. Brasses to husband and wife, c.1525 (chancel s), 18 in. figures. – Thomas Anscell † 1591 and family. Alabaster tablet with three columns and kneeling figures.

COLLEGE FARMHOUSE in the High Street, ¼ m. NW, is C18, red brick, of two and a half storeys, and has a pedimented doorway.

BRIDGE. The bridge is partly of the C15. Unfortunately it has new brick parapets. Seventeen irregular arches, cutwaters only upstream.

0030

HARLINGTON

ST MARY. Perp ironstone tower with sandstone dressings and higher stair-turret. The rest is rendered. Embattled aisles. The church is essentially late C13 to early C14. The very tall four-bay arcades are still C13. Quatrefoil piers and double-chamfered arches. The chancel arch is of the same details. Dec the chancel windows and the N aisle E (reticulated tracery) and W windows (tracery broken out). Above the chancel piscina a good head. Also three Perp stone corbels for the nave roof. Elaborate niches l. and r. of the E window, different in the details. – FONT. Octagonal, on eight shafts. On the bowl eight shields and below an unusual crenellation frieze. It is probably Dec too. – BENCHES. Perp, just with little buttresses against the ends. – PLATE. Cup of 1742; Paten of 1802.

MANOR HOUSE, by the main crossing. Timber-framed. The main front is late C17, with two projecting wings. The plastering is done rustication-fashion. Wooden cross-windows.

9050

HARROLD

ST PETER. The original church received a raw N arcade in the early C13. Parts of the wall were made into pillars and given stiff-leaf capitals. The arches were left unmoulded. Of the same time the chancel, with an equally rough arch. The chancel is clearly shortened. Of the windows one lancet survives, showing by its position that the chancel must have been longer. In the late C13 the S arcade was built. This is of two bays only and has semicircular responds, but an octagonal pier. Dec N chapel with one very tall arch. Dec W tower with Perp recessed spire. The tower pinnacles are connected with the spire by thin flying buttresses. Three tiers of lucarnes. The walls of the aisles are late C13 N, with intersected tracery and three stepped lancet lights, and Dec S, with reticulation. Perp clerestory. – PULPIT. With Perp panels from the rood screen. – SCREEN. With a nice Jacobean dado. – The woodwork around is Jacobean. – PAINTING. Saint, very bad, in the N aisle. From a screen dado. – LECTERN. Also with re-used Perp bits. – BENCHES. The usual Perp type with buttressed ends, but also some panelled. – COMMUNION RAIL. Of c.1675, characteristic strong turned balusters. – PLATE. Chalice 1699; Flagon given in 1726; Paten given in 1728. – MONUMENTS. Tomb-chest of Oliver Boteler † 1657. Plain. – Large tablet to Dame Anne Jolliffe † 1732. Reredos-type. Bust on a sarcophagus. Side pilasters and broken pediment on the top.

All along the E approach to the church new well-to-do HOUSING, by *John Gedge*.

In the High Street THE OLD MANOR, of c.1600, with mullioned and transomed windows. (Inside a wooden overmantel with blank arches and strapwork. MHLG)

On the GREEN a stone LOCK-UP, circular, with conical roof, and larger than most. Also the open, octagonal, wooden MARKET CROSS. It is a handsome, tree-planted green, not too large.

BRIDGE and CAUSEWAY. Of eleven arches in all, five pointed and eight round. Partly C14. Cutwaters.

(HARROLD HOUSE. Tall, symmetrical Victorian–Jacobean villa. NMR)

Of the Augustinian Priory nothing is left. Buck in 1730 still shows quite substantial remains.

HAYNES

ST MARY. C14 to C15 W tower with higher stair-turret. Nearly all the rest externally by *Woodyer*, 1850. His most personal contribution is the rose window of the Carteret Chapel with a six-cornered star. Inside, the S arcade (of four bays) is original work of c.1300. Quatrefoil piers, double-chamfered arches. A puzzling feature is the chancel which, with its thin rib-patterns, looks decidedly early C19. – SCREEN to the Thynne Chapel. Iron, by *Poole & Son*; very attractive. – By the same, designed by *Scott*, the FLOOR of the Thynne Chapel. – STAINED GLASS. The E window of *c.*1850 by *O'Connor*. Crucifixion. Small figures, still in strong, simple colours. – Other glass by *Clayton & Bell*. – (ALTAR CLOTH. The gold cloth on which Queen Victoria knelt at the Coronation.) – MONUMENTS. Anthony Newdegate † 1568. Kneeling brass figure in a broad, very well detailed stone surround which must be about fifty years earlier. But the inscription of *c.*1568 is also still in black-letter. – First Lord Carteret † 1826. By *Westmacott*, with a telling portrait head in an oval recess. White marble. – Second Lord Carteret † 1838. Grecian tablet. – Lady Thynne. By *H. H. Armstead*, 1868. Recumbent white effigy of the young woman, praying. The alabaster canopy was designed by *Sir G. G. Scott*. The Rev. Lord John Thynne was responsible for the new church building. His grandfather, the first Marquess of Bath, had a Carteret as his mother.

(The former SCHOOL is dated 1850 and has the same rose window as the church. So it is obviously also by *Woodyer*. GMCH).

HAWNES. Large, square mansion, built partly *c.*1720, partly in 1790.* The later work was done for Lord Carteret, the earlier for Earl Granville. This earliest part is the W range, thirteen bays long and very characteristic of its date. Red brick with broad giant pilasters to mark the slightly projecting angle pairs of bays and the three-bay centre. Segment-headed windows. The S and E fronts are of stone, the E front plain except for a Greek Doric porch. This front is of 1849–50 by *Cubitt's*. The S front of 1790 is distinguished by two bows l. and r. and a giant Corinthian order of pilasters for the centre. The capitals are excellently carved. The windows have raised stone surrounds. Top balustrade. The spacious staircase of *c.*1725 has fluted columns as balusters and a swagger newel post as its start. Of the furnishings of 1790 the best are the entrance hall with its discreet stucco decoration and the room behind it with two apses, charmingly decorated with foliage trails.

9020   HEATH AND REACH

ST LEONARD. A poor specimen. 1829 with pointed windows except for a short C16 W tower, and an apse of 1866, yellow

* The work of 1790 is attributed to *James Lewis*.

brick with red bands, polygonal. The s porch is similar and of 1876. Inside not more of interest.

HEATH MANOR. The five-bay brick front of the early C18 with the rusticated pilasters and the ill-informed triglyph frieze does not prepare one for the earlier events of the house. On the N side C16 timber-framing and brick infilling, on the s side a stately C17 doorway with round arch and columns set below a Dutch gable, and inside several Elizabethan or Jacobean chimneypieces and Jacobean carved woodwork, notably the huge lintel of the kitchen fireplace. But the *clou* of the house is the sumptuous, almost oversized staircase, also Jacobean. Vertically symmetrical balusters, sturdy posts.

STOCKGROVE PARK, 1½ m. NW of the church and just across the border in Buckinghamshire. A large neo-Georgian mansion of brick with plentiful outbuildings. By *W. Curtis Green*, 1929, for F. M. Kroyer Kielberg.

HENLOW

1030

ST MARY. Clunch tower and N aisle, the rest ironstone. In the Victorian N chapel a re-used small Norman window from the original aisleless church. Of this building the nave NE quoin can also still be seen (inside the Victorian chapel). The N arcade is of *c.*1300. Three bays, but formerly four – see the place where the tower buttress touches the pier. Octagonal piers, double-chamfered arches. The s arcade is also of three bays, but the w bay is separated from the others by the place where the original w wall of the building ran. The E bays are early C14, the w bay is Perp. Perp w tower with higher stair-turret. Perp chancel. – PILLAR PISCINA (s aisle E). With a Norman capital. – REREDOS (N aisle E). Of the Perp aisle reredos remains one band of quatrefoils. – PAINTING. The Preparation for the Passover. By *Frederic Shields*, after an unfinished drawing by Rossetti, given by Ruskin to the Ashmolean Museum. The painting, which is mentioned in a letter in 1889, and was then probably recent, used to belong to the Rev. A. Gurney of St Barnabas, Pimlico. It is iconographically very interesting. St John as a child buckling the sandal of the Child Jesus. Jesus holds the bowl of blood for the Passover. St Joseph in the distance carries the lamb, the Virgin gathers herbs, and Zacharias paints the door with blood.* – PLATE. Cup 1700; Flagon 1766; Paten 1824; Cup 1827. –

* I owe the information on this picture to the Rev. R. I. Howard.

MONUMENTS. Very many tablets, from 1675 into the C19. The quality is high. The best perhaps are † 1688 (convex cartouche) and † 1712.

HENLOW GRANGE. A fine three-storeyed brick house of five bays with originally low three-bay wings. The date is probably c.1700. Chequer brick, broad giant angle pilasters, parapet. Garden doorway with carved brackets. The entrance doorway perhaps later. Ionic columns and a pediment. Staircase with twisted balusters and a string to hide the treads. That looks late C17 rather than early C18. The lavish S loggia dates from c.1930. Front garden with piers, and iron fence and gates.

HENLOW CAMP (Royal Air Force), 2 m. S. The principal buildings date from 1930–6. The building of the church of St Andrew is actually to a large part the Gymnasium.

1030   HIGHAM GOBION

ST MARGARET. Much of the exterior is Victorian (*Burton & Wood*, 1879–80; PF): the W tower (except for the arch to the nave), the N aisle, and the chancel E wall entirely. Inside, on
45   the other hand, the N arcade is good work of c.1300. Three bays, quatrefoil piers with thin shafts in the diagonals, double-chamfered arches. The chancel arch is of the same type, but has two sunk quadrants in the arch itself. SEDILIA and PISCINA again are largely Victorian. – PLATE. Cup and Paten of 1681. – MONUMENT. Dr Castell † 1674, Professor of Arabic at Cambridge. The last line of the inscription is in Arabic and reads: He elected to be buried in this spot in hopes of a better (Collier). Tablet with prettily carved emblems of death on the frame.

Immediately E of the church a timber-framed HOUSE with narrowly spaced uprights. A large new house has recently been added to it.

(MANOR FARM, behind the church. Inside a wooden Elizabethan chimneypiece. NMR)

9060   HINWICK

88   HINWICK HOUSE. Built in 1709–14 for Richard Orlebar. The house is still in the same family, and the building events are exceptionally fully documented. E front of seven bays, scanned by giant pilasters into 2–3–2. The pilasters are Corinthian. The house is of two and a half storeys with a top balustrade. Brown stone almost as small as bricks and buff

stone dressings. The windows have moulded surrounds, the elegantly slender doorway a foliage frieze and an open scrolly pediment. Round the corner to the s there are five bays and the scanning is by two tiers of niches thus: 2 – niches – 1 – niches – 2. Above the centre and awkwardly placed against the attic storey is a steep pediment of Diana and her cortège. This is by *John Hunt* of Northampton, who has also been credited with the design of the house, but on insufficient evidence. The carving of the pediment is robust, not delicate. The top half-storey differs in material from the rest, and so the pediment may have been commissioned before it was decided to have the attic storey. To the w are two projecting wings and a doorway with an apsed hood on nicely carved brackets. The wings must be an afterthought, as the way proves in which they cut into the window surrounds of the recessed centre. The w side faces the walls of the pre-Reformation manor house, which was converted into stables. The bell-turret with cupola has the date 1710. So has the beautiful rainwater-head of the house, made in all probability by the same craftsman as the contemporary ones at Kimbolton in Hunts. Spacious entrance hall with four of the niches so typical of the Queen Anne style, two in the N, two in the S wall. The staircase hall is also generously large. The balusters of the staircase are exceptionally slim for their date. In one of the bedrooms is a French chintz wallpaper, assigned to as early a date as *c.*1720. The Victorian N wing of the house is of 1859–66. The architect was *F. C. Penrose*. He did his job very self-effacingly, and the choice of the Georgian style for reasons of conformity is remarkable too.

HINWICK HALL. Hinwick Hall is much older than Hinwick House. The w side is essentially of *c.*1540, even if the windows are all renewed. They have the arched uncusped lights of the time of Henry VIII. The front also has a number of gables, but no clear idea of the original appearance can be obtained, and there are no C16 features inside. The best-preserved element is the big chimneybreast on the S side. Early in the C18 General Livesay turned the house round and gave it a new E front. This has some of the same motifs as Hinwick House, but they are handled more rustically and conservatively. Seven bays, two storeys, angle pilasters, and a square porch flanked tightly by pilasters too, but here by two tiers, a 1660 rather than 1700 motif. The doorway has the same open curly pediment as that of Hinwick House, and the windows have moulded surrounds. On top of the façade an awkward square wooden cupola. A fine wrought-iron grille in axis with the front. It may be by *Thomas Warren*, who worked at Hinwick House and at Clare College, Cambridge. A straight avenue leads to the house. It is accompanied by two canal-like sheets of water. The interior of Hinwick Hall does not have much to single out. The best element is the staircase, with turned balusters and carved tread-ends. Two Tuscan stone columns, now inside, must once have been outside, and may have belonged to a porch.

HOCKLIFFE

9020

ST NICHOLAS. Rendered w tower. The rest Totternhoe and ironstone. Mostly Perp. Aisleless nave. In the chancel C14 PISCINA and EASTER SEPULCHRE and also two niches in the E wall.

HOCKLIFFE HOUSE. Early C19 red-brick house of three bays with a doorway with Tuscan columns. The kitchen exit has a finely moulded Perp arch from the former Hospital of St John.

HOLCOT

9030

ST NICHOLAS. A rarity indeed – a church built entirely about 1590.* Yet in general outline it might be medieval. Only the windows are all mullioned and transomed, in the Elizabethan way, mostly of two lights. The E window alone still has the arched lights of Henry VIII's tradition. Inside, the tower arch is specially Perp. The ceiling on the other hand is white and tunnel-vaulted. The church contains the MONUMENT to Richard Chernocke † 1615 who 'reedified his parish Church'. It is a family monument in three tiers. In the large middle one his father Robert with two wives are seen kneeling. Above, a narrow strip with himself and his wife also kneeling and fourteen small kneeling children. In the bottom strip ten kneeling children of Robert. – FONT. An undersized C18 piece with a column as support. – (WOODWORK. In the choir stalls and on the nave walls panels of the C16 and C17, linenfold, Early Renaissance and Jacobean. GMCH) – COMMUNION RAIL. With thin twisted balusters; early C18. – DOOR. With stud decoration including Chernocke's initials, R. C. – PLATE. Cup and Paten on foot, 1641; flat Paten, 1685; Flagon, 1739.

* Two BELLS have the date 1593.

– MONUMENT. Edward Harvey † 1796. By *Robert Blore Sen.*
  With the usual woman by an urn.
Opposite, the former RECTORY with an odd portico of four
  attached giant columns and a steep pediment. Is it Late
  Georgian ?

HOUGHTON CONQUEST

0040

ALL SAINTS. Perp w tower. The contract of 1393 exists for it,
  with a mason of Dunstable and a mason of Totternhoe, the
  cost to be 10s. a foot for foundations and 13s. 4d. plus six
  quarts of frumenty for work above ground. The work was to
  be completed in three years. Nave and aisles embattled.
  Battlements and clerestory are Perp. Perp chancel with two-
  storeyed vestry. The s doorway is a very fine Perp piece with
  two orders of thin shafts carrying intricate foliage. The N aisle
  is high and has windows with Dec tracery, one design being
  specially interesting which consists of an arch-head on three-
  light intersecting lights. Dec also the exceptionally tall four-
  bay arcades. The piers are quatrefoil with four thin shafts in
  the diagonals. Hood-moulds on small head-stops. Double-
  chamfered arches. The roof is Perp, with carved bosses. The
  chancel arch is like the arcade piers. The chancel is Perp but
  much renewed and has niches l. and r. of the E window. Also a
  DOUBLE PISCINA. The chancel roof is by *Sir G. G. Scott*, a
  rather alien hammerbeam roof with wind-braces. – FONT.
  Dec, hexagonal, with cusped and crocketed ogee arch-heads
  in the panels. – SCREEN. Recently nicely painted. Not much
  of the woodwork is old. – STALLS. With good poppy-heads:
  an angel and a dragon, a grotesque with two dogs, and one
  with two deacons and two heads. – BENCHES. Some are Perp. –
  PAINTING. Over the chancel arch a large C14 Doom, Christ
  in the almond-shaped glory with angels l. and r. – Also a 16-
  ft-high St Christopher over the N doorway. This is C15. – (In
  the s aisle traces of a St George with the Dragon.) – STAINED
  GLASS. Original bits in many windows. – PLATE. Cup and
  Paten 1618; oval Paten on foot 1827. – MONUMENTS. Outside
  the chancel a plain recess with four-centred arch for Thomas
  Awdley (?) † 1531. – In the chancel tomb-chest with brasses
  of Isabel Conquest † 1493 and her husband and her son. It is
  worth thinking about the fact that nobody can have cared for
  the two men to be seen in brass as they had really looked.
  Instead of that they are identical even in the features. The
  figures are 28 in. long. – In the chancel floor brasses to Richard

Conquest † 1500 and wife (13 in. figures). – Monument to Dr
Thomas Archer, put up in his life-time in 1629. The device is
Sustine et Abstine, and the Latin inscription is worth reading. Alabaster. Frontal demi-figure, preaching, i.e. with a
cushion lying in front of him and a book held in his hand.

Houghton Conquest church, brass to Isabel Conquest † 1493 and
husband and son

HOUGHTON HOUSE *see* AMPTHILL

HOUGHTON REGIS

ALL SAINTS. A stately church. The general impression is Perp
from outside. Much flint and stone chequer, except for the
w tower. The church is embattled, the tower has two two-

light bell-openings to each side. In the tower w wall are two niches l. and r. of the main w window. Most of the windows of the church are of the restorations of 1856 and 1867. The arcades are of five bays with octagonal piers and arches with sunk quadrant mouldings. That points to the early C14 and goes with the internal shafting of the aisle windows. – FONT. Of tub shape; Norman. The base is in the form of a flat single-scallop capital with carved lunettes. The bowl is fluted; two bands of decoration. – SCREEN. Little original Perp work. One-bay divisions. – PULPIT. Stone, with characteristically High Victorian panels of c.1890. – COMMUNION RAIL. Twisted balusters; c.1700. – MONUMENTS. In the s aisle late C14 Knight, his feet against a big lion. In an ogee-gabled recess. Tomb-chest front with four quatrefoils. – In the chancel floor brasses to John Waleys, priest, † 1410 (demi-figure 12 in. long), and to Sir William Walley, priest, † 1506.

Houghton Regis is near enough to Dunstable to take part in that town's renewal. Recent shopping E of the church. See p. 413

BAPTIST CHAPEL. A gruesome Victorian piece with a debased tower and vaguely Gothic, oddly arranged façade windows. It is supposed to have been built about 1864.

HOUGHTON HALL. A fine five-by-five-bay chequer-brick house of c.1700. Raised red-brick quoins. Hipped roof with pedimented dormers. The doorway is Victorian, but what may have been the pediment of the original doorway (open and scrolly) is now above the window of a canted bay which forms part of an C18 extension of the s front. Pretty outhouse of c.1700 with pyramid roof and lantern. The staircase has three twisted balusters to the tread and carved tread-ends. Good panelling in several rooms.

HOWBURY HALL see RENHOLD

HULCOTE see HOLCOT

HUSBORNE CRAWLEY

9030

ST MARY. Has any other church such green greensand as the w tower of Husborne Crawley, where it appears mixed with iron-stone? The w tower is Perp with two two-light bell-openings on each side and a higher stair-turret. Next to the s doorway a large stoup. Much of the church is Victorian restoration. Three-bay arcades of standard elements, s low and C13 (or

at least its capitals), N higher and Perp. The tower arch
has nicely decorated capitals. In the S aisle E wall a pretty
niche. – PLATE. Chalice and Paten, 1636; Flagon given in
1638; Chalice, undated. – MONUMENTS. John Thompson
† 1597(?). Large standing alabaster monument with badly
carved effigies and much better strapwork cartouches on the
base. Five columns, two back, three front, carry a studded
ceiling. Achievement at the top. – Talbot Williamson † 1765,
of coloured marbles, with urn before obelisk.

BEDFORD ESTATE HOUSING in groups of four gabled red-
brick houses.

MANOR FARM HOUSE, by the church. Late C16, timber-
framed with brick infilling.

CRAWLEY PARK. 1777–8. Five bays, red brick, with three-bay
pediment. Pretty doorway. In 1806 two canted bay windows
were added and two complete bays to the l. with another
canted bay window. (Inside, the Drawing Room has an
Egyptian Regency wallpaper and a good chimneypiece.
MHLG)

ICKWELL

ICKWELL BURY. Free neo-Georgian by *A. G. S. Butler*, 1938–40.
The adjoining STABLES are of 1683. Ten bays and a square
cupola. The DOVECOTE is also C17.

GREEN. A very spacious green. Most of the houses are low, the
best being on the W side. At the N end a more formal C18
five-bay house, a nice effect. Near this the Smithy, standing
on the green. One new house alas breaks the scale of the
green mercilessly.

KEMPSTON

ALL SAINTS. In a perfectly villagey setting, although most of
Kempston is now a suburb of Bedford. Short Perp W tower,
short Perp nave with clerestory, lower chancel. Two-storeyed
Perp S porch with a tierceron-star vault. But in the S wall
of the tower one Norman window, and in the chancel a blocked
Norman S and traces of a blocked Norman N window. Indeed,
upon entering one sees that the church has a Norman tower
arch as well as a Norman chancel arch, the former larger than
the latter. One impost of the chancel arch has tiny saltire
crosses. The three-bay arcades are both E.E., the N arcade
earlier than the S arcade. On the N side round piers with very
simply moulded capitals and only slightly double-chamfered

arches, on the s side octagonal piers and normally double-chamfered arches. – FONT. Square, with chamfered corners, Dec. Low, broad, crocketed ogee arches with single figures in them. – PAINTING. Two panels (nave w wall) with Creation of Eve, Temptation, Discovery, and Expulsion. Rustic C15, and no reason not to call it English. – STAINED GLASS. The E window is characteristic of its date: 1852. – MONUMENT. Large coffin lid with a cross with curious small ornamental motifs in places on it. C13 no doubt.

ST JOHN. The church has been demolished.

KENSWORTH

ST MARY. Perp w tower with higher stair-turret. The rest, except for an E extension of the chancel, Norman, and quite early. The chancel has its herringbone flint courses exposed. On the N side are small Norman windows in chancel and nave. The s doorway is original too. One order of shafts, in one capital fox and crane, in the other close interlace. The arch face has rows of small saltire crosses. Also one big roll. There was a w doorway as well, still high and narrow. Its decoration is very similar to that of the s doorway, but it now of course leads into the tower. The nave was quite spacious. The chancel arch has scalloped capitals, and there are only two scallops to the main capitals. That also is early. The chancel E window is Perp, and l. and r. of it are two niches. – COMMUNION RAIL. In parts. It must be of c.1630–40. – PLATE. Set of 1731.

LYNCH HOUSE, I m. SE. Late C18, brick, of seven bays with a three-bay pediment. Porch with thin Roman Doric columns.

KEYSOE

ST MARY. w tower of the C14 and after. High arch to the nave, pairs of transomed two-light bell-openings, four pinnacles, recessed spire with three tiers of lucarnes in alternating directions. Dec N arcade of three bays with standard elements, Dec N aisle windows, Perp two-bay N chapel with Perp windows. Dec chancel with the appropriate windows (intersecting tracery with ogee) and a PISCINA with sweet small-scale tracery. Only the s doorway and the s chancel doorway are much earlier, i.e. late C12 Transitional. – FONT. Of what date is that strange powerful base? It has thick, heavy spurs and eight gables with a ball finial. It has an inscription in French:

Trestin* qui par ici passerez
Pour l'ame de Warel priez
Que dieu par sa grace
Vraie merci li fasse. Amen.

Can it be early C13 ? – BENCHES. Panels with a broad flat ogee
arch and a small cresting above. Not the Beds run-of-the-mill.

KNOCKING KNOLL LONG BARROW

see SHILLINGTON

0060   KNOTTING

ST MARGARET. The unbuttressed w tower is dated 1615 on the
solid parapet. The bell-openings are plain two-light mullioned
windows. But the nave is Norman, see one small s window,
and also the flat buttresses at the w end, the remains of a
Norman w window, earlier than the tower, and the chancel arch
with zigzag. The VCH points out that the w window is set in
such thick masonry that it probably carried a bellcote. The
tower arch is parabolic and barbaric and quite undateable
The chancel was rebuilt, the s transept built, and alterations
made in the nave at the end of the C13 – see the pointed-trefoiled lancets and the window with three stepped lancet
lights. – PULPIT. A simple Jacobean two-decker. – BENCHES.
Of the C16 and the C17, both dates of the same straight-
topped simple type. – CHANCEL GATES. 1637. Set up after
cock-fighting had been indulged in in the chancel on Shrove
Tuesday in the presence of rector and churchwardens. –
PLATE. Cup and Paten of 1629. – CHURCHYARD CROSS. The
base has a quatrefoil frieze. The top is not original.

1040   LANGFORD

ST ANDREW. Of brown cobbles. An uncommonly uniform Dec
church. Nave and aisles and short s porch tower. The s aisle
has flowing, reticulated, and also still geometrical tracery
(three spherical triangles in the head). The N aisle tracery
is flowing and over-restored. The nave w window has reticulated tracery again (four lights). The arcades have finely
moulded capitals and double-chamfered arches. The chancel
arch is of the same type, but the chancel is Perp. – PULPIT.
Plain, but nice; C18. – BENCHES. The nave front rows Perp

* Professor Bony suggests that trestin = trestous, superlative of tous.

with buttressed ends. – STAINED GLASS. Old fragments in several windows. – BRASS to Thomas Hundon, vicar, † 1520 (18 in.).

LEAGRAVE *see* LUTON, pp. 116, 119

LEIGHTON BUZZARD *see* LEIGHTON LINSLADE

LEIGHTON LINSLADE*   9020

The river Ouse divides Leighton Buzzard from Linslade, and it was only in 1966 that the two were made one town. On the Linslade side runs the Grand Junction Canal connecting the town with London and the North. The town had a market as early as the late C11. After 1164 a Benedictine cell of Fontevrault existed at Leighton Buzzard, but it was never of any size, and nothing remains of it.

ALL SAINTS. A large ironstone church. Its pride is its crossing steeple, E.E., with single lancet bell-openings flanked by blank lancets and a high spire with big broaches, three tiers of lucarnes in the same four directions, and small pinnacles on the broaches. The former E.E. roof-lines are visible against the tower. The rest of the exterior is nearly all Perp, with transepts and aisles, a chancel only 2 ft 6 in. shorter than the nave, and a two-storeyed N vestry. The only earlier feature is the Dec W doorway. Inside it is different, negatively and positively. The crossing arches are not E.E., or at least so ill-treated as not to be recognizably E.E. now. But in both transepts the E wall has a niche with a pointed-trefoiled head, and that is probably late C13. The church was consecrated by Bishop Oliver of Lincoln in 1288, and from the same year dates a bequest for its completion. Of this time also are probably the four-bay arcades of standard elements. – FONT. E.E. Of cauldron shape, on five round supports. – SCREEN. Tall, of broad single-light openings, cusped. – STALLS. Probably from St Albans Abbey. Complete MISERICORDS. They have mostly heads and foliage. – Traceried BENCHES with poppyheads. – PULPIT. Given in 1638. Panels typical of the mid C17. Also carved back panel. – LECTERN. A beautiful wooden eagle on a shaft, assigned to the late C14. – WEST DOOR. With excellent ironwork, mostly scrolls, a little looser and sparser than at Eaton Bray. It could be by *Thomas of*

* Formerly Leighton Buzzard.

Leighton, who in 1294 made the iron grille for Queen Eleanor's tomb in Westminster Abbey. – STAINED GLASS. Very much by *Kempe.* It ranges from 1887 (w and one in the s aisle), 1888 (two s transept), and 1889 (one N aisle) to 1905 (also N aisle). The clerestory is of 1896. – The s transept s and N transept N windows are of 1863 and 1865 and represent the pre-Kempe era. – SCULPTURE. In the crossing piers are a number of interesting sgraffiti and carvings. The one really exquisite one is the master-mason's precise drawing of a four-light window

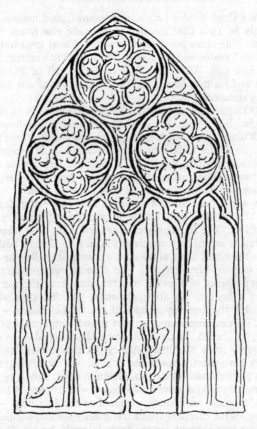

Leighton Linslade church, sgraffito of four-light window with geometrical tracery

with geometrical tracery: a cinquefoiled circle above the quatrefoiled ones (SE pier to the SW). More entertaining is the so-called Simon and Nellie story about first boiling and then baking a cake. She is threatening him with a spoon (SW pier). – MONUMENTS. Robert Wyngate † 1603 and wife. Tablet with

Leighton Linslade church, sgraffito of 'Simon and Nellie' story

the usual kneelers. – Elizabeth Leigh † 1704 and Anne Holt † 1697. Columns, a pediment, and, framed by these, an open book as large as the Tables of the Law. – John Welles † 1645. Tablet with frontal demi-figure, one hand on a book, the other on his heart. Quite small.

ST ANDREW, Church Street. 1866–7 by *J. Neate*. 'Lamentably bad', writes Goodhart-Rendel. Ironstone, with a NW tower with octagonal top of limestone. Eight big lucarnes crowd round the foot of the spire. Much very ungainly plate tracery, but W and E also bar tracery of the geometrical kind. (Inside, the SE corner of the tower is just an extra-fat round pier. Arcades of low piers and high arches, unattractively detailed. GR)

ST MARY, Linslade, 1 m. N, close to the canal. Early C12 nave masonry. Of the same date the unmoulded chancel arch. C15 W tower, early C16 chancel. No aisles. Yellow limestone and ironstone. The nave is embattled. To the N of the chancel arch

a Perp recess; to the s of the E side of the chancel arch a recessed early C13 SEAT, round arch, two stone arms – a very
unusual piece. – FONT. Late C12, circular, with a band of
scrolls and beasts. – SCREEN. Remains of a C15 screen. –
BRASS to a Civilian with three wives. 14 in. figures (W wall).

ST BARNABAS, Linslade. By *Ferrey*, 1848, originally only with a s
aisle. N aisle of 1905 etc. by *J. T. Lawrence*. Front with SW
tower with pyramid roof. – STAINED GLASS. In two N aisle
windows glass by *Kempe*, the Annunciation 1878, the other
1885. – PLATE. Cup of 1568.

BAPTIST CHAPEL, Lake Street. 1864, in the Italian Romanesque
style, but without a campanile. Plum brick, with red and
yellow brick and stone. Front with a wheel-window and a
Lombard frieze climbing the gable.

METHODIST CHAPEL, Hockliffe Street. 1864 by *Bellamy &
Hardy*. Grey brick, three bays, with big pediment and giant
blank arches.

FRIENDS' MEETING HOUSE, North Street. Of 1789, with
wooden cross-windows. Happily simple interior with the usual
seating.

TOWN HALL (now Fire Station), Market Place. 1851, red brick,
Gothic touches. Wholly undistinguished.

CORN EXCHANGE (given up), Lake Street. 1862 by *Bellamy &
Hardy*. Victorian at its most irresponsible. Gay and vulgar,
with a two-storeyed middle porch adorned with upper atlantes
and caryatids. The style is a kind of dissolute Renaissance.

LEIGHTON INSTITUTE, Lake Street. 1845, yet still purely
Grecian. Small and very pleasant, with four attached unfluted
Ionic columns and a pediment.

PERAMBULATION. CHURCH SQUARE is oddly Londonish
Early Victorian. Tall houses, one a terrace of six houses by
W. C. Reed, 1855 (GS), and at the corner of Bridge Street a detached five-bay house, now the CEDARS SCHOOL. Also by
Reed and also 1855. Behind this is the school's Assembly Hall
and Library, formerly the MUSIC ROOM of the Prebendal
House. Mid C18. Blue brick with red dressings, including red
lacing and stone quoins. Portico of four Roman Doric columns
with pediment lower than the wall. Hipped roof. The interior has a boldly coved ceiling and stucco decoration.
From this corner the HIGH STREET rises a little and widens a
little towards the Market Place. It is a good, if uneventful
street. On the N side the WESTMINSTER BANK, formerly
London & County Bank, built in 1856 by *A. Parnell* (GS).

Grey brick, with arched ground-floor windows. On the s side
the SWAN HOTEL, of perhaps c.1840, but still classical.
White, with a porch. So to the MARKET CROSS. This is an 58
uncommonly fine C15 piece, pentagonal, with the lower stage
vaulted and the recessed upper stage with quite well preserved statues. Top pinnacles. To the N and s the MARKET
PLACE has some good, quite early, C18 houses, blue and red
brick, and also BARCLAYS BANK, built by *Waterhouse* for
Bassett & Co. (*see* below). Bath stone, Gothic, two-storeyed,
with dormers. Turn s into LAKE STREET, where, apart from
the Corn Exchange and the Institute, the UNICORN HOTEL,
a late C17 brick front with raised brick quoins, nine bays long
with a recessed five-bay centre. Three storeys; in the top one
three round windows. Also an Early Victorian stuccoed house
with two giant pilasters and two blue and red brick C18
houses.

N from the Market Place runs NORTH STREET. On the w side
HOLLY LODGE, the most impressive house of Leighton
Buzzard and hence, as so often, derelict. Blue and red brick.
Centre and two cross gables; later C17. A little further N, past
the Quaker Meeting House, the WILKES ALMSHOUSES,
1857 and 1873, yellow brick with gables; modest Jacobean. N
of North Street, and N of Church Street, along Plantation
Road to The Plantation, an enviable wood. In it THE KNOLLS,
built by *Norman Shaw* in 1880 for F. Bassett, the banker.
Plenty of tile-hanging, but run-of-the-mill Shaw.

E of the old church of Linslade is MANOR FARMHOUSE, a fine
early C18 house of five bays and two storeys, with one-bay
additions. Vitreous and red brick. The centre bay is flanked
by two sturdy giant pilasters. Doorway with pediment on
rusticated Doric pilasters.

LIDLINGTON   9030

OLD ST MARGARET has been pulled down.

ST MARGARET. 1886, a Bedford Estate church, by *R. Macpher-
son* of Derby. Ironstone, spacious, E.E., with transepts and a
bellcote on the nave E gable. Lancet windows, but the crossing
details taken rather from c.1300. – BRASS. William Goldington, c.1500. Length of the plate 31 in.

LIMBURY *see* LUTON, p. 116

LINSLADE *see* LEIGHTON LINSLADE

LITTLE BARFORD

St Denis. Norman s doorway, in the arch very elongated lozenges fitted to make a continuous chain similar to zigzag. Hood-mould with dogtooth. Also a Norman window in the nave on the s side and in the n aisle w wall (re-set?). Dec n arcade of standard elements and no special interest, and better Dec s chapel. The arcade is of two bays, the pier of the quatrefoil type. The e bay was filled in by *Street* with a screen wall with a very large, bald quatrefoil. In the s chapel an oddly boxed-out PISCINA. – FONT. Probably later C13. The panels of the bowl have just a plain beading. The supports are square with moulded bases and capitals. – SCREEN. One-light divisions. On the dado painted (re-painted) big roses. – STAINED GLASS. The w window by *Kempe*, 1887. – PLATE. Cup and (modernized) Paten, 1571. – BRASS (nave floor) to Thomas Perys † 1535 and wife (12 in.).

POWER STATION. 1945–7 by *Farmer & Dark*. Brown brick, still in the tradition of Scott's Battersea Power Station, but already more cubic and less ornamental. Farmer & Dark's power stations were going to develop a good long way beyond Little Barford in the 1950s.

LITTLE STAUGHTON

St Margaret. The church lies away from the village and makes a fine picture from the s. Limestone and brown cobbles. w tower with recessed spire. Two tiers of lucarnes in alternating directions. Embattled s side. s aisle, clerestory, porch, and chancel all Perp. But the three-bay s arcade is of *c.*1300 – see *25* the quatrefoil piers and their capitals.* Double-chamfered arches. Raw Perp nave roof on good stone corbels, e.g. a bagpiper. In the chancel a C14 tomb recess with crocketed gables and buttress shafts, also raw. – PULPIT. C18. – BENCHES. Of the plain panelled type. – SOUTH DOOR. Traceried; C15. – STAINED GLASS. Bits in several windows. – PLATE. Cup and Paten in a wooden case, 1740.

LOWER GRAVENHURST

Our Lady. In the chancel is a brass inscription to Sir Robert de Bilhemore 'qe fiet faire cette eglise de nouele'. He died *c.*1360, and yet the church is still entirely Dec – see especially

* But Mr McHardy points out the strangeness of the e bay and especially the trefoil pier.

the s side with cusped Y-tracery and simple flowing tracery. In the chancel SEDILIA and PISCINA and an embattled shelf. A very odd feature is the absence of any chancel arch. No aisles. The church is of ironstone. w tower with pyramid roof. Roof with thin tiebeams and kingposts. Pleasant old flooring, and altogether a pleasantly unimproved interior. – PULPIT. Jacobean, with sounding-board. – SCREEN. One-light divisions. Dado with remains of floral painting. – Attached to the screen is an HOURGLASS STAND. – BENCHES. The majority are original. Ends with plain buttressing. – STAINED GLASS. Fragments in one N window, including a head of Christ. – PLATE. Chalice and Paten of c.1600. – 'Early' silver-gilt Shroud-Pin. – MONUMENT. Benjamin Pigott † 1606 and family. The open scrolly pediment cannot be so early. Back wall with kneeling brass figures. They were kept when c.1650 or so the monument was remodelled.

LUTON

0020

INTRODUCTION

Luton, with nearly 150,000 inhabitants, is by far the largest town in Bedfordshire, but it is a town of very little architectural interest. Not that the reason is its relatively recent growth – there were only c.3000 inhabitants in 1820 and only 36,000 in 1901; there is not merely, except for the parish church, a lack of worth-while old buildings, but the C19 and early C20 are weak too, and, although Luton prospers, it has demolished very recently its finest Georgian mansion, Stockwood, and has totally neglected its one and only medieval manor house, Moat House.* It tells of the same lack of visual responsibility that the parish church is set against immediately adjoining cooling towers of a power station and that the new College of Technology refuses to form any picture with the church. As this potential visual centre has been muffed, so throughout the Luton of today there is an absence of visual character. Yet – to say it again – the town is prosperous. It was famous for straw-plaiting and straw-hat-making. Evidence for the introduction of this trade in the C17 is tenuous. In the later C18 it certainly existed, but it became the chief source of wealth only in the C19. When straw hats went out engineering works took their place in the economy of Luton, and now Vauxhall Motors alone (1963) employ 25,000.

* But cf. p. 118.

CHURCHES

ST MARY. The large church of a wealthy town (182 ft long) externally predominantly Perp and much restored (by *Street* 1865–85*). The surfaces are largely flint and stone chequerwork. W tower with higher stair-turret, nave and aisles of five bays, transepts, E of them two prominent chapels, Hoo S and Wenlock N, chancel not projecting far beyond them, and two-storeyed N vestry. The chronology of the church is complex. The oldest features are inside: the arch from S aisle to S transept, simply and only slightly chamfered, say of *c.*1190, and the arch from N aisle to N transept with lush, mature stiff-leaf capitals, i.e. of *c.*1230. So the church already then had transepts and substantial aisles. Of the C13 chancel part of one shaft with capital of some wall arcading has been exposed on the N side. Much was done in the early C14. The W tower in its lower parts is Dec, see the fine W doorway with fleurons in the arch mouldings, the W window with cusped intersecting tracery, and the tall arch to the nave with close leaf in the capitals. Of the same period the whole crossing and the two bays between N transept and Wenlock Chapel. A little later the two bays between S transept and Hoo Chapel (octagonal pier). Dec again the EASTER SEPULCHRE in the chancel with fleurons in a moulding, and Dec the small aisle W windows and the pretty S aisle PISCINA. Dec finally the N vestry, a room with a round pier in the middle and each bay vaulted with diagonal and ridge-ribs. The ribs have one long chamfer. The arcades between nave and aisles are a problem. The W responds on both sides belong to the tower, i.e. the early C14. But then, on the N side three piers were erected with the side to the nave in a continuous chamfer. The rest here and the whole S side have normal octagonal piers and normal double-chamfered arches. The NW parts come, so it seems, after the responds, but before the rest, the rest being Perp in character. The Perp, as has already been observed, dominates the exterior and particularly the fenestration. But it has also contributed more to the interior than has so far been noted. The major contribution is the splendid two-bay opening between chancel and Wenlock Chapel (on the monuments *see* below). It is very high and two tiers in depth, with the reveals and the arches all panelled and with quite elaborate, though not refined, details above the arches. Opposite is the small sunk

56

* By him the E wall of the chancel in the E.E. style.

chantry chapel of Richard Barnard, vicar from 1477 to 1492, a
charming piece with an ornate vault and a separate entrance
from outside through a lobby. E of the Barnard Chapel are the
SEDILIA, late C14.

FURNISHINGS. FONT. Octagonal, of Purbeck marble,
c.1330–40. – Of about the same date the majestic FONT
CANOPY, also octagonal, with eight richly crocketed steep 42
gables and inside a vault with eight radial ribs and eight
ridge-ribs. Big figural boss. – SCREENS. Between S transept
and Hoo Chapel the former rood screen, over-restored. –
Between N transept and Wenlock Chapel a richer screen, but
made up of various parts and also over-restored. In the dado
linenfold panels, at the top broad cornice and cresting. It
must be early C16. – STALLS. In the chancel, with heads
carved on the upper arm-rests. – SOUTH DOOR. With splendid
tracery, including a mouchette wheel; probably C14. –
STAINED GLASS. Original fragments in the Wenlock Chapel
E window. – PLATE. Cup 1610; Flagon 1669; Paten and
Almsdish 1815. – MONUMENTS. There are so many that they
are to be registered by position. – In the chancel in the openings to the Wenlock Chapel William Wenlock, Master of the
Farley Hospital at Luton, † 1392. Large effigy on a big tomb-
chest with inscription. It is worth looking for the abstract
pattern of his robe, seen from the E. – Lady Alice Rotherham
c.1490(?). Tomb-chest with lozenges, brass effigy, 3 ft long
under elaborate but fragmentary canopy. – In the Wenlock
Chapel two tomb recesses, one with the chest with lozenges
and brasses formerly against the back wall, the other of the
familiar Purbeck type with a recess with flat panelled top and
panelled sides. – Brass of Hugo atte Spettyl † 1416 (floor).
The figure is 13½ in. long. Also a husband with two wives
(20 in. figures), a Priest (18 in.), a layman (20 in.), and, by the
rood-stair, a Civilian (18 in.) and a Lady (24 in.).* – In the N
transept lively brasses of John Acworth † 1513 and wives. The
figures are 24½ in. long. Enormous helm with cresting behind
his head. Below are members of the Fraternity of Holy
Trinity. – Also in the N transept Thomas Waller † 1845.
Signed: *Pietro Costa* Fiorentino sculpì, 1847. Urn on a high
pedestal, a genius on the l., a mourning woman on the r. – In
the S transept on the floor brasses to John Sylam † 1513 and
wives (29 in.). – Brass to Edward Sheffield, priest, † 1525–6

---

* In the Wenlock Chapel are two HELMS, C16 and C16 to C17, with C15
chin-guard.

(24 in.). – In the s aisle two C14 tomb recesses, one very low, the other with a four-centred arch and in it the effigy of a priest, very badly preserved.

ALL SAINTS, Shaftesbury Road. 1922–3 by *W. D. Caröe*. More conventional than Caröe was earlier in life. Only the big bellcote remains in one's memory. Plum brick, the fenestration Dec, Perp, and even Elizabethan.

ST ANDREW, Blenheim Crescent. 1931–2 by *Sir Giles Gilbert Scott*. Light brick, with a massive w tower, big sloping buttresses without set-offs, narrow aisle passages, and clerestory windows in groups of eight arched lights. Inside prominent transverse arches.

CHRIST CHURCH, Upper George Street. 1856–60 by *H. Elliott*, the tower and s aisle 1864, the chancel by *G. Vialls*, 1881. Brick, of disjointed parts with a clumsy tower. The details in the style of 1300. Indifferent interior.

ST CHRISTOPHER, Round Green. 1936–7 by *Sir Albert Richardson*. The chancel of 1959. Pleasant, though very reactionary. The side windows under deep segmental arches. Roof with dormers. No tower.*

ST FRANCIS, Carteret Road. 1959–60 by *P. Dunham, Widdup & Harrison*. – The PAINTING behind the altar by *Mary Adshead*. Expressionist.

ST JOSEPH (R.C.), Gardenia Avenue. By *J. E. Sterrett*, 1958–60. This Early Christian style in brick was popular and conservative twenty years earlier. For 1960 it is almost beyond belief.

ST LUKE, Oakley Road, Leagrave. By *Lord Mottistone (Seely & Paget)*. Consecrated 1956, and in its architectural style startlingly out of touch with the age. Strangely secular-looking façade. – (PAINTING. Mural by *Norman Blamey*.)

ST MATTHEW, Havelock Road. 1875–6 by *G. Vialls*. Brick, without a tower. Dignified, though dull. Small lancets, polygonal apse.

ST PAUL, Hibbert Street. 1890 by *T. N. Laslett*. Brick, without a tower. High interior with exposed brick. – STAINED GLASS. E by the *Glasscraft Guild*, 1927.

ST SAVIOUR, Russell Street. 1897–1905 by *Micklethwaite & Somers Clarke*. Brick, without a tower. Good N view with even windows high up. Wide, low nave, piers and arches typical of *c*.1900. The s aisle not yet built.

HOLY TRINITY, Limbury (Biscot). 1867–8 by *T. Nicholson* of

* Internally, the roof is supported on wooden piers, not on the walls, Mr F. M. Gardner tells me.

Hereford. Yellow brick, red brick, and stone. Dec details. Bellcote. – PULPIT. Of stone, semicircular, typically High Victorian.

CHAPELS. A selection only. The UNION CHAPEL, Castle Street, of 1836–44 is one of the best buildings of Luton (one of only two graded II by the MHLG). Three bays with three-bay pediment and an entrance with giant Greek Doric columns *in antis*. Egyptianizing front windows. All stuccoed. – The former Wesleyan Chapel, now INDUSTRIAL MISSION, in Chapel Street is of 1851–2 (by *W. W. Pocock*), large, with arched windows, and on the verge from Classical to Italianate. – Fifteen years later, the CONGREGATIONAL CHURCH in Stuart Street, 1865–6 by *J. Tarring* (cost £4,663 with the schools etc.; GS) has turned late C13 Gothic and is made more prominent by a tower with spire.

PUBLIC BUILDINGS

TOWN HALL. 1934–8 by *Bradshaw, Gass & Hope*. Proud, but lifeless. Portland stone, the fag-end of the Classical Re-Revival. With a symmetrically placed tower.

ART GALLERY AND MUSEUM. This is WARDOWN, a wealthy, but uninspired, gabled brick house of 1875. The architect was *T. C. Sorby* and the tender £10,070 (GS).

PUBLIC LIBRARY, Bridge Street. By the Borough Architect, *M. H. G. Blackman*, 1960–2. Remarkably large, and pleasant externally and internally.

COLLEGE OF TECHNOLOGY, Park Square. By *Norman & Dawbarn*, 1957–9. The centre of the town, but not a memorable building, though reasonable and not marred by gimmicks.

GENERAL POST OFFICE, Dunstable Road. 1957–8 by *T. W. Winterburn*. A sensible, modern job – just compare it with the new building of Vauxhall's (*see* p. 118).

STATION. 1937 by *W. H. Hamlyn*. One of the relatively few stations of between the wars which were designed in the international style of the thirties. The brick and the block-grouping here derive probably from Holland.

AIRPORT TERMINAL BUILDING. 1964–6 by *Yorke, Rosenberg & Mardall* (*Brian Henderson*). A sound, simple, and logical design, all one-storeyed and under one big, flat roof.

WATER TOWER, West Hill Road. 1901 by *Henry T. Hare* (consultant). One of the most enjoyable buildings of Luton. Decidedly Arts and Crafts and resourcefully handled.

PERAMBULATION

It is no good pretending that a perambulation is possible. On the general character or lack of character of Luton enough has been said in the Introduction. Now all that can be done is to pick out a few buildings of interest.

In PARK STREET WEST (Nos 21, 23, 29, 31) and in LANGLEY STREET (No. 20) are still very minor late C18 or early C19 houses with doorways with fluted pilasters of semi-elliptical section. They ought not to be allowed to disappear.

In the triangle that was once MARKET HILL and is now nothing definable (between Park Square and George Street) is the CONSERVATIVE CLUB, 1908, of red sandstone with two porches, very characteristic of c.1900, and a fancy Dutch gable.

The VAUXHALL MOTOR COMPANY came to Luton from Lambeth in 1905. It turned to motor cars in 1907. The payroll in 1935 was c.7,000, in 1963 c.25,000. The Offices in Kimpton Road are by *H.B.Cresswell*, 1907–15, neo-William-and-Mary, of brick, with brick quoins and a doorway with a big semi-circular pediment. Extensions in the same style. The main factory building is by *Howard, Fairbairn & Partners*, 1957–8. It covers 1½ million square feet. The most recent building is the STYLING CENTRE, by the same architects, 1962–4. It is itself irritatingly overstyled. A long, four-storeyed façade, all forward and backward in saw-tooth fashion, with restless pre-cast concrete members. The porch is big enough for Gog and Magog to call.

For the new Whitbread premises in Oakley Road *see* Dunstable, p. 79.

At BISCOT in MOAT LANE is still MOAT HOUSE, but it is derelict at the time of writing. Yet it was the one remaining medieval house of Luton, built, it is assumed, in the late C14 (and with a fine roof of c.1500. Collar-beams and arched braces. The collars and purlins are embattled. The roof was the former hall roof. In the N wall of the house two original two-light windows with segmental arches. Austin).*

½ m. E of Vauxhall's but accessible via Copt Hall are the ruins of SOMERIES CASTLE, the house first of the de Someries and then the Wenlocks. Lord Wenlock, who fell at Tewkesbury, or his successor at Someries, Bishop Rotherham of Lincoln (cf. Buckden, Hunts.), built the house whose ruins stand. They date from the middle or the late C15. What remains is the brick

* At the time of going to press it seems certain that the house will be restored and the roof exposed.

gatehouse, to its E the brick chapel, and to its W some more
brick walling. The gatehouse has bold and broad polygonal
projections and to the r. of the carriage entrance a pedestrian
doorway which, however, leads into the main gateway, i.e.
has no separate exit into the former courtyard. In the extension
to the E is a spiral stair with a sunk handrail. The chapel E
window was of four lights and had a segmental arch. There was
a S chapel or chamber; for the squint from it towards the
altar remains. The building is the earliest in the county to use
brick.

1 m. ESE of Someries, at CHILTERN GREEN FARM, is a square
dovecote of brick and timber-framing.

DRAY'S DITCHES, 3 m. NNW. This linear dyke has a length of
approximately ½ m. and runs roughly at right angles to the
Icknield Way. Its ends have been largely obliterated by
ploughing on the W and by the construction of the South
Bedfordshire golf course on the S. Originally the double bank
and ditches ran from a barrow (destroyed) on Old Warden
Hill in the direction of Great Bramingham, in the area now
covered by St Margaret's Home. The only major portion of the
bank now visible, which survives to a height of 4 ft, lies approximately ½ m. E of the Home. Excavations conducted in this
central area revealed two hitherto unrecognized Bronze Age
boundary ditches, which contained sherds of Early Bronze
Age collared urns, and three main Iron Age ditches. Sherds
of Iron Age A pottery came from the latter. Between the central
and S ditch were located the post-holes of a double palisade
with intervening tie-beams. These earthworks probably
mark the SW limit of a tribal territorial area.

WAULUD'S BANK, ½ m. N of Leagrave railway station. This is a
univallate earthwork inside a broad, flat-bottomed ditch 30 ft
wide and 8 ft deep, abutting on the river Lea on the W and
enclosing a D-shaped area of 18 acres. Excavation revealed
traces of a timber-built hut on the outer edge of the ditch,
and sherds of Late Neolithic Rinyo–Clacton pottery and
flintwork were found on the floor of the ditch.

LONG BARROW, ¼ m. SE of Sundon Park in the recreation
ground. The barrow is 110 ft long and 56 ft wide at its broader
E end, where it still stands over 7 ft in height.

LUTON HOO

1010

The splendour of Luton Hoo is its celebrated collections and
its park by *Capability Brown* of 1,500 acres with its two lakes.

He began this grandiose job in 1764, one year after *Robert Adam* had started drawings for the house. It belonged to the Earl of Bute, then Prime Minister. He had bought it in 1762 with a brick house built in the early years of the C17. But the thrill of the house as it now stands is not Robert Adam, nor *Sir Robert Smirke*, who remodelled what was there c.1827 etc., but *Mewès* of Mewès & Davis who remodelled it once again in 1903 for Sir Julius Wernher, diamond magnate in the heroic years of the diamond and gold discoveries in South Africa. The architectural history of the house is complicated and not fully known. Adam made plans and began work, but the old house remained, and, though there was a fire in 1771, Mrs Delaney in 1774 still went through principal rooms of the old house to reach the new and especially Adam's sensational Library, 144 ft long and facing S. The house was apparently not fully completed till Smirke came. Moreover, there was a fire in 1843 which gutted it. Redecorating was done, but almost entirely replaced by Mewès.

The house is of ashlar stone throughout. The W, i.e. the entrance, side is essentially by Smirke, although it tallies in some major features with what Adam designed and probably built. It has a far-projecting centre with a giant hexastyle portico and a pediment. Recessed parts of four bays l. and r. and then two angle bows. The bows and the portico are as in Adam's drawings. In the middles of the recessed parts are two odd set-pieces, Grecian-Mewès, and Mewès repeated them on the S and E fronts as well. They are of browner stone than the rest and consist of four Doric pilasters only one storey in height and crowned by a frieze with wreaths. The S side, facing a sunk garden with two domed pavilions, Edwardian no doubt, has preserved from Adam the two slender Greek Doric columns *in antis* in the middle but has otherwise been changed by Mewès (cf. the illustration of 1819 in Neale's *Seats*). The house has always been three-storeyed here, whereas the W side and also the E, i.e. the lake, side are of two storeys, or at least now appear to be. The N side has giant columns carrying projecting pieces of entablature. This may be* work by *Sydney Smirke* after the fire of 1843. Towards the E Adam built a middle bow and wrapped a hexastyle portico round it. Thus the front was at the time of the fire. After that it was reduced to the bow with attached columns as we now see it. The view to the distant lake is not easily forgotten.

* So Mr Urwick Smith suggests.

The interior is, to say it again, neither his nor Adam's. The CHAPEL is the one main room older than 1900. It was done in a kind of Byzantine style by *G. E. Street* in 1875. The blank arcading along the walls has almost entirely gone, but the alabaster-faced apse remains, and the ceiling painted in rather joyless colours. Of *Mewès'* remodelling the *clou* is the oval staircase hall, French *Beaux Arts* at its most convincing 103 and indeed its most splendid. White walls, the staircase rising in a dashing sweep, its balustrade of massive wrought iron to contrast against the whiteness of the rest. Sculptured groups in niches high up, 'L'Amore degli Angeli' by *F. Borgonzoli* at the foot. Discreet decoration of the walls and the door surrounds. Oval skylight. There are more rooms on this scale and of this sumptuousness of decoration – the Blue Hall or Entrance Hall with a screen of two columns and again a skylight; the Dining Room with the central E bow, marble walls in two colours, one for the panels, one for the framing, tapestries, and mirrors; the present main Drawing Room with four marble columns, *boiseries*, and again skylighting; and the Ballroom, all white and gold, instead of Adam's Library. This has two bows which appear outside as the two square projections between which are the Doric columns.

Mewès & Davis were the architects of the Ritz, the former Carlton, and the Waldorf. To say that is not a slight on Luton Hoo, but a compliment to the Ritz. The combination of Edwardian riches with an exacting French training brought about interiors – at Luton Hoo as at the Ritz – which are of the very highest quality in their own terms. That they were not the terms of the 'Pioneers', i.e. those that led into the new century and its new style, is neither here nor there. At Luton Hoo display was demanded, and it was provided with a *panache* of which no one after the First World War would have been capable.

In one of the rooms not shown to the public are wood-carved garlands, birds, etc. by *Grinling Gibbons*, brought from Cassiobury, the house begun in 1674 by Hugh May.

In the basement is the TEAROOM painted by *Mary Adshead* with the illusion of a marquee.

The STABLES are by *Adam*. A quiet front with three pediments, the middle one on two pairs of Doric pilasters.

LADY BUTE'S LODGE, near the E end of the Lime Avenue, 1¼ m. S of the house, must, with its mullioned windows and gable, date from 1850 or perhaps a little later, but incorporates a genuine Late Norman doorway with colonnettes and a moulded arch. It probably comes from a church demolished or drastically restored at the time and may have been a priest's doorway.

LYNCH HOUSE *see* KENSWORTH

MARSTON MORETAINE

9040

The landscape is determined for miles by the uncountable chimneys of the London Brick Works.

ST MARY. The church, like Elstow, has a detached tower. This is Dec, see the bell-openings. The buttresses have many set-offs, the ground-stage is vaulted. Quadripartite vault with very strongly chamfered ribs. Dec also is the ironstone chancel – see the one N window, cut into by the N aisle. And Dec finally is the vestry. Very handsome sexpartite vault, also with single-chamfered ribs. The Perp contributions dominate. Six-bay arcades, slender piers of standard moulded section, moulded two-centred arches. The W bay is shorter than the others, an error in the calculation presumably. The chancel arch matches the arcade arches. Good nave roof with angels and carved bosses. Perp aisles, and a fine high Perp N porch with pinnacles (later than the aisle – see the base moulding of the latter). The N doorway has tracery in the spandrels. The nave W window is of five lights with panel tracery just a little out of the ordinary. – SCREENS. At the W end is a small screen, with one-light divisions and dainty tracery. – In the N aisle at the E end part of a screen dado with four painted prophets – the East Anglian type and as bad as most of them are there. – BENCHES. Ends, backs, and fronts with good tracery and below it linenfold. – PAINTING. Above the chancel arch Doom, unrecognizable. – STAINED GLASS. In a chancel S window three large figures by *Morris & Co.*, i.e. by *Burne-Jones*, c.1893. – Bits of ancient glass in the N aisle E window. – PLATE. Cup and Cover Paten of 1614; Paten on foot presented in 1806. – MONUMENTS. In the chancel brasses to Walter Papley, rector, † 1420, a demi-figure, 12 in. long, and to Thomas Reynes † 1451 and his wife, 3 ft 1 in. figures. He began the Perp rebuilding of the church. – Thomas Snagge and his wife, erected some time between 1593 and 1626. Standing alabaster monument with recumbent effigies under a five-column tester. His feet are set against his gaunt-lets. The children kneel in relief against the back wall.

MOAT FARMHOUSE, ¼ m. NW. Timber-framed with two front gables. Only the W side is C16. Much was restored and modernized in 1880.

MAULDEN

0030

ST MARY. 1858–9 by *B. Ferrey*, except for the W tower and the W part of the N wall, with the N doorway. Of ironstone, the tracery of the windows geometrical to Dec. Thin piers inside with naturalistic capitals. In the aisles much shallow ornamental relief decoration. – STAINED GLASS. The E window by *Clayton & Bell*, 1858 (TK), not yet in their usual colouring. – PLATE. Cup, 1619. – The interest of the church is the MAUSOLEUM of the Bruces. It is a Gothic building of 1859. Beneath is a crypt with a quadripartite rib-vault and a plain FONT of the late C12. Above three memorials. In the middle the large MONUMENT to Diana, Countess of Elgin, erected in 1656. It is a big, rather stark architectural composition with a strigillated frieze and rising to a strigillated oblong basin. Out of this appears the demi-figure of the Countess in her shroud, meant to be floating up at the sound of the last trump. One hand is on her heart, the other points upward. The whole is a typical mid C17 conceit. No wonder Horace Walpole found it 'the most ridiculous that ever was imagined'. At the bottom large cartouches also of characteristic mid C17 forms. – In the corners of the room two busts of excellent quality: Thomas Bruce, Earl of Elgin, † 1663 and Edward Bruce, † 1663 too, seventeen years old. *Burman*'s and *Bushnell*'s names have been suggested. The busts, however, are by a different and a better hand than the Countess's figure. On the Bruces *see* Houghton House, Ampthill.

HILLFORT, Maulden Firs. *See* Barton-le-Clay.

MELCHBOURNE

0060

ST MARY MAGDALENE. A Georgian church with a medieval W tower. But the Georgian chancel has medieval masonry, including traces of a low-side lancet, and the nave is so wide now that it must have had a S aisle. On the other hand the buttresses l. and r. of the Perp pairs of transomed two-light bell-openings appear too thin to be medieval. The Georgian date is 1779. Large, even, arched windows. However, when would the N porch have been attached to this building? It is obviously Jacobean, with its Roman Doric columns and

frieze, its round entry-arch, and its oval side windows.
According to Mr Collier it is said to come from Woodford in
Northamptonshire. Arcades of Tuscan columns and a coved
ceiling inside. – Also a PULPIT with discreet inlay, BOX PEWS,
and, alas, STAINED GLASS by *Mayer* of Munich in the E window, as late as 1902 or later, yet in its gaudy Holbeinesque
style utterly out of sympathy with either the church or any
style of 1900. – PLATE. Silver-gilt Set of 1788.

THE STREET is the name of the long row of thatched C18
estate cottages leading towards the church.

MELCHBOURNE PARK. Built *c.* 1610 for Lord St John as a replacement of the out-of-date Bletsoe Castle and remodelled in
1741. Red brick. Of the former date only the two gables at the
back with their mullioned windows and probably the H-plan
and the big chimneybreast on one of the short sides. The
façade of 1741 has two projecting wings with big canted bay-
windows, a recessed five-bay centre, and a low parapet. All
first-floor windows have alternating triangular and segmental
pediments. Porch of two pairs of Tuscan columns. The large
staircase hall has a ceiling with dainty plasterwork on four
shallow pendentives and the staircase itself a restrained iron
handrail. (Fine gallery on the second floor with pedimented
doorheads and overmantels.)

MEPPERSHALL

ST MARY. Of ironstone, with a Norman crossing tower – see the
one original s window. But the top of the tower is Perp. The
crossing arches are in different states of preservation, the best
being the w arch with one angle roll. The transepts are Norman too – see the blocked E arches. Can they have led to
apsidal chapels? Or do they only represent altar recesses?
In the southern one there is indeed now a Perp REREDOS with
panels and tracery. The chancel is early C13, though much renewed. The lancet windows, three stepped ones in the E wall,
five originally N and s, are shafted inside. The buttressing outside is still of the flat Norman kind. Nave and N aisle are by
Sir Arthur Blomfield, 1875–6. Three wide bays, so wide that
two thin lancets in the clerestory correspond to one bay. The
piers are round, and the capitals are not at all strictly E.E. The
aisle has an uncommonly steep lean-to roof. – PLATE. Two
Cups and a Paten, 1673. – MONUMENTS. Brasses to John
Meptyshale † 1440 and wife (18 in.) and to John Boteler † 1441

and wife (18½ in.). – Timothy Archer † 1672. Badly done demi-figure, frontal, the usual type for clergymen, and he was vicar here. The top is an open scrolly pediment.

ST THOMAS' CHAPEL, Chapel Farm, ¾ m. ENE. Nave and chancel. Late Norman N doorway of two orders. The capitals are decorated scallop and decorated waterleaf. In the arch lozenges, each slightly folded across the middle. All that means a date c.1170–80. One Dec two-light window.

MANOR HOUSE, by the church. One of the most impressive timber-framed façades in the county. Two big gables with timber decoration of the familiar concave-sided lozenges, and between them smaller gables, the middle one over a canted bay. On the front of this just one pargetted thistle and crown. The date is probably early C17.

THE HILLS, SW of the church and manor house. Motte and bailey castle. The original bailey is E of the motte. The second bailey followed farther E. The motte is only c.30 ft in diameter.

MILLBROOK

0030

ST MICHAEL. On a hill. The S arcade is late C13, the N arcade Perp. Both have standard elements. Externally the church looks predominantly Victorian. A thorough restoration was done by *Butterfield* in 1857 and 1864. Undisturbed are the N doorway and the N aisle E window. The S doorway is bigger and, as also a small S aisle lancet, goes with the S arcade. The church is of ironstone. In the N aisle NE corner an image niche. – REREDOS. By *Sir Albert Richardson* (of Ampthill). – BENCHES. Perp, with a knob on the top, a knob on the top of the arm, and a third on top of the back. – MONUMENTS. William Huett and his wife, both † 1602, on the same day. Two defaced recumbent stone effigies. Back tablet with a very pretty surround: curling-up strapwork, flowers, a death's head, and emblems of death.* – Lord and Lady Holland † 1840 and 1845 and Georgiana Anne Fox † 1819 aged ten. By *Westmacott*. White marble. L. and r. two busts on columns. Read his inscription and you will understand why *The Ecclesiologist* called it 'flagrantly Whig'. In the centre big square base with a relief of Christ and the children. The child's bust at the top.

* It is not certain that the effigies and the back tablet belong together. The effigies were dug up in 1919.

MILTON BRYAN

ST PETER. Norman nave and chancel, but far too drastically treated by *Cottingham* in 1841–3. One w window, one chancel s and one chancel N window, and two nave N windows are Norman. Some Perp details also (N doorway). By Cottingham the NW tower with single lancet and pairs for the bell-openings, solid and four-square. Inside there is one very curious feature, a Norman nook-shaft half-way along the chancel. As the chancel arch is Norman too, also with nook-shafts, can the other nook-shaft mean an apse arch? – STAINED GLASS. One w window is a memorial to Sir Joseph Paxton, born in this parish. It was presented in 1867 and is by *Wailes*. – PLATE. Cup and Paten of 1611. – MONUMENTS. Large coffin lid with

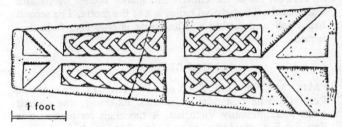

Milton Bryan church, coffin lid, twelfth century

a strangely stylized cross and close interlace. C12. – Sir Hugh Inglis. By *Chantrey*, 1832. White marble. Recumbent effigy, his head on the half-rolled-up mat favoured in Elizabethan and Jacobean monuments. The monument cost £1,000.

MILTON ERNEST

ALL SAINTS. The church has an Early Norman chancel – see the small N and s windows. The bold chancel arch of two sweeping continuous mouldings, however, is C13. The w tower is C13 too, still unbuttressed, with a w lancet and bell-openings with Y-tracery. Dec N aisle windows and, inside, a splendid tomb recess, with crocketing and large cusping and subcusping and big leaves in the cusps. The N windows are straight-headed, the w window has intersecting tracery. Dec also the N as well as the s arcade. They have the standard elements, but differ in details. Perp clerestory and nave roof with bosses, two-storeyed s porch, its entrance with traceried spandrels, and s aisle wall. At the tops of the buttresses pretty bits of decoration. – FONT. Octagonal bowl on eight buttress supports. The panels have simple Dec tracery. – SCREENS. One C15 screen in the N aisle; a fine low, early C19 iron screen in the tower arch. – BREAD CUPBOARD. 1729. With three tiers of four arched pigeon-holes each and a steep pediment. – BENCHES. By *Butterfield*, and typical of him. – CHANDELIER. 1728. Of brass, two tiers of curly arms. – STAINED GLASS. The church was restored in 1864–5 by *Butterfield*, and the characteristic glass in the s aisle w, tower w, chancel E, and chancel side windows must be by *Gibbs*, whom Butterfield patronized. The clear, watery colours are typical, and the strong, bold leading. – PLATE. Cup and Cover Paten of 1570. – MONUMENTS. Tablet to Christopher Turnor † 1675 (s aisle). – In the churchyard, E of the church, William Butterfield † 1866, the architect's father. A foliated cross slab.

MILTON HALL. By *Butterfield*, 1856, and extremely characteri- stic of him. No-one would call the house engaging, but it is done with a grim determination and an unfaltering conviction. Buff stone and red brick trim. Both main façades are extremely asymmetrical. Motifs include bay-windows, very steep dormers, pairs of windows with shouldered lintels, and of course also large and serious Gothic windows. (In the staircase hall are two-light inner windows, the lights with ogee heads.)*

MOGERHANGER

ST JOHN EVANGELIST. 1860–1 by *Slater*. A serious, bold, and austere exterior. Bands of brown and buff stone. Chancel tower with pyramid roof and a high polygonal apse immediately abutting on it. Nave and aisles, the arcades with their French C12 foliage capitals less original. Low paired aisle windows. They are pointed-trefoiled.

MOGERHANGER PARK (Park Hospital). By *Soane* for Godfrey and after 1805 Stephen Thornton of the Clapham Sect. Godfrey was a director of the Bank of England. The house was first designed much more simply in 1791, but finally designed in its present form in 1809. It is rendered. The facing material was originally 'Parker's Metallic Stucco'. The garden side of seven bays has a wooden veranda. In the centre is a very shallow pediment on pilaster-strips with sunk panels. The

* Information kindly given me by Dr Paul Thompson.

entrance side is more eventful. Low centre with a semicircular porch of Greek Doric columns of the Delos type. The end bays of the façade have on the ground floor arched windows with heavy, broad Grecian pediments over. Behind the porch is a square entrance hall once with a shallow dome. Behind that rises the staircase, square and high. It is all cantilevered and has the simplest iron balustrade just of reversed Ss. On the first floor off the staircase an apsidal or exedra vestibule followed by a room with two apses or exedrae. The main room on the ground floor has lost its four pillars. There are two Soanian chimneypieces.

1040

NORTHILL

ST MARY. Of ironstone and Totternhoe clunch and all too drastically restored. Much is Dec and much is Perp. Dec N and S aisle W windows (reticulated tracery), Dec two-storeyed S porch with a two-bay vault with diagonal and ridge-ribs. Dec S doorway with three orders of thin colonnettes. Dec the high tower arch (three sunk-quadrant mouldings), and Dec also the high four-bay arcades. Piers quatrefoil with four thin diagonal shafts, arches with two sunk quadrants. Similar, but C19, the chancel arch. On the other hand Perp the aisle windows and the chancel windows.* The chancel may have been rebuilt when Henry IV in 1404 made the church collegiate. The strange vestry group with the rose window dates from 1862 and is by *Woodyer*. – STALLS. For the college. With carved arm-rests and poppy-heads. The MISERICORDS are very plainly carved. – SCREEN. With some old elements. – STAINED GLASS. This is what will stay for ever in one's memory. Two splendidly large-scaled windows of 1664, commissioned by the Grocers' Company, patrons of the church. They are signed by *John Oliver* and are heraldic and ornamental; bold, rich, and very secular. – W windows all three by *Clayton & Bell*. – One N aisle and one S chancel window by *Kempe*, 1897 and 1906. – PLATE. Cup of 1569; Paten on foot of 1689; smaller Paten on foot; Flagon of 1696. – MONUMENT. Tablet to J. Harvey † 1793 by *T. King* of Bath. Oval inscription beside a draped urn. – (CURIOSA. Sixteen leather BUCKETS and a BIER. In the porch parvis.)

THE GRANGE. A fine house, unfortunately not well kept at the

* The tracery of the windows of the church, says the VCH, is 'almost entirely modern'.

time of writing. The date must be *c*.1700. Five bays, with an apsidal door-hood on carved brackets. Staircase with twisted balusters and still a string hiding the tread-ends.

(In HOMEWOOD is a rectangular earthwork with a motte, probably Norman.)

OAKLEY   *0050*

ST MARY. Late C12 W tower – see the small slit-windows half-way up. The tower was unbuttressed too. Perp top. The arch to the nave has a little nailhead, i.e. is of *c*.1300. The nave was originally one bay shorter than it is now. Early C13 N arcade of two bays, with round piers and moulded arches, C13 S arcade, totally re-done, except for the responds. The E respond was re-used when the E bay was added with its double-chamfered arches. The S doorway of two continuous hollow chamfers is of the C13 too. The rest of the exterior is Perp. Two-storeyed S porch, its entrance with traceried spandrels. Battlements everywhere. The chancel has a Late Perp four-light E window, but is throughout over-restored. – FONT. Octagonal, Perp, with tracery motifs. – SCREENS. One (N chapel W) with one-light divisions, coving, and loft, and on the coving PAINTINGS of stars and Christ seated on the rainbow, another (S chapel W) with four-light divisions as at Felmersham, and remains of the rib-vaulted coving. – BENCHES. A complete set of the standard buttressed type, quite a rarity in Bedfordshire. – STAINED GLASS. In the E window two roundels with suns. – More fragments in several windows. – MONUMENT. Coffin lid with a defaced foliated cross growing out of an animal (cf. Pavenham). – Effigy of a Lady, early C14, also defaced, in a low, later tomb recess with bold pointed trefoiled cusping.

OAKLEY HOUSE. Remodelled by *Henry Holland* out of a late C17 house with hipped roof. (Verandas on the S, E, and W sides. Inside, the doorway in the hall comes from Fineshade Abbey. MHLG)

ODELL   *9050*

ALL SAINTS. All Perp, except for the lower part of the W tower (see the doorway). The tower is an unusually monumental piece of four stages with clasping buttresses, paired transomed two-light bell-openings, a tracery frieze, and pinnacles. In the S porch a tierceron-star vault. Spacious interior. Four-bay arcades with slender Perp piers of standard

section. The same type for tower arch and chancel arch. –
FONT. Octagonal, Perp, with simple arched panels. – PULPIT.
Jacobean. – SCREENS. Under the tower arch excellent screen
of 1637, with two tiers of balustrading of thick, vertically
symmetrical balusters. – Of the Perp rood screen little is old. –
BENCHES. The standard type of buttressed ends.* – HOUR-
GLASS STAND. On a nice bracket. – STAINED GLASS. In the S
aisle E window. C15 figurines of angels. – Also fragments in a
chancel S window. – PLATE. Large silver-gilt Chalice and
Paten of 1637; Paten of 1685; Paten of 1728. – MONUMENTS.
To the Alston family, probably of 1678. Large, richly decorated
tablet with open pediment. By the same hand as the monument of 1678 at Bletsoe. – Thomas Alston † 1807. By *John
Bacon Jun.* Hope stands by an urn on a pedestal. Landscape
relief meant to represent Montevideo.

ODELL CASTLE has been replaced by a recent house. Originally
this was a motte and bailey castle. Later stone buildings were
put up, and they were in ruins in Leland's time. The keep was
still used in the C17, and new building was done in the Thorpe
Hall style. Of the outbuildings of this much remains.

OLD WARDEN

ST LEONARD. Of brown cobbles. Late C12 to early C13 W
tower, see externally the absence of buttressing and the tiny
lancets. The nave is in a poor state, the chancel is almost
entirely Victorian and of no special interest. There is nothing
in this exterior to prepare for the shock in store upon entering.
One can only just register the high unmoulded Norman tower
arch, the early C14 S arcade of standard details and slightly
earlier chancel arch before going under in the mass of woodwork indiscriminately got together by Robert Henley, Lord
Ongley, in 1841 etc. It oppresses you from all sides; it is
utterly disjointed, and can only here and there be read con-
secutively. An example is the PULPIT with biblical scenes and
the Signs of the Evangelists on the corner posts. This was
bought in Scotland much later than 1841. It is probably
Belgian C18, and Belgian, it is said, is also most of what Lord
Ongley assembled. In trying to take it in, one is all the time
up against the Early Victorian connecting pieces, often far
more than mere connecting pieces. For instance it can be
assumed that the wavy tops of the BENCHES are due to Lord
Ongley. One can compare the wavy timbers forming part of

* Some incorporate Jacobean panels (G Mc H).

the elaborate and indeed thrilling roof of the nave. The bench ends with their Gothic tracery also look Early Victorian. Similarly the Gothic FONT COVER is no doubt English and of the 1840s. In the SOUTH GALLERY the blank-arched panels are English and may be genuinely Elizabethan or Jacobean. The BOX PEW beneath the monument by Mabey has thin open-work acanthus scrolls, typically Belgian late C17 or early C18. Another of the box pews has some ogee-headed panelling, ogee also at the foot, which may be Belgian early C16. The many panels with the letters AC are said to come from the House of Anne of Cleves at Bruges. (What has Anne of Cleves to do with Bruges?) They have indeed some discreet strap-work. Many of them are the frontal of the ALTAR. In the panelling behind the altar young caryatids. Hanging garlands are everywhere, small scenic reliefs everywhere. The total impression is as stuffy as are those houses which Early Victorian squires have crowded similarly with the fruits of their travelling.

Of other FURNISHINGS the FONT is large and originally had twelve shafts. It will be of the early C14. – STAINED GLASS. In one N window much-restored figures and surrounds of the early C14 from Warden Abbey. – PLATE. Paten on foot of 1822; Paten and Flagon, Spanish, c.1720.

MONUMENTS. Sir Samuel Ongley † 1726, signed by *Scheemakers* and *Delvaux*, or rather P. Chiemaker en L. Delvaux Inventor et Fecit. It must be Delvaux's spelling, and whose is the Latin? Standing Emperor with two putti l. and r. Reredos back. A pity it is crowded out by the woodwork. – Lord Ongley † 1814. Tablet with a drape and a coat of arms. – Caroline Jane Shuttleworth † 1899. This monument, signed *C. H. Mabey* Sc., succeeds in the end in outdoing all the collecting of 1841. In the SE angle of the nave, high up, appears a white Magdalen – no, probably Faith – life-size, in the Baroquest of attitudes. It looks as if it were Belgian and real Baroque too. Alabaster surround. Putto heads at the top.

QUINT'S HILL. Just to the N of the church are the much overgrown remains of a bivallate earthwork only the NW portion of which survives; the remainder was presumably destroyed in laying out the park to the SE. The site is unexcavated but is probably Early Iron Age in date.

OLD WARDEN PARK. 1872 for Joseph Shuttleworth by *Clutton*. Of yellow brick, large, compact, three-storeyed, Jacobean, but with an asymmetrically placed tower. The clock is surrounded by an odd openwork grille of stone, an original motif. Large, centrally placed entrance hall. Staircase hall with glazed lantern. Library with white and gold ceiling and sky-lights.

At the approach to the church a very pretty terrace of thatched cottages roughcast a delightful honey colour.

WARDEN ABBEY, 1 m. WSW. Warden Abbey was founded in 1135 by Walter Espec, who had founded Rievaulx before. Like Rievaulx it was a Cistercian house, and the monks came from Rievaulx. It must have been quite a large house, but nothing of it is visible. All that remains is one part of the successor house of the Gostwicks. Brick, Early Tudor, small and quite irregular. Two ground-floor windows set back under deep arches. Next to them a chimneybreast and a decorated stack with star top, and next to this a stone doorway with crocketed ogee gable. At the back a stair-turret. There is no knowing the context of this fragment. The house seems to have been built shortly after 1537, the year of the dissolution of the abbey.

DRAY'S DITCHES. See Luton.

₉₀₅₀

PAVENHAM

ST PETER. W tower with stone spire. Low broaches. Two tiers of lucarnes. (Fine C13 s porch, re-set. Good capitals and good arches. GMCH) Not much else remarkable outside. Three-bay Perp N arcade of standard elements. One-bay Perp s transept. Two niches in the E wall, but a PISCINA of c.1300, proving the masonry of the transept to be older. In the N chapel N wall a fine, re-set pair of large crocketed ogee niches. Where do they come from, and what was their function? (At the E end of the N aisle an excellent Green Man corbel, and in the N aisle E arch a yet better corbel. GMCH) – The church is full of WOODWORK, mostly Jacobean and collected from chimney-pieces, beds, etc. It was all given to the church in 1848 and now adorns the pulpit, lectern, stalls, altar wall, side walls, w gallery, etc. – COMMUNION RAIL. Of cast iron; early C19. – STAINED GLASS. One C15 roundel in the N aisle W window. – PLATE. Silver-gilt Cup and Paten of 1569. – MONUMENT. Coffin lid of the C13 in the chancel floor. Foliated cross growing out of a lion (cf. Oakley), the foliation being asymmetric-ally arranged.

STAFFORD BRIDGE, across the Ouse. Originally of four arches and C13.

PEGSDON see SHILLINGTON

PERTENHALL   0060

ST PETER. The earliest evidence is the three-bay N arcade.
This is of c.1190 – see the only slightly chamfered arches, the
round piers with square abaci, and the bits of dogtooth on one
arch. The chancel received a N chapel of two bays (only one
survives) in the early C14. In 1848 the chancel E window was
provided in the then decidedly reactionary way with a round
arch and intersecting tracery. Of the same date obviously the
vestry and one N window. Perp W tower with a broach spire
with low broaches and two tiers of lucarnes, and also Perp the
large transomed S windows of the nave. – SCREEN. An uncommonly good piece with one-light divisions, little restored.
The inscription above the doorway refers to the Transfiguration. – COMMUNION RAIL. Good, late C17, with dumb-bell
balusters. – BENCHES. The standard Beds kind. – ORGAN. A
charming case of 1783. – PAINTING. On the N aisle E wall
traces of a seated figure, to its l. a female Saint, to its r. a male
Saint and an angel. – STAINED GLASS. Many fragments in a
chancel S window. – PLATE. Cup of 1684; Paten on foot of
1719. – MONUMENTS. (In the N chapel damaged C13 effigy
of a Knight, cross-legged. GMCH) – A number of worthwhile
tablets: in the vestry † 1685, in the chancel, all four very similar, † 1732, 1742, 1747, and – consciously archaic no doubt –
† 1825.

OLD RECTORY, E of the church. A C16 or C17 house refronted
in 1799. Red and rubbed brick. Three storeys, five bays, with
a three-bay pediment. The ground-floor windows l. and r. of
the doorway have blank arches.

MANOR HOUSE, SW of the church. C17 and C19. In one ground-
floor room Elizabethan panelling and an overmantel with two
broad blank arches.

Former MORAVIAN CHAPEL, ⅝ m. NE. Built in 1827. Two-bay
building with a truncated pyramid roof and a lantern. Low
one-bay gabled pavilions with a circular window. A wooden
veranda between.

PODINGTON   9060

ST MARY. The chancel is Norman, see the one blocked S window. Of the Norman nave nothing is visible. It received a S
arcade of three bays about 1190, see the square abaci of

the round piers, the elementary leaves of a capital, and the pointed arches with just one slight chamfer. Much was done in the C13. Externally this can be seen in the W tower with the long (later lengthened) W lancet, the plain N doorway, the N aisle E lancet, and the chancel lancet, side by side with a window with Y-tracery indicating a late C13 date. The interior confirms all this. The N arcade has round abaci with nailhead and hood-moulds with coarse nailhead, and in the chancel the windows are shafted inside and the PISCINA has continuous rolls with keels and a fillet. The unfeeling geometrical tracery of the E window is patently Victorian. The S aisle E and W windows are Dec, the tower top is Perp. The spire is slightly recessed and has low broaches, crockets up the edges, and three tiers of lucarnes. The pinnacles have mostly disappeared. – FONT. The font is Norman, of drum-shape, decorated with close, big zigzags, and also with blank arches and lozenges. – SOUTH DOOR. Traceried. – BENCHES. Perp, plainly buttressed. – STAINED GLASS. In a chancel S window by C. A. Gibbs of London. – PLATE. C17 Chalice and Paten. – MONUMENTS. In the chancel N wall at the time of the S windows, i.e. late in the C13, four tomb recesses were apparently made. They were all filled in in the C17 with blocking and inscription slabs of very good lettering. The dates commemorated are 1647, 1658, 1666, and (a different type of slab) 1681. The naïve, extremely odd finials must date from the same time. But what is that time? Can the bands of post-C13 ornament and the finials be indeed as late as the mid C17? The ornament looks decidedly Elizabethan. So perhaps there was a preceding appropriation.* – Brass to John Howard † 1518, 18 in. in length (nave floor, opposite the entrance). – Mrs Diana Orlebar † 1716.‡ By *John Hunt*. Tablet with two crying putti. Open scrolly pediment.§ – Richard Orlebar † 1803. By *Lewis* of Cheltenham. A female figure kneels by the sarcophagus, which incidentally has a small Gothic quatrefoil. – Richard Orlebar † 1833. By *Humphrey Hopper*. Tablet in a Gothic surround, the sort of thing Hopper repeated time and again.

Opposite and to the W of the churchyard ESTATE HOUSING of c.1773–5, in terraced groups, two with steep middle gables and

---

* Mr McHardy suggests that the two inner recesses are late C13, the two outer ones later (C16? C17?) copies.

‡ Because of her name the pediment at Hinwick House represents Diana.

§ As over the doorways of Hinwick House and Hinwick Hall.

one of these quite an ambitious little composition with two concentric arches in the centre below the gable, the smaller one above a narrow passage to the back, the larger one bracketing this and two adjoining doorways.

CASTLE, behind Manor Farm. Motte-and-bailey type, with an outer enclosure, large enough to circumscribe the whole village.

HINWICK. *See* p. 98.

POTSGROVE 9020

ST MARY. 1880 by *J. D. Sedding*, but with some old masonry. Nave and chancel; NW bell-turret. In the N wall, built in, some Norman and later bits. – SCREEN. C14, though much restored. Shafts with rings instead of mullions, and typical Dec tracery. – STAINED GLASS. Many figural fragments. – BRASSES. Richard Saunders † 1535 and wife, 15½ in. figures. – (Also William Saunders † 1563, a palimpsest of Flemish-type canopy-work, the remains of a plate, not a cut-out figure.)

POTTON 2040

ST MARY. A large church of brown cobbles. W tower, nave and aisles. N transept, chancel, S chapel, and two-storeyed N porch with access from W as well as N. The porch is further E than customary. Embattled clerestory, embattled chancel and S chapel. The oldest feature is a lancet in the chancel N wall. Then, late C13, the S arcade of five bays. Square piers with broad semicircular projections. Double-hollow-chamfered arches. The abaci are not all the same. Two are chamfered squares set diagonally. The N arcade is C14. Standard elements. The details of the transept are Perp, and so is, Late Perp no doubt, the S chapel. Note the design with continuous mouldings to N and S, capitals only to E and W. – STALLS with plain MISERICORDS. – STAINED GLASS. One S aisle window by *Powell*, 1874; very characteristic. – PLATE. Cup of 1717; Paten probably of 1717; small Almsdish of 1718; two Almsdishes of 1720. – Many rustically and delightfully carved GRAVESTONES in the churchyard.

VICARAGE. Georgian. Red brick, five bays, two storeys, hipped roof.

The MARKET PLACE is specially attractive (compared with Biggleswade for instance). Mostly red-brick C18 houses. In the middle the recent, forgivably neo-Georgian CLOCKHOUSE of 1956. Otherwise e.g. on the s side No. 21 with a nice pedimented doorway and No. 23 of 1697, seven bays long. On the w side, statelier (but with shops on the ground floor), Nos 3–4, three-storeyed, and No. 5, stuccoed and also three-storeyed, on the N side the ROSE AND CROWN with two canted bay windows. At the start of KING STREET is THE HOLLIES, neglected at the time of writing. This is early C19, of yellow brick with a dainty porch and dainty one-storey bay windows. The upper middle window is tripartite.*

w of Potton is the conspicuous ANGLIA TELEVISION MAST, 750 ft high.

PULLOXHILL

ST JAMES. Mostly 1845–6 by *J. T. Wing*. Ironstone, w tower, nave and chancel. Windows with geometrical to flowing tracery. w rose window. Most of the chancel of the medieval building remained – see the roof. The nave roof is an elaborate Victorian piece. – PLATE. Cup, Paten, and Chalice of 1700; Salver of 1808. – MONUMENT. Sir William Bryers † 1653. Very characteristic of its date and of high quality. The centre is a bust in an oval recess with garlands. The surround is broad, high, and massive, with volutes up the half-pilasters and a kind of broken scrolly pediment at the bottom.

On the N of the church a late C17 house of seven bays chequer brick, with a hipped roof and a doorway with a hood on carved brackets.

RAVENSDEN

ALL SAINTS. Over the s doorway inside is a Norman tympanum with chequerboard pattern. w tower with small recessed spire. N aisle with two cross-gables. The chancel s wall and the s porch are of brick, probably late C17. One s window is Dec, and Dec also is the N arcade. Three bays, quatrefoil piers, double-chamfered arches. The church has a kingpost roof. – PULPIT. Jacobean; plain.

RENHOLD

ALL SAINTS. Perp w tower with small recessed lead spire. Perp s side and chancel; brown cobbled walls. The N aisle has Dec windows and also a Dec arcade. Three bays, quatrefoil piers, arches with sunk wave mouldings. – FONT. Norman, drum-

* Since demolished.

shaped, with two palmettes being the beginning of an ornamental band, never continued. – PULPIT. Mid C17, with
typically detailed panels. – BENCH FRONTS. Two, with
simple arched panels (N aisle). – STAINED GLASS. Old bits in
N windows. – PLATE. Flagon 1674; Paten 1683; Cup and
Cover Paten 1725. – MONUMENTS. Tomb-chest with richly
cusped quatrefoils. Barbaric writing on the rim, no longer
black-letter. On the lid brasses of Edmund Wayte † 1518 and
wife (14 in.). – Tablets to the Becher family, specially good
William † 1694 with the usual urn in an open scrolly pediment,
the cartouche to Mrs Elizabeth † 1701, and the larger piece to
William † 1751. – Robert Graham Polhill † 1854. By *I. Evan
Thomas*. Sarcophagus with the inscription ALMA and standing
by it a young genius with an extinguished torch.

HOWBURY HALL, 1¼ m. SE. 1849, but still quite pre-Victorian.
Five-bay front plus canted angle bay-windows. The latter
have first-floor cast-iron balconies. Top balustrade. (Inside
proof of an earlier date than 1849. Staircase with rustic
columns as balusters and the wall with stucco of apparently
*c.*1730–40.)

At SALPH END, 1 m. w, is ABBEY FARMHOUSE, a largish and
good C17 house, timber-framed, with two slightly projecting
gables l. and r. of the centre.

RIDGMONT

9030

ALL SAINTS. 1854–5 by *Sir G. G. Scott*. A Bedford estate
church and a competent piece, though not as original nor as
grand as Clutton's Woburn. Goodhart-Rendel called it
'respectable, solid and handsome'. Ironstone is used for
minor decorative enrichment. Late C13 style, with w tower
with broach spire and one tier of prominent lucarnes. Clerestory windows quatrefoil, piers of the arcades quatrefoil in
section. Hood-mould stops with a variety of naturalistic
foliage. Texts in big black-letter on the aisle walls.

Ridgmont is the typical Bedford estate village, with groups of
gabled brick houses of many dates. Between them the BAP-
TIST CHAPEL of 1811 with a broad dissolute stucco façade
which looks Early Victorian.

RISELEY

0060

ALL SAINTS.* The church appears baffling as long as one has
not seen one special point about its architectural history. The

* The Rev. F. J. C. Davis tells me that very recently, embedded in the E
wall, part of a Saxo-Norman arch has been found.

s aisle was originally the nave: hence the width of the E.E. arch to the present chapel, then chancel, and hence the lancet in the chapel N wall now looking into the chancel. This original nave, early in the C13, received an aisle of a width unknown to us. But the arcade is there. Four bays, round piers, base spurs, flat square capitals, one with small-scale stiff-leaf, double-chamfered arches. Early in the C14 the then chancel, i.e. the present s chapel, was given a new E window with reticulated tracery and also a N chapel (i.e. part of the present chancel). It is of one bay and has typical details. The reorganization of the whole came in the C15, and included the new clerestory, the ashlar s porch, and the upper part of the w tower, which is of ashlar too. Pairs of transomed two-light bell-openings. The lower part of the tower is C14. – BENCHES. The usual buttressed kind. – PLATE. Set presented in 1788.

The recent four-storeyed block of FLATS is by *E.H.C. Inskip & Son.*

RISINGHOE CASTLE *see* GOLDINGTON

ROXTON

ST MARY. Short w tower, nave and chancel. Brown cobble walls. The s aisle has a doorway of c.1300 and a three-bay arcade of the same date. Octagonal piers, semicircular responds, double-chamfered arches. The tower was built into the existing nave. The N windows of the nave are irregular. Perp two-bay s chapel. – SCREEN. Perp. On the dado painted saints, the East Anglian way.* – PAINTING. Italian Rood, early C15, the ends of the arms with decoration of c.1600.‡ – MONUMENTS. Lady, early C14(?), in a plain recess in the nave N wall. – Tomb-chest to Roger Hunt † 1438. On the chest shields in cusped arches. No effigy.

CONGREGATIONAL CHURCH. Founded in 1808. A most unusual and a delightful design, thatched with a tree-trunk veranda. The style is that of Metcalfe estate housing in the vicinity.

YARDWOOD. Traces of a mysterious earthwork in a solitary motte or mound, c.40 ft in diameter.

SALFORD

ST MARY. The most striking features are *William White's* of 1867: the N porch, open, of heavy timbers (one beam with

---

* Mr McHardy queries that the screen is all of a piece.

‡ The Rood is said to have been brought from the Crimea.

dogtooth and some ornament is genuine C13 work), and the
bellcote of equally heavy timbers in curved crossings as if for a
Victorian lychgate. The bellcote is for three bells and carries
a spirelet. The church itself is mainly of *c.*1300, see the w
window with bar tracery of three uncusped circles, the N windows, the small s lancet, the s window of three stepped lancet
lights, and the s aisle E window, which has cusped intersecting
tracery. With this goes the s arcade of quatrefoil piers with
moulded capitals. The capitals are perfectly normal, except
that their bottom member is drawn in to fit the piers. Yet all
seems of the same date. Had the masons made a mistake? In
the chancel a priest's doorway which, with its unmoulded
pointed arch, looks older than the rest, and a Dec E window
with reticulated tracery. The chancel arch goes with the s
arcade.* – BENCHES. A few are pre-Reformation. – PLATE.
Chalice and Paten, 1638; Salver, 1763; Flagon, 1802. –
MONUMENTS. In the s aisle cross-legged Knight, in all probability he who built the s aisle. The fragmentary canopy is
later. – Brasses to John Peddar † 1505 and family, 28 in.
figures.

SALPH END *see* RENHOLD

SANDY

ST SWITHUN. Essentially by *W. G. Habershon,* 1860 (PF). Ironstone, large, with aisles and transepts. Inside the chancel,
the chapel arcades, the chancel arch, and the roof corbels all
have naturalistic foliage. The aisle arcades have arches of
dark ironstone. The octagonal s piers are genuine Perp work.
The w tower is medieval too.‡ – STAINED GLASS. One s chancel
window by *Charles Gibbs,* with medallions. – SCULPTURE. In
the chancel a small fragment of a C15 alabaster panel of the
frequent Nottingham type. It belongs to a scene of Christ in
the Garden of Gethsemane. – PLATE. Chalice given in 1661;
Paten 1739. – MONUMENTS. Several tablets, e.g. two with
urns, † 1775 and † 1788. – Statue of white marble of Captain
Sir William Peel, hand on his sabre. By *W. Theed,* 1861.
SANDY PLACE, s of the church. Mid C18. Red brick. Five bays
in a 2–1–2 rhythm. Parapet partly balustraded. Horrid porch.
Round the corner another five-bay façade with a three-bay

* The church had a w tower into the C19.
‡ So are SEDILIA and PISCINA (GMcH).

pediment and a later wide single-storey bow. New school buildings, by *S. V. Goodman*, then county architect, *J.C. Barker*, the present county architect, and *K. P. Roberts*. One or two of the buildings are specially pleasant.

SANDY LODGE, 1¼ m. SE. 1869–77 by *Clutton*.* Yellow brick, Tudor, the stables with a fanciful cupola.

Sandy is probably the site of a small Roman settlement on the Roman road between Godmanchester and Verulamium. Miscellaneous Roman remains have been found in the neighbourhood, but structures are wanting.

HILLFORT, NE of the railway station. The fort is of univallate construction and encloses 7 acres of a spur overlooking the Ivel. The site has been considerably damaged and now presents the appearance of a slight earthwork.

9030   SEGENHOE

OLD CHURCH. Derelict and ivy-hung, yet a church of considerable archaeological interest. The chancel is C11 with two small N windows and a plain chancel arch which is unmoulded but has just a little flat zigzag on the abacus of the responds. One of the windows has a lintel stone with the arch cut into and very elementary decoration, three crosses in circles and two saltire crosses. It looks Saxon at first. The (re-set) S doorway is Early Norman too, with a tympanum whose bottom is cut segmentally. The windows of the church and all the details of the W tower are Georgian, but the N arcade is partly C13, partly early C14. The ironstone E bay represents the former, the rest the latter date. Octagonal pier first, quatrefoil piers with thin shafts in the diagonals later. Oddly triple-chamfered arch first, arches of two sunk quadrants later. – PLATE. Cup of 1689.

9050   SHARNBROOK

ST PETER. The W tower is Dec below – see the flowing tracery of the W window – but the recessed spire connected by thin flying buttresses with the corner pinnacles is Perp.‡ The parapet between the pinnacles is of pierced quatrefoils. The rest of the exterior is Perp, except for the C13 S doorway with two continuous hollow chamfers and the N doorway with many

---

* So Professor Welsh kindly informed me.
‡ Three tiers of lucarnes in the same directions (GMcH).

fine mouldings, which is Dec again. Internally the story is
different. Both arcades are E.E., i.e. go with the s doorway.
Round and octagonal piers and double-hollow-chamfered
arches with broaches. The chancel arch of the same date, but
the N chapel Dec – see its arch to the chancel and also the
SEDILIA and PISCINA. The arcades are linked by a Perp bay
to the tower after this had been built sufficiently high. – FONT.
Octagonal, Perp, with a buttressed shaft and quatrefoiled
lozenges broken across the corners. Fleurons on the underside. – SCREENS. The rood screen has one-light divisions, but
with a broad ogee-headed entrance with panel tracery over. –
The screen to the N chapel has kept old tracery bits. – RERE-
DOS. Probably of c.1855 (restoration), with stone inlay and
glass mosaic – a typical piece. – STAINED GLASS. The E window, still pictorial, of c.1855–6. – MONUMENTS. Brasses to
William Cobbe † 1522, wife and son, 18 in. figures. – Sir
William Boteler, 1618. Tablet with two columns and strapwork on the top (N chapel). – William Lee Antonie † 1815. By
Flaxman. Portrait in medallion and a landscape with a lion
below. – Hollingworth Magniac and wife, put up in 1867. Very
different from the run of English monuments, and indeed decidedly French. Huge neo-Rococo tablet with much stone
inlay and iron railings curving out in section. Their style is
that of say c.1700. – In the churchyard is the MAGNIAC
MAUSOLEUM, equally exotic. The style here is the English
style of c.1660, an improbable choice. The date seems to be
c.1891–2. – CHURCHYARD GATES. Wrought iron; early C18.
They led to the avenue to Sharnbrook House.

BAPTIST CHAPEL. 1865. A typical front – yellow brick with
red-brick trim. Three bays wide with arched windows with
Venetian tracery. Pediment along the whole façade.

SHARNBROOK HOUSE, High Street. Early C18, originally with
a recessed front and projecting wings. Hipped roof. In the
centre a pediment. Much altering and adding.

TOFTE MANOR, ½ m. NW. Partly of 1613. To this date belong
the four gables; the higher castellated part is an addition of
1902.

COLWORTH HOUSE, now UNILEVER, 1 m. WNW. The house,
built by Mark Antonie, is Early Georgian, of ashlar, three-
storeyed, seven windows wide, with a three-bay pediment.
The top storey has segment-headed windows. The quoins of
even length are characteristically Early Georgian. The staircase has a rich neo-Rococo railing. The house then belonged

to the Magniacs. Good recent buildings to the r. They were put up in 1863–6.

IRON AGE SETTLEMENT. See Felmersham.

SHARPENHOE see STREATLEY

1030

SHEFFORD

ST MICHAEL. Of ironstone. Built in 1822, except for the lower parts of the C14 NW tower.* The Perp tower arch also remains. In 1850 a second nave was added, and about 1928 the arcade was rebuilt. The windows are of the early C19 type, with Y- and intersecting tracery. Prettily remodelled roofs by *Mallows & Grocock*, 1907 (GR).

ST FRANCIS (R.C.), a little w. 1884 by *S.J. Nicholl*. The plan is oblong with two narrow chancel aisles formed by two-bay arcades within the (ritually) E parts of the rectangle. The brick façade is not detached to the l. and r. It has an asymmetrically set bellcote. – REREDOS. 30 ft high.

Attached to the Catholic church is ST FRANCIS' HOME, established in 1869 and designed by *Nicholl*. Lower l. part with the dates 1879 and 1884, higher r. part, as high as the church, with two wooden gables. This latter is the PRESBYTERY.

There is little else of note at Shefford. In HIGH STREET Nos 36–38 half-timbered and over-restored, and in NORTHBRIDGE STREET the timber-framed house, now BARCLAYS BANK, more picturesque than genuine. The very pretty ground floor e.g., which is a passage of the pavement below the front of the house, is recent.

0060

SHELTON

ST MARY. A rough building, and wonderfully unrestored inside. The principal external features are Dec, though the s doorway, with two slight continuous chamfers, must be early C13, and the chancel arch seems C13 too. Dec especially the two uncommonly enterprising E windows; of the chancel, five lights, and of the N chapel, three lights straight-headed. Inside, the arcades are evidently earlier, but they are puzzling just because no Victorian do-gooder has tidied them up. The NE respond is Late Norman with a multi-scalloped capital and a

---

* And even there the large window is evidently of 1822 (GMCH).

square abacus, the next pier is of the same date, round with a square abacus, but the W pier is Dec with a charming, nodding-ogee upper stop-chamfer. The S arcade is partly probably of the late C12 too, but much pulled about. The N chapel – see above for the E window – has indeed a two-bay Dec arcade. Perp S aisle windows and Perp clerestory. – PULPIT. C16. Plain panels. – SCREEN. Perp, of one-bay divisions. – BENCHES. The usual buttressed type. – PAINTINGS. St Christopher, N wall. – To the E of this two frontal figures, said to represent St Michael with the scales and the Virgin pressing down one scale. – STAINED GLASS. Many bits, including heads, and the Symbol of the Trinity. – PLATE. Cup with foliage band, 1569.

SHELTON HALL. A plain, long, rendered front, but said to be medieval in origin and one range of a former quadrangle (VCH).

SHILLINGTON

ALL SAINTS. Quite large; of ironstone, and impressive in its length with closely set grey stone buttresses, no division of chancel from aisles visible externally, and with two square E turrets (cf. Tingrith, Wymington). Internally there is a chancel arch, dividing four-bay nave arcades from three-bay chapel arcades. Quatrefoil piers with hollows in the diagonals, sunk quadrant mouldings, i.e. Dec. The details of bases and abaci differ. The E bay of the chancel chapels has always been blocked by a screen wall. The insides of the aisle windows and the E window also Dec. The E window was reduced in size as early as the C15. The S and the smaller N doorway are Perp. Is the arch between the nave and the W tower again C14, though later than the other C14 work? The upper part of the tower is of brick, dated 1750. Arched bell-openings. For the earlier C14 build a date is available: Bishop Burleigh of Lincoln in 1333 issued a commission to compel the parishioners to repair the nave. Does that mean that he had then finished rebuilding the chancel? Owing to the position of the church the E end has a crypt under. This looks late C13 rather than Dec. Round middle pier, slim wall-shafts, vault with eight radiating, single-chamfered ribs. – FONT. With Perp foot. – SCREENS. An exceptional wealth. The chancel screen is very high, with one-light divisions and crocketed ogee arches. – Several parclose screens, specially pretty the one between chancel and N chapel with alternating tracery patterns. – The corresponding S screen is a little simpler. – Of the chapel W screens that of the S chapel is nearly all new, that of the N chapel has some pretty dado panels. – BENCHES. Many, with plain buttressed ends. – ARCHITECTURAL FRAGMENTS. The stiff-leaf capitals of a double column in the crypt. – PLATE. Paten inscribed (16)77; Cup 1702. – MONUMENTS. Very good brass to Matthew Asscheton, priest, † 1400, a 4 ft 4 in. figure. – Brass to a priest, late C15, an 18½ in. figure. (Both N chapel floor.) – John Briscoe † 1766 and members of the Longueville family. Large tablet, of elegant workmanship. Putti at the foot.

(MANOR HOUSE. Inside, a timber ceiling dated 1581 and panelling. They come from a house at Droitwich. NMR)

ROUND BARROW, in Tingley Wood, Pegsdon. The mound is 20 ft in diameter and 4 ft high. No record survives of any excavation carried out on the site, and its overgrown state makes examination difficult.

KNOCKING KNOLL LONG BARROW, Pegsdon, 1 m. SSW of Pirton. The barrow is approximately 100 ft long and 10 ft high at the broader W end. Considerable damage has been done to the mound, which now resembles two round barrows. The site was partially excavated in the C19, but no record survives of the results of this work.

SHORTSTOWN see CARDINGTON

SILSOE

0030

ST JAMES. An astonishing job for its date: 1829–31. The architect, *Smith* of Hertford (GR), achieved an antiquarian accuracy here extremely rare ten years before Pugin, i.e. in the years of Commissioners' Gothic. Nave and aisles, W tower with higher stair-turret, long (not short) chancel. All ironstone, all embattled. The two-light windows, it is true, are too monotonous to be genuine, but otherwise, and even in the arcade piers inside, this is the image of the local Perp church.

LOCKUP. Octagonal, with a pointed head to the doorway.

WREST. *See* p. 172.

SOMERIES CASTLE see LUTON, p. 118

SOULDROP

9060

ALL SAINTS. The unbuttressed W tower is of *c.*1275 and has a contemporary broach spire which has two tiers of lucarnes. It

is the oldest spire in the county. The rest is by *Clutton,* 1861.
His chancel is stone-vaulted; so is the porch and the adjoining
organ chamber, which has a rose window. The chancel side
windows are in pairs with detached mid-shafts. The arrangement for the SEDILIA is especially noteworthy. The capitals
are French, not English, Early Gothic (cf. Woburn). Weird
detailing throughout. – STAINED GLASS by *O'Connor,* 1865–9.

SOUTHILL

ALL SAINTS. The W tower, the chancel E and SW windows, two
N aisle windows, and the N doorway are C15. Only the N aisle
NW window seems to be older. Its tracery looks *c.*1300. All the
rest of the church is of 1814–16. Long nave and long chancel
with low parapets. The arcades cut into by the tower must
with their quatrefoil piers repeat the Dec arcades that were
there. The clerestory on the other hand looks wholly Late
Georgian. Pretty brick flooring. – (FONT. A fine piece with
a shallow bowl, by *Sir Albert Richardson,* 1937 – WEST
GALLERY. Of 1814–16; see the inscription. – MONUMENTS.
Lots of tablets, e.g. † 1710 by *Edward Stanton* (Gunnis), † 1800
by *King* of London, and – the handsomest – † 1777 with a
succinct and beautifully designed inscription (chancel S).*

SOUTHILL. Southill is one of the most exquisite English under-
statements. That so refined and reticent a house could be demanded in 1795 by a brewer is a telling illustration of the
rarely admitted cultural possibilities of the Industrial Revolution of the Georgian Era. For a brewery surely is an industrial
establishment. It is true on the other hand that the brewers
were ahead of the ironmasters and millowners in matters of
intellectual and social ambition. The Thrales in London, the
Whitbreads here – they have no parallel among the founders
of other enterprises. Samuel I Whitbread of Cardington had
opened the brewery in 1742. He was M.P. for Bedford from
1768 to 1790 and died in 1796. One year before, his son
Samuel II, M.P. for Bedford from 1790 to 1815, had engaged
Henry Holland to remodel the mid C18 house at Southill,
which was of about of the same size as now. Between 1796 and
1801 he spent over £53,000 on it. Holland had done Brooks's
Club in 1777. He had begun his memorable remodelling of
Carlton House for the Regent in 1783 and had worked at
Althorp in Northamptonshire from 1787 till 1791. In 1787 also

---

* The signature A....s is convincingly connected by Mr McHardy
with *John Atkins.*

he had begun the alterations and additions at Woburn Abbey.
So Samuel Whitbread knew exactly what he was going to get,
and must indeed have preferred it to the graces and the showy
intricacies of the followers of Robert Adam.

Southill is a long house with a moderate-sized core, and
two angle pavilions connected by straight links with the core.
The house is of stone, in smooth ashlar blocks except for the
smooth rustication of the ground floor of the centre and the
whole of the pavilions, where rustication was used visually to
strengthen the ends of the house. In the centre Holland added
the polygonal bay on the N side in the place where anybody
would expect the main entrance. This, incomprehensibly, is
pushed two bays to the r. and given no emphasis at all. On the
S side Holland added the portico and the colonnades of the
links. He also created the corridors behind these colonnades
to secure easier access to the rooms. For Holland was a careful planner, as he was a careful detailer in every respect. On
the N side the centre is of five bays with a three-bay pediment.
The polygonal bay ends in a pediment too – and that is all.
Bareness here was clearly considered a virtue. The garden side
is more relaxed, but the pairs of unfluted Ionic columns are of
course also far from ornate. There are a balustraded balcony
over the centre colonnade and balustrades over the link
colonnades. Beyond that, once more – nothing.

The interior for the same reason is not easily described,
except in general mood. The restraint in quantity and character
of motifs is admirable. Thin friezes, thin cornices, strictly
rectangular frames to the wall panels, and no fear of panels
left entirely bare. Holland's sources are partly Roman – he
used drawings made by *Heathcote Tatham* in 1794–6 and
published in 1799. But the Paris of the Late Louis XVI
meant more to him, especially Neufforge. The present entrance
hall is in light blue and white. The overdoors with horses,
bulls, camels, lions, and deer are by *George Garrard*, a protégé
of Samuel Whitbread. The former entrance hall, now drawing
room, has a ceiling divided into three parts by flat bands of
guilloche. Except for the characteristically spare structural
decoration there is a decorative accent only in the frame of
the mirror above the fireplace and in the white, frontal caryatids of the chimneypiece. Originally the walls were crimson
and the curtains apple-green. The hall is separated from the
dining room by a narrow passage. The dining room is in pale
green with brown vertical strips. The bay window, polygonal

outside, is semicircular inside. The main staircase is simple to the verge of the puritanical. The library on the other hand is the stateliest room. It is divided into an ante-library and the library proper. The connexion is a perfectly plain arch. The largely recessed shelves are plain too. Of the other rooms nothing need be said individually, and the *Gainsboroughs*, the *Romneys*, the other paintings and the furniture and the busts are not the business of *The Buildings of England*. In front of the house a Dog on a pedestal. This is again by *Garrard*.

The GATES of the North Terrace have the Byng arms – the Byngs owned Southill before the Whitbreads – and were brought back *c*.1900 from a butcher's yard at Shefford. The grounds were landscaped by *Capability Brown*, Holland's father-in-law, in 1777, i.e. still for the Byngs (Lord Torrington). The lead STATUES are by the *Cheeres*. They were sold at John Cheere's death and bought *en bloc* by Samuel II Whitbread in 1812. On the way to the Fishing Temple is a one-arch BRIDGE, ascribed to *John Smeaton*, who worked for the brewery. The FISHING TEMPLE itself lies at the head of the present lake but was originally between two lakes. It has Tuscan four-column porticoes to front and back, with pediments. The back portico is reached from the sides through two arches and along an arcaded wall.

Pleasant ESTATE COTTAGES, rendered in a honey colour and thatched. They carry dates 1796 (several), 1797, 1800, 1815, etc.

BROOM HALL, 2¼ m. ENE. Late Georgian. Three-storeyed with parapet. Semicircular porch with thin Tuscan columns. Tripartite upper windows. A fine cedar-tree on the l.

STAGSDEN

ST LEONARD. Unbuttressed C13 W tower with a W lancet and an arch to the nave with two continuous chamfers. The upper parts Perp. Short lead spire. C13 also the S doorway. But the S arcade is early C14, of five bays, with low quatrefoil piers and double-chamfered arches. The N side has no aisle, but the windows are also Dec, and so is the low tomb recess inside. Perp clerestory, Perp niches in the E wall of the S aisle – four of them. The N chapel of two bays is C14, between Dec and Perp. Double-hollow-chamfered arches. Two-storeyed Perp S porch. – FONT. Square, with chamfered corners, Dec. In two panels small single figures, re-cut probably in the C17. On the underside ballflower and some other decoration. –

SCREEN. A good Perp piece, with four-light divisions, the mid-mullion reaching right up into the apex. – PLATE. Cup of 1825.

STANBRIDGE

9020

ST JOHN BAPTIST. Of ironstone, except for chancel and s aisle, which are Totternhoe. Mostly Perp, especially w tower and clerestory, but Dec the N doorway and probably the tiny quatrefoil N aisle w window. Late C13 chancel, see the arch to the nave, the PISCINA, and the one-light N window. The arcades are a little later. Four bays, octagonal piers, double-chamfered arches. The piers differ. The N side comes first. The arches are indeed very similar to the chancel arch. – FONT. The base of three short shafts is E.E. – PULPIT. Partly Elizabethan. – PLATE. Cup of 1683.

STEPPINGLEY

0030

ST LAWRENCE. Built in 1859–60 by the Duke of Bedford and the rector. w tower with higher stair-turret, nave and N aisle, chancel. Ironstone. The architect was *Clutton*. Note his over-pronounced cusping of the round heads of the window lights and their curious combination with panel tracery in the bell-openings. Even odder the small pointed-quatrefoiled N aisle windows and the large rose window in the present organ chamber, which has five circles enclosing such pointed quatre-foils. Just as odd are all the details: the excessive chamfering, the hood-mould stops, the BENCH ENDS. All the wood and stone carving was done by *Thomas Earp*. From the old church the pretty PISCINA in the chancel. – PLATE. Cup, 1569.

SCHOOLROOM. Built c.1870. Also by *Clutton*, also ironstone, small, but unusually monumental. Embattled Tudor with two doorways, two chimneybreasts up the façade, and flanking the l. two single-light windows, flanking the r. two four-light windows. The SCHOOL HOUSE with the upper timber-framed floor belongs to the group of church and schoolroom too.

STEVINGTON

9050

ST MARY. The church boasts an Anglo–Danish w tower. It is recognizable outside by the long-and-short quoins, and inside by the extremely narrow arched opening into a former *porticus*. Also two double-splayed windows. The tower-top is Perp. The exterior of the church otherwise is confusing. Both chancel chapels have been unroofed but left standing. Inside, the S arcade is of *c.*1300, with high quatrefoil piers with deep continuous hollows in the diagonals and sunk quadrant arch mouldings. The S doorway is contemporary. The N arcade is later Dec: filleted quatrefoil piers with thin shafts in the diagonals. Arches again with sunk quadrants. The same motifs are used in tower arch and chancel arch. What is left of the chancel chapels is Dec too. Perp nave clerestory with good roof and figures holding shields with the emblems of the Passion and also woolpacks and the initials of two merchants. – SCREEN, now under the tower. High, Perp, of one-light divisions. – BENCHES. The poppyheads of the front benches are early C16. Two men kneeling and drinking, two semi-reclining, one seated, one writing, and three animals. – PLATE. Cup and Cover Paten 1569. – BRASS. Thomas Salle † 1422. His head on a large helmet. The figure is 32 in. long.

VILLAGE CROSS, at the main crossing. In the base four small pointed-trefoiled niches. Shaft, re-tooled foliage capital, and big finial.

WINDMILL. Put up in 1783* and rehabilitated in the last ten years. It is a wooden post-mill, though the post is now a stone base. New sails have been attached, and all is complete, though not in working order.

STEWARTBY

0040

The garden estate on the doorstep of the London Brick Company's large brick works. They are said to be the largest brick works in the world and can produce *c.* 650 million bricks a year. The small administration building looks over a semicircle with on one side the VILLAGE HALL, neo-Colonial by *E. Vincent Harris*, 1928–30, with a wooden pediment on square pillars and a cupola, on the other side the CLUB, with a plainer front with arched windows, also by *Harris*, 1933–4. A little further E the SECONDARY MODERN SCHOOL by *Oswald P. Milne*, 1936–7, also with a cupola, and along a very large crescent facing a field OLD PEOPLE'S HOMES by *Richardson & Houfe*, 1955–6. The hall for these homes has a veranda all round and a roof with concave hips – all rather Swedish of the 1920s type. The estate was begun in 1927.

* But *Industrial Archaeology in Bedfordshire*, 1967, p. 9, says *c.*1765–70.

STOCKGROVE PARK see HEATH AND REACH

2030
STOTFOLD

St Mary. A curious building, externally Perp except for the late c13 s aisle w window (bar tracery with a spherical triangle). w tower, the bell-openings pairs of two lights. Inside one is at first baffled. The N aisle has two bays, a bit of wall, and a third bay, the s aisle one bay, a bit of wall, and then two bays. The story is presumably this. At first the nave had no aisles. Then, c.1300, a N chapel was built. The responds are half quatrefoil, the arch has two sunk quadrants. Then a s aisle was built, of two bays to the then w wall. This has early c14 quatrefoil piers with thin shafts in the diagonals, similar arches to the N side, and hood-moulds with head-stops. The decision was then taken to lengthen the nave, and on the N side the chapel was extended to form a N aisle. The clerestory is Perp. The chancel was rebuilt in 1890. – FONT. Octagonal, Perp, with quatrefoils. – STAINED GLASS. Old bits in a N window. – PLATE. Cup of 1739.

STRATTON PARK see BIGGLESWADE

0020
STREATLEY

St Margaret. Mostly c14. Four-bay arcades with standard elements. The e and w aisle windows and the N doorway are c14 too. So is the tower arch, though other features of the tower are later. Higher stair-turret. Victorian chancel, short, of brick. – FONT. The stem of the font is E.E., and it has vertical strips of dogtooth. The bowl, however, is a mystery. It is octagonal, with foliage motifs largely stiff-leafish. One panel moreover has a blank three-light window with geometrical tracery, i.e. typical late c13. But can the other panels be – in spite of their stiff-leaf? The only possible solution seems to be drastic re-cutting and even re-modelling in the c17. – PULPIT. With linenfold panels and a Georgian sounding-board. – BENCHES. With linenfold and also with Jacobean panels. – PLATE. Cup of 1685.

E of the church an c18 HOUSE of chequer brick, nine bays long. (At SHARPENHOE, 1¼ m. N, BURY FARM has a timber-framed, aisled barn, probably pre-Reformation.)

LONG BARROW AND ROUND BARROW CEMETERY. The earliest monument in the group, the long barrow, is 300 ft long and 40 ft wide at its broader E end. The site was badly mutilated in the C19 and has only recently been re-discovered from the air. Four round barrows are visible on the same hillside, and further sites have been detected from the air. The largest of the group is 20 ft in diameter and 5 ft high. This site produced a number of secondary Saxon burials.

STUDHAM 0010

ST MARY. An unpromising cemented exterior. W tower, nave and aisles and chancel, the windows Late Perp with straight hood-moulds. Inside the story is very different. Four-bay arcades of c.1210–20. The church was indeed consecrated in 1220. There are two puzzling facts. One is that three bays were built at one go and reached as far as the former W wall and a fourth bay was added as an extension to the W, but apparently at once, as there is no stylistic difference at all. The other puzzlement is that the broad and good stiff-leaf capitals 23 of arcades and (rebuilt and widened) chancel arch look just before 1220 indeed, but that there are also very big and coarse scalloped varieties which appear 1190–1200 rather. Yet they are not confined to any one place. One must assume that an old man and a young man worked together. – FONT. A round Norman bowl with a band of leaf trail and dragons on a curving-out base with E.E. stiff-leaf.* – Old TILES by the font. – BENCHES with linenfold panelling. – STAINED GLASS. In the chancel a single light with *Kempe* glass of 1903. – PLATE. Cup of 1674.

SUNDON 0020

ST MARY. Nearly all Dec, and uncommonly impressive inside. Pre-Dec, i.e. C13, the arcades of high square piers with four half-round projections and arches of one chamfer and one sunk chamfer. These arcades embrace the W tower, which is noticeable inside only by the W arches of the arcades being bigger and by a cross-arch. The aisles are also crossed by arches (cf. Luton). The clerestory has round, quatrefoiled windows, a Dec sign. The aisle windows are Dec too, with one curious exception – the N aisle E window, which is again a generation earlier (geometrical tracery) and much more delicate in the mouldings. Dec again the S transept. Large reticulated

---

* Is this an inverted capital (cf. Westoning)? (GMcH).

transept s and transept E windows. Crocketed ogee niches to l. and r. of the latter. Dec finally the W tower too, with another large reticulated window. But the doorway is Perp, and so is the tower top. Chequer pattern. Higher stair-turret. In the chancel the E window is Perp, but there is a low-side lancet and the niches l. and r. of the E window and the PISCINA (all ogee arches) are Dec once more. Single-framed chancel roof. Along the aisle walls runs a stone bench. – FONT. Octagonal, of Purbeck marble, with two flat, pointed arches to each side; C13. – SCREEN. Of one-light divisions, Perp, modest. – BENCHES (nave W). Plain, with buttress-shafts. – STAINED GLASS. Fragments in the N aisle E and s transept s windows. – PLATE. Cup of 1628.

2040   SUTTON

ALL SAINTS. The C13 is the first represented in the church. To it belong the s doorway and the s arcade of four bays. The square piers with broad semicircular projections are as characteristic as the hollow-chamfered arches. Next in order of time is the N arcade of quatrefoil piers with plain double-chamfered arches. This is followed by the Dec chancel arch (responds of the type with thin diagonal shafts and the arch with two sunk quadrants). Rich SEDILIA and PISCINA. In the s aisle also a Dec PISCINA. Dec chancel windows, those on the s side with segmental arches. Perp tower of ironstone. Tall arch to the nave. The rest of the church brown cobbles. All castellated, except for the chancel. Perp s porch with two-light windows. – PULPIT. 1628, with sounding-board. – COMMUNION RAIL. Later C17. – BENCHES. The ends buttressed. – BOX PEWS. C17 and later. – PLATE. Cup and Paten 1569. – MONUMENTS. John Burgoyne † 1604. Large standing monument of stone. Recumbent effigy. Much lively strapwork. Two columns, and at the top achievement and two obelisks. – Sir Roger Burgoyne † 1679. By *Grinling Gibbons*. Urn on a strigillated sarcophagus with putti l. and r. All this is high up above a large inscription tablet with garlands. The garlands are the one item that might make one think of Gibbons. – John Burgoyne † 1709. Reredos type with two mourning cherubs. By *E. Stanton* (Gunnis). – William Burgoyne † 1835. By *G. Oldfield* of Ashford in Derbyshire. Small tablet with two colonnettes. – CURIOSUM. The church possesses a BARREL ORGAN which is in use.

In the middle of the village is a humped PACKHORSE BRIDGE with two pointed arches.

JOHN OF GAUNT'S HALL. A broad and deep moat marks the site of what is traditionally supposed to have been a manor house of John of Gaunt.

SWINESHEAD

ST NICHOLAS. An impressive Dec church. The W tower started Dec, though the bell-stage with pairs of two-light openings and the recessed spire rising behind an openwork quatrefoil frieze is Perp. Two tiers of lucarnes, transparent from a distance. The distinguishing feature of the tower is the shallow W porch with a gable and angle buttress-shafts. Springing of a former vault inside. The tower arch has three chamfers dying into the imposts (cf. Oundle, Raunds, Rushden, all in Northants and all E.E.). The Swineshead tower, however, comes relatively late in the Dec story. It was preceded by a unified plan of nave, aisles, chancel, and NW tower. The aisle, even the S porch, and the chancel are all pulled together by the same pretty trail-frieze below the parapet, with heads etc. (cf. Yelden; also Abbotsley Hunts). In the S aisle the S windows and the S doorway are typically Dec; in the chancel the specially nicely detailed S windows ought to be sampled. The E and N chancel windows are Victorian. But the N aisle windows are Dec again. The E window is in two tiers and small and corresponds indeed to a former two-storeyed vestry which still has a (blocked) fireplace. The projection of wall in the W bay represents the thickness needed for a tower. Inside, the projected tower is marked by the thickening of one pier of the N arcade and the springer of an arch across the aisle from that pier. The S arcade has no such break. Both arcades are Dec, with standard elements and the most characteristic Dec bases. Pretty image niche in the S aisle E wall with a nodding ogee canopy. The chancel is beautifully fitted up, with shafting of the windows, leaf capitals to the shafts, an ANGLE PISCINA, the chancel arch (later re-set and widened) on two excellent busts, and SEDILIA with stepped seat, but simply a blank lowering of the sill of a S window. In the N wall a sumptuous EASTER SEPULCHRE or tomb recess, cusped and subcusped, with much leaf. A tiny stair and passage connects it with the former vestry. – SCREEN. Partly Perp. – STALLS. With a little carving on arms and MISERICORDS. – BENCHES.

The buttressed standard type. – WEST DOOR. Dec, with bold, broad tracery. – PAINTING. On the s aisle E wall, unrecognizable. – STAINED GLASS. Some bits in a chancel s window. – PLATE. Elizabethan Cup.

TEMPSFORD

ST PETER. Not much to interest in the exterior, except for the predominance of horizontal banding of brown and buff. Much repair was done in 1621; is all the banding of that date? As for features, the w tower is Dec, and the aisle E windows are Dec. Otherwise mostly Perp. Perp also the four-bay arcades of the wide nave. Standard elements, but different N from S. The two niches in the s aisle E wall may be Dec. The nave roof is Victorian, but has its wall-plate with egg-and-tongue from the work of 1621. – PULPIT. Perp, of wood, with traceried panels. The door is preserved. – SCREEN. Old parts in the dado. – SCULPTURE. Good Virgin by *Lucy E. A. Turner*, 1951. – PLATE. Cup and Paten 1660.

Immediately N of the church GANNOCK HOUSE, a good timber-framed C15 house, with big bracing, ogee members.

TEMPSFORD HALL, across the A1. Quite a big gabled red-brick house in the Elizabethan style. 1898. A new building by *F. Heather Hughes & J. P. Lomax* has been added recently.

BRIDGE. By *James Savage*, 1815–20. With three round arches.

GANNOCK'S CASTLE. An earth enclosure, 115 by 85 ft, probably C12.

THURLEIGH

ST PETER. The crossing tower is Anglo-Danish, that is certain from the proportions of the doorway on its s side which must have led into it from outside or from a *porticus*. The tympanum with Adam and Eve, the tree, and the serpent may be a Norman addition or not. The rest is Perp, except for the early C13 N doorway and the ogee-headed low-side window, which seems Dec. Deep s porch with two two-light windows E and two W. In the chancel Late Perp ironstone windows. Four-bay arcades of standard elements. At the time of writing the whole nave was derelict. – FONT. Perp, octagonal, shields on the shaft. – STAINED GLASS. Bits in the s aisle w window. – PLATE. Cup of 1577 with foliated band. – BRASS to John Harvey, *c.*1420, the figure 3ft 10 in. long and much rubbed off.

BURY HILL. Considerable remains of a motte and bailey castle, SSW, S, SE, and E of the church. The motte is E of the church and the moat is *c.* 20 ft deep and 25 ft wide. An outer enclosure circumscribes nearly the whole village.

TILSWORTH   9020

ALL SAINTS. The S arcade is C13, three bays, with standard elements. But the arcade was longer to the W. The ironstone W tower has been built into it and been given its own arch into the aisle. The E arch of the tower looks *c.* 1300 (VCH: C15). Nave and chancel have single-framed roofs. Externally the church is a mixture of ironstone and Totternhoe. On the N side one large three-light window with flowing tracery. The N doorway is Dec too. – FONT. Of cauldron-shape, on an E.E. four-shaft foot. – (PULPIT. Usual Jacobean type with blank-arched panels. GMCH) – STAINED GLASS. In a N window fragments including a C15 head. – SCULPTURE (all N aisle). Three detached statuettes of soldiers and part of a fourth. They are certainly C13. What kind of group did they belong to? – Lower part of a seated figure of the mid C13; beautiful drapery. – Fragmentary Pietà; C15. – Also a stiff-leaf capital. – PLATE. Cup of 1823. – MONUMENTS. In the chancel big and beautiful, 63 effigyless monument to Gabriel Fowler † 1582. Canopy on four slender fluted columns, good leaf-trail frieze, top achievement. On the base typical elements of Elizabethan ornament. – Sir Henry Chester † 1666. The same type, but with unfluted columns and (already) an open curly top pediment. In the frieze three elementary cherubs' heads, but nothing like as abysmally elementary as the kneeling effigies. – In the nave N wall Dec recess with a late C13 effigy of a priest; poor quality.

GATEHOUSE to Manor Farm House, S of the church. C15, of ironstone, with a one-light window to the N, a two-light window to the S. The gateway is unvaulted. C18 hipped and half-hipped roof.

WARREN KNOLL. Simple, poorly preserved motte and bailey castle.

TINGLEY WOOD *see* SHILLINGTON

TINGRITH   0030

Along the church approach bargeboarded houses, one dated 1838, another 1841.

St NICHOLAS. Of ironstone, Perp, over-restored in 1845–6. W tower, embattled nave and aisles. The chancel E wall with two short polygonal angle turrets (cf. Wymington, also Shillington). Impressive three-light clerestory windows with panel tracery. Better preserved the S doorway with large-leaf spandrels. The arcades, also excessively renewed, have the standard Perp section, here in the details still C14-looking. In the S aisle SE corner an image niche with a grotesque head as its bracket. – STAINED GLASS. Much in the chancel, Early Victorian (one date 1846). – PLATE. Cup and Paten, 1771.

TODDINGTON

St GEORGE. A big Perp church with a crossing tower. The church is all embattled, and below the battlements runs a frieze with lots of beasts and grotesques: an otter, a pair of fishes, a hawk, a fox, a hound, a sow, peacocks, a bull, a horse, a swan, a griffin, a mermaid, a wyvern, and so on. The costume of a human figure allows one to date all this (and most of the exterior of the church) early C16. The church has aisles and transepts. Chancel windows of three lights N and S, of four E; nave W window of five lights. To the N of the chancel is a three-storeyed vestry, on the upper floors originally the priest's dwelling. The tower bell-openings are pairs of two lights on each side. In the N porch an elaborate canopied Perp STOUP. The only external detail which suggests earlier work is the S doorway, which must date from the late C13. Inside one can go back yet a little more. The S transept PISCINA, a double piscina, looks mid C13 at the latest (two pointed arches set in a round arch). The crossing arches are low and have big semi-octagonal responds and plain two-step (i.e. unmoulded) arches. That also is C13, as is no doubt the plan with the transepts. To the W, above the crossing arch, is a lancet window. The roof-line before the Perp clerestory (of three lights) is also visible. (Inside the tower, on the stage above the present ceiling, is C13 blind arcading.) The nave arcades of four bays may have been added about 1300 or a little later. High octagonal piers, one on the S side with a little nailhead in the capital. Double-chamfered arches. Perp roofs of chancel and nave with angels and bosses. Shields refer to Thomas Peyre, † 1429. The Perp fenestration makes the whole church and particularly the chancel very light. – PAINTINGS.

In the s aisle dim fragments of scenes under arcades, also a more clearly recognizable band of medallions with lions' heads and swans. Also figures of Christ and two women. – On the N side two trees, one with a bird and several figures. Band with tools (hammers, nails, pincers, etc.). – MONUMENTS. In the s transept effigy of a Knight, early C14, much damaged. – Two Perp recesses in the s wall, with early C15 effigies of Knight and Lady, probably Thomas Peyre † 1429 (*see* above) and his wife. – Dame Anne Cheyne † 1561. Stone effigy. – Alabaster effigy of Henry Lord Cheyne † 1587. His head is on a half-rolled-up mat. His legs are lost. – Lady Cheyne † 1614. Alabaster too. All three on tomb-chests. – In the N transept Maria Wentworth † 1632, but later in style. 72 Frontally seated figure under baldacchino with two putti. Of very good quality. – Opposite Lady Henrietta Wentworth † 1686. Grey and black marble. Of reredos type with an open segmental pediment. Two allegorical figures and a gruesome still-life of death. The head, now loose, may have belonged to a bust.

CONGER HILL, E of the church. Motte, 92 ft in diameter at the top. Also remains of earthworks farther E.

THE SQUARE. The church lies at the N end of a spacious green of delightfully irregular shape. There are no bad houses or cottages around it, and some very good ones. The best is OLD WENTWORTH HOUSE of *c.*1700, chequer brick, of seven bays, with the middle three lying slightly back, and a top parapet. The doorway with fluted pilasters and a pediment must be mid C18.

PARKFIELDS SCHOOL. 1962–3 by the county architect, *J.C. Barker.*

Near by, also in PARK ROAD, a new house, TWO WATERS, by *Keith Miller*. Grey brick, on pilotis; good.

MANOR HOUSE. Toddington Manor, built *c.*1570–80 and recorded on a map in 1581 and again on a somewhat larger scale by *John Thorpe* early in the C17, was a quadrangular mansion round a spacious inner court. It had three storeys, mullioned and transomed windows, and round angle towers. All that survives now is a small oblong block with a hipped roof, *c.*1830 in appearance, but containing evidence that it was the Elizabethan kitchen, a round tower, and a low extension of old brick behind the oblong block. It may be connected with the NE corner and an attached outbuilding and in any case tells little.

TOFTE MANOR see SHARNBROOK

TOTTERNHOE

Here were the principal quarries of the neighbourhood in the Middle Ages and also much later (Woburn Abbey). The stone is a clunch and weathers badly.

ST GILES. Quite big, mostly of local stone, in ashlar blocks. Low w tower. The church is embattled and appears Perp. Pretty N vestry. The chancel E wall has flushwork and battlements. Perp arcades, octagonal piers, triple-hollow-chamfered arches. Against the NE respond a very handsome demi-figure of an angel holding a shield. The sharp angular folds of the drapery spell late C15 or early C16, the shield contains a rebus for Ash-well (VCH). Very fine original nave roof with moulded purlins, carved beams, and bosses. The aisle roofs are original too. There also appears the Ashwell rebus. – SCREEN. Under the tower arch, partly Perp and probably once the rood screen. Single-light divisions. – BENCHES. Some with linenfold panels. – STAINED GLASS. Fragments in a s aisle window. – BRASS. John Warwekhyll, vicar, † 1524 (chancel floor; c.6 in. long).

LANCOTBURY, N of the church. A handsome timber-framed manor house with closely set studs; C16 probably.

CASTLE. In a very impressive position at the end of a promontory. Small motte; baileys to its NW, N, and E. This was once the strongest of the early castles of Bedfordshire. The oldest building is that NW of the motte.

SETTLEMENT SITE. Chalk quarrying ¼ m. E of the castle mound has revealed traces of a Late Bronze Age/Early Iron Age settlement site marked by a series of pits containing occupation debris including sherds of large situlate vessels and an enclosure ditch which produced a bronze vase-headed pin of West Alpine type datable to the C6 B.C.

The banks of CELTIC FIELDS, probably associated with this settlement, can be seen on the slope of the ridge NE of the quarry.

TURVEY

ALL SAINTS. A large and very rewarding church. The nave is in its masonry still Anglo-Danish, as is proved by the remains of double-splayed windows above the s arcade. The tower is Anglo-Danish too, and this is visible in the doorway high up

in its E wall, i.e. towards the nave. The nave no doubt went
as far as the pieces of solid masonry in the present arcades.
The lancets in the W tower to N and S on the other hand are
E.E., and so is the arch towards the nave. The W tower now
ends in a rather blunt pyramid roof. Next follows the W part of
the S arcade. Three bays, octagonal piers, moulded arches –
say late C13. Then a N arcade was built, and at the same time
the nave was extended round the former Saxon chancel.
Hence the different details of the octagonal piers and the
double-chamfered arches in the E bays of the S arcade as well.
This work may be c.1320. The S aisle doorway with continuous
mouldings and the fenestration go with the earlier work: i.e.
intersecting tracery and three stepped lancet lights. But such
a window also repeats in the part of c.1320, and the SEDILIA
and PISCINA, fitted from the beginning under it, are undoubtedly still C13. So one must assume that all this was moved
from the former chancel when the aisles were extended. Most
of the windows of the church are over-restored or Victorian.
The latest in style are those towards the E end of the N aisle.
Two-storeyed Perp S porch, originally vaulted. Perp clerestory and roof with angels and bosses. The chancel is of
1852–4, by *Sir G. G. Scott.* The three-arch organ arcade with
polished granite piers lavish and impressive.* – FONT. Is this
c.1200? The supports look E.E., but the four lobes of the
bowl have Norman voluted designs. – SOUTH DOOR. With
excellent iron scrollwork and knockers of the same type as at 36
Leighton Linslade and Eaton Bray. The date is no doubt
that of the doorway. – PAINTING. In a recess in the S aisle an
exquisite early C14 painting of the Crucifixion. Dark green
background with a pattern of small flowers. The twisted figure
of Christ is especially characteristic and moving. – STAINED
GLASS. In the chancel apparently by *Hardman.* The date is
c.1854. – PLATE. Silver-gilt Set of 1788. – MONUMENTS. A
most impressive collection. Brasses in the S chapel to a Priest,
c.1500 (2 ft figure), and a Civilian, c.1480 (19 in. figure). – In
the S aisle Sir John Mordaunt † 1506 and wife. Tomb-chest
of Purbeck marble with twisted angle colonnettes and highly
cusped lozenges. On it the two effigies of alabaster. His head
lies on a helmet with the crest of a screaming man.‡ – Between

* Mr McHardy calls the chancel in its totality 'the finest mid-Victorian
ecclesiastical ensemble in Bedfordshire' and refers among elements to PUL-
PIT, STALLS, floor TILES, and even the painted ORGAN pipes.
‡ Or a biting man, *un homme mordant*?

62 chancel and s chapel the first Lord Mordaunt † 1560, among
    very early Elizabethan monuments one of the most important
    in the county. It is by *T. Kirby*. Alabaster effigies and stone
    surround. Coupled Roman Doric columns and an arch
    decorated with chains of squares and circles. Victories in the
    spandrels. The solid upper storey has two caryatids, and the
    whole is finished by a solemn pediment. The monument is
    the same to chancel and to chapel. – Second Lord Mordaunt
    † 1571 and his two wives. Eight-poster with Tuscan columns.
    The three effigies lie side by side, but he in the middle raised
    higher than his wives. The straw mats on which they lie are
    rolled up at the feet, and the way his feet balance on the spurs
    he is wearing is surprising. Coffered ceiling of the tester. –
    Third Lord Mordaunt † 1601. A rare conceit. Tomb-chest
    with a black cloth of stone hanging down like a pall and the
    inscription plate in white on it. The most similar monument is
    Maximilian Colt's of Princess Sophia † 1606 in Westminster
    Abbey with the cradle cover of stone hanging down on the
    ground.* – In the churchyard MAUSOLEUM of the Higgins
    family. Victorian, with the motif of the pinnacles borrowed
    from Turvey Abbey and that of the balustrade with big
    lettering from such houses as Castle Ashby.
TURVEY ABBEY. A Jacobean house, with dates 1603 and 1608,
    gabled and quite irregular. It is made interesting externally
    by the balustrades and pinnacles brought over from Easton
    Maudit in Northamptonshire about 1801. From Easton
    Maudit also the two monumental double-transomed windows
    towards the garden. The window to the l. of these is larger
    still and has a surround of about 1700. At that time the room
    behind it was made – see e.g. the door pediments and the
    beautiful bolection-moulded chimneypiece. But another
    chimneypiece is of the time of the house. It has the same
    chains of plain geometrical ornament as the monument of
    1562. – Late medieval oblong DOVECOTE. – STABLES with a
    fine Georgian cupola, square below and round above. – At the
    end of the garden the so-called CHAPEL, a Gothick summer
    house of 1829.
TURVEY HOUSE. 1794. The house has an extremely swagger
    façade, decidedly Empire in flavour and hardly possible at so
    early a date. Only seven bays, but widely spaced. The angle

    * Mr McHardy draws my attention to the monument to Charles Longuet-
    Higgins † 1885, signed by *Armstead*. Two angels by a sarcophagus, against
    a blue mosaic background.

bays are flanked by giant Corinthian pilasters, the recessed
centre has giant pilasters instead. In the angle bays the ground-
floor window is set in an aedicule, above the upper window
is a small Grecian relief. The top of the façade is a rich foliage
frieze with tiny cherubs in it and above this an attic. In the
middle this is crowned by an eminence with an acroterion.
The entrance side is unimpressive, but has a four-column
porch of Tuscan columns with pediment. Inside there is at
once an apsed room. In the centre of the house is the spacious
staircase hall with a coffered dome with lantern on four segmental arches. The staircase leads up to a landing with two
columns, and behind this is another domed room. Also in the
house is a cast-iron spiral staircase which comes from the
Crystal Palace.

BRIDGE and CAUSEWAY. Sixteen arches in all, half of them
pointed, the others round. Cutwaters only upstream. The
oldest parts of the bridge are ascribed to the C13, but most of
what one sees is of 1795 and the 1820s. Close to the bridge on
the island midway two C18 pieces of SCULPTURE, one alleg-
edly Jonah, the other a man with a three-cornered hat. The
latter was put up only in 1953.

UPPER GRAVENHURST   1030

ST GILES. Ironstone. Norman the nave walling and the N doorway with its one-step arch. Perp the W tower. Much of the
detailing Victorian. Inside, the chancel arch has Victorian
columns and arched side openings, but the zigzag is mostly
original. – PLATE. Cup of 1569.

UPPER STONDON   1030

ALL SAINTS. 1857. Short, with a slightly higher chancel than
nave, a S porch tower of three storeys, with pyramid roof,
looking distinctly domestic, and a N transept opposite. The
one ancient piece is a modest C13 doorway.

WARDEN ABBEY see OLD WARDEN

WAULUD'S BANK see LUTON

WESTONING   0030

ST MARY MAGDALENE. Perp W tower with later lead spire.
The rest mostly early C14 – see the (very renewed) windows

and the mouldings of the N doorway. See also the arcades and
the chancel arch. Among the windows there are some with
stepped lancet lights and two with a cusped and subcusped
circle in the top of the tracery. Two-storeyed s porch. – FONT.
Cauldron-shaped, with big bold rolls – obviously C13. The
foot may have been made for a pier capital. – ARCHITECTURAL
FRAGMENTS. In the S aisle wall. – PLATE. Cup of 1655;
Paten of 1777.

MANOR HOUSE. 1843, red brick, Jacobean, with shaped porch
gable. (Inside much woodwork from Wrest Park and the
Palace of Westminster. VCH)

WHIPSNADE
0010

ST MARY MAGDALENE. It is delightful to find this combination of a C16 brick W tower with an C18 chequer brick nave.
The W doorway is of stone. The nave windows are arched, and
the N door surround is rusticated. On the S side the angles of
the former stone church have been kept. The chancel is of
1866. – PULPIT. Jacobean, with back panel and sounding-
board. The usual short blank arches abound. – COMMUNION
RAIL. Of c.1700, with slim twisted balusters.

ZOO. The zoo was opened in 1931. In 1934–5 *B. Lubetkin &
Tecton* built some animal houses and other buildings which
were among the most uncompromisingly modern ones then
put up in England. The ELEPHANT HOUSE has aged specially
well. It is not, like the GIRAFFE HOUSE or one very good, long,
low SHELTER, in the straightforward International style of the
thirties, but with its four circular white pavilions with skylighting uncommonly sculptural and dramatic and thus pro-
phetic of the style of today. In the sixties *Peter Dunham,
Widdup & Harrison* designed a SHELTER (1962) and *F.A.P.
Stengelhofen*, the architect to the Zoological Society, the main
ENTRANCE and new OFFICES (1963).

Also in the neighbourhood two excellent bungalows designed by
Lubetkin & Tecton. They are reached through the zoo and
face the Ivinghoe Downs. They were built in 1933–4.

GREEN CATHEDRAL, c.150 yds N W of the Green. A plantation of
20 acres with trees of twenty-five different species. It is not in
the least laid out as a cathedral, but services are held in it.

WILDEN
0050

ST NICHOLAS. Tall Perp W tower. In one spandrel of the doorway an owl. Three-light Perp nave windows, but on the S side

also one Dec window. Lower Perp chancel. – FONT. Octagonal.
Perp, with a flower, a shield, a quatrefoil, etc. – SOUTH DOOR.
With charming C15 ironwork, especially a circle treated like a
rose-window. – STAINED GLASS. In the E window two C15
figurines. – PLATE. Cup of 1628; Paten of 1715. – MONUMENT.
Modest alabaster tablet to Jasper Fisher † 1643.

WILLINGTON

1040

ST LAWRENCE. A historically important church, as it is all[51]
Late Perp. It is built of buff stone. W tower; high S side with
the porch set symmetrically between two large transomed
four-light windows. The lights are cusped below the transom
but uncusped above. The porch entrance has a basket arch
with a lozenge frieze looking Early Gothic Revival rather
than Latest Perp. S chapel with three-light windows. The E
end impressive, with the flat expanse of N chapel and chancel
wall with their two large windows and their battlements. No
roof visible here. Inside, the chancel E window (five lights)
is shafted; the shafts stand on a head and on two quadrupeds with one head. The N chapel windows high, of three
lights. This chapel, and probably the whole church, was built
by Sir John Gostwick, Master of the Horse to Cardinal
Wolsey and later Treasurer of the First Fruits and Tenths
under Henry VIII. He bought the manor in 1529 and died in
1545. The arcades inside deserve attention too. The aisle arcade is high and has the standard moulded type of piers with
two-centred arches. The chancel arcade has the same type of
piers but four-centred arches. – BENCHES. Some with C16
tracery. – TILES in the chancel. They are typical of the moment after the Minton type of the mid C19. They date from
1876–7 (restoration under *Clutton*) and are rather orientally
inspired.* – HOURGLASS STAND. Nave NE corner. – PLATE.
Paten on foot presented in 1685; Paten Lid of 1685; Cup of
1686; Flagon of 1691. – MONUMENTS. First of all Sir John
who died in 1545. A big plain tomb-chest between chancel
and N chapel. The inscription contains the date 1541 and
refers to him as having caused 'this work' to be done, meaning
probably the chapel, if not the whole church. – A second completely plain tomb-chest in the NE corner of the chapel. – Two
HELMETS, one worn by Sir John at the Field of the Cloth of
Gold, the other a fighting helmet and tabard of a few years

* Also some medieval tiles. They are in the N chapel (G MC H).

later. – Sir William Gostwick † 1615. Alabaster tomb-chest and effigy. His head on a half-rolled-up mat. Low wooden tester. – Sir Edward Gostwick † 1630 and his wife † 1633. Very elaborate alabaster monument with kneeling figures in the usual composition.

MANOR HOUSE. Of Sir John Gostwick's manor house in which he entertained Henry VIII in 1541 two minor buildings of buff stone are all that survives. One is the DOVECOTE, an oblong structure with two nesting chambers and stepped gables oddly arranged because of some vertical shuttering half way up along the roof. That makes the stepped gables start with a coping and above the vertical part continue with a second coping. The other building was emphatically not the great hall. It has always been two-storeyed. It has a large entrance and l. and r. of it one five-light window with straight head. On the opposite side is a three-light window on the upper floor and also a flat projection. The building has stepped gables too.

Many yellow-brick Bedford ESTATE COTTAGES, and many more bungalows of recent date.

WILSHAMSTEAD

ALL SAINTS. Early C14 S arcade of four bays. Quatrefoil piers with four thin shafts in the diagonals. Double-chamfered arches. The N arcade uses late C13 piers with abaci chamfered and set diagonally and with double-hollow-chamfered arches. But the bases are Perp. Good nave roof with carved bosses. Nave and aisles are embattled. The W tower is of 1852 (VCH), and the chancel of 1873 (by *Sir Arthur Blomfield*; GS). – PLATE. Cup and Cover Paten of 1626; Paten of 1723. – MONUMENTS. Brass to William Carbrok, priest, *c.*1430, a 14 in. demi-figure. – Tablet to William Tompson † 1596. With a steep pediment and the tiny kneeling figure of the deceased on it.

WOBURN

ST MARY, Park Street. By *Henry Clutton*, 1865–8, for the 8th Duke of Bedford. The typical estate church, even if here conveniently placed in the village and not somewhere in the park. Solidly and expensively built, large and so much all of a piece that atmosphere is hard to come by. The church is in the late C12 style, with some of the details deliberately broad and summary, and others – e.g. the shaft in the middle of the

E wall – deliberately wilful. S tower with richly shafted bell-openings. The spire alas proved unsafe in 1890 and was not replaced. Tall aisle and chancel windows. The interior is amazing. It is not wilful at all, but extremely bold in its handling of French late C12 material. First of all, this is a hall church, and that was unusual in France as well as England. Did Clutton look to Anjou and Poitou? His piers are double columns set in depth, and provided with shaft-rings. The capitals are of the crocket type, and there is throughout solid stone vaulting. Money was evidently no object. The chancel has shafted windows and a flat E wall. – REREDOS by *Caröe*. – PAINTING by *Maratta*. – STAINED GLASS. E window 1894 by *Kempe*. – PLATE. Silver-gilt pairs of Chalices, Patens, and Almsdishes of 1802.

Woburn is a perfect C18 village with the character of a small town. The centre is the MARKET HOUSE, neither perfect nor C18. It is red brick, Gothic, with an oriel, an asymmetrical turret, and dormers. *Blore* is the architect, 1830 the date. From the Market House N runs the HIGH STREET and BEDFORD STREET, with one pleasant C18 brick house after the other. At the corner of Park Street and continuing along High Street three-storeyed early C18 fronts, blue brick with red dressings and segment-headed windows with aprons. Two have giant pilasters as well. Between the first and the other two is a late C18 house with two shallow canted bay windows. A little further on is a bijou front with a balcony on iron posts. One of the early C18 houses has two charming Late Georgian shop-fronts. Opposite this group is a less eventful but equally pleasing row. This ends with the OLD RECTORY, mid C18, also brick, though now whitewashed. It is much statelier than the other houses, with a centre with pairs of banded columns, and pairs of columns above. Attic over this centre with pediment. The side of the house looks over the forecourt of the cemetery.

The CHAPEL was built in 1868. Next to it the stump of the tower of the medieval church of Woburn. On it *Blore* placed an upper part also of ironstone and then a stone top, a very pretty piece of confectionery, with an open octagonal stage, pinnacles, and a crocketed spirelet. In the chapel MONUMENT to Sir Francis Staunton and wife † 1630, and their family. Two tiers of kneelers, the lower tier without inscription. Alabaster. *Blore* also built, again of ironstone, the OLD SCHOOL next to the chapel, a restoration job really, as the building is partly

originalElizabethan,with mullioned windows. Two storeys and
dormers. The porch towards the street is of course by *Blore*.
Opposite a five-bay brick house with stone quoins and a pedimented doorway on Tuscan columns. More nice houses to
follow. The end along here is two ranges of yellow brick
ALMSHOUSES, dated 1850, with many thin Jacobean stepped
gables.

In the other streets departing from the main crossing less
happens. In GEORGE STREET is the quiet, long white front
of the BEDFORD ARMS HOTEL and then THE CHESTNUTS,
three wide bays with plenty of ogee arches, even to Venetian
windows, in LEIGHTON STREET is one good five-bay brick
house, and in PARK STREET is the church and then the Park
Gate to Woburn Abbey.

9030
WOBURN ABBEY

It is known that houses were open to suitable visitors as early
as the C18. Mr Ketton Cremer has drawn attention to the case
of Holkham Hall in Norfolk, where one party was waiting while
another was shown round, and Horace Walpole in 1763 wrote
that he had so many visitors at Strawberry Hill that he ought to
put up a sign The Gothic Castle. He gave out tickets and hid
himself from the sightseers. In cases like Holkham and Strawberry Hill a high tip went to the butler or another servant. However, a recognition of the fact that visitors can be made a source
of substantial income for the maintenance of the house and
otherwise came only after the Second World War. The Marquess
of Bath at Longleat was the pioneer. He opened his home in 1949,
but ever since the Duke of Bedford opened Woburn Abbey to
the public in 1955, Woburn has become the case *par excellence*
of mass attraction. In 1965 *c.* 475,000 visitors were counted, and
the side-shows included a zoo with e.g. bison and many species
of deer, a pets' corner, model soldiers, and sailing. It goes without saying that the majority of the visitors care more for the
entertainments (including a glimpse of the Duke) than for
the house, yet Woburn Abbey is among the stately homes of
England one of the stateliest. It stands in vast grounds (3,000
acres), it has lakes, woods, and plenty of park furnishings, and
the house itself is vast, was vaster still till 1950, and has vast
adjoining outbuildings.

Woburn was a Cistercian abbey founded in 1145 from Fountains.
The cloister was probably where the courtyard between the
three wings now is; but more is not known. In 1547 the priory

buildings were granted to John Lord Russell of Chenies, an
executor of Henry VIII and later first Earl of Bedford. However, nothing of the house is older than the time of the fourth
Earl, i.e. *c.*1630, and very little of features is as old as that. What
we now see is mostly of the C18. So Woburn Abbey is not a
house of all periods like Drayton or Boughton. But it is not as
unified as Houghton or Holkham either. The house is – or
was, before the E range was pulled down – oblong, 148 by
138 ft, with E of it two large square stable quadrangles. They
were visually linked by the Riding School and Tennis Court
range no longer in existence. But between the two courts still
stands a glorious cedar tree.

The demolitions were undertaken by the twelfth Duke in
1950, and are very unfortunate. The ranges between Riding
School and Tennis Courts were by *Henry Holland*, one of the
most sensitive and discriminating English architects of the
late C18, and by him also was the E range of the house, which
came down together with about a third of the N and S ranges.
The new ends of the N and S ranges were treated by *Sir
Albert Richardson* as a display of his brand of C20 classicism
(though he deplored the demolitions). All this is regrettable,
but what remains is enjoyable and admirable enough.

EXTERIOR. The N range is essentially of the late C17, as
is visible from the S. It is two-storeyed, of brown stone. The
three-bay centre is pedimented, and Richardson had to pile
something on the new E end to match the fine bay W of the
pedimented part.

As for the other ranges, the W range was built by *Flitcroft*
for the fourth Duke and dates from 1747–61, and the S range
is by *Holland*, for the fifth Duke, of 1787–90. Holland also did
the Conservatory in the S range of the S service court. But
what did *Chambers* do ? We know that from *c.*1767 to 1772 he
was concerned with the house, rooms inside, and a bridge. To
this we shall revert later. The fifth Duke was twenty-one when
he called in Holland.

The stones used at Woburn Abbey are Ketton oolite
and Totternhoe clunch. *Flitcroft*'s WEST RANGE is the principal range. It cost *c.* £85,000 to build. To the courtyard it is of
eleven bays and two storeys with a three-bay centre where
giant Ionic pilasters carry a pediment with achievement. To
the gardens the front of this range is the most monumental of
the house. The centre here is raised by a half-storey, and has
attached giant Ionic columns carrying the pediment. The

angle pavilions are of two and a half storeys as well. They have
a Venetian window each with a tripartite lunette window over.
The lower parts of the front are balustraded, and the whole
ground floor has smooth rustication. It is a dignified façade,
faultless, but not moving. The N range has already been mentioned. To the N it has an odd rhythm, owing to the fact that
much of the masonry of c.1630 is preserved. Its W corner belongs to Flitcroft's angle pavilion, its E corner to Richardson.
Holland's s range towards the courtyard is quite simple, but
towards the s it has a character quite different from Flitcroft's.
It is of two storeys, and was before the mutilation thirteen bays
divided into 2–9–2, without any emphasis on the centre. The
whole is terminated by a long balustrade, and the angle
pavilions are singled out only by slight projection. The
ground-floor windows are all pedimented, and in the angle-
pavilions they are set in blank arches. That is all.*

In the courtyard are four STATUES by *J. V. Legterin*, of
c.1700 (MHLG).

INTERIOR. The rooms will be described as they are seen by
visitors, but rooms are included which are not shown. In the
N range on the ground floor are rooms with Rococo ceilings,
the BOOK ROOM with a good late C17 ceiling with garland decoration, and then the GROTTO, the one surviving room of
about 1630. The decoration with bands of shells and of rocky
stalactite stuff, a big niche and small niches is highly typical
of the date and may be by *Isaac de Caus*. It includes masks and
garlands and nymphs in rocky mosaic. On the two doorways
lie flat-faced putti. The grotto is followed by another room
with a late C17 ceiling. The chimneypiece here, however,
looks mid C17, and the Jacobean overmantel might well have
belonged to the work of c.1630. Attributed to the same time
is the N corridor, known as PATERNOSTER ROW. Up the C18
STAIRCASE with a simple iron railing to the first floor. On
that floor in the N range the E room has a Chinese wallpaper
bought in 1753 and a Rococo ceiling. The chimneypiece has
rams' heads. The ROOM OF THE FLYING DUCHESS has a
chimneypiece by *John Deval* with young frontal caryatids and
a fine overmantel. The Rococo ceiling of the YELLOW DRAW-
INGROOM is one of the most gorgeous in the house. The centre

* Mr John Harris attributes this front to *Chambers*: 'The somewhat
monotonous range of windows is just what Chambers liked. I think Holland
gutted Chambers's apartments and gave the front a little more movement
by inserting the end windows on the projections in blank arches.'

has a big face in sun rays. Similar but smaller in its form is the ceiling of the adjoining room. Then the STATE BEDROOM in the NW corner. Here the ceiling has a big bold circular centre and surrounding it heavy octagonal coffering (derived from Wood's *Palmyra*, published in 1753). Good white chimneypiece and overmantel by *Deval*, bought in 1756 for £100. We have entered Flitcroft's range.

The QUEEN'S DRESSING ROOM is in the same style, with classical Greek-key bands. The BLUE DRAWING ROOM is also dateable to 1756. The fireplace by *Deval* has a plaque by *Rysbrack*, and the overmantel is enriched by an eagle between the scrolly shanks of a pediment. The STATE SALOON in the centre of the range has a broadly coved ceiling and two white 91 chimneypieces by *Rysbrack* with frontal caryatids. The total cost of the decoration of this room was £1213 18s. Displayed here are two of the Mortlake tapestries made in 1664 for the predecessor room. The STATE DINING ROOM has guilloche bands and the caryatids of the chimneypiece (by *Deval*) are in profile. So to the SW corner, i.e. the celebrated CANALETTO ROOM, remodelled by *Holland* to contain twenty-two Venetian views by *Canaletto* – previously at Bedford House in London, which was demolished in 1801. Parallel to the E with these state rooms in the W range runs the LONG GALLERY, divided into three parts by pairs of columns and with pediments to doorway and overmantel. The gallery dates from 1754–6. The fireplaces are again by *Deval*. They cost £120 each.

Before describing Holland's rooms in the S range, the ENTRANCE HALL in the W range must be mentioned, with unfluted Ionic columns in pairs and two splendid chimneypieces by *Deval* with reliefs by *Rysbrack* (1756).

The SOUTH RANGE contains a corridor all along its N side (early C19 glass) and on its S side as its centre the long tripartite LIBRARY, i.e. Ante-Library, Library proper, and 93 Wood Library. The stucco ceiling is ornate, and very different in style from both the earlier Flitcroft and the contemporary Adam. Fireplace of 1818 by *Sir Richard Westmacott*. Overdoors by *Biagio Rebecca*.★

★ Miss Gladys Scott Thompson, the historian of the house, has recorded that in 1748 a water closet was put up for His Grace in the N garden, that in 1760 there were three more, one of them in the house, that there were then also baths with piped water supply, and that in 1753 and 1756 pottery stoves were imported from France.

The STABLES are by *Flitcroft*. The centre of the fronts towards the house of both quadrangles has an octagonal dome. The entrances have attached coupled columns or pilasters and at the angles is the motif of the tripartite lunette above the Venetian window as we have found it in the W range. In the S range of the S courtyard *Holland* created his Conservatory, later converted into the SCULPTURE GALLERY. It has arched French windows and in the middle a Venetian French window. Above this a pediment set against an attic block raised above the rest of the building. The centre was emphasized inside by *Wyatville* in 1818 to make use of eight antique columns. It was also given a shallow dome and an apse. *Holland* in 1801–3 added at one end of the conservatory a tetrastyle Ionic temple front, at the other end *Wyatville* in 1818 added a coffered rotunda with a glazed centre to the ceiling. This was for *Canova*'s Three Graces. Good, blocky exterior.

Most of the sculpture has had recently to be removed. There are too many hooligans among 475,000 visitors. Apart from Roman statuary there were works by *Thorwaldsen*, *Westmacott*, *Chantrey*, and others.

The CAMELIA HOUSE with its large windows forms a quadrant E of the Sculpture Gallery. It is assigned by Miss Stroud to *Repton*.

In the grounds the following items deserve notice.

CHINESE DAIRY. By *Holland*. Polygonal, with a pagoda roof; all of wood. Pretty ceiling inside with Chippendale-Chinese trellis motifs and culminating in an octagonal lantern. Furniture similar to the mock-Chinese furniture in the Brighton Pavilion. Painting almost certainly by *John Crace*. Gallery along the lake.

BASIN BRIDGE. By *Chambers*, c.1770. Of three arches. Rebuilt.

PARIS EXHIBITION HOUSE, ¾ m. SW of the house. Built by *Cubitt*. Shown at the exhibition of 1878. Half-timbered.

THORNERY, ¾ m. N. Square, with four gables. Of stone, with a thatched roof and tree-trunk veranda. In the basement a tunnel-vaulted room, tiled white. Probably for preparing food to be consumed inside or outside the upper room.

CHINESE TEMPLE in the maze, 300 yds SE. Octagonal, with a pagoda roof and ogee arches.

GROTTO, 500 yds NE. Like an igloo. Walls decorated with shells, quartz, etc. Pointed windows.

TEMPLE in line with the centre axis of the house, but 350 yds E.

ICE HOUSE, 500 yds S. Circular and embattled, with a brick dome.

LONDON LODGE. This is the main approach to the house. It is placed in the centre of a sweeping semicircle of walls. *Holland* was the designer; 1790 is the date. Triumphal arch with three arches through. Unfluted Ionic columns carrying projecting pieces of entablature. Raised attic over the centre with short pilasters and volutes – all oddly unclassical and more demonstrative than one would expect Holland to be.

PARK STREET GATE, towards Woburn village. Just piers with rocky rustication and lions on top.

GATES from this road towards the house, with a polygonal middle lodge.

VILLAGES. The villages around the Woburn Abbey estate with their estate cottages are listed separately (*see* Husborne Crawley, Lidlington, Ridgmont, Willington). Charles Greville in his *Diary*, i.e. about the middle of the C19, writes that the Duke of Bedford then had 450 employees.

WOBURN SANDS*   *9030*

Development began probably when the railway came in 1846.

ST MICHAEL, the parish church. *See* Aspley Heath.

The STATION is charming, *ornée*, with bargeboarded gables, and then Victorian houses and terraces followed up the street to Woburn in all manner of moods.

HENRY VII LODGE, ¼ m. E of Aspley Heath church, i.e. in Beds. On the A50. By *Humphry & J. Adey Repton*, 1810–11, for the Duke of Bedford, in an attempt to create the perfect late C15 house. The motifs were taken from 'some curious specimens of Timber houses [communicated] to the Society of Antiquaries in 1810': 'The hint of the lower storey' was taken from Eltham Palace, the hints for the brick-nogging from a house at King's Lynn, for the arches at the top of the narrow panels from a house near Kelvedon, for the barge-boarding from a house at Bury St Edmunds, for the pinnacles from a house at Shrewsbury, for the oriel from Norwich, and for the chimneys from Wolterton Manor House, Barsham, Norfolk (Repton's *Fragments*).

* Really in Buckinghamshire.

WOODSIDE

ST ANDREW. 1890 by *J. R. Brown & Son*. Plum brick, aisleless, with transepts, a bell-turret, and plate tracery.

WOOTTON

ST MARY. Chiefly a Dec church. This is patent first of all in the arcades with quatrefoil piers and double-chamfered arches. The arcades are of a height exceptional for a parish church. The chancel arch goes with them. So that will be c.1300. The tower arch is a little later. The tower w window has cusped intersecting tracery. The w bays of the aisles, embracing the tower, are an early C19 addition – see its plaster rib-vaults and also that in the tower. However, the heavy plate tracery of the aisle w windows must belong to the restoration of 1860. The tower has a recessed lead spire. The chancel is Dec too, and so is the N vestry. Large four-light Perp aisle windows. – (FONT. Perp, octagonal, with panelled stem and traceried bowl. GMCH) – SCREEN. Perp, but nearly all 1896. – PLATE. Flagon of 1684. – MONUMENTS. In the chancel tablets to Sir Humphrey Monoux † 1685 and Philip Monoux † 1707, the latter by *Edward Stanton* (Gunnis). They are very similar and both excellent. The tops are open scrolly pediments with an urn set in.

WOOTTON HOUSE, w of the church. Late C17, of eight bays with a hipped roof. Red brick, quite plain. The porch of course is a late addition.

VICARAGE, SE of the church. Early C18, of seven bays, also red brick, and also plain.*

WREST

The manor of Wrest was held by Reginald de Grey as early as the late C13. At the time of Edward IV the de Greys were made Earls of Kent. The house preceding the one now standing lay a little to the s and was Jacobean or older. *Leoni* remodelled it for the twelfth Earl, who became Duke of Kent in 1710. He was also Lord Lucas. He died in 1740 (cf. Flitton). The estate then went to his grand-daughter, Jemima, Marchioness de Grey and Baroness Lucas in her own right, who married the second Earl of Hardwicke. In 1833 her grandson Thomas Philip, third Lord Grantham, succeeded to the title.

* Since demolished.

He became also first Earl de Grey, and incidentally first President of the (Royal) Institute of British Architects.

This is curious, as the house as it now stands and as it was built in 1834–6 was designed, it seems, by an otherwise unknown French architect, *Cléphane*,* and is absolutely French in style – something unique in England at that time. There had been odd occasional French *intérieurs* by Benjamin Wyatt in the twenties, but a French country house with all the rooms in the Louis XV style has no parallel. For interiors one's mind turns to the fifties and the Rothschilds. The house has a thirteen-bay front of stone, two-storeyed, with segment-headed windows, their glazing bars originally gilt, and mansard and pavilion roofs. The centre on the entrance side projects ovally and has a fancy pavilion roof. On the garden side 98 the centre is flat and there are fifteen bays. The entrance hall has putto reliefs all round, high up. It leads into a grand and elegant staircase hall with the stairs in two arms and with iron 99 handrail. Glazed lantern. Behind the staircase facing the garden is the library, with ceiling paintings. Most of the decoration is white and gold.

From the library one looks in a straight axis across the parterre with four lead statues of *c*.1730 (by *Carpentière* ?) and along the Long Water to Archer's celebrated pavilion, nearly ½ m. away. The pavilion is only one of many garden ornaments, and they will now be described in the order of an easy tour. What distinguishes the garden more than anything is that it has remained basically formal, in spite of a compliment paid to *Capability Brown*, who worked at Wrest in 1758–60. The gardens were begun in 1706. The main avenues are radially arranged from the parterre and from the pavilion. Originally they were lined by high hedges.

First, s w of the parterre, the ORANGERY, also by *Cléphane* and also assigned to 1836, a very dissolute design, again in this ahead of its date. Eleven bays. End bays with square French domes. Strange pilasters with basket capitals and little mats hanging from them. Entrance between a caryatid and an atlas.

Behind the Orangery the BATH HOUSE, two rooms, cyclo- *See* pean, half-ruined-looking, the first domed, the second lower $_{413}^{p.}$ down the cold bath itself. The building is ascribed to *Brown* by Horace Walpole.

s of the Orangery a large group, called HUNTING SCENE. A

* But cf. Ampthill workhouse.

young lady on horseback and two youths. Who was the sculptor? E of this group is the site of the old house.

Further s the BOWLING GREEN HOUSE. This must be of *c.*1740. Tuscan colonnade of six columns with triglyph frieze and balustrade. At the back towards the canal plainer arcade with groin-vaults. The room inside is splendidly decorated in the William Kent taste. Fine doorway with Corinthian columns and pediment, fine chimneypiece opposite with rich, broad volutes. Wall panels with hanging garlands. L. and r. of the Bowling Green House two lead VASES by *Nost*, 1725.

So by way of WEST HALFHOUSE, a small pedimented exedra of brick, to *Archer*'s PAVILION. This is a very curious conceit, more Borrominesque than one would expect in England, except from so travelled a gentleman as Archer. The principle of the plan is that of Borromini's S. Ivo. It is the principle of a star of three identical motifs front and diagonally back and three other identical motifs back and diagonally front. The former motifs in Archer's case are rectangular, the latter semicircular. The whole centre room is round and domed, with a lantern. The curved triplet has flat brick pilaster strips, the oblong triplet quoins of even length. At the junction of the curved parts with the centre are tiny semi-domes. The entrance unit is open. It has Ionic pilasters. Inside there are painted statues and a painted coffered ceiling. These are signed *Handuroy* 1712. The doorway is most characteristically Archer. It might be described like this. Take two pairs of pilasters, streak them vertically, and turn the outer outward, the inner inward, and continue this in the pediment. It is a device specially favoured in Vienna, Salzburg, and Prague at Archer's time, and Archer may well have known any of them. The date of the pavilion is 1709–11. The surprisingly large room inside has five windows in the five projections and in addition three round windows in the attic.

In front of the pavilion stands a lead STATUE of William III, by *Andrew Carpentière*.

To the NE of the pavilion is the EAST HALFHOUSE, like its companion but a little larger, i.e. with blank side pieces. From here straight N to the COLUMN commemorating *Capability Brown*, who worked here (cf. previous page): an urn on a Tuscan column, weirdly girt by two square rocky blocks. Brown gave the wilderness its wiggly paths and added the serpentine canal all round the gardens. N of this is the CHINESE BRIDGE of 1874, not specially Chinese-looking but meant to compose with trees into the Willow Pattern come true. Finally at the s end of the parterre the Victorian MARBLE FOUNTAIN (and off, along what is called the Old Road, up Cain Hill, to the COLUMN put up in 1831 to the memory of Jemima, Marchioness de Grey).

To the E of the house the STABLES with a short tower, free-English-Classical and not French. To the W of the house is the very large WALLED GARDEN, with gateways so undisciplined that again they look 1850 rather than 1835. The WEST LODGES are square and French with their mansard roofs.

WRESTLINGWORTH   2040

ST PETER. Of brown cobbles. In the chancel N wall a small Norman window. Short Perp W tower with higher stair-turret. The aisle windows are Dec and straight-topped with reticulation units. The s arcade and the s doorway are late C13, but the doorway has lost its shafts, and ornamental carving has taken the place of the capitals. The N arcade is a little later. Both have standard elements. Dec chancel, see the arch with responds of half-quatrefoil section with the familiar thin shafts in the diagonals. Arch of two sunk waves. Dec also the transomed low-side windows of the chancel, and the PISCINA. Perp clerestory. – PULPIT. Pretty, early C18 stair with twisted balusters. – WEST GALLERY and BOX PEWS probably early C19. – PLATE. Cup inscribed 1633.

WYMINGTON   9060

ST LAURENCE. Not a large, but an ambitious church, mostly Dec, and mostly built by the munificence of John Curteys, who died in 1391. The W tower is Dec up to the bell-openings (pairs of two-light transomed windows with ogee arches below the transoms and a flower trail in the surrounds) and Perp above. Top frieze, decorated battlements, crocketed spire whose lowest tier of gabled lucarnes gives the effect of an octagonal stage below the spire proper. The top lucarnes are also gabled. The aisles and chapels are all Dec, with straight-headed windows. The E end is a fine sight, with one low embattled roof above chapels and chancel and higher angle-turrets (cf. Tingrith; also Shillington). The E window of five lights with flowing tracery is said to be a facsimile of what was there before the restoration of c.1844. The chancel was then probably shortened a little. The s porch is uncommonly lavish too.

It is two-storeyed, with a rib-vault with diagonal and ridge-ribs and a Green Man boss. The interior is oddly tight, or in other words, crowded with motifs. The arcades inside are identical, of four bays, with standard elements and recognizably Dec details. The tower arch is unusual. The responds are one broad splay, divided by three niches into four parts. The tops of the niches are tiny arches like stop-chamfers. In the tower are the remains of a vault too. Arches from the aisles into the chapels and from the chancel to the chapels. On the N side it is only one bay (since 1845), on the s side one plus the Curteys Monument (*see* below). SEDILIA and PISCINA are obviously Dec, the piscina with a nodding canopy. Another such canopy above the s chapel PISCINA. In the s chapel also, in the angle of the SE window, a niche with ogee arches but Perp panel tracery over. Next to it an angel-bracket. The chancel roof has traceried braces. The aisle roofs are of 1923. – FONT. Octagonal, probably Dec. The stem with quatrefoils, the bowl strongly moulded, and at the top a small frieze of ogee arches. – PULPIT. Jacobean, with back panel and sounding-board. – SCREEN, in the N chapel. Jacobean, with small balusters. – BENCHES. A set of the buttressed Perp type, some with C17 pull-out auxiliary seats. – PAINTING. On the s aisle E wall high up a late C14 Trinity. This is suggested to be the earliest painting in the church. – Of the C15 the large, faint Doom over the chancel arch and extending into the nave.– Also some ornamental painting in the s chapel (N wall). – MONUMENTS. Between chancel and s chapel John Curteys † 1391, Mayor of the Staple of Calais, 'qui istam ecclesiam de novo construxerat', and wife. Brasses, 34 in. long, the earliest in Bedfordshire; on a tomb-chest with Perp blank tracery. The tomb-chest is placed under a large ogee arch. The capitals have small foliage strips and small angels. – Sir Thomas Brunflet † 1430 and his wife 1407 (chancel floor). He is 6 ft long, she 3 ft. Above his head a long inscription in Latin hexameters. – John Stokys, rector, c.1510 (s chapel, floor). The figure is 22 in. long.

SCHOOL, by the church. 1878 by *John Bird*. Remarkably good recent additions by *Oliver Carey* in the idiom of the sixties: engineering bricks e.g.

YELDEN

ST MARY. Externally mostly Dec, but certain disjointed features are E.E., i.e. the s aisle doorway with one order of shafts, the chancel s doorway, the piece of string-course above it inside, a re-set PISCINA in the chancel N wall, the plain blocked nave N doorway, the remains of an E lancet in the s aisle, and the s arcade except for the Perp responds. The s aisle w window looks *c*.1300, i.e. earlier than the Dec features of the church. To these belongs the w tower, with bell-openings with flowing tracery and a delightful corbel-frieze with a tendril connecting flowers, animals, heads etc. (cf. Swineshead not far away). Short broach spire with two tiers of lucarnes. Dec also the chancel, see the windows, the arch towards the nave, the SEDILIA and PISCINA with their ogee arches, and a N window in the nave. Perp clerestory. – FONT COVER. Perp. Conical and crocketed. – PULPIT. Perp, of wood, similar to that at Dean. – BENCHES. The usual buttressed type. – PAINT-INGS. On the s wall a St Christopher and much painted ashlaring with a flower in the middle of each block. Also on the aisle E wall a Saint, probably St James. – PLATE. Cup and Cover Paten 1629; Paten probably of the same date. – MONUMENTS. In the nave N wall simple ogee recess and effigy of a Civilian holding his heart. Early C14. – Larger and more splendid tomb recess in the s aisle. Cusped and subcusped arch with leaf in the spandrels and crockets on the gable. Buttress-shafts l. and r. Two of the cusps are heads of Knights. – Brass to J. Heyne, rector, † 1433. A 19 in. figure. – Also an oblong brass plate with the figure of Christopher Stickland † 1628, and a square brass plate with the kneeling figure of Thomas Barker † 1617.

CASTLE. Considerable earthworks remain on the s bank of the river E of the village. The motte is oblong, *c*.130 ft by 90 ft in size at the top. In addition two large baileys and more en-closures farther away. The principal bailey is w and sw of the motte. During excavations in 1881 stone foundations were discovered, including the bases of two small round towers in the sw corner of the bailey. A little to the w of this, on a small island mound, was another round tower, this one 30 ft in dia-meter.

THE COUNTY OF
HUNTINGDON AND PETERBOROUGH

*

INTRODUCTION

HUNTINGDONSHIRE until 1965 was one of the smallest counties
of England – in population it was the last but two, in size the
last but four (including London). It had no big town, it was re-
mote and had all the attractions of peace and quiet and intimacy.
The 1965 shot in the arm is changing all that. Peterborough
with 60,000 inhabitants at present – Huntingdonshire has
80,000 – is a lustily growing town, and the Ministry of Housing
and Local Government want to blow it up to double its population.

In architecture also the merger has brought it a massive body
of monuments of the first order: Peterborough Cathedral,
Barnack, Castor, Longthorpe Tower, Thorpe Hall – Huntingdonshire had nothing or hardly anything of that calibre.

On the landscape side on the other hand the Soke of Peterborough is no gain. The attraction of Huntingdonshire still remains the modest rolling country of the s and – for those who
understand it – the fen country of the n.

Geology as the science showing what – literally – underlies
landscape and architecture is summed up on p. 29. Here it is
enough to say that most of the county's churches are of brown
cobbles, i.e. carstone, but that the fringe towards Northamptonshire partakes of the best English building stone, the oolitic
limestone, as quarried e.g. at Barnack but also across the Rutland
border at Ketton. Hence – to anticipate – Huntingdon and
Peterborough is a spire county. The total – including three no
longer surviving – is over forty. Barnack amongst them is one of
the earliest in England.

But Barnack at this stage of an architectural summary of
Huntingdon and Peterborough means the C11, not the C13. It
means an Anglo-Saxon church, not an E.E. spire. Nor does
Barnack stand at the beginning of ANGLO-SAXON ARCHITEC-
TURE in the county. The Hedda Stone at Peterborough and the
eminently interesting and in several ways enigmatic bits of a
frieze at Fletton just outside Peterborough go back to the early
C9. Connected with them is a small stone at Castor. What can

the purpose of the Fletton frieze – and the closely related frieze at Breedon-on-the-Hill in Leicestershire – have been? The scale is so small that it must have been displayed close to the eye, and the effects also are intimate and miniature. The technique is highly curious, with the scooping out as if into clay and the leaving of thin ridges, a technique in which the negative of flecky space counts almost as much as the positive of tendril, bird, and quadruped. There is nothing quite like it, not only in England but also in the Carolingian empire.

Late Anglo-Saxon architecture is, compared with the Continent, backward and provincial rather, and the confidence that we have that the carvers of Peterborough and Fletton knew exactly what they wanted to achieve has no parallel in the early C 11 buildings, powerful as their impact may be. One need only remember St Pantaleon at Cologne, St Michael at Hildesheim, St Mary-in-Capitol at Cologne, and Jumièges to admit that. The 31 thin pilaster-strip work of the Barnack tower with the strips starting without any worry on the apexes of arches is a timber-people's misunderstanding of the properties of stone. On the other hand, the most elementary power of stone is brought out 10 in the massive chancel arch of Wittering. The most advanced piece of architecture of that moment in England is Great Paxton; for here the Anglo-Saxon mason built a real crossing such as St Michael at Hildesheim and Jumièges possessed, i.e. with transepts as wide and as high as nave and chancel, not just *porticus* or narrower or lower transepts, and moreover he built a nave 9 separated from aisles by real compound piers not just chunks of wall (as at Brixworth and Lydd). They are odd piers, lacking in logic, but they also possess that sense of mass which makes the whole church unforgettable. Of other pre-Conquest features Wittering has angles in long-and-short work, Woodston some little masonry with a small double-splayed window, Elton and Peakirk have crosses or cross fragments with interlace, Castor a cross-base with interlace, Fletton a cross with some animals, two set in medallions, and Stanground a defaced cross, and 11 Barnack one of the finest pieces of C 11 figure carving in England, a seated Christ. Its softness of modelling distinguishes it from C 12 work, just as the harder precision of modelling of two small figures inside Fletton church marks them as Norman rather than C 11 Anglo-Danish.

So to the NORMAN STYLE. Here of course Peterborough 12 p. Cathedral, or rather the Benedictine abbey of Peterborough, 306 must take precedence over anything else. For Peterborough became a cathedral only in 1541. It had been founded about 650 and rebuilt after Danish raids about 965. It was given at that time wide transepts and a straight-ended chancel. This church was destroyed by fire in 1116, and so the present cathedral has nothing above ground earlier than that date. The choir with its wide apse, accompanied by the side apses of the choir aisles, which ended externally in straight walls, was built between 1118 and c.1150, the nave and aisles in the second half of the C12. The style is therefore High and Late not Early Nor- 14 man. The zigzag as a decorative enrichment e.g. appears from the outset. So does the motif of alternating circular and polygonal piers, a motif accepted widely only in the late C12 and early C13. Especially precocious is the use of zigzag at r. angles to the wall surface, which begins at Peterborough about 1130 or 1135 at the latest, although it is as a rule a sign of Late Norman date. The capitals on the other hand still have heavy scallops at first, and the arches heavy roll mouldings. The system of elevation is that almost universally adopted in Anglo-Norman major architecture: arcade, spacious gallery, clerestory with inner wall-passage, flat ceiling. The ensemble is tall, forceful, and consistent.

The other great abbeys were Thorney and Ramsey, both also Benedictine and both also Anglo-Saxon foundations: Thorney founded about 670 and refounded after the Danes in 972, Ramsey founded afresh c.969. Both are in the fenland, and the 'ey' of Thorney and Ramsey means island. At Thorney all that survives is part of the nave deprived of its aisles. It is somewhat earlier than Peterborough. The church was begun, at the missing E end no doubt, c.1085, and the nave must have been started ten years later at the latest. It was completed in 1108, though consecration only took place ten years after Peterborough was begun. The system at Thorney is arcades with alternating supports, but mast-like shafts, just as at Ely, running up to the ceiling in front of every support. The gallery, as against those of Peterborough and Ely, was unsubdivided. Capitals are mostly scalloped, but there are some also of the primitive volute type characteristic of Early Norman. The W front is preserved too, though much chopped about. The Norman evidence makes it likely that Thorney had three giant niches like Lincoln. At Ramsey nothing remains of before 1180, and what does remain will concern us a little later.

For the moment this is the place to interpolate a quick survey of the MONASTIC HOUSES of Huntingdon and Peterborough

altogether. They are as follows. Peterborough must of course have precedence. This Benedictine house had before the Black Death about 60 to 65 monks. The cathedral is its major remains,
p. but of the monastic quarters also plenty survives. Their climax
321 is the seven-bay infirmary. The other principal abbeys were Ramsey, also Benedictine and also large in numbers (c.80 in the C12 and C13), and Thorney, again Benedictine, but only about half the size of the other two or less (c.30 monks in the C14). Of Ramsey there is only the Lady Chapel (in a position like that
60 of Ely and Peterborough), the sumptuous gatehouse (partly at
17 Hinchingbrooke), and the spectacular late C12 *hospitium*, a hostel for guests or a hospital, but not the monastic infirmary, as it was outside the gates. It is eight bays long plus the chancel and became the parish church in the C13. The other monastic houses were small, and little or nothing of them survives. Hinchingbrooke was founded before 1087 for Augustinian nuns. Only traces of the plan and featureless masonry are preserved. Benedictine were the small priories of St Ives and St Neots, both of which have disappeared, whereas the priories of Huntingdon and Stonely near Kimbolton were Augustinian. At Stonely there is one cottage as the only reminder of the medieval buildings. Of the Cistercian Sawtry nothing is left, nor is there of the only two friars' houses, the Austin Friars of Huntingdon and Whittlesey Mere.

Of the two monumental hospitals just mentioned, a little more must be said, and a third must be added to them. The Peterborough infirmary dates from c.1250–60, but the Hospital
16 of St John at Huntingdon, now the Cromwell Museum and formerly the Grammar School, right in the middle of the town, is Late Norman. The length was also seven bays and a chancel. The details of the two remaining bays, piers and arches, are
17 just like those of a parish church. And the *hospitium* at Ramsey founded c.1180 and built rapidly till c.1190 is late C12 architecture at its most monumental. The chancel is heavily rib-vaulted and still fully Norman. The nave arcades demonstrate the precise moment of transition from Norman to E.E. The piers have a glorious variety of shapes, the capitals exhibit waterleaf and even crockets, and the arches are pointed.

But we have not yet looked at NORMAN PARISH CHURCHES at all. The chancel arches at Haddon, Stibbington, and Sutton can be assigned to the early C12. Of the first quarter probably and dated by the unique survival of the dedication inscription is
13 Castor with its spectacular crossing tower. This of course came

at the end of operations, i.e. about 1120, as the dedication date is 1124. Castor is a cruciform church. The detail is very different from that at Peterborough. It is gay, with ornamental fancies. Their detail, thanks probably to work done by the Castor workshop, is also met in some village churches, notably the capitals of Haddon and the pier bases of Morborne and Maxey. The figural details of the Castor capitals are entertaining, but no-one would call them great art, such as are the capitals, say, of the Moissac cloister. And as regards Norman tympana, where they do not confine themselves to geometric all-over ornament (Bury, Folksworth, Peakirk, Southoe, Wistow), they are outright barbaric. This is less true of the affronted quadrupeds of Conington, as of the incredible mermaid and quadrupeds of Stow Longa and the Christ, the animals, and the cross of Little Paxton. The doorway with the greatest number of motifs piled on is at Southoe. Among the most interesting Norman doorway motifs (not at Southoe) is what goes under the name beakhead. It appears just once in the county, in a re-set fragment at Little Stukeley. But there and also at Spaldwick and at Toseland is a stylized version of it in which head and beak have become unrecognizable. Another decorative motif, and one of even greater interest, is the lion at Sutton which once carried a colonnette. That is an Italian motif entirely, but it did occur in England originally on the Prior's Doorway at Ely.

Other sculptural Norman work worth inclusion here is the bronze door knocker at Warboys and the font at Wansford – one of very many of less interest – with the Baptism of Christ, two Knights fighting, etc. There is no complete Norman tower in Huntingdon and Peterborough, and at least three churches, all in the Soke of Peterborough, have or had bellcotes instead (Werrington, Northborough, Peakirk, and – c13 – Sutton). As for arcades, there are plenty of them, all Late Norman, and often on the verge of E.E. The typical Norman form such as it survives e.g. at Eynesbury has round piers with square multi-scalloped capitals, square abaci, and round arches. The various forms the transition to E.E. can take have been described in the introduction to Bedfordshire on p. 16. The most characteristic motif of this transition is the waterleaf capital.   22

For the EARLY ENGLISH STYLE again the great abbeys or at least two of them take first place. At Ramsey the Hospital, a 17 paradigm of the way into Early English, has already been mentioned. The Lady Chapel must date from about 1240–50 and has pointed-trefoiled, deeply moulded arcading (cf. Westminster

Abbey in the same years) and mature stiff-leaf capitals. At Peterborough the whole confused story of the W extension of the Norman building with its ultimate unsatisfactory end falls, almost exactly as at Ramsey, into the years between c.1180 and the consecration of 1238. If the layman's vision of the C13 is that of the climax of medieval nobility and harmony, a glance at the Peterborough façade is sufficient to impress him with the degree of discordance which this great Gothic century was ready to accept, at least in England. Perhaps the highest beauty of the façade is the twin portal with the *trumeau* – to use the French word – and the relief both agitated and nobly carved. It is carved in Purbeck or probably rather Alwalton marble,* a con-
18 glomerate really. Of the same material are the abbots' monuments inside the cathedral, a most instructive series if one wants to understand the development of the funerary effigy from about 1195 to about 1225. There are other effigies of the same materials and the same and the following decades in the county; an abbot (upper part only) at Great Staughton and the outstanding so-
28 called Ailwin in the abbey gatehouse at Ramsey, both mid-C13. Of local stone is the priest at Morborne whose feet are supported by two human heads.

Of EARLY ENGLISH CHURCHES the best all-round in the county is Leighton Bromswold, now cruciform, though originally with narrow aisles, beautifully proportioned and puritan in its bare surfaces, even before the C17 started its sympathetic remodelling. The only spectacular piece of equipment is the double piscina with a round arch intersected by two half-arches in such a way that not only the arches but the very mouldings are interwoven. The same motif exists at Hemingford Grey
35 and St Ives, and also in Jesus College and St John's College, Cambridge, at Histon, and in three other places in Cambridgeshire, and moreover at Barnston in Essex. The most complete E.E. church is probably Etton. It has an E.E. spire too, and one of the earliest in the county. The earliest of all,
31 and one of the earliest in England, is, as we have seen, Barnack, where there is also a porch of the very beginning of the century. The porch is vaulted, and vaulting in England was still an exception at that time, not only in parish churches. It remains noteworthy that even Peterborough Cathedral was satisfied about 1220 with a wooden nave ceiling, however memorable in its lozenge-pattern. It is one of the most important medieval

* Where in the gazetteer Purbeck marble is mentioned, it may well be Alwalton instead (cf. *Country Life* CXXXVIII, p. 620).

ceilings in Europe. As for the spires, that at Barnack has low
broaches with big pinnacles set on them, that at Etton also low
broaches, and so has Warboys, another E.E. spire, but the E.E. 34
Buckworth and Alconbury have high broaches. So the two types 33
developed side by side. A speciality of the county are extremely
long lancets in towers. They are to be seen at Bury, Warboys, 32
Chesterton, and (bell-openings) Alconbury. Alconbury is an- &
other church predominantly E.E. The chancel remains in one's 30
memory for the noble, close-set shafting up the N and S walls enclosing the windows. The same was done with plain giant arches
of continuous mouldings at Brampton, Great Gidding, and
Molesworth. The last named is mid C13, the two former late
C13.* One late C13 church is datable with some probability:
Yaxley, where an interesting and moving heart-burial monu- 38
ment is likely to record an abbot of Thorney called William de
Yaxley who died in 1293. The late C13 windows at Yaxley of
stepped lancet lights and stepped lancet lights under one super-
arch have a parallel about twenty-five years earlier in the transepts of Peterborough. Another motif appearing at that time is
windows or arches which are pointed-trefoiled. You find them at
Longthorpe, where the start of building was in 1263–4, and, as
we have seen, the Lady Chapel of Ramsey Abbey.

Apart from the Yaxley monument, the only other of special
quality is the Franciscan tertiary of about 1300 at Conington, 39
sensitively characterized and carved. There are other MONU-
MENTS of these years – late C13 to early C14 – but they need no
individual singling out. The best perhaps is a Knight at Orton
Longueville. A coffin lid at St Neots with a foliated cross growing out of an animal (is it a dog?) has its parallel at Oakley and
Pavenham in Bedfordshire. The uncommonly large indent in the
slab to a priest at Great Gransden is of c.1330 and a reminder
that brass as a new material had now arrived.‡ But the earliest P.
surviving brasses in the county are of c.1400 (Tilbrook, Sawtry). 334
However, before the C14 can be summarized a postscript is
necessary on C13 and early C14 CHURCH FURNISHINGS. There
are not many, but they are nearly all worth-while: the coffin
chalice found at Stanground, the minor iron scrollwork on doors,

---

* The motif goes on in the Perp churches of Abbots Ripton and Bluntisham.

‡ In Peterborough Cathedral is the indent of a large brass to an abbot who
died in 1321. There is nothing in Huntingdon and Peterborough like the
wooden effigies of the late C13 and early C14 in Northamptonshire. The only
wooden piece, and a very striking one, is the C15 cadaver at Keyston, part of
a monument no doubt such as that of Bishop Fleming at Lincoln.

e.g. at Orton Longueville,* the stone seat or throne at Farcet,
21 the Barnack font with pointed-trefoiled arches and leaf decoration,
the beautiful stall fragment of *c*.1235 at Peterborough Cathedral,
37 the two lecterns at Peakirk and Bury, both early C14, and the
latter outstanding, the Dec screen at Offord Darcy and the Dec
doors at Brampton and Castor, and the wall paintings at Old
Weston and, far more rewarding, at Peakirk. Included among
the themes represented is that of the Three Quick and the Three
Dead.

43   This theme repeats in the wall paintings at Longthorpe
Tower, perhaps the most interesting of their date, *c*.1330, in
the country. They were only discovered after the Second World
War and have therefore been neither over-restored nor neglected.
They give the most vivid impression of civilized life in a manor
house. Of other SECULAR BUILDINGS Huntingdon and Peterborough have quite some of more than local interest, foremost
the late C12 upper hall of Hemingford Grey Manor House with
its twin windows, and Northborough Manor House of about
1330–40 with its gatehouse and its hall. The hall has tall windows with reticulated tracery, and still the three doors inside
which led to buttery, kitchen, and pantry. At Longthorpe the
hall also exists. It dates from the late C13, and the tower with
the frescoes was added about 1300. It is rib-vaulted on two
floors. Of the late C13 is the only more castle-like building: the
fragment of Woodcroft Castle. Bodsey House was a house of the
abbots of Ramsey. The C14 chapel survives, and traces of the C13
in the domestic quarters N of the chapel. The chapel has no
features of special interest, but there are parish churches
to tell us what the DECORATED STYLE was like in the
county.

The transition from E.E. to Dec is fluid. In tracery it lies
where the ogee arch comes in. Thus e.g. W towers in the later
C13 had here and there in addition to normal windows and bell-
openings intermediate windows of a more decorative kind. They
are quatrefoil at Orton Longueville, trefoiled-circular at Stanground, quatrefoiled-circular at Alconbury, sexfoiled-circular
with the foils enterprisingly cusped at Buckworth, but of
40 lozenge-shape with flowing, i.e. ogee, tracery at Spaldwick and
Keyston. The Keyston tower, moreover, has the distinguishing
feature of a recessed W porch. Dec windows in the county are

---

* With these scrolls one can compare the stone ornament in the tympanum
of a chancel window at Haddon, and to this one might append the small
incised rose-window-like mass dial in Godmanchester church.

unusually often straight-headed, and straight-headed are even three windows of *c.*1300 – i.e. pre-Dec – at Hemingford Abbots. To pier shapes applies what has been said in the Bedfordshire Introduction on p. 18. The most usual section is octagonal, the most usual arch-shape double-chamfered. This is what in the gazetteer is termed 'standard elements'. Few buildings call for special notice. At Northborough a big rebuilding began in the early C14. The S transept S window has fascinating flowing tracery. Another major example of flowing tracery is the E window of Yaxley. Bluntisham is remarkable for its polygonal apse – a great rarity in England. We have no date for it, and dates are indeed rare for the C14. The proud chancel of Fenstanton was provided by the man who was rector from 1345 to 1352, the chancel of Wistow was consecrated in 1347, and the N chapel at Maxey was started in 1367. Fenstanton and Wistow are Dec, Maxey is the earliest datable Perp.

Fenstanton has a broach spire, and so a little more may now be said about SPIRES, from the C13 to the end of the Middle Ages. The total of over forty has already been referred to. They occur pretty evenly throughout the county, and apart from broach spires (with low or high broaches) there is the type of the spire recessed behind the battlements or parapet of the tower. Of the latter there are nine, one of them with the little flying buttresses connecting it with the tower pinnacles. A few of the broach spires are recessed as well. A specially fine group of spires is W of Huntingdon, with Easton, Ellington, and Spaldwick. The tower of Houghton turns octagonal for a short top bit before starting on the spire, and Grafham and Old Weston have a similar though more compromising arrangement.

In the C15 and early C16 the blunt, straight end of a tower was preferred, and we may just as well begin the account of the PERPENDICULAR STYLE with the monumental W towers of St John at Peterborough of 1402–7 with polygonal buttresses and four-light bell-openings, Buckden of *c.*1430–40, Eaton Socon, Elton, Glatton, Great Staughton, St Mary at Huntingdon, St Ives, and so to St Neots of *c.*1490–1535 and Conington of *c.*1500. These towers mostly have decorative quatrefoil friezes, and St Neots, Great Staughton, and quite a few others (e.g. Buckden, Eaton Socon) have pairs of transomed two-light bell-openings. St Mary at Huntingdon is specially ornate, but not high. It seems of before 1400. Conington, like St John at Peterborough, has polygonal buttresses and four-light bell-openings. Several of the others have clasping buttresses. With these towers most

of the leading Perp churches have been named. But a good deal
still needs filling in.

48   St Neots is a complete major Perp church. When the tower
was begun, the rest of the church was complete. The character
is uniform and solid. The piers are of the section with four
shafts and four hollows in the diagonals which will, in the
gazetteer, be called the 'standard moulded section', and the
roofs are standard too, of the type by far most frequent in
Huntingdon and Peterborough, i.e. of very low pitch with tie-
beams on shallow arched braces and with bosses at the intersection of principals with ridge beam and purlins. There are also
often figures of angels against the intermediate principals and
other figures against the wall-posts. As for piers, the most inter-
eating ones are those – and there are about ten of them in the
county – which have shafts with capitals only to the arch openings but more or less complicated continuous mouldings to nave
and aisle. Such was done e.g. at Conington, Godmanchester,
Great Gransden, Wistow, and Yaxley. At Stilton the tower arch
is a short tunnel-vault, Hail Weston has an impressive timber-
framed W tower of the type famous in Essex. St Ives possesses
2 one of the very few surviving bridge chapels in England (the
32 altar was dedicated in 1426), Bury a mysterious W addition to
the W tower, probably a chapel. It had a tunnel-vaulted undercroft. Otherwise vaulting in parish churches was confined to
towers (and there often intended and not executed or later removed) and to porches (Buckden e.g.).* So the one major Perp
47 stone vault in the county is the sumptuous retrochoir of Peterborough. The vault is a fan-vault, and it may have been designed
by *John Wastell*, who designed the fan-vaults of King's College
Chapel at Cambridge. Finally the NW tower of All Saints at
Huntingdon, the W tower and S porch of Diddington, and the
NW tower and clerestory of Southoe are of brick, the first C15,
the other two of *c.*1530.

But the earliest major display of brick in the county was
Buckden Palace, the finest by far of the late medieval SECULAR
BUILDINGS. Buckden was a palace of the bishops of Lincoln,
and what remains was built about 1475–90. It is the gatehouse,
59 a piece of curtain wall, and the so-called Great Tower, a keep,
one is tempted to say, built for living, though a great hall
and other domestic quarters are known from excavations to
have existed. The Great Tower was apparently built on the
pattern of that, some thirty years earlier, of Tattershall in

* But Glatton has a vaulted vestry (cf. Bedfordshire).

Lincolnshire. The red brick is used with dark blue vitrified bricks in diapers and more elaborately ornamental patterns. But what there is at Buckden is serviceable rather than splendid. One need only compare with the abbey gatehouse of Ramsey, now partly at Hinchingbrooke, to remember how sumptuous Perp display about 1500 could be. Yet another gatehouse, much simpler and still machicolated, is at Elton, where also the rib-vaulted undercroft of the chapel remains, in the same range, i.e. not the hall-range, of the house. Private stone or brick houses are absent, but the plentiful timber-framed houses of the county go back to the C15. More research on their dating and their interiors must be done. They go on without any drastic change into the C17.

It is curious altogether that there is, in other fields as well, no drastic change at the time of the Reformation. In some counties it is easy to lay one's finger on the very places where Italian Renaissance forms first appeared. Not so in Huntingdon and Peterborough. Take CHURCH FURNISHINGS, which, for the C15 and early C16, have not yet been reported. Metal first. Bells are not fully included in the gazetteer, but it may be worth mentioning that there are four of the C14. Plate begins with a Spanish dish of the early C15 at Upwood and an Italian processional cross of c.1500 at St Ives. Also of c. 1500 are the patens of Farcet and Stow Longa, the latter the earliest piece in the country with a London hallmark. The eagle lectern at Little Gidding is of brass, made in East Anglia, and of a type famous on the Continent. The wooden lectern at Ramsey has a stem of four buttress-like members set crosswise. Of paintings the best (or the most easily recognizable) is the St Christopher at Orton Longueville. Stained glass has nothing much to offer: a complete window at Wistow and a window looking more complete than it is at Diddington. That leaves woodwork. The best set of stalls with misericords is unquestionably at Godmanchester, but the best individual pieces are the three at Brampton. The best set of benches with poppyheads is at Glatton, another good set at Eynesbury. Screens are on the whole uneventful. The best is, again unquestionably, that at Tilbrook with its well-preserved ribbed coving. The Kimbolton screen has painted figures on the dado which, in their mannered elegance, are much above average. St Neots has pretty openwork vine scrolls over the entrance. The pulpit at Fenstanton introduces linenfold panels. Linenfold is an early C16 motif, and on the Farcet pulpit it appears side by side with Early Renaissance.

So there we have arrived, but we do not know at what date. We do not for instance know the date of the very typical Early Renaissance panels with heads in profile in medallions which are displayed at Elton Hall. In short, the ELIZABETHAN STYLE is upon us without our knowing in the county when and how it came about. And this is so, although evidence of the mid C16 is by no means lacking. Only it is not very articulate. About 1550 Sir Richard Williams, alias Cromwell, began to remodel for his secular purposes the abbeys of Ramsey and Hinchingbrooke. On the former the Cromwells worked in stone, on the latter in brick. At Ramsey the house seems to have assumed an E-plan at once, though with towers over the top and bottom strokes. The windows – one has recently been uncovered in a good state – were mullioned and transomed and already without arches at the top of the lights. Several problems remain unsolved, but the impression is that this house was fully Elizabethan. Hinchingbrooke never assumed any regularity, but again there were 61 windows without arches to the lights, and there were also canted bay windows.* The little Grammar School at Godmanchester is of c.1559, also of brick, and has unarched window-lights too. Work on Hinchingbrooke and Ramsey must still have gone on when William Cecil, future Lord Burghley, began to remodel 64 and soon to enlarge out of recognition Burghley House outside Stamford. When he had finished with it in the eighties it was, one might well say, the grandest of all Elizabethan mansions. He began in the mid fifties with the E range and left it irregular. The kitchen still has a Gothic rib-vault, the great hall buttresses, arched lights to the large transomed windows, and a double-66 hammerbeam roof. But the fireplace in the great hall, which may be dated c.1562, is, with its crowning pediment, purely 65 classical, and so is the Roman Staircase of a year or two later. The pattern, especially for the tunnel-vaulting, is no doubt such French staircases as Lescot's in the Louvre, and we know indeed that Burghley was fully aware of what went on in France and also the Netherlands. In the late sixties Burghley concentrated on Theobalds near London rather than on the distant Burghley House, but in the seventies he returned, and now built at one 67 go the three grandiose W, N, and S fronts. They carry dates 1577, 1585, and 1587. With its turrets and its innumerable chimneystacks, Burghley is the most improbable apparition in the gentle landscaped grounds outside Stamford. In size and in

68   * The generous bow window is dated 1602 and originally had an open ground floor.

THE PLATES

*

In the captions, Bedfordshire is abbreviated (B), Huntingdon (H),
and the Soke of Peterborough (P).

1 *Townscape*: St Ives (H), church

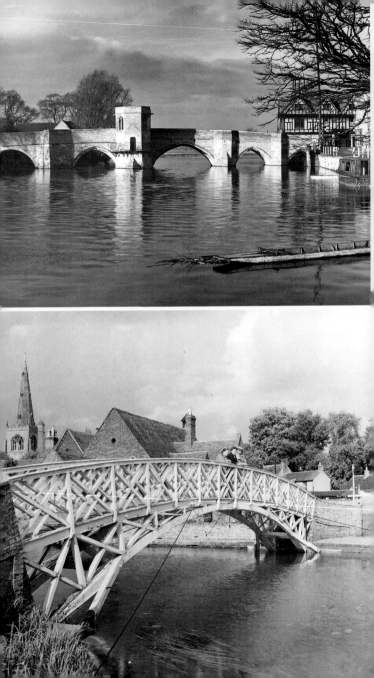

2 (above left) *Townscape*: St Ives (H), bridge, *c.*1415
3 (below left) *Townscape*: Godmanchester (H), Chinese Bridge, 1827
4 (above) *Townscape*: Woburn (B), High Street

(left) *Windmill*: Stevington (B), 1783

(below left) *The Fens*: Near Upwood (H)

(right) Peterborough Cathedral (P), Hedda Stone, *c.* 800

(below right) Fletton (H), church, friezes, ninth century (first half)

9 (left) Great Paxton
(H), church, north
arcade, c. 1000

10 (below) Witter-
ing (P), church,
chancel arch Saxon,
arcade arch Norman

11 (right) Barnack
(P), church, Christ
in Majesty,
c.1000–50

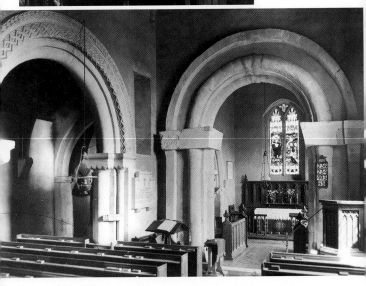

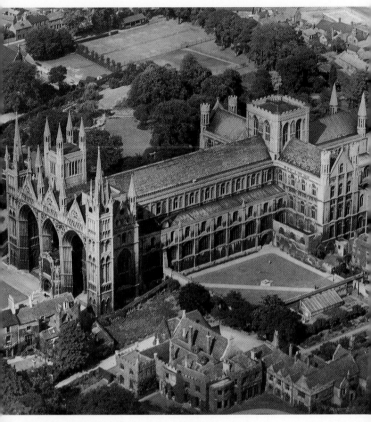

12 Peterborough Cathedral (P), begun 1118

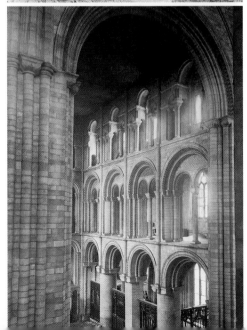

15 (left) Dunstable
Priory (B), nave,
c. 1150–60 and
c. 1180–90

16 (right)
Huntingdon (H),
Cromwell Museum,
c. 1170–90

17 (below) Ramsey
(H), church,
c. 1180–90

18 (left) Peterborough Cathedral (P), monument to an abbot, c. 1200

19 (below left) Dunstable Priory (B), font, Norman

20 (right) Eaton Bray (B), church, font, c. 1235–40

21 (below right) Barnack (P), church, font, thirteenth century

22 (left) Chesterton (H), church, south arcade, waterleaf capital, *c.* 1200

23 (below left) Studham (B), church, consecrated 1220, stiff-leaf capital

24 (left) Eaton Bray (B), church, south arcade, c. 1220, leaf bracket

25 (below left) Little Staughton (B), church, south arcade, c. 1300, capital

26 (left) Felmersham (B), church, west front, *c.* 1220–30/40

27 (above) Dunstable Priory (B), north-west doorway, mid thirteenth century.

28 Ramsey Abbey (H), gatehouse, monument to Ailwin, c. 1230

29 (left) Eaton Bray
(B), church, north
arcade, c. 1235–40

30 (below left)
Alconbury (H),
church, chancel,
c. 1300

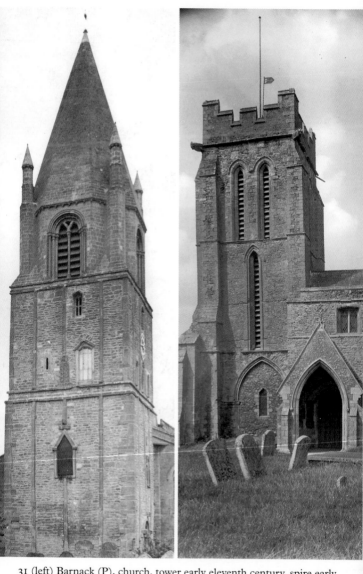

31 (left) Barnack (P), church, tower early eleventh century, spire early thirteenth century
32 (right) Bury (H), church, tower, thirteenth century

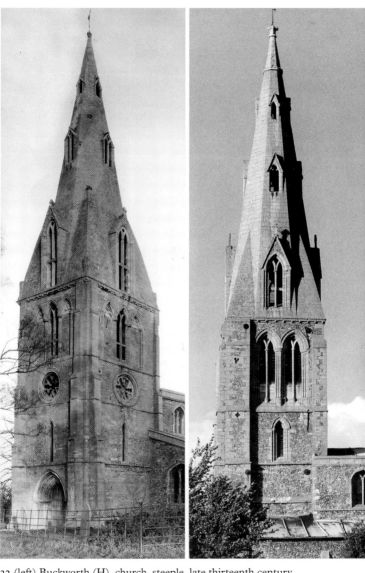

33 (left) Buckworth (H), church, steeple, late thirteenth century
34 (right) Warboys (H), church, steeple, thirteenth century

35 (left) St Ives (H), church, double piscina, mid thirteenth century(?)

36 (below left) Turvey (B), church, south door, thirteenth century

37 Bury (H), church, lectern, early fourteenth century

38 (left) Yaxley (H), church, heart burial of William de Yaxley (?) †1293

39 (below) Conington (H), monument to a Franciscan tertiary, c. 1300

40 (right) Spaldwick (H), church, east window, latest thirteenth century

41 (below right) Fenstanton (H), church, east window, c. 1350

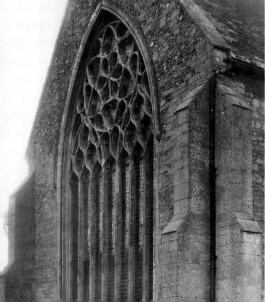

42 (left) Luton (B), church, font canopy, *c.* 1330–40
43 (above left) Longthorpe Tower (P), wall painting, *c.* 1330
44 (above right) Blunham (B), church, alabaster Virgin, fourteenth century

45 (left) Higham Gobion (B), church, north arcade, *c.* 1300

46 (below left) Marston Moretaine (B), church, north arcade, Perpendicular

47 (right) Peterborough Cathedral (P), retrochoir, begun *c.* 1500

48 (left) St Neots (H), church, mainly complete by 1486

49 (below left) Conington (H), church, *c.* 1500

50 (right) Eaton Socon (H), church, Perpendicular

51 (below right) Willington (B), church, *c.* 1530–40 (?)

52 (left) Clifton (B), church, alabaster monument, early sixteenth century
53 (below left) Stevington (B), church, bench end, early sixteenth century
54 (below) Wilshamstead (B), church, nave roof, Perpendicular
55 (bottom) Tilbrook (H), church, screen, Perpendicular

56 (left) Luton (B), church, Wenlock Monument, Perpendicular

57 (below left) Totternhoe (B), church, north-east respond, c. 1500

58 (right) Leighton Linslade (B), market cross, fifteenth century

59 (above) Buckden (H), Great Tower, *c.* 1475–90, and church tower,
c. 1430–40
60 (above right) Hinchingbrooke (H), gatehouse from Ramsey Abbey,
c. 1500 (*Copyright Country Life*)
61 (right) Hinchingbrooke (H), north front, bay windows, mid sixteenth century with materials of *c.* 1500

62 (left) Turvey (B), monument to the first Lord Mordaunt †1560, by T. Kirby

63 (right) Tilsworth (B), church, monument to Gabriel Fowler †1582

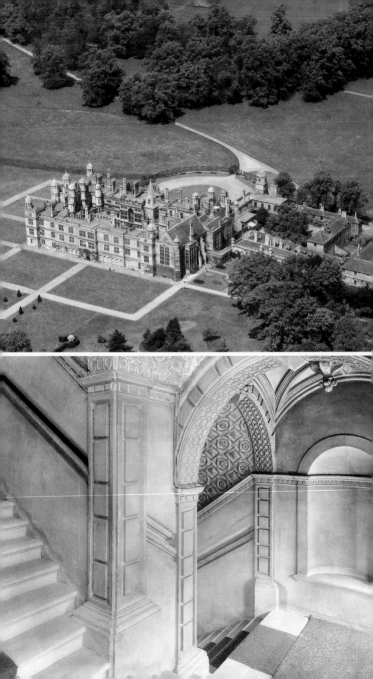

64 (above left) Burghley House (P), *c.* 1555–*c.* 87
65 (left) Burghley House (P), Roman Staircase, 1560s(?) (*Copyright Country Life*)
66 (above) Burghley House (P), fireplace in the Great Hall, *c.* 1562(?) (*Copyright Country Life*)

67 (above) Burghley House (P), west front, c. 1577 etc.

68 (left) Hinching-brooke (H), south front, bow window, 1602

69 (above right) Stibbington Hall (H), façade, 1625

70 (below right) Ampthill (B), Houghton House, begun c. 1615 (?), centre peices c. 1635–45. Engraving

71 (left) Great Staughton (H), church, monument to George Wauton †1606

72 (below left) Toddington (B), church, monument to Maria Wentworth †1632, probably mid seventeenth century

73 (right) Colmworth (B), church, monument to Sir William Dyer, 1641

74 (above) Camptor (B), monument to Sir Peter and Sir John Osborn, by John Stone, 1655

75 (left) Conington (H), church, monument to Sir Robert Cotton, c. 1675

76 (right) Leighton Bromswold (H), church, pulpit and reader's desk, c. 1630

GOD GRAVNT GRACE. MARGARETE SLANEY

THO^S HVSSEY
ESQ^R M^r
IOHN LAWSON
WARDEN
IACOB BONELL
WARDEN
IOHN MYNN
WARDEN

Oliver fecit.

77 (left) Northill
(B), church, stained
glass, by John
Oliver, 1664

78 (right) Leighton
Bromswold (H),
church, tower, 1634

79 (below) Thorpe
Hall (P), by Peter
Mills, 1653–6

80 (above) Thorney Abbey (H), overmantel, *c.* 1660 (*Copyright Country Life*)

81 (above right) Burghley House (P), overmantel in the Jewel Closet, by Grinling Gibbons, late seventeenth century

82 (right) Cockayne Hatley (B), church, stalls from Aulne, 1689

83 (above left) Kimbolton Castle (H), courtyard, *c.*1690(?)

84 (below left) Kimbolton Castle (H), east range, probably by Sir John Vanbrugh, 1707–10 (*Copyright Country Life*)

85 (above) Kimbolton Castle (H), painting in the staircase hall, by G. A. Pellegrini, *c.*1710

86 (right) Wrest (B), pavilion, by Thomas Archer, 1709–11

87 (above left) Little Gidding (H), church, façade, 1714
88 (below left) Hinwick House (B), 1709-14 (*Copyright Country Life*)
89 (above) Bedford (B), town hall (Harpur's School), 1756

90 (above) Woburn Abbey (B), west front, by Henry Flitcroft, 1747–61 (*Copyright Country Life*)

91 (left) Woburn Abbey (B), state saloon, by Henry Flitcroft, 1747/61

92 (above right) Bedford (B), Swan Hotel, by Henry Holland, 1794

93 (below right) Woburn Abbey (B), library, by Henry Holland, 1787–90

94 (left) Cardington
(B), church, monu-
ment to Samuel
Whitbread †1796,
by John Bacon, 1799

95 (below left)
Buckden (H),
church, monu-
ment to Robert
Whitworth †1831,
by Thomas
Rickman

96 (right) Carding-
ton (B), monument
to Samuel
Whitbread †1815,
by H. Weekes, 1849

97 (below right)
Flitton (B),
monument to the
Countess de Grey,
by Terence Farrell,
1853

TO THE MEMORY OF
SAMUEL WHITBREAD, OF SOUTHILL, IN THIS COUNTY,
ONLY SON OF SAMUEL WHITBREAD, OF BEDWELL PARK, HERTFORDSHIRE,
BORN 18TH JANUARY 1758, MARRIED 27TH JANUARY, 1788, DIED 6TH JULY, 1815.
ELECTED MEMBER OF PARLIAMENT FOR THE BOROUGH OF BEDFORD 1790,
WHICH SERVED HE AS REPRESENTED TO THE TIME OF HIS DEATH.
A STATESMAN OF UNBLEMISHED INTEGRITY, A RAY OF TRUTH, CONSCIENCE, AND VIRTUE,
BY LOVED FREEDOM AND PEACE,
AND APPLIED IN THEIR HIGHLY TALENTS ELOQUENCE, ENERGY AND PERSEVERANCE,
SINCERE IN HIS ATTACHMENT TO THE CHRISTIAN FAITH,
HE ESCHEWED ALL PERSECUTION AS UNJUST, CRUEL AND UNRIGHTEOUS,
HE NEVER SWERVED IN HIS ENDEAVOURS
TO PROMOTE THE EXTENSION OF RELIGIOUS AND POLITICAL LIBERTY,
THOSE WHO CLAIMED TO BE FOLLOWED HIM BY A FAITHFUL GUIDE,
THOSE WHO DIFFERED FROM HIM RESPECTED HIM AS AN HONEST MAN.

ALSO TO THE MEMORY OF ELIZABETH, HIS WIFE,
DAUGHTER OF CHARLES, FIRST EARL GREY,
BORN 7TH APRIL, 1765, DIED 26TH NOVEMBER, 1846.
SHE WAS INNOCENT, VIRTUOUS, AND CHARITABLE, HER DUTIES WERE HER PLEASURES,
AND DREW FROM HER RELIGION,
HER SWEETEST COUNSEL IN PROSPERITY, AND HER CHIEF CONSOLATION IN AFFLICTION.

98 (above) Wrest (B), by Cléphane, 1834–6, garden front

99 (left) Wrest (B), by Cléphane, 1834–6, staircase hall

100 (above right) Milton Ernest (B), Milton Hall, by William Butterfield, 1856

101 (right) Woburn (B), church, by Henry Clutton, 1865–8

102 (above) Bedford (B), High School for Girls, by Basil Champneys, 1878–82
103 (right) Luton Hoo (B), staircase hall, by Mewès. 1903

104 (above) *Industrial Scenery*: Brogborough (B), brick-works
105 (below) *Industrial Scenery*: Chicksands (B), Antenna

swagger it can compete with any contemporary palace this side
of the Alps. The work includes the vault of the western entrance,
which is Gothic Survival (or Revival?), the fantastic frontispiece in the courtyard crowned by spiky obelisks, open arcading
in the courtyard and on the s front, and interior marvels of
which we know next to nothing.

That nothing in the county can compete in scale or splendour
with Burghley House goes without saying, although Milton of
shortly after 1594, with its long front of seven bay windows and
a porch, makes a proud display. The porch has superimposed
orders of Tuscan and Ionic columns. This motif was taken up,
probably after 1620, at Chesterton, whose porch now stands at
Alwalton, and at Stibbington Hall, dated 1625. Both the 69
Chesterton and the Stibbington porches have big shaped gables,
and a rather more bulbous shaped gable was still built at Glinton
about 1630–40. They were soon to be replaced by Dutch, i.e.
pedimented, gables, and the earliest of these, of the mid C17, is
at Gransden Hall, Great Gransden, but shaped gables, especially
end gables, run on locally till after 1700 (Broom Lodge, Hemingford Grey). Stibbington Hall is a perfect example of the Jacobean manor house on an E-plan and of moderate size. Toseland
Hall is interesting because of its compact plan of three by three
bays, a type of plan which John Thorpe in his book of drawings
experimented with. The house that Sir Gervase Clifton intended to build at Leighton Bromswold before 1608 and that
John Thorpe drew and probably designed, was never built. But
its gatehouse of 1616 is there, with four square, higher angle
towers and a frontispiece with columns and short odd pilasters
and finials over.

The architectural decoration of such houses is mostly closely
matched in FUNERARY MONUMENTS. One need only think of
Lord Burghley's own monument in St Martin's at Stamford
(*see The Buildings of England: Lincolnshire*) or his wife's in
Westminster Abbey to agree. But as for churches there is not a
single church or part of a church of between the Reformation
and 1600, and there are no church furnishings either, except for
the one, probably Late Elizabethan, pulpit at Orton Waterville
which is a gorgeous piece.* The best monuments in village

---

* And except of course for CHURCH PLATE; for here the Elizabethan
Settlement demanded the replacement of chalices and patens by cups and
cover patens, and so about 1570 large numbers of them were commissioned.
If one takes a Cup as one, a Paten as one, but a Cup and Paten together also
as one, the figures are 1559–60 one (Godmanchester), 1564–5 one (Abbotsley,
perhaps foreign), 1568–9 two, 1569–70 fifteen, c.1570 two, 1571–2 two.

churches are either of the four-poster type with recumbent effigies (Upton near Ailsworth † 1633) or of the newer type with kneeling figures facing one another across a prayer-desk. The Dyer Monument at Great Staughton probably of about 1605 has two such couples, with three columns and a lot of rather stiff strapwork on top. The Beville Monument at Chesterton probably of 1611 is similar, but the figures kneel, two facing the other two, and there are only two columns and a pendant in the middle. At Barnack is one of these kneelers' monuments of 1612, and this is signed by *Thomas Greenway* of Derby, a very rare thing still at that time. About 1600 at Conington two Cotton monuments were put up facing across the church two memorials to the Scottish royal family.

Early in the C17 the desire arose among sculptors to get away from standard types and express new conceits. Thus the George
71 Wauton † 1606, at Great Staughton, has the recumbent effigy placed on a slab carried by two caryatids – a Netherlandish motif by origin. Even more original is Mrs Armyne of 1629 at Orton Longueville; for here the monument itself is a black slab on pink alabaster legs, and the rest is just an inscription tablet behind. About fifteen years later the first Earl of Manchester at Kimbolton was commemorated by a black slab on arches and columns with a white cushion on it carrying the inscription and behind two columns and a third high up on a bracket in the middle.

The second quarter of the SEVENTEENTH CENTURY saw much in art and architecture that was new, and we have to examine it in some detail. First of all CHURCHES and church furnishings come back into the picture. The chancel at Helpston has some strange windows dated 1609. They are tall, of two lights, straight-headed, and have a pointed quatrefoil at the top of each light. That indicates the intention not to break away from the Perp tradition. The windows of the Dove Chapel at Upton near Ailsworth are also still entirely Gothic, although the balustrade inside has vertically symmetrical balusters. Nor is the intention to break new ground noticeable in the early C17 brick tower of Morborne and the towers of Godmanchester (1623) and St Thomas Ramsey (1672), both built with the use of old materials. When Thorney Abbey church was restored in 1638, the tendency was the same, and imitation Gothic forms were used. Denton, on the other hand, in 1629 introduced normal i.e. domestic, mullioned and mullion-and-transomed cross windows, i.e. left Gothic conventions behind. The same is true on a much

more monumental scale of Leighton Bromswold. When the
Duke of Lennox rebuilt the tower in 1634, he used, it is true, 78
clasping buttresses and pinnacles, but the pinnacles are obelisks,
and the windows and doorway have round arches on pilasters.
Leighton Bromswold and, side by side with it, Little Gidding
are among the most interesting C17 churches in the whole of
England. This is due to religious and literary reasons as much as
artistic. The incumbent (deacon, not priest) at Leighton Bromswold from 1626 till 1630 was George Herbert, the poet, and
Little Gidding was the place chosen by Nicholas Ferrar and his
mother and then his married brother and married sister for their
religious colony. They went there in 1626, and Nicholas was
ordained deacon. His inspiration came chiefly from the Cambridge Platonists and Juan de Valdes. The Ferrars restored a
small existing church for their purposes. George Herbert restored his large church too, and put a new roof on. A rainwater
head gives the date 1634. Of FURNISHINGS he was responsible
for the pulpit with sounding-board and also the reader's desk 76
of the same design and placed as an exact counterpart; for
Prayer and Sermon must be given equal right. At the same time
new stalls came in, deliberately in no way different from the
benches, and a low, deliberately not a high, screen, and also
plate. At the same time at Little Gidding the reredos was given
with brass plates for the texts, the choir panelling, and the seating and the delightful little brass font with its delightful crown-
like brass cover. Of brass also is the chandelier of Dutch type
in Catworth church which has the – for England early – date
1666.* Otherwise of these years only the pulpit at Yaxley
dated 1631 deserves a place here.

So much for ecclesiastical art and architecture. But in
DOMESTIC ARCHITECTURE just as much was happening. Here
the key buildings are of the mid C17: Thorpe Hall outside Peter- 79
borough, 1653–6 by *Peter Mills*, and Thorney Abbey formerly
in Cambridgeshire, 1660 etc. by *John Lovin* of Peterborough,
may be to Mills' designs as well. Both are superficially of the
new type established by Inigo Jones and brought to perfection
in Roger Pratt's Coleshill begun about 1650. They are square
blocks with large hipped roofs and dormer windows. The windows have (or had) mullion-and-transom crosses, and some at
Thorpe Hall have pediments. That far they are indeed like

* Brass chandeliers of the Dutch types went on unchanged for a long time.
We find them at Somersham with the date 1787 and at Little Gidding even
of 1853 (a copy of a predecessor ?).

Coleshill. But then – even more in the garden piers at Thorpe and the wooden doorcases inside the same house – odd, Mannerist details come in, and they multiply in the panelling and
80 chimneypieces: pilasters vertically halved, lugs or ears in unexpected places, volutes, and also fat garlands. The Haycock Inn at Wansford, an uncommonly large and architecturally serious inn, of probably about 1670, partakes of some of these mannerisms.

The staircase in Thorpe Hall belongs to the most progressive type of its time. It has richly carved openwork foliage panels instead of balusters. The same motif, yet richer, occurred in the staircase of Hinchingbrooke which dated from c.1663 and of which only single panels survive. These were major buildings; locally the current forms were not quite the same. The Guildhall of Peterborough of 1671, the first public building (apart from the little Godmanchester Grammar School) here to be introduced, is admittedly not provincial in style. Its Tuscan columns for the open ground floor, its cross-windows, and its hipped roof are up-to-date, though the steep middle gable was perhaps old-fashioned, but if one goes into the villages, one sees different things; first, about 1670–80, three-bay brick houses with square porch and either two tiers of brick pilasters (The Limes, Spaldwick) or a framework of broad vertical and horizontal brick bands (Manor Farm Sawtry, 1672, with shaped end-gables; Swan and Salmon Little Stukeley, 1676). It is entertaining to watch how this kind of house gradually gets classical. A doorway at Farcet of 1684 has a pediment, but not yet quite a classically correct one. The doorway of Ivy House, Spaldwick of 1688 has the real thing and also giant angle pilasters, though in the middle still two tiers.* The classical type, i.e. the type say of Eltham Lodge by May rather than of Coleshill, is accomplished at Walden House Huntingdon with its row of giant pilasters and the Dutch garlands below the first-floor windows. It is also accomplished more simply but on a much larger scale in 1690 in the stables of Milton – eleven-bay centre, four-bay wings – and there the architect was probably *Talman*, i.e. the man who was second in command during these years under Wren in the Office of Works. The courtyard of Kimbolton Castle on the other hand, possibly by the joiner *William Coleman* and probably of about 1690, is provincial, with its schematic leaf

* Similarly one can watch the longevity of mullioned windows: to 1685 in Model Farm House, Upton near Ailsworth, and even to 1708 in Manor Farm, Walton, though by then they are symmetrically placed.

decoration above the windows. The finest room inside is the White Hall with its panelling and pilasters and hanging garlands. But the finest late C17 rooms in the whole county are of course those in Burghley House. Here *Grinling Gibbons* himself carved 81 his floral and foliage displays, and here *Verrio* and *Laguerre* painted (not so well).

In CHURCHES hardly anything of the mastery of the wood carvers appears. There is just one pretty pulpit at Eynesbury, late C17 in date, and there are the reredos with coupled Ionic pilasters, the altar table on wrought-iron supports, the pulpit, and the handsome three-arched screen at Chesterton. All this is of *c.*1730, when the church was remodelled with arched windows and the porch received its entrance with a Gibbs surround. Much more interesting is Little Gidding, not Nicholas Ferrar's church, but its replacement of 1714, eminently suited, however, to the pervading mood. The small façade is quite out of the 87 ordinary, stone-faced with angle pilasters carrying little obelisks, a doorway a little Archerish in its details, and an odd bellcote with a steep pyramid on top pierced by three precisely oblong holes. The panelling etc. inside is in self-conscious imitation of that of Nicholas Ferrar's time, and the seating is college-wise. One would dearly like to know if that also followed Nicholas Ferrar's precedent.*

We have now only to bring the FUNERARY MONUMENTS up to date, and then we shall be ready for the Georgian style. There are few of note, really only about half a dozen. The first is in All Saints Huntingdon and is interesting only because it has the open scrolly pediment typical of about 1700 and after and yet commemorates a death in 1636. The second is at Marholm and commemorates a boy who died in 1646. He is recorded with a free-standing bust in front of a black needle-obelisk. Such busts became fashionable at about that time, and at Conington two Cottons who died in 1631 and 1662 are represented by busts, but apparently not before about 1675. Both are good also in the surrounds, but the bust of Sir Robert is of a quality not 75 often matched at that early date in the whole of England. The fourth is by *Grinling Gibbons* (Conington † 1702), but nothing very special. The fifth, at Hemingford Abbots, commemorates a Regius Professor of Greek at Cambridge and hence has an inscription partly in Greek. The surround includes a baldacchino

---

* One Early Georgian NONCONFORMIST CHAPEL is worth recording, though for its early date only: the Baptist Chapel at Great Gransden of *c.*1735–40, quite a plain three-by-three-bay house with a hipped roof.

and the familiar cherubs' heads. He died in 1712. Seven years later Earl Fitzwilliam died, and he is portrayed standing on his monument at Marholm. This had become a fashionable way of providing monuments about 1700. The Fitzwilliam Monument at Marholm is by *Fisher* of Camberwell. *Robert Taylor Senior*'s monument in Peterborough Cathedral on the other hand, though the death commemorated is 1720, goes on with the semi-reclining effigy.

The GEORGIAN AGE had begun in 1714. It has nothing more to contribute to churches and church furnishings than has already been said, and hardly anything to church monuments. That leaves us with the development of secular architecture. At the beginning all interest is focused on *Vanbrugh*'s Kimbolton Castle, the fourth Earl of Manchester's mansion. This was of course a remodelling job. Parts of the castle and the

83 whole of the courtyard were there. Vanbrugh in 1707–10 provided

84 the rather austere façades, castellated mostly to make it, as he wrote, 'a masculine show', but with the E front partly higher and provided with a two-column giant portico *in antis*. The columns are Tuscan, as Wren and Vanbrugh liked it. This probably excludes *Alessandro Galilei*, who was consulted in 1714 and in some details followed by the Earl. More festive is the entrance to the E range from the W, i.e. the courtyard. Here there are giant pilasters, and the wide staircase with its wrought-iron railing leads up to a pedimented doorway. Inside *G.A.*

85 *Pellegrini* painted the staircase, the boudoir, and the chapel. They are about the finest decorative painting of the whole period in England. The large and monumental gatehouse is by *Robert Adam c.*1765, and it is gratifying to see how this great and agile designer expressed his respect for Vanbrugh.

Kimbolton has segment-headed windows. Wren had used these at Hampton Court, i.e. in 1689 etc. In Huntingdonshire they appeared for the first time at Hemingford Grey House in 1697 and then, together with giant pilasters, panelled parapets, staircases with twisted and then slender and ornamental turned balusters, in several Queen Anne and Early Georgian houses. The finest George II staircase is in Little Paxton Hall. It dates, like the beautiful doorway and the plasterwork, from 1738. Another excellent, if less spectacular, house of those years (1746) is Farm Hall at Godmanchester. The Town Hall of Huntingdon of 1745 with an extension of 1817 must also be mentioned in this context, and the ample plasterwork and one very grand chimneypiece, all of *c.*1760, at Elton Hall. About ten or fifteen

years earlier Milton had received its new s front, the Huntingdon and Peterborough companion-piece to the s front of Woburn
Abbey in Beds. Both are by *Flitcroft*, both are strictly Palladian,
and both have gorgeous rooms with partly Kentian and partly
Rococo decoration. *John Carr* about 1800 added a room with an
ample bow and Adamish decoration. In the gardens *Chambers*
put up a Temple with a Corinthian front in 1774–6, but there
are also Gothick buildings. The earliest appearance of the
GOTHIC REVIVAL in the county is *Capability Brown*'s Orangery
at Burghley. This dates from before 1763. Whether his neo-
Jacobean Bath House is so early as well, we cannot say. Some
Gothic remodelling took place at Elton Hall about 1783, and
Soane's minor alterations at Ramsey Abbey made in 1804–6
use pointed windows too. Capability Brown had bought himself
the manor of Fenstanton, and there he is buried. His monument
– he died in 1783 – is plain though not small and also Gothic in
detail.* That of his widow, dated 1793, was made by *Coade*, i.e.
is of Coade stone. The modelling is no doubt by *Bacon*. Bacon
also did two monuments († 1781 and † 1790) at Warboys. The
alternative Classical–Gothic in MONUMENTS remained throughout the C19. *Westmacott*'s monument at Bainton († 1805) is
Grecian, *Flaxman*'s at St John Peterborough († 1826) is Grecian
too, and *Chantrey*'s at Orton Longueville (1827) at any rate
classical (and rather cold), but *Rickman*, the amateur architect
and inventor of the terms E.E. – Dec – Perp, signed a large
Gothic triptych tablet at Buckden with a date of death of 1831. 95
Gothic finally is the most ambitious of funerary monuments of
the VICTORIAN AGE in the county, that to Mr and Mrs Rowley
at St Neots. It was designed by *F. A. Walters* and carved by *Earp*
and is as late as 1893. By that time one might expect a deeper
understanding of what the Middle Ages meant and no longer a
mere imitation of all the details. *William Morris* had preached
this from the seventies and worked in that spirit already much
earlier. His stained glass at Peterborough Cathedral is as early as
1862 and yet already far forward on the way out of historicism.
It stands alone in its superb quality. VICTORIAN ARCHI-
TECTURE has nothing to offer in the secular field – what *Blore*
did at Hinchingbrooke and Ramsey lacks distinction – and
nothing in the ecclesiastic, save for one church by *Butterfield*:
Waresley of 1857. This was preceded by two jobs carried out in

---

* One reminder of the CHINOISERIE fashion of the C18 is the two bridges
at Godmanchester of which the more prominent and better preserved one 3
is as late as 1827.

the neo-Norman fashion in the 1840s (the E end of Thorney by *Blore* of 1840–1 and the former St John Evangelist at Huntingdon by *W. G. Habershon* of 1845) and by Pugin's small Catholic church of 1843 at St Ives, re-erected from its original site at Cambridge and an endeavour towards a correct C13 vocabulary. Butterfield's Waresley has one great moment inside, and in its chancel exhibits to perfection his faith in structural polychromy. *Scott* did a successful addition to All Saints at Huntingdon in 1859, *Temple Moore* the sensitive, quite original design for All Saints at Peterborough in 1894, and *Stokes* a less interesting design for All Souls, also at Peterborough, in 1896.

And with that church of seventy years ago we can stop. Nothing has since appeared in Huntingdon and Peterborough that ought to prolong this introduction – recent serviceable schools yes, a few recent office buildings at Peterborough yes, but there would be no justification in commenting on them individually.

FURTHER READING

The Victoria County Histories (VCH) have done Huntingdonshire completely (1926–36). In addition there is the volume of the Royal Commission on Historical Monuments (1926), complete or intended to be complete to 1714 but silent for anything after that. For the Georgian century the best source is *Country Life* with its detailed articles on important houses. In addition Hunts matters are dealt with in the *Transactions of the Cambs. and Hunts. Archaeological Society* and the *Proceedings of the Cambridge Antiquarian Society*.

For individual places, Huntingdon and Godmanchester have Mr P. G. M. Dickinson's excellent *Official Handbook* (1964), and Mr Dickinson has written a number of pamphlets on other Hunts places, all valuable.

GEOLOGY

See Introduction to Bedfordshire, p. 29.

PREHISTORY OF HUNTINGDON AND PETERBOROUGH
BY DEREK SIMPSON

No field monuments in the county can be ascribed with certainty to the prehistoric period. Intensive cultivation and gravel quarrying have obliterated surface traces of sites in the river valleys where small finds indicate the main weight of settlement. A number of these sites destroyed by cultivation can still be detected from the air, and doubtless detailed aerial reconnaissance work of the type carried out on the gravels of the Welland and Warwickshire Avon would reveal a great many more such sites. At present, however, the prehistory of the area is revealed by small finds rather than sites, and this introduction to the prehistory of Huntingdonshire will necessarily be brief.

The earliest evidence of human activity is provided by numerous finds of flint hand-axes of Acheulean type from the gravels of the Nene and the Ouse. One of the most prolific areas is Woodston, where hand-axes and other flint tools have been found in association with bones of mammoth, cave bear, horse, and reindeer. A number of these bones appear to have been split by human agency, presumably for the extraction of marrow. Other Palaeolithic tools have been recorded from Old Fletton, Orton Longueville, and Orton Waterville.

For the appearance of early farming communities in the area from c.3000 B.C. the evidence is even more scanty. To this period belong the polished stone axes from Pondersbridge, Godmanchester, Hartford, and Brampton. In the Nene valley stray finds of leaf-shaped arrowheads and other flintwork attest to the presence of Neolithic communities in the area, and at Little Paxton a flint working site has been located. The Late Neolithic Beaker groups (from c.2000 B.C.) are represented by a series of burials in the county. That from Ramsey St Mary's accompanied an inhumation burial in a gravel hillock, possibly a round barrow. At Somersham a large domestic form of Beaker and a handled Beaker mug, probably imitating a wooden form, were recovered.

The rite of single grave burial continues into the Bronze Age. Food vessels accompanying inhumation burials are recorded from Fletton and Elton gravel pit; at the latter site the vessel lay between the skulls of two skeletons. Contemporary cremation burials in collared urns, reflecting a continuance of Neolithic burial and potting traditions, are known from Cross Keys Inn (Woodston), accompanied by five shale beads, Fletton, Somersham, and Stibbington. At the latter site the burial lay in a stone cist, in contrast to the more normal pit grave in this area. For the Late Bronze Age one has stray finds of metalwork (e.g. socketed axes from Horsey, Whittlesey Mere, Pidley, and St Neots) and two bronzesmiths' hoards from Horsey (Stanground) containing worn and broken objects intended for melting down and re-casting.

A number of sites in the county have produced haematite-coated pottery and other, coarser Early Iron Age A wares. These finds come from grain storage pits re-used as rubbish pits and indicate the presence of farmsteads, although none have been scientifically excavated (e.g. Woodston; Wrayhouse Farm, Little Paxton). The most interesting discoveries come from a brickyard at Fletton, where a brushwood platform secured by wooden piles provided a living area. Finds from this site, other than pottery, included a hafted iron knife and an axe and spear ferrule of antler. The final phase of prehistory in the century before the Roman Conquest is marked by the appearance of Belgic wheel-turned pottery (e.g. Weybridge Farm, Alconbury) and coins of Tasciovanus and his son Cunobelin indicating the incorporation of the area in the territory of the powerful tribe of the Catuvellauni.

ROMAN REMAINS

See Introduction to Bedfordshire, p. 34.

THE COUNTY OF
HUNTINGDON AND PETERBOROUGH

*

ABBOTSLEY

ST MARGARET. Of brown cobbles; Dec and Perp. Dec the N
aisle, according to the two-light windows with reticulation
units, and the four-bay arcade with quatrefoil piers and thin
shafts in the diagonals. Dec, though much restored, the S
aisle too. The doorway anyway is reliable, and the S arcade
with standard motifs looks in its detail even earlier than the
N arcade. In the aisle is an ogee-headed recess with crockets
and buttress-shafts. The long tendril with flowers in one
moulding is reminiscent of Swineshead and Yelden in Bedfordshire. In the vestry W wall outside a re-set niche of very
pretty details. Perp W tower, the figures of the pinnacles sup-
posedly Elizabethan. The chancel is by *Butterfield*, 1861, with
the N vestry and N porch, but there is nothing that could reveal
him at once. – SCREEN. Under the tower arch. Partly (dado)
Perp. – PAINTING. Interesting Flemish late C15 Adoration
of the Magi. The scene is in demi-figures, which is rare. –
STAINED GLASS. In the N aisle E window old bits. – The E window and the one N and two S windows in the chancel must be
by *Gibbs*, Butterfield's protégé. – PLATE. Cup of 1564–5, an
early date.

ABBOTS RIPTON

ST ANDREW. Externally all Perp, of different materials and
dates, with windows with two-centred arches and panel
tracery, and four-centred arches, and also – in the tower W –
uncusped. The bell-openings of the tower may well be post-
Reformation. E.E. S doorway and E.E. S arcade piers. But the
spacing of the bays is too wide for E.E. work, and the arches
are Perp. So is the W respond. The N arcade is Perp throughout, with capitals to the shafts towards the openings, a moulded
continuous order, and the outer order or hood-mould given
its own minor shafts with capitals towards nave and aisle. In
the S aisle the Perp windows are set internally in much wider
blank arches. Perp one-bay N chapel. The chancel roof has

figures against the wall-posts. – FONT. Octagonal, Perp, with plain quatrefoils. – PLATE. Plate of 1656–7; Flagon of 1744–5; two Cups of 1828–9. – BELL. One bell is of *c.*1400, by *William Dawe.*

(ABBOTS RIPTON HALL. Said to be C18, but the appearance dominated by what *Salvin* did in 1856.)

1090

AILSWORTH

ROMAN VILLA. The site of a house of the corridor type lies SW of the station beside the Nene, *c.* ½ m. upstream of the ford. It was found by E. T. Artis in the C19. The general layout (only the NE wing was excavated), with hypocausts, mosaic floor, and further tessellated pavement, seems to have been similar to that of the villa at Apethorpe (Northamptonshire).

1070

ALCONBURY

ST PETER AND ST PAUL. An E.E. church of high quality, certainly in two of its elements, the steeple and the chancel. The steeple has a W lancet, then a circular window with a quatrefoil, long bell-openings of two lights with bar tracery, and a spire with high broaches and three tiers of lucarnes. The lowest ones are large and of *c.*1300. The arch to the nave is small and triple-chamfered.* The chancel is late C13 too. The windows are lancets – three very slightly stepped in the E wall – or have Y-tracery. The N doorway has a rounded-trefoiled head. Traces of a S doorway can also be seen. The buttresses are slightly chamfered, and the chamfers end charmingly in a little concavity at the top. Inside, the chancel
30 is quite excellent. It not only has rich shafting to the E lancets, but all along the N and S walls close high blank arcading on shafts – six full arches and at the W and E end the baffling half- and two-thirds arches which the E.E. style never minded, though they contradict so much an ideal of purity which we cannot help attributing to it. Below the E window are three recesses, arranged symmetrically – cupboards probably. The chancel arch matches. The nave arcades cannot have been done much after the tower, yet must be later, though not later than the chancel. This dating is based on the fact that the tower in its position presupposes the S arcade where it is, but a N arcade some feet further S. On the other hand, the chancel

* The base of the tower was rebuilt in 1877 by *Ewan Christian.*

arch is centred with the nave. So, when the arcades were
built, that to the N was set further N than a preceding N arcade
or nave N wall had been. The details of the arcades (standard
elements) are hardly later than 1300. The clerestory has
plain Y-tracery, and that also means late C13. In the S aisle are
a W lancet, a late-C13-looking doorway with fine mouldings,
and a window with bar tracery. The nave buttresses are
chamfered, as in the chancel. There is also a Perp and a Dec
window, the latter with reticulated tracery, and a low tomb
recess. The N aisle has more reticulated windows, and a doorway with continuous mouldings. So that will be c.1330. Good
Perp roofs of chancel and N aisle. In the chancel angels against
the intermediate principals, in the aisle figures against the
wall-posts, holding shields and various other things. – (PUL-
PIT. With some original Perp tracery. GMCH) – PLATE. Cup
of 1634–5, gilt inside, and Paten Cover of the same date.

BRIDGE. In the middle of the Green. C15, with four pointed
chamfered arches.

DIRECTION STONE. In the middle of the A1, near the Alconbury Weston turning. Square, with a ball-finial. Hands point
in different directions, and inscriptions tell you how far it is to
Huntingdon, Cambridge, Buckden, and Sutton, and how far
to London *via* Huntingdon, *via* Cambridge, and *via* Buckden.

ALWALTON   *1090*

ST ANDREW. A church rich in interest externally as well as internally. The W tower is early to late C13, with clasping buttresses, several lancets, an arch to the nave with keeled main
shafts to the responds, the simplest moulded capitals, and
double-chamfered arches, twin bell-openings with mid-shaft
and plate tracery and a blank arch either side of each twin.
Corbel-frieze, battlements, spirelet. The transepts are later
than the tower, but still C13. They each have at their end a
large three-light window with three trefoiled circles in bar
tracery. To the E they have Y-tracery. That is clearly late
C13. The chancel was done at the same time. Y-tracery with
cusping and a foiled circle in the fork of the Y and similar
motifs. But the E window has reticulated tracery, i.e. is a
generation later. However, the oldest feature of the exterior is
the S doorway, which combines the Norman motif of zigzag
at r. angles to the wall with a pointed arch. This may be called
late C12. The interior takes us back yet farther. The N arcade

is of about 1170. Four bays, low round piers, the capitals with pre-Gothic leaf volutes or crockets, the abaci square with nicked corners. Round arches of two chamfers with broaches. The abacus of the W pier is octagonal and has a waterleaf capital. This represents a lengthening of the arcade at the time the tower was begun. The S arcade is still early C13, three bays, for the same length as the N arcade's four. Slender round piers on water-holding bases, still round arches. The chancel was originally vaulted in two bays. Traces are recognizable. In the chancel simple SEDILIA and recess opposite. The area round the crossing is confused and has not yet been sufficiently explained. The present arches to the transepts are Perp, but they look makeshift. What was in this place before? Also l. and r. above the chancel arch are quoins. What do they represent? Even more puzzling is a blank arch above the blank tower doorway high up in the tower E wall. – STAINED GLASS. Bits in one chancel S window. – PLATE. Cup and Cover Paten of 1569–70; Salver of 1688–9; Cup of 1818–19.

A COTTAGE NE of the church is dated 1645 and has mullioned windows, but the doorway-head straight and no longer four-centred. NE of this is the rebuilt PORCH of Chesterton, the Dryden mansion, demolished in 1807. It must be of c.1625 (cf. Stibbington Hall). It has two-storeyed Tuscan columns and the round-arched doorway below, Ionic columns and a three-light window with transom above, and is surmounted by a shaped gable. In the gable and on the pedestals of the upper columns simple geometrical patterns of an Elizabethan type.

MANOR HOUSE, NE of the porch. This must be of c.1700; for it combines a type of wooden casement characteristic of c.1660–80 with window surrounds of smooth rustication in alternating sizes which belongs rather to the beginning C18. The casements are of three lights, the side lights transomed, the middle light arched without a transom. It is a popular variation on the motif of the Venetian window.

LYNCH FARM, 1 m. NE. The L-shaped house is said to incorporate windows and other details from Chesterton. The windows are mullioned and mullioned-and-transomed. The bay window may also be imported (cf. Elton Hall), and even the small gable. But can the round corner turret be, or is this not rather a piece of Gothic fancy like the round turrets at Elton Hall?

BAINTON
Soke of Peterborough

oooo

ST MARY. The interior first. N arcade early C13. Three bays, circular piers, circular capitals and abaci, double-chamfered round arches. The w bay is later (pointed arch) and was built as a link with the new w tower. This is Dec. Angle buttresses. Each side in addition treated as a giant sunk panel. w window with Y-tracery but ogee details, tall tower arch towards the nave, bell-openings with Y-tracery, ballflower frieze. Spire with two tiers of lucarnes. Dec also the s doorway and the windows l. and r. of it. Dec finally the N chapel (one bay, sunk quadrant mouldings). Late C13 rather than early C14 the two splendid PISCINAS, both not *in situ*: in the E wall of the chancel with a tall gable with naturalistic oak leaves and acorns; in the E wall of the N aisle with crocketed gable and big finial. Perp chancel. In the E wall two brackets for images. – PLATE. Cup and Cover Paten, 1650. – MONUMENTS. Mary Henson † 1805. By *Sir Richard Westmacott*. With a seated mourning young Grecian.

VILLAGE CROSS. Four big square steps and a fragment of the shaft.

ROMAN SITE. *See* Helpston.

BARHAM

1070

ST GILES. Nave, narrow N aisle, and chancel; no tower, but a bellcote of 1842. The s doorway and the three-bay arcade are Transitional between Norman and E.E. The doorway has one order of polygonal shafts, scallop capitals, zigzag set diagonally, and the arch just pointed (an alteration?). The arcade has round piers with square abaci and round arches with only a slight chamfer. The hood-mould also has a slight chamfer. But the capitals are one of the Late Norman waterleaf the other of the E.E. crocket variety. The E bay is wider than the others. The chancel is late C13 with Y- and intersecting tracery. – BOX PEWS. – C17 BENCHES with knobs on the ends (cf. Leighton Bromswold). – PLATE. Cup with bowl of *c.*1570.

BARNACK
Soke of Peterborough

oooo

ST JOHN BAPTIST. Without any doubt one of the most rewarding churches in the county, with interesting work of all periods, none more interesting than that of the early C11 W

31   tower. The exterior has irregular long-and-short quoins, the
        familiar thin, unstructural lesenes or pilaster strips, starting
        in quite an insouciant way even on top of arches or triangles,
        windows with arched and triangular heads, the typical un-
        moulded block-like abaci, the flat bands placed parallel with
        jambs and arch of an opening but at some distance from it,
        and in addition the most curiously moulded tower arch, an
        example of how unstructural Late Saxon architectural detail
        was. One ought to observe specially how, between capitals and
        abaci of the responds (if these terms can be used), the mould-
        ing recedes and rounds the corner instead of forming an
        angle. The form is almost streamlined. At least as noteworthy
        the decorative slabs outside the tower with scrolls branching
        off a stem symmetrically to the l. and r. and birds, one a cock,
        at the top.* The original entrance into the tower was from the
        s. The w recess can never have been more than a recess, as one
        of the lesenes runs up the wall outside behind it. The s door-
        way is now blocked inside by the work done in the C13. This
        consisted of an internal strengthening e.g. by a rib-vault on
        corbels (single-chamfered ribs leaving a large bell-hole open)
        and the addition of the octagonal upper part of the steeple.
        Two big bell-openings of two lights with round arches, triple-
        shafted jambs and a pierced spandrel (i.e. the Y-motif), low
        broaches and, standing on them, tall, plain, polygonal angle
        pinnacles, short spire, or perhaps rather steep-pitched octagonal
        roof. If it is called a spire it must be one of the earliest in
        England. The angles of the Saxon nave, which was aisleless,
        can also still be seen. It was a little wider than the nave is now.
        In the SE angle a mysterious small arched niche which looks
        almost as if it had been a piscina. The Saxon roof-line appears
        on the E wall of the tower.
            The Norman style is missing, except for a capital and a head,
        re-set in the former rood stair in the s aisle.
            Next in time come the N aisle and N chapel. The chapel is of
        one bay. The capitals of the responds indicate a late C12 date.
        The arch is round but double-chamfered. The arcade is of
        three bays and has slender circular piers and crocket and volute
        capitals with small heads.‡ Square abaci with the corners
        nicked. Round arches, still with zigzags on the wall surface
        and at r. angles to it. The N doorway still has a waterleaf capi-
        tal. So the date of all this is probably the late C12. Small

        * One such bird also now below an image bracket in the s aisle E wall.
        ‡ On one capital an entwined serpent.

clerestory windows are visible from inside the aisle. Only a little later the s aisle and s porch. The arcades now have fine quatrefoil piers with subsidiary shafts in the diagonals and shaft-rings. The capitals have upright stiff-leaf. The arches are still round but have many fine mouldings. The s porch is a superb piece, tall and gabled with a tall entrance flanked by three orders of columns with stiff-leaf capitals. Pointed arch with many mouldings. The sides inside with tall blank arcading again with stiff-leaf capitals. s doorway with once more three orders, stiff-leaf capitals, and a round arch with many mouldings. The stiff-leaf is all early, that is upright with separate single stems. So the date will be within the first twenty years of the century. An odd rib-vault rises right into the gable (single-chamfered ribs). Shortly after the completion of the porch work must have started on the tower, and must have continued slowly.

The chancel dates from *c.*1300–30. At the same time the s aisle was widened E of the porch. Pretty windows with segmental arches and ballflower above them. Simpler Dec the windows in the aisle wall w of the porch and in the chancel. The chancel E window, however, is a true showpiece: five steeply stepped lancet lights and below the arch of each light a cusped arch with a crocketed gable over – a very rare motif (but cf. Milan Cathedral, late c14). Of the same phase the chancel arch, the SEDILIA (hood-mould on heads and also one head with arms held up), the PISCINA (pointed-trefoiled arch leaning forward, as they do above the heads of c13 effigies, and crocketed gable), and also the N aisle windows. Perp vestry of two storeys, Perp s chapel (Walcot Chapel) with richly decorated parapet and battlements. Quatrefoil frieze at the base. Simple windows. Very wide arch to the chancel. In the E wall brackets and very tall richly panelled canopies for images.

FURNISHINGS. FONT. C13. Octagonal. Leaf decoration in segmental lunettes at the foot of the bowl and also as a top band. In between single flowers. The supports are pointed-trefoiled arches of openwork with continuous mouldings. – SCULPTURE. Seated Christ in Majesty, relief, Late Saxon, and of exquisite quality. The draperies are managed as competently as never again anywhere for a century or more, and the expression is as human, dignified, and gentle as also never again anywhere for a century. – Annunciation, under a canopy, SE chapel. The message is carried on rays emanating not from the angel but from the Trinity. Late C15. – STAINED

GLASS. Many windows by a former rector, *Marsham Argles*, one dated 1873. They are remarkably good. – PLATE. Cup and Paten, 1569; Almsdish, 1683; Cup, Paten, and Breadholder, silver-gilt, 1707. – MONUMENTS. Cross-legged Knight, defaced (N chapel). – Lady of *c.*1400; this must have been of fine quality (N chapel). – Grey marble tomb-chest, with recess above and cresting. The recess has a straight lintel on quadrants. Early Tudor (S aisle). – Similar tomb with recess of *temp.* Henry VIII to a member of the Walcot family. Richly quatrefoiled tomb-chest, recess and four-centred arch. The arch is panelled inside. The back wall has one big shield and above it diapering. Top cresting. – Francis Whitestones † 1598 and family. Signed (a rare thing at the time) by *Thomas Greenway of Darby*; 1612. With two groups of small kneelers.

Barnack was known throughout the Middle Ages for its quarries. Peterborough Cathedral is built of Barnack stone. So is e.g. Ely Cathedral. The quarries were exhausted in the C18.

HOUSES. Many enjoyable houses in all directions. (N of the church remains of the MANOR HOUSE, which until 1830 had an aisled C12 hall similar to that at Oakham, Rutland.) SE of the church KINGSLEY HOUSE (Old Rectory), big, mostly Victorian Gothic, but with, at the back, pre-Reformation features such as big buttresses and a pretty oriel window. A house just S of the church is Georgian, of three bays with rusticated surrounds to the doorway and all windows. To the NE of the church, close to the disused railway station, LITTLE-FIELD, a *mixtum compositum* with a canted bay window from a house at Stamford, a small arched Saxon window probably from the church, and a C13 fragment. To its W a cottage (No. 7) with a C13 arch-head with five roses below. (Nos 23–24 has a blocked traceried window hidden by a lean-to. MHLG)

(FEOFFEE COTTAGES, Millstone Lane. C15 with a later E wing. Traceried gable-end. Two arched doorways, two cross-slit windows. MHLG)

WINDMILL. A tower-mill, of Barnack stone, derelict.

WALCOT HALL. *See* p. 360.

HILLS AND HOLES. The area S of the village marks the site of the stone quarry used from Roman times.

BLUNTISHAM

3070

ST MARY. Rubble and brown cobbles. The amazing thing about the church is that it has a polygonal apse which is a genuine Dec piece. That, as everyone knows, is an extreme rarity in

England. The windows are small and of two lights. Dec also the arches from the tower into the embracing aisles; they have three wave mouldings. The tower carries a recessed spire. Perp the high four-bay arcades with a typical pier section. The chancel arch matches. The four-centred aisle windows, another unusual trait (of East Anglian origin), are internally placed under much broader blank arches. So here – which is also not at all usual – the whole of nave and aisles is one unified design. The nave roof stands on good stone corbels, mostly of angels with shields or musical instruments. – FONT. Perp, octagonal. Panelled stem, quatrefoiled bowl, big flowers and also a Green Man on the underside. – SCREEN. Three divisions of the dado kept under the tower. Two are painted crudely with St George and the Dragon and St John Baptist. – STAINED GLASS. In the apse by *Wailes*, 1851. – PLATE. Chalice and Cover of 1569; Paten on foot inscribed 1693; Plate of 1702; Flagon of 1705; undated Salver.

RECTORY. A five-bay, three-storey, early C19 front of yellow brick, but re-used in it a splendid late C17 doorway. The door surround has big lugs and is framed by fluted Corinthian columns carrying a broken straight hood. In the lintel large crossed palm-leaves. The doorway comes from Old Sleep Hall, St Ives. Inside, a fine panelled dining room.

BAPTIST CHAPEL. 1874. Unusual is the best one can say. Red brick with two gables. Lower porch with three gables. The details Gothic.

Opposite a Georgian house of five bays with a door-hood on scrolly brackets.

BODSEY HOUSE

2080

1½ m. N of Ramsey

A country house for the abbots of Ramsey, and as such provided with a chapel (S) and a dwelling (N). In the dwelling part is a corbel with dogtooth decoration, and next to it a lancet window. So that is C13. The chapel seems a hundred years later. It has its SW buttresses and two blocked S windows. In the N wall the entrance arch, detailed in such a way that the outer side is the S side, i.e. that inside the chapel. Also the original wooden bar was fastened on the N side. This means that the doorway was seen as the entrance to the house, not to the chapel, which was probably open to laymen. On the upper floor a main living room with a timber wagon roof and a very large C16 chimneypiece.

2070

BRAMPTON

ST MARY. Perp mostly. But the chancel is late C13, with geometrical tracery, Y-tracery, and similar forms in the windows which are framed inside by giant blank arcading. The coarse PISCINA is late C13 too. The w tower is Dec, though the date 1635 appears over the door. It has set-back buttresses, a doorway with continuous mouldings, pairs of transomed two-light bell-openings, a nice frieze over, and no spire. The arch towards the nave has castellated capitals. Dec also the s doorway, with continuous mouldings too. But the arcades of five bays are Perp, with piers of the standard moulded section and two sunk waves in the arches. Also Perp the four-light aisle windows with uniform panel tracery, the clerestory windows, and the ornate s porch with niches l. and r. of the entrance and a small third niche above the entrance arch. The latter contains the lily-pot of the Annunciation. Good nave and aisle roofs with stone corbels. – FONT. Octagonal, with pointed quatrefoils etc. – ROOD SCREEN. Dec, of one-light divisions, the doors each with two ogee arches carrying a circle with flowing tracery. – The STALLS have MISERICORDS, the best in the county. They represent (a) a man writing – a Knight and lady with a shield – an animal, (b) a carpenter – a man and a woman haymaking (wool-combing?) – a sheep shearer, (c) a woman gleaning – a man reaping and a woman with a sickle – sheaves of corn. – COMMUNION RAIL. Jacobean. Imported into the church. – SOUTH DOOR. With bold Dec tracery. – STAINED GLASS. Much of *Kempe & Tower*; none of much interest, considering the late dates. – PLATE. Cup of Britannia silver, 1721–2; Cup, 1724–5; undated Paten on foot; undated Plate; Flagon, 1743–4; late C16 German brass Almsdish with the Annunciation and stags and hounds, engraved. –MONUMENTS. Sir John Bernard Robert † 1679. According to Gunnis by *William Kidwell*, c.1690. It has a remarkably good bust on top. – J. and T. Miller † 1681 and 1683. Cartouche tablet in the tower. – Mrs Jackson † 1689. Slab in the s aisle. She was Pepys' sister, the last of the Pepys family in the parish.

PEPYS HOUSE. This is the farmhouse where Samuel Pepys was born. It is NE of the church, on the s side of the A-road.

BRAMPTON PARK. Not enough is known of this house. It was rebuilt in 1821–2 by *Thomas G. Whitwell* and much altered in 1825 by *J. B. Papworth* (Colvin). Then there was a fire in 1907,

and a smaller house was built. But a considerable part of the
house is obviously not of 1907 and might well be of the 1820s.
It is castellated and has steep gables and decorated Tudor
chimneys. (Sumptuous interiors of 1907.)

SIGNPOST at the Brampton turn of the A-road. It is a triangular
obelisk of C18 date with hands pointing on one side to Huntingdon and Thrapston, on another to London.

BRINGTON   0070

ALL SAINTS. Slender Dec w tower with low-broached spire.
Three tiers of lucarnes. The bell-openings are of two lights
with a transom. There is a frieze above them. The steep roof
of the chancel is higher than the embattled aisleless nave. The
nave has on the s side an attractive Dec window of uncommon
details. The chancel is mostly 1868 (*Slater*), but the DOUBLE
AUMBRY is C13 work. – FONT COVER. Jacobean. Simple,
conical, with a ball finial. – STAINED GLASS. Bits in one s
window. – PLATE. Plate of 1638–9 (or 1678–9); Cup of 1663–4.

BROUGHTON   2070

ALL SAINTS. Stone w tower with broach spire. Two tiers of
lucarnes. Mostly Perp. Contributions to the building are
mentioned in 1528. Exceptions are the E.E. chancel (see the
remains of the low-side s lancet and the DOUBLE PISCINA),
the nave s doorways of *c.*1300, and the Dec four-bay arcades
of standard elements, but the arches starting with broaches. –
FONT. Square, Norman, with blank arcading. – BENCHES.
Perp and plain. – COMMUNION RAIL. C18. – PAINTING.
Doom; above the chancel arch; C15. The rising of the dead is
most clearly visible. – Also, round the s corner, Expulsion,
and Adam delving and Eve spinning. – PLATE. Cup of 1597;
Paten inscribed 1620. – BRASS. Laurence Marton and wife,
*c.*1490. Only his head, the lower part of his body, and a
shield with rebus are preserved. The figures were 33 in. long.

LOCKUP. Of brick, oblong, and of not much interest.

HOUSE, SW of the church. Late C17, with a square porch. Over
the doorway a frill cut into the bricks. Shaped end-gables.

BUCKDEN   1060

The church with its stone steeple and the dark brick of the
Bishop of Lincoln's palace form an unforgettable picture. The

church is only a few feet away from the Great Tower of the palace, just like Lambeth parish church and Lambeth Palace.

ST MARY. The w tower is Perp. It has set-back buttresses, pairs of two-light bell-openings, and a recessed spire with three tiers of lucarnes. The tower buttresses are built into the church. So the tower came before the nave. As for this and most of the rest, it can be dated by the arms of Bishop Alnwick (1436–9) on a corbel of the nave roof and by known benefactions of his predecessor Bishop Gray (1431–6). More-over, an inscription in the E window referred to John Deeping, Prebendary of Buckden in those years. Externally the em-battled aisles and clerestory belong to them, and the large transomed windows on the S and E sides, the ornate two-storeyed S porch with a quatrefoil base frieze, a niche over the entrance, and battlements and pinnacles. Below the battle-ments a frieze of genre-scenes of animals and on the battle-ments wavy tracery. Inside the porch is a tierceron-star vault with five bosses, the middle one showing the Assumption, i.e. the Virgin surrounded by rays. The nave is divided from the aisles by five-bay arcades, their piers of standard moulded section. The chancel arch matches the arcades. The chancel roof has angels at the feet of the intermediate principals and stone corbel-angels. The nave roof, restored in 1649, is sup-ported on the same type of corbels. The aisle roofs are Perp and similar too. However, a few features are earlier, i.e. the S doorway with two orders of shafts (the slenderer ones keeled), carrying stiff-leaf capitals, and fine arch mouldings, the priest's doorway in the chancel, the SEDILIA and the very wide PISCINA, and the small chancel N doorway. All this is E.E. – FONT. Octagonal, Perp, with pointed quatrefoils con-taining shields. – PULPIT. With good Jacobean tiers of the usual broad blank arches and lozenges in them. – READERS' DESKS. With eight later C16 Flemish reliefs of scenes from the Passion. – STAINED GLASS. In the heads of the S aisle W and E windows original figures. – PLATE. Tall Cup of 1607–8; large Cup and Paten on foot of 1679–80; Paten on foot of 1745–6. – MONUMENTS. In the chancel Bishop Barlow † 1691. Big, black marble inscription plate with a stone surround with garlands. – Bishop Green † 1779. With a very fine roundel at the foot, showing a female figure reading. – Bishop Pelham † 1827. By *E. H. Baily*. White marble, large kneeling woman with a bible on the ground. Rather cold. – Robert Stuart Hurst

Whitworth † 1831. Large white Gothic triptych without 95 figures. Signed *T.Rickman*, architect.* – In the churchyard large obelisk on square base to William Whitworth, c18.

BUCKDEN PALACE. What remains of Buckden Palace is the fragment of something very much larger. The estate was the bishops' of Lincoln already in Domesday, and that palace was in existence certainly in the middle of the c13; for Bishop Grosseteste died at Buckden. What survives is the outer gateway and walling near it, the inner gatehouse, and the so-called Great Tower. They are of red brick with diapers of dark blue vitrified bricks and were built by Bishops Rotherham (1472–80) and Russell (1480–94). In addition excavations have shown NE of the Great Tower the Great Chamber, NE of that the chapel, and SW of that the great hall, probably about 90 ft long. Behind the recent CHAPEL‡ is some masonry of the chapel, built up – when ? – with a pediment on top. To the N of the new chapel is BUCKDEN TOWERS, built in 1872 of red brick, with a porch tower and mullioned and transomed windows.§

The principal building is the GREAT TOWER. It is oblong, 59 three storeys high, with polygonal angle turrets of yet another storey. Is it a keep then ? The question is not easily answered. The best way to decide is to look to Lord Treasurer Cromwell's Tattershall in Lincolnshire, built some forty years earlier and no doubt the pattern on which the Great Tower was modelled. At Tattershall one can prove that the tower was meant to be defensible but at the same time had large and well-equipped living apartments and windows too large for a real keep. Also brick would in any case not be the safest material. So it will be the same at Buckden – the tower was intended apotropaically as much as for its military potential. The tower has to the N a small basement entrance and a ground-floor entrance with a stone four-centred arch. The windows are all of stone and have cusped lights and straight tops. They are of one, two, and three lights. On the ground floor to the W is a window of two plus two lights. There is an elaborate design of blue bricks on the N side, lozenges and a cross, repeated twice. In the W wall is a large cross in blue

* Whitworth is called in the inscription 'of St John's College, Cambridge', and that, as Mr McHardy points out, may explain the presence of Rickman.
‡ The cloister bay in front picks up the motif of the curtain-wall arches – *see below*.
§ In one room inside handsome TILES with women's heads, very probably by *Walter Crane*.

bricks. A large chimneybreast projects from the s wall. The largest chimneypiece is on the ground floor too (four-centred arch), but there is nothing to match the elaboration of plan and detail at Tattershall. The only surviving staircase is in the NE turret. A second existed in the NW turret. The garderobes are placed in the SE turret.

w of the Great Tower is a piece of CURTAIN WALL, rather low to be of much use. The wall-walk behind the battlements stands on shallow segmental arches. The wall connects the tower with a short brick range which in its turn connects directly with the inner gatehouse. The range ends to the s in a stepped gable, and below this is a big, decorative ogee arch. The windows of this range are of brick, two lights and straight-headed. The INNER GATEHOUSE is three-storeyed, with dia-gonal buttresses. The archway has a four-centred head, and there are rooms l. and r. The windows are of two lights, except for one of three. They are again of stone, and the lights are cusped. The top has battlements. To the N is a Victorian extension ending in a stone pavilion dedicated to Napoleon III by the then owner, Miss Eddleston. Her idea was to start here a museum to the Emperor.

The OUTER GATEWAY is plain with a four-centred head and battlements.

A good deal of the OUTER WALL is preserved too, also em-battled.

In the HIGH STREET are a number of pleasant brick houses. One group is N of the palace, the best being JESSAMINE HOUSE of five bays. s of the palace and sw of the church at the main crossing the LION HOTEL, timber-framed, of c.1500, with, in the entrance lounge, moulded beams and a big boss with the Agnus Dei. Opposite the GEORGE HOTEL, a long, three-storeyed C18 brick range, totalling fifteen windows. Top parapet. C17 parts behind.

In CHURCH STREET the VICARAGE, yellow brick, with two canted bay windows, and then the MANOR HOUSE, timber-framed and plastered, of the late C16 and the early C17, though the wall to the street may be medieval. (Several late C16 or early C17 chimneypieces.) Further on in Church Street BRIDGE HOUSE of five bays, Georgian, and opposite it the modest yellow brick ALMSHOUSES of 1840, Tudor style, with the inscription Industry rewarded, Age protected. Then w into SILVER STREET for FIELD HOUSE, again brick, five bays, but with a parapet and a good doorway.

STIRTLOE HOUSE, Stirtloe, 1 m. S, has a semicircular stone porch of columns with fluted capitals. So it dates probably from the late C18.

BUCKWORTH

ALL SAINTS. The church has a splendid late C13 W steeple. Set-back buttresses, a doorway with three orders of columns and a handsome moulded arch, a sexfoiled, cusped rose-window, bell-openings of two lights with Y-tracery, and to their l. and r. one blank cinquefoiled arch. In the heads of these arches are carvings of three radially placed heads and foliated cusps. The spire has high broaches with three tiers of lucarnes. The first tier is very high, transomed and with Y-tracery. Quadruple-chamfered arch towards the nave. The S arcade is late C13 too. Three bays, round piers, double-chamfered arches. The N arcade with octagonal piers is a little later. The N doorway goes with it. Whether the chancel is still C13 or just after the turn of the century must remain open. It has to the S intersecting tracery in one window and a corresponding priest's doorway. The vestry doorway from the chancel is obviously Dec (ogee arch). So are the N aisle W window (reticulated tracery) and the S doorway. Perp S aisle windows and clerestory windows. Perp nave roof with large bosses. But the nave E angles are the oldest thing in the church. They are Norman. – PLATE. Cover Paten of 1671–2.

BURGHLEY HOUSE
Soke of Peterborough*

William Cecil was born in 1520. In 1535 he entered St John's College Cambridge, in 1541 Gray's Inn. His first wife had been a sister of John Cheke of St John's College, the Greek scholar, his second was Mildred Cooke, sister of Edward VI's governor, as Cheke was his tutor. Another sister became the mother of Francis Bacon. When Edward VI ascended the throne and Somerset became Protector, William Cecil was made Somerset's secretary, and, after two months in the Tower in 1550, a Secretary of State. He was knighted at the age of thirty-one, in 1551, became Chancellor of the Garter in 1552, and, after an eclipse in the years of Mary Tudor, Chief Secretary of State in 1558 and Lord Burghley in 1571.

* Stamford St Martin is also in the Soke of Peterborough, but in *The Buildings of England* it is treated as part of Stamford, i.e. in the Lincolnshire volume.

Burghley's father had bought the manor of Burghley at about the time when William was born. His mother lived there, and if any parts of the house still represent the state it was in before William started enlarging and remodelling it, they would be the rooms in the E range facing the E cloister and the courtyard. He was certainly busy already in the 1550s, though he did not finish till the 1580s, interrupted or held up, it seems, by his purchase of Theobalds near London in 1563 and the building of the prodigious house there. Theobalds as well as Burghley show Lord Burghley as a disciple of Protector Somerset, whose Somerset House of c.1548–52 is the watershed in English C16 architecture. Sir William Sharington, also a protégé of Somerset, followed his example at Lacock about 1550, Sir John Thynne, again a protégé, at Longleat. Thynne's brother-in-law was Sir Thomas Gresham, and in his Exchange in London ties with Somerset's architectural tastes are also traceable. Of William Cecil's personal interest in architecture there can be no doubt. Correspondence exists between him and Gresham, who was then English Resident at Antwerp. From this it is clear that Flemings were involved in the work for him, whether at Theobalds or at Burghley. From later correspondence with Sir Henry Norris it is also clear that he knew French architectural books. He refers once to Delorme and to an unnamed book which he had seen in the library of Sir Thomas Smith of Hill Hall Essex, yet another protégé of Somerset. Smith owned e.g. four editions of Vitruvius and Philander's commentary on Vitruvius. Burghley is one of the largest of the Elizabethan mansions. It is an oblong, 240 by 125 ft, with originally two wings projecting N by another 115 ft and, apart from the forecourt between them, a large oblong centre courtyard. The house was in this respect of the type of Longleat. Theobalds, like Somerset House, Holdenby Northants, and the later Audley End Essex, had two courtyards; Wollaton, Hardwick, and Hatfield, none. Burghley has the exciting skyline of Henry VIII's Hampton Court or the Richmond and Greenwich of the earlier Tudor period. Its short square towers, ogee-capped turrets, frilled balustrade, and countless tall chimneyshafts in the form of Tuscan columns are unforgettable, even if they will not easily be remembered in detail. The motifs are those of the Somerset circle, but their combination in this profusion remains unique at Burghley. Moreover, Burghley presents itself in supreme self-confidence on the wide lawns of its C18 garden.

The building is mostly of Barnack stone, three storeys high 64
and characterized by even, large, unadorned, mullioned and
transomed windows. They are the *continuo* which sets off the
other motifs. The style of the whole is uniform in spite of the
variety of elements and motifs, except for the E range, which
is clearly older than the rest, though equally clearly not much
older.

The history of the buildings, as far as published dates help,
begins in 1556 with letters from Cecil's mason and clerk of
the works mentioning the dormer windows of an inner court,
bay windows, the hall, its future screen, and the pantry and a
gallery, both under construction. The kitchen roof also is referred to as a major piece of work yet to be done. The first two
items cannot be linked up with any surviving work, but the
rest most probably connects with the present hall and the
present KITCHEN at the NE corner, which has a stone rib-
vault. The kitchen is extremely lofty, and has a central louvre
towards which the ridge-ribs and the three pairs of tiercerons
in each pair of cells run, and mighty fireplaces. Its Gothic
character would fit a large and utilitarian piece of work of the
1550s. The GREAT HALL to the S, lying twelve steps higher
up, partly due to the contours, partly because of a vaulted
basement beneath,* corresponds stylistically, and it is indeed
called 'half sealed with plaster' in 1561. It still has buttresses
and also arched lights at the top of its three- and four-tran-
somed windows. There are a six-light S window, a very large
bay window to the E, and to the N of this two more large E windows, both however blocked. The steep double hammerbeam
roof, though with Renaissance pendants, has Gothic tracery
in the spandrels.‡ The huge and noble fireplace on the other 66
hand, with its big fluted volute corbels, its broad, bulging
frieze with leaf and geometrical ornament, and its tall concave-
sided chimneybreast ending in a pediment, is purely classical,
and this was going to be the hallmark of further work at
Burghley. Even the circle round the coat of arms with the
four bars connecting it with the four sides of the chimneybreast is a hallmark occurring right to the last stages of work
at Burghley. The motif is derived (once more) from Somerset
House. The fireplace is placed so that the two windows to the
N of the bay had to be blocked. It is therefore either not *in situ*

* The vault is now apparently of the late C17.
‡ The bookcases are Victorian, the twisted columns Belgian, from
Tongerlo, and Baroque.

or, more probably, an afterthought. The flue also had to be taken up diagonally to reach a chimneybreast. An afterthought also could be the two coffered archways to the w, now both blocked at their ends. They could be connected with the continuation of Cecil's building activity in the s range. Of this internally there is now only one indication: the fragment of a ceiling with pendants in the se corner bay of the s range, adjoining the hall and now part of the Grand Staircase. One would like to connect the s arch with a staircase from the high table and the N arch with the screens passage. A letter of 1564 in fact discusses the staircase, the high-table end of the hall, and the s range. But the present screens passage, if thus it can be called, is N of the hall in the centre of the E range, i.e. the axis as seen from the courtyard. The coffered arches here however look Victorian. Wherever the screens passage was, it connects in the accepted way with the kitchen. As one enters the COURTYARD through the present screens passage one finds all ties with the Gothic past cut. The dependence on Somerset House, however, is once again obvious. The centre is a 'frontispiece' of three storeys crowned by a fabulous top storey supported by lions and an obelisk – all this a later addition dated 1585. The main obelisk may well be a reminiscence of Delorme at the chapel of Anet. Two smaller obelisks stand at the corners behind the lions. If all this is of 1585, the storeys below, perhaps up to the beginning of the second, seem to date from c.1562–4, and they repeat the 'triumphal arch' motif which Alberti and Bramante had used in Italy and which had then migrated to Fontaine-bleau and Anet. It is the most characteristic and advanced motif of Somerset House, and appears there, as at Burghley, with pairs of columns separated by niches. The archway in the centre is repeated on the first floor by a deep, coffered giant niche (of Fontainebleau derivation). On the second floor however there is a canted bay window instead, marking a turn from the Franco-Somerset style to the more indigenous mature Elizabethan. The fantastical top follows. The arcades to the l. and r. of the frontispiece were originally open, and this motif of the open colonnade, a continuation really of the medieval cloister, had of course been a universal feature of the Italian Renaissance courtyards. It also was the motif of Gresham's Exchange of the 1560s. At Burghley it seems to have been the work of an Antwerp mason, *Hendrik*, whom Gresham had introduced to Cecil in 1563. The colonnade was converted into a corridor in 1828 (*see* below). As purely

French and Renaissance as the frontispiece is the ROMAN [65]
STAIRCASE N of it and W of the kitchen. The initial source of
this is the typical Florentine and Roman Renaissance staircase,
but the more immediate source is probably the staircase of
Henri II in the Louvre, begun in 1546. The Burghley staircase
has solid walls, with the handrail moulded and partly recessed
into them and tunnel-vaults with geometrical patterns made
up of circles and squares connected by bands, the same that
occur on the Dormer Monument at Wing (Bucks.) in 1552 and
in Northamptonshire houses about 1570 and after. The land-
ings however are still rib-vaulted with pendants. No date is
known for the staircase.

The dating at Burghley is complicated by the fact that, when
Cecil began Theobalds in 1563, he seems to have lost interest
for a while in Burghley. We do not know how far work had
proceeded by then. At any rate the time between c.1575 and
c.1587 must have been very busy again. Cecil's master mason
then was probably *John Symonds*, who, we know, drew a
'plat', i.e. made a design, in 1578. The date 1577 is on the
vault of the W entrance, the date 1587 on the parapet over the
N entrance. It can be assumed that Cecil first intended the W
entrance to be the principal access, in the same relation to the
hall range as e.g. at Kirby and indeed the standard medieval
English manor house. It is also the relation between the two
parts of St John's College. The N entrance came later, and
became by its grandeur the state approach. All these later
parts can now be described topographically.

We shall look at the three remaining façades first, the
courtyard second, the interiors third, the surroundings last.

The WEST FRONT, which carries the date 1577 inside the [67]
gateway, is more conventionally Tudor in plan than the S and
N fronts. The motif of the gatehouse, higher than the rest,
and with four yet higher polygonal turrets, is familiar from
Hampton Court, St James's Palace, Layer Marney, and so on.
The square angle projections occur e.g. at Syon House and
Osterley Park c.1550–75. The even fenestration to which
reference has already been made, and the bay windows in the
recessed portions of wall between the angle projections and
the gatehouse, connect these later fronts of Burghley with
the slightly earlier Longleat. The openwork cresting also can
be compared with Longleat motifs. The archway is closed by a
pair of exquisitely beautiful wrought-iron GATES. These
were seen by Celia Fiennes in 1687 and are probably by *Tijou*.

The SOUTH SIDE is quieter in its rhythm. In the middle it has on the ground floor a nine-bay arcade, originally open, but closed in the late C17, and in its centre provided with a late C17 segmental pediment. In the pediment a shield with thick garlands. The NORTH FAÇADE was completed last. It has a date 1587. Its centre is the unique motif of a triple projection. The first step is square on the ground floor and treated as a loggia with open arches to N, W, and E, but a quarter-circle above; the second is a normal step; the third rectangular on the ground floor and a semicircular bow above. The portal has Tuscan columns. And whereas the N façade (like the S side) has a plain balustrade at its top (cf. Somerset House and Longleat), the bow and the quarter-circle have a varied, more fanciful cresting with little obelisks. To the l. of the N façade is a low projecting wing ending in a four-storeyed tower with an octagonal fifth storey and a cap. A corresponding wing to the r. was pulled down, probably in the C18. Semicircular forecourt and fine iron railings.

The COURTYARD has as its focal point the frontispiece of the E range already described. The fantastic obelisk spire, the two supporting lions in the openwork, and the smaller obelisks behind them make a splendid if somewhat gross final flourish. To the l. and r. of the frontispiece arcading of two bays with Tuscan columns, also originally open. Balustraded balcony on it, recessed first floor, again with balustrade in front of the further recessed second floor. The N and S ranges have a centre motif as spectacular as was the frontispiece before it received its crown of 1585. Tall triple arches flanked and separated by Tuscan columns. Above the middle bay on the first floor a big coffered niche corresponding to, but much higher than, the upper niche of the frontispiece. To its l. and r. big transomed four-light windows (two plus two lights), much taller than those of the wall l. and r. of the centre, i.e. appearing somewhat like bay windows. These less stressed walls are now flush with the centre. But that is an alteration of 1828, made by *Gandy-Deering*. The arcading here did not originally exist, and the walls were plain. The W side has the gatehouse in its centre, balancing, or rather calling for, the frontispiece opposite. The portal again has Tuscan columns, and there is arcading l. and r. which again belongs to 1828. Above the portal bay a curious motif, also frontispiece-like but less classical. Columns above the columns below, but in the middle a transomed window of five lights of which the centre three come forward as a narrow bow in the tradition of Windsor, Henry VII's Chapel, and Thornbury. Big attic with simple geometrical decoration. To the l. and r. lower and simpler first floor with balustrade. The second floor recedes as it does on the N and S sides. Polygonal stair-turrets with caps in the NW and SW angles, adding yet more excitement to this exciting piece of Elizabethan scenery.

As for the INTERIOR, most of what remains of William Cecil's time has already been mentioned. The interiors are mostly by the fifth Earl, executed during the 1680s and 1690s. The Earl was first cousin to the Duke of Montagu, who remodelled Boughton at the same time, and brother-in-law of the Duke of Devonshire, who rebuilt Chatsworth again at the same time. Starting from the Roman Staircase and turning first E, then W, one sees first the CHAPEL. This has an altar painting by *Veronese*, delightfully lively and daring wood-carving, according to Vertue by *Grinling Gibbons*, pretty fitments of *c*.1770 including ten lampholding Virgins of *Coade* stone, a sumptuous scagliola fireplace brought from the monastery of Passo de Arcos near Lisbon, and a ribbed Elizabethan plaster ceiling more probably of 1828 than of William Cecil's time. To the W of the Roman Staircase along the N range the main rooms are the BILLIARD ROOM, with a Gothick stucco ceiling, probably part of work undertaken by *Capability Brown* at Burghley from 1756 onwards, and the BALLROOM lying in the centre, at r. angles to the front and projecting N. Its ceiling and walls were painted by *Laguerre* in 1698. The pictures represent Anthony and Cleopatra, the Continence of Scipio, and the Battle of Cannae. The way in which painting runs without any caesura from ceiling into walls is typical of English painting of the late C17, and it is never satisfactory. After the ballroom rooms with stucco and wood-carving, according to Vertue by *Grinling Gibbons*.* Splendidly free garlands and fruit, birds, etc. The W range, also on the first floor, was originally filled entirely by the long gallery. It was divided into rooms by the fifth Earl, and the most remarkable are the MARQUETRY ROOM with its French furniture, the BROWN DRAWING ROOM with stucco and a *Gibbons* overmantel, the BLUE AND SILVER ROOM, the BLACK AND YELLOW BEDROOM, and the JEWEL CABINET. The latter is in the SW corner. The silver and steel fireplace

* The Marquis of Exeter kindly informed me that a bill of payment has recently been found for £50 to Grinling Gibbons.

interiors of *c.*1750–60 are especially magnificent. Turning round the corner from the Jewel Cabinet one is in the State Rooms.

The STATE ROOMS on the first floor are known as the George Rooms. They are distinguished by much painting, unfortunately not of a distinguished quality. *Verrio* did most of the work, but *Chéron* some too (according to Vertue). The rooms from W to E are as follows. First the DRESSING ROOM. The ceiling represents Morning chasing Night; the chimneypiece is by *J. A. Richter*, *c.*1780, the woodcarving of the *sopraporte* belongs to the Gibbons group. Second the JEWEL CLOSET, again with a *Gibbons* overmantel. The ceiling shows Fortune blindfolded and tied to a wheel. Then the STATE BEDROOM. Its ceiling depicts the Rewards of Virtue. The fireplace was made in Rome to a design by *Piranesi*. The bed was made for Queen Victoria in 1844. Next the DRAWING ROOM (ceiling of 1691: Reunion of Cupid and Psyche), the DINING ROOM (ceiling: Feast of the Gods, 1692, fireplace in the Adam style), and the HEAVEN ROOM (ceiling an Assembly of Gods, painted walls with giant colonnading, E wall Cyclops' Forge). Finally the HELL ROOM. Its ceiling dates from 1696–7, but the staircase was built into it in 1785, the floor was taken out for the purpose, and the wall paintings were done by *Stothard* in 1801 in a remarkably Rubensian vein. The stair rail is no more than a simple, graceful trellis. The landing rests on Tuscan columns. The *Gibbons* garlands are not *in situ*. They probably belong to the fireplace of the Hell Room.

The rooms on the ground floor, not open to the public, are no less splendid. The climax here is the MARBLE HALL in the centre of the S front, with a prodigious plaster ceiling, and the two rooms adjoining it to the E and W, the former with a screen of four Corinthian columns across, the latter with a gorgeous gilt Rococo overmantel of *c.*1750. The suite of rooms remodelled about 1680–90 continues into the W front and the N porch. Even the small room in the NW corner turret has a stucco ceiling. There are also *Gibbons* chimney friezes and overmantels in several rooms. Other rooms on the N side, including the central SCAGLIOLA HALL, were redecorated some time after 1760.

While one is thus amply compensated for the loss of William Cecil's original interiors, one yet remains intrigued as to what they might have looked like. The only indication is the ENTRANCE HALL across the centre of the W range, for this has a tierceron-vault, a little incorrect in its details, but once more essentially Gothic, although provided with the date 1577. It is continued by a second tierceron-vaulted room, forming the centre towards the courtyard, and from this radiate tunnel-vaulted and coffered arches of the same type as in the Roman Staircase and the w arches of the great hall. Sir William Cecil and his designers did not feel any clash between Perpendicular and Renaissance.

Of outbuildings the ORANGERY lies to the E of the E front. It is Gothick, by *Capability Brown*, and was seen by Horace Walpole in 1763. Eleven bays, four angle turrets, Perp panelling, battlements. The STABLES run along three sides of a courtyard. They have nine bays, the windows are mullioned with arched lights, and there is a hipped roof. Fine BRIDGE of three arches.* About ¼ m. to the SE *Brown*'s BATH HOUSE, overlooking the lake and framed by splendid cedar trees. This is neo-Jacobean, which is a rarity at so early a date, small, with a pierced strapwork cresting and finials. The BOATHOUSE on the opposite side of the lake is neo-Jacobean too, but its date seems unrecorded. The WEST GATES from the A1 road are also neo-Jacobean. They are however a much grander affair, with three archways. They were designed by *Legg* in 1801. Brown's presence at Burghley was more concerned with the remodelling of the grounds than with the design of the buildings. He began shortly after 1756, and when he had finished, he had created one of the most perfect landscape settings in England.

BURY

HOLY CROSS. A large church, and puzzling in one or two ways. It has an excellent C13 w tower with very long paired lancet bell-openings and yet longer single lancets on the stage below. It also had a fine w doorway with mature stiff-leaf and appendages N and S to which the arches are blocked. Moreover, there is a W annex, and that is completely mysterious. It was evidently Perp, see the niches in its E (i.e. the tower w) wall with their little vaults and the E jambs of the E windows. Also this annex has a tunnel-vaulted undercroft of which the springing courses remain. So the tower doorway was then blocked. What was the purpose of this annex, and can the N and S

* The LIONS on the bridge are, so Mr John Harris informs me, by *Henry Gilbert* of Stamford.

appendages simply have been embracing w bays of aisles? When the w tower was begun, i.e. before *c.*1240, the church wall was made the tower E wall. This w wall was Norman and still has its Norman w portal, with two orders of colonnettes carrying decorated scallop capitals, an arch with rolls, and a tympanum with the plainest trellis pattern formed by the joints of the stones. The Norman chancel arch also remains, and shows that the Norman nave was quite long, with triple responds, crudely decorated capitals, and two thick rolls in the arch. Peterborough is the source. The N arcade dates from the years when the tower was begun, or perhaps just a little earlier. Three bays, octagonal piers, big stiff-leaf capitals in which however the individual leaves are still static. The arches were re-done about 1500. Perp s side of the church, but the s doorway again C13. – SCREEN. Perp, of not too narrow one-light divisions.* – LECTERN. Of wood. An outstanding piece of the early C14. Ogee-trefoiled arcading on one outer side, oak leaves and acorns on the other; on the side covered by the book a symmetrical middle panel of big leaves and a border of small foliage with a Green Man in the centre. – BENCHES. Plain, straight-topped, Perp. – SHUTTERS. The N and s low-side windows in the chancel have medieval shutters. – SCULPTURE. The foot of the lectern is a C13 stone with leaf decoration on top and on all four sides. What was it? – STAINED GLASS. Ancient fragments in a chancel N window and some N aisle windows. – PLATE. Elizabethan Cup with engraved ornament. – BELL. One bell is of the C14 and possibly by *William Rofford.*

ROUND BARROW. A possible round barrow lies $\frac{1}{4}$ m. s of the church. The site is 75 ft in diameter and 6 ft high.

BYTHORN

St LAWRENCE. An unhappy sight. The tower has recently lost most of its spire, and what remains looks like a tower-mill with its cap and without sails. The broaches are there too, and one tier of lucarnes. The bell-openings are of two lights, and there is a quatrefoil frieze over. The w window is Dec; so is the spherical triangle window above it. The chancel with its steep roof is higher than the embattled nave, and that does not make things better. The plain N and s doorways are of *c.*1200, the N and s arcades of *c.*1300. They are of four bays. N has alternating round and octagonal piers, s all quatrefoil. Both have

---

* Does the cresting belong? (GMCH)

double-chamfered arches. N probably precedes S by a little. The two-bay N chapel arcade is elementary Perp. – PLATE. Cup with Steeple Cover of 1614–15.

CALDECOTE

ST MARY MAGDALENE. 1874 by *Edward J. Tarver*. Nave with double-bellcote and chancel. The chancel lancets and the shafts of the chancel E window are C13. So is the handsome DOUBLE PISCINA with a fleur-de-lis in the spandrel and the bracket opposite. The chancel arch responds are made up of twin-scalloped Norman capitals. The W window has a late C13 quatrefoil in the spandrel. – PULPIT. 1646. Plain panels and small arabesque panels over. – SOUTH DOOR. With C13 iron straps and scrolls.

CASTOR

Soke of Peterborough

ST KYNEBURGA. The dedication is unique in England. St Kyneburga was the daughter of Peada, King of Mercia and founder of Peterborough Abbey. The church of Castor is the most important Norman parish church in the county. It extends with original parts from the spectacular crossing tower to W, N, S, and E. To the W it includes the W end, where there is a shafted Norman window, and the fine S doorway (re-set ?) which has two orders of shafts with capitals decorated by beaded interlace, an arch with roll mouldings, and an outer billet frieze (the nailhead border is a C13 addition). It also includes the N transept, whose masonry with Roman brick is Norman, and where part of a N window remains (with billet decoration), the S transept, which has a fragment of a Norman W window (with roll and a billet frieze), and of the chancel at least the famous inscription which records the consecration of the church in 1124. The stone is tympanum-shaped, but its bottom line rises in the middle in a smaller semicircle. Another Norman tympanum, not *in situ*, is in the S porch gable. This has a demi-figure of Christ blessing. But the glory of the church is its tower. It rests on four sturdy Norman arches with demi-shafts and roll mouldings. The steep bases have a very flat zigzag decoration and the capitals beaded interlace decoration in addition to stalks, leaves, birds, beasts, monsters, and small figures including a combat and a vintage scene. The arches have a moulding including two rolls and a small hollow.

To the outside the tower rises in four stages. First a plain

Castor church, inscription recording the consecration of
the church, 1124

storey up to the ridge of the roofs and finished by a corbel
table. Then a stage with large two-light windows, the lights
having zigzag arches (the only zigzag proper at Castor) and
the windows billet surrounds. The windows are framed by
two-light blank arcading. The next stage has the bell-openings,
three tall, slim two-light openings, framed by one blank arch
l. and one r. Finally the Norman top corbel table, and above
it a C14 parapet and a short spire with two tiers of lucarnes.
At the same time the tower was strengthened inside by a plain
rib-vault with ridge ribs.

Next in order of time comes the C13. It did much. The
chancel was rebuilt early on, with its S doorway still with a
round arch (segmental rere-arch), with its SEDILIA still
round-arched, the PISCINA with much dogtooth decoration,
and with lancet windows. The S aisle must be of about the
same time. It has three bays, with round piers and round abaci,
a little nailhead decoration, and pointed double-chamfered
arches. The W window is a lancet, and the E arch is round.
The S transept was rebuilt with an E aisle about 1280. The
windows have bar tracery with circles, except for those to the
E, which have Y-tracery. A small tomb recess outside the S
wall. The arches are double-chamfered. Dec N arcade (octagonal piers, double-chamfered arches), Dec window in the S
aisle (reticulated tracery). Dec probably also the tomb recess

outside the s aisle. The only Perp contribution of interest is the big E window, which replaces a group of three lancets.

FURNISHINGS. REREDOS. N aisle. Five blank arches. – DOOR. The s door is of the C14 and has a foliate border with an inscription to 'Ricardus Beby Rector Ecclesie de Castre'. No such rector is recorded at Castor, though one at Whittlesey in Cambridgeshire. – WALL PAINTINGS (N aisle). C14. Three scenes of the Life of St Catherine, one above the other. St Catherine and the Wheel, the Execution of the Philosophers, Maxim's Entry into Alexandria(?). – SCULPTURE. Small Saxon stone with a man standing under an arch and fragment of a second. Only 19 in. tall. The style is connected with that of the Hedda Stone at Peterborough, but somewhat harder and more linear. The suggested date is the mid C9 (chancel). – Base of a Saxon Cross with interlace and also two dragons, originally probably a Roman altar (N aisle E). – PLATE. Silver-gilt Cup and Cover Paten, 1632; two silver-gilt Breadholders, 1673; silver-gilt Flagon, 1774. – MONUMENT. Coped coffin lid with, at the head end, bust of a Priest, his head surrounded by a rounded-trefoiled canopy; early C13.

CASTOR HOUSE, at the E end of the village. Georgian, of five bays and two storeys. The gatepiers with niches seem mid C17.

THE CEDARS, E of the Fitzwilliam Arms (No. 32). With a Greek Doric porch without pediment.

VILLAGE FARMHOUSE, at the w end of the village. The house has one Saxon window above the side entrance and an ogee-headed archway inside.

ROMAN REMAINS. The large group of buildings excavated by Artis in Castor village was centred round a courtyard which lay in the area of the parish church. It measured c.600 ft square. In the sw corner a separate bath house was included. It contained a group of mosaic-decorated rooms on the N side; one polychrome mosaic has been removed to the dairy at Milton. A section of herringbone brickwork is visible just s of the church, and the columns in the N chancel wall are also Roman.

ROMAN VILLA. At Mill Hill, ½ m. SE of the village, on the gravel terrace above the Nene, crop marks indicate the site of a two-winged corridor house with attendant buildings. The NE section was excavated by Artis in 1822. The E part of the house contained at least three fine mosaics; a small separate building next to it, with apsidal feature, hypocausts, and tessellated paving, may well have been the bath house.

0070

CATWORTH

ST LEONARD. A late C14 church, except for the half-destroyed
E.E. DOUBLE PISCINA in the chancel and the lavish E.E. S
doorway with three orders of shafts carrying mature stiff-leaf
capitals and an arch of three hollow chamfers. The W tower is
slender, ashlar-faced and well detailed. A W window which is
a spherical triangle with six spokes as tracery is still essentially
Dec, and so are the two-light bell-openings with transom.
But the top frieze, the battlements, and the recessed spire
(with two tiers of lucarnes) are Perp.* The arcades of four
bays inside are quite typical of the late C14, i.e. the standard
Perp moulded pier-section but still rounded bases and capitals
and still sunk-quadrant mouldings in the arches. The chancel
arch matches. Later clerestory and nave roof (almost entirely
renewed) with traceried spandrels of the braces and carved
bosses. Bosses also on the S aisle roof. – PULPIT. Of wood;
Perp. – SCREEN. Perp, of three-light divisions. – SCULPTURE.
A stiff-leaf bracket in the N aisle. – CHANDELIER. Of brass,
dated 1666 and inscribed by Brasenose College. – STAINED
GLASS. Fragments in the chancel S windows. – PLATE. Cup
of 1568–9; C17 Paten; Jug of 1771–2; Plate of 1778–9. –
MONUMENTS. Tablets with simple urn at the top to Elizabeth Booth † 1846 by *Maile & Son* and to Sir Felix Booth
F.R.S. † 1850 by *S. Manning Jun.*

1090

CHESTERTON

ST MICHAEL. A fine E.E. W tower with a small blocked C18
doorway, chamfered buttresses with stop-chamfers, two
extremely long lancets to W and S, twin bell-openings under
one pointed arch, fully shafted, a corbel-frieze of small heads,
and a spire with low broaches and two tiers of lucarnes. Of the
same time the S doorway, with early stiff-leaf of not very high
quality (including one small head) and an arch of many
mouldings. This doorway was provided at the same time as the
S aisle and S arcade. The piers alternate between round and
octagonal and three capitals have waterleaf, early stiff-leaf,
and real stiff-leaf crockets. The N arcade is later C13, of standard elements. The clerestory is Dec. In the C18, probably
about 1730, the chancel was rebuilt of ashlar with round-

22

---

* The gargoyle on the N side is re-used and marks the outlet of a flue from
a recess inside, probably for baking the communion wafers.

arched windows and a doorway of flat rustication of alternating sizes, the s porch was built, its entrance with a Gibbs surround, and some new aisle windows were put in. It is not known when all this was done. Internally the Georgian work in the chancel is very complete, a SCREEN of three arched openings, a broad REREDOS with coupled Ionic pilasters and a wide open pediment, an ALTAR TABLE on wrought iron supports, a COMMUNION RAIL, and also the PULPIT on a broad base, with a little inlay, and the baluster FONT. – BELL. One is by *John Walgrave*, i.e. of *c.*1420–30. – PLATE. Cup and Cover Paten of 1569–70; two undated Cups. – MONUMENTS. Plain tomb-chest to William Beville (Beivele), 1483–4 (anno regis Richard tertii 1°). – Large standing stone monument to Robert Beville † 1602 and wife and Sir Robert † 1634 and wife. The date is probably that of the death of Sir Robert's wife, i.e. 1611. Two kneeling couples, husband and wife facing one another, the children small below. The couples kneel under pendant arches, and there are columns l. and r. Big top achievement. – John Driden † 1707. A fine piece of reredos type. White and veined marble. Pilasters and hanging garlands. No figures. Original iron railings. – Richard Edwards † 1730. Large oval inscription tablet.

CHESTERTON HOUSE, the Dryden mansion, was demolished in 1807. For re-used parts *see* Elton Hall and Alwalton.

DUROBRIVAE. *See* Water Newton.

COLNE

3070

ST HELEN. 1896–1900 by *Fawcett* of Cambridge, with materials of the old church, e.g. the piers and arches of the arcade, the PISCINA in the s aisle, a tower lancet, etc. The tower is at the sw end and has a lead spike. – ORGAN CASE. A pretty, early C19 piece.

OLD CHURCH, 600 yds WNW of the new church along a lane. All that survives is the s porch. The entrance has a basket arch.

CONINGTON

1080

The draining of the fens began in earnest in 1630 on the initiative of the fourth Earl of Bedford. He and his Co-Adventurers received their charter in 1634. In 1639 Sir Thomas Cotton started on the Conington Fen. The Cottons had been at Conington ever since 1460.

ROUND HILL, 1¼ m. WSW of the church. A five-sided enclosure

of 17½ acres with a moat. The earthwork was probably made for a house to be built by Sir Robert Cotton.

CONINGTON CASTLE has been totally demolished. It was the principal mansion of the Cotton family, built mostly by Sir Robert early in the C17. The church monuments remain as a family memorial.

49 ALL SAINTS. A large and important church, all of c.1500, with a w tower truly monumental. It is ashlar-faced and of four stages and has panelled polygonal buttresses (cf. Cambridge), a base frieze and a panelled top frieze, a surprising recessed doorway with a small pointed tunnel-vault, a transomed (over-restored) w window of five lights, then, above small two-light windows, round windows, looking C17 in their details, four-light bell-openings under four-centred arches, and big pinnacles re-done in 1638 by Sir Thomas Cotton. The rest of the church is cobble. Embattled nave and aisles, four-light aisle windows, three-light clerestory windows (except for the much wider w bay, which has five-light windows), a higher rood-stair turret, and a chancel only projecting by one bay beyond the chapels. Internally the greatest surprise is due to the restorations of the C19. The tower was originally open to the nave by a high arch, and at that height there was a vault. Now there is a low w entrance hall with a tierceron-star vault and as high up as the original vault a plaster vault. The arcades are of four bays with a very complex Perp section to the piers and capitals only towards the arch openings. The aisle roofs stand on the wall side on shafts carried up from the floor. The chancel chapels are of only one bay. In the chancel very handsome SEDILIA, straight-topped with three little hanging vaults. The seat front has a frieze of reticulation units. The PISCINA has a shelf. – FONT. Octagonal, Late Norman, with intersecting pointed arches on colonnettes. – SCREENS. To the s chapel, of broad one-light divisions with ogee arches. – To the N chapel simpler. – (CHAIR. High-backed Gothic armchair, probably late C14. The back has a blank panel with a cusped and subcusped arch.)* – PEWS. 1841, and characteristic of the date. – (FRONTAL. Parts of two Italian C17 maniples and two stoles. Silver embroidery on pink silk.) – PLATE. Large foreign Plate; Paten on foot of Britannia silver, 1702–3; Britannia silver Cup, 1711–12.

* As the brackets indicate, I have not seen this chair. Mr McHardy doubts that it is medieval. He thinks it may belong to the pews. Photographs make me inclined to believe the date of the RCHM, but with the proviso of heavy restoration about 1840.

MONUMENTS. Conington is uncommonly rich. The series starts with the memorable Purbeck-marble effigy of a Fran- 39 ciscan tertiary, a young face, perhaps someone who joined, as was not unusual, shortly before he died to be buried a religious. It is a noble, very sensitive piece. The date must be about 1300. – Then, all of about 1600, the memorial tablet between two columns to Thomas (inscribed XIII) Cotton † 1519 and his wife and in the same position in the other aisle that to Prince Henry of Scotland,* and one much larger to Thomas (XV) and Thomas (XVI) Cotton and their wives with two arches and columns and an upper display of strapwork and heraldry, and opposite it in the other aisle that to David King of Scotland in two tiers with columns. In the upper part lies just a crown in the arch between the two columns. – Sir Robert Cotton † 1631, the famous antiquary whose collection of manuscripts is now in the British Museum, and Sir Thomas † 1662, both erected by Sir John about 1675 or thereabouts. The composition and details of the two tablets are identical except that Sir Robert's bust is in an oval recess and the gar- 75 land below is of laurel, whereas Sir Thomas's is in a circular recess, and the garland is different. In spite of the identity in so many ways, the sculptural quality differs. The bust of Sir Thomas is good, that of Sir Robert outstanding. Who was capable at the time of characterizing so strikingly and model-ling so perfectly? – Sir John † 1702 and his wife, also † 1702, two identical tablets with portrait medallions at the top. Very similar to the Cotton monument at Conington, Cambridge-shire, dated 1697 and signed by *Grinling Gibbons*.

COVINGTON   0070

ST MARGARET. A grey, aisleless church of small size. The earliest part is the tympanum of the N doorway. This is Norman, with its two affronted quadrupeds: a lion and a wingless griffin(?). More evidence of the Norman church is to be found built into the S wall of the vestry, e.g. some zigzag and the fragment of a colonnette. Then follows the priest's doorway, which must be c.1200. Good early C13 S doorway with one order of shafts with shaft-rings and leaf capitals. Arch with many mouldings including rolls with fillets. Good late C13 chancel S windows with simple but attractive geo-metrical tracery. The chancel arch corresponds to them.

* Members of the Scottish royal family were lords of the manor in the C12 and early C13.

Above it two deep recesses in the nave E wall. A former s chapel has Dec details. The small w tower is Dec too – see the arch towards the nave* and the w window. The tower originally carried a spire. – FONT. Octagonal, Norman, with scalloped base and underside. – BENCHES. Three Perp ones, of the buttressed type. – PLATE. Cup of c.1570 and matching Cover Paten.

1000

DEEPING GATE
Soke of Peterborough

BRIDGE across the river Welland into Lincolnshire. Three nearly semicircular arches with two slight chamfers. Cutwaters. Probably C17.

1080

DENTON

ALL SAINTS. In ruins. It was essentially a C17 church. Nave and chancel, and a small, short SW tower. Certain minor old parts were re-used (e.g. the C13 chancel arch), but the windows – three lights with transom in the nave, two lights in the chancel – are of 1629, and the mouldings of the chancel arch responds too. The N porch (not the mouldings of the entrance) is of 1665, the w tower of unknown date. The E window tracery looks c.1800. The work of 1629 was paid for by Sir Robert Cotton, the antiquary (cf. Conington), the work of 1665 by his grandson Sir John.

1060

DIDDINGTON

ST LAWRENCE. A brick w tower and a brick s porch, both Henry VIII and rare in the county. E.E. chancel, cut short and finished off in yellow brick later. It has s and N lancets and a two-light low-side window which is Dec. The three-bay N arcade is also E.E. Round piers and double-chamfered arches. On the s side only a two-bay chapel. This is Perp and probably of c.1505 (see below). Octagonal pier, the responds corbels in the form of a knot (cf. Little Paxton). – SCREEN. Original dado with tracery. More tracery used in the lectern. – BENCHES. Many, with traceried ends, better than most in the county. – STAINED GLASS. The s chapel sw window looks more complete than it is. It dates from the C15 and contains two female saints and made-up parts from a Resurrection etc., also a kneel-

* The VCH calls it c.1500 with re-used stones from c.1330.

ing *donatrix*. All recently restored. – In the neighbouring window Netherlandish c16 and c17 roundels etc. – MONU-MENTS. In the s chapel tomb-chest with shields and fleurons and against the back wall kneeling brass figures of William Taylard † 1505 and wife (11 in.). The brass must once have been very handsome. There was a Trinity above, and there still are framing strips l. and r. each with three figures. – Alice Taylard † 1513. Kneeling figure, 12 in. long.

DULOE HILL *see* EATON SOCON

DUROBRIVAE *see* WATER NEWTON

EARITH

SCHOOL. 1839. Yellow brick, one-storeyed, of seven bays with a three-bay pediment and a cupola.

WOODLANDS, in the main street. Yellow brick and red-brick dressings. Five bays. Nice doorway with Doric pilasters and a pediment. A Venetian window over.

At Earith start both the Old and the New Bedford Rivers, two of the principal enterprises in the draining of the fens. The OLD BEDFORD RIVER was begun in 1631, an enterprise of the fourth Earl of Bedford and thirteen co-adventurers. The NEW BEDFORD RIVER, or Hundred Foot River, dates from 1651 etc. They run in straight diagonals to Salter's Lode Sluice and Denver Sluice in Norfolk, whereas the Ouse me-anders on from Earith to the E to Ely until at the two sluices it receives the drains again and carries the water N to King's Lynn.

THE BULWARK, 150 yds N of the bridge. Probably an earthwork of the Civil War, as it is square with four arrow-shaped angle bastions. It comprises 4¾ acres.

EASTON

ST PETER. The w tower is of especially fine proportions. Set-back buttresses, pairs of two-light transomed bell-openings, a top frieze, and a spire with low broaches and three tiers of lucarnes. The s arcade is of *c.*1300, four low bays, round piers and double-chamfered arches. Perp nave N side with a large three-light and a large two-light window, both transomed. Perp three-light clerestory. Good nave roof with the date 1630. In the N wall, built in, the head of a small Norman win-dow. – SCREEN. Perp, of broad one-light divisions. – BENCHES.

Three old ones remain. – PULPIT. C18, of mahogany with a little inlay. It comes from South Shields. – PLATE. Cup with bowl and foot, without a stem; 1669–70.

SE of the church a HOUSE with an Early Georgian brick front of five bays. Segment-headed windows, doorway with straight hood on brackets.

1060 EAST PERRY

For GRAFHAM WATER see p. 252.

For GAYNES HALL see p. 257.

SAILING CLUB. By *S. Johnson-Marshall* and *Kenneth Buffery* of *Sir Robert Matthew, Johnson-Marshall & Partners*, 1965–6. A nice, fresh, nautical-looking job – in its style carrying on from the thirties rather than succumbing to the Brutalist fashion of the sixties.

1050 EATON SOCON

50 ST MARY. The church was gutted by fire in 1930 and restored and partly rebuilt by *Sir Albert Richardson*.* The S arcade of five bays remained, with early C14 (re-used) arches, but otherwise Perp, and the S clerestory, and of course the W tower. It is a high tower with set-back buttresses and pairs of transomed two-light bell-openings. The SEDILIA consist simply of a seat with as its back wall the window above having its jambs and sill taken lower down. – FONT. Square, Norman, of Purbeck marble, painted white. The decoration is intersecting arches. – COMMUNION RAIL. Of *c.*1640, curving forward. Balusters, and between them sharp pendants.‡ – In the N chapel SPIRAL STAIR by *Richardson* in a very enjoyable wooden cage. – ARCHITECTURAL FRAGMENTS. Found after the fire. Large parts of the arch of a main doorway with zigzag. – Also E.E. pieces. – STAINED GLASS. In the S chapel E window four Flemish(?) roundels. – TAPESTRIES. One large scenic Flemish C17 piece, and one smaller foliage piece with a pelican. They were obtained for the church in 1932 by Sir Albert Richardson. – PLATE. Cup and Cover Paten, inscribed 1609; Plate dated 1609; Paten 1635; C17 Cup and Paten. – BRASSES to a Civilian and his wife, *c.*1450. Also scrolls. The figures are 19 in. long.

METHODIST CHAPEL. 1850. Yellow brick, terribly businesslike. Just arched openings with bits of brick decoration.

---

* The consecration took place in 1932.
‡ This is the rail for the Lady Chapel.

Lockup, s of the church. c19. Oblong, of brick, with an arched doorway. There are two cells inside.

In the main street, called Great North Road, as anybody will find appropriate who has tried to cross it, there are s of the church No. 117, timber-framed and gabled with overhang and (at the time of writing) derelict, the White Horse, a red-brick building with one Early Georgian range with panelled parapet to the street and a later five-bay range with a very pretty doorcase at r. angles to it, and the Old Plough, low, timber-framed with closely set studs. N of the church is the former Workhouse, yellow brick, of 1842, with the usual octagonal centre and wings. It is not strictly classical, but in its utilitarian way certainly not yet anti-classical.

Windmill, Duloe Hill, 1 m. N. A tower mill without sails. A cottage is attached to the tower.

The Hillings, on the w bank of the Ouse. A post-Conquest earthwork. Excavations in 1949–50 and 1960 have shown that the castle was of three periods: the D-shaped enclosure first, then the two others, one c11, the other c12. The s bailey was the innermost defence, as there was no motte.

ELLINGTON

1070

All Saints. A very fine, slender Perp w tower with set-back buttresses, pairs of two-light transomed bell-openings, a top frieze, and a broach spire with low broaches and three tiers of lucarnes in alternating directions. Inside, it is evident that the tower was built independent of the church. The start of a vault in the tower is preserved. The chancel is later c13, i.e. the Victorian geometrical tracery of 1863 (by *Scott*) represents the style correctly. Original are the shafts of the E window, the chancel arch with stiff-leaf capitals, a little of the sill-frieze, and the priest's doorway. Of the same date approximately is the re-set N aisle doorway. But the aisle itself and the s aisle, both embattled, and the embattled clerestory and the N porch (with leaf spandrels to the entrance) are all Perp. The four-bay arcades have piers with the standard moulded section and arches with two sunk-quadrant mouldings. Good nave roof with carved braces, embattled collars, angels against the feet of the secondary principals, and figures against the wall-posts. The N and S aisle roofs are similar, but also have ornamented bosses. – Font. Octagonal, Perp, with quatrefoils and one other simple motif. – Stalls. Victorian, and, curiously enough, in the E.E. style. – Bell. One by *John Walgrave*, *c.*1420–30. – PLATE. Cup of 1725–6. – MONUMENT. Badly defaced effigy of a Lady, C14, the effigy carved on a coffin lid and the coffin preserved too.

ELTON

ALL SAINTS. Outside Perp dominates, inside it is the decades around 1300. Proud ashlar-faced W tower with clasping buttresses, a base frieze, a doorway with traceried spandrels, a three-light W window with a niche over, three-light transomed bell-openings, a frieze below them and another at the top. No spire. High arch to the nave. Ashlar-faced also the S porch. Late Perp aisle windows. The aisles embrace the tower. Only the chancel points to what the interior has to say. Here is a window with bar-tracery (quatrefoiled circle), a window with cusped Y-tracery, and one later one with flowing tracery. Inside, the chancel arch is definitely some time before 1300. Triple shafts and nailhead. The SEDILIA and PISCINA and the AUMBRY opposite have cinquecusped arches. Then the arcades. Four bays. Quatrefoil piers, differing a little in the details. Arches S with one chamfer and one hollow chamfer, except the easternmost, which, like the N aisle, already has two sunk quadrants. – FONT. Octagonal, with simple cusped blank arches, *c.*1300 too. – BENCHES. The ends with traceried blank arches and also some linenfold. – CROSSES. In the churchyard two Anglo-Danish Crosses with wheel-heads and interlace. – STAINED GLASS. By *Morris & Co.* chancel S († 1891), tower W (1893), and S aisle W (1901). – PLATE. Two Cups and Cover Patens 1571–2; two Patens on foot and Flagon 1669–70. – MONUMENTS. In the S aisle N wall a carved coat of arms and inscription to Sir Richard Sapcote (*see* Elton Hall). – Robert Sapcote † 1601, a large incised slab (S aisle floor). – Tablets of black and white marble with columns to Sir Thomas Proby † 1689 and Sir John † 1710. – Lord Proby † 1858. Tablet by *Tyley*. Georgian-looking seated female figure in front of a grey, summarily indicated mausoleum with arched entrance.

ELTON HALL. Huntingdonshire mansions are composite affairs. That applies to Elton Hall as much as to Hinchingbrooke and Ramsey Abbey. At Elton Hall work of the C18 and C19 is overlaid over work of the late C15, whereas of the important work of 1664 no features have been allowed to remain.

The late C15 work was done for Sir Richard Sapcote and perhaps his son Sir John. It consists of the gatehouse and in

the same range the chapel undercroft. The GATEHOUSE has
a four-centred arch, and two quadripartite rib-vaults inside,
preceded by a shallow entrance bay with two quadripartite
vaults placed across, not along, i.e. rising to a middle ridge,
each with its own apex. There are two tiers of two-light windows, and the top is embattled and strongly machicolated.
Work preserved goes on a little to the E. The CHAPEL UNDER-
CROFT is in the same range to the W. Of the chapel itself above
the undercroft, some masonry no doubt survives, and also the W
end-gable and its pinnacles. The undercroft consists of two
chambers each of two bays of rib-vaulting, the single-chamfered ribs growing out of the wall-shafts without capitals and
forming tierceron stars. The bays are separated by four-centred
transverse arches. Nothing is known for certain about the
further extent of the house. One can assume that the Sapcotes'
hall range lay N of the surviving range, separated from it by a
courtyard. The property was sold in 1617 and was ruinous by
the time of the Restoration. Sir Thomas Proby then pulled
down most of it and built the NW range, smaller however than
it is today. We know from Buck's engraving of 1730 that it was
to the E of seven bays and two storeys with a hipped roof.
What we see now from this side, and even statelier from the W
side, is by *Henry Ashton*, 1856–60, and is remarkably tactful.
The window details are different; a mansard roof with dormers
is introduced, and the N end is a new three-storeyed extension.
There is also a porch with two pairs of Tuscan columns on the
E side of the range.

But Ashton did more in other parts, and others had done
yet more before him. It is indeed the C18 work which con-
fuses the appearance of the house and is by no means fully
elucidated yet. Starting from the SE corner, there is here a
C19 service extension of unknown date. Then follows the gatehouse and then the C18. Inside, on the principal floor, that
is easily seen, but outside it is all bits and pieces. The centre
of interest is of course the ashlar-faced part with the canted
bay window and the outer staircase. This stands above the
chapel undercroft, i.e. takes the place of the chapel. The wide
pointed windows and the whole general character make a
later C18 date probable, and this is indeed a time when work
went on (*see* below). But to the r. of this part is a canted bay
window brought over from Chesterton when that house was
demolished in 1807. To the l. of the ashlar part is rough C17
masonry to the end, and a mullioned window is just round the

corner. But the features of this part are not C17: they belong
to the remodelling of the late C18 and early C19, and have as
their centre a small embattled gable between buttress-shafts
and at the very W end of the whole range a pair of round
towers. Behind appears a tower, originally also Gothick, but
now Victorian Gothic. This remodelling is not by Ashton but
of c.1870 by *S. Inskip Ladds* and (or ?) *H. F. Traylen*. Placed
against the wall of this range are two small Angels. They were
brought over from the damaged part of the Houses of Parliament after the Second World War. The W side starts with the
pair of round towers just referred to, continues with an C18
stretch of three storeys, undisguised, and then with Ashton's
principal range, a doubling in length of the range of c.1665.
Finally the N side of the principal, i.e. S, range. Here also the
thickness of the original, in this case C15, work was doubled,
but the theme of the chapel was taken up about 1860 and the
dining room N of the chapel given three large three-light
Gothic windows.

So to the INTERIOR. Here the interlocking of C18 and C19
is even more puzzling, especially since *Ashton* was evidently
bent on conforming in decoration with the C18. As for the
C18, dates are missing, except for a 1783 in the stained glass
in the Octagon Room W of the former chapel. This is a Gothick
room, and the date is what one would expect. It would suit
the fenestration of the former chapel itself, i.e. the centre room
with the broad bay window. But the room, the principal drawing room of the house, received its bay window and decoration earlier. From the details of the stucco ceiling one would
assign it to c.1760. However, the wall treatment is Ashton's.
The spectacular chimneypiece of the drawing room with overmantel is now in the dining room, where the rest of the decoration may well also be imitation-classical. The room between
the drawing room and the C15 gatehouse has an C18 ceiling,
but in the coving charming floral painting of c.1860. Of the
latter date is of course the staircase with its cast iron hand-rail.
The wall and ceiling decoration is not mid C18 either, although
the tower to which it belongs was there at least by the early
C19, i.e. is not a Victorian creation. Ashton's detailing in the
Georgian manner is remarkably competent throughout. In
the range of c.1665, i.e. the one facing E, there is more mid
C18 work, but the middle room is panelled in the C17 manner.
However, that panelling is import of after 1916. It comes from
Glenart in Ireland and is supposed to be Dutch of c.1600.

In the garden is a DORIC TEMPLE à la Athenian Treasury
at Delphi. It looks Georgian at first, but is in fact by *Hope
Bagenal* and quite recent.

THE VILLAGE. Elton is a village of stone-built houses and
cottages. There are two main streets, Over End and Middle
Street, the former N–S, passing the church, the latter E–W. In
OVER END several C17 houses with mullioned windows and
two Georgian ones, the BLACK HORSE of five bays, and, on
the other side, a battlemented one with two canted bay windows. In MIDDLE STREET again some mullioned windows,
No. 14 e.g. This is of three bays, symmetrical, and must be
later C17. On the other side is a stately five-bay house dated
1727. Yet it still (if they are original) has wooden cross-windows. At the W end is the METHODIST CHURCH, dated
1864, but still with arched windows. However, the Jacobeanish
gable would rule out a much earlier date. Turn r. into DUCK
LANE. At the far end is *Sir Guy Dawber*'s BURY LEAS, built
about 1930 in his sensitive neo-Cotswold style with mullioned
windows and gables.

ENCLOSURE, ¾ m. NNE of the church and just to the E of the
B671. Aerial photography has revealed a pit alignment with a
sub-rectangular enclosure abutting on it. The site is unexcavated and cannot be precisely dated.

ETTON
Soke of Peterborough

ST STEPHEN. Memorable as a completely C13 church. W tower
with flat angle buttresses, lancet windows, and bell-openings
of two lights with a circular shaft between and under a shafted,
still round arch. This is remarkably late for a round arch.
Frieze with heads, stiff-leaf, and a horizontal figure. Shortish,
simple broach spire with low, broad broaches and two tiers
of lucarnes in alternating directions. They are just single-
chamfered lancets. The aisle windows are of two lights with
circles over (originally they were foiled). The blocked N doorway has a pretty trefoiled head. The S porch entrance is round-
arched with a chamfer and a hollow chamfer. In the chancel
the E window is of five steeply stepped lancets under one arch,
and the S windows have two lights and a trefoiled circle. There
are no N windows. A blocked arch in the N wall shows that
there was a chapel here. Inside the church, the tower arch is
pointed and double-chamfered. The C13 roof-line can be seen
above it. The quatrefoil clerestory windows are therefore

later (C14?). The arcades, not in axis with the tower arch, are of three bays. Circular piers, circular capitals and abaci (different s from N), pointed double-chamfered arches. Some nailhead ornament on the s side. The chancel arch has two hollow chamfers. PISCINAS in chancel and s aisle. SEDILIA in the chancel, pointed-trefoiled. – PLATE. Cover Paten, 1610.

MANOR HOUSE, E of the church. Elizabethan, on a not quite regular E-plan.

WOODCROFT CASTLE. *See* p. 367.

WOODCROFT CASTLE. *See* p. 367.

2000

EYE
Soke of Peterborough

ST MATTHEW. 1846 by *Basevi*, one of his last works. The steeple built shortly after by *F. T. Dollman*. Cruciform, the w tower carrying a broach spire. Lancet windows. Dull. – FONT. C14. Octagonal, on eight supports not set back. The spaces between the supports form recesses, and the decoration of the bowl is their ogee gables. – STAINED GLASS. E window 1863 by *Gibbs* (TK). – PLATE. Paten, 1798; Cup, 1809.

Straight village street with many houses of yellow brick.

WINDMILL, 75 yds from the church. A tower-mill, eight storeys high, visible for miles around. It is still working, but by machinery, without sails.

EYEBURY FARM, ¾ m. s. Probably late C17. Four by three bays with hipped roof. The windows are symmetrically arranged but have mullions and transoms. The doorway looks a little more classical.

NORTHOLM, 1 m. N. Dated 1704, yet traces show that there were still mullioned windows.

BARROWS. Three barrows of Bronze Age date lie on the s edge of the parish, E of Oxney House. A food vessel was found in one.

EYEBURY FARM *see* EYE

EYEBURY FARM *see* EYE

1050

EYNESBURY

ST MARY. Of brown cobbles. The s tower has the date of 1688, but it was in all probability rebuilt with E.E. materials. E.E. also the s doorway. Otherwise mostly Perp and much re-done in the C19. But on entering one is at once faced with much more ancient history. The N arcade is partly Late Norman and partly earliest E.E. Round piers, square abaci, five bays. The Norman part has multi-scalloped capitals. Then follows one capital with flat stylized pointed leaves and then stiff-leaf. The capitals are low, and the stiff-leaf is on a small scale with the arrangements symmetrical. The s arcade is of the late C13, with octagonal piers, arches with two hollow chamfers, and broaches at the start. The aisle is narrow, as the s tower determined its width. The arch from the tower to the aisle is C13 too. Small nailhead in the respond abaci. Again of the same time the chancel arch.* – PULPIT. An unusually beautiful late C17 piece, the panels with a little inlay, the angle posts carved with cherubs' heads and garlands. – BENCH ENDS. An excellent set (N aisle). Traceried fronts and ends modestly decorated with palms or an edging of fleurons and with bold poppyheads of leaf in plain outlines far from the usual fleur-de-lis type. Also human heads, stags, a sitting hen, a camel, and other animals and birds and monsters.

At the s end of Montagu Street, MONTAGU HOUSE, late C18, brick, three widely spaced bays, pedimental gable with an arched window reaching up into it. Pretty doorway.

(COUNCIL HOUSING. By *Barry Parker*, probably *c.*1920–1.‡)

FARCET

2090

ST MARY. The w tower is Late Norman and E.E. Clasping buttresses. The lower windows are still round-headed lancets, but the bell-openings have two pointed openings under a round arch. Corbel-frieze, small recessed lead spire. The low arch towards the nave, however, is already pointed. The pointed arch was usually adopted structurally before it became accepted decoratively. The s arcade has octagonal piers looking fully E.E. but round, if double-chamfered, arches. The chancel arch has one chamfer and one hollow chamfer. All this is C13 and not late, and so is the one-bay s chapel. The N aisle and clerestory date from 1852. The nave roof no doubt also does, but used in it are some C15 heads and angels. – SEDILE. A C13 stone throne, partly original. At the top of the arm a flower in a roundel. – PULPIT. An Early Renaissance piece still with linenfold but also with arabesques including mermaid-like creatures. The remaining fragment of the back panel carries

* The Rev. P. J. Bond tells me that before the restoration of 1857 the chancel had a flat roof and the nave an E window. He wonders whether the details of the chancel arch are not of 1857. Mr Bond also mentions ballflower decoration of the lintel of the N doorway.

‡ Information kindly conveyed to me by Mr A.V. Mountfort, the St Neots Librarian.

the date 1612, but that cannot apply to the parts described. –
BOX PEWS in the N aisle. – STAINED GLASS. The N aisle E
window by *Kempe & Tower*, *c*.1920. – PLATE. Parcel-gilt
Paten with the monogram of Christ, *c*.1500; Cup and Cover
Paten of 1692–3.

A HOUSE in the main E–W street running towards the church has
a doorway dated 1684. This is on the way to being classical,
but has not quite arrived yet. Pilasters against a rusticated
background, but instead of a real pediment a hood starting
straight and going segmental only in the middle.

3060   FENSTANTON

ST PETER AND ST PAUL. The most interesting part of the
church is the chancel. It is higher than the nave, and has a
41   proud seven-light E window and high three-light side windows
with reticulated tracery such as also appears prominently in the
E window. The priest's doorway is well moulded, and the
SEDILIA and PISCINA have an even row of ogee arches. Now
this chancel was built by William of Longthorne, whose brass
– now only the indent – is in the middle of the floor, and he
was rector from 1345 till 1352. The lettering on the tomb-slab
incidentally is still Lombardic. So here is a dated piece of the
mature Dec. The w tower cannot have been started much
later. The w doorway is also still Dec. To it belong the two
fragmentary windows to s and N cancelled when the mason of
the Perp church decided upon aisles to embrace the tower.
The head corbels of these new s and N arches look C13, but
they must be re-used. The church is of rubble and brown
cobbles. The ashlar spire with low broaches is Perp. Two
tiers of lucarnes in alternating directions. Perp aisles and
clerestory, Perp arcades of three wide bays, the piers with four
polygonal projections and four diagonal hollows. Tower arch
and chancel arch more or less match, though the bases of the
chancel arch are E.E. As early as this is the s porch entrance,
re-set no doubt. This has dogtooth and an almond-shaped
recess above. – PULPIT. With linenfold panels of the early
C16. – PLATE. Silver-gilt Cup of 1619–20. – MONUMENTS.
For William of Longthorne *see* above. – Lancelot Brown †1783,
i.e. Capability Brown, the celebrated garden designer. He was
Lord of the Manor. The monument is a flat tomb-chest on
steps with a back plate with modest Gothic detail. The inscription reads:

Ye Sons of Elegance, who truly taste
The Simple charms that genuine Art supplies,
Come from the sylvan Scenes His Genius grac'd,
And offer here your tributory Sigh's.
But know that more than Genius slumbers here;
Virtues were his which Arts best powers transcend.
Come, ye Superior train, who these revere
And weep the Christian, Husband, Father, Friend.

– Mrs Brown, by *Coade*, 1793, i.e. made of Coade stone, and apparently designed by *Bacon*. Mourning woman by an urn on a pedestal. The pretty corbel is of Coade stone too.

CONGREGATIONAL CHURCH, Chequer Street. 1874–5 by *Tait* (GS). In a fanciful Gothic, rock-faced, and looking more like a school than a chapel. N transept or chamber with a rose-window and N porch at the W end with a turret like a bold chimney.

LOCKUP. Square, of brick, with a clock-turret. The RCHM dates it late C17.

There are plenty of pleasant houses at Fenstanton, notably GROVE HOUSE, W of the lockup, Early Georgian, brick, with segment-headed windows, a segmental pediment for the doorway, and a parapet curving up to the corners, FENSTANTON MANOR, opposite the Congregational Church, later C17, with a square two-storeyed porch and wavy end-gables, and the early C18 MANOR FARMHOUSE, to the N of the A45 bypass. This is of seven bays, also red brick, and has a hipped roof, four giant pilasters to accentuate the façade, and a staircase with twisted balusters and fluted columns as newel posts. The staircase starts from the entrance hall behind a screen of two columns.

FENTON HOUSE *see* PIDLEY

FLETTON   *1090*

Fletton has become the industrial suburb of Peterborough. Factories and housing grow against the background of the brick-makers' chimneys. The parish churches of Fletton, Woodston (*see* p. 368), and Stanground (*see* p. 346) are all submerged. Nothing villagey has remained around the first two. Stanground is still holding out.

ST MARGARET. How many people realize that Fletton has not only a national but an international claim to be visited? Its ANGLO-SAXON REMAINS, even admitting that some are 8 closely linked with Breedon in Leicestershire and others with the Hedda Stone in Peterborough Cathedral, are startling in style, and have no parallel in earlier or late Anglo-Saxon art, and none in contemporary Continental art. Their date, thanks to Breedon, is certain: the first half of the C9, i.e. the time of Charlemagne and his immediate successors. As they are discoloured pink by fire it is quite likely that they come from Anglo-Saxon Peterborough Abbey, which had a conflagration in 1116. The remains are small in scale, minute, one might well say, and their original position and purpose remain a mystery, as do those of the Breedon pieces. They are now built into the E buttresses of the church, and most of them must have belonged to a frieze or friezes. Only one has human figures – three heads under arches, just like the figures on the Hedda Stone. But at Fletton the whole fragment is a mere 18 in. wide. The others, as at Breedon, are ornamented with weird little birds and quadrupeds, and they are scooped out in a peculiar technique so that just the ridges remain. The style is lively, even humorous, and not really primitive at all. They are not great sculpture, like the Ruthwell and Bewcastle Crosses well over a hundred years earlier, but they are done by someone who knew exactly what he wanted to do and found his means to achieve it. The two panels with saints inside the church, though generally considered part of the same scheme, are more likely Norman and come quite close to French sculpture of the early C12. They are precise in their carving, whereas the Anglo-Saxon artist modelled softly, as though in clay.*

Now for the church itself. The N arcade, chancel arch, and N chapel arcade came first. They are of about 1160. The N arcade originally had four bays, but one pier was removed at some time and a wide arch introduced. The remaining piers are sound and sturdy, with square abaci nicked at the corners and round arches with two very slight chamfers. The chancel arch received its pointed form later. All capitals are multi-scalloped. 1160 is a date that might also suit the two panels referred to. The chancel was Norman too, as is shown by the corbel-table, one blocked S window, and the buttressing. The present S windows are Dec. The S arcade is probably early C14. The thin octagonal piers carry capitals with polygonal projections which do not seem to fit (but cf. Stanground and Orton Longueville). Back to the end of the C13 with the S

* Until c.1900 they also were outside.

aisle W and E and the N aisle W window, all with three lancet-lights under one arch. Other S aisle and the clerestory windows must be C17. The N aisle dates from 1899. Again late C13 the W tower with Y-traceried bell-openings. Broach spire with high broaches and two tiers of lucarnes. – FONT. Probably of c.1661–2. Octagonal, of plain panels, four of them just vertically fluted. – CROSS. In the churchyard an Anglo-Saxon Cross. The shaft has the familiar two handles. The cross-head is of the wheel type. On the sides roundels with a quadruped, on the E face also a larger animal (Agnus Dei ?). The inscription is in Norman lettering. It reads Radulph Filius Wilielmi. Maybe the cross was appropriated to his memory. Recently Mr Clive L. George has discovered two more fragments of the cross.

FOLKSWORTH 1080

ST HELEN. Nave, chancel, and S transept. A steep bellcote on the W gable. At first it all seems Victorian, but then one realizes that the masonry and the buttressing are medieval, and one is not surprised to find a Norman N doorway. One order of shafts with scallop capitals. Arch with a roll, tympanum with a pattern of gridiron and pellets. The chancel arch is indeed also Norman. It is quite high and has thick zigzag in the arch. The capitals are decorated, two with small heads, the others with volutes. The arch to the S transept has two continuous chamfers and may well be contemporary with the buttressing. The Victorian work is of 1850, especially the blatantly neo-Norman chancel. – PLATE. Cup and Cover Paten, 1569–70; Paten on foot of Britannia silver, 1697–8.

THE ELMS, SSW of the church. An L-shaped brick façade, rendered, with a late C17 projecting wing and an early C17 main part. This has a square porch. But surely the two buttresses to its r. must be pre-Reformation.

GAYNES HALL see GREAT STAUGHTON

GLATTON 1080

ST NICHOLAS. A proud, ashlar-faced Perp W tower. The doorway has traceried spandrels, and the quatrefoil base-frieze runs right round it. Above it a four-light transomed window, then a blank crenellation frieze, to the W with quatrefoils, to the W also a beautifully rich transomed four-light window over, and above that, to the same design, the bell-openings. Top

frieze, battlements, pinnacles with animal supporters on them.
The body of the church is embattled. The aisles embrace the
tower. The s aisle is of *c.*1290–1300 externally – see the
intersecting tracery in the W and E and the Y-tracery in the s
windows. The chancel has one low-side window with Y-
tracery too, but the rest is Perp, over-restored in 1857. The N
transept is again of the date of the s aisle – see the E windows
with a quatrefoil placed diagonally above two lights. On the
N vestry to the E another quatrefoil frieze. As for the interior,
the chancel arch goes with the chancel, but the three brackets
above it for the rood are Perp. And the arcades are earlier
than anything outside, though much changed. They were
built about 1200, but were then considerably lower. They are
of three bays with round piers and moulded octagonal capitals
– except for one which is still many-scalloped. That is a
Norman motif, but so are the round arches. They already have
double chamfers. In the transept is a big bracket with nailhead – i.e., like the window, late C13. The vestry is vaulted
in two bays of quadripartite ribbing. The clerestory is of
course Perp; large three-light windows. The windows are
unusually large for Huntingdonshire clerestories. – SCREEN.
High, Perp, with one-light divisions. Ogee arches and panel
tracery – all almost entirely C19. – BENCHES. A specially
good set of poppyheads on the ends, including e.g. a bearded
man and a woman with a square headdress. – PAINTING. On
the nave E wall, N St Mary Magdalene, standing, against a
background with ornamental crowns, s Christ rising from the
tomb, a kneeling priest round the corner on the nave s wall.
Both are of *c.*1500. – PLATE. Cup of 1695–6. – MONUMENT.
Large, unidentified hanging monument with two arched recesses with shell tops between three columns. On the columns
weird short pilasters of bulgy outline. The most likely date is
*c.*1600.

GLINTON
Soke of Peterborough

ST BENEDICT. Norman W window in the N aisle. Early C13
chancel chapel. One bay, semicircular responds, capitals with
single upright leaves, remodelled pointed arch with one
chamfer and one wave moulding (C14 ?). Of *c.*1300 the s porch
entrance, with dogtooth in the arch, and the s aisle windows.
Perp arcades (octagonal piers, castellated abaci) and clerestory.
Big figures as supports of the former roof beams. Short Perp

w tower with a spire recessed behind battlements and taller
than the tower. Two tiers of lucarnes. The outline of the spire
has a marked entasis. – FONT. Square, Norman, with decoration
of squares, saltire crosses, etc. – PLATE. Cup, 1710; Paten on
foot, 1711. – MONUMENT. Stone effigies of a Forester with
horn and a Lady, early C14, very defaced. Perhaps from
Northborough, in which case the man might be Geoffrey
Delamare, supposed to have been Forester of Kesteven.

MANOR HOUSE, E of the church. Built probably by the Wilde-
bore family. The date is c.1630–40. Two-storeyed with mullioned windows and ogee gables of different sizes, the smaller
ones drawn in at the foot so as to make a bulbous shape (cf.
Stanway, Gloucestershire). The porch is at the r. end, but
was probably originally in the centre of a symmetrical façade
of which to the r. of the porch only a fireplace and some walling
survive. The porch has a doorway with a rusticated surround.
The doorway is arched and has a keystone with weird curly
rustication similar to C18 vermiculated rustication. Rusticated
square chimneyshafts.

BALCONY HOUSE, NE of the church. With a porch of ashlar.
Arched doorway, mullioned window, top balcony with fine
vertically symmetrical balusters which look post-Inigo-Jones.

HOUSE, No. 31, s of the Manor House. Fairly symmetrical front
with mullioned windows. Only the centre window on the first
floor has a transom. It is of four lights and placed under a big
gable. Near the top of this an oval window. Is the date c.1660?

GODMANCHESTER 2070

Godmanchester was, as the last syllables of its name show, a
Roman station, and we know something of its plan (*see* below).
The size of the church proves its importance in the Middle Ages
as well, and in the C17 it was called 'a very great county Toune'.

ST MARY. The w tower is exceptionally interesting, as it is
Perp in appearance and yet of 1623, though with the use of
the materials from the C13 tower which is recognizable by
the stiff-leaf responds of the arch towards the nave. The
Stuart modifications of the Perp style come out in the w doorway and the windows above it. But the pairs of two-light
transomed bell-openings and the recessed spire with its three
tiers of lucarnes are Huntingdonshire Perp obviously. The
tower is ashlar-faced, the rest of the church is of brown cobbles.
Perp are the N and s windows, the big two-storeyed s porch

with a broad entry flanked by niches and the not so big N porch, and Perp also the original chancel windows. But the chancel is an E.E. piece; this is shown by the buttressing and the exquisite MASS DIAL on one of them, in the form of an incised rose-window with trefoiled arches between the spokes. The vestry lancet could be re-set from that chancel. The arcades are Perp as well, with a complex continuous moulding to the nave and capitals only to the shafts towards the arch openings. But the E bay of the arcades stands in place of a crossing tower. The two small lancets above the present chancel arch prove that. They were in the tower E wall. The tower no doubt soon turned out to be unsafe and so was replaced by the W tower. – REREDOS and ROOD SCREEN are by *Bodley*, 1901. – STALLS with a good set of MISERICORDS, said to come from Ramsey Abbey. They show e.g. a WS referring to William Stevens, vicar in 1470–81, a fox and goose, a wyvern, a falcon, a cat, a dog, a rabbit, a monkey, a lion, a horse. – STAINED GLASS. One S aisle window by *Morris & Co.*, c.1896; nothing special. – Much by *Kempe* (S aisle S 1889; S aisle W 1894; N aisle NE 1896; chancel S 1901; S aisle SW 1903; N aisle NW c.1911). – PLATE. Silver-gilt Cup and Cover Paten 1559–60; Elizabethan Cup. – MONUMENTS. Brass to a Civilian, early C16, a 14 in. figure. – Tablet, † 1696, in the S aisle, rustic but attractive.

PERAMBULATION. The centre of Godmanchester is the small widening W of the meeting of Cambridge Street with Post Street and Causeway. Here the Town Hall and Queen Elizabeth's Grammar School flank the approach to the delightful CHINESE BRIDGE, Chinese meaning Chippendale-Chinese. Its date is surprisingly as late as 1827. The bridge leads to the islands in the river Ouse which make the view W so enchanting. The TOWN HALL is of 1844, by *Abbott & Habershon*, and was then just a small rectangle of yellow brick with a big shaped gable. An addition was built in 1899.* Queen Elizabeth's GRAMMAR SCHOOL was founded in 1559. The original building is small, of red brick, with a square porch. The back part is of 1851.

We move N first. In POST STREET on the E side HATTON HOUSE, C17, a pretty timber-framed house with overhang and two pedimented Georgian doorways. Then opposite ISLAND COTTAGE, also C17, also with overhang. Its neighbour is ISLAND HALL, lying back from the street, a large red-brick

* INSIGNIA. Late C13 Seal; Mace of 1740–1, made in London.

house of three bays and two and a half storeys with pediment and lower two-bay wings. A very fine arch between entrance hall and staircase and the staircase itself with its mostly twisted balusters suggest a date *c*.1750, but the external details, except for the Tuscan porches, have been victorianized, perhaps about 1850. Front and back of the house are identical. Behind the house is a second CHINESE BRIDGE, but this one is desperately neglected at the time of writing. Next to Island Hall is ERMINE COTTAGE, double-gabled, of 1887, and THE HOLME, three-storeyed, early C18, of yellow and red brick, with segment-headed windows.

A short move E from the hub to see one timber-framed house in CAMBRIDGE STREET, dated 1611 and 1613. Closely set studs and a gable with curved brackets.

Now S, i.e. along THE CAUSEWAY, all the time open to the river basin on the W side. On the E side No. 10 is timber-framed with closely spaced studs. The date 1597 is not genuine. Then No. 13, yellow brick, Late Georgian, with a nice doorway.

Before turning into West Street, we continue S to see a timber-framed house in OLD COURT HALL, with wonderfully phoney decoration, and then by London Road into EARNING STREET for a house on the E side dated 1625 and with two gables to the street, then PLANTAGENET HOUSE with a bargeboarded gable and an oriel window also with bargeboards, and then TUDOR HOUSE, the best timber-framed house in Godmanchester, built in 1600–3 (dates inscribed), with gabled wings l. and r. of the centre. There is an overhang all along, and a second for the gables.

Finally into WEST STREET from the S end of the Causeway. No. 1 is timber-framed with a Georgian doorway, No. 45 on the N side has an overhanging upper floor. No. 44 is mid-Georgian, of red and rubbed brick, quite narrow, but with two Venetian windows, one above the other. The type is the same as Farm Hall (*see* below). After that THE CHESTNUTS, yellow brick of 1873 with some Gothic features, and so to Farm Hall, the finest house in Godmanchester.

FARM HALL. Built in 1746 for Charles Clarke, Recorder of Huntingdon. A plain parallelepiped, except for a short projecting SW wing which is probably a little older. The front is of three storeys, red and rubbed brick, of five bays with a pedimented three-bay projection and a parapet. Tuscan porch with pediment. Contemporary cast-iron railings. The garden side has seven bays, and the centre here has a group of three windows on the first floor, which is a simplified version of a Venetian window. A splendid lime avenue runs away from this garden side. Towards the river is another avenue and a canal. They are separated from the entrance side of the house by a garden wall with two gates also of *c.*1746. The plan of the house is interesting in that it has a cross corridor. Otherwise there is little of special note, except for some extremely fine marble chimneypieces. Elegantly detailed staircase, oddly inconspicuous. Good doorcases on the first floor. The rooms are higher than those below, i.e. we have here a *piano nobile.*

The polygonal outline of the ROMAN TOWN, 24 acres in extent, is shown up well by the present-day roads which encircle the Roman nucleus. Of the defences there is little to be seen. The s gate was, however, examined recently, when blocks of flats were built in PIPER'S LANE, and found to consist simply of two gate-towers flanking a 30-ft-wide road which is thought to have been spanned by a single arch. The buildings of the town are not well known, but BATHS discovered near Pinfold Lane deserve mention. The bath suite, with its rooms arranged linearly in strip form, was built at the beginning of the C2 and continued in use, with modifications, throughout most of the Roman period. Its moderately large size might suggest that it was attached to a *mansio* (official guest house). To the N traces of a second building, apparently a courtyard house of C2 date, were uncovered.

1060
GRAFHAM

ALL SAINTS. Not a large church. The w tower turns octagonal at the very top, for the short length above the springing of the arches of the bell-openings. The spire has two tiers of lucarnes in alternating directions. On the square lower part are four C17 obelisk pinnacles. Late C13 chancel with Y-tracery, and intersecting tracery, the E an adaptation of this tracery made probably in 1803. The DOUBLE PISCINA is late C13 too, and so is the N arcade of four low bays with round piers and double-chamfered arches. The s arcade of standard elements is Dec. – FONT. Octagonal, Dec, with quatrefoils of three varieties and simple blank-arched panels. – ARCHITECTURAL FRAGMENTS in the s porch. – BELL. One by *W. Dawe*, *c.*1400. – MONUMENT. Upper part of an early C14 effigy of a priest (s porch).

GRAFHAM WATER. A reservoir, begun in 1961. The water surface created is at the highest level 1,570 acres; the deepest depth at that level is 70 ft. The dam has a length of 5,600 ft, but is quite low.

SAILING CLUB. *See* East Perry.

GREAT GIDDING

1080

ST MICHAEL. Early C13 s doorway, later C13 arcades with round piers, octagonal abaci, and double-chamfered arches, and much more interesting late C13 chancel. The chancel has windows of three stepped lancet lights (and one Dec one with reticulated tracery), a low-side lancet, a simple N doorway, and inside giant blank arches, one for each bay. On the inner walls also are stone-carved shields. They refer to the Watson family and their relations. The Watsons bought the estate *c.*1546. Good PISCINA. The w tower is Dec. It has pairs of transomed two-light bell-openings and a recessed spire with two tiers of lucarnes. The rest is Perp, except for one Dec s aisle window (with reticulated tracery). – COMMUNION RAIL. Early C17. Two tiers, the lower one short, stubby balusters, the upper arches with pendants. – Octagonal wood PANEL dated 1614 with the words: SATOR ARIPO TENIT OPERA ROTAS, which is intended to read the same forwards and backwards. – PLATE. Cup and Cover Paten of 1638–9.

BAPTIST CHAPEL, Chapel End. 1790. A plain oblong house of three bays frontage with a hipped roof. Three galleries on wooden columns. The BOX PEWS, PULPIT, etc. are all preserved, including the brass CANDLEHOLDERS.

GREAT GRANSDEN

2050

ST BARTHOLOMEW. Of brown cobbles, and Perp throughout. Embattled throughout as well. w tower of four stages with pairs of two-light bell-openings and a spike. Three-light windows and a rising NE turret in the clerestory. Doorways with traceried spandrels. Arcade piers (four bays) with capitals only to the shafts towards the openings, not to the moulded projections towards the nave. Handsome roof with figures. – PULPIT. Of *c.*1660, with characteristic cartouches on the panels. – SCREEN. Partly Perp. – BENCHES. The simple buttressed type of ends, and fronts with plain arched panels. – STAINED GLASS. Old fragments in one chancel window. – CLOCK. The carillon and chimes mechanism is said to have been added in 1683. – PLATE. Cup, Paten, and Paten on foot of 1634–5. – MONUMENT. Very large indent slab with Lombardic lettering to Thomas de Neusum, priest, *c.*1330.

Round the church an exceptionally satisfying triad of houses: to the W the VICARAGE, a plain five-bay house with hipped roof, to the E RIPPINGTON MANOR FARMHOUSE, brick, on an H-shaped plan with an enormous stone chimneybreast of the C16, to the S COLLEGE FARMHOUSE, brick, with a five-bay front of *c.*1700 and the gable-ends still in a late C17 fashion, i.e. with S-curves up to a raised parapet.

GRANSDEN HALL is a similar case, but the two periods are kept neatly apart. The two-bay side-pieces of the front have massive Dutch gables carried by giant pilasters, and that will be mid C17, but the centre has a panelled parapet curving up in the middle to a higher centre part, and that belongs to a re-modelling of 1716.

BAPTIST CHAPEL. Shortly after 1734. A plain brick house of three by three bays with a hipped roof. The furnishings are not contemporary.

WINDMILL, ½ m. E. A weatherboarded post-mill, still on its post. Decrepit sails.

₂₀₆₀   GREAT PAXTON

HOLY TRINITY. There are very few Anglo-Saxon buildings one can call grandiose. Stow in Lincolnshire is one, Great Paxton is without doubt another. Yet on approaching the building, no-one can form any idea what is in store. Here is a church of grey stone and brown cobbles with a Perp W tower, Perp windows and S doorway, and a Perp chancel, except for one N window with intersecting tracery, i.e. of the late C13. The clerestory is Perp too, but there a hint at the interior is given. Some windows on both sides are round-arched (in ironstone) and double-splayed. That is Saxon.

But the interior is not only a surprise, it is also an architectural shock of a high order. This was a cruciform church with a true crossing, and it was an aisled church. Both in pre-Conquest times are extreme rarities. The date of the church is not known, but it is not likely to be earlier than 1000. As for the crossing, a true crossing means that it is as wide as the nave, as the chancel, and as the transepts. This was a matter of course in Romanesque architecture on the Continent at that date, but it does not even apply to Stow.* It does, however, apply to Great Paxton, as is fully displayed in the N transept arch.

---

* Nor to Norton-on-Tees, which has crossing arrangements similar to Stow, but is smaller (transept arches *c.* 14 ft. wide at Stow, *c.* 11 ft at Norton, *c.* 15 ft at Great Paxton).

The responds are four big demi-shafts with thin shafts between. They carry lumpy, shapeless capitals and a plain abacus, and then the unmoulded arch is thrown across at a height unparalleled in early English architecture. The same arrangement applied to the other arches, even if the responds are not so well preserved and the arches are on the s and e side triplechamfered of the late c13. Moreover, as a kind of framing to these groups of four shafts side by side, a thin pilaster strip ran up and no doubt continued all round the arch. This is a usual Late Anglo-Danish thing (cf. e.g. St Benet, Cambridge), and it is visible in several instances.

The nave is just as amazing. The only other Anglo-Saxon aisled naves are Brixworth and Lydd, and the arcade piers of both are just untreated chunks of wall. But at Great Paxton there are proper compound piers, even if they are of a very strange kind, as if Continental compound piers had been misunderstood. The easternmost piers are quatrefoil in section, placed diagonally and with thin shafts between the foils so that they come out in the cardinal directions. The westernmost piers have spurs instead of the thin shafts. The arcade went on to three instead of the present two bays. One w respond was re-used in the new place. This and the two e responds are much more acceptably detailed than the capitals and abaci of the piers: capitals as bulgy as those of the crossing and one-step abaci. The arches are single-step too. The responds are built up of long and short stones rather like Late Anglo-Saxon quoins. The date of the chancel is confirmed by the SEDILIA. – SCREEN. Under the tower arch. Perp. It originally had the Virgin of the Assumption above the entrance, but only the rays which surrounded her survive. – BENCHES. The ends of the plain buttressed type. – SOUTH DOOR. With c13 ironwork, not of the elaborate scroll type as in Bedfordshire. – STAINED GLASS. Old fragments in one chancel n window. – PLATE. Cup of 1813–14.

GREAT STAUGHTON

ST ANDREW. The w tower is Perp and more ambitious than most, with its quatrefoil base frieze and its quatrefoil top frieze and its pinnacles. Set-back buttresses. Pairs of transomed two-light bell-openings. Earlier is the chancel, say early c14. One window has cusped Y-tracery, and the low-side window of two lights even a reticulation unit. Definitely Dec is the

s aisle. Again reticulated tracery. The s doorway is something
special, with its dainty foliage capitals and the many mouldings
of the arch. The tower must be later than the s aisle. This is
obvious by the aisle w window. Inside, the arcades (of five
bays) are both older than anything outside. First come three
bays on the s side (round piers and abaci), then the rest of the
s arcade and the whole N arcade. Round piers and the abaci
chamfered squares set diagonally. All arcade arches are double-
chamfered. But the chancel arch and the tower arch are Perp.
The N chapel dates from *c.*1455 and has a tomb recess with a
panelled vault. – SCREEN. Under the tower arch. It consists
of two parts, the lower panels from a C17 pulpit (with one
inlaid panel), but the upper, once a bench-back, with an
inscription to Olyver Leder and his wife and the date 1539.
– COMMUNION RAIL. Late C17, of strong, twisted balusters. –
(STAINED GLASS. C16 and C17 heraldic glass from Gaynes
Hall in the N aisle E window. GMCH) – BELL. One bell is by
William Dawe; *c.*1400. – PAINTINGS. Two icons brought
from Chanak(?) in Anatolia in 1923. One the Virgin, the other
a saintly King. – PLATE. Cup, Paten on foot, and Almsdish,
all 1751–2. – MONUMENTS. Upper part of a C13 monument
to an abbot. Alwalton (rather than Purbeck) marble. The head
in a pointed-cinquefoiled surround. The monument used to be
in the garden of Gaynes Hall, and its provenance is unknown.
It should be compared with the abbots' monuments of
Peterborough Cathedral. – Large stone monument to Sir
James Dyer † 1582, in judge's robes, and his wife, and Sir
Richard † 1605 and wife. Two kneeling couples, husband facing wife across a prayer-desk (but Sir Richard has put his helmet on it). Three columns and pendant arches. Big strapwork
on the top, and obelisks. – George Wauton † 1606. Recumbent
effigy, the slab on which he lies supported by two free-standing
atlantes with short skirts. – Sir Baldwin Conyers † 1731. A
conservative composition for its date. An urn on a small
sarcophagus in a shell-headed niche. Roman Doric columns
and a pediment broken back in the centre. Two cherubs on it
and two cherubs' heads at the foot.

PLACE HOUSE, opposite the church. One range of a formerly
larger mansion. Red brick. The present front is flat and has
mullioned and transomed windows, widely spaced. Two pretty
BARNS, timber-framed with brick infilling.

At the N entrance to Staughton House is a group of C18 COTTAGES
neatly arranged on two sides of a square lawn. The E piers to

the garden of Staughton House are uncommonly fine and probably of *c*.1760–70.

VILLAGE CROSS, Staughton Highway. A fluted pillar with a square sundial and a ball-finial. 1637.

GAYNES HALL, 2¼ m. NE. By *George Byfield*, *c*.1800. Yellow brick, of seven bays and two and a half storeys. Semicircular porch of unfluted, not at all elegant Ionic columns. The ground-floor windows are set in blank arches, and the pedimented middle window and the attic window above it are included in one blank arch. On the middle of the eaves an urn. Oval entrance hall and staircase hall with a circular skylight.

EARTHWORK at Old Manor Farm, 1 m. SW. Perhaps the remains of a motte and bailey castle.

Great Staughton is the site of a recently excavated ROMAN VILLA. Two separate buildings were found close together. Both were of the corridor villa type, one (the northern) containing several mosaics, the second possessing simple hypocausts.

GREAT STUKELEY

2070

ST BARTHOLOMEW. Substantial Perp w tower with clasping buttresses chamfered towards the middles of the four sides of the tower. Low post-medieval pyramid roof. On the chancel N side a pair of E.E. lancets. Internally the evidence is earlier. Arcades of four bays. N differs from S in interesting ways, suggesting only a small difference in time. On the S side the piers and abaci are round, and one capital has early stiff-leaf. The arches are pointed, of one step and one slight chamfer – say 1190. But the W bay has two slight chamfers, i.e. is a little later. On the N side the abaci are octagonal, and arches two and three are of the earlier, arches one and four of the later variety. The arch from tower to nave is Perp, and a vault was begun inside the tower. The ribs rest on figural brackets, one of a frightening frog creature. – STOUP. Square and gabled. Mr Sisson suggests that it may be part of a pinnacle. – PLATE. Cup and Cover Paten 1624–5.

HADDON

1090

ST MARY. The church has a mighty Norman chancel arch of the early C12. Capitals with interlaced bands (cf. Castor), thick rolls in the arch. Along the hood-mould and down the jambs saltire crosses, like flattened-out dogtooth. Then, still Norman, the N aisle w window, and after that, early C13, the S aisle w window and both arcades. They are of three bays and have round, double-chamfered arches. Octagonal piers. N comes before s. Some nailhead on the s side. The arches from the aisles into the transepts are contemporary. The transepts are clearly contemporary too (see the N transept N lancet), as is also the w tower with its lancets below. The curious twin rising arches to the w ending on a long mid-shaft must indicate that in the C13 a bellcote and not a tower was planned. The top stage is indeed Perp. The N porch is a puzzle. Can it also be early C13? The twin side openings still have round arches. The doorway is pointed, with slight chamfers. The entrance has nailhead. The N doorway is like the s doorway. In the s transept s wall is a three-light window with cusped intersecting tracery, i.e. of c.1300, and the N and s aisle windows of three stepped lancet lights under one segmental arch are most probably of such a date too. The chancel is c.1300 at the latest, but more probably c.1275. It has twin lancets under one blank arch to N and s. That on the N side has in the blank tympanum a charming foliated cross, just like those on coffin lids or indeed like the ironwork on C13 doors. Re-fixed against the nave roof are men and angels probably from the roof's predecessor. – PAINTINGS. Over the chancel arch C15 figures, hardly recognizable. – STAINED GLASS. E window by *Kempe*, 1901. – PLATE. Paten on foot of 1648–9; Cup, Cover Paten, and Plate of 1798–9.

HAIL WESTON

1060

ST NICHOLAS. A sweet building with its cobbled walls, its one big old tiled roof over nave and chancel, and its totally shingled w tower, whose pyramid roof starts lower than the ridge of the tile-roof. Architecturally the tower is of great interest. It represents a type familiar in Essex but unique in Huntingdonshire. It is entirely timber-framed, with heavy posts along the s and N walls, four tie-beams, two across the space, two against the E and w walls, and scissor-bracing as well as wind-braces against the walls. The impression is confusing but powerful. Is the tower of c.1500, or earlier? Dating in Essex has recently gone earlier – thanks to radio carbon. The building itself is E.E. – see the chancel N lancet with continuous outer mouldings and the small DOUBLE PISCINA. The nave N doorway has a finely moulded arch. – BENCHES. With summarily shaped poppyheads. – (SCREEN. Original dado. GMCH)

HAMERTON   *1070*

ALL SAINTS. It is odd that the s porch windows should be late
C13, with bar tracery. Do they come from a porch preceding
the present one? The w tower is ashlar-faced and Perp, with
set-back buttresses, a w doorway with traceried spandrels,
bell-openings in pairs of two lights each, a quatrefoil frieze
over, and no spire. Embattled s and N aisle and clerestory, all
Perp. But the s doorway seems to be of *c.*1300 (continuous
mouldings) and the chancel of about the same date, though
over-restored. Windows with Y-tracery and two low-side
windows, that on the s a prolongation below a transom of one
light of a two-light window. Early C14 N and s arcades of four
bays, tall piers, standard elements. The nave roof has figures
on the wall-posts and angels against the intermediate principals,
the N and s aisle roofs only the former. – FONT. A big, ambitious Perp piece. Panelled stem, bowl with alternating patterns.
– PLATE. Cup and Cover Paten of 1674–5; Paten on foot of
1837–8. – MONUMENTS. In the s aisle two large, uncouth
standing monuments, both no more than an inscription tablet
in big letters with strapwork around or on top. Mawde
Bedell † 1587, dated 1597, and Sir John Bedell † 1613.

HARTFORD   *2070*

ALL SAINTS. In a delightful position by the Ouse with a landing place to the E and the trees of Hartford House. Perp w
tower with battlements and pinnacles, the middle merlons on
all sides connected by thin ogee arches. The s doorway has
traces of E.E. origin; all other external features are the restorer's. But internally there is something of interest. First the
restorer's work, *Hutchinson*'s of 1861, i.e. the imitation-Norman chancel arch and chancel E wall. Then the four-bay
arcades, both late C12, but N in characteristic ways just a little
earlier. Both sides have round piers and round abaci already,
but the N arches are round, of one step and one slight chamfer,
the s arches pointed and of two slight chamfers. – PULPIT.
High Victorian, i.e. probably of the sixties. Stone with pink
marble colonnettes and nice metal tracery. – PLATE. Cup of
1694–5; Paten on foot of 1749–50.*

HARTFORD HOUSE. Early Georgian, of five bays and two
storeys plus parapet; red brick. The lower windows are segment-headed.

* The plate is now in the Fitzwilliam Museum at Cambridge.

MANOR HOUSE, a little NE of Hartford House, on the other side of the road. The suggested date is *c.*1500. Hall-house type with two gabled wings, the l. gable jutting on brackets. The gabled porch is in the traditional way not in the middle of the hall part.

At SAPLEY, 2 m. NNW, is an earthwork with moat, probably the fragment of a motte and bailey CASTLE. The motte is now only 9 ft high.

HELPSTON
Soke of Peterborough

ST BOTOLPH. Norman W tower rebuilt in 1865. The lowest parts are said to have had Saxon long-and-short work. This was exposed in 1865. Early C12 arch towards the nave with scallop capitals. The pointed arch is a remodelling. Arches also to N and S. These have the original thick roll mouldings. The tower turns octagonal at the clerestory level. C14 bell-openings. Very short spire with one tier of lucarnes. Of the early C13 the S arcade of two bays with circular pier and circular capitals and abaci. Round arches with two slight chamfers. Mid C13 N arcade with octagonal pier and double-chamfered pointed arches. Then *c.*1300 the chancel and the E bay connecting it with the arcades. The chancel arch has filleted shafts. Original also the SEDILIA and PISCINA, and on the original lines the E window. The other chancel windows are strange replacements of 1609 (date on one of them). Tall, of two lights, straight-headed, with a pointed quatrefoil at the top of each light. Early C13 S doorway with one order of colonnettes and one waterleaf capital and one with upright leaves. Pointed arch. In spite of this, the doorway could go with the S arcade. The porch entrance is early C14. Early C14, i.e. Dec, also the pretty S aisle E window. – PLATE. Cup, 1768(?); two Patens, 1828; Flagon, 1830.

VILLAGE CROSS. Circular steps. Tall polygonal base with crocketed gables and battlements.

CLARE MONUMENT. 1869. In an undisciplined Gothic. John Clare was born and buried at Helpston.

COLLEGE HOUSE, S of the church. Two buttresses to the N. Other medieval fragments are a slit window (now inside) and a four-centred archway. Several other handsome houses, e.g. HELPSTON HOUSE (100 yds uphill from the village cross), with gables, dormers, and a canted bay window.

ROMAN BUILDING. Pail Grounds, on the E side of the road, ¾ m. s of the village, is a site recorded in 1827 as containing at least one fine mosaic. The mosaic in the chancel of Helpston church may have possibly come from this or from another Roman site in Lawn Wood, Bainton, w of King Street.

HEMINGFORD ABBOTS

2070

A village of attractive houses, but, as at Hemingford Grey, a recent rash of small private houses.

ST MARGARET. Of brown cobbles. W tower with clasping buttresses with chamfers towards the middles of the sides and a recessed spire with two bands and two tiers of lucarnes in alternating directions. Interesting N aisle with windows and doorway of c.1300. All three windows are of two lights and straight-headed, which is remarkable, and the E window is just as remarkable, provided it is not interfered with. The chancel is of yellow brick, probably of c.1800. The interior has arcades of three bays (standard elements) plus a truncated fourth into which the tower now cuts. The E bay represents a former crossing. This is evident from the thicker octagonal piers, the half-arches, i.e. flying buttresses, across the aisles, and the thickening of the upper nave walls. Another disturbance in the clerestory walls is the replacement of two-light by three-light windows. Fine decorated rood-bay of the nave roof. Decorated bosses also in the N aisle roof. The S porch entrance is E.E. Could it belong to the date of the arcades, or must it be earlier? And is it re-set? – STAINED GLASS. In the N aisle E window good C18 heraldic glass. – In a N aisle window glass by *Tower*, of 1928, incredibly reactionary.– PLATE. Salver on foot of Britannia metal, 1719–20; two Cups and a Flagon, 1795–6; Paten on foot, 1800–1. – MONUMENTS. Joshua Barnes † 1712. Baldacchino above the inscription; putto-heads and palm-fronds at the bottom. He was Regius Professor of Greek; so the inscription is partly in Greek. – Jacob Maxey † 1710. Tablet with a little bust on top.

HEMINGFORD GREY

2070

ST JAMES. The w tower faces the Ouse. It is a pretty position. The history of the building begins with the N arcade. The middle arch is round with one step and one slight chamfer. The piers are round and sturdy, the abaci square and nicked at the corners. The capitals have small decorated scallops.

That makes it c.1180. E bay and W bay are later, late C13 and late C14 respectively. The meeting of two responds W of the E bay deserves a good look. The S arcade has one arch almost identical with the earliest on the N side, but probably some twenty years later. The piers now have round abaci. The E and W bays are as above. The S doorway is over-restored but matches the S aisle. The chancel is mid C13 – see the two N lancets and the lovely DOUBLE PISCINA with its intersecting not only arches but mouldings (cf. Introduction, p. 184, for other examples). The arches stand on Purbeck shafts. Opposite a plain DOUBLE AUMBRY. Finally the details of the Perp W tower. Clasping buttresses, turning diagonal higher up. Ball finials of the C18 on the buttresses, and a truncated recessed spire also crowned by ball finials. The rest of the spire was blown down in the hurricane of 1741. – STAINED GLASS. One window of the S aisle by *Kempe*, 1906 (still without his future partner Tower). – PLATE. Cup and Paten on foot, 1684–5. – MONUMENTS. Enjoyable cartouches, one inside † 1682, one outside † 1715.

MANOR HOUSE, ¼ m. SW of the church, with its garden extending to the river. The house is of very special interest, because its whole centre is a C12 hall. The hall is on the upper floor, and there was in all probability a chapel wing attached to its E side. Norman two-light windows are preserved in the W, S, and E walls. The arches are decorated with pellets at the l. and r. starting-points and the apex, almost anticipating cusping. The jambs and the intermediate pier are single-chamfered. The entrance was on the S side, where the doorway remains. This is one of the short sides, which is unusual (but cf. King John's Hunting Box, Romsey, Hants). There must have been wooden steps up to the doorway. On the same side is a narrow, straight-headed window on the ground floor. Also on the ground floor, to the E, is a doorway which was originally an arched window. The finest internal feature is the mighty chimneypiece with two Norman columns with two-scalloped capitals. Segmental arch of one slight chamfer. Are the tiles at the back of the fireplace Norman too? A MOAT surrounds the house on three sides; on the fourth is the river.

Immediately N of the church is HEMINGFORD GREY HOUSE, built in 1697. Red brick, two storeys, five bays, with segment-headed windows and hipped roof. Apsed door-hood on well-carved brackets. An addition to the r. By the river one of the largest plane trees in England, planted in 1702. Five foot from the ground the girth is over 20 ft.

The HIGH STREET runs from close to the Manor House towards the E. At the start RIVER HOUSE, late C18, of yellow brick. Five bays, and a handsome doorway. At the corner of Braggs Lane another five-bay house called BROOM LODGE. This, though early C18, still has shaped end-gables. Much further E GLEBE COTTAGE, dated 1583, timber-framed with closely set studs and thatch.

Hemingford Grey, which even ten years ago was still perfectly rural, has recently suffered from an invasion of small speculative private houses and bungalows. It is a great pity.

HILTON

2060

ST MARY MAGDALENE. C14 W tower, the rest Perp. Brown cobbles. The arcades of four bays have typical Perp piers with capitals only to the arch openings. In the chancel a bracket on a head, in the S aisle a very pretty but mutilated vaulted niche. – SCULPTURE. Small, strange stone of keyhole shape now in the W wall of the tower. In the upper part the Crucifix, in the lower defaced foliage. – STAINED GLASS. In a chancel N window a head of Christ. – The E window by *Wailes* of Newcastle, 1861, the W window by *Constable* of Cambridge; both bad. – Also two windows by *Kempe*, 1896 and 1898. – PLATE. Cup and Cover Paten 1571–2; Paten on foot 1681–2. – MONUMENT. Two alabaster pieces from a tomb-chest, one with two quatrefoils enclosing shields, the other with two kneeling angels holding a shield.

On the GREEN is a nicely kept grass MAZE, first cut in 1660. In the middle a PILLAR with a ball finial to record the death of William Sparrow, who had it cut. He died in 1729.

E of the maze the fine BARNS of the GRANGE, weatherboarded, and one of seven, the other of six bays.

(ST JOHN'S COLLEGE FARM, on the road to Graveley. C15 hall house, altered and enlarged in the C17. Parts of the hall roof remain. RCHM)

(HOUSE, 600 yds N of the church. By *Dyson & Hebeler*, 1937–8. In the 'International Modern' of the most progressive English houses of those years. Specially typical the glazed semicircular projection of the staircase and the long window boards. – By *W.P.Dyson* also a much more recent house, 650 yds NW of the church, cubic, and with a giant Ionic portico.)

HINCHINGBROOKE

Hinchingbrooke started life as an Augustinian nunnery. It was founded before 1087 and soon moved here from Eltisley in Cambridgeshire. It was never large, and at the time of the suppression had only its prioress and three nuns. In 1538 the site was given to Sir Richard Williams *alias* Cromwell, who one year later also received Ramsey Abbey. He died in 1544, and shortly after his son began to adapt and build. The house grew through the C16 and C17. It was sold by Sir Oliver Cromwell in 1627 to Sir Sidney Montagu. Sir Sidney's son became Viscount Hinchingbrooke and Earl of Sandwich. He was Pepys's second cousin.

The house makes an exceptionally varied picture – 'old, spacious, irregular, yet not vast or forlorn' is how Horace Walpole describes it – but in spite of what the centuries have done, the conventual core is still recognizable. The principal range has an inner hall with skylight. This before the C19 was a courtyard and represents the cloister of the nunnery. Medieval walling exists to its s, where the church lay, and also to the W and E. But visible features begin only with the Cromwells, and as they are scattered, it is more useful to walk round the outside and then the inside and sample them as they come.

One enters by the GATEHOUSE, and this is not germane to Hinchingbrooke at all. It was taken over by the Cromwells from Ramsey Abbey after the Dissolution. It dates from c.1500 and has to the outside a carriage way and a pedestrian way. The duplication of the pedestrian archway is not medieval. The main archway has traceried spandrels, two wild men with clubs to the l. and r. and a quatrefoil frieze over. Battlemented top. The pattern repeats to the inside, except that pedestrians are here no longer segregated.

As one has passed through the gateway one faces in front the back of the former brewhouse and bakehouse and to the l. the N side of the principal building. The former are of Tudor brick with blue-brick diapers, and there are in the s half five buttresses, set close to each other and connected at the top by shallow arches. The NORTH FRONT of the principal building has two two-storeyed canted bay windows, both of the mid C16, but both built with ornamental materials of c.1500. The two differ one from the other. The l. one has altogether nine lights, the r. seven, and the arch-heads, all uncusped, are not the same. Between the ground-floor and the first-floor openings is decoration including Cromwell heraldry. The battlemented tower further r. is C19, probably of the thirties etc. when, after a fire *Blore* remodelled the house drastically.

The EAST FRONT in its N part was ashlar-faced and re-done by *Blore*, but must be C16 (*see* below). Then C16 brickwork appears again, with the blue, vitrified bricks forming diapers. The gable is old too and seems to have been stepped from the start. The canted bay window is also C16, though the pointed windows must be of *c*.1800. Round the corner the first feature of the SOUTH FRONT is an ample semicircular bay window, 68 and this is dated 1602. It belonged originally to the N part of the E front, was deeper than it is now, and the ground floor had open arcading. The S front otherwise is of *c*.1830. Between this range and the SW tower is re-used old ashlar work with a brick parapet. The SOUTH-WEST TOWER itself is mid C16, but has windows of the C18 and later. The WEST SIDE is below all C16, but above late C17 brick with cross-windows. This includes the square projection to the W. But at the N end of this side, where the short C17 wing begins – there was formerly here a long C19 wing – appears a medieval buttress, a reminder of the nunnery. The doorway of the wing is late C17 with a straight hood on carved brackets. So to the W side of the brewhouse and bakehouse. This is of brick and stone mixed with a row of small timber-framed gables. The detached LAUNDRY range NW of the brewhouse and bakehouse is C16 too.

At the S end INSIDE the brewhouse and bakehouse is the KITCHEN, with a large N fireplace and a W fireplace arch. The main rooms of the house are all by *Blore*, and nothing is specially grand. He was a dull man; Hinchingbrooke confirms it. Of the C16 there remain only a few doorways with four-centred heads and some lush openwork panels of the main STAIRCASE, made by the King's Joiner *Kennard*, *c*.1663. In the LIBRARY is a chimneypiece with two caryatids, dated 1580. On the first floor some Georgian chimneypieces. The courtyard roof dates only from 1909.

NENE AND OUSE WATER BOARD, S of the grounds of Hinchingbrooke. 1962–5 by *H. J. Smith* of *Pick, Everard, Keay & Gimson*; good.

NUNS' BRIDGE. C18. The three E arches are of the C15 or C16. Cutwaters on the S side. The rest is mostly C18.

1080
HOLME

ST GILES. 1862 by *Edward Browning*. Rock-faced, with a
double bellcote. Dec in style, even the round clerestory windows with flowing tracery. The even, straight-headed three-
light aisle windows look well from inside. Inside old materials
were re-used. The E respond and two pier capitals N and S are
medieval, S with a scalloped C12 capital and a moulded C13
capital, N with C13 octagonal capitals. – PLATE. Cup of
1709–10.

HOLME WOOD HOUSE. 1873–4 by *William Young* (GS). Rather
Waterhousish. Red brick and red terracotta. Mullioned and
transomed windows. Gables. Good big cast-iron garden gates
and railings.

1070
HOLYWELL

ST JOHN BAPTIST. The W tower is a mystery. It is said to date
from 1547 and to be built of stone from Ramsey Abbey. What
does that statement involve? The tower is broad and substantial and built of regular stone blocks. Its buttresses start
with chamfers, i.e. semi-polygonal, and the W window is indeed
Tudor. But the bell-openings are Dec, and the doorway with
its broadly rounded-trefoiled head and the big cusped tracery
motifs of the spandrels defeats dating. The arch towards the
nave is Dec anyway, and in the N and S walls are thin blank
arches which are Dec too and fulfil no useful function in their
position. Is it then all re-used Ramsey material? The body of
the church is stone and cobbles, and the features are over-
restored. The chancel is a beautiful early C13 piece with
paired lancet windows, with a detached middle shaft between
them inside and a rib rising from the shaft to the rere-arch,
an unexpected personal touch. The aisle windows are Early
Dec. So are the three-bay arcades with their standard elements.
The roof of the nave is of 1862, but figures from the old roof
are displayed in the church. – PLATE. Cup 1822–3; Paten
on foot 1834–5.

1070
HOUGHTON

ST MARY. Of brown cobbles. Partly Dec and partly Perp. Early
C14 the chancel with windows from the cusped lancet to reticulation. The DOUBLE PISCINA indeed looks no later than
*c.*1300. Early C14 also the N arcade of standard elements. Perp

w tower of unusual shape (but cf. more than half a dozen in Cambridgeshire, the centre of course being Ely). The buttresses stop below the bell-openings, and above them the tower turns octagonal to carry the stone spire. The spire has two tiers of lucarnes, the square part of the tower very prominent pinnacles, the top parts of which unfortunately were blown off in the hurricane of 1741. The N aisle wall is a cheap brick rebuilding of 1871. – SEDILE. Stone seat, with arms like that at Stanground; C13 (N aisle, W end, not *in situ*). – PLATE. Early C17 Cup.

UNION CHAPEL. 1840. Yellow brick with arched doorway and windows, a pediment across the façade, and a small pediment over the doorway.

HOUGHTON GRANGE, 1 m. w. By *Ransome*, 1896–7. Elizabethan in the free latest C19 way, i.e. for example with a big segmental pediment over the porch and above it a square bay window of altogether eleven lights. Two nice identical free-Tudor lodges on the A-road.

HUNTINGDON

INTRODUCTION

Huntingdon was a Saxon burgh. In 1068 William the Conqueror ordered a castle to be built and the burgh repaired. A monastery was founded before 1092, perhaps before 973. In 1113 it became Augustinian. Its site was where the cemetery now is. The Benedictine nunnery of Hinchingbrooke just outside to the W was also founded before 1100. Before 1265 came the Austin Friars. At that time the town had sixteen parish churches. Deterioration of the Ouse and the Black Death did much damage, and the town declined. Early in the C16 there were only four parish churches left. Yet John Evelyn called Huntingdon a fair town, and so did Cowper, who lived there from 1765 to 1767.

CHURCHES

ALL SAINTS. Along the Market Place. The E end is close to the High Street. The church is varied in outline and fits well into its surroundings. The tower is placed at the NW corner. It was set into an existing building, as its S wall stands on the first bay of an E.E. N arcade, the oldest remaining feature.* That it was an arcade and not a tower arch is evident from the fact that the W respond of the arch is a respond indeed – it has stiff-leaf decoration – but that the E respond is simply a round pier with an octagonal abacus. The upper parts of the tower are of brick, rebuilt after the Civil War, and the very top is Victorian. Otherwise the church is essentially Perp, except for the N aisle windows, which with their crocketed arches and tracery look Dec, and the organ chamber and vestry, which are by *Sir G. G. Scott*, of 1859. The organ chamber is the prettiest feature of the church, with its angel at the apex playing on a positive organ. The arcades, of four (on the N side of course three) bays, are characteristically Early Perp. Piers of standard moulded section, arches of two sunk-quadrant mouldings, the arch tops slightly ogee. The E window of the S aisle has mullions carried down blank to form a reredos. In the SE corner charming niche on a foliated corbel and with a canopy. Good Perp chancel roof with carved bosses. – STAINED GLASS. The clerestory windows are of 1860, by *Clayton &*

---

* But some N walling is Norman.

Bell. – By the same the former chancel E window, now in the
w wall of the s aisle. It shows the Te Deum in the presence of
Prophets, Apostles, and Saints, and also the Venerable Bede,
William of Wykeham, Archbishop Cranmer, Bishop Ridley,
George Herbert, Newton, Handel, Queen Victoria and Prince
Albert, and the Duke of Wellington. – The w window is by
Kempe, 1900 (with his wheatsheaf). – The E window is by
Tower, Kempe's successor, *c.*1920. – PLATE. Flemish Chalice
of *c.*1750; silver-gilt. – MONUMENT. Alice Weaver † 1636.
Tablet with kneeling figures in relief. The top has already –
very early – an open scrolly pediment. – Good Victorian
CHURCHYARD RAILINGS.

ST MARY, High Street. The w tower is the most ornate piece of
the church, Perp, with a doorway flanked by niches and decorated with quatrefoils in spandrels, buttresses clasping and at
the same time set-back and enriched by gablets, and niches
for images on brackets with e.g. a Pelican and a Green Man,
bell-openings as pairs of two-light openings, two quatrefoil
friezes, and battlements and pinnacles. On the ground stage to
the N was originally large gabled blank arcading. But the
earliest parts of the church are first the remains of flat Norman
buttresses in the SE corner of the nave and the SW corner of
the s aisle – proving the existence of a large, aisled Norman
church – and then the chancel, early C13, with a priest's doorway which still has waterleaf capitals and also two lancet windows, shafted inside. The N one is re-set in the vestry; the
other re-set window has Y-tracery and is hence of the late
C13. The position of the priest's doorway shows that the
chancel was originally longer. The present E wall is of 1876.
Aisles and clerestory appear Perp externally, but the arcades
tell a different story. They are both E.E., s perhaps of *c.*1240,
N of *c.*1260. Much of the N side and some of the s, however,
are a C17 rebuilding after the tower had partly collapsed in
1607. The s arcade has a variety of supports. The w respond
of the s arcade has a stiff-leaf capital on a short triple shaft,
two piers are octagonal, one is round, and one consists of four
keeled major and four minor shafts. The arches are of many
fine mouldings, and the stops of the hood-mould are pretty
stiff-leaf balls. The N arcade is simpler, mostly of standard
elements, i.e. for instance double-chamfered arches. In several
places are C17 inscriptions. – PLATE. Cup 1569–70; Cover
Paten 1624–5; early C17 Cup and Cover Paten; three engraved
Plates 1684; Flagon 1726. – MONUMENTS. Tablets under the

tower, the largest to the Carcassonnett family, 1749, assigned to *Scheemakers* (two pilasters, open pediment). – Also some enjoyable cartouches, e.g. † 1729.

ST MICHAEL (R.C.), Hartford Road. 1900–1 by *A.J.C. Scoles*.* Brick and stone, round-arched.

METHODIST CHURCH, High Street. 1878 by *R.Hutchinson*. Rock-faced, geometrical tracery, no tower.

CEMETERY CHAPEL, Priory Road. 1855 by *Hutchinson*, a 'rogue' job, as cemetery chapels often are. L-shaped, of ironstone, with a totally asymmetrically placed angle turret.

PUBLIC BUILDINGS

TOWN HALL, Market Hill. 1745. Red brick, of seven bays and three storeys. The strong three-bay projection with pediment is an addition of 1817. So is the porch of two pairs of Tuscan columns and the extension with cupola behind. In it the Assembly Room on the second floor with Venetian windows. On the ground floor on the E side a Tuscan loggia. There were originally such loggias on three sides. The Courts of Justice have their original fitments. – INSIGNIA. Mace with Stuart arms; Seals of 1628 and 1634.

16 CROMWELL MUSEUM, formerly Grammar School – the one attended by Cromwell, and originally the W end of the long infirmary hall of the Hospital of St John. What survives is the two W bays of nave and aisles, but there were seven bays and the premises of the master, the refectory, etc., round a courtyard to the N. The remaining fragment is of *c*.1170–90. The S arcade was built before the N arcade. On the S side are round piers with multi-scalloped capitals and square abaci. The arches are round, and one has zigzag at r. angles to the wall. Also there is a hood-mould with nutmeg. On the N side the abaci are round, the arches pointed, and one capital has stylized upright leaves. These details can now be seen from outside as well as inside, as the outer aisle walls have disappeared. The façade has the portal not in the centre but to the r., with a small window on its l. However, before the N aisle was built it was central. The portal has two orders of colonnettes and the arches zigzag, also at r. angles to the wall. Above is a frieze of five large shafted arches containing two windows, but otherwise blank. The whole building was completely rebuilt 3 ft higher up in 1878.

---

* According to Mr Dickinson.

TECHNICAL COLLEGE, California Road. 1963–5 by *Twist & Whitley*. Glass, grey brick, and black granite chippings. Nicely grouped and only one to two storeys high.

SCHOOLS. It is quite interesting to follow the development of style from the free Tudor with three identical gables of the SECONDARY MODERN SCHOOL ANNEX in Brookside of 1905 to the Interwar-Tudor with William and Mary hipped roofs but mullioned and mullioned-and-transomed windows of the GRAMMAR SCHOOL of 1939 in the Brampton Road and the Anglo-Dudok of ST PETER'S SCHOOL of as late as 1957 in St Peter's Road (it looks as if it were done in the thirties) and so to the best of the most recent ones, the COUNTY JUNIOR SCHOOL in Mayfield Road of 1963–4, yellow brick and very well grouped. This is by *K. G. Sparrow*, county architect, and *K. G. Dines*.

COUNTY HOSPITAL, Brampton Road. 1852–4 by *T. Smith* of London. Yellow brick. Thirteen bays. Latest Classical, going free, i.e. still with a pediment, but with arched as well as segment-headed windows, and with garlands in the pediment, i.e. a touch of the English Classical as against Roman or Greek. – In front the charming SANDWICH MEMORIAL FOUNTAIN, 1889 by *Edis*. Terracotta with strapwork top like the Cambridge conduit.*

PETERSFIELD HOSPITAL, the former WORKHOUSE, St Peter's Road. Yellow brick, in plan not of one of the standard types. The workhouse was probably built in the 1830s.

FIRE STATION, Hartford Road. 1964–5 by *K. G. Sparrow*, the county architect. A good-looking job.

COUNTY GAOL (former), St Peter's Road. 1828. Yellow brick, classical. The gatehouse is demolished. Two pavilions l. and r., and between and behind the octagon which was the watching-centre.

PERAMBULATION

MARKET HILL is the natural start. The bronze MONUMENT ('the brooding soldier') is by *Lady Scott*. The best house no doubt is WALDEN HOUSE behind the church, a late C17 design of red brick, five bays and two storeys, with hipped roof, giant Ionic angle pilasters, raised window surrounds, and Dutch garlands below the first-floor windows – a tradition from the Hugh May generation. Next to it WYKEHAM HOUSE,

The fountain has recently been destroyed.

early C19, yellow brick with a porch of heavy pillars. On the other side, i.e. No. 110 High Street, is an Early Georgian three-bay, three-storey house with giant brick pilasters and both mid-windows round-arched. Parapet with cypher and the date 1727. Next to it No. 111, a six-bay house with two-bay pediment and a Venetian mid-window.

We continue down the HIGH STREET to the bridge. On the N side a PEDESTRIAN SHOPPING STREET has recently been made (by *Parkinson, Hull & Fawcett,* 1961). A pity it is architecturally not a little more distinguished. At its far end, at the time of writing, GOVERNMENT OFFICES are being built to the same architects' designs. Opposite in the High Street is the small entrance to the churchyard of St Benet. The church has long disappeared. Next, on the same side, the LITERARY AND SCIENTIFIC INSTITUTE, 1840, stuccoed, of three bays, with giant pilasters and a statue of Pallas Athene on the top. Nos 36–38 is a Late Georgian group of two-and-a-half-storey houses in grey brick. Nos 28–32 are a long group of red two-storeyed houses with modillion frieze.

The climax is COWPER HOUSE, where Cowper, the poet, lived. This has a steep three-bay pediment and on the first floor window-lintels with brick frills. This front is early C18. Another house of the group has a touch of Gothick in the doorway. Inside a fine room with fireplace, doorcase, etc., the details suggesting *c.*1720. Hidden by the panelling fragments of Elizabethan paintings with large flowers and leaves and a dog. Recently some smaller leaf painting has been discovered in an upper room as well.

Opposite St Mary's church is CASTLE HILL HOUSE, standing on its own. It is of yellow brick, of 1787, with a good pedimented doorway. Behind the house and visible from the High Street nearer the bridge lie the earthworks of Huntingdon CASTLE. It was established by William the Conqueror and went out of use hardly more than a hundred years later. The inner bailey lay along the Ouse, the motte to its W, now only 12 ft high, and an outer bailey followed W of both. In moving on towards the bridge more Late Georgian yellow-brick houses, No. 151 and No. 154–5, which was the GAOL. It has giant pilasters.* No. 152 between the two has a nice late C18 doorway. Then, back on the S side, the OLD BRIDGE HOTEL with a specially good late C18 doorway. Corinthian columns, finely detailed frieze, pediment.

* (Beneath is the condemned cell with a vault on a brick pillar.)

The BRIDGE is of the early C14. It is called 'lately built' in 1332. It has cutwaters to both sides. Their tops differ s from N, an indication of two authorities building from their sides at the same time. The bridge chapel of St Thomas Becket stood on the E side.* Next to the bridge a new PEDESTRIAN BRIDGE, 1965–6, by *R. E. C. Dorling*, engineer and county surveyor, crossing the river with an elegant sweep. (E of the bridge end of the High Street on the river is the oldest remaining factory in the county. It dates from *c*.1820 and has a square chimney. P. G. M. Dickinson) On the s side of the bridge the HUNTINGDON HOSIERY MILLS. Along the river two three-storeyed ranges, the one nearer the bridge bigger and more important. Behind, a later seven-storey range with tiers of giant pilasters. The buildings were probably erected shortly after 1857. They were at first a flour mill.

That completes the SE walk. Now NW, along the other half of the HIGH STREET. The first building of note is the GEORGE HOTEL. Its three-storeyed yellow-brick front of eleven bays is of 1865 (by *R. Hutchinson*). It is vaguely classical, with a pedimented gable and segment-headed ground-floor and round-arched first-floor windows. The yard behind still has its late C17 gallery along one side. The shape of the balusters allows the dating. The back of this range is of brick and looks a little later.

Turn into GEORGE STREET for the Conservative Association, i.e. the former church of ST JOHN EVANGELIST, neo-Norman of 1845 (by *W. G. Habershon* of St Neots). Yellow brick but with an ornate portal. Then WINDOVER'S factory, also yellow brick, with giant pilasters. This is Late Victorian. Next to this the ALMSHOUSES of *c*.1852, again yellow brick; Tudor and humble.

So back to the HIGH STREET. Next the WESTMINSTER BANK of *c*.1867, three-storeyed, of yellow brick, with a columnar Gothic ground floor – a townish job. Opposite is a passage at the end of which rises MONK'S HOUSE, a narrow, white, Soanian house, only one bay wide, the windows with hood-moulds on head-stops and yet Soane's free Grecian mannerisms. Then the churchyard of ST JOHN BAPTIST. Back to the E side for a derelict late C18 doorway. Then, again on the other side, FERRAR HOUSE, early C18, red brick, of seven bays with hipped roof and arched middle window. The elegant staircase has been moved. It was originally where there is still the

* Of the Huntingdon portion, says Mr Dickinson.

characteristic Venetian window at the back. Twice in the course of this stretch of the High Street Georgian brick houses stand across the vista, an always welcome townscape effect. The first is WHITWELL HOUSE, dated 1727, of five bays and three storeys with segment-headed first-floor windows. Pretty railings to the front garden. The second is MONTAGU HOUSE of about 1800, also of five bays. This has a pretty doorway and a Venetian window over. Opposite – the street is now called ERMINE STREET – is first CROMWELL HOUSE, the house where Cromwell was born. Externally it is not of interest, but it was converted. Then a terrace of three three-bay houses of yellow brick, early C19, with pedimented doorways. The middle one is distinguished by columns, the other two have pilasters only. Further on in Ermine Street one more good doorway: No. 14, late C18, well detailed.

KEYSTON

ST JOHN BAPTIST. Of grey stone. The w tower is highly un-usual and also poses a problem. Its w doorway with continuous mouldings is recessed behind a porch which is, however, flush with the wall. This porch has a high ogee arch beneath a gable with billet, cusped and subcusped and with buttress-shafts. Figure of a man above the ogee top; carved spandrels (a head, bust of a goat). Above it is a lozenge-shaped window with flowing tracery. All this is clearly Dec. The bell-openings are Perp – pairs of two lights with transom, and the blank arcad-ing above is of course Perp too. But the broach spire (with high broaches) has three tiers of lucarnes in alternating direc-tions, and they are as clearly C13 in style. The explanation is a rebuilding and remodelling of the spire in the favourite Victor-ian 'Middle Pointed', done in 1882. The tower buttresses are of the set-back type. The arch towards the nave has three chamfers and may well be Dec. Vaulting springers are pre-served inside the tower. As for the rest of the church, the chancel is late C13, see the pointed-trefoiled priest's doorway with stiff-leaf capitals and the chancel arch, the window with Y-tracery, and the good SEDILIA and PISCINA. Of the same time the arcades. They have piers alternatingly round and octagonal, and not only along but also across the nave. The S arcade is entirely a Victorian rebuilding or re-tooling. The N doorway with one order of (missing) colonnettes is E.E. too. Dec s porch entrance, Late Perp transepts, and Perp windows of specially nice design in the westernmost windows of the chancel and in the s transept and aisle. The N transept N window has an embattled transom. Good N transept and good nave roofs. – LECTERN and READING DESK. With Jacobean pieces. – BENCHES. A few are old, and one of them carries the date 1608. – STAINED GLASS. In one N and one s chancel window, including one small figure. – More in the N transept. – PLATE. Cup and Cover Paten of 1735–6; Plate of 1775–6. – MONUMENT. Leaning in the s aisle oaken cadaver from a C15 tomb (cf. Bishop Fleming at Lincoln).

KIMBOLTON

0060

The little town stretches N–S between the church and the mansion. The HIGH STREET is wide, neat, well-kept, and has no positively unattractive houses. Several have nice doorways, notably the WHITE HOUSE, CLANCARTY HOUSE, and KIMBOLTON HOUSE which is all covered by close dark green trellis-work. EAST STREET runs parallel with the High Street, and the doorway of No. 5 is the prettiest at Kimbolton. *See* p. 413.

ST ANDREW. The w tower is a fine piece, early C14 throughout, including its broach spire – see the details of the three tiers of lucarnes. The w portal has thin shafts with deep mouldings between them, and each group of mouldings has ballflower. The w window and the bell-openings have Y-tracery. At the top of the tower itself is a frieze of small heads. Perp s aisle and handsome s porch with, at the entrance, openwork tracery spandrels and on the side walls wide blank arches enclosing the (now blocked) small windows. The N aisle is Perp too, but the clerestory is still Dec and has handsome figured stone corbels as the roof supports inside. The chancel s wall is of brick, probably of 1748, but inside in the N wall is a blocked late C13 window with formerly intersecting tracery. The chancel arch matches such a date. The N and s chapels, however, are Perp, and both have their original roofs with carved figures. The nave roof is original too. The oldest feature of the church is the arcades. Four bays. The s arcade has round piers and arches of one chamfer and one slight chamfer, i.e. early C13. The N arcade with alternatingly round and octagonal supports has a little nailhead in the capitals and a big nailhead hood-mould. The arches are of one chamfer, one slight chamfer, and a third chamfer. So that may be later C13. However, the NW respond is earlier than either arcade. With its

single fleur-de-lis-like leaf motifs it looks *c.*1200. The tower
arch has three continuous chamfers, which suggests *c.*1300,
and that agrees with the external evidence. – FONT. From
Little Stukeley. Very large and very uncouth. Consequently
called Saxon, though more probably C12. No decoration at
all. – SCREENS. The screen to the S chapel is uncommonly
good. It has broad ogee-headed divisions with tracery above.
Four of the panels of the dado have PAINTINGS of *c.*1500.
Note the mannered elegance of St Edmund. – The screen to
the N chapel is a little simpler. – SOUTH DOOR. With C14
tracery. – SCULPTURE. Small group of the Virgin and Child
with the Baptist. White marble, by *P. Romanelli,* 1859. It is a
copy after Raphael's Belle Jardinière in the Louvre. – STAINED
GLASS. In the S chapel one small complete figure; in the N
chapel E window a few bits; C15. – PLATE. Large Cup, late
C16, with engraved scenes of Daniel in the lions' den and
Habakkuk guided in the air by an angel; Cup of 1655; Almsdish of *c.*1660 with repoussé flowers and leaves; Paten C17;
Silver-gilt Flagon 1750. – MONUMENTS. First Earl of Manchester † 1642. Standing wall-monument with the impressive
conceit of a marble table with an arched front but angle
columns, a black top slab, and on it a white marble cushion
with an inscription. Against the back wall, and as though quite
a separate monument, the commemorative inscription flanked
by two black columns. A third column stands on a bracket
above and is crowned by a helmet with crest.* – To the l. and
r. of this identical cartouches to his two wives: *c.*1658. The
fleshy, gristly details are characteristic of the date. – Many
tablets, the best to George Montagu † 1780, signed *J. Wilton,*
very sparse and elegant, with an urn on top. Put up by
Frederick Montagu. – Consuelo Duchess of Manchester;
1912. White marble relief in the *schiacciato* technique, very
Paris-Salon in style. She is seen surrounded by clouds and
reaches up to two angels.

KIMBOLTON CASTLE. *Vanbrugh* had turned to architecture
with spectacular suddenness in 1699, when he designed
Castle Howard, the largest country house of the period up to
that date in England. Among the first letters referring to the
building is one to the fourth Earl of Manchester.‡ So when the
Earl, in 1707, decided to remodel Kimbolton, he invited
Vanbrugh to design and supervise the work. The choice was

* Over the monument is a CEILURE, apparently *ex situ* (GMCH).
‡ He was created the first Duke in 1719.

even more understandable if one remembers that meanwhile
Vanbrugh had also designed Blenheim. The job at Kimbolton
must at first have appeared unpromising. There had been a
castle on the site in the Middle Ages. This castle had been rebuilt shortly after 1525 and again in 1617–20 with four ranges
round a courtyard. Of the Tudor building a few minor mullioned windows and one piece of exposed wall in the room s of the
White Hall still tell us.* The c17 house and probably the castle
before occupied the same area as today's Kimbolton Castle.
The early c17 building was remodelled about 1690, perhaps by a
local joiner *Coleman* of whom we know nothing. Due to *c.*1690,
and stylistically quite incompatible with Vanbrugh, are the interior façades of the courtyard. They are of exposed brick,   83
basement and two storeys except for the E range, which has large
windows through both floors, and the windows have lintels
decorated with two leaf volutes meeting in the middle.‡ To
the W is a big archway, to the E a monumental portico.

We hear that in 1707 the SE corner collapsed. So Vanbrugh
went in July, taking *Hawksmoor* with him who was his chief
assistant and collaborator at Castle Howard and Blenheim, and
they and Coleman agreed on the design. Coleman was apparently the resident clerk of works; for Vanbrugh says that,
if only they had such a man at Blenheim, it would save £1,000
a year. Coleman, in return, said about Vanbrugh: 'If their is
anay Credet Gayned In this Bulden, I beg that he may have it'
(L. Whistler in the *Sunday Times* 10 May 1953). Building went
on quickly. In 1708 the battlements were reached. In 1709
work went on on the s side and the E side. In 1710 the W front
went up, and probably the E portico. But for the latter there
are no building accounts left, and this is where a complication
comes in. Vanbrugh at the beginning had apparently thought
of three giant arches instead of the portico. We have a sketch
of this, in all probability by Vanbrugh himself. Moreover, in
1714 *Alessandro Galilei* came to England from Rome, and a

* This wall and the N wall of the s range, towards the courtyard, were left
by Vanbrugh. It is here also that the mullioned windows are. Moreover, Mr
Sisson tells me of two arched doorways, one in this same wall, the other in
the return wall at the E end. This again opened into the courtyard. In the *See
early 1950s, in addition, in the White Hall, behind the family portrait –   p.
see* below – some Tudor wall-painting came out which Mr Dickinson dates   413
*c.*1560, and below it a fireplace.   *See*
‡ This decoration has much in common with *Henry Bell*'s decoration of p.
the Sessions House at Northampton. This observation was made by Mr 413
Martin Archdale (*Country Life*, vol. CXL, 1966, p. 615).

letter of 1719 exists in which the Earl refers to the front towards the town as finished, to 'what you designed over ye
gate', to two pairs of stairs to be made in the middle of the
colonnade, 'as you first proposed it', and to chimneypieces
being made in London 'according to your design'. There
is also in the County Archives a drawing of the great E portico
inconspicuously initialled *A. G.** What does all this amount
to ? Its significance has in my opinion been overrated. Galilei,
the architect of the famous façade of S. Giovanni in Laterano,
of the Corsini Chapel in the same church, and of the façade
of S. Giovanni dei Fiorentini was only twenty-three when he
reached England and twenty-eight when the letter reached
him. The three works in Rome date from 1732 and after.
Moreover, Kimbolton by 1714 was finished. As for comments
concerning the details of the letter we shall see later; for no
description of the building has yet been given.

84   We start with the E front. It is of thirteen bays, coming forward from the angles in two steps to reach the portico, the
most monumental feature of the house, though of course nothing like as grand as that at Blenheim or indeed as dramatic.
That is the remarkable thing. Kimbolton is very severe and
of few words. The portico has two giant Tuscan columns *in
antis* and closed bays l. and r. with giant pilasters flanking two
tiers of niches. There is a triglyph frieze and a balustrade. A
wide staircase leads up to the portico. That is all. The recessed wings are lower and have a basement and two floors,
segment-headed windows with flat raised surrounds, angle
quoins of equal length or, if you like, rusticated giant pilaster
strips, and top battlements. They are a surprise after the
strictly classical portico. But we know that Vanbrugh liked
medieval evocation, and in this case we have Vanbrugh's letter
to the Earl telling him that this 'castle air' would give the
building the 'masculine' character which he wanted. He did
indeed continue in the same vein, with a S front of the same
design, only prevented from uniformity by a projection of the
three middle bays and by a big portal with Tuscan columns,
a triglyph frieze, and a straight hood. To the W there are eleven
bays, and the centre is a giant archway. This façade has an
unexpected rhythm. The two angle-bays are three-storeyed,
the rest is lower, perhaps another allusion to medieval castles.
The N side is less formal. In front of this were the offices; for

* Mr Marshall Sisson kindly drew my attention to this. The two initials
are hidden l. and r. of the scale of feet.

here is a low colonnade of depressed arches on the ground floor. The attic storey, so Mr. Burkett tells me, was put on only in 1869. The battlements, however, though different from Vanbrugh's, appear already in a print of 1831.

Now what of all this can be by Galilei? The decoration over the W entrance may have been. But the portico – no, in spite of the drawing which may just as well represent the then existing portico. Style forbids the attribution to Galilei. The portico is convincingly similar to that illustrated in *Vitruvius Britannicus* in 1717 as 'A New Design for a Person of Quality in Dorsetshire' and has nothing at all of the festive swagger of Galilei's later designs.

The only place at Kimbolton where something like festiveness appears is in what must be regarded as the main entrance, i.e. the entrance to the E range inside the courtyard. But that also is not Italian in style. *Talman* had done something very similar at Drayton, just a few years earlier. A wide staircase with a splendid wrought-iron handrail leads to a portal with unfluted Ionic columns and a segmental pediment with recessed centre and some carving. There is a coat of arms above it. This whole bay is stone-faced, the rest of the courtyard is, as we have seen, red brick. Also the whole five-bay side of the courtyard has giant pilasters above the basement. The lead down-pipes are among the finest in all England.

The two entrances into the E range from the courtyard and the giant portico lead into the principal room, the WHITE HALL, white until 1938. It is of Coleman's (or Bell's) time, not Vanbrugh's – i.e. in the Gibbons tradition. Panelled walls, wood pilasters with garlands hanging down them, a wooden leaf cornice, and a plain ceiling. The entrance is not in the middle of the hall. In this we can still recognize the fact that here was the hall already in the Tudor building. This position is in the medieval tradition; neither Coleman nor Vanbrugh would have chosen it; and the position of the chimneypiece does in fact try to neutralize it. Above the chimneypiece is the family of the Earl painted by *Giovanni Antonio Pellegrini*, the Venetian painter who had been brought to England by the Earl in 1708 and began at Kimbolton in 1709. It does not prepare one for the brilliance of his work in other rooms of the house.

On the r. nothing of importance, except a pretty Jacobean back staircase. On the l. (s) the Drawing Room (in which the patch of earlier walling is exposed) and then, at the

SE corner, the Green Drawing Room. The Green Drawing Room is followed by Vanbrugh's principal room, the PARADE ROOM. The chimneypieces in the house are mostly of a straightforward bolection-moulded type – the standard type of the earliest C18 – but here is a more splendid piece with a big shell and garlands. That may well be to *Galilei*'s design. The N quarter of the room is treated as an alcove with a screen of two columns close to the pieces of solid projecting wall. The ceiling is Victorian. The SW corner on the other hand, the Boudoir, has the first of the *Pellegrini* ceilings, and this is a delightful piece, with Venus and Cupid against a light blue sky and vases and garlands in the coving.

Vanbrugh made this range 'double-pile', i.e. deep enough not only for an inner corridor, but also for the principal staircase to go into the inner NE corner. This arrangement admittedly did not leave him quite enough space, and it is worth noting the fact that at Castle Howard and Blenheim also he found surprising rather than spacious plans for his staircases. At Kimbolton the flight runs up E to W and fills the S half of a relatively narrow space. It has a wrought-iron handrail, and it leads through an upper arch to the landing. To the r. of the arch is a second arch with a railing to look down. The two arches are separated by one pilaster – a daring solecism. The r. arch stands on another, at main floor level, which contains the access from the W-E corridor. Below the single pilaster is a hanging garland. On the two main walls are Trionfi of *Pellegrini*'s, in the spirit of Mantegna rather than Veronese, and darker and heavier than he usually is (over-painting?). The ceiling on the other hand has all Pellegrini's sparkle. It was completed by 1710 and is thus pre-Rococo at its most exhilarating. Only Sebastiano Ricci could do likewise at so early a date. The ceiling represents Bellona pointing to a portrait medallion of William III with fame floating and blowing the trumpet. Against the outer wall between the windows are trophies and single figures, and here, close to the eye, one can fully appreciate Pellegrini's *tocco*, i.e. his rapid, sketchy technique. Another enchanting Pellegrini ceiling is above the upper landing of the staircase. It is datable to 1719, because putti are playing about with the successive coronets which the Montagus had acquired, including the new ducal one. Also female figures in niches, a monkey, a parrot, trophies, drapery, and flowers.

Finally the CHAPEL, in the W wing, reaching as far N as the great archway into the courtyard. The room was remodelled,

85

it is said, before Vanbrugh. This applies to the arched w gallery, the s balcony, the door with its heavy surround with drapery, and also to the altar, but *Pellegrini* painted above the altar and on its sides the Transfiguration, and on the two window walls the four Evangelists (only three are by Pellegrini). There is, however, no ceiling decoration at all.

Of other buildings only one deserves description, the GATEHOUSE designed by *Robert Adam* and built about 1765, i.e. early in his career. The most interesting thing about it is that it must be meant as a conscious compliment to Vanbrugh. It is square and more solemn than Adam is otherwise. The composition is tripartite. The centre is an archway with one window either side. They have Gibbs surrounds, which is also a backward-looking motif. The archway has coupled Tuscan columns and the surround is rusticated. On the top is a balustrade. Three-bay links connect the centre with pedimented angle pavilions. They are windowless to the outside and have just a niche and angle pilasters. The surrounds of the niches are again rusticated. The composition is more or less the same towards the house. Inside the gatehouse, in its N part, was the BREWHOUSE, and remarkably complete equipment was found in it in the 1950s.

The gateway in the middle of the w front of the castle had originally been nearly axial to the village street. The Adam gatehouse did not keep that up, and now it is the N angle pavilion that closes the view from the village, or – more effectively – a cedar tree which neither Vanbrugh nor Adam could have counted on.

The EAST GATES along the London Road have square rusticated pillars and wrought-iron gates.

GRAMMAR SCHOOL. 1877 by *Ladds*.

STONELY. *See* p. 349.

ROUND BARROWS, 700 yds NW of the church. These two barrows have diameters of 50 ft, the larger being 5½ ft high. Both are surrounded by quarry ditches.

KINGS RIPTON

2070

ST PETER. A rough building. w tower, nave with N aisle, and chancel. The chancel PISCINA is of the second third of the C13, but the exterior of the chancel is faced with early bricks, mostly headers. Perp N arcade of three bays; standard elements. – FONT. Square, with tapering sides. Norman stylized leaves on the sides, including on three sides colonnettes to separate the leaf motifs.

1070 LEIGHTON BROMSWOLD

ST MARY. This is a wonderful church, thanks to the E.E. architects, and a highly interesting church, thanks to the patrons of the first half of the C17. What faces the visitor first of all is
78 the C17, a strong W tower, ashlar-faced, cream-coloured, and dated 1634. It exhibits no Gothic yearnings, except that from a distance its general shape is traditional. But the W doorway and the W windows are round-arched, and so are the twin bell-openings. There are battlements and pinnacles, but the pinnacles are obelisks. However, behind that tower, there is the C13 at once, in its details and even more in its clear plan of the noblest simplicity: nave, transepts, chancel. In fact, as the roof-line against the W walls of the transepts proves, the E.E. church had narrow aisles, and the two doorways must have belonged to them. The N doorway with a bold, rather blunt semicircular moulding and two orders of colonnettes may – so the RCHM suggests – even be *in situ*. The S doorway is the more splendid, with four orders and fine arch mouldings, one of them occupied by dogtooth. In the transepts no E.E. features remain, except the buttresses. The large E windows with their reticulated tracery are Dec. But the chancel is wholly of the latest C13. Its two large, clear S windows with intersecting tracery make the room beautifully light. The E window with panel tracery, almost entirely uncusped, is Late Perp, but has something of the same spirit. Late Perp also one chancel S and one N window. There is no more to be said about the architecture. The interior is one of large unbroken surfaces. To go into details, the chancel arch stands on triple shafts which start high up, i.e. presuppose a low stone screen. The arch is double-chamfered. In the chancel is the finest of all E.E. DOUBLE PISCINAS, square-headed with a large round arch intersected, even in the individual mouldings, by two half-arches. (For other cases cf. Introduction, p. 184.) Opposite is an AUMBRY with a shelf. Of the E.E. transept details there are only the E responds of the arches towards the former crossing.* The roofs transport us to the C17. They are original in transepts and nave, with tiebeams on short straight braces and arched braces up to the collars, and also wind-braces. The tower arch has C17 responds too, though the arch is pointed.

* Two round E.E. capitals have been cut to make them suitable as a FONT.

The C17 dates, as far as we know them, are as follows. The church was ruinous about 1600. The S aisle was demolished in 1606. The nave was then roofless. In 1626 George Herbert, the poet, was ordained deacon and became prebend. In 1630 he was ordained priest and took over the parish of Bemerton. In 1633 he died and left the manuscript of his *The Temple* to Nicholas Ferrar of Little Gidding. In Herbert's years the N aisle was demolished and the church re-roofed. The furnishings also belong to that time. The Duke of Lennox was Lord of the Manor and paid for the W tower. Other benefactors were Nicholas and John Ferrar. – The FURNISHINGS just referred to are these. PULPIT and READER'S DESK. Two 76 identical pieces with sounding-boards, l. and r. of the chancel arch – like Early Christian ambos. – STALLS. Just long benches with open front and open ends. Balusters for the front, knobs for the arms. – The BENCHES in the body of the church are the same. In the transepts they face inwards, college-wise. – SCREEN. Only 5 ft high, also open, and also with knobs. – The screened-off part of the S transept, the LECTERN, the LITANY DESK, and the TOWER SCREEN all have original C17 parts. Those of the lectern come from Stow Longa Manor House. – RAINWATER HEADS. They are very fine, and one is dated 1634. – PLATE. Cup and Cover Paten of 1627–8. The cup has the Lennox arms. – MONUMENTS. Sir Robert Tyrwhitt † 1572 and wife. Alabaster effigies, defaced, on an alabaster tomb-chest with stiff standing figures of children and in the middle the coat of arms. – Lady Darcy, daughter of Sir Robert, † 1567. By the same hand, and also defaced.

GATEHOUSE, E of the church. This was the gatehouse to Leighton Bromswold Castle, originally a prebendal manor house of the late C15, then the seat of Sir Richard Tyrwhitt, of his son-in-law Sir Henry d'Arcy, and then of d'Arcy's son-in-law Sir Gervase Clifton. The Duke of Lennox mentioned above was Clifton's son-in-law. Clifton, before 1608, intended to build an up-to-date mansion. *John Thorpe* either designed it or drew it, but it was not built. All that was done was the stately gatehouse. This dates from 1616. It is large and oblong, with four square projecting corner towers and of red brick. The centre is a wide and high stone archway, now cruelly hidden in its lower part by a modern addition. The arch is flanked by Tuscan columns carrying a highly incorrect triglyph frieze and above that short pilasters with a simple geometrical pattern of chains of pyramidal lozenges. The top is

a balustrade of vertically symmetrical buttresses. The towers
are three storeys high and have cross-windows. The back is
not identical, but very similar. However, it lacks the attic
storey with the pilasters.

The long AVENUE which leads from the W to the church seems
to have been laid out in the C17. The medieval village was E of
the church.

LITTLE GIDDING

1080

Nicholas Ferrar was the son of a wealthy merchant. He was born
in 1593 and studied medicine. He went abroad, to the uni-
versities of Padua and Leipzig, and returned home in 1618.
He was a man of a mystic bent, impressed by the Cambridge
Platonists, Juan de Valdes, and the Arminians. The idea of
forming a religious community came to him in 1624. His
mother felt as he did, and they decided to buy a house at
Little Gidding. Nicholas Ferrar was ordained deacon in 1626.
The community numbered about thirty to forty, and Nicholas's brother John Ferrar with wife and two children and their
sister with husband and sixteen children also joined. There
was a school with three schoolmasters, and there were alms-
people. The discipline was demanding, three services a day
and only two meals for the adults, but no vows were prescribed.
Nicholas Ferrar worked on Concordances or Harmonies of
the Bible, i.e. biblical materials presented as consecutive
stories. The books were written and bound by hand. Embroidery was cultivated too. The community was in close
touch with George Herbert at Leighton Bromswold and Sir
Robert Cotton at Conington. Charles I visited them three
times, the last time on his flight. Bishop Williams of Lincoln
also paid them a visit (from Buckden). Mrs Ferrar died in
1634, Nicholas Ferrar in 1637, and the nephew whom he had
regarded as his successor in 1640. In the mood of the forties
the community was decried as popish. In 1646 Little Gidding
was attacked and sacked. The fifties saw the end.

St JOHN EVANGELIST. The community did not build a new
church: they remodelled a dilapidated old one. Excavations in
1921 have shown that this old church was larger than the
present one. Anyway the present church is very small. It
consists of nave and chancel only. It lies with trees l. and r.
looking into spacious fields and towards the gently rolling
country. The building is of brick and only its façade is of
stone. This façade is dated 1714. It is a strange façade, not in

87

any Queen Anne tradition. If a big name were to be connected with its style, it would be Archer rather than Hawksmoor. The façade is quite narrow and has two giant angle pilasters with small obelisks on. The doorway has a kind of pilaster strips with sunk panels carrying big corbels for the straight hood instead of capitals. In the middle is a bellcote of rusticated pilasters, and on that a flat obelisk or steep pyramid with a ball finial and three mysterious pierced oblong openings. – The most interesting feature of the interior is the arrangement of the SEATING in the nave college-wise. This is decidedly a Puritan tradition, and one would like to attribute it to Nicholas Ferrar's time. If so, it can only have applied to the church preceding this, and the argument that the household and other population was too big to allow for such an arrangement would only be fully valid if the dimensions of the preceding church were known. The STALLS in the nave have thick balusters and the backs high detached baluster-like columns carrying segmental arches. In the chancel the PANELLING has long balusters too. This may well be of 1714, in imitation to a certain extent of the time of Nicholas Ferrar. But can the stall-fronts also be 1714 and not c.1625? Or can they possibly be *Clutton*'s, who restored the church in 1853 and must have done the job extremely well? – REREDOS. One panel of the Jacobean reredos with one of the usual broad blank arches is now S of the altar. – The present REREDOS of brass tablets with the Creed, the Commandments, and the Lord's Prayer dates from c.1625. – Also of c.1625 the FONT, a brass baluster with a delightful brass cover surrounded by a kind of crown. – Of the same time also the HOURGLASS STAND. – But the CANDLE SCONCES of slender turned balusters, extremely well grouped, are an exceedingly good Arts and Crafts job of c.1920, designed by *W. A. Lee*. – The LECTERN is the one medieval piece in the church. It is of brass, of a well-known East Anglian type, of the late C15. The same moulds were used for the lecterns of e.g. Urbino Cathedral and Oxburgh in Norfolk. It was presented by Nicholas Ferrar and is a splendid eagle, the moulded stem is splendid too, and the little lions at the base are pretty enough. – CHANDELIER. Little Gidding is a confusing church. This piece of a familiar Baroque type is of 1853. It might just as well be 1753. Is it perhaps a copy of a predecessor? – STAINED GLASS. Probably of 1853. The Crucifixion in the E window still has the 'prearchaeological' glaring colours and pictorial composition. –

EMBROIDERED CUSHION COVER of the Ferrar Community. – Also three BOOK-BINDINGS. – PLATE. C17 Paten on foot; Flagon of 1629–30; Almsdish of 1634–5; C17 Crucifix.

LITTLE PAXTON

1060

ST JAMES. Barbaric and entertaining Norman tympanum with a cross in the middle, on the l. Christ and the Lamb (?), on the r. two indefinable animals. In the chancel s wall the head of a Norman window. The chancel arch responds are Norman too, square with an angle shaft. So nave and chancel were once Norman. Perp w tower with its buttresses inside the church. Perp s arcade of four bays, very rough. Octagonal piers, but the responds just corbels in the form of a knot (cf. Diddington). – PLATE. Cup and Cover Paten inscribed 1569; Plate 1685–6. – MONUMENT. In the churchyard N of the N porch plain coped stone to the architect *John Buonarotti Papworth* († 1847), architect to the King of Württemberg, as the inscription tells you. Paxton Park, which he built, has been demolished.

PAXTON HALL. The front and the finest interiors are of 1738. The house was built for the son of Bishop Reynolds of Lincoln. Finely detailed brick front of nine bays with slightly projecting two-bay side parts. Two storeys, hipped roof with dormers behind a low parapet. The windows have raised and moulded stone frames, and the doorway a pediment on beautifully carved brackets. The staircase starts in the entrance hall. It is spacious and also beautifully detailed. Balusters with bulbous foot, carved tread-ends, on the top landing Greek-key frieze. Stucco ceiling with ornament and in medallions the four seasons. In the dining room an excellent stone chimneypiece. Above it an open pediment and in this the profile of a young man. Can he really mean Bishop Reynolds's son?

LITTLE RAVELEY

2070

ST JAMES. Nave and chancel, no bellcote. Perp, but the two-light E window and the chancel arch Dec. – FONT. Perp. Against the underside an eagle, a tree(?), and two unidentified figures. – STAINED GLASS. Small fragments in one nave N window. – PLATE. Cup and Cover Paten, late C16.

LITTLE STUKELEY

2070

ST MARTIN. The most interesting thing about the church is that *R. Hutchinson*, who restored it, collected earlier remains carefully and displayed them to advantage. Thus in the s wall of the tower outside are Norman column-shafts, and inside the tower whole collections including an arch with proper beak-head, an arch with beakhead stylized to excess (cf. Spaldwick), two Norman window-heads, and lengths of a battlement frieze and billet, in the N aisle N wall outside quite a length of Norman corbel-table, and in the N chapel s arch a whole order of short Norman rolls or tubes set at r. angles to the arch. Something similar seems to have been done by Hutchinson inside the nave, where carved friezes of Early Renaissance foliage are used to form a vertical strip (N), a cross (S), and a square set in a lozenge (E). Due to Hutchinson may possibly also be the wealth of corbels. A large winged man is attached to the N arcade, and there are plenty of smaller ones. Now for the church itself. The w tower is short and has big pinnacles but no spire. There is a top quatrefoil frieze. Perp windows in the s and N aisles, the clerestory, and the chancel (E). The s porch has the date 1652, but it is Perp, and the s doorway inside is quite ornate, with the stoup in a niche on the r. and a bracket on the l. The two-bay arcades of standard elements are Perp also. The SE respond is a monster devouring a man, the deed performed horizontally. The chancel arch and the one-bay N and s chapels are contemporary with the arcades. – FONT. Octagonal, with quatrefoils. Leaves on the underside. – GUERIDON. By the altar. Domestic, and probably of c.1730–40. – STAINED GLASS. In the s chapel parts of canopies made up as canopies.

SWAN AND SALMON INN (former). Dated 1676. A coarser version of The Limes at Spaldwick, i.e. with a square porch, giant pilasters so rustic that they stop being pilasters, and broad raised brick surrounds to the windows. The pilasters in fact belong to a system of raised verticals and horizontals articulating the front.

LOLHAM

1000

1¼ m. WSW of Maxey
Soke of Peterborough

LOLHAM HALL. Inside the house three medieval stone archways.

LOLHAM BRIDGES. Five bridges in line from N to s on King Street, a branch of Ermine Street. They do not go across a river but across meadows liable to floods. (Inscriptions of

1652 and 1721 according to the VCH, of 1641 and 1790 according to Jervoise.)

LONGTHORPE
Soke of Peterborough

ST BOTOLPH. Permission for the rebuilding of the church was given by the Abbot of Peterborough to Sir William de Thorpe in 1263–4. Nave and aisles and bellcote. No structural division between nave and chancel. The windows have pointed-trefoiled lights; the W window has a quatrefoiled circle over its two lights. Wide nave of three bays. Slender circular piers with circular capitals and abaci. Single-chamfered arches with hood-moulds. – PLATE. Cup and Paten, 1817.

LONGTHORPE TOWER. About 1300 the tower was added to a late C13 hall. The hall survives, but has no internal features of interest. The N window is of two lights divided by a shaft and has a quatrefoil in plate tracery. Access to the ground floor as well as the upper floor of the tower was only from the hall, not from the outside. The tower is square, and has walls 6 to 7 ft thick and square turrets on the corners. The windows are small, of single lights, with trefoiled heads or shouldered lintels. Some early C17 alterations. The ground-floor room has a quadripartite rib-vault. So has the room on the principal floor. The ribs are single-chamfered and stand on corbels. The second-floor room has no vault. It is reached by a straight staircase in the thickness of the S wall.

The outstanding interest of Longthorpe Tower is the WALL PAINTINGS in the principal room, which were discovered only after the Second World War. They date from *c.*1330 and are more extensive than any of so early a date in any house in England. Subjects are taken from the Bible, as well as moralities such as the Three Quick and the Three Dead. Also a monk teaching a boy (the inscription here is in French), the Wheel of the Seven Ages of Man, the Wheel of the Five Senses (figured as animals), the Labours of the Months, and plenty of birds and flowers. In the vault figures of musicians and the Signs of the four Evangelists.* As for the style, it has been compared by Mr E. Clive Rouse with such somewhat earlier illuminated manuscripts as Queen Mary's Psalter and the Bestiary at Corpus Christi College Cambridge.

* A detailed description will be found in the leaflet published by the Ministry of Public Building and Works.

VILLAGE STREET. Several good houses, especially one NW of the church, timber-framed with a handsome porch with open balustered sides. The proposed date is c.1560.

(RAILWAY STATION. In the Old English style. By *Mr Livock*, 1845.)

THORPE HALL. *See* p. 353.

STANDING STONE. *See* Peterborough, p. 329.

The site of a ROMAN FORT lies on the N bank of the Nene, 2 m. W of Peterborough. It was revealed by air photography to be nearly 28 acres in extent, with a smaller, presumably later, enclosure within. Its date is unknown, but presumably is C I.

LYNCH FARM *see* ALWALTON

MARHOLM
Soke of Peterborough

1000

ST MARY. The visual memory of the church is of four cedar trees to the W and three to the E, and of the contrast between the ambitious chancel and the rest. Short Norman W tower with clasping buttresses and slit-windows. Tower arch narrow, single-stepped, with responds carrying late C12 crocket capitals. C13 arcades and chancel arch. The arcades have quatrefoil piers and double-chamfered arches. The aisles externally mostly C19. The chancel was rebuilt by Sir William Fitzwilliam of Milton, who died in 1534 and wished to be buried in the chancel 'lately edified' by him. Ashlar-faced to the S. Five-light E and four-light side windows. – STAINED GLASS. Some of the original glass is preserved in the chancel. – FONT. Octagonal, probably of the 1660s, with panels each with a leaf and a rose. – PLATE. Breadholder, 1633(?); Cup and Cover Paten, 1687; Flagon, perhaps German, c.1750. – MONUMENTS. In the nave recumbent effigy of a Knight, the tomb-chest mostly C19. The effigy is of c.1400. – Sir William Fitzwilliam † 1534. Kneeling brasses against the back wall of a recess. The architectural parts of plaster. Tomb-chest with ornate quatrefoils. Colonnettes with raised lozenge pattern. Four small ogee arches. – Sir William Fitzwilliam † 1599. Two recumbent effigies. – Edward Hunter alias Perry † 1646. Bust of a boy in front of a black needle obelisk. Below a cartouche with weeping putti and an inscription commemorating him as a 'courteous soldier', 'grassante bello civili', and ending with

> 'Noe crucifixe you see, noe Frightfull Brand
> Of superstitions here, Pray let me stand.'

– William, first Earl Fitzwilliam, † 1719 and wife. By *James Fisher* of Camberwell. Standing white marble figures. Unusual, restless draperies. Grey surround with detached Corinthian columns and a broken, open, segmental pediment. The *magnum opus* of this little-known sculptor.

MARHOLM FARM. In spite of the date-stone 1633 this must be essentially late C17. H-shaped, with mullioned windows with pediments, triangular as well as occasionally segmental. Also an oval window. One window curiously tucked across a re-entrant angle. One re-set, small medieval ogee-headed window.

MAXEY
Soke of Peterborough

ST PETER. The church lies away from the village, grey, broad, and of irregular blocks of varying age and shape. Broad Norman W tower. Flat, thin buttresses strengthened in the C14, when a pretty ogee-headed stair doorway was inserted inside. Corbel-table and above it tall two-light bell-openings flanked by pairs of blank arches.* The top is Perp. The arch to the nave makes an early C12 date certain. Shafted responds with demi-column. Steep bases with a flat zigzag (cf. Castor). Decorated capitals. The arch was remodelled later. The original church was aisleless, see the W angles. Norman also and not much later (cf. Peterborough) the N arcade of two bays. Big circular piers with many-scalloped capitals and heavy square abaci. Arches with thick rolls. The S arcade is Norman too, but later, say *c.*1175–95 (cf. Peterborough). Circular piers and square abaci, less heavy. More busily scalloped capitals, nicked at the corners. Arches with two chamfers and a big outer nailhead. The Norman church had a clerestory. Its small windows can be seen from inside the aisles. Of the C13 the chancel arch; the chancel windows seem later, about 1290. Y-tracery cusped, also two lights with a foiled circle over. Perp E window. Attached to the chancel on the S side a treasury of the late C13 or a somewhat later date. It is a small chamber with lancet windows, some of them still with iron grilles, and has a vault. This has diagonal and ridge ribs (sunk wave moulding). Finally the ambitious N chancel chapel, founded as a chantry in 1367. Two bays, four-light E and three-light N windows, with transoms; Perp. Battlements. Arch to the chancel with two sunk quadrant mouldings. The E respond shows that a C13 chapel had existed before. Tall arch to the

* (Blank arcading inside this stage. VCH)

aisle, splendidly cusped and subcusped in pierced work.
SEDILIA and PISCINA with ogee arches and crocketed gables.
In the chancel a Perp EASTER SEPULCHRE, ogee-arched, with
much quatrefoiling, etc. – PLATE. Cup, 1570; Cup and shallow Bowl on baluster stem, silver-gilt, secular, 1601.

MAXEY CASTLE, Castle End. Licence to crenellate granted to
Sir William de Thorpe in 1374. The Lady Margaret lived
here. The castle has disappeared. A house called THE FRIARY,
Castle End Road, has a C15 doorway and an angle fireplace in
the former Parlour.

(CASTLE FARM. In a gable-end two pairs of two-light windows
in two storeys. Straight-headed, with arched lights. NMR)

Crop-marks ½ m. S of the post office, including two concentric
circles, may represent a possible Neolithic or Early Bronze
Age HENGE MONUMENT.

A Saxon site of some importance lies just NE of the church. It has
timber-framed long houses (the first of the period to be found
in this area), hearths, and rubbish pits. Of the six houses discovered so far, the largest measured 51 by 23 ft. Iron Age and
Romano-British material has also been excavated around here.

MILL HILL *see* CASTOR

MILTON
Soke of Peterborough

1090

William Fitzwilliam, of an old Yorkshire family, bought Milton
in 1502. It was his grandfather who had established relations with this region by marrying a Greene of Drayton.
William, who was a merchant of London, became High
Chamberlain to Cardinal Wolsey, Alderman of the City, and
Master of the Merchant Taylors' Company. He was knighted
in 1522 and died in 1534. He had a son William and a grandson Sir William who died in 1599, was Lord Deputy of Ireland
till 1594, and lived mostly over there, except for the years
1573–88, which he spent at home. The earliest work surviving
at Milton is therefore likely to be either of the 1580s or of
after 1594. The latter date is more probable, and Sir William's
son William no doubt continued. The house is still Fitzwilliam
property now.

The earliest work is the N front. It dates from *c.*1600. It is a
curious composition, long, two-storeyed, with eight projections of which the third contains the porch, the others being

bay windows. To the r. of the porch all is symmetrical, with
the middle bay coming forward more than the others and the l.
and r. (i.e. the fourth and eighth) being treated as one-storeyed
with three transoms and all the lights arched. The other windows are of the normal mullioned and transomed kind. The l.
of the tall one-storeyed windows corresponds to the hall dais,
the r. to the former chapel. It is possible, but not certain, that
these two windows represent a state of the house earlier than
the end of the C16. The porch has Tuscan columns below,
Ionic columns above. The Late Elizabethan work is embattled.
Behind the battlements an attic was contrived in 1773 by *Sir
William Chambers*. Behind the four main accents, i.e. bays one,
four, six, and eight, he placed tripartite lunette windows, but
chose to give them Gothic detail. No interior of the period
about 1600 remains.

To the E of the N front lies a monumental STABLING
RANGE occupying three sides of a quadrangle. This is dated
1690. Its designer was *William Talman* (or *John Sturges*?).
The recessed centre has eleven bays, the projecting wings four
plus, on the r., i.e. connecting with the house, two more. Two
storeys, cross-windows, quoins, hipped roof. The centre has
its own quoins, a pediment, and a lantern. Doorway with a
pediment with a three-centred top, i.e. the form the French
call *anse de panier*. Staircase with dumb-bell balusters. Two
rooms have William and Mary panelling, one of them in the
link to the house, which must therefore be contemporary with
the work of 1690. In the wall between the work of *c.*1590 and
the link of *c.*1690 a former external window survives.

In 1720 a back range was added to the stables. It also consists of three ranges, centre and wings. In the courtyard thus
created stands an octagonal harness-house.

Then, about 1745–50, a new S front was built. Its designer
was *Flitcroft*, and it is therefore Palladian in style. Nine bays,
two and a half storeys, ashlar-facing. The first and last bays
project and have canted bay windows. The centre bay projects slightly, has a Kentian doorway, a Kentian window above
this, a tripartite lunette window in the half-storey, and a pediment. W front of three bays with a canted bay window. To the
E of the S front two more bays by Flitcroft or remodelled by
him, then an ample bow window of *c.*1800 by *Carr*, and then
offices by *Flitcroft*. In Flitcroft's time the room behind the
Carr window had been a courtyard, and a Venetian window
which looked into this from the N has recently been found. In

addition, E of the house the laundry of c.1690, with cross-windows and hipped roof.

The INTERIOR is mostly Georgian, of the Flitcroft, the Chambers, and the Carr periods, i.e. of c.1750, c.1770, and c.1800. The ENTRANCE HALL is a fine example of the style of c.1750. Coved ceiling, chaste stucco work. Sumptuous fireplace, if restrained in its motifs. Open curly pediment. To the r. the DINING ROOM with a Rococo ceiling, then the SMALL DINING ROOM with a specially lovely ceiling, and a room with a pretty Gothick cornice. The stucco decoration of c.1750 continues along the W side. The centre of the S front is the PILLARED HALL, tripartite with Tuscan columns as division. This room is in axis with the symmetrical part of the Elizabethan front. Accessible from here and from the entrance hall is the STAIRCASE. Wrought-iron hand-rail with S-motifs decorated with leaf. The motif is the same as was used by Kent at No. 44 Berkeley Square. Sumptuous stucco ceiling. Glazed lantern. The room made by *Carr* out of Flitcroft's yard has beautiful Adamish decoration. It was built as the LIBRARY, and Carr also did the SMALL LIBRARY next to it. Behind the Small Library a connecting LOBBY by *Tatchell* with an oval opening to an upper miniature colonnade and an oval lantern. The porch-bay of the hall can be reached from here.

On the upper floor the LONG GALLERY lies above the Pillared Hall. It was redecorated by *Chambers*. It is five bays long and tripartite, with delightful segmental vaults and a shallow dome over the middle. The main doorway has Ionic columns and a pediment. Two chaste fireplaces. The style is instructively different from Flitcroft's before and Carr's after. The adjoining rooms were also re-done by Chambers. In the (present) Library the Savonnerie carpet repeats the pattern of the ceiling. The PETERBOROUGH DINING ROOM is the most interesting of these rooms. Its ceiling has an oblong panel and a broad frame with a diagonal trellis.

On the first floor facing N a BEDROOM of Flitcroft's time and another (formerly Boudoir) with a Chinese wallpaper dated in Chinese 1749. Very prettily decorated chimneypiece and doorcase, the latter with an open scrolly pediment.

The GARDEN was remodelled by *Repton* in 1791. Divers garden furnishings, notably the ORANGERY of seven bays with Tuscan columns, the outer ones coupled, the TEMPLE by *Chambers* (1774–6) with a tetrastyle Corinthian front,* the

* To be re-erected NW of the house.

KENNELS of 1767 in the form of a ruined medieval gatehouse, and the GOTHIC LODGE, near the SW entrance. This has a polygonal front, a rose-window, and a gable with the peculiar Norman scallop frieze seen at Peterborough Cathedral. The WALLED GARDEN has a gate towards the lake with fine C18 ironwork and the DAIRY with a segmental rusticated arch and a cresting. In the room next to this a ROMAN PAVEMENT found at Castor. Another GOTHIC LODGE near Ferry House.

FERRY HOUSE, named after Gunwade Ferry and formerly an inn, stands by the main road. It is of the C17. (In its garden an Anglo-Saxon CROSS-HEAD.) Opposite it, across the main (A) road, a BRIDGE of three arches, with cutwaters and a date 1716.

⅛ m. W, opposite the entrance to the Peterborough Golf Course, just off the road to the S, LITTLE JOHN and ROBIN HOOD, two standing stones, 18 ft in height, leaning slightly W. Where dateable, standing stones are generally of Late Neolithic or Bronze Age date (cf. Peterborough, p. 329). These are supposed to mark a privileged roadway free of toll for the cartage of Barnack stone to Gunwade Ferry for shipment via the Nene to Bury St Edmunds (MHLG).

MOLESWORTH

ST PETER. Short W tower without spire. Aisleless nave. The steep chancel roof is higher than the nave. The chancel, though it looks all Victorian, is in fact a genuine and fine design of the C13.* This is evident from the chancel arch and the beautiful blank giant arches enclosing the windows, single lancets and triplets of lancets. Externally the buttresses are original too; on both N and S they continue as a framing band at the top of each bay. The nave S doorway is C13 as well. It has one stiff-leaf capital, and the arch starting with broaches. The rest is Perp. – PULPIT. Early C18; plain. – ARCHITECTURAL FRAGMENTS. They include a spiral-fluted Norman column-shaft and a piece of Norman abacus. – PAINTINGS. Large St Christopher (N wall). Note the timber-framed house in the middle distance on the l. Although the painting is of c.1500, the house has the kind of braced panels making concave-sided lozenges which one would not expect before c.1575. – St Anthony and the pig (S wall); unrecognizable. This painting is late C15. – PLATE. Cup and Cover Paten of 1569–70.

* It was demolished and rebuilt in 1884–5.

MONKS HARDWICK

2060

2 m. NE of St Neots

Of c.1830, with a pedimented Tuscan porch. The back wing is much older, late C16 probably, and timber-framed. The chimneybreast on the W side is very mighty.

MORBORNE

1090

ALL SAINTS. The most prominent part is the early C17 brick tower. The W window has a pediment. Of the same time also probably the low mullioned windows with uncusped lights and the porch entrance with four-centred head. The oldest feature dates from c.1140, namely the chancel arch with big scalloped capitals, fat rolls, and abaci and bases with a flat zigzag decoration as at Castor. That the arch is pointed must be a late improvement. After that several parts of c.1190, i.e. the priest's doorway and the N and S doorways, with waterleaf capitals and arches of one step and one chamfer. Of c.1240 is the N arcade. Three bays, round piers with base-spurs, double-chamfered arches. Of c.1260 the S arcade, similar but with a little nailhead. The bases of both arcades are of the waterholding variety. Then the SE chancel window of c.1275: two lights with plate tracery and inside an attached mid-shaft. The DOUBLE PISCINA belongs to this, with the three curious recesses in the tympanum. Can they have been for relics? The S transept S window of three lancet lights, very slightly stepped, looks late C13 too. Nothing medieval is later. – PLATE. Cup of 1728–9. – MONUMENT. Almost totally defaced effigy of a Priest, first half C13, his feet placed against two human heads.

MASTS. On Morborne Hill a long, slender mast, and a shorter, broader one of lattice work – both for BBC Television.

ROUND BARROW, 1¼ m. E of the church. The mound is 50 ft in diameter and 6 ft high. Traces of the surrounding quarry ditch are still visible.

NEEDINGWORTH

3070

LOCKUP. Brick, early C19(?), decrepit.

THE CHESTNUTS. Red brick, dated 1710. Of that date convincingly the l. wing with its hipped roof. The recessed r. part has had the doorway and windows remodelled later.

NORMAN CROSS

1090

The ENGLISH GARDEN HOTEL is a Late Georgian red-brick house of five bays with a central Venetian window. The ground

floor is changed. Opposite, the NORMAN CROSS HOTEL has
recently added a circular two-storeyed part for motel purposes.
The date is 1962–5, the design came from Messrs. *Charrington's
Architects' Department*. On the road to Yaxley on the l. is a
three-storeyed, three-bay house with parapet walls l. and r.
curving up to it. This may be the COMMANDANT'S HOUSE
of the former Barracks, built for French prisoners of war about
1796–7.

¼ m. N of Norman Cross is a MONUMENT to these prisoners
erected early in the C20 by the Entente Cordiale Society. It is a
bronze eagle on a column.

1000

NORTHBOROUGH
Soke of Peterborough

ST ANDREW. The general impression is more curious than
beautiful – a small church like many others in the neighbourhood and the fragment of an enlargement so bold that it would
have given Northborough one of the biggest parish churches
in the county. The original building is late C12 to C13. Late
C12 the W end with the bellcote. Four thin buttresses, two
open bell arches with continuous roll mouldings, and a gable.
C13 the S doorway (orders of colonnettes, moulded arch with
very wilful details, a little stiff-leaf and two head-stops), the
S and N aisle windows, the arcades inside (three bays, circular
piers, circular capitals and abaci, double-chamfered arches),
and the SEDILIA and PISCINA in the S aisle. The chancel is
Dec – see the chancel arch with fillets on the responds and
knobbly leaves on one capital – and the N and S windows. Dec
also the start of the great renewal. The work was paid for by a
member or members of the Delamare family. In the new S
transept end wall, two large tomb recesses are provided, and as
the effigies have disappeared (cf. however Glinton) one cannot
now say which of the Delamares was the benefactor. Geoffrey
died in 1327, Henry in 1340. The transept is two big bays long
and ends in a wall with a big five-light window between two
polygonal turrets. The window has flowing tracery of original
design under a four-centred arch. The E and W windows are
equally interesting. They have segmental arches, and the
tracery beneath them is of arch heads standing on the apexes
of the arches of the lights. The arch heads are filled with
minor tracery motifs. The transept is embattled and has a frieze
of ballflower below the parapet. The W wall is obviously not

in its final form. To the N of the window it recedes, and there is an arch there rising only partly above the roof of the old aisle. This arch must be intended to be the connexion between the new work and a new, much higher aisle, i.e. a completely new W arm.

In the interior the incompleteness is even more noticeable. Arch into the chancel with continuous mouldings (two waves). Another, much too high, into the aisle. But as the transept W wall lies a little further to the W, this arch rests on a detached pier, and thus a narrow passage is formed between the main vessel of the projecting part of the transept and its W wall. The pier is slender and has a square core with four demi-shafts. Moulded capitals, arch mouldings as in the other arches. At the S end the arch stands on a small horizontal human figure. The window is shafted inside, the other windows have head-stops. In the E wall between the two windows, and originally no doubt above the altar, two brackets for statues and two rich canopies. The two tomb recesses have already been mentioned. The work is lavish throughout and done in excellent masonry. – PLATE. Cup and Cover Paten, 1776. – MONUMENT. James Claypole † 1594. Big, rather bare standing monument with a plain arch. No effigy. The Claypoles owned Northborough Manor House. Cromwell's daughter married a Claypole. His widow also lived at Northborough.

MANOR HOUSE. A remarkable survival of hall and gatehouse of a major manor house of c.1330–40. Much alteration in the earlier C17. The gateway has broad N and S arches with one chamfer and one wavy chamfer. From the N there is inside first a very narrow bay formerly rib-vaulted, then a cross-wall with entrances for carriages and pedestrians (cf. Abbot's Gate Peterborough), then a wider rib-vaulted bay. The entrances in the cross-wall have a simple rounded moulding. The hall of the C14 can easily be picked out from the C17 surroundings. It has to the N two tall two-light windows with straight heads and blocked reticulated tracery. To their r. is the doorway behind the Jacobean porch. The doorway has a filleted roll moulding. The back doorway is also preserved, and there are two hall windows to the back as well, though one of them is not in line with the front window. To the r. of the screens passage one can still see the three low doorways which, according to the standard arrangement of the English manor house, must have led into buttery, kitchen, and pantry. They have crocketed ogee heads below taller ogee gables. Especially rare is the survival of the W gable of the hall range with bold leaf crockets and the chimneyshaft at its apex.

In a COTTAGE, 400 yds E of the church and Manor House, John Clare lived for ten years (cf. Helpston).

NORTHOLM *see* EYE

2060

OFFORD CLUNY

The village is so called because the famous Cluny Abbey in Burgundy was lord of the manor from the C11 to the early C15.

ALL SAINTS. Primitive C13 S arcade with octagonal piers and single-chamfered arches. N arcade of three bays with round piers, octagonal abaci, and double-hollow-chamfered arches with broaches. That must be late C13. The chancel arch matches. Otherwise a Perp church, built of cobbles, with a W tower, a clerestory and a nave roof with six carved figures. The minimum brick chancel is of 1726. – PULPIT. Elizabethan with two tiers of the familiar broad blank arches. – COMMUNION RAIL. 1752. – LECTERN. With minor Jacobean panels. – (STAINED GLASS. E window, 1850, and typical of that date. GMCH) – PLATE. Cup of 1756–7.

MANOR HOUSE, E of the church. A stately nine-bay front with somewhat projecting two-bay wings. Brick, two storeys, hipped roof. It was built about 1704.

2060

OFFORD DARCY

ST PETER. The N arcade is Norman, with square piers with angle shafts. E of the arcade was a recess in the N aisle which was later converted into an opening. The chancel is C13, with a S and a smaller N lancet and a pointed-trefoiled PISCINA. The E window is Perp. Then follows the late C13 S arcade with quatrefoil piers with fillets and double-chamfered arches. Handsome ANGLE PISCINA with a vault and a boss. Externally the church is of cobbles. The W tower seems c.1300. It has clasping buttresses and a recessed stone spire, and the bell-openings and lucarnes look early. – SCREEN. Dec – which is rare; with ogee arches and foiled circles. – STAINED GLASS. Bits in a chancel S window. – PLATE. Cup inscribed 1569; later Cover Paten. – MONUMENTS. Brasses to Sir Laurence Pabenham † 1400 and two wives. Demi-figures, c.22 in. long. According to Mill Stephenson c.1430 (S aisle). – Brass to Dr William Taylard, priest, † 1532. Kneeling figure, 23 in. long (nave floor). – Civilian and Wife, sunk stone effigies, her

draperies very confused. The suggested date is late C14 (N
aisle). – R. Nailour † 1616 and family. Kneeling parents above,
children below. Alabaster (S aisle).

MANOR HOUSE, to the SW. The front is C18 and irregular in its
fenestration. In the middle it has a curious giant niche or recess. (The house was, however, built between 1606 and 1608
and has interior features of that time. RCHM)

OLD HURST   3070

ST PETER. Nave and chancel in one. Space for two bells in the
gable.* The building is E.E., see the S doorway with a pointed-
trefoiled head, the lancets and pairs of lancets as windows, and
the Y-tracery of the E and W windows. Perp tiebeam roof with
crown-posts. – FONT. Octagonal. Probably of c.1300. Blank
windows with intersecting tracery on all eight sides. – PILLAR
PISCINA (SE corner). Norman, with decorated stem. – PLATE.
Cup and Paten, late C16.

MANOR FARM. 'Externally of little interest, but retains a fine
original staircase' (MHLG). Vertically symmetrical balusters,
newels with terminals and pendants. Jacobean.

OLD WESTON   0070

ST SWITHIN. The W tower has an odd top. It starts with
broaches, but then there is another string-course. Two tiers of
lucarnes, the lower three-light Dec. The bell-openings however are Perp, of two lights with transoms. The earliest part
of the church is the plain N doorway, which must belong to
c.1200. The chancel follows. Its Y-traceried windows indicate
the late C13. A little later are the four-bay arcades. Octagonal
piers and double-chamfered arches. One has a little nailhead,
and so has the one pier with round abacus. The S doorway with
continuous filleted mouldings belongs to the arcades. Straight-
headed Dec N aisle and clerestory windows. In the S aisle is a
specially pretty three-light Perp window with traceried
spandrels to connect a four-centred arch with a straight top. –
BOX PEWS. – PAINTINGS. In the S aisle C14 scenes: the en-
thronement of one bishop by two others, the beheading of a
Saint, and in the jambs of the E window St Margaret and St
Catherine. – PLATE. Cup of 1727–8.

* Mr McHardy points out that on the nave E gable is a very odd rood, the
figures of the Virgin and St John being replaced by foliage of roughly human
shapes.

ORTON LONGUEVILLE

HOLY TRINITY. The earliest part of the church is the N chapel. It has a one-bay opening to the chancel which looks about 1275 (arch with two hollow chamfers). Of the same date may be the chancel N window E of the chapel. This has bar tracery with a quatrefoil, and that confirms *c*.1275. The W tower is only a little later. It has an arch to the nave of one chamfer and two continuous chamfers, and in its mid-stage walls quatrefoil windows. No spire. But most of the church is Dec, i.e. the chancel fenestration with a large E window with elongated reticulated tracery, an ogee-headed chancel S doorway, two big odd niches in the S wall outside, and a length of ballflower in the chancel S wall inside. In the W wall l. and r. of the chancel arch also two flat niches. They contain seats. The N aisle windows have cusped Y-tracery, the S aisle is very wide and has two E windows both with three stepped lancet lights under one arch, with the middle one to one's surprise ogee-headed. The S windows have basket arches almost semicircular. In the N chapel there is an E window with two intersecting ogee arches. The three-bay arcades are Dec too, though the bases (with spurs) are older. Octagonal piers with capitals with polygonal projections or brackets, the brackets displaying some ballflower and carrying the outer of the two chamfered orders of the arch. – FONT. Octagonal; plain decoration. – CHANCEL DOOR. Good original, i.e. early C14, scroll-work. – BELL. One with the stamps of *John Walgrave*, i.e. *c*.1420–40. – PAINTING. St Christopher, early C16, good. Only the upper part is preserved. – STAINED GLASS. Fragments in the N aisle W and N and the tower W window. In the N aisle W window some C13 foliage scrolls. – PLATE. Cup of Britannia silver 1711–12; Paten on foot 1829–30. – MONUMENTS. Most of them in the N chapel. Effigy of a cross-legged Knight, late C13; damaged. – Elizabeth Talbot (Mrs Armyne), 1629. Black marble table-top on five alabaster legs. Back panel with arched head and inscription. No figures, but many armorial shields. – Lady Mary Seymour. By *Chantrey*, 1827. Rather cold compared with other monuments of his. Seated young woman against Grecian background. All white marble. – Countess of Aboyne † 1839. Large standing Gothic monument, an extremely rich Dec tomb-chest with canopy. The inscription will be read with profit. The monument is for its date (unless it was made five or ten years later) surprisingly accurate in its use of the Dec style. – Lords Bertrand and Lewis Gordon † 1869 and 1870. Tomb-chest with Gothic inscription. – FUNERAL HELM, early C17. – Monuments not in the N chapel: Sir Charles Cope † 1781. A charming tablet of coloured marbles. – Lord Douglas William Cope Gordon † 1888. By *H. H. Armstead*. Portrait in a roundel set in a Quattrocento surround. – Marie Antoinette, Marchioness of Huntly, † 1893. Alabaster, in an interesting neo-1630. With two angels flanking the inscription.

ORTON HALL. Not enough is known about the architectural history of this house of the Gordon family, Marquesses of Huntly, Earls of Aboyne. The first Earl of Huntly belongs to the C15, the first Marquess died in 1636. One of his younger sons became Earl of Aboyne in 1660. The fourth Marquess was made Duke of Gordon in 1684. The dukedom became extinct in 1836. The ninth Marquess died in 1853, and Orton Hall in its present form is most probably of the last Duke's or the ninth Marquess's time. The house has a flat entrance side with mullioned and transomed windows and ornate Gothic details such as chimneys and a turret. Mid-century quite probably also the remarkable conservatory with its iron hammerbeam roof. But there is a doorway re-set between the house and an outbuilding which has a coat of arms in a florid strapwork setting. The doorway came from Fotheringhay, the outbuilding is dated 1654 on a chimney.* Also, as regards the dating within the C19, *Willement* records that he did the heraldic glass on the staircase in 1831. In the dining room is an assembly of woodwork, C16 to C17 and English as well as foreign.

ORTON WATERVILLE

ST MARY. Unbuttressed, i.e. early, W tower with a small arch to the nave. Perp top with quatrefoil frieze and cusped lancets in the battlements. E.E. S porch entrance with fillets on the principal respond shafts and two hollow chamfers in the arch. This porch belongs to the four-bay S arcade, which has standard elements except for one capital with good stiff-leaf. The N arcade is Perp and poor. Dec N and S aisle walls. C17 chancel. – PULPIT. An exceptionally sumptuous Elizabethan piece with dogtooth (an interesting touch) in the usual blank arches,

* I owe the information on this date to the Headmistress of Orton Hall School.

full-bosomed caryatids, and arabesque decoration of pilasters and panels. The pulpit is supposed to come from Great St Mary at Cambridge, Pembroke College being the patrons. – More such panels re-used in the N aisle REREDOS. – (ROYAL ARMS. Stuart; of wood, exceptionally fine. GMCH) – PLATE. Cup and Paten of 1683–4; Bowl, late C17.

MANOR FARM, W of the church. The house is a C16 hall house of stone. In the hall, re-used, a doorway dated 1571, with two steep pediments above the inscription and l. and r. two shapes like goblets with domed lids in a somewhat barbaric but not unimpressive design.

PAIL GROUNDS *see* HELPSTON

¹⁰⁰⁰

PASTON
Soke of Peterborough

ALL SAINTS. W tower of c.1300 with a big quatrefoil window, bell-openings of two lights with encircled motifs in bar tracery, and a broach spire with two tiers of lucarnes. The finest piece in the church is the triple-chamfered tower arch towards the nave. It rests on two splendid horizontal figures. But the earliest part of the church is the N chancel chapel. Two bays, semicircular responds, octagonal pier, single-chamfered arches. One stiff-leaf label stop. The date may be c.1225. Of the late C13 the SEDILIA in the chancel. The straight-headed chancel windows look as if they were Perp, but in spite of the Perp principle of panel tracery the details are mid C14 – and extremely pretty at that. Perp arcades of four bays with octagonal piers and double-chamfered arches. Perp chancel arch, aisle windows, and clerestory windows. – SCREEN. Tall, Perp, with one-light divisions. – SCULPTURE. Inside the E bay of the S aisle fragments of very small blank arcading. – PLATE. Cup and Cover Paten, 1715; Almsdish, 1807; Cup, 1836. – MONUMENT. Edward Mountsteven † 1635. Tablet with kneeling figure between black columns.

OLD RECTORY. Mostly c.1620–30, with gables with finials and mullioned windows. But a row of four splendidly decorated brick chimneys proves that the house dates from the time of Henry VIII.

The village has much changed recently. Most of it is now Peterborough–Suburban.

PAXTON HALL *see* LITTLE PAXTON

PEAKIRK
Soke of Peterborough

1000

ST PEGA. A unique dedication. St Pega was the sister of St Guthlac of Croyland across the Lincolnshire border. The w wall belonged to an aisleless Norman building. The bellcote is Norman too. It has two plain arches on plain imposts and one above them. Gable with one set-off to allow for the two lower arches. Norman also the ornate s doorway. One order of slim colonnettes. Tympanum with three fan-motifs, two horizontal from the bottom corners spreading to the centre, the third vertically rising in the middle. Arch with zigzag on the surface as well as at r. angles to it and with other motifs. The outer porch entrance is Dec (cf. Werrington). The N doorway is plain, round-arched, and single-chamfered. Of the C13 the w lancets. Internally the C12 is represented by the N arcade of three bays. Circular piers with many-scalloped capitals and square abaci. Round arches with roll mouldings. A little later the N chancel chapel. The responds still have many-scalloped capitals and the arch still has rolls, but it is pointed. The tall chancel arch cannot be later either, yet it is pointed too. The capitals of the responds have late C12 leaves. Fully E.E. the s arcade. Circular piers, circular moulded capitals, and abaci with a little nailhead decoration. Double-chamfered pointed arches. – LECTERN. The wooden stem is of the early C14 – a rarity. It has slender attached shafts. – SCULPTURE. Two pretty C14 head corbels in the E wall of the N aisle. – WALL PAINTINGS. Mostly C14. Cycle of the Passion above the N arcade in two tiers (top l. the utensils on the table of the Last Supper, below Scourging of Christ; then a later St Christopher interrupting the cycle; then Christ washing St Peter's feet and Crucifixion and Deposition below, followed by Entombment and Resurrection; at the E end Mocking of Christ and the Noli me Tangere below). Below both tiers a zigzag band painted in perspective. In the s aisle (SE corner) one unidentified representation, in the N aisle (near the NE corner) also an unidentified representation. In addition, in the N aisle E of the N door the Three Quick and the Three Dead (cf. Longthorpe Tower). The upright corpses and the insects around them are very horrible. Also a scene representing a Warning to Gossips. Two women sit whispering to one another. A devil presses their heads together. – STAINED GLASS. E window by *Kempe & Tower*, c.1914. – PLATE. Cup, 1710, and Paten, 1711 Almsdish, 1791.

THE HERMITAGE, E of the church. The chapel is the successor of St Pega's cell. Nave C15, but restored into a C13 shape; chancel c.1300, see the three-light window with trefoiled lights and small trefoils between them. – SCULPTURE. Fragment of a Saxon cross-shaft with interlace, and some foliage.

PETERBOROUGH

INTRODUCTION

Peterborough grew up outside the gates of the monastery. The monastery is now a cathedral, and the small town is no longer so small. In 1801 it still had only 3,580 inhabitants. Now (1967) there are nearly 80,000. The growth is due to the Fletton brick works, whose tall chimneys form almost a palisade along the s fringe of Peterborough. There can be few places in England where one can see so many chimneys at one glance.

The immediate future looks promising for Peterborough. The Ministry of Housing and Local Government has suggested the town for expansion. A study of possibilities was made in 1963 and another, by *Tom Hancock*, in 1966. The proposed figures of population for 1981 vary from 150,000 to 170,000. According to Tom Hancock the main growth should be directed to the w and should go nearly as far as the w boundary of the former Soke, i.e. to Wansford. It would include Castor and Ailsworth.

THE CATHEDRAL*

INTRODUCTION

Henry VIII raised Peterborough to Cathedral rank in 1541.[12] Until the time of the Reformation it had been a Benedictine

* A number of fragmentary inscribed Roman slabs of Barnack rag were found during the restorations of 1884 and 1888. As the site of Durobrivae belonged to the medieval monastery, it is possible that this may have been the source of the slabs.

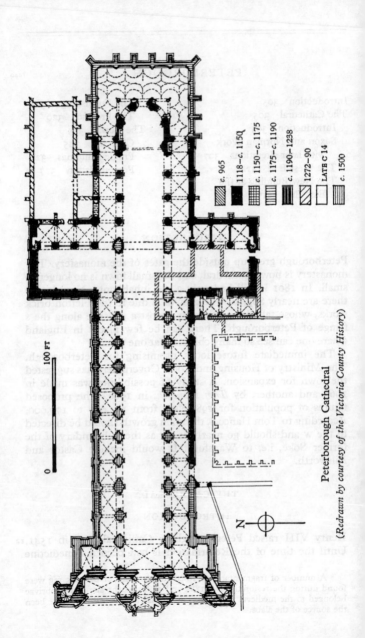

c. 965
1118–c. 115q
c. 1150–c. 1175
c. 1175–c. 1190
c. 1190–1238
1272–90
LATE c 14
c. 1500

100 FT

0

N

Peterborough Cathedral

(Redrawn by courtesy of the Victoria County History)

monastery. As such it was founded by Peada, King of Mercia,
about the year 650. The monastery was sacked by the Danes in
870, re-colonized and rebuilt c.965, and sacked again by Hereward in 1070. The church was however spared. It was burnt in
the great fire of 1116. Rebuilding started in 1118 under Abbot
John de Séez. He died in 1125, and little can have been done between 1125 and 1132. In 1143 at the latest services were held in
the new building. One can assume therefore that by then the
chancel was usable. The nave probably dates from c.1150 etc. Its
w end cannot have been reached before 1177; for the Chronicle
tells us that Abbot Benedict built (i.e. probably completed) the
whole nave *usque ad frontem*, and he ruled the monastery from
1177 to 1194. Finally, after many changes of mind the present w
front was complete by the time of the great consecration in 1238.
After that a Lady Chapel was built E of the N transept in 1272
etc. (consecration 1290) and a chapel between this and the
chancel aisle about the same time. Both have since been pulled
down. The Norman crossing tower was replaced by a lower and
less ambitious one c.1315, a porch was added to the w front in
the late C14, windows were renewed almost entirely in the C14
and C15, and the retrochoir was erected E of the Norman E end
c.1496–1508. The principal restoration, including the rebuilding
of the crossing piers and the crossing tower, took place in
1882–6. The architect responsible was *J. L. Pearson*.

The church consists of nave and aisles, a w porch, a crossing
with tower, transepts with E aisles, a chancel with chancel aisles,
and the retrochoir. The Norman work survives exceptionally
complete. Only the ground floor of the main apse and the two
side apses at the end of the chancel aisles have disappeared. The
cathedral is built of Barnack stone. It is 481 ft long and 81 ft high
inside. The tower rises to a height of 143 ft.

SAXON AND NORMAN WORK WITH LATER ALTERATIONS

Of the SAXON CHURCH the wide transepts and the straight-
ended chancel have been excavated and can be seen below the
floor of the present s transept and part of the crossing. The
Saxon church had a w steeple which was consecrated in 1059.

The NORMAN CHURCH was begun in 1118. Its E end largely
remains. It has three apses, one wide at the end of the chancel
which exists except for the ground floor, and two smaller at the
ends of the chancel aisles. These side apses do not survive. Of the
EXTERIOR of the ground floor of the main APSE all that can now
be seen is a stretch of wall E of the former aisle chapels with a

zigzag course on the level of the window sills. It is always said
that such zigzag decoration, which became the main stand-by of
the Anglo–Norman style when it came to enrichments, was
introduced c.1110. At Peterborough it occurs, as this course
shows, from the very beginning, i.e. from 1118. Above the ground
floor there are windows in two tiers with a frieze of intersecting
blank arcading between the two tiers. Intersecting arches are
found at Durham as early as 1093. The windows have Dec
tracery, the upper ones under segmental heads. The bays are
separated by demi-shafts. The parapet has medallions with
busts. These belong to the C13. Norman spirelets stress the
point where the chancel adjoins the apse.

The CHANCEL is four bays long. Its aisles have a zigzag
course at the sill level of their windows. One N window alone
has its original shape preserved, with a zigzag and a billet surround. The others on the S side are of the late C13 (five stepped
lancet lights under a segmental arch). On the N side they are
Perp. A second zigzag frieze runs above the top of the windows.
The gallery windows have flowing tracery on the N side and
simpler Dec tracery on the S. The bays are separated by broad
Norman buttresses with shafts at the angles. On the S side they
are strengthened by small C14 buttresses. On the N side the
blocked arch in the style of c.1300 belongs to the CHAPEL OF ST
THOMAS, erected shortly before 1298. The two lower blank
arches to the E of it with the springers of a vault belong to the
same. The chapel formed the link between the chancel and the
former Lady Chapel (see below). The clerestory of the chancel
has tripartite bays, the side pieces being blank arches. The bays
are separated by demi-shafts. The windows are now Perp.
Norman corbel-table and Perp parapet with blank quatrefoils.

Norman evidence about the TRANSEPTS must be pieced together from the S as well as the N arm. The transepts have E
aisles. Their E windows were probably like the chancel N and
S windows, with zigzag and billet surrounds. A zigzag ran at
sill level, as is indicated by remains in the S transept. The windows have all been replaced, on the S by larger ones of c.1260–75
with three stepped lights and three foiled circles over, on the N
by one of the same type and the two former entrance arches into
the late C13 Lady Chapel. The present Perp-looking windows
here are C19. The gable of the Lady Chapel can still be seen.
The gallery windows are Norman in the N transept (with blank
lower coupled arches l. and r.), except that one (and the aisle
gallery window to the N) is replaced by late C13 windows with a

large pointed trefoil above three stepped lights. The s transept has Dec gallery windows. The sill course of the gallery has zigzag on the N as in the chancel, but no longer any zigzag on the s clerestory and parapet as in the chancel.

The transept end walls have on the ground floor windows like those in the aisles, i.e. with zigzag and billet surrounds (see s wall). A doorway to the s also has zigzag in the arch. It has three orders of colonnettes. The upper windows are all Perp in Norman surrounds. Much blank arcading, especially small arched friezes above the first and the second upper windows. The walls end in gables flanked by polygonal turrets. In the w wall, which is exposed only on the N side, the windows are all Perp, but the surrounds remain in their Norman form. There is again much blank arcading of the same system as on the s and N sides. At the clerestory level the shafted buttresses change into demi-shafts to comply with the aisled chancel and the aisled E side of the transepts. The w wall of the s transept is in its lower parts hidden by the VESTRY built in the second half of the C12.

The CROSSING TOWER was originally work of *c.*1160–70 and higher than it is now. The present tower is a rebuilding of 1883–6 of a replacement of *c.*1325. This was crowned by a wooden octagon just like the crossing at Ely. The tower has polygonal panelled buttresses, two three-light bell-openings with transom, and, flanking them, blank two-light and four-light windows. The parapet is panelled.

The NAVE continues the Norman system of the E part for two bays, though certain changes in various points show that work proceeded gradually and slowly. Such changes are that the zig-zag frieze at the sill level of the aisle windows goes on for three bays on the N side but is discontinued on the s side at once. Also the buttresses drop their shafts at the level of the window sills of the gallery on the N side, but at the level of the sills of the ground-floor windows on the s side. Moreover in the clerestory the rhythm of the bays of the transept w wall is continued for two bays on the N side, for only one on the s. All this, and the former remarks about the zigzag at gallery level in the transepts, proves that work on the N side preceded that on the s. Of details the following ought to be noted. Near the middle of the N aisle is a doorway with three orders of colonnettes and capitals with decorated scallops. The arches have exceptionally much zigzag, both on the front and at r. angles to it. The details look mid C12. On the s side there are two doorways which originally led into the cloister. The Canons' Door is in the first bay from the E. It has four orders with block capitals. In the inner arch moulding fleur-de-lis foliage is set in the triangles of a beaded zigzag – the only occurrence of Norman foliage at Peterborough (cf. Ely). The Bishop's Door to the w walk of the former cloister is a C13 insertion. Four orders of colonnettes, big dogtooth between. Finely moulded arch. The ground-floor windows of the aisles with their five stepped lancet lights under depressed arches are typical work of the late C13. The gallery windows are Dec (segmental heads) but still flanked by small blank Norman arches. Clerestory and corbel-table carry on the system of the E parts. The windows are Perp, the parapet now has cusped wavy decoration. The continuation of the exterior to the w will be described in the next section (p. 313).

Now the INTERIOR. Generally speaking, the impression, as one enters from the W, is strong and consistent, thanks to the survival of Norman work all the way from W to E and the absence of any obstacle to the eye in trying to penetrate to the apse. The architecture is robust and determined, reiterating its simple statement with conviction. In detail the bays of the APSE are separated by triple shafts. The ground floor is altered (*see* below p. 317), but some capitals of former blank arcading remain. The wall-passage at first-floor level round the apse has against the back wall blank intersecting arcading, at the same height as the same motif occurs outside. The upper storeys of the straight bay between the former apse arch and the apse proper continue the system of the chancel, but in a painfully lopsided way. On both levels the bay has only two-thirds of a tripartite arrangement. It is remarkable how little C12 and C13 masons worried about such incongruities. The former arch between apse and chancel has triple responds too. The arch itself has disappeared, and the verticals of the piers are continued instead by ogee-headed niches. There are many small discrepancies on the top level of the apse indicating that it may originally have had a vault leaning against the former apse arch. The date of the alteration (C14? *c.*1500?) is not certain.

The CHANCEL is four bays long. The piers of the arcade are octagonal, circular, and dodecagonal. The responds are triple groups like the shafts of the apse. The aisles are rib-vaulted, an early occurrence for England and indeed Europe. The earliest rib-vaults in existence are at Durham of *c.*1095–1100. In France they appear *c.*1100–20. The date of the design at Peterborough is, as we have seen, 1118. The transverse arches have a rectangular section with rolls along the angles, the ribs have a demi-roll on a rectangle. The mouldings are big and bold. The outer walls have large intersecting arcading. The capitals are of the block type, or varieties of heavy scallops. They are all big and bold, as far as the piers are concerned, but more playful in the wall-shafts of the aisles (where of course they might well be the result of re-carving). The arches have heavy roll mouldings and a billet frieze round the outer edge. On the side towards the nave shafts rise in front of the piers to the ceiling. They were probably originally meant to carry transverse arches. There is no indication that a rib-vault was ever intended. The original ceiling was replaced in the C15 by a complicated wooden ceiling-cum-vault, i.e. a panelled ceiling, four square cross-ribbed panels wide, on a deep coving with tierceron ribs. The ceiling has many bosses. Among them are the Crucifixion, the Assumption, Christ in Majesty, the Annunciation.

The gallery has large arched openings subdivided by a tall shaft helping to carry two sub-arches. The piers alternate between a compound shape and a circular one with demi-shafts on rectangular projections. The capitals are busier than below. The tympana have different fillings, starting on the N side with a pierced circle and a group of four pierced circles, on the s side with one plain tympanum. The others have diapering in relief and no piercing. A frieze at the floor level of the gallery has zig-zag coming forward at r. angles to the wall plane. The outer moulding of the arch has the same motif. Horizontal zigzag or zigzag at r. angles to the wall plane is usually regarded as a Late Norman motif. Here it can hardly be later than c.1135. At the floor level of the clerestory zigzag was begun at the E end on the s and the w end on the N side, but was soon discontinued and replaced by an undecorated course. The clerestory has a wall passage with the tripartite stepped arcading familiar in English Norman buildings (e.g. Winchester, Ely, Durham transepts).

The CROSSING piers differ. Those to the E and w have responds with three shafts in a line and arches altered in the C14, those to the N and s triple responds as we have found them in other places and arches with zigzag at r. angles to the wall plane. The tower has a lierne-vault of timber. The central boss shows Christ in Majesty, the other bosses the Signs of the four Evangelists and the Instruments of the Passion.

The E sides of the TRANSEPTS are aisled and continue the design of the chancel, though with significant changes. The alternation of round and octagonal piers remains, but the shafts up to the ceiling are no longer in front of the arcade piers, but start above them. The arcade responds are segments of circular piers. The billets of the arches are coarser. Above the arcade runs a course with horizontal zigzag just as in the chancel. The gallery piers alternate as in the chancel. The gallery tympana have on the s side the same relief diapering as in the chancel (except that the southernmost tympanum is left plain). On the N side the first bay has diapering in the flat, the second in relief, the others again in the flat. Below the clerestory the string course has a little zigzag in the N transept and none in the s. In the clerestory there is no change against the chancel. Between the aisle bays of the s transept low separating walls are inserted to divide them into chapels. Towards the chancel aisle is a low arched recess on short Norman columns. Above this, at the top of the wall, runs a small frieze which seems zigzag at first, but is in fact nutmeg (as is also the frieze in one bay of the chancel N aisle). In the middle chapel is flat intersecting arcading. The s chapel has normal blank arcading like the rest of the transepts. The N wall of the aisle in the N transept contains a small doorway with fish-scale decoration in the tympanum. The other walls of the transepts have tall blank arcading on the ground floor, shafted windows in two tiers, and the familiar tripartite stepped arcading of the wall-passage on the clerestory level. The bays are divided by tall demi-shafts. In the blank arcading of the s transept s wall one capital is a big monster head. The string course above the blank arcading again has nutmeg instead of zigzag decoration. This applies to the end and w walls of both transepts. The s transept has a doorway in its s wall. The transepts both have original CEILINGS. They are flat, of wood, and have bold lozenge patterns.

Adjoining the w wall of the s transept is the VESTRY. This dates from the late C12. It is entered by a Dec doorway with an ogee arch. The vestry is of three bays, with low cinquepartite rib-vaults (quadripartite plus an extra rib). The ribs have a slight chamfer, the transverse arches a rectangular projection and keeled rolls at the angles. The arches and ribs rest on short piers with scalloped capitals.

The NAVE goes on without change of system, though changes of detail are as noticeable inside as they are outside. The blank arcading resumes the intersecting of the chancel. The capitals on the s side are as simple as those of the chancel and transepts, which indicates that the s aisle wall was carried up very early, probably in connexion with work on the claustral parts. On the N side the capitals are more decorated and clearly later. They

play on forms of scalloping, of little volutes, etc., and beasts'
heads with wide open mouths. The aisle vaults occasionally have
very small bosses at the intersection of the ribs. The arcade piers
resume the shafts towards the nave. In shape the piers differ
from those in chancel and transepts. They begin from the E with
a respond with clustered shafts, then follows a circular form with
attached shafts on flat projections in all four directions – a form
developed from the piers of the gallery in chancel and transepts –
then the clustered pier is repeated, i.e. the principle of alternation
continued. After that however this principle is abandoned and
all piers are like the second, i.e. they are circular with projections
on all four sides consisting of a rectangle with a demi-roll. The
capitals are busier. Small changes in the details of the bases within the nave are noted in the VCH. The arch mouldings change at
once E of the crossing. They contain one more roll moulding to
the nave. The gallery tympana have relief diapering only in the
first two bays from the E. After that they are plain. An odd, un-
explained anomaly is the crocket capitals of the third gallery pier
from the crossing on the N side. They must be an alteration of
c.1200 or later. Perhaps the capitals had at first been left un-
carved.

The NAVE CEILING is a very precious survival. It must date
from c.1220. It is canted, decorated with lozenge patterns like
those of the transept ceilings, and retains its original colouring.
In the lozenges are figures of kings and queens and saints, a
Janus head, a monster feeding on the bleeding limbs of a man,
figures with musical instruments including an animal playing
the harp, an architect with L-square and dividers, a monkey on a
goat, etc.

The WEST END is an area of so many changes and problems
that a separate section must be dedicated to it. What is certain is
that the Norman nave was intended to be nine bays long with W
towers over the ninth aisle bays. This appears from the greater
width of the piers between the eighth and ninth bays, which is
specially noticeable on the gallery level. The outer wall of the
bay in question is thicker too, and a buttress on the S side is
much wider. On the gallery one can also see that a transverse arch
ran across, of which the N respond survives and a lump of stone
where the S respond was. Close to this there is a spiral staircase
whose W wall was clearly bonded originally against a cross wall.
In spite of this, when the decision was taken to continue the nave
to the W, the system was still not changed. Yet by then 1175
must have been reached.

THE WEST END

The history of the west end with its w transepts and its deep niches is complicated. Sir Charles Peers has tried to elucidate it in the VCH, and the following account follows his explanations. He distinguishes four stages. The first has been discussed. It is the beginning of Norman w towers over the ninth bay from the E. The second stage was a lengthening by one more bay and a w transept, on the lines of Ely and Bury St Edmunds, though with two towers instead of one. The third stage was the addition of giant niches one bay deep and as wide as the transept. They were to be divided into seven bays with the middle one widest and to have three openings just like Lincoln. The last stage was a revision in the design of the niches by which they received their present rather unfortunate form, that is five bays in width instead of seven, with the outer openings consequently wider than the middle one, and with four angle turrets to project beyond the line of the transept and give the effect of a wider screen, comparable e.g. to Salisbury.

In detail the following can be seen. When it was decided to lengthen the nave – a decision which must have been taken c.1180 – the Norman system was still not given up. So bay ten and even the openings from the aisles into the w transept keep to the elements already described. The wall arcading on the s side now at last takes up the lively forms of capitals which had been used on the N side from the E end of the nave onwards; on the N side the tenth bay has for the first time waterleaf capitals. Sir Charles Peers can point out many more small changes, but they are not of great relevance. The first major change is the fact that the arches across the transepts are pointed. Their details are typical Latest Norman with big, rich zigzag and similar more complicated and even bigger motifs set at an angle. The vaults are quadripartite with the much finer details and more delicate members of the E.E. style. In the bays below the towers bellholes are left, that under the N tower being surrounded by playful ribs. The centre bay has a boss with stiff-leaf foliage. To the E springers can be seen in the first nave bay, proving that the intention existed of vaulting the nave in the new style. The w wall is purely E.E. in its motifs, except that the three doorways are still round-headed. But they have finely moulded arches and stiff-leaf capitals, and there is pointed blank arcading at the ground level, and the upper windows (altered Perp) are set in tall blank E.E. arcading too. In the projecting bays of the transept the change is also made to E.E. forms and proportions, but even here the windows behind the gables follow the system of the Norman clerestory. One must assume that the W, N, and S walls of the transept were completed first, and that the W wall and the vaulting followed.

To the outside, i.e. the niches, which will be described presently, the middle portal has a *trumeau* or middle post of Purbeck marble with a beautifully carved relief round the circular base, which is also of Purbeck marble.* This represents a man upside down and tormented by devils. He has been interpreted as Simon Magus. The portal had five or six orders of colonnettes, the side portals have five orders. The W wall (before the addition of the giant niches and the Perp porch) had in addition tall blank arcading with sub-arches sharing their outer mouldings with the super-arch, then a frieze of small trefoil-headed arches, and then again tall arcading broken by the windows. Here the rhythm goes restless owing to the necessities created by the altered design of the front.

The exterior of the W transept essentially continues the system of the W wall. But the windows with their cusped intersected tracery are a late C13 alteration of former windows which must have been lancets.‡ The tall, narrow E windows have Perp tracery. The gables have a many-foiled circular window each and up the slope of the gable a frieze of lunettes. The gables are flanked by polygonal turrets. On their top storey zigzag still occurs. Of the W towers only that on the N side was built. It lies awkwardly behind the later porch, and can only be seen and appreciated in its original meaning if one stands far enough away from the cathedral. The tower has lancet windows on two storeys and blank arches to their l. and r. The pinnacles are polygonal.

Of the plans for the giant niches before the idea of the projecting turrets was accepted we can see only one indication. Immediately W of the start of the W buttresses of the transepts on their N and S sides the wall projects a little and has a shaft at the angle just like those of the transept buttresses. The projection reaches up only a few feet and is then discontinued.

The GIANT NICHES in their final form are an unhappy addition, though they proceeded from a grand conception. This conception was no doubt based on Norman Lincoln, where three deep niches, the central one wider and taller than the others,

---

* Or is it the marble from Alwalton used for the abbots' tombs, *see* p. 319.
‡ Inside the S transept is a DOUBLE PISCINA of the same date.

receive the faithful. At Peterborough this same motif was developed into recesses which were to be a full bay deep and endowed with quadripartite vaults in seven bays of which the outer corresponded to the transept projections, three of the others to the portals, and the remaining two to the spaces between the portals. In execution however all this was changed. Turrets were added outside the area of the original composition. The seven vaulting-bays were reduced to five, with the outer bays much wider than the central one, and the outer arch openings or portal niches consequently much wider than the middle niche. A worrying rhythm is thus created for the front proper, and nonsense is made of the former W wall with its details. Nonsense is incidentally also made of the three gables above the entrance arches. The details must be seen to judge of the truth of this indictment. The most painful thing is the way in which the wide side openings lead to side portals appearing out of axis. In detail the three truly monumental giant portals have six orders of shafts each with three shaft-rings. The centre arch has tufts of stiff-leaf rising in subsidiary orders between them (a Lincoln motif). The arches are decorated with a bobbin motif, foliage, and dogtooth. The turrets have the usual blank arcading, including a frieze of trefoil-headed arches such as had occurred on the W wall behind the niches. Higher up there is an interesting motif of blank intersection with zigzag decoration set in front of blank arcading. This motif may well be inspired by the angle turrets of the façade of Ely Cathedral. The tops of the turrets were completed only in the C14 – not to the benefit of the former conception of the whole W end; for they compete with the W towers diagonally behind them, and the general effect from far enough away is one of profusion – it is true – but also of confusion. The top of the S turret is the more elaborate of the two. The angle shafts turn into square pinnacles set diagonally, and behind these rises an octagonal spire with one set of lucarnes and four spirelets accompanying it and linking it to the angle pinnacles. These spirelets have an open bottom stage and are crocketed. The N turret is simpler. The angle shafts here end with taller pinnacles, and the spirelets are missing. The gables above the portals have the most haphazard assembly of motifs, quatrefoil in circles, trefoil pointed arch-heads, niches with statues (gradually being replaced by work of *Alan Durst*), foiled circles with heads, wheels with six or eight spokes, etc. Moreover, the strong shafts which are set between the three portals are suddenly replaced by turrets. All this shows the disastrous effects of the change of plan from the narrow–wide–narrow to the wide–narrow–wide rhythm for these portals. Inside the niches the top storey of the W wall of the church is affected equally disastrously by this change. Because he had reduced them from seven to five and widened the outer ones, the designer chose to give these quadripartite vaults an additional W–E rib running against the façade wall of the church. This plays havoc with the blank arcading and fenestration at that stage.

Finally, to do yet more damage to the W view, a Perp PORCH was tucked into the middle opening of the C13 porch, filling it in width but not in height. This work was done in the later C14. It is two bays deep and two storeys high. It has tierceron-vaults with ridge ribs (star-vaults) on the ground floor* and an upper floor with a large Perp window. The upper floor is reached by two spiral staircases which project in front of the C13 jambs.‡ The doorway has a depressed arch. The spandrels have blank tracery decoration. The gable above the Perp window is of low pitch and embattled.

THE NEW BUILDING AT THE EAST END

Abbot Robert Kirkton, whose rebus, initials, and other signets appear all over it, erected a new retrochoir. He ruled the monastery from 1496 to 1528. The retrochoir is two bays deep and as wide as the church nave and aisles. The new work links up with the old in the following way. The aisle apses of the Norman church (which must have been remodelled in the C13 – see their elegant quadripartite rib-vaults and the handsome DOUBLE PISCINA in the N bay) were removed and the aisles connected by two new bays with the retrochoir. It is here that the exterior of the main Norman apses shows inside the new building. The apse windows were continued to the ground and these new openings linked up by arches and new triangles to the retrochoir. There is plenty of enjoyable tracery here to conceal the awkward junction. The apse arches have cusped four-centred arches with tracery over, and the triangles are also marked by four-centred arches with tracery over. Moreover, the beginning of the retrochoir proper is marked by a broad arch with big, heavy fleurons in the deep main moulding both to the W and E. The retrochoir has four-light and three-light windows with panel tracery, separated

* The two main bosses illustrate the Coronation of the Virgin and the Trinity.

‡ On one of these, for no known reason, a fireplace with a flue has been built in.

by buttresses. The set-offs of these are decorated with fleurons. The work is crowned by an openwork parapet very similar to that of King's College Chapel, Cambridge, and seated figures on the tops of the buttresses which must have been of good quality when they were newly made. Inside, the windows are continued 47 by blank panelling with stone benches. The vault is a very handsome fan-vault carried on slender shafts. The new building is internally no higher than the aisles, and the closely panelled vaulting at that height gives it a sense of comfortable as well as rich enclosure. Mr Harvey has suggested that *John Wastell*, who began in 1508 at King's College Cambridge and built the fanvaults there, may have been the designer.

THE FURNISHINGS*

7 RETROCHOIR. SCULPTURE. Hedda Stone. An extremely important piece of Anglo-Saxon sculpture to be dated *c*.800 by comparison with illuminated manuscripts, High Crosses, and also such work as is preserved at Breedon-on-the-Hill in Leicestershire. Grey stone with a pitched roof. Against the long sides standing figures of the apostles in close-fitting arcading. The short sides are defaced. The roof is pitched like that of a metal shrine and has scrollwork with interlace, affronted pairs of animals, and also what has been called an 'inhabited scroll', i.e. a vine scroll with an animal inside. The figures are stiff, mostly frontal, and have the fluffy carving and the deeply drilled eyes characteristic of their date. Comparable work is also to be found at Castor and at Fletton.‡ – The three bays of a BASE, Perp, with a quatrefoil frieze at the foot, panels and canopied niches, and a cresting with a frieze of little beasts, belong probably to the Shrine of Hedda. – STAINED GLASS. Southernmost E window by *Clayton & Bell* (TK). – MONUMENTS. Abbot, probably R. Kirkton † 1528. Recumbent effigy of stone; defaced. Two angels by the pillar. – Orme Family, early C17. Hanging monument almost completely ruined. Of the figures only one small group survives. – Bishop Cumberland † 1718. Signed by *Thomas Green* of Camberwell. Hanging monument with open segmental pediment above the inscription plate and standing putti to its l. and r. – Thomas Deacon † 1720. Signed by *Robert Taylor* (*Sen.*). Standing monument. White and greyish marble. Semi-reclining,

* From E to W.
‡ As Abbot Hedda was killed by the Danes in 870, the stone can have nothing to do with him.

well carved effigy with wig. Reredos background with Corinthian pilasters and an open segmental pediment. – Dean Ingram. Recumbent effigy of white marble. By *H. R. Ingram*, 1903.

CHANCEL. BALDACCHINO. 1894, probably by *J. L. Pearson*. – TAPESTRIES. Two of the late C16; probably Flemish. – STAINED GLASS. In the apse some pieced-together fragments of Perp glass.

SOUTH CHANCEL AISLE. MISERICORDS. Three of the C14. – MONUMENTS. Four Abbots all of Alwalton marble, and all made within the thirty years from *c.*1195 to *c.*1225. Of only one, the first from the E and in date the latest (supposed to be Alexander of Holderness † 1226), the tomb-chest is preserved. It has short columns and quatrefoil panels (cf. the Marshall Monument in Exeter Cathedral). The effigy is flanked by shafts carrying a projecting pointed trefoiled canopy. Stiff-leaf ornament. The third of the series alone has a rounded-trefoiled canopy over his head, also carried on shafts. It is much defaced. The second has a rounded cinquecusped canopy which is very depressed and carries bits of buildings. The curly hair and beard are a sign of an early date. The fourth is in higher relief. It has no flanking shafts. Two angels at his head, a dragon at his feet. – Also of the C13 a coffin lid with foliated cross. – Joseph Stamford † 1683. Pretty cartouche with cherubs' heads. – Archbishop Magee of York † 1891. By *J. Forsyth*. White recumbent effigy on a tomb-chest in classical Elizabethan forms.

NORTH CHANCEL AISLE. CHEST. C15, with elaborate tracery. – STAINED GLASS. One window († 1856) by *Wailes* (TK). – MONUMENTS. Another early Abbot of the same material and date as those in the S aisle. Beardless head under a rounded-trefoiled arch. Shafts by his sides with capitals clearly still of the C12. A dragon at his feet. – Dean Duport † 1679. Very classical, with open pediment with curly ends and garlands. Small. – Constance May † 1681. Cartouche with fine flower carving.

CROSSING. Large brass LECTERN, late C15, English. With inscription referring to Abbot William de Ramsey (1471–96). The same pattern as at St Nicholas King's Lynn, Christ's College Cambridge, St Mark's Venice, etc.

SOUTH TRANSEPT. SCREENS. Late C15. – SCULPTURE. In the w wall a small C13 panel with two figures under arches. – In the low excavated space of the Saxon S transept several Saxon stones with interlace ornament. – STAINED GLASS. S wall, lowest tier, easternmost. By *Morris, Marshall & Faulkner*, 1862, i.e. a very early work by William Morris and his Pre-Raphaelite friends. Predominantly red and brown. – Next to this to the w by *A. Gibbs* (TK), 1861.

NORTH TRANSEPT. SCREENS. Perp with much tracery. Not *in situ*. – STALLS. Fragments of two units of the original choir stalls of some time between 1233 and 1245. Slender double shafts with stiff-leaf capitals. Remodelled in the late C16 or early C17. – STAINED GLASS. N wall, lowest tier, first and second from E: *Clayton & Bell*, 1860, 1863; tier above this from E to W: *Cox & Son*, c.1849, *O'Connor*, 1865, *Heaton, Butler & Bayne*, c.1852; top tier 1865.

NAVE. STALLS, c.1894. – PULPIT AND LECTERN, Neo-Georgian, by *Leslie T. Moore*.

WEST TRANSEPT. FONT. C13 bowl on C19 support. The bowl has twelve shallow projections or undulations decorated with stiff-leaf. – PAINTING (w wall). So-called Old Scarlett († 1594).

PORCH. Fine and elaborate IRON GATES.

PLATE. Silver-gilt Cup and Paten, 1569; silver-gilt Paten, 1634; silver-gilt Cup, Paten, and two Flagons, 1638; silver-gilt Almsdish, c.1650; silver-gilt Cup, 1836.

THE PRECINCT

The precinct is entered from the Market Place by the OUTER GATE. This was built by Abbot Benedict (1177–94) and considerably altered in 1302–7. The Norman work consists of the two archways (columns with scalloped capitals, arches with roll mouldings), the blank wall arcading raised above the doorways to N and S), and the rib-vault of the same elementary moulding as in the Norman work in the church. The early C14 placed a higher arch in front of the Norman W arch. The upper parts are also C14. Panel-motifs and two turrets. To the S of the Outer Gate some vaults connected with the KING'S LODGING and the ABBOT'S PRISON. The best piece is a late C12 room with a short circular pier and slightly chamfered arches and ribs. Another vaulted room to the E of this. The range continues with Victorian building and then the ABBOT'S GATE. This is of the early C13, projects squarely to the N, and has square turrets. Two-centred archways to N and S; four orders of colonnettes with moulded capitals. To the N as well as the S are original figures, deserving to be better known than they are. The upper windows (Knights' Chamber) altered in the Jacobean style. Inside the gateway from N to S first one bay with slender blank arcading very similar to that of the W wall of the church and a quadripartite rib-vault, then a cross-wall dividing the traffic into pedestrians (two-centred

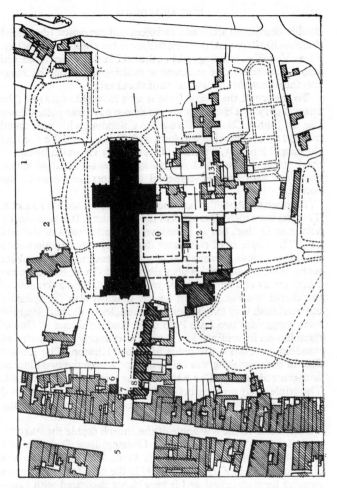

Peterborough Cathedral: Precinct

1. Tout Hill
2. Deanery
3. Prior's Gate
4. Priory Gate
5. Market Place
6. St Thomas's Chapel
7. Outer Gate
8. King's Lodging and Abbots' Prison
9. Abbot's Gate
10. Cloister
11. The Palace
12. Refectory
13. Infirmary

(Redrawn by courtesy of the Victoria County History)

double-chamfered arch) and carriages and horsemen (depressed double-chamfered arch). Then two more bays much as the N bay. More Victorian building, and at the end of this range a blocked single-chamfered C14 arch and a vaulting-shaft. So the range continued towards the SW angle of the church.

To the NE of the Outer Gate is ST THOMAS'S CHAPEL, the chancel only of a church of *c*.1330 whose nave was pulled down (*see* St John's Church). Five-light E window with reticulated tracery, three-light side windows with Dec tracery. To the N of the chapel Nos 3–5, a terrace of three Early Georgian houses of three storeys, yellow and red brick, segment-headed windows, doorways with broken segmental pediments on pilasters, top parapet.

Through the Abbot's Gate one reaches the BISHOP'S PALACE. This was the ABBOT'S HOUSE of the monastery. It is now mostly Victorian Gothic, but in it survive two undercrofts of the mid C13. The larger is of two naves divided by circular piers with moulded capitals. Arches and ribs are chamfered. The smaller room, now the chapel, is also rib-vaulted. In it Expressionist STAINED GLASS by *Patrick Reyntiens*, 1958. The E window of the chapel is an original slit lancet. Original also the splendid buttress, with very long set-offs. At r. angles to the hall wing the solar wing, with two Late Perp oriel windows facing N. One of them has on its under-side a church, very nicely portrayed, and standing on a tun – the rebus of Abbot Kirkton. The ground floor of the solar wing was originally open – see the two blocked four-centred arches. The E wall of this wing was not exposed. The triple shaft on a corbel (late C12) belonged to the monks' kitchen, i.e. linked up with the premises surrounding the cloister (*see* below).*

From close to the NW angle of the church façade the PRIORY GATE leads to the former Prior's Lodging, later Deanery, and now a private house called Prior's Gate. The GATEWAY was built under Abbot Kirkton, i.e. early in the C16. It has a separate opening for pedestrians and is very richly decorated with blank tracery etc. Another gateway, at r. angles to this, formerly led into the monastic graveyard. The house, i.e. Prior's Gate, contains little that is medieval. Only the E wall of the hall, with a former spiral staircase, exists. The windows, now of two pointed-trefoiled lights with a circle over, might well reproduce the

---

* In the bishop's garden (and only visible from there) one can also see the interior of the refectory (*see* below) and the remains of the misericord (*see* below).

original late C13 work. They have original depressed rere-arches.
Most of the house is by *W. J. Donthorne*, 1842. In the garden
to the E TOUT HILL, a mound heaped up by Abbot Thorold in
the late C11. There are no signs that it ever carried more than
wooden fortifications. To its SW a picturesque ARCH made up in
the C20 of fragments from the cathedral.

The CLOISTER can be reached from the E end of the range
containing the Abbot's Gate by a passage along the S side of the
W parts of the church, or direct from the church by the two portals already described (p. 309). The cloister walks survive nowhere, and against the church there are not even any traces of
the bays and their vaults left. The existing W wall was the E wall
of the cellars. In it there are some blocked early to mid C12 doorways, and also, at the N end, one well-preserved one with one
order of columns and one continuous roll moulding. The arch
has a big outer billet moulding, similar to those of the transepts.
There is also a small C14 doorway with flowing tracery, one Perp
doorway with a four-centred arch, and one doorway with Late
Norman arch fragments (crenellation, frieze of lobes – cf. the
gables of the cathedral). The remains of the arcading are superimposed on all this. They are Perp.

The SOUTH RANGE has remains partly E.E., partly Perp.
E.E. the blank arcading with sub-arches, whose outer mouldings
are those of the super-arch as well, and also two doorways, at the
E and W ends. The W doorway is round-arched. It has four
orders of colonnettes and a beautiful arch with extremely fine,
deeply cut stiff-leaf. Tympanum with a quatrefoil and two
dragons. This doorway leads into the REFECTORY, of which no
more stands than the very wall we have just looked at. Towards the
interior, i.e. the S, it has blank arcading with very varied paterae
in and above the spandrels. They contain much stiff-leaf. Of
the refectory E wall the N springer of some taller blank arcading
is the only sign of decoration. The C13 arcading of the S wall of
the S range was replaced in the five bays next to the refectory
doorway during the C15 by a renewed LAVATORIUM of very
rich Perp panelling. The E doorway of the S range of the cloister
has a segmental arch and a quatrefoil above this. Fine mouldings;
stiff-leaf detail. The doorway led into the Hostry Passage. Of the
E range nothing at all survives. Part of its place is taken by two
Georgian stone houses of three storeys. Doorway with pediment
on Tuscan columns.

The HOSTRY PASSAGE was a long vaulted passage running
along the E wall of the dormitory wing, which exists no longer.

The passage was vaulted, and the details of blank tracery etc. point to *c.*1330–40. To the W of its S end there is a square vaulted building of the later C12 (two oblong quadripartite rib-vaults, chamfered ribs) which formed part of the undercroft of a W attachment to the S end of the dormitory (misericord?). The little building is neglected at the time of writing. To its N are signs of a vaulted C14 passage, and one unit of blank Dec arcading like that in the Hostry Passage (i.e. on the opposite side of the same wall). From the S end of the Hostry Passage one has to turn E to visit the impressive remains of the INFIRMARY. This was built by an abbot who ruled from 1250 to 1262. It is a large building with a nave and aisles, seven bays long, and an unaisled chancel. The arcades have tall, slender, but strong piers with a square core and four semicircular shafts with fillets giving the impression of a quatrefoil section. The arches have many deep mouldings, and there is excellent stiff-leaf enrichment. The W responds stand on corbels, and these are carried by a human figure and a grotesque. Blank arcading below the W window of the nave. Blank arcading on a higher level (why?) also in the W wall of the S aisle. Remains of a spiral staircase at the W end of the junction of S aisle and nave. The outer aisle windows are tall and shafted with shaft-rings. This evidence has to be pieced together from two separate houses built into the aisles. Inside one of them a round-headed doorway leading from the S aisle to the S. The chancel arch has slender blank arches l. and r. of the beautifully moulded arch. Of the chancel itself remains are in yet another house, partly C13 (buttresses, re-used mask-corbels) and partly C14 alterations. The house itself is Georgian.

Close to the infirmary are two small detached buildings, Table Hall and what is supposed to have been the Infirmarer's Lodging. TABLE HALL stands just to the NE of the NE corner of the infirmary N aisle. It is a C15 building and has a fireplace to the N and a roof with collar-beams on braces and wind-braces. The INFIRMARER'S LODGING is more interesting. This is of the late C13, and has windows consisting of two pointed-tre-foiled lights with a trefoil or a quatrefoil in plate tracery. The lights are separated by a polygonal shaft, not a mullion.

S of the Infirmary is the present DEANERY, formerly known as the Archdeaconry House, and originally, it is suggested, the HOSTRY or guest house. The building is largely Victorian (probably *c.*1875–80 and probably by *Sir G. G. Scott*), but con-tains valuable early evidence. The E half was a late C13 hall. The windows are tall, shafted, with shaft-rings, and have two lights with a plain circle over. It is doubtful however whether they are original or *in situ*. But further W is a fine room (kitchen?) with a large N fireplace and a splendid wide late C12 arch. This rests on shafts with waterleaf capitals. Further evidence of the C12 to C17 in the building is scanty and confused.

More outbuildings to the SW of this; also, to the S, further away, a STABLE(?) with a building attached to the E. This has tall transomed one-light windows of *c*.1300.

Remains of the PRECINCT WALL in many places, chiefly the W and the E. Its age is uncertain.

THE TOWN

CHURCHES

ST JOHN BAPTIST. The church was E of the cathedral until it was rebuilt on its present site, in 1402–7, using material from the old church and the nave of St Thomas W of the cathedral (*see* p. 322). Mostly Perp, the oldest parts at the foot of the W tower. Rubble and ashlar for the upper parts of the tower and the clerestory. The tower is embraced by the aisles, and the tower E, N, and S arches are in their mouldings and responds earlier than the work of 1402, though probably not earlier than the C14. Re-used also the W doorway and the window above it. The rest is all of a piece. Large Perp four-light windows,* tower bell-openings of four lights with transom. The tower buttresses are polygonal. Decorated parapets; pinnacles.‡ S porch of two storeys and two bays deep, the outer bay open to the W and E as well as to the S. Tierceron-vaults with ridge ribs and bosses with Annunciation and Crucifixion. Interior of seven bays, tall arcades with slender piers of the usual section with four shafts and four hollows. The chancel arch of the same type, the E chapel arches too. – FONT. Big, Perp, octagonal, with quatre-foil panels. – EMBROIDERY. Cruciform piece of the C15 with the Crucifixus and two angels; English. – STAINED GLASS. One N aisle window by *Kempe*, 1896. – PLATE. Flagon, Breadholder, and Spoon, 1675; Flagon, 1703; silver-gilt Almsdish, 1704; silver-gilt Paten, 1711; Patens, 1731 and 1734; two silver-gilt Cups, 1799. – MONUMENTS. William Wyldbore † 1781, by *Richard Hayward*. Standing monument. Obelisk with urn in relief, two female allegories in relief to the

---

* The tracery is all renewed. The intersecting tracery cannot be regarded as authentic even in design.

‡ A spire was removed in the C19.

l. and r. (SE chapel). – John Image † 1786, by *Edward Bingham*.
With a female figure by an urn (S aisle). – William Squire
† 1826, by *Flaxman*. A mourning Grecian by a tall pedestal
with a medallion showing the heads of Mr and Mrs Squire in
profile.

ALL SAINTS, Park Road. 1894 by *Temple Moore*, a sensitive
design and quite original. In the Dec style. The tower stands
beyond the S chancel aisle at its E end. The S aisle is uncommonly wide, and there is no N aisle.

ALL SOULS (R.C.), Fitzwilliam Street. 1896 by *Leonard Stokes*.
Of small squared rubble with only a small polygonal bellcote.
This is at the W end, where the Priest's House is attached.
Interior with aisle of no more than passage width. Tall aisle
windows. The arcade arches are so tall as to embrace them.

ST BARNABAS, Taverners Road. 1900 by *W. Bryer* (GR). Brick;
no tower. No interest inside.

ST MARK, Lincoln Road. 1856 by *E. Ellis*. Quite an original and
picturesque design. Early Dec style with a NE tower and spire.
Nave with stone dormers with fanciful circular windows.
Also a half-timbered dormer.

ST MARY, Boongate. 1859 by *Ewan Christian*. E.E., rock-faced,
with apse. Steeple of 1883 with a saddleback roof.

ST PAUL, Walpole Street. 1868 by *James Teale* ('bullied by
Lord Grimthorpe', GR). In the E.E. style, with lancet and Geo-
metrical windows. Big central tower open to the inside. Apse.
Quite an impressive, though a coarse design. – STAINED
GLASS. Several windows by *Cakebread*.

CEMETERY CHAPEL, Eastfield Road. 1850. With a gateway
crowned by a spire, attached to the chapel.

METHODIST CHURCH, Wentworth Street. 1874–5 by *Johnson*.
Yellow and red brick. With three angle towers with spires
and arched windows with Venetian tracery.

TRINITY PRESBYTERIAN CHURCH, Priestgate. Built *c*.1864
into a Georgian house of five bays. The centre received a
tower with a low spire of somewhat Vanbrughian proportions
and detail.

PUBLIC BUILDINGS

OLD GUILDHALL, Market Place. 1671. Three by two bays with
an open ground floor on Tuscan columns and arches. Upper
windows of cross type. Steep hipped roof and steep gable
towards the square.

TOWN HALL, Bridge Street. Designed in 1928 by *E. Berry*

Webber. Neo-Georgian, brick with stone dressings. The choice of the style at so late a date may be deplorable, but the building is tactfully fitted into the street architecture of Peterborough. The architect has resisted the temptation to set his work up as a monument to compete with the cathedral. Thirteen-bay centre with a narrow portico of four tall giant Corinthian columns. Turret with detached, diagonally set columns and cupola. The parts to the l. and r. of the portico have widely spaced tall arched windows. In addition long, lower, two-storeyed wings ending in giant arches and fitting the building into the street frontages to the l. and r. and opposite. Spacious staircase hall of a kind of Quattrocento character.

TECHNICAL COLLEGE, Eastfield Road. 1952 by *David Jenkin* and 1957–8 and 1964–5 by *Portress & Richardson*.

MUSEUM, Priestgate. 1816. Fine, plain, three-storeyed ashlar front, with a one-storey portico of pairs of Greek Doric columns. Supposed to have been built as a private house. Later an infirmary, before it became a museum.

ST JOHN'S CLOSE, Thorpe Road. Now a hospital, originally the WORKHOUSE. Front Latest Classical, of 1836. Three-bay centre with cupola, and five-bay lower wings. Later additions. Behind the gaol entrance (*see* below) is a new large block running w–e (1963–7 by *Guy Aldis*).

TELEPHONE EXCHANGE, Trinity Street. By *M. H. Bristow*, 1963–5.

POLICE, Bridge Street. 1957, nicely designed. By *L. M. Robjohn*.

GAOL, Thorpe Road. 1842 by *W. J. Donthorne*. Norman, symmetrical, with gatehouse in the middle.

(EAST STATION. Tudor style. By *Livock*, 1845.)

GOODS DEPOT. *See* p. 328.

POWER STATION. 1951 by *T. H. Eley*. Brick, in the accepted modern idiom created at the Battersea Power Station in London. The position is unfortunate. It ruins the view of the cathedral as one approaches Peterborough by train from the s.

PERAMBULATION

There is surprisingly little of interest in the town, in spite of its age. It is hard to make up a perambulation. The natural start is the Market Place, which lies just outside the w gate to the cathedral precinct. The way in which the gatehouse and the Old Guildhall face one another is telling. To the r. and l. of the gatehouse the NATIONAL PROVINCIAL BANK, 1928–9 by

F. C. R. Palmer and *W. F. C. Holden,* in the style of Kirby Hall, and LLOYDS BANK, 1913 by *Alan Ruddle,* in a more restrained neo-Tudor and apparently of Portland stone. The Market Place itself has recently been newly laid out in an attempt at easing traffic and at the same time achieving prettification. The Gothic PEARSON GATES MEMORIAL FOUNTAIN was set up in 1898.* From the Market Place to the W along CHURCH STREET, where the new NORWICH UNION BUILDING (by *Feilden & Mawson,* 1964–6) clashes most painfully with the tower of St John. Round the corner in QUEEN STREET No. 10 is Georgian, five bays, of brick, with a stumpy Venetian window in the centre. A little to the W, in CUMBERGATE, the OLD WORKHOUSE, C17, with rubble ground floor and oversailing timber-framed upper floor.

From the E end of Cumbergate N to the end of The Causeway, where at the corner of MIDGATE a new office block, HEREWARD HOUSE, 1963–6 by *Douglas Stephen & Partners.* High slab on a two-storeyed podium. A passage leads through this towards St Peter's Training College. This is now called PETERSCOURT. It was built in 1856–64 by *Sir G. G. Scott.* Red brick, Gothic. E of Peterscourt, in ST MARY'S STREET, are new council flats by *Ruddle & Wilkinson.* The W continuation of Midgate is WESTGATE. The BULL HOTEL has a low, two-storeyed front of nine bays, probably early C18. The ROYAL HOTEL is a handsome, plain Georgian house of five bays. WORTLEY'S ALMSHOUSES are of 1837. They are in the Tudor style, but the cartouche above the entrance comes from the previous building of 1744. From the W end of Westgate to the North Station and opposite it the GREAT NORTHERN HOTEL, a large, simple, Latest Georgian building with eleven bays to the garden. Only the rocky rustication of the ground floor betrays the real date: 1852 (extension 1855). To the N, in WESTWOOD STREET, a new GOODS DEPOT. This is a small part of a complete renewal of the station. Off the Lincoln Road 226 COTTAGES were erected in 1854–66 for railway workers. The plan is a primitive grid. The estate was called New England.

More in Bridge Street, which runs S from the Market Place towards and across the river Nene. Immediately after its beginning we must turn W into PRIESTGATE, where the best Georgian houses of Peterborough are, though not one of them needs singling out. Also YORKSHIRE HOUSE, L-shaped, C17,

* At the time of writing it has disappeared, but it will be re-erected.

and partly of stone, partly timber-framed. Mullioned windows; much renewed. At the corner of Priestgate and BRIDGE STREET the ANGEL HOTEL, Georgian, three-storeyed, of brick and plain. Original staircase inside. Wing in Priestgate of 1899, gabled. At the N end of the bridge the former CUSTOMS HOUSE (now Sea Cadets), rubble with quoins, three widely spaced windows, hipped roof, and cupola, probably of c.1700. At the S end of the bridge the premises of the MITCHELL ENGINEERING CO., 1955 by *Howard Lobb & Partners*. Brick and glass, L-shaped, with the N wing three-storeyed and overlooking the river, the W wing two-storeyed and containing the main entrance. The N wing has a ground floor of brick and curtain walling for the upper floors. The W wall of this block is completely flush and faced with a large relief by *A. J. Ayres*. 'Arranged round a central group depicting Administration, Design and Works, are various historical and mythical figures including Archimedes, Minerva and Isaac Newton'(*Journal R.I.B.A.*).*

See p. 414

STANDING STONE. At the W end of Longthorpe village, on the S side of the main road, is a standing stone, presumably of prehistoric date (cf. Milton, p. 294).

SETTLEMENT. Fengate, a site showing occupation from Neolithic to Roman times, lies on a gravel promontory beside the river Nene, bounded on the W side by the first section of Car Dyke. An oval ditch measuring 38 by 28 yds included both Beaker inhumations and a large number of cremations in urns of Middle Bronze Age type. Early Iron Age occupation material was also recovered from a number of pits.

BARROW. A barrow which contained a flint knife dagger and quartzite axe hammer lies ¼ m. S of Newark.

PIDLEY

307b

ALL SAINTS. 1864–5 by *William Fawcett* of Cambridge. Nave and chancel. W tower with tiled broach spire. Small lancet windows. Inside exposed brick. – PLATE. Cup of 1576–7; Cover Paten of 1758–9.

STANLEY FARMHOUSE, at the start of the road to Old Hurst. Early C18. Five bays, red brick, with segment-headed windows and a hipped roof. Doorway with hood on carved scrolly brackets.

FENTON HOUSE, I m. NNW. Early C18, H-shaped, but with the

* Compare also Woodston, p. 368.

façade along one of the arms of the H. Steep one-bay pediment. Doorway with upright scrolls as the brackets for the hood.

2090 ## PONDERSBRIDGE

ST THOMAS. 1869. Yellow brick, lancet-shaped windows, with a s transept and a polygonal NW turret to add the High Victorian touch. Polygonal apse.

2080 ## RAMSEY

RAMSEY ABBEY, like Ely on an island in the fens, was founded c.969 and dedicated in 974, i.e. four years after the older Ely was rededicated after the Danish troubles. It developed into one of the important English monastic houses and seems to have had about eighty monks in the C12 and C13 and still thirty-four at the time of the Dissolution. The premises then, together with those of Hinchingbrooke nunnery, were given to Sir Richard Williams *alias* Cromwell. In the Elizabethan decades stone from Ramsey Abbey was used for Caius, King's, and Trinity Colleges and in the C17 for the towers of Ramsey, Godmanchester, and Holywell churches. In the late C16 and early C17 the Cromwells built or decisively improved the house on the site of the former Lady Chapel. In 1737 the Fellowes family took over who became Lords De Ramsey in 1887. In 1937 the house became a grammar school, and the new occupiers are proud of it. So while the following report must be divided into the Middle Ages, the time about 1600, and the early C19, to the unwary the whole building must now appear to belong to the latter period. The architects acting for the Fellowes family were *Soane* in 1804–6 and *Blore* in 1838–9.★

The principal medieval remains are the Lady Chapel of the mid C13 and the gatehouse of c.1500. The LADY CHAPEL was not, as usual, at the E of the church, but as an independent building to the s of the chancel, just as at Ely and Peterborough. Externally what can be seen is the buttresses along the s side with chamfers and stop-chamfers. For some one must specially look. There is also part of the arch of the s doorway. The N buttresses are inside the house, but the E buttresses appear in all their monumentality, and a pinnacle marks the NW corner. Two pairs of the N buttresses are connected by Tudor arches

★ The following account is based on the RCHM volume, but Mr T. A. Edwards now queries much of this, and I have added references to what he wrote to me in February 1967.

and to the W of them is a round-arched Tudor doorway.* Inside, the chapel is surrounded by a dado of blank pointed-trefoiled arcading. The colonnettes have been robbed or broken, but stiff-leaf capitals remain. The arches are richly moulded. The S doorway has to the inside a segmental arch on short vertical pieces. The transept of the church probably lay W of the chapel, and the thick W wall of the chapel may represent the E wall of the N transept. More of the church or the monastic quarters cannot be said.

When the Cromwells came, they must have made some part of the premises habitable. It is likely that the present house was always their principal or only range. Their building activity is not documented. A date 1620 scratched in in the wine cellar must be the *terminus ante quem*. The house of *c.*1600 survives, but mixed up with many confusing additions, and it is the latter which must first be anticipated. The Cromwell house was built on the usual E-plan facing N.‡ The two wings have diagonal buttresses (as a compliment to the medieval abbey?) and are developed as towers, but the middle porch no longer appears as a porch, because *Soane* put in front of it an odd truncated circular porch or lobby. He also added a corridor with pointed windows but round rere-arches from the NE wing N of the Lady Chapel and running on to the NW wing. The round-arched doorway in the basement already referred to is the inner doorway of the Cromwell porch. The outer doorway is also there, but of course also in the basement. It corresponds to the S wall of Soane's lobby. The Cromwell porch went on to the full height of the house, as a small gable still shows. This porch led no doubt to the great hall. But on what level was the Cromwell hall? One of its N windows has recently been exposed. It is of four lights with a transom, and to its E is part of a large chimneybreast (standing on the two arches already mentioned). The arches are in the basement, the fireplace must have been one storey up,§ and so is the win-

* Mr Edwards writes that there is an E.E. doorway here in line with the S doorway, but that it has a Tudor arch.

‡ Mr Edwards now reports that in Soane's drawings there is no indication at all of the church transept and there is only the NE Tudor tower and the N porch S of Soane's porch (*see* below). So the E-plan was introduced by Soane. The thickness of the wall between Soane's work and the C13 work is due to a brick thickening by Soane. In a Soane drawing the W wall of the Lady Chapel has four tiers of windows, those of the two main stages having transoms.

§ 'It was', writes Mr Edwards. He has found it recently behind the book-cases of the library. It has stone jambs and a brick arch and is directly opposite the big S bay window.

dow. But if therefore the Cromwell hall was on that level, where was the staircase ?

The height of the tower-like NE wing is original, as is proved by the mullioned windows on four floors in the E face. The tower at the NW end of Soane's work is by him. The openwork balustrade here and otherwise is by *Blore*. Blore also remodelled the kitchen and service wing W of the main building. On the E front Blore's is the big canted bay window.

The S façade is more of a jigsaw puzzle. The final result looks prevalently *Blore*, completely asymmetrical, with the W part, i.e. the presumed former N transept, highest. Of the Cromwell era are the two-light basement windows and the big rectangular bay window. This has windows in two tiers. Was the Cromwell hall only one-storeyed then, with a chamber above ? The porch a little further W is pre-Soane, i.e. Cromwell era, though altered by Blore, but the big bay window in the former transept part is again by Blore.

There is yet another puzzle connected with the Cromwell hall. The N and S porches are in line. They no doubt corresponded to the screens passage. But there seems to have been one more bay W of the porches. And did the big bay window correspond to the dais end ? It would mean an oddly short hall or else a hall going on to the E wall of the Lady Chapel and thus resulting in a bay window in an odd place.

Blore was responsible for the whole present top storey and the main staircase.* But the apsed subsidiary staircase is most probably by *Soane*.

The GATEHOUSE is an uncommonly ornate piece. Part of it is now at Hinchingbrooke (*see* p. 264). What remains is E of the original carriageway. It has a small doorway‡ from the inner side with a two-light oriel window over, all with fleuron and quatrefoil friezes. The buttresses are panelled. In the gatehouse on the ground floor is the MONUMENT to Ailwin who founded the abbey. It is of Purbeck (Alwalton ?) marble and dates from about 1230, and resembles the abbots' monuments of Peterborough. The head is in a cinquefoiled pointed arch. The face has a short beard. Stiff-leaf crockets run up the edges. – Also a Norman(?) stone with blank arcading and some bosses found in the churchyard wall. They may be C14 work.

ST THOMAS OF CANTERBURY. This is not the original dedica-

---

* Though Soane's drawings have the staircase in this place.
‡ Originally a window.

tion; there was none, and with this is connected the sensational impact of the building. It was not built as a church at all; for at the time to which most of its details point, the laymen had parochial rights in the abbey church. It was built as a HOSPITIUM, i.e. a guesthouse or maybe a hospital. Such a hospital was founded *c.*1180 and seems to have been dissolved before 1291. A dedication date 1237 for the parish church appears in the literature but seems unconfirmed. As a guesthouse-hospital its position is not unusual (cf. Sawtry). Its size appears spectacularly large, but it is not larger than other hospitals, e.g. the former Hospital of St John at Huntingdon (*see* p. 270) of a few years earlier. The details of the building point to dates between *c.*1180 and *c.*1190. Work proceeded from E to W. The chancel is pure Norman, and it is distinguished by a heavy rib-vault with broad, unmoulded ribs. 17 The chancel arch has triple responds, the main shaft keeled, and scallop capitals. There were S and N two-bay chapels as well. That is recognizable from outside (i.e. for the N from the vestry). The supports have keeling again, and apart from scallop capitals one with some kind of waterleaf. The E wall has three lancets, still round-headed and inside with a continuous roll, but an almond-shaped window above and a small round-headed one in the gable. But the chancel arch is again pointed. The aisle walls have all Late Perp windows, but inside the Late Norman or rather Transitional story goes on. There are seven bays of large, spacious arcading, and there were formerly eight. The arches are all of one step and one slight chamfer and pointed, and the piers are a most instructive assortment of late C12 possibilities. They ought to be looked at one by one. The sections from E to W go as follows: triple respond with keeling, quatrefoil with thin shafts rather indistinctly attached to the foils, quatrefoil with subsidiary diagonal shafts, round, quatrefoil with subsidiary shafts all keeled, octagonal, eight keeled shafts. The capitals are as varied. They still comprise many scallops (E responds, but also pretty far W), waterleaf of several varieties, and crockets of several varieties but none of French purity. The W doorway ends this story. It is probably re-set. Even here there is still waterleaf, and even some more conservative Late Norman capital types. The arch here, with several rolls, is still round. There are three orders of shafts, with shaft-rings. The doorway is built into a W tower which in its present form, ashlarfaced and big, is of 1672. But the bell-openings and other places, e.g. the arch to the nave, show clearly the re-use of C13 materials. If then a W tower was built into the hospitium by then, the use must have changed and the building become a church. – FONT. Hexagonal, absolutely plain, and of some species of dark marble. Probably C13 too. The existence of a font, as Mr Dickinson remarked to me, would also point to parochial use in the C13 – i.e. if the font is in its original habitat. – LECTERN. The stem is C15, with diagonally set, openwork, traceried supports. The rotating top is mostly C19. – PAINTING. Dim remains of a man and an angel in the nave above the N arcade. – STAINED GLASS. Much of *Morris & Co.*, but all, except the S aisle Adoration of the Child, of after the deaths of Morris and Burne-Jones. The dates recorded are about 1920. – There is also completely indifferent glass in the S aisle signed by *Morris & Sons*, but there is no risk of confounding the one with the other. – PLATE. Cup and Cover Paten of 1568–9; Cup and Paten on foot of 1648–9; Britannia silver Flagon of 1712–13; Cup and Cover Paten of 1730–1; Paten on foot and Almsdish of 1838–9. – MONUMENTS. W. H. Fellowes † 1837. Large, ornate standing monument in the Gothic style with two small allegorical figures. By *Hopper*. The Fellowes family had been lords of the manor since 1737. – (Memorial to Edward Fellowes, 1843–4. Cartouche with garlands à la Gibbons. This and the leaf decoration look very improbable for 1844. GMCH)

SALEM CHAPEL, High Street. 1857. Of four bays, with arched windows and a big pediment. Two recessed entrances. Note the giant pilasters and the naughty way they are given two eaves brackets each to carry instead of capitals. A fine monkey-puzzle in front.

BAPTIST CHAPEL, Great Whyte. 1894, yet still in a mid-Victorian mixed Italianate. Two pedimented entrances. A group of narrow round-headed windows and a pedimental gable with a kind of Lombard top-frieze.

METHODIST CHAPEL, High Street. 1898–9. Only four years later, but now with the pretty free-Gothic details of the Arts and Crafts generation. Yellow brick with a square SW turret.

N of the abbey gatehouse is ABBEY GREEN, N of the church CHURCH GREEN. On the N side of the latter one five-bay Georgian house and next to it the ESTATE OFFICE, probably of after 1873, one-storeyed, of nine very closely set bays. Abbey Green has on its W side a symmetrical group of gabled yellow-brick estate housing dated 1863, and on its N side two

similar symmetrical groups, r. the former Elementary School
of 1848, also yellow brick, also gabled, l. the Almshouses of
1839, stone, but again gabled.

The HIGH STREET has nothing of note. The ABBEY ROOMS
look like a chapel, i.e. yellow brick with red dressings, and
arched windows. (In the GEORGE HOTEL a nice staircase of
c.1630 with heavy balusters.) The wide, market-like GREAT
WHYTE meets the High Street at a T. It has no greater
interest than the High Street. In the middle is a CLOCK on a
cast-iron column with typical leaf decoration – typical of its
date: 1888. It is signed by its makers, *McFarlane* of Glasgow.
Of houses there is Nos 1–5, early C19, yellow brick, with
giant pilasters, and there is Nos 66–8, one of the only two at
Ramsey given grade II by the MHLG and hence (at the time of
writing) derelict. That is all.

BOOTH HILL. Overgrown small C12 motte-and-bailey castle.

RAMSEY MERE   3080

One mile N of Forty Foot Bridge on the Old Nene is the tower
of a former DRAINAGE MILL.

RAMSEY ST MARY'S   2080

ST MARY. Built in 1858 at the expense of Miss Emma Fellowes
(cf. Ramsey). It is a strikingly large church for its situation in
the sparsely populated fenland. But churches in such neglected
parts were specially urgently needed (cf. e.g. the Parts of
Lindsey in Lincs.). Yellow brick with a NW tower, nave, aisles,
and chancel. Tracery of before and after 1300. The
chancel arch rests on demi-figures of angels with a positive-
organ and a lute. The STAINED GLASS is original.

ROUND HILL see CONINGTON

ST IVES   3070

St Ives was a cell of the Benedictine Priory of Ramsey. The
buildings lay at the E end of the market space (*see* p. 338). The
prosperity of the town in the Middle Ages was founded on
the Easter Fair, granted in 1110. It was one of the four busiest
fairs of England (with Winchester, Northampton, and Boston).

CHURCHES

ALL SAINTS. In an enviable position by the Ouse and normally ¹
reached by a footpath from The Waits. It is a large church

built mostly between c.1450 and c.1470, and its steeple is
exceptionally fine in its proportions. The bell-openings are
pairs of slender two-light openings, Perp, and the spire is recessed but has low broaches behind the battlements and
pinnacles. Two bands run across it and contain the lucarnes,
the upper ones being just quatrefoils. The w door is very elaborate, with two niches l. and r. The aisles and the chancel are
also all Perp, except for the C13 N doorway with a hood-mould
on head stops and the latest C13 S aisle E window of five lights
with intersecting tracery broken at the top to allow for an encircled quatrefoil. Inside the S aisle is a splendid DOUBLE
PISCINA with a surround of big dog-tooth. Each half has a
pointed arch, but they are taken together by a round arch.*
The date could be as late as that of the E window, but is more
likely to be earlier in the C13. The interior is as obviously Perp
as the exterior. Arcades of high thin piers and thin arches;
four bays. Against the piers a whole series of brackets for
images, all decorated, some with foliage, one with a dog,
another with a bull baited by a dog. High tower arch and
tierceron-star vault in the tower. Embracing aisles. Two
niches in the S aisle E wall. – FONT. Octagonal, Norman, with
blank intersecting arches. – PULPIT. Elizabethan, with very
elongated blank arches and panels with elementary geometrical
motifs. – The vast ORGAN, in the Bodley tradition, is by
Comper, 1893. – He also did the imitation-German STATUES
on the brackets. – STAINED GLASS. Much by *Wailes*, also one
window by *Kempe*, 1903 (chancel S) and one by *Comper*, 1896
(S aisle). – PLATE. Two large engraved Flagons of 1779–80;
Processional Cross, Italian, C15 or early C16; bronze and
brass Altar Cross, Venetian, c.1540. – MONUMENTS. Many
tablets, e.g. a bulgy cartouche † 1728 (a late date for the type).
A tablet † 1857 has a kneeling Hope by a Bible and an urn
(also late for its type).

ST LAWRENCE (Bridge Chapel). *See* p. 338.

SACRED HEART (R.C.), Needingworth Road. By *Pugin*, 1843
and transferred here from Union Street Cambridge in 1908.
Brick with stone dressings and not large. Nave and aisles and
flat E end; bellcote. The windows are small lancets or have low-
pitched triangular heads and often appear in pairs. Three E
lancets, stepped. Mid-buttress with a lancet W. Inside round
and octagonal piers, i.e. an endeavour towards a correct C13
vocabulary. Vestry annex.

* For other examples, *see* Introduction, p. 184.

FREE CHURCH, Market Hill. By *John Tarring*, 1862–3. A fussy façade with not enough space l. and r. It is simply one of a terrace of buildings. Dec detail, embracing aisles, steeple of 156 ft. The interior with thin iron columns and no galleries. Just one unified room, but with an apse. Windows of three lights with geometrical tracery.

METHODIST CHURCH, The Waits. 1905 by *Trower*. In a heavy-handed fancy Gothic.

PUBLIC BUILDINGS

Neither the TOWN HALL (built as Stanley House) nor the CORN EXCHANGE (1864 by *R. Hutchinson*; GS) nor the POST OFFICE (1887) nor really the NORRIS MUSEUM (one-storeyed Tudor, by *S. Inskip Ladds*, 1932) needs comment.

LIBRARY, North Road. By *K. G. Sparrow*, County Architect, 1964.

COUNTY JUNIOR SCHOOL, Ramsey Road. By *K. G. Sparrow*, County Architect, 1964.

PERAMBULATION

St Ives has put its river, the Ouse, to good use visually. The river is indeed good enough to be made a feature of. It is in view along The Waits and again along The Quay.

Starting the walk from the church BARNES HOUSE is to the NW; late C18, with two canted bay windows and a very pretty doorway with Gothick quatrefoils in the spandrels, but Doric pilasters and a pediment. Then the main walk, all straight, through the town from W to E. A little to the N the pleasant new CLARE COURT, housing by *E. Fawcett*, 1965, in the Span style. THE WAITS is an agreeable street. The only notable house is BURLEIGH HOUSE, five bays, white, with a Tuscan porch and a Venetian window above it. The continuation is BROADWAY, a market-like widening. No special houses, but two ambitious doorways with columns (Nos 11 and 18). In the middle MONUMENT to Queen Victoria's Jubilee, 1897, but looks like Sir G. G. Scott about 1860. Then the walk splits, Merryland on the r., CROWN STREET on the l. In Crown Street No. 5 is Early Georgian, of three storeys, red brick and rubbed brick trim, segment-headed windows, and a door-hood on carved brackets. Off to the N in CROWN YARD the former PUBLIC INSTITUTION, 1848, one-storeyed, stuccoed, with giant pilasters.

Then turn s along BRIDGE STREET. Two more Early Georgian

houses, both of only three bays but three storeys, both with segment-headed windows and panelled parapets. The first has a doorway with pilasters in front of rustication, the second has giant pilasters. The MANOR HOUSE by the river with three gables that side and four to the street is too much restored to be enjoyable. It dates from *c.*1600 and has ornamental barge-boards and moulded bressumers.

2 The BRIDGE is the most memorable monument of St Ives. May the temptation be resisted to sacrifice it to a through-traffic which should not at all rush along here. The bridge is still narrow and has preserved its cutwaters on both sides. It dates from about 1415. Midway along it is still a bridge chapel, one of only three in England, the others being Wakefield and Rotherham. The chapel is dedicated to ST LAWRENCE, and its altar was consecrated in 1426. It has an E apse and below the main room a lower one. No features or furnishings to report.

The other side of the bridge is BRIDGE HOUSE, early C18, of five by five bays, with to the street a doorway with a big seg-mental pediment, to the river a round-arched middle window. All other windows are segment-headed.

Back to CROWN STREET. There follows now a nice Victorian shop front (the MHLG says *c.*1885) and then the Market Place, called MARKET HILL, but the houses along the N side THE PAVEMENT. In the middle bronze STATUE of Cromwell by *F. W. Pomeroy*, 1901. No houses of great interest. (In the pas-sage by No. 7 Pavement a re-set early C16 beam with the arms of Ramsey Abbey flanked by an ox and sheep and a crown, a rose, and the name W. Wesbyche. RCHM) Opposite a five-bay Later Georgian house of three storeys. Doorway with Tuscan pilasters.

From the end of the Market Place S into PRIORY ROAD. St Ives Priory was founded as a cell of Ramsey in the C11. All that is left is two lengths of wall of a BARN. The house called THE PRIORY is of 1870, by *Robert Hutchinson* (GS). It is intensely Gothic and rather grim. Yellow brick and stone dressings. From the Market Place N in the NEEDINGWORTH ROAD is CROMWELL TERRACE, yellow brick, Early Victorian, a long terrace with a broken pediment in the middle.

ST NEOTS

1060

St Neots was the place of a Benedictine PRIORY, founded according to tradition *c.*972–5 and re-founded as a dependency

of Bec in Normandy *c*.1081. It lay along the river, N of the
bridge, and the town developed *ante portas*. Recent excavations
have shown that the church lay s of Priory Lane, partly where
the back premises of the Cross Keys hotel are, that the
cloister was N of the church and of Priory Lane, and was of
C15 timber-work, that the dormitory undercroft was two-
naved and dated from *c*.1250, that the refectory was in the
N range and had a two-naved undercroft and a pulpitum,
as usual (the substructure was found), and that the kitchen
stood w of the refectory and was 68 by 22 ft in size with three
massive piers along its middle axis. They dated from the C12.
N of the claustral parts was apparently the infirmary (not in
axis). Nothing of all this is visible. The gate-house stood complete until 1814.

ST MARY. One of the largest, most uniform late medieval 48
churches in the county. Apart from one early C13 lancet window in the N wall of the chancel, better visible from the vestry,
all is Perp. The body of the church was apparently complete
by 1486, the porches were added in 1489, and the w tower begun at about the same time. Wills refer to work on the top
pinnacles in 1526–35. The tower is the most impressive element of the church, 130 ft high and broad, with uncommonly
high and substantial pinnacles. There are intermediate pinnacles on merlons as well, decorated with the signs of the
Evangelists. The parapet has faces and paterae. The buttresses
are of the set-back type and have gablets applied to them. They
end in their own pinnacles, detached from the body of the
tower – a Somerset trait. Doorway with tracery spandrels and
little double-X motifs in one moulding. They repeat in the
moulding of the broad middle mullion of the large four-light
w window which has a castellated transom. Large blank three-
light N and s windows. The bell-stage has pairs of two-light
openings, again with a castellated transom. There are decorative friezes as well at base, top, and in between. It is all entirely of a piece and done without faltering. The rest of the
church is embattled. All the windows are large, the buttresses
have gablets, the s porch is two-storeyed with pairs of windows
to the E and w, and the s doorway has traceried spandrels. The
N porch is similar but a C19 rebuilding, with much original
material re-used. Both it and the N doorway have traceried
spandrels. Three-light clerestory windows. Short chancel.
The arch from the tower to the nave is extremely high. The
nave is separated from the aisles by high five-bay arches with

piers of the standard moulded section. The arches still have
the two sunk quadrants of the Dec style. At the E end of the S
arcade an arch starts into the chancel arch. How did that come
about? It is probably the one-bay S chapel which interferes.
To the N its W arch dies into the impost, to the S there is a
respond, so it may be that the chapel was there earlier and a
plan existed to do away with it. However, if so, it was given up;
for the arch to the chancel is Perp like the arcades, and also
like the corresponding and the W arch of the N chapel. Original,
exceptionally ornately decorated roofs in the nave, the N and
S aisles, and both chapels. They have crested cornices and
ornaments, plenty of angels with shields, and in addition in all
sorts of places angels, monsters, a mermaid, camels, dogs,
lions, fishes, an eagle, an elephant, fox and goose, hare and
hound, and so on. Pretty niche with a nodding ogee arch in
the N wall. – PULPIT of 1846–8. – STALLS of 1860, but a few
of the C15 or early C16 from Milton Ernest. Carved arms,
misericords with shields and inscriptions. – COMMUNION
RAIL. C18, of wrought iron. – SCREENS. Several Perp screens,
the most attractive the W screen of the N chapel, with lovely
transparent vine scrolls over the entrance. – The others have
broad ogee-arched one-light divisions. – In the N aisle moreover a few fragments from painted panels of a screen dado. –
STAINED GLASS. Much by *Clayton & Bell* (e.g. tower W
c.1868–70) and by *Hardman* (e.g. Woman of Samaria, S aisle,
exhibited at the Paris Exhibition in 1878). Also by Clayton &
Bell the Transfiguration, also by Hardman the Widow of Nain.
– PLATE. Set of 1754–5. – MONUMENT. The monument to
G.W. Rowley and his wife is a fabulous piece of display. The
recumbent effigy of Mrs Rowley † 1886 by *Thomas Earp* is
hardly visible behind a grille of the closest, most ornate decoration, and the canopy rises, with statuary and canopies and
pinnacles, to the roof. It was designed by *Frederick A.
Walters* and put up in 1893. – (In the N chapel on the floor a
defaced C13 slab with a foliated cross supported by a dog; cf.
e.g. Pavenham, Beds.)

CONGREGATIONAL CHURCH, High Street. 1887–8 by *Edward
J. Paine* (GS). Red brick with a W steeple. Perp. (Original
fittings.)

PERAMBULATION. The centre is the MARKET PLACE, long,
spacious, and not too rigid in its alignments. Along its N side
runs the main traffic to the BRIDGE and into Bedfordshire.
The bridge was replaced in 1963–5 by a long concrete

structure, part bridge, part causeway. It is of no special
interest (architectural consultant *F. Gibberd*). At the corner
of the bridge and market place is the BRIDGE HOTEL.
(Inside this some panels of wall-panelling of *c.*1600, with
strapwork and roses. RCHM)

In the centre of the market place is a tapering Doric PILLAR of
1822, with four thick scrolly arms in the main directions.
There are no houses of great merit around, but nothing has
gone wrong either. On the N side off in Priory Lane THE
PRIORY, three bays with a pedimented doorway and across the
end a four-bay house. Then in the market place the CROSS
KEYS, low, with two canted bay windows. Opposite a row of
uniformly acceptable frontages. The centre is the former Bull
Inn, late C18, yellow brick, of seven bays and three storeys
with a broad archway – several more houses here have these
archways, most of them also of yellow brick – a Venetian window over and a pediment with an arch rising into its base. To
its r. a five-bay red-brick house with a panelled parapet,
Early Georgian probably, to its l. a mid C18 red-brick house
with raised stone window surrounds and a stone cornice and
to the l. of that a timber-framed later C17 house with four
gables.* On the E side of the market place an early C19 house
with paired pilasters on the first floor.

Turn into SOUTH STREET for the KING'S HEAD, with the
curious brackets for the door-hood growing straight out of
demi-columns, the type occurring here and there at Ampthill,
Bedford, and around there. Then round the corner BROOK
HOUSE, W of the church, seven bays, three storeys, with a
hipped roof: *c.*1700. (Staircase with slim twisted balusters
and carved tread-ends. NMR) Again round the corner and up
CHURCH STREET for the VICARAGE of 1849, but with
gabled Tudor enlargements of *c.*1855–60. To its l. C18 walls
and GATEPIERS with a very fine set of wrought-iron GATES.
Opposite more C18 gatepiers. This takes us to the High Street.

In the HIGH STREET, starting from the market place first, at
the corner of SOUTH STREET the PAVILION, the former
CORN EXCHANGE, yellow brick with a rounded corner and
close and jolly cast-iron work. 1863 by *Bellamy & Hardy* of
Lincoln.‡ Then in the High Street a red-brick building of two

* In No. 20 handsome plaster in the staircase hall: roses, cherubs and
musical instruments.
‡ Originally the building had a tower (*Illustrated London News*, October
1863).

bays, free Jacobean with a big gable. After that a low C16 half-timbered house with closely spaced studs and opposite, at the end, an early C19 seven-bay house of yellow brick. A Venetian window cuts into the pediment.

(CROMWELL GARDENS. Council housing by *Barry Parker*, c.1920–1.)

SAPLEY see HARTFORD

1080

SAWTRY

SAWTRY ABBEY, 2½ m. SSE of the village, was founded in 1147 for Cistercians. It was colonized from Warden in Bedfordshire. Nothing remains above ground, but the site has been excavated. The church was of the standard Cistercian type with a square-ended chancel and two square-ended chapels E of either transept. The nave had aisles. The refectory was placed in the S range, running N–S, as was also Cistercian standard. An aisled guesthouse stood SSW of the claustral precinct, not in axis with it.

ALL SAINTS. 1880 by *Sir A. Blomfield*. With a very steep bellcote of tricky details. Old materials were much used, e.g. the two-bay arcade of the N chapel, the late C13 N aisle W window with bar tracery, and one straight-headed N window. – Inside, from Sawtry Abbey, a number of C13 ARCHITECTURAL FRAGMENTS, and also some TILES, C13 and C14. – STAINED GLASS. In two chancel windows, fragments from Sawtry Manor House, C15 and C16, including ten heads. – MONUMENTS. Four coffin lids with foliated crosses are displayed. – Brasses to Sir William le Moyne † 1404 and wife. Outstandingly good, in line-work as well as interpretation. The figures are 4 ft 6 in long.

SAWTRY VILLAGE COLLEGE. 1961–3 by *S. M. Holloway*, then county architect. The conception of the village college was taken over from Henry Morris's Cambridgeshire village colleges.

MANOR FARM, Judith Lane, ¾ m. s. Brick. The house has a date 1672 inside. To that date belongs the curious flat framework of pilaster strips and horizontal bands. Big shaped end-gables.

SIBSON MANOR HOUSE see STIBBINGTON

3070

SOMERSHAM

ST JOHN. An almost completely E.E. church, perhaps so sweepingly done because at Somersham was a palace of the

Sawtry church, brass to Sir William le Moyne †1404 and wife.

Bishops of Ely. Externally the chancel has single widely spaced lancets along its sides and a group of over-restored lancets in the E wall. The S and the N aisle doorways have mature stiff-leaf (N badly preserved) and arches of many mouldings. The windows of the aisles are Perp, as is the clerestory. Only the W tower with its spike is later. One W window looks *c.*1300, and the bell-openings are Dec. Internally the four-bay arcades have piers of four shafts and four thin polygonal shafts in the diagonals and typically E.E. moulded capitals. The crenellation is of course a Perp re-cutting. The bases, except those of the responds, are also re-cut. Double-hollow-chamfered arches with a step between the chamfers. Moreover E.E. tower arch with keeling, chancel arch with keeling, and PISCINAS in the chancel, S aisle, and N aisle. In the chancel the SEDILIA have responds in the form of stiff-leaf corbels. The chancel side lancets are surrounded by a continuous thin roll, but the E lancets are fully shafted. The nave roof is Perp and has a large number of carved bosses. The structure consists of tiebeams on arched braces, the braces sweeping up in the same curvature to the ridge-piece, a very fine effect. – CHANDELIER. Of brass. 1787. Two tiers of arms. The centre is of a very Baroque, baluster-like shape. – PLATE. Cup 1569–70; Flagon 1638–9; Paten 1812–13; Plate undated. – BRASS. Priest, early C16, 2 ft long (chancel floor).

SOUTHOE

ST LEONARD. A Norman S doorway with about as many motifs as could be accommodated. One order of shafts with trellis decoration. In the l. lozenges one pellet each, in the r. a cross of pellets. One capital with a kind of stylized upright shrubs, the other with the same trellis with pellets. Abacus with a lozenge-chain, roll moulding covered with saltire crosses or lozenges, extrados with saltire crosses, hood-mould with billet, tympanum with chequer and inside with zigzag for good measure. The chancel arch is Norman too. Responds with angle-shafts, small, coarse scroll capitals. Pointed arch with a step and two slight chamfers, perhaps a little later. Of the late C13 the chancel, which has not only lancets but also Y-tracery. Of the same time the S arcade: three bays, round piers, double-chamfered arches. The N arcade is Perp, of standard elements – the E side externally is a little more ornate than the rest. Late Perp the brick clerestory and the brick NW tower. The church otherwise is of cobbles. – MONUMENT. (Coffin lid with a foliated cross, but the cross-head replaced by the bust of a man. GMCH)

SPALDWICK

1070

ST JAMES. A fascinating w tower of the mid C14, 152 ft high. The doorway has continuous mouldings, and on the stage above are lozenge-shaped windows to N, S, and W with flowing tracery, a typically Dec conceit. Above, two-light transomed bell-openings and a broach spire with three tiers of lucarnes. (The stair-turret has a stone vault with chamfered ribs and a boss. RCHM) The oldest part of the church is the Norman N doorway with continuous mouldings, including one of stylized beakhead. Hood-mould with billets. The masonry on this side (brown cobbles) is Norman too. The chancel is latest C13 – or is the chancel arch a little earlier ? The windows have excellent tracery, of the stage just before ogees appeared, i.e. 40 pointed-trefoiled lights, pointed trefoils but also a large circle and rounded trefoils. The S arcade is of *c.*1300. Four bays, round piers with round or octagonal abaci, bits of nailhead, double-chamfered arches, and coarse nailhead in the hood-moulds. Wide Late Perp s aisle and s chapel. One-bay arch to the chancel. – SCREEN. To the s aisle, Perp, only bits original. – STAINED GLASS. Fragments in the s aisle E window. – PLATE. Silver-gilt Cup and Cover Paten, 1628–9. – Also the Chalice and Paten of 1570 from Woolley.

FREE CHURCH. 1844. Quite big, with a pediment across the front and beneath it a group of three arched windows.

At the w end of the village is a small C15 BRIDGE of three arches, the middle one with chamfered ribs.

Along the main street, E of the church, first the GEORGE INN with, on the upper floor, paintings of single figures about 31 in. high. The best-preserved figure carries a long bow and a long arrow. The date must be *temp.* Henry VIII. Then THE LIMES, late C17, red brick, with a square porch. This and the angles of the house have brick pilasters in two tiers. IVY HOUSE, a little further on, is more advanced, i.e. has a flat five-bay front and giant angle pilasters. Also its doorway carries a pediment. But the middle bay is still flanked by two tiers of pilasters, and the windows have broad raised brick surrounds. The house is dated 1688; so The Limes may be of 1675 or 1680.

STAMFORD ST MARTIN

Stamford St Martin is in the Soke of Peterborough, but in *The Buildings of England* it is treated as part of Stamford, i.e. in the Lincolnshire volume.

STANGROUND

2090

ST JOHN BAPTIST. A church almost entirely of the latest C13 to early C14. The W tower starts with such a motif as circular trefoiled windows and ends with a ballflower frieze. Broach spire with high broaches and two tiers of lucarnes. The chancel has high windows with Y-tracery. The five-light E window with intersecting tracery is over-restored. Below the SW window is a curious low-side window of three uncusped lights. Very pretty DOUBLE PISCINA. SEDILIA under one long segmental arch. The arch is hollow-chamfered. The chancel arch has two hollow chamfers, the tower arch even three. The aisle windows are characteristic of *c.*1300 too, i.e. they have intersecting tracery and three lancet lights under one arch. In the N vestry is even a slightly earlier-looking window, i.e. bar tracery with a foiled circle. Only the arcades of four bays are later. The thin octagonal piers with the curious capitals with polygonal projections carrying the outer chamfer will be early C14 (cf. Fletton and Orton Longueville). The three leaf capitals on the N side with their nobbly leaves are typical of such a date.* But the recess in the S aisle is once again late C13. – – SEAT. In the chancel on the N side a stone seat with low arms (cf. Houghton). – BENCHES. The ends with poppyheads, including human heads. – CROSS. In the churchyard an Anglo-Saxon cross, much defaced. The wheel-head is incomplete. But the two 'handles' (cf. Fletton) are preserved. Of carving one can recognize small round arcading and a simple geometrical pattern: a circle and a larger saltire cross across it. – PLATE. Fragment of a C13 Coffin Chalice; Cup of 1703–4. – MONUMENT. John Forster † 1752. Tablet with a lively bust on top.

STAUGHTON HIGHWAY *see* GREAT STAUGHTON

STEEPLE GIDDING

1080

ST ANDREW. The steeple is rather underfed. The narrow arch towards the nave is of three chamfers and dies against the im-

* The RCHM reports that the base of the NW respond is a re-used Norman capital from Fletton. The E bays of the S arcade have re-used C13 bases.

posts. This, and the whole tower, is Dec. Recessed Perp spire;
shortish and with two tiers of lucarnes. Dec also the s arcade
of four bays (standard elements), and the chancel, the s aisle,
the clerestory, and the straight-headed N nave windows. The s
aisle E window still has intersecting tracery. Only the s doorway is much earlier. It is partly late C12 and partly early C14.
Outer arch with zigzag at r. angles to the wall. Inner arch
pointed. The capitals of the colonnettes have one normal stiff-
leaf, the other oddly stylized and interlocked stiff-leaf. –
BELLS. Three by *Henry Jordan*, i.e. *c.*1450–60. – ALTAR
CLOTHS. One large mid C16 piece, Flemish, with the Virgin
and angels, and one small, early C17 one, also Flemish, with
a hunting scene. – PLATE. Cup of 1569–70; Paten on foot of
Britannia silver 1697–8. – MONUMENTS. Mrs Mary Kinyon
† 1714, wrongly assembled, with a bust on top. – Sir John
Cotton † 1752. Large, but mostly an inscription plate.

STIBBINGTON

St JOHN BAPTIST. The church as a whole represents 1848–9.
To this date belong the idea of the broad three-gabled front
and the lancet fenestration of the sides and also the N transept.* Medieval are the chancel and a very little of the Norman
W doorway with two orders of columns, rolls, and billet. But
the chancel arch is a real, serious early C12 piece. The responds have big, heavy two-scallop capitals and the arch one
step and one big half-roll. As for the chancel, the E wall has
two long lancets and a large quatrefoil over. Rere-arches inside.
But inside more is medieval, namely the later C12 N arcade and
the late C13 s arcade. The former has two, the latter three bays,
but the Norman arches cannot originally have been as wide as
they are now. The piers are round, the abaci square with
nicked corners, the arches single-stepped. The s arcade has
standard elements. – FONT. Octagonal, with arched panels,
the arches standing on thin colonnettes sunk into the angles.
The date may be the late C12. – PLATE. Late C16 Cup, partly
gilt; Flagon 1659–60; Salver and Paten on foot 1667–8. –
MONUMENT. In the chancel the defaced effigy of a priest,
probably C14. – (Captain John Wright † 1785. Tablet with
Adamesque and Gothick elements. GMCH)
STIBBINGTON HALL. The house has the finest Jacobean

---

* The work, the Rev. C. Witts tells me, was done by the Duke of Bedford's
architect for this area. His name was given as *Protheroe*.

69 façade in the county. It is dated 1625 on the porch, and the inscription 'Deo trin-uni sit Gloria' is added. The façade is on the E-plan with gables, canted bay windows in the wings, dormers in the recessed parts, and a shaped gable on the square porch. All windows are mullioned and transomed. The house is altered and enlarged on all other sides and has inside just some panelling and some fireplaces. In the hall some domestic panels of c.1535 with heads in medallions and a Jacobean overmantel with caryatids and some inlay. A very handsome gateway led into the front garden. It has strapwork bordered by ogee curves on the top.

The RECTORY, S of the church, and STIBBINGTON LODGE FARM HOUSE, W of the church, have flat fronts with mullioned and mullioned-and-transomed windows.

The same is true of SIBSON MANOR HOUSE, ¾ m. SSE, on the A1. The fenestration here is perfectly even, but the doorway is not yet placed centrally. The house must be of the mid C17.

ROMAN POTTERIES. See Water Newton.

1080 STILTON

ST MARY. Tall Perp W tower. The arch to the nave is nicely interpreted as a short tunnel-vault between two pairs of responds whose capitals are castellated. The chancel is of 1808, but in all its details of 1857. It was then also that most of the other external features received their present appearance. Inside it is different. Both the three-bay arcades are of the early C13, N a little before S; for N has single-step arches, S double-chamfered ones. But both are still round. The piers are round on the S, octagonal on the N side. The W arches however are later, in order to connect with the tower, but it should be noted that the SW respond has nailhead, i.e. cannot be later than c.1300. – PLATE. Cup 1626–7; Paten on foot 1630–1; Cup 1810–11; Paten on foot 1822–3.

Stilton is now by-passed by the A1. By-passing has done a lot of good to places like Stamford, Grantham, and Newark. But it seems to have left Stilton in a sad state of dereliction and dispiritedness. The two finest buildings are given up at the time of writing, the stone-built former BELL INN with its canted bay windows, one rising into a dormer – all C17 work, and the former ROYAL HOTEL opposite, of brick, three-storeyed with a Venetian and a lunette window, once no doubt in the middle of the façade. The lovely wrought-iron sign of the Bell Inn now graces the STILTON CHEESE hotel a little further N, in NORTH STREET. At the start of that street, next to the Bell, is a well-kept Georgian stone house of five bays.

STIRTLOE see BUCKDEN

STONELY
1 m. SE of Kimbolton

1050

Opposite the Bell Inn is the COTTAGE ORNÉ which Captain Welstead, one of Nelson's captains, built for himself. The best view is from Hatchet Lane. It is thatched, with a bargeboarded gable and a tree-trunk veranda.

½ m. N of the main road is the site of the small Augustinian PRIORY of Stonely. All that is visible of it now is a stone-built cottage of *c.*1500 with a single-chamfered doorway. The arch is four-centred. The masonry is all original, but no-one can say what the function of the building was.

(WARREN HOUSE. A late C17 'standing' built with C16 and early C17 materials. Brick and stone. Small and square. The doorway and the main window are round-arched. MHLG)

STOW LONGA

1070

ST BOTOLPH. The church is outside the village. It is quite large. The Norman tympanum of the priest's doorway is more barbaric than almost any other. The centre is a mermaid, and l. and r. are quadrupeds. Coarse zigzag surround, wildly detailed capitals of the colonnettes below. W tower with pairs of transomed two-light bell-openings. No spire. The tower can be dated *c.*1500 from an inscription to Robert Becke (S wall) and the arms of Bishop Smith of Lincoln (1496–1514; W wall). E.E. S doorway with three orders of colonnettes with very damaged stiff-leaf capitals. Arch with hollow chamfers. The arcades are E.E. too, N being a little earlier than S. Four bays, round piers, double-chamfered arches, those of the S arcade with broaches. The N aisle was never widened. The aisle windows partly straight-headed Dec, partly Perp. E.E. again the chancel arch. The respond shafts start high up; there was probably a stone screen here. – FONT. Octagonal, but the round support made up of two E.E. capitals. – SCREEN. Perp, with wide one-light divisions. – REREDOS. This incorporates one panel with reticulated tracery brought in from an Oxfordshire church. – (STALL END. One, with a poppyhead. GMCH) – SOUTH DOOR. With a little tracery. – SCULPTURE. One stone with interlace, rather from a coffin lid than a cross;

CII or CI2. – STAINED GLASS. Small bits in two N aisle windows. – BELL. One bell by *Henry Jordan,* i.e. *c.*1450–60. – PLATE. Paten with head of Christ engraved; hallmarked 1491–2. This is the oldest known London hallmark. – Cup of 1577–8. – MONUMENT. Tablet to Sir Thomas Maples † 1634. Stone surround and brass indent.

VILLAGE CROSS. Moulded base and part of the shaft.

⁰⁰⁹⁰
SUTTON
Soke of Peterborough

ST MICHAEL. Little of interest externally, except for the bell-cote, which, with the tall lancet window below, is, it seems, of the CI3. Inside fine Norman chancel arch with strong shafts, capitals with beaded interlace, arches with fat rolls. The date probably *c.*1130. S arcade of *c.*1200. Two bays, circular pier, simple moulded capital, square abacus, double-chamfered round arches. A little later the S chapel. One bay, semi-octagonal responds, pointed double-chamfered arch. – SCULPTURE. Recumbent Lion, Norman. The back shows that this carried a shaft originally. It was thus probably connected with a portal of the type of the Prior's Door at Ely. Columns on recumbent lions are a North Italian Romanesque motif. – PLATE. Beaker, *c.*1650 (imitation of the foreign beaker at Upton).

(VICARAGE. The vicarage is of the CI9, but re-set in its walls is a two-light CI3 window. VCH)

ROMAN POTTERY. *See* Water Newton.

²⁰⁵⁰
TETWORTH

ST SYLVESTER. By *St Aubyn;* consecrated in 1886. Red brick. Nave and chancel in one, bell-turret a little E of the W gable. S transept, polygonal apse, small lancets.

TETWORTH HALL. A fine early CI8 house of red brick. Five bays, two storeys, hipped roof, giant stone angle pilasters, parapet. Big doorway with pilasters and a segmental pediment. To the l. of the entrance hall behind a screen of two fluted columns the staircase with twisted balusters.

WOODBURY HALL. The appearance of the house is Late Georgian. In fact* it is CI8, but received divers Victorian additions which *Philip Tilden* removed in 1931, and then suffered from a fire in the Second World War. After that, in 1954, it was given its present form by *Sir Basil Spence.*

* So Mr R. J. V. Astell kindly tells me.

THORNEY

ST MARY AND ST BOTOLPH. A monastery was founded here
c.670. It was destroyed in the Danish raid of 870 and re-
founded in 972 for Benedictine monks. After the Conquest
Abbot Guenther rebuilt the church. He must have begun
immediately after he had been elected in 1085; for in 1089 the
monks could move in. By 1098 the chancel and crossing tower
were ready. The church was completed in 1108, though consecrated only in 1128. All that remains of it is part of the nave,
shorn of its aisles and of its E end. The total original length was
nearly 300 ft. However, the crossing, with crossing tower, the
transepts and chancel, and practically all the monastic buildings have disappeared. The present E end is by *Blore*, in the
Norman style, 1840-1. The original fragment, inadequate as it
may be, is yet very impressive, owing chiefly to its tall W front.
This is a composite structure to which the C12, the C15, and
the C17 have contributed. Norman are the angle turrets,
starting as broad buttresses and continued octagonal. They
end in Perp battlements. These buttresses originally separated
the W end of the nave from that of the aisles. Their stepped
plan makes it probable that the Norman W front of Thorney
had three giant niches on the pattern of C11 Lincoln. Perp W
window partly blocked; probably Perp the doorway. In 1638
the ruined church was restored as the parish church of Thorney.
It was then that, to the l. and r. of the doorway, blank arcades
were carved with ogee heads and a frieze above decorated with
heads like fleurons. All this is in a typical imitation-Perp of
which a contemporary example is e.g. Peterhouse Chapel at
Cambridge. The Perp W window may belong to the same date.
Along the N and S sides the design of the Norman arcades can
be studied, as the arcade openings were blocked in 1638, when
the aisles were pulled down. One bay of the Norman clerestory
also survives, a plain arched window (blocked) on the S side,
but decorated by billet friezes on the N. The interior elevation
is quite evident when one enters the church. The arcades are
designed with alternating supports, but the principal motif,
the shaft rising without interruption from floor to ceiling, is
the same everywhere. The design towards the arch openings,
however, differs between segments of fat circular projection
and three stepped shafts – just as at Ely. The arches are single-
stepped, but the capitals are scalloped. The gallery openings
are not subdivided (cf. e.g. Colchester St Botolph). They are

now filled with C15 tracery, perhaps from the former clerestory. The piers have two shafts towards the openings, and the
arches two roll mouldings. The capitals are mostly of the
primitive volute type, but others are also scalloped. – STAINED
GLASS. German or Swiss panels in the nave E windows. –
The E window is a copy from Canterbury. – PLATE. Cup and
Paten of 1709; Almsdish of 1750.

The cloister of the abbey was where now lies the pretty turfed
square to the S of the church. On the E side of the square two
stately houses, the VICARAGE, stone, late C17, probably with
older remains, possibly of the abbey, and the house S of it,
also C18, also stone, with two projecting wings. On the W side
of the Green a five-bay house also called Thorney Abbey which
is the most important house in the village.

THORNEY ABBEY. The house consists of two parts, one later
C16, with gables and mullioned windows and a shallow canted
bay window, the other of 1660, connected with the older by a
short range inside which some short round piers are said to
be a memory of the monastery. If that is true they must have
been much altered. For the house of 1660 the contract exists
between the Duke of Bedford, who owned the abbey lands and
the village, and one *John Lovin* of Peterborough. The house is
square, stone-built, with two storeys, a hipped roof, dormer
windows, and one central chimney. The quoins are hewn
stone, and so are the windows, with mullion-and-transom
crosses and broad frames. The doorways have odd broad
corbels carrying flat pediments. The eaves cornice is of a
characteristic shape, deep and coved. Inside, the dining room
has its original panelling incorporating a big fireplace surround
with odd and wilful volutes and eared panels. Similar fireplaces in other rooms. The staircase has sturdy balusters with
leaves growing up their lower moulding, and heavy square
newel-posts decorated by hanging-down garlands. The doorcases are again in the style of the fireplaces, a style characteristic of East Anglia at that particular moment and matched at
Wisbech Castle in Cambridgeshire and at Tyttenhanger and
Balls Park in Hertfordshire. It is a style recently identified
with that of *Peter Mills* of London, the architect who designed
Thorpe Hall, and Thorney Abbey may be his design too, in
which *Lovin* would be only the executing builder. On the
other hand the style may just as well be rather regional than
wholly personal. Sturdy square rusticated GATEPOSTS (cf.
Wisbech Castle) towards the village.

In the village some small but ornate buildings of the mid C19 erected by the Duke of Bedford (e.g. the store N of the church, formerly post office) and much plain white brick Bedford housing in terraces. A little to the N, the most conspicuous accent of Thorney, in spite of the church, the WATER TOWER in the Jacobean style, with a higher polygonal stair-turret. It was built in 1855.

S of the Wisbech Road, lying back somewhat, PARK HOUSE, with a big shaped and pedimented C17 (Dutch) gable.

WINDMILL. Derelict tower-mill with date-stone 1787. It had seven storeys, and the diameter at the base is 26 ft.

At WILLOW HALL, 3 m. SW, three good houses, all C18: BAR PASTURE FARM, brick, stone-slated, L-shaped, WILLOW HALL, with a five-bay front with stone-framed window frames terminating in keystones and a pedimented doorway, and PRIOR'S FARMHOUSE with a similar front.

THORPE HALL
Soke of Peterborough

1090

Built in 1653–6 by *Peter Mills* for Chief Justice St John. Peter Mills was bricklayer to the City of London and a man of considerable competence and reputation. After the Fire of London he was appointed with May, Pratt, and Wren, all three younger men, to supervise the rebuilding. He also designed the Selden end of the Bodleian Library at Oxford, Hitcham's Building at Pembroke College Cambridge, and possibly a group of other houses in the area between Cambridge and Peterborough (e.g. Thorney, Wisbech) which have the same characteristics as Thorpe Hall. They determine a place for Mills aside from the direct development of classical architecture from Inigo Jones to John Webb, May, Pratt, and Wren. He was, it seems, the leader of a lively, mannered, somewhat fantastical style which Sir John Summerson has christened Artisan Mannerism. It runs parallel with and sometimes overlaps the equally lively and equally uninhibited local mid-century Baroque of such buildings as the portal of St Mary at Oxford and the additions to Bolsover.

Thorpe Hall stands foursquare and solid, with walled gardens to the N, S, and E and stables to the W. The walled gardens have GATES with Mannerist details, especially those to the N and S, where tall slender niches are partly filled by pedestals in relief carrying vases in relief which end in Ionic capitals. The E gate, to give another example, has a pilaster against the

rusticated pier which stands on a volute. The gates from the
garden to the stables introduce one of Mills's favourite motifs, a
pilaster halved vertically and placed l. and r. of the big, heavy,
eared door-frame. In this particular case the pilasters again
start out of volutes, but here volutes in profile. In the same
wall also an exedra, and, in the garden, s w of the house, a free-
standing tripartite archway, based in its design on the motif
of the Venetian window. The side parts and the big voluted
and pedimented attic have oval openings.

79   Now for the house itself. Its N and S fronts are identical.
Seven bays, two and a half storeys, quoins, and a hipped roof.
In the roof dormers with alternatingly triangular and segmental pediments. On the roof originally a lantern or belvedere (see the staircase inside), just as at Coleshill by Pratt, and
at Wisbech, Tyttenhanger, and many other houses of the second
third of the C17. Also on the roof square groups of four-
square rusticated chimneyshafts. Porch on Tuscan columns
and with a balcony. The S porch has a stuccoed ceiling. The
window above the porch has a segmental pediment and a
broad eared frame, again with halved pilasters on volutes in
profile. To the l. and r. of this central window the other central
windows, i.e. those of bays two and six, are stressed by triangular pediments. The windows probably had mullion and
transom crosses and in the half-storey mullions only. This can
be guessed from the state of the W side.

The E side is the most remarkable side of the house. There
is a terrace here with a balustrade of dumb-bell balusters, and
the wall has three instead of the expected five bays. These
three bays are treated on both main floors in a tripartite
rhythm, bays one and three as bay windows, the middle bay
flat but wider than the others. The centre has a segmental
pediment, the centres of the bay windows triangular pediments. The Venetian motif is of the normal kind (first introduced into England by Inigo Jones) in the middle bay, but in
the bay windows there is a variation which was to become
specially popular in the 1660s and 1670s. The spaces above the
lower side lights are opened so that the side lights can be
called transomed, the transom being discontinued under the
middle light because of the higher arched opening. All pilasters
of these tripartite openings have sunk panels. The whole
composition strikes one as oddly Victorian-looking, and Sir
Gyles Isham may well be right in attributing it to the years
1850–2, when the then owner, the Rev. William Strong,

employed *Francis Ruddle* of Peterborough to restore and alter
the house. 'The restoration and alteration of the stone framework' of the E side appears indeed under 14 April 1851 in a
journal of work done.

The plan of Thorpe Hall is very clear and simple. Nothing
of the medieval and Elizabethan principles remains. The house
is what Pratt called a 'double pile', i.e. has rooms in two rows,
one facing N, the other S. A passage runs through between
them from E to W. There are in the E half a large room behind
each of the bay windows and the principal staircase behind
the broader centre bay. The W half is divided into smaller
rooms and a broad passage to a secondary staircase. Where the
N–S and the E–W axes meet, the crossing is marked by columns.
On the principal landing is a tripartite stone screen which is
similar in style to the bays of the E front. It does indeed date
from 1850 and is also by *Ruddle*. In the top storey right in the
middle of the house a spiral staircase goes up to the former
belvedere. The principal staircase has a broad balustrade with
heavily and richly carved openwork foliage panels, a little
more advanced in style than those of Lamport Hall. The
turned balusters of the subsidiary staircase make use of the
motif of leaves growing up the bulbous bottom part of the
baluster. The principal rooms have equally heavily and richly
decorated fireplaces and plaster ceilings. The motifs here are
those typical of Peter Mills. Only examples can be given to
characterize the style: wall panelling with curiously carved
panels, stuck one into another, frames on volutes in profile
turned inward as well as outward, pilasters with garlands
hanging down them and over the front of a volute which replaces the base of the pilaster. Plaster ceilings with oval or
circular centres framed by fat wreaths. In the entrance passage
two stone tables on stone feet.

The STABLES have similar motifs, the centre of the S front,
e.g., a big pedimented dormer with volutes l. and r., and the
small window below it small volutes and ears.

TILBROOK

0050

ALL SAINTS. A good Dec church. The most telling exception is
the N aisle. The arcade is hard to understand. It was first a
matter of three bays added to a Norman nave. The Norman
piers are round, the abaci square but chamfered, the arches
pointed with just a slight chamfer. That makes the work
c.1190. The W bay was later cut into by the tower, but the W

respond was found in 1930. Then, in the late C13, the arcade was extended E with circular piers whose abaci are alternatingly octagonal and round, double-chamfered arches, and a little nailhead enrichment. The W wall of the chancel (whose arch is Dec) cuts into this lengthening, so that the easternmost of the late C13 piers now acts as a respond for the one-bay N chapel, which is also Dec. But externally the N doorway seems early C13, and the N aisle W lancet and the NW window of two separate lancets with a tiny blank quatrefoil over belong to the late C13 build. However, externally it is the W tower that dominates. It is Dec and has two-light bell-openings with transom and a recessed broach spire with low broaches and two tiers of lucarnes. The nave S windows are Dec but Victorian. The chancel and N vestry appear Perp, but the eaves-frieze includes ballflower; so that is Dec too, and Dec is indeed the ANGLE PISCINA in the chancel. Late Perp the clerestory, Late Perp a head-corbel and the brackets l. and r. of the chancel E window, and Late Perp the N aisle roof with angels against the intermediate principals. – (FONT. In the churchyard the bowl of a Perp font with quatrefoils. GMCH) – SCREEN. Perp, of three-light divisions and without doubt the best in the county. It still has its ribbed coving with three patterns of ribbing and much original colour. On the dado painted Saints no longer clearly recognizable. – STALLS. Two have old poppyheads. – SCULPTURE. In the S porch a Cross of the C12, probably not from Tilbrook. On one narrow side a bishop standing on a colonnette rendered in relief. On one broad side fluting but with two big flowers. – Above the S porch entrance a man with a pig; C12? – STAINED GLASS. Fragments in a chancel S window. – In the E window two early C16 roundels. – BRASSES. Under the organ brasses of a Civilian and wife, c.1400. The sizes of the figures seem unrecorded.

TOSELAND

ST MICHAEL. By *Arthur Blomfield*, 1873. Neo-Norman, of nave and chancel with W bellcote. But the masonry is mostly original Norman work, and there are a Norman S window and a Norman S doorway, evidently late. Two orders of shafts, single- and double-scallop capitals, undecorated tympanum but a band of rosettes round it, zigzag arch, the zigzag also placed at r. angles to the wall. The chancel arch is Norman too, but here the capitals have volutes and also – foreshadowing waterleaf – inturned volutes. In one abacus a little decoration. Single-step arches. – Outside the s wall lies a large Sarsen stone.

TOSELAND HALL. An exceptionally compact and symmetrical red-brick house of about 1600. It is two storeys high plus an attic storey in the gables. The front has three gables, and to them correspond two canted bay windows and a middle porch. The windows are transomed except in the gables. The fenestration is perfectly symmetrical, except that on the l. of the porch is an extra two-light window, just enough to state that on that side lies the hall. The sides also have three bays, but only two gables. The position of the middle window on one side demonstrates where the staircase is. The windows on the sides have no transoms, but that may be a later alteration. The kitchen lay at the back. – The BARN is of about the same time. It is aisled and has tiebeams on braces and collar-beams.

UFFORD
Soke of Peterborough

oooo

ST ANDREW. The chancel comes first. Two E windows (their tracery C19), N and s windows with a variety of Y-tracery, SEDILIA and PISCINA, and chancel arch all point to the late C13 or c.1300. Two s windows renewed. Dec with segmental arches. Dec also the aisle windows. Rood turret on the N side. The arcades (three bays) are Early Perp. The slender piers are typical, still with a square core and four demi-shafts, but Perp-looking capitals. Arches with sunk mouldings. Perp w tower. On the clasping buttresses concave-sided gables in relief. Tall two-light bell-openings with transom. Battlements. – FONT. Tall, octagonal, Perp, with shields, etc. – COMMAND-MENT TABLES and ROYAL ARMS. Signed by *John Everard* of Stamford, 1790. Ionic pilasters with Gothic arches as frames. – STAINED GLASS. Much of c.1910. One pane is signed *T.F. Curtis, Ward & Hughes* 1910.* – BELLS. Two are medieval. They are assigned to *Richard Hill* (VCH). – PLATE. Cup and Cover Paten, 1619. – MONUMENTS. Bridget Lady Carre † 1621. Semi-reclining on her side. Back arch with well-carved gristly cartouche. Columns l. and r. – Three good tablets (s aisle), dates 1689, 1705, 1790. That of 1705 is, according to Le Neve, by *Edward Stanton*. Excellent ornament and three cherubs' heads at the top.

---

* But according to local tradition these windows were designed by Miss *Erskine* of Stamford.

OLD RECTORY. Close to the church, to the SE. The most prominent external motif is two tall imitation church windows in the
style of *c.*1300. They may date from the early C19. (But inside
remains of the roof timbers of a C14 hall. VCH)

GATES. Below the church to the N are gates to the Ufford Hall
grounds. They are also perhaps early C19. The style is a mixture of Gothic and Jacobean, with old bits.

UFFORD HALL. Rainwater-heads of 1751. A strangely disjointed composition, owing probably to an addition on the
entrance side. Garden side plain: five-bay centre of two
storeys plus a half-storey above the cornice, wings of two bays
and two storeys. The five-bay centre is rusticated below the
cornice. To the entrance most of this centre is hidden by a
double-canted projection, or one canted bay on either side and
a further-projecting canted bay window. In this lies the
entrance, and it leads straight to the (later) staircase. The most
noteworthy rooms are the dining room and drawing room,
which fill the two side wings completely. Their decoration is
Late Georgian.

UPTON

1 m. N of Ailsworth
Soke of Peterborough

ST JOHN BAPTIST. A very odd but very engaging church.
Intensely domestic front. Nave and N aisle of the same width
and height and with the same gables and domestic windows.
The windows are straight-headed, of arched lights. A third
smaller gable in the middle with a buttress up its centre. The
other windows also all straight-headed. Chancel rebuilt 1842.
The rest looks C17 Gothic – and such it is indeed. All the more
surprising is the interior. For now we are transported into
a much earlier time. The chancel arch has early C12 shafts
with scalloped capitals with decoration and a C17 arch. N
arcade of two bays, late C12. Shortish circular pier, square
abacus. Capitals with upright leaves and crockets. Arches C17.
The C17 work is connected with the erection of the MONU-
MENT to Sir William Dove † 1633 and his two wives. The
monument stands in the N aisle, and the aisle was rebuilt to
receive the monument. The floor is raised by four steps, and
the space is separated by a big classical balustrade with vertically symmetrical balusters. The monument is a four-poster.
Three recumbent effigies, that of the second wife († 1665) in

wood, i.e. made after the rest of the monument. One would like to date it from the balustrade and the big open segmental pediments as *c.*1650–60 rather than *c.*1633. – COMMUNION RAIL. Jacobean with flat openwork balusters. – PULPIT. Jacobean, elaborate, with tester. – PLATE. Slender Beaker, *c.*1610 (German ?); Paten, 1680; Cup, 1769.

(VICARAGE. In its two chimneypieces of the C13 from the Priest's House at Sutton. Information kindly supplied by the Rev. John Price.)

MANOR HOUSE, S of the church. Of the house of the Dove family very little remains: three bays, two storeys. Doorway with four-centred arch. The ground-floor windows with arched lights. The most probable date is late C16 to early C17. In the garden, buried in nettles at the time of writing, a SUN-DIAL, nearly 6 ft high.

MODEL FARMHOUSE, at the W end of the village. Dated 1685. The hipped roof with oblong moulded chimneyshafts goes well with that date, but the windows are still mullioned, though now symmetrically placed.

UPTON
1070

2 m. NW of Alconbury

ST MARGARET. Not a large church. The W tower has a short broach spire with two tiers of lucarnes. The big mid-buttress is odd, but the RCHM has an explanation for it. The S doorway is the oldest feature. With its thin angle-shafts it is undoubtedly Late Norman. Then follow the arcades. They are mid C13, with round piers, round abaci, and double-chamfered arches. There were originally three bays, but the tower was built into the nave. The tower W wall was once the nave W wall. The RCHM suggests that when this received its two ogee-headed lancets, the big buttress was also built to receive a bellcote. But is the buttress not fully justified by the fact of a tower being raised on a mere W wall? The chancel is E.E. too, see the lancet giving into the vestry, the priest's doorway with its rounded-trefoiled head, and the tomb recess. However, the chancel arch is Perp. Straight-headed Dec S aisle and clerestory windows. The N aisle is by *Scott*, 1870–1. – FONT. A tremendous Norman piece like a two-scalloped capital. It stands on nine (renewed) E.E. supports. – PLATE. Cup and Cover of 1634–5.

UPWOOD

St Peter. The nave has a Norman N arcade, but above it
appear the traces of two Norman windows from the time before the arcade was built. The arcade is later C12. Round piers,
cruciform multi-scalloped capitals, one-step arches with two
tiny chamfers. The w bay was rebuilt when the tower was
built, but the Norman pier shows that such a bay had existed
already in the C12. Norman also the chancel arch, depressed
rounded. In the chancel N and S walls a long round-headed
lancet, i.e. late C12. The tower is late C13, see the bell-openings with two sub-arches on a polygonal shaft. To the w a
small Dec niche with a kneeling figure and a soul in a napkin.
The s arcade is ambiguous. The arches are C13, but the capitals
Perp. – (FONT COVER. Jacobean, with nicely decorated ribs.
GMCH) – SCREENS. Modest screens of one-light divisions to
chancel and N chapel. – STAINED GLASS. In two S aisle windows good C15 canopies. – PLATE. Spanish silver-gilt Dish
ornamented in repoussé, the centre engraved with an Annunciation, partly enamelled. Early C15. – Cup and Cover Paten
1613–14. – MONUMENTS. Tablet to Peter Phesaunt † 1649,
still Elizabethan in style. Latin inscription. – Tablet to Sir
Richard and Lady Bickerton. She died in 1811. Urn above
inscription.

Upwood House, w of the church. Of the later C17. Front of
red brick with two projecting wings. They have giant angle
pilasters. Giant pilasters also to emphasize the middle bay of
the recessed centre. They carry a steep gable with an oval
window in it. Towards the garden five bays. Against one of the
short sides two big flat stone chimneybreasts probably older
than the façades.

WALCOT HALL
¾ m. SE of Barnack
Soke of Peterborough

Nine by five bays, of ashlar, two-storeyed. Quoins of even length,
hipped roof with pedimented dormers, four square rusticated
chimneys. That far the house goes well with the date 1678 on
two rainwater-heads. But there are others of 1767, and they
may refer to the present shape of the windows, their alternating triangular and segmental pediments, and the three-bay
pediment on the garden side. Fine terraces. In the garden a

Rotunda and two Temples. The latter two, in memory of a son who died young, are by *W. H. Ansell*, designed shortly after 1941. – Good C17 GATEPIERS.

WALTON
2 m. NW of Peterborough
Soke of Peterborough

1000

MANOR FARM. Dated 1708. Still with mullioned windows, although they are now regularly placed and have hoods. A house SE of this (No. 1103 Lincoln Road) is dated 1668 and still has all the traditional Jacobean features.

At the corner of Sage's Lane (No. 1066 Lincoln Road) is a three-bay HOUSE which looks Georgian, but has a doorway with a big straight hood on excessively voluted brackets which seems to be of the time and style of Thorpe Hall. (Inside the date 1600 on a beam.)

WANSFORD

0090

ST MARY. The church is N, the village S of the Nene. In the W wall a Saxon window which now looks into the C13 tower. This has lancet windows, bell-openings of two lights with a separating shaft, a dogtooth frieze, and a not too tall broach spire with two tiers of lucarnes in alternating directions. The spire seems early C14. The S wall of the nave and the porch redone in 1663 and hence very domestic-looking. But the coarse S doorway is of *c.*1200: two orders of shafts and a round arch. A little later the N arcade of two bays. Short quatrefoil pier, a little nailhead decoration, round double-chamfered arches. The chancel is of 1902. (The PULPIT and SEDILIA have Jacobean panels. GMCH) – FONT. Circular, Norman. Primitively carved figures under arches. A border of leaf-trail above. The figures include a Baptism, two Knights fighting, two other groups in communication. Dr Zarnecki supports *c.*1120 as the date. – PLATE. Cup, *c.*1570; Cover Paten dated 1570.

The village is of the one-street type, because it was on the Great North Road. Hence the amazing spaciousness of the HAYCOCK INN. Its date must be *c.*1670. The building has a five-bay centre and two-bay wings. The fenestration was originally no doubt cross-windows. The doorway and the window above it have pediments and details with those curious mid C17 mannerisms which culminate at Thorpe Hall, e.g. the square blocks in the middle of the pilasters. And what on the pilasters is capital, what abacus? The staircases have those fully-fashioned balusters which again characterizes 1660 to 1680.

WANSFORD BRIDGE. A splendid specimen, in spite of the irregularity of its arches. On the village side there is after a small round arch a very wide one, dated 1795, and then the cutwaters begin on both sides. The next three arches are of 1672–4, the following seven of 1577 (dated). These latter have stepped arches.

(RAILWAY STATION. Jacobean, symmetrical, with shaped gables.)

A little further s than the Haycock is the drive to STIBBING-TON HOUSE, a late C18 house with a three-bay front, a belvedere on the roof, and a charming iron veranda. The doorway is broad for its date and has fluted Ionic pilasters.

3080

WARBOYS

ST MARY MAGDALENE. A stately church of brown cobble, but how could they, in 1832, rebuild the chancel in yellow brick, 34 even if they chose lancets to match the superb C13 w steeple – C13 to the top of the broach spire? The tower is high and has broad flat buttresses with shallow set-offs, a lancet window, once it seems not divided across but of its whole astounding length in one. The next stage has a cusped w lancet, shafted. Then the bell-openings, pairs of the lights each with Y-tracery with a foiled spandrel and much shafting. The lowest of the three tiers of lucarnes is in exactly the same style. The broaches are quite low. After this most impressive piece one must look at the oldest piece: the Norman chancel arch, with scalloped capitals to the triple responds, a tiny tree motif on one of the capitals, and an arch with two rolls and zigzag. Then, still chronologically before the tower, both arcades. They are of four bays and quite different one from the other; yet both date from the early C13. N has round and octagonal piers and arches with one chamfer and one more complex moulding including keeling, s has round piers, round capitals, and round abaci and double-chamfered arches, i.e. a more conventional *parti*. Very good bases. Then, to continue chronologically, the tower. What has not yet been said is that the arch to the nave goes with all the rest, and so do the lower N and s arches. So embracing aisles were provided for, although they (see the E arches) and most of the fenestration of the church are Perp. Nice N doorway of *c*.1300. – FONT. The font was obtained at

the time when the enlargement by aisles took place. It is of
table-top form and has stiff-leaf of the mature kind to the N.
All the other sides are re-cut out of recognition. – DOOR
KNOCKER. Chancel N. A small C12 piece with a lion's head,
and the ring made into two dragons fighting. – PLATE. Set of
1841–2. – MONUMENTS. John Leman † 1781. By *Bacon*. Hope
pointing to an urn. – Mrs Strode † 1790. Also by *Bacon*.
Mourning woman by an urn. On the pedestal a fine small
relief of the Good Samaritan.

MANOR HOUSE, N of the church. Mid C17. Red brick with two
large shaped gables. The brick is laid in Flemish bond already.

(OLD RECTORY, E of the church. Large, early C19, of yellow
brick, but with a broken scrolly door pediment on scrolled
brackets. In the garden a part of a large pier said to come from
Ramsey Abbey. RCHM)

THE CHESTNUTS, Ramsey Road. Early C19. The gates are
handsome Grecian cast iron.

CLOCK TOWER. In the centre of the village. 1887, and of no
merit. Yellow and red brick, Gothic below, square above, with
a pyramid roof.

WARESLEY 2050

ST JAMES. By *Butterfield*, 1857. Built together with the Duncombe Mausoleum, which connects with the interior of the
church by a wall with a window of three stepped lancet lights
with foiled circles over. The E wall of the mausoleum has two
strange blank arches with blank sexfoiled almond-shapes
hanging from their apex. This is the only oddity of the church.
Otherwise it is all normal late C13 detail, and the N porch
tower (which is unexpected) is slender and noble, with its
sheer, steep shingled spire with just a suspicion of broaches.
Gothic well-house by the street. Inside, the chancel is one of
the most perfect examples of Butterfield's structural polychromy: stone, red tiles, green tiles, and a little yellow – all in
elementary geometrical patterns. – (FONT COVER and
BENCHES are excellent and typical. GMCH) – STAINED GLASS.
The E and S windows of the chancel, judging by their style,
must be by *Gibbs*, but the N window is a mystery. The background of broad patches of ruby, lilac, and dark mauve is
entirely out of the ordinary. Young *Burne-Jones* is the name
that would come to mind, but the style of the figures is not his.

WARESLEY PARK. 1934 by Guthrie of *Wimperis, Simpson &*

Guthrie. Large villa with a round towered centre and wings projecting at an angle. Big roofs.

WATER NEWTON

ST REMIGIUS. 'Water' here means the Nene, on whose bank the church lies. Ashlar-faced E.E. W tower with a niche on the W side in which stands a small praying figure. The inscription beneath reads: Vous ke par issi passez pur le alme Thomas Purdew priez. Long twin bell-openings with shaft and re-set Norman zigzag on the super-arch. The latter comes from the chancel of Castor church. Broach spire with two tiers of lucarnes.* E.E. also the S arcade. Three bays, the first pier octagonal, the second quatrefoil. Round single-chamfered arches. The same in the N arcade of octagonal piers, which is E.E. too. To the S arcade belongs in style the S doorway and the S porch entrance, to the N arcade the little trefoil in the W wall of the aisle. The clerestory has Y-tracery, and so is of the end of the C13. But most of the windows of the church are of the C17. This applies to the chancel throughout. Yet the SEDILIA and PISCINA are E.E., and there are traces of the pre-C17 windows. – FONT. Perp, octagonal. – SCREEN. Perp, of high and narrow one-light divisions. – DESK. The two ends have poppyheads, each with two little human heads. – BELL. One bell probably by *William Rufford*, C14. – PLATE. Cup of 1636–7; Cover Paten C17. – MONUMENT. Defaced effigy of a Civilian, late C13 (S aisle).

E of the church a WATERMILL of 1791 and the LOCK KEEPER'S COTTAGE, a picturesque group.

WATER NEWTON HOUSE, SSW of the church, has a regular C18 front, but mullioned windows at the back.

The site of the Roman town of DUROBRIVAE lies on the triangle of land S of the River Nene, between Billing Brook and the Great North Road. It clearly owes its existence partly to the fact that here the Roman Ermine Street crosses the river Nene, and partly to the vast pottery industry that grew up here-abouts. Originally its 44 acres were defended by a wall, bank, and ditch; all are now much reduced, but most of the circuit is picked out by modern field-boundaries. Little is known of the internal arrangements of the town, but aerial photography shows the existence of a somewhat irregular grid of streets set

---

* The arch towards the nave is small, and the blocked triangular head above it remains a mystery.

askew to the line of Ermine Street, which bisects the walled area. To the s of the town considerable traces of ribbon development, consisting of strip houses, were examined when the Great North Road was widened.

w of Billing Brook is the site of a ROMAN FORT guarding the river-crossing. It is known, from air photographs, to measure 510 ft by 460 ft and to be defended by double or treble ditches.

Nearly 1¼ m. N along Ermine Street is a small ROMAN CAMP, visible only from the air.

Between Durobrivae and Water Newton are the traces of an extensive Roman pottery industry, consisting of kilns, workshops, and other buildings. Similar structures are known to cover a considerable area N of the Nene, E of Castor station. The pottery produced in these centres varied from coarse wares, for the local market, to pots of very high technical and artistic quality, which from the c2 to c4 were exported to all parts of the country. Other pottery-making centres in the area are known at Stibbington, Sibson, and Sutton Field.

WERRINGTON
Soke of Peterborough

1000

ST JOHN BAPTIST. Primarily a Norman church, see the s doorway with one order of colonnettes carrying decorated scallop capitals and an arch with an outer zigzag at r. angles to the wall plane; see also the chancel arch, which is narrow and has responds of two shafts with decorated scallop capitals; and see finally the s aisle w window with its deep splay. The double bellcote with continuous roll mouldings around the arched openings and a gable may be a little earlier, but is also no doubt still c12. The arcades of three bays are early c13. That on the s side has piers with four shafts and in the diagonals four rectangular projections. The moulded capitals are simple but have a little nailhead. The bases have angle spurs. The arches are round, double-chamfered, and have stiff-leaf label-stops. The N arcade is much simpler: round piers, round capitals and abaci, round double-chamfered arches. Also of the early c13 the chancel chapel. One wide, round, double-chamfered arch on semicircular responds. Fine stiff-leaf details. Wide Dec chancel with four-light E window.* Reticulated tracery. Beautiful head-corbels inside to its l. and r. Dec also the outer entrance of the s porch (cf. Peakirk). – FONT. Plain c13 bowl, octagonal, on shafts with moulded

* The chancel was rebuilt with the old materials in 1901–2.

capitals. – PLATE. Breadholder, 1723; Cup and Cover Paten, 1758.

WILLOW HALL see THORNEY

WINWICK

1080

ALL SAINTS. Perp w tower with broach spire. Two tiers of lucarnes. The s doorway is a C13 re-use of Late Norman zig-zag set at r. angles to the wall. But the s aisle is of the early C14 – see one window with intersecting and one with reticula-ted tracery. The s transept has a Dec PISCINA, but a large Perp window. The chancel is a good C13 piece, with chamfered buttresses similar to those at Leighton Bromswold, and two N lancets. The large E window dates from the restoration by *Slater & Carpenter*, 1864. They are also responsible for the round, octofoiled clerestory windows. The arcades are late C13 and early C14. Four bays, low, on the s alternating round and octagonal piers with a little nailhead, on the N octagonal piers. The chancel arch responds are C13 too; the arch has two hollow chamfers. The N aisle and transept roofs have carved bosses. – SCREEN. Wide one-light divisions with ogee arches and busy details. Mostly C19. – PLATE. Cup inscribed 1569, made at Norwich; the Cover Paten matches.

WISTOW

2080

ST JOHN BAPTIST. Of cobbles, but the Late Perp w tower of stone. Is it post-Reformation ? Perhaps the top part. Perp also the high and wide two-bay arcades. Piers of continuous mouldings to the nave, shafts with capitals to the arch open-ings and fleurons in the mouldings. To each bay corresponds a pair of two-light clerestory windows. A higher rood-stair turret at the E end of the clerestory. The nave roof has figures against the wall-posts and against the sub-principals. The N aisle roof has figures on the wall-posts only. The chancel arch corre-sponds to the arcades, the tower arch is plainer. In the chancel ogee-headed SEDILIA and a low-side window of two lights with a transom. The lights are ogee-headed too, and the chan-cel was indeed consecrated in 1347. Close to the s doorway is evidence of the church preceding this: a fragmentary Norman tympanum with diapering of four-petalled flowers and a bit of zigzag. – SCREENS. In the s chapel of three- and four-light divi-sions. – Under the tower arch plainer, of one-light divisions. –

SOUTH DOOR. Symmetrical sparse iron scroll-work of the early C14. – STAINED GLASS. The S aisle W window is complete, with figures of the Virgin of the Annunciation and the Resurrection and small angels below and in the tracery head. It is all early C15 and was originally in the chancel E window. How is it no-one smashed it up? – In the chancel N and S windows glass by *Wailes*. – PLATE. Two Chalices of 1809–10. (LIMETREE FARM, 350 yds SW. Timber-framed, early C16. In a ground-floor room early C18 painted panelling. RCHM)

WITTERING
Soke of Peterborough

6000

ALL SAINTS. People who visit the church come to gaze at the Saxon chancel arch, which, in its cyclopean crudity, is without equal. A half-roll in the respond, a half-roll just outside the angle, a rectangular projection further out. Combined capital and abacus block 18 in. tall and tapering out towards the top but without any moulding whatever. The three mouldings or bands are carried on round the arch. It all makes even Barnack look refined. Yet of its rude force there can be no question. Perfect long-and-short work is preserved at the angles of the chancel and the nave (the NE angle to be seen inside). Mid C12 arcade of two bays with big circular pier and square abacus. Many-scalloped capital. Similar triple-shafted responds. Arches with one big roll and an outer band of zigzag combined with lozenges and lozenges broken at r. angles. Late C13 W tower, see the pointed-trefoiled windows and the bell-openings of two lights with a quatrefoiled circle. Short spire with two tiers of lucarnes in alternating directions. Of about the same time the chancel S window and the S doorway of the nave. Early C14 N chapel, opening to the chancel in one arch of two chamfers, the inner on a head corbel. Early C14 also the tomb recess in the chapel. – STAINED GLASS. E window by *Kempe*, 1903.

WOODBURY HALL *see* TETWORTH

WOODCROFT CASTLE
1¼ m. S of Etton
Soke of Peterborough

1000

A fragment of a late C13 castle with later alterations and additions. The present front has a stout circular tower on the l.

and had an identical one on the r. Gateway in the middle. There was originally probably a courtyard and perhaps two more towers, on the pattern of Barnwell and also Harlech. The windows with shouldered lintels and transom are in fact characteristic of the Welsh Edwardian castles ('Caernarvon arches'). The ranges between towers and gateway have a cornice above the upper floor, and this is taken up to include the second upper floor of the gatehouse. Gateway with segmental double-chamfered arches. Behind the remaining tower an Early Tudor range. Windows with arched lights and hoodmoulds. (One big medieval fireplace inside. NMR)

3070

WOODHURST

ST JOHN BAPTIST. Chancel, nave, s aisle, and weatherboarded bell-turret. The blocked N doorway is basically Norman, the s arcade E.E. Four bays, round piers, double-chamfered arches. The s windows are Perp, the clerestory post-medieval, and the chancel C19, unfortunately of yellow brick. – BENCH ENDS. Four, with elementary poppyheads. – PLATE. Cup, Paten, and Paten on foot, all 1763–4.

At the E end of SOUTH STREET is a late C17 brick house of seven bays with hipped roof and a modillion frieze.

N of this, at the E end of the main street, the MANOR HOUSE, also brick, but a little later. Five bays, hipped roof, doorway with segmental pediment.

1090

WOODSTON

ST AUGUSTINE. In the W tower is a recess on the W side, where Anglo-Saxon masonry is exposed and a small double-splayed window. The rest of the tower and the church are of 1844, 1884, and 1896, but the Norman twin bell-openings with a thick roll on the Peterborough example and the nutmeg frieze below are original. So is the s transept s window of three stepped lancet lights, i.e. c.1280–1300. Inside, the s arcade with octagonal piers is C14 work. – FONT. Late C13. Five supports, the four outer ones acting as knobs or spurs to the plain octagonal bowl. – PLATE. Cup and Cover Paten 1569–70; silver-gilt Bowl 1630–1; Paten on foot 1671–2; Flagon 1727–8.

The MITCHELL CONSTRUCTION COMPANY have their four-storeyed head offices opposite. The block has curtain walling and a zigzag canopy over the entrance. Architects: *H. V. Lobb & Partners*. Date: 1961–2.

WOOD WALTON

2080

ST ANDREW. Outside the village, by the railway line. Dec w
tower with pyramid roof. Dec chancel with straight-headed
windows, including a low-side window. The s arcade is E.E.,
of four bays with two round piers and arches of one step and
one chamfer. The w pier and w respond and the E respond are
Perp. Perp also the N arcade. The piers are double-chamfered,
the outer chamfers continuous, the inner with capitals, two
with shields, two with crenellation. – STAINED GLASS. In a
chancel N window two complete C14 figures. – PLATE. Cup of
1821–2. – MONUMENTS. An unusual number of early coffin
lids with foliated crosses.

CASTLE HILL, c.700 yds NNE. A motte and bailey, the motte
being c.135 ft in diameter.

WYTON

2070

ST MARGARET AND ALL SAINTS. Brown cobbles and externally mostly Perp. The label-stops of the s doorway are specially
pretty. However the following are not Perp. First the SW
steeple, by *Hutchinson*, 1865–6 – rather starved. Then the
priest's doorway, with a little dogtooth, and the paired lancets
in the chancel. They are early C13. A very little later is the N
doorway, with stiff-leaf capitals looking c.1230–40 and a keeled
roll moulding. The doorway goes perfectly with the N arcade,
which is a beautiful design. Four bays and two different pier
shapes: octagonal, and four keeled shafts and four minor
shafts. Deeply moulded arches, including keeled rolls. Very
bold and animated stiff-leaf capitals, all different. The Perp
roof-corbels of the nave deserve notice: foliage, grapes, a rose-
sprig, heads. The three incongruously placed gargoyles in the
outer wall of the N aisle come from the tower of 1846 which
preceded the present one. – NORTH DOOR. With sparse C13
iron scrolls. – STAINED GLASS. In a N window *Kempe* glass of
1906.

THREE JOLLY BUTCHERS. Timber-framed and plastered.
Dated 1622. (Inside a room with a beam with scroll ornament
and some recently discovered, somewhat crude wall paintings
with arcades, the arches supporting pendants.)

YAXLEY

1090

ST PETER. Yaxley church is one of the most rewarding in
Huntingdonshire. It is large, and it represents all medieval

styles after the Norman and yet does not lose its unity. One
niche in the E wall of the S transept with a round head and
a continuous roll moulding might even be accepted as Late
Norman, but it is most probably re-set. The transepts themselves are E.E., see the E lancets and, in the N transept, a W
lancet too. But the N transept in its N wall received a three-
light window of stepped lancet lights with trefoils in the
tracery, which is typical of *c.*1300, and the same type also occurs
in the N chapel. The S transept on the other hand had its S
window replaced early in the C14 by a large window with
elongated reticulated tracery. To the late C13 belongs the W
bay of the S aisle, which now embraces the later tower. The
windows are of three stepped lancet lights as in the N chapel
but without tracery, and it is incidentally worth noticing how
wide this S aisle already was. Such wide aisles only came in in
the later C13 (cf. e.g. Grantham). Again late C13 the S doorway. It has three orders of thin shafts with rings and three
orders of thin roll mouldings, two with fillets. Of *c.*1300 the
two E windows of the N aisle. They have three stepped lancet
lights with tracery under one arch. The other aisle windows,
N and S, are Perp. Three stepped lancet lights under one arch
and with tracery occur also in the S chapel, but the dominating
window here is that in the E wall, which has lively flowing
tracery of, say, *c.*1330–40. Also flowing tracery, but much more
exuberant (and much more restored), in the chancel E wall.
Five lights, a delightfully sinuous pattern, and inside the window two high niches with ogee canopies. The interior in fact
largely confirms the exterior. Late C13 chancel arch, late C13
two-bay N chapel arcade with quatrefoil piers and double-
chamfered arches, three-bay S chapel arcade with quatrefoil
piers with fillets. Double-chamfered arches again. In the N
chapel also good late C13 SEDILIA and PISCINA (pointed-
trefoiled arches under gables). There now only remains the
Perp contribution, and it is considerable: not only the S porch
with the three niches above the entrance and three supporter
beasts on the gable, but four-bay arcades (of piers with
characteristic mouldings and capitals only on the shafts towards the arch openings) and the clerestory, and of course the
grand W tower. This is high, ashlar-faced, and kept together
by clasping buttresses with many shallow set-offs, and it has
large three-light bell-openings and a recessed crocketed spire
with two tiers of lucarnes. The spire is steadied – so the eye
feels – by the delicate flying buttresses with openwork quatre-

foils which connect it with the pinnacles in the four corners of the tower. The arches towards nave and aisle W bays are all Perp too. – FONT. Octagonal, the panels simply bordered by a thin roll-moulding. This probably represents the late C13. – PULPIT. Dated 1631. With back panel and sounding-board. The patterns are mostly stylized leaf. – STALLS. The kneeling-desks are Perp, with arched panels in front and poppyheads on the ends. – SCREEN. Tall, of one-light divisions. – Above it rises the large ORGAN GALLERY and CASE, 1904–10 by *Temple Moore*, who then restored the church well. – Much plain WOODWORK is re-used in benches, the N screen, etc. – DOOR to the rood-loft, with linenfold panels. – PAINTINGS. Nothing any longer that would be enjoyable. Above the arcade on the S side of the N chapel are late C14 scenes from the Resurrection. Above the chancel arch early C16 Doom. On the W wall of the nave C17 texts, a gravedigger, a skeleton, a man in Roman armour, etc. – STAINED GLASS. In the S chapel E window humble but characteristic glass of 1849. – The E window, alas just as characteristic of its date (in its refusal to accept the C20 at all), is by *Comper*, and of 1947. – MONUMENT. In the N transept one arched panel with sunk carving [38] of two arms holding a heart. This represents a heart burial, and the small tubular box found behind it contained the heart. The burial is convincingly attributed to William de Yaxley, Abbot of Thorney, who founded a chantry at Yaxley in 1291 and died in 1293. The chantry foundation may in fact help to date the large amount of ambitious late C13 work in the church.

SE of the church is a brick HOUSE with the kind of flat framework of vertical and horizontal raised brick bands typical of *c.*1675.

The MAIN STREET is E of the church and runs NE – far from straight. Nos 215–17, SE of the church, at the start of the street, has again such a raised brick framework. There are also two blank ovals placed vertically, and they were just as popular about 1675. However, the broad doorway with its Doric pilasters and triglyph frieze looks 1700 rather than 1675. Further on an C18 house with two canted bay windows on the ground floor, tripartite windows above them, and a doorway with columns and a broken pediment. Turn into CHAPEL STREET for a house dated 1649, which has of course mullioned windows. The fenestration is symmetrical, but the entrance is just l. of the centre and the shield above just r. of the centre, thus still preserving the Jacobean and older asymmetry of house fronts. Back in the Main Street the SCHOOL, dated 1848. It is of yellow brick and Gothic and has, to one's surprise, a triangular porch. The METHODIST CHAPEL is dated 1812. It is also of yellow brick. Three bays' width, pyramid roof.

2060

YELLING

HOLY CROSS. Of brown cobbles. The three-bay N arcade is of *c*.1190, i.e. the piers are round, but the abaci square and the capitals still of the multi-scalloped kind, but the arches, though unmoulded, are pointed. The S arcade of four bays with standard elements (but broaches at the start of the arches) looks *c*.1300. So do the S aisle windows (Y-tracery, still geometrical tracery with a quatrefoil and a trefoil in a circle) and S doorway (two continuous chamfers). A plain, low tomb recess in the aisle wall inside. Again, the chancel is of *c*.1300 or has work of that date. The SEDILIA fit it, but the chancel arch looks a little later. Late C14 W tower, but still with Dec bell-openings. The tower had a spire up to the C19. Most of the rest is Perp.

BAPTIST CHAPEL. 1850. Yellow brick, three by three bays. Segment-headed windows (a solecism in 1850), pilaster strips, a triglyph frieze of brick, very incorrect, and a big pediment across the façade.

CHURCH FARM HOUSE. An interesting, late C17 brick job, five by three bays. Angle pilasters and pilasters flanking the middle, all in two tiers. A re-set pediment from a former window or doorway.

GLOSSARY

ABACUS: flat slab on the top of a capital (q.v.).

ABUTMENT: solid masonry placed to resist the lateral pressure of a vault.

ACANTHUS: plant with thick fleshy and scalloped leaves used as part of the decoration of a Corinthian capital (q.v.) and in some types of leaf carving.

ACHIEVEMENT OF ARMS: in heraldry, a complete display of armorial bearings.

ACROTERION: foliage-carved block on the end or top of a classical pediment.

ADDORSED: two human figures, animals, or birds, etc., placed symmetrically so that they turn their backs to each other.

AEDICULE, AEDICULA: framing of a window or door by columns and a pediment (q.v.).

AFFRONTED: two human figures, animals, or birds, etc., placed symmetrically so that they face each other.

AGGER: Latin term for the built-up foundations of Roman roads; also sometimes applied to the banks of hill-forts or other earthworks.

AMBULATORY: semicircular or polygonal aisle enclosing an apse (q.v.).

ANNULET: *see* Shaft-ring.

ANSE DE PANIER: *see* Arch, Basket.

ANTEPENDIUM: covering of the front of an altar, usually by textiles or metalwork.

ANTIS, IN: *see* Portico.

APSE: vaulted semicircular or polygonal end of a chancel or a chapel.

ARABESQUE: light and fanciful surface decoration using combinations of flowing lines, tendrils, etc., interspersed with vases, animals, etc.

ARCADE: range of arches supported on piers or columns, free-standing: or, BLIND ARCADE, the same attached to a wall.

ARCH: round-headed, i.e. semicircular; pointed, i.e. consisting of two curves, each drawn from one centre, and meeting in a point at the top; segmental, i.e. in the form of a segment;

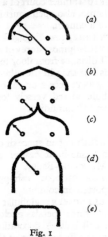

Fig. 1

pointed; four-centred (a Late Medieval form), *see* Fig. 1(a); Tudor (also a Late Medieval form), see Fig. 1(*b*); Ogee (introduced *c.*1300 and specially popular in the C14), see Fig. 1(*c*); Stilted, see Fig. 1(*d*); Basket, with lintel connected to the jambs by concave quadrant curves, see Fig. 1(*e*) for one example; Diaphragm, a transverse arch with solid spandrels carrying not a vault but a principal beam of a timber roof.

ARCHITRAVE: lowest of the three main parts of the entablature (q.v.) of an order (q.v.) (see Fig. 12).

ARCHIVOLT: under-surface of an arch (also called Soffit).

ARRIS: sharp edge at the meeting of two surfaces.

ASHLAR: masonry of large blocks wrought to even faces and square edges.

ATLANTES: male counterparts of caryatids (q.v.).

ATRIUM: inner court of a Roman house, also open court in front of a church.

ATTACHED: see Engaged.

ATTIC: topmost storey of a house, if distance from floor to ceiling is less than in the others.

AUMBRY: recess or cupboard to hold sacred vessels for Mass and Communion.

BAILEY: open space or court of a stone-built castle; see also Motte-and-Bailey.

BALDACCHINO: canopy supported on columns.

BALLFLOWER: globular flower of three petals enclosing a small ball. A decoration used in the first quarter of the C14.

BALUSTER: small pillar or column of fanciful outline.

BALUSTRADE: series of balusters supporting a handrail or coping (q.v.).

BARBICAN: outwork defending the entrance to a castle.

BARGEBOARDS: projecting decorated boards placed against the incline of the gable of a building and hiding the horizontal roof timbers.

BARROW: see Bell, Bowl, Disc, Long, *and* Pond Barrow.

BASILICA: in medieval architecture an aisled church with a clerestory.

BASKET ARCH: see Arch (Fig. 1*e*).

BASTION: projection at the angle of a fortification.

BATTER: inclined face of a wall.

BATTLEMENT: parapet with a series of indentations or embrasures with raised portions or merlons between (also called Crenellation).

BAYS: internal compartments of a building; each divided from the other not by solid walls but by divisions only marked in the side walls (columns, pilasters, etc.) or the ceiling (beams, etc.). Also external divisions of a building by fenestration.

BAY-WINDOW: angular or curved projection of a house front with ample fenestration. If curved, also called bow-window: if on an upper floor only, also called oriel or oriel window.

BEAKER FOLK: Late New Stone Age warrior invaders from the Continent who buried their dead in round barrows and introduced the first metal tools and weapons to Britain.

BEAKHEAD: Norman ornamental motif consisting of a row of bird or beast heads with beaks biting usually into a roll moulding.

BELFRY: turret on a roof to hang bells in.

BELGAE: Aristocratic warrior bands who settled in Britain in two main waves in the CI B.C. In Britain their culture is termed Iron Age C.

BELL BARROW: Early Bronze Age round barrow in which the mound is separated from its encircling ditch by a flat platform or berm (q.v.).

BELLCOTE: framework on a roof to hang bells from.

BERM: level area separating ditch from bank on a hill-fort or barrow.

BILLET FRIEZE: Norman ornamental motif made up of short raised rectangles placed at regular intervals.

BIVALLATE: Of a hill-fort: defended by two concentric banks and ditches.

BLOCK CAPITAL: Romanesque capital cut from a cube by hav-

Fig. 2

ing the lower angles rounded off to the circular shaft below (also called Cushion Capital) (Fig. 2).

BOND, ENGLISH or FLEMISH: see Brickwork.

BOSS: knob or projection usually placed to cover the intersection of ribs in a vault.

BOWL BARROW: round barrow surrounded by a quarry ditch. Introduced in Late Neolithic times, the form continued until the Saxon period.

BOW-WINDOW: see Bay-Window.

BOX: A small country house, e.g. a shooting box. A convenient term to describe a compact minor dwelling, e.g. a rectory.

BOX PEW: pew with a high wooden enclosure.

BRACES: see Roof.

BRACKET: small supporting piece of stone, etc., to carry a projecting horizontal.

BRESSUMER: beam in a timber-framed building to support the, usually projecting, superstructure.

BRICKWORK: *Header:* brick laid so that the end only appears on the face of the wall. *Stretcher:* brick laid so that the side only appears on the face of the wall. *English Bond:* method of laying bricks so that alternate courses or layers on the face of the wall are composed of headers or stretchers only (Fig. 3*a*). *Flemish Bond:* method of laying

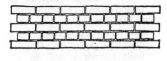

(a)

(b)
Fig. 3

bricks so that alternate headers and stretchers appear in each course on the face of the wall (Fig. 3*b*).

BROACH: see Spire.

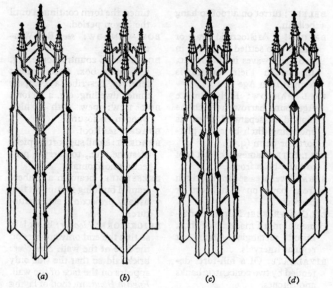

(a)   (b)   (c)   (d)

Fig. 4

BROKEN PEDIMENT: see Pediment.

BRONZE AGE: In Britain, the period from c.1800 to 600 B.C.

BUCRANIUM: ox skull.

BUTTRESS: mass of brickwork or masonry projecting from or built against a wall to give additional strength. *Angle Buttresses:* two meeting at an angle of 90° at the angle of a building (Fig. 4a). *Clasping Buttress:* one which encases the angle (Fig. 4d). *Diagonal Buttress:* one placed against the right angle formed by two walls, and more or less equiangular with both (Fig. 4b). *Flying Buttress:* arch or half arch transmitting the thrust of a vault or roof from the upper part of a wall to an outer support or buttress. *Setback Buttress:* angle buttress set slightly back from the angle (Fig. 4c).

CABLE MOULDING: Norman moulding imitating a twisted cord.

CAIRN: a mound of stones usually covering a burial.

CAMBER: slight rise or upward curve of an otherwise horizontal structure.

CAMPANILE: isolated bell tower.

CANOPY: projection or hood over an altar, pulpit, niche, statue, etc.

CAP: in a windmill the crowning feature.

CAPITAL: head or top part of a column.

CARTOUCHE: tablet with an ornate frame, usually enclosing an inscription.

CARYATID: whole female figure supporting an entablature or other similar member. *Termini Caryatids:* female busts or demi-figures or three-quarter figures supporting an entablature or other similar member and placed at the top of termini pilasters (q.v.). Cf. Atlantes.

CASTELLATED: decorated with battlements.

CELURE: panelled and adorned part of a wagon-roof above the rood or the altar.

CENSER: vessel for the burning of incense.

CENTERING: wooden framework used in arch and vault construction and removed when the mortar has set.

CHALICE: cup used in the Communion service or at Mass. *See also* Recusant Chalice.

CHAMBERED TOMB: burial mound of the New Stone Age having a stone-built chamber and entrance passage covered by an earthen barrow or stone cairn. The form was introduced to Britain from the Mediterranean.

CHAMFER: surface made by cutting across the square angle of a stone block, piece of wood, etc., usually at an angle of 45° to the other two surfaces.

CHANCEL: that part of the E end of a church in which the altar is placed, usually applied to the whole continuation of the nave E of the crossing.

CHANCEL ARCH: arch at the W end of the chancel.

CHANTRY CHAPEL: chapel attached to, or inside, a church, endowed for the saying of Masses for the soul of the founder or some other individual.

CHEVET: French term for the E end of a church (chancel, ambulatory, and radiating chapels).

CHEVRON: Norman moulding forming a zigzag.

CHOIR: that part of the church where divine service is sung.

CIBORIUM: a baldacchino.

CINQUEFOIL: *see* Foil.

CIST: stone-lined or slab-built grave. First appears in Late Neolithic times. It continued to be used in the Early Christian period.

CLAPPER BRIDGE: bridge made of large slabs of stone, some built up to make rough piers and other longer ones laid on top to make the roadway.

CLASSIC: here used to mean the moment of highest achievement of a style.

CLASSICAL: here used as the term for Greek and Roman architecture and any subsequent styles inspired by it.

CLERESTORY: upper storey of the nave walls of a church, pierced by windows.

COADE STONE: artificial (cast) stone made in the late C18 and the early C19 by Coade and Sealy in London.

COB: walling material made of mixed clay and straw.

COFFERING: decorating a ceiling with sunk square or polygonal ornamental panels.

COLLAR-BEAM: *see* Roof.

COLONNADE: range of columns.

COLONNETTE: small column.

COLUMNA ROSTRATA: column decorated with carved prows of ships to celebrate a naval victory.

COMPOSITE: *see* Order.

CONSOLE: bracket (q.v.) with a compound curved outline.

COPING: capping or covering to a wall.

CORBEL: block of stone projecting from a wall, supporting some feature on its horizontal top surface.

CORBEL TABLE: series of corbels, occurring just below the roof eaves externally or internally, often seen in Norman buildings.

CORINTHIAN: *see* Order.

CORNICE: in classical architecture the top section of the entablature (q.v.). Also for a projecting decorative feature along the top of a wall, arch, etc.

CORRIDOR VILLA: *see* Villa.

COUNTERSCARP BANK: small bank on the down-hill or outer side of a hill-fort ditch.

COURTYARD VILLA: *see* Villa.

COVE, COVING: concave undersurface in the nature of a hollow moulding but on a larger scale.

COVER PATEN: cover to a Communion cup, suitable for use as a paten or plate for the consecrated bread.

CRADLE ROOF: *see* Wagon roof.

CRENELLATION: *see* Battlement.

CREST, CRESTING: ornamental finish along the top of a screen, etc.

CRINKLE-CRANKLE WALL: undulating wall.

CROCKET, CROCKETING: decorative features placed on the sloping sides of spires, pinnacles, gables, etc., in Gothic architecture, carved in various leaf shapes and placed at regular intervals.

CROCKET CAPITAL: *see* Fig. 5. An Early Gothic form.

CROMLECH: word of Celtic origin still occasionally used of single free-standing stones ascribed to the Neolithic or Bronze Age periods.

Fig. 5

CROSSING: space at the intersection of nave, chancel, and transepts.

CROSS-WINDOWS: windows with one mullion and one transom.

CRUCK: big curved beam supporting both walls and roof of a cottage.

CRYPT: underground room usually below the E end of a church.

CUPOLA: small polygonal or circular domed turret crowning a roof.

CURTAIN WALL: connecting wall between the towers of a castle.

CUSHION CAPITAL: *see* Block Capital.

CUSP: projecting point between the foils in a foiled Gothic arch.

DADO: decorative covering of the lower part of a wall.

DAGGER: tracery motif of the Dec style. It is a lancet shape rounded or pointed at the head, pointed at the foot, and cusped inside (*see* Fig. 6).

Fig. 6

DAIS: raised platform at one end of a room.

DEC ('DECORATED'): historical division of English Gothic architecture covering the period from *c.*1290 to *c.*1350.

DEMI-COLUMNS: columns half sunk into a wall.

DIAPER WORK: surface decoration composed of square or lozenge shapes.

DIAPHRAGM ARCH: *see* Arch.

DISC BARROW: Bronze Age round barrow with inconspicuous central mound surrounded by bank and ditch.

DOGTOOTH: typical E.E. ornament consisting of a series of four-cornered stars placed diagonally and raised pyramidally (Fig. 7).

Fig. 7

DOMICAL VAULT: *see* Vault.

DONJON: *see* Keep.

DORIC: *see* Order.

DORMER (WINDOW): window placed vertically in the sloping plane of a roof.

DRIPSTONE: *see* Hood-mould.

DRUM: circular or polygonal vertical wall of a dome or cupola.

E.E. ('EARLY ENGLISH'): historical division of English Gothic architecture roughly covering the C13.

EASTER SEPULCHRE: recess with tomb-chest, usually in the wall of a chancel, the tomb-chest to receive an effigy of Christ for Easter celebrations.

EAVES: underpart of a sloping roof overhanging a wall.

EAVES CORNICE: cornice below the eaves of a roof.

ECHINUS: Convex or projecting moulding supporting the abacus of a Greek Doric capital, sometimes bearing an egg and dart pattern.

EMBATTLED: *see* Battlement.

EMBRASURE: small opening in the wall or parapet of a fortified building, usually splayed on the inside.

ENCAUSTIC TILES: earthenware glazed and decorated tiles used for paving.

ENGAGED COLUMNS: columns attached to, or partly sunk into, a wall.

ENGLISH BOND: *see* Brickwork.

ENTABLATURE: in classical architecture the whole of the horizontal members above a column (that is architrave, frieze, and cornice) (*see* Fig. 12).

ENTASIS: very slight convex deviation from a straight line; used on Greek columns and sometimes on spires to prevent an optical illusion of concavity.

ENTRESOL: *see* Mezzanine.

EPITAPH: hanging wall monument.

ESCUTCHEON: shield for armorial bearings.

EXEDRA: the apsidal end of a room. *See* Apse.

FAN-VAULT: *see* Vault.

FERETORY: place behind the

high altar where the chief shrine of a church is kept.

FESTOON: carved garland of flowers and fruit suspended at both ends.

FILLET: narrow flat band running down a shaft or along a roll moulding.

FINIAL: top of a canopy, gable, pinnacle.

FLAGON: vessel for the wine used in the Communion service.

FLAMBOYANT: properly the latest phase of French Gothic architecture where the window tracery takes on wavy undulating lines.

FLÈCHE: slender wooden spire on the centre of a roof (also called Spirelet).

FLEMISH BOND: see Brickwork.

FLEURON: decorative carved flower or leaf.

FLUSHWORK: decorative use of flint in conjunction with dressed stone so as to form patterns: tracery, initials, etc.

FLUTING: vertical channelling in the shaft of a column.

FLYING BUTTRESS: see Buttress.

FOIL: lobe formed by the cusping (q.v.) of a circle or an arch. Trefoil, quatrefoil, cinquefoil, multifoil, express the number of leaf shapes to be seen.

FOLIATED: carved with leaf shapes.

FOSSE: ditch.

FOUR-CENTRED ARCH: see Arch.

FRATER: refectory or dining hall of a monastery.

FRESCO: wall painting on wet plaster.

FRIEZE: middle division of a classical entablature (q.v.) (see Fig. 12).

FRONTAL: covering for the front of an altar.

GABLE: *Dutch gable:* A gable with curved sides crowned by a pediment, characteristic of c.1630–50 (Fig. 8a). *Shaped gable:* A gable with multi-curved sides characteristic of c.1600–50 (Fig. 8b).

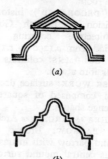

(a)

(b)

Fig. 8

GADROONED: enriched with a series of convex ridges, the opposite of fluting.

GALILEE: chapel or vestibule usually at the W end of a church enclosing the porch. Also called Narthex (q.v.).

GALLERY: in church architecture upper storey above an aisle, opened in arches to the nave. Also called Tribune and often erroneously Triforium (q.v.).

GALLERY GRAVE: chambered tomb (q.v.) in which there is little or no differentiation between the entrance passage and the actual burial chamber(s).

GARDEROBE: lavatory or privy in a medieval building.

GARGOYLE: water spout projecting from the parapet of a wall or tower; carved into a human or animal shape.

GAZEBO: lookout tower or raised

summer house in a picturesque garden.

'GEOMETRICAL': see Tracery.

'GIBBS SURROUND': of a doorway or window. An C18 motif consisting of a surround with alternating larger and smaller blocks of stone, quoin-wise, or intermittent large blocks, sometimes with a narrow raised band connecting them up the verticals and along the face of the arch (Fig. 9).

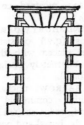

Fig. 9

GROIN: sharp edge at the meeting of two cells of a cross-vault.

GROIN-VAULT: see Vault.

GROTESQUE: fanciful ornamental decoration: see also Arabesque.

HAGIOSCOPE: see Squint.

HALF-TIMBERING: see Timber-Framing.

HALL CHURCH: church in which nave and aisles are of equal height or approximately so.

HAMMERBEAM: see Roof.

HANAP: large metal cup, generally made for domestic use, standing on an elaborate base and stem; with a very ornate cover frequently crowned with a little steeple.

HEADERS: see Brickwork.

HERRINGBONE WORK: brick, stone, or tile construction where the component blocks are laid diagonally instead of flat. Alternate courses lie in opposing directions to make a zigzag pattern up the face of the wall.

HEXASTYLE: having six detached columns.

HILL-FORT: Iron Age earthwork enclosed by a ditch and bank system; in the later part of the period the defences multiplied in size and complexity. They vary from about an acre to over 30 acres in area, and are usually built with careful regard to natural elevations or promontories.

HIPPED ROOF: see Roof.

HOOD-MOULD: projecting moulding above an arch or a lintel to throw off water (also called Dripstone or Label).

ICONOGRAPHY: the science of the subject matter of works of the visual arts.

IMPOST: bracket in a wall, usually formed of mouldings, on which the ends of an arch rest.

INDENT: shape chiselled out in a stone slab to receive a brass.

INGLENOOK: bench or seat built in beside a fireplace, sometimes covered by the chimneybreast, occasionally lit by small windows on each side of the fire.

INTERCOLUMNIATION: the space between columns.

IONIC: see Order (Fig. 12).

IRON AGE: in Britain the period from c. 600 B.C. to the coming of the Romans. The term is also used for those un-Romanized native communities which survived until the Saxon incursions.

JAMB: straight side of an archway, doorway, or window.

KEEL MOULDING: moulding whose outline is in section like that of the keel of a ship.

KEEP: massive tower of a Norman castle.

KEYSTONE: middle stone in an arch or a rib-vault.

KING-POST: see Roof (Fig. 14).

KNEELER: horizontal decorative projection at the base of a gable.

KNOP: a knob-like thickening in the stem of a chalice.

LABEL: see Hood-mould.

LABEL STOP: ornamental boss at the end of a hood-mould (q.v.).

LACED WINDOWS: windows pulled visually together by strips, usually in brick of a different colour, which continue vertically the lines of the vertical parts of the window surrounds. The motif is typical of c. 1720.

LANCET WINDOW: slender pointed-arched window.

LANTERN: in architecture, a small circular or polygonal turret with windows all round crowning a roof (see Cupola) or a dome.

LANTERN CROSS: churchyard cross with lantern-shaped top usually with sculptured representations on the sides of the top.

LEAN-TO ROOF: roof with one slope only, built against a higher wall.

LESENE or PILASTER STRIP: pilaster without base or capital.

LIERNE: see Vault (Fig. 21).

LINENFOLD: Tudor panelling ornamented with a conventional representation of a piece of linen laid in vertical folds. The piece is repeated in each panel.

LINTEL: horizontal beam or stone bridging an opening.

LOGGIA: recessed colonnade (q.v.).

LONG AND SHORT WORK: Saxon quoins (q.v.) consisting of stones placed with the long sides alternately upright and horizontal.

LONG BARROW: unchambered Neolithic communal burial mound, wedge-shaped in plan, with the burial and occasional other structures massed at the broader end, from which the mound itself tapers in height; quarry ditches flank the mound.

LOUVRE: opening, often with lantern (q.v.) over, in the roof of a room to let the smoke from a central hearth escape.

LOWER PALAEOLITHIC: see Palaeolithic.

LOZENGE: diamond shape.

LUCARNE: small opening to let light in.

LUNETTE: tympanum (q.v.) or semicircular opening.

LYCH GATE: wooden gate structure with a roof and open sides placed at the entrance to a churchyard to provide space for the reception of a coffin. The word lych is Saxon and means a corpse.

LYNCHET: long terraced strip of soil accumulating on the downward side of prehistoric and medieval fields due to soil creep from continuous ploughing along the contours.

MACHICOLATION: projecting gallery on brackets constructed on the outside of castle towers or walls. The gallery has holes in the floor to drop missiles through.

MAJOLICA: ornamented glazed earthenware.

MANSARD: see Roof.

MATHEMATICAL TILES: Small facing tiles the size of brick headers, applied to timber-framed walls to make them appear brick-built.

MEGALITHIC TOMB: stone-built burial chamber of the New Stone Age covered by an earth or stone mound. The form was introduced to Britain from the Mediterranean area.

MERLON: see Battlement.

MESOLITHIC: 'Middle Stone' Age; the post-glacial period of hunting and fishing communities dating in Britain from c. 8000 B.C. to the arrival of Neolithic communities, with which they must have considerably overlapped.

METOPE: in classical architecture of the Doric order (q.v.) the space in the frieze between the triglyphs (Fig. 12).

MEZZANINE: low storey placed between two higher ones.

MISERERE: see Misericord.

MISERICORD: bracket placed on the underside of a hinged choir stall seat which, when turned up, provided the occupant of the seat with a support during long periods of standing (also called Miserere).

MODILLION: small bracket of which large numbers (modillion frieze) are often placed below a cornice (q.v.) in classical architecture.

MOTTE: steep mound forming the main feature of C11 and C12 castles.

MOTTE-AND-BAILEY: post-Roman and Norman defence system consisting of an earthen mound (the motte) topped with a wooden tower eccentrically placed within a bailey (q.v.), with enclosure ditch and palisade, and with the rare addition of an internal bank.

MOUCHETTE: tracery motif in curvilinear tracery, a curved dagger (q.v.), specially popular in the early C14 (Fig. 10).

Fig. 10

MULLIONS: vertical posts or uprights dividing a window into 'lights'.

MULTIVALLATE: Of a hill-fort: defended by three or more concentric banks and ditches.

MUNTIN: post as a rule moulded and part of a screen.

NAIL-HEAD: E.E. ornamental motif, consisting of small pyramids regularly repeated (Fig. 11).

Fig. 11

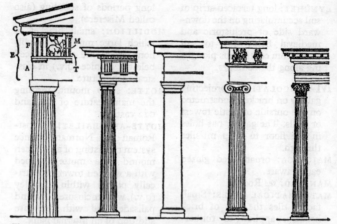

Fig. 12. Orders of Columns (Greek Doric, Roman Doric, Tuscan Doric, Ionic, Corinthian) E, Entablature; C, Cornice; F, Frieze; A, Architrave; M, Metope; T, Triglyph.

NARTHEX: enclosed vestibule or covered porch at the main entrance to a church (*see* Galilee).

NEOLITHIC: 'New Stone' Age, dating in Britain from the appearance from the Continent of the first settled farming communities *c.* 3500 B.C. until the introduction of the Bronze Age.

NEWEL: central post in a circular or winding staircase; also the principal post when a flight of stairs meets a landing.

NOOK-SHAFT: shaft set in the angle of a pier or respond or wall, or the angle of the jamb of a window or doorway.

NUTMEG MOULDING: consisting of a chain of tiny triangles placed obliquely.

OBELISK: lofty pillar of square section tapering at the top and ending pyramidally.

OGEE: *see* Arch (Fig. 1c).

ORATORY: small private chapel in a house.

ORDER: (1) *of a doorway or window:* series of concentric steps receding towards the opening; (2) *in classical architecture:* column with base, shaft, capital, and entablature (q.v.) according to one of the following styles: Greek Doric, Roman Doric, Tuscan Doric, Ionic, Corinthian, Composite. The established details are very elaborate, and some specialist architectural work should be consulted for further guidance (*see* Fig. 12).

ORIEL: *see* Bay-Window.

OVERHANG: projection of the upper storey of a house.

OVERSAILING COURSES: series of stone or brick courses, each one projecting beyond the one below it.

OVOLO: convex moulding.

PALAEOLITHIC: 'Old Stone' Age; the first period of human culture, commencing in the

Ice Age and immediately prior to the Mesolithic; the Lower Palaeolithic is the older phase, the Upper Palaeolithic the later.

PALIMPSEST: (1) *of a brass:* where a metal plate has been re-used by turning over and engraving on the back; (2) *of a wall painting:* where one overlaps and partly obscures an earlier one.

PALLADIAN: architecture following the ideas and principles of Andrea Palladio, 1518–80.

PANTILE: tile of curved S-shaped section.

PARAPET: low wall placed to protect any spot where there is a sudden drop, for example on a bridge, quay, hillside, housetop, etc.

PARGETTING: plaster work with patterns and ornaments either in relief or engraved on it.

PARVIS: term wrongly applied to a room over a church porch. These rooms were often used as a schoolroom or as a store room.

PATEN: plate to hold the bread at Communion or Mass.

PATERA: small flat circular or oval ornament in classical architecture.

PEDIMENT: low-pitched gable used in classical, Renaissance, and neo-classical architecture above a portico and above doors, windows, etc. It may be straight-sided or curved segmentally. *Broken Pediment:* one where the centre portion of the base is left open. *Open Pediment:* one where the centre portion of the sloping sides is left out.

PENDANT: boss (q.v.) elongated so that it seems to hang down.

PENDENTIF: concave triangular spandrel used to lead from the angle of two walls to the base of a circular dome. It is constructed as part of the hemisphere over a diameter the size of the diagonal of the basic square (Fig. 13).

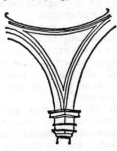

Fig. 13

PERP (PERPENDICULAR): historical division of English Gothic architecture covering the period from c.1335–50 to c.1530.

PIANO NOBILE: principal storey of a house with the reception rooms; usually the first floor.

PIAZZA: open space surrounded by buildings; in C17 and C18 England sometimes used to mean a long colonnade or loggia.

PIER: strong, solid support, frequently square in section or of composite section (compound pier).

PIETRA DURA: ornamental or scenic inlay by means of thin slabs of stone.

PILASTER: shallow pier attached to a wall. *Termini Pilasters:* pilasters with sides tapering downwards.

PILLAR PISCINA: free-standing piscina on a pillar.

PINNACLE: ornamental form crowning a spire, tower, buttress, etc., usually of steep pyramidal, conical, or some similar shape.

PISCINA: basin for washing the Communion or Mass vessels, provided with a drain. Generally set in or against the wall to the s of an altar.

PLAISANCE: summer-house, pleasure house near a mansion.

PLATE TRACERY: *see* Tracery.

PLINTH: projecting base of a wall or column, generally chamfered (q.v.) or moulded at the top.

POND BARROW: rare type of Bronze Age barrow consisting of a circular depression, usually paved, and containing a number of cremation burials.

POPPYHEAD: ornament of leaf and flower type used to decorate the tops of bench- or stall-ends.

PORTCULLIS: gate constructed to rise and fall in vertical grooves; used in gateways of castles.

PORTE COCHÈRE: porch large enough to admit wheeled vehicles.

PORTICO: centre-piece of a house or a church with classical detached or attached columns and a pediment. A portico is called *prostyle* or *in antis* according to whether it projects from or recedes into a building. In a portico *in antis* the columns range with the side walls.

POSTERN: small gateway at the back of a building.

PREDELLA: in an altarpiece the horizontal strip below the main representation, often used for a number of subsidiary representations in a row.

PRESBYTERY: the part of the church lying E of the choir. It is the part where the altar is placed.

PRINCIPAL: *see* Roof (Fig. 14).

PRIORY: monastic house whose head is a prior or prioress, not an abbot or abbess.

PROSTYLE: with free-standing columns in a row.

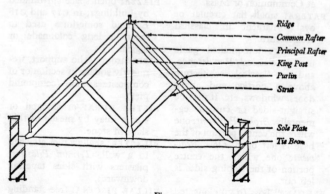

Ridge
Common Rafter
Principal Rafter
King Post
Purlin
Strut
Sole Plate
Tie Beam

Fig. 14

PULPITUM: stone screen in a major church provided to shut off the choir from the nave and also as a backing for the return choir stalls.

PULVINATED FRIEZE: frieze with a bold convex moulding.

PURLIN: see Roof (Figs. 14, 15).

PUTHOLE or PUTLOCK HOLE: putlocks are the short horizontal timbers on which during construction the boards of scaffolding rest. Putholes or putlock holes are the holes in the wall for putlocks, which often are not filled in after construction is complete.

PUTTO: small naked boy.

QUADRANGLE: inner courtyard in a large building.

QUARRY: in stained-glass work, a small diamond- or square-shaped piece of glass set diagonally.

QUATREFOIL: see Foil.

QUEEN-POSTS: see Roof (Fig. 15).

QUOINS: dressed stones at the angles of a building. Sometimes all the stones are of the same size; more often they are alternately large and small.

RADIATING CHAPELS: chapels projecting radially from an ambulatory or an apse.

RAFTER: see Roof.

RAMPART: stone wall or wall of earth surrounding a castle, fortress, or fortified city.

RAMPART-WALK: path along the inner face of a rampart.

REBATE: continuous rectangular notch cut on an edge.

REBUS: pun, a play on words. The literal translation and illustration of a name for artistic and heraldic purposes (Belton = bell, tun).

RECUSANT CHALICE: chalice made after the Reformation and before Catholic Emancipation for Roman Catholic use.

REEDING: decoration with parallel convex mouldings touching one another.

REFECTORY: dining hall; see Frater.

RENDERING: plastering of an outer wall.

REPOUSSÉ: decoration of metal work by relief designs, formed by beating the metal from the back.

REREDOS: structure behind and above an altar.

RESPOND: half-pier bonded into a wall and carrying one end of an arch.

RETABLE: altarpiece, a picture or piece of carving, standing behind and attached to an altar.

RETICULATION: see Tracery (Fig. 20e).

REVEAL: that part of a jamb (q.v.) which lies between the glass or door and the outer surface of the wall.

RIB-VAULT: see Vault.

ROCOCO: latest phase of the Baroque style, current in most Continental countries between c.1720 and c.1760.

ROLL MOULDING: moulding of semicircular or more than semicircular section.

ROMANESQUE: that style in architecture which was current in the C11 and C12 and preceded the Gothic style (in England often called Norman). (Some scholars extend the use of the term Romanesque back to the C10 or C9.)

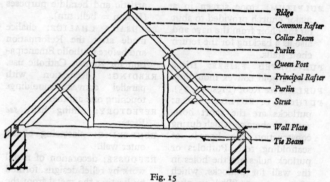

Ridge
Common Rafter
Collar Beam
Purlin
Queen Post
Principal Rafter
Purlin
Strut
Wall Plate
Tie Beam

Fig. 15

ROMANO-BRITISH: A somewhat vague term applied to the period and cultural features of Britain affected by the Roman occupation of the C1–5 A.D.

ROOD: cross or crucifix.

ROOD LOFT: singing gallery on the top of the rood screen, often supported by a coving.

ROOD SCREEN: *see* Screen.

ROOD STAIRS: stairs to give access to the rood loft.

ROOF: *Single-framed*: if consisting entirely of transverse members (such as rafters with or without braces, collars, tie-beams, king-posts or queen-posts, etc.) not tied together longitudinally. *Double-framed*: if longitudinal members (such as a ridge beam and purlins) are employed. As a rule in such cases the rafters are divided into stronger principals and weaker subsidiary rafters. *Hipped*: roof with sloped instead of vertical ends. *Mansard*: roof with a double slope, the

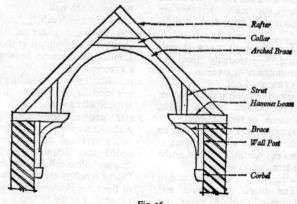

Rafter
Collar
Arched Brace
Strut
Hammer Beam
Brace
Wall Post
Corbel

Fig. 16

lower slope being larger and steeper than the upper. *Saddleback:* tower roof shaped like an ordinary gabled timber roof. The following members have special names: *Rafter:* roof-timber sloping up from the wall plate to the ridge. *Principal:* principal rafter, usually corresponding to the main bay divisions of the nave or chancel below. *Wall Plate:* timber laid longitudinally on the top of a wall. *Purlin:* longitudinal member laid parallel with wall plate and ridge beam some way up the slope of the roof. *Tie-beam:* beam connecting the two slopes of a roof across at its foot, usually at the height of the wall plate, to prevent the roof from spreading. *Collarbeam:* tie-beam applied higher up the slope of the roof. *Strut:* upright timber connecting the tie-beam with the rafter above it. *King-post:* upright timber connecting a tie-beam and collar-beam with the ridge beam. *Queen-posts:* two struts placed symmetrically on a tie-beam or collar-beam. *Braces:* inclined timbers inserted to strengthen others. Usually braces connect a collar-beam with the rafters below or a tie-beam with the wall below. Braces can be straight or curved (also called arched). *Hammerbeam:* beam projecting at right angles, usually from the top of a wall, to carry arched braces or struts and arched braces. (*See* Figs. 14, 15, 16.)

ROSE WINDOW (or WHEEL WINDOW): circular window with patterned tracery arranged to radiate from the centre.

ROTUNDA: building circular in plan.

RUBBLE: building stones, not square or hewn, nor laid in regular courses.

RUSTICATION: *rock-faced* if the surfaces of large blocks of ashlar stone are left rough like rock; *smooth* if the ashlar blocks are smooth and separated by V-joints; *banded* if the separation by V-joints applies only to the horizontals.

SADDLEBACK: *see* Roof.

SALTIRE CROSS: equal-limbed cross placed diagonally.

SANCTUARY: (1) area around the main altar of a church (*see* Presbytery); (2) sacred site consisting of wood or stone uprights enclosed by a circular bank and ditch. Beginning in the Neolithic, they were elaborated in the succeeding Bronze Age. The best known examples are Stonehenge and Avebury.

SARCOPHAGUS: elaborately carved coffin.

SCAGLIOLA: material composed of cement and colouring matter to imitate marble.

SCALLOPED CAPITAL: development of the block capital (q.v.) in which the single semi-circular surface is elaborated into a series of truncated cones (Fig. 17).

Fig. 17

SCARP: artificial cutting away of the ground to form a steep slope.

SCREEN: *Parclose screen:* screen separating a chapel from the rest of a church. *Rood screen:* screen below the rood (q.v.), usually at the W end of a chancel.

SCREENS PASSAGE: passage between the entrances to kitchen, buttery, etc., and the screen behind which lies the hall of a medieval house.

SEDILIA: seats for the priests (usually three) on the S side of the chancel of a church.

SEGMENTAL ARCH: *see* Arch.

SET-OFF: *see* Weathering.

SEXPARTITE: *see* Vault.

SGRAFFITO: pattern incised into plaster so as to expose a dark surface underneath.

SHAFT-RING: motif of the C12 and C13 consisting of a ring round a circular pier or a shaft attached to a pier.

SHEILA-NA-GIG: fertility figure, usually with legs wide open.

SILL: lower horizontal part of the frame of a window.

SLATEHANGING: the covering of walls by overlapping rows of slates, on a timber substructure.

SOFFIT: underside of an arch, lintel, etc.

SOLAR: upper living-room of a medieval house.

SOPRAPORTE: painting above the door of a room, usual in the C17 and C18.

SOUNDING BOARD: horizontal board or canopy over a pulpit. Also called Tester.

SPANDREL: triangular surface between one side of an arch, the horizontal drawn from its apex, and the vertical drawn from its springer; also the surface between two arches.

SPERE-TRUSS: roof truss on two free-standing posts to mask the division between screens passage and hall. The screen itself, where a spere-truss exists, was originally movable.

SPIRE: tall pyramidal or conical pointed erection often built on top of a tower, turret, etc. *Broach Spire:* a broach is a sloping half-pyramid of masonry or wood introduced at the base of each of the four oblique faces of a tapering octagonal spire with the object of effecting the transition from the square to the octagon. The *splayed foot spire* is a variation of the broach form found principally in the south-eastern counties. In this form the four cardinal faces are splayed out near their base, to cover the corners, while the oblique (or intermediate) faces taper away to a point. *Needle Spire:* thin spire rising from the centre of a tower roof, well inside the parapet.

SPIRELET: *see* Flèche.

SPLAY: chamfer, usually of the jamb of a window.

SPRINGING: level at which an arch rises from its supports.

SQUINCH: arch or system of concentric arches thrown across the angle between two walls to support a superstructure, for example a dome (Fig. 18).

SQUINT: a hole cut in a wall or through a pier to allow a view of the main altar of a church from places whence it could not otherwise be seen (also called Hagioscope).

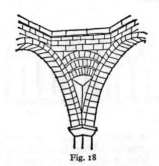

Fig. 18

STALL: carved seat, one of a row, made of wood or stone.

STAUNCHION: upright iron or steel member.

STEEPLE: the tower of a church together with a spire, cupola, etc.

STIFF-LEAF: E.E. type of foliage of many-lobed shapes (Fig. 19).

Fig. 19

STILTED: *see* Arch.

STOREY-POSTS: the principal posts of a timber-framed wall.

STOUP: vessel for the reception of holy water, usually placed near a door.

STRAINER ARCH: arch inserted across a room to prevent the walls from leaning.

STRAPWORK: C16 decoration consisting of interlaced bands, and forms similar to fretwork or cut and bent leather.

STRETCHER: *see* Brickwork.

STRING COURSE: projecting horizontal band or moulding set in the surface of a wall.

STRUT: *see* Roof.

STUCCO: plaster work.

STUDS: the subsidiary vertical timber members of a timber-framed wall.

SWAG: festoon formed by a carved piece of cloth suspended from both ends.

TABERNACLE: richly ornamented niche or free-standing canopy. Usually contains the Holy Sacrament.

TARSIA: inlay in various woods.

TAZZA: shallow bowl on a foot.

TERMINAL FIGURES (TERMS, TERMINI): upper part of a human figure growing out of a pier, pilaster, etc., which tapers towards the base. *See also* Caryatid, Pilaster.

TERRACOTTA: burnt clay, unglazed.

TESSELLATED PAVEMENT: mosaic flooring, particularly Roman, consisting of small 'tesserae' or cubes of glass, stone, or brick.

TESSERAE: *see* Tessellated Pavement.

TESTER: *see* Sounding Board.

TETRASTYLE: having four detached columns.

THREE-DECKER PULPIT: pulpit with Clerk's Stall below and Reading Desk below the Clerk's Stall.

TIE-BEAM: *see* Roof (Figs. 14, 15).

TIERCERON: *see* Vault (Fig. 21).

TILEHANGING: *see* Slatehanging.

TIMBER-FRAMING: method of construction where walls are built of timber framework with the spaces filled in by plaster

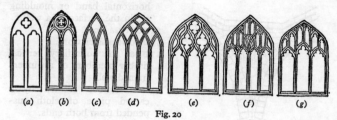

(a)   (b)   (c)   (d)   (e)   (f)   (g)

Fig. 20

or brickwork. Sometimes the timber is covered over with plaster or boarding laid horizontally.

TOMB-CHEST: chest-shaped stone coffin, the most usual medieval form of funeral monument.

TOUCH: soft black marble quarried near Tournai.

TOURELLE: turret corbelled out from the wall.

TRACERY: intersecting ribwork in the upper part of a window, or used decoratively in blank arches, on vaults, etc. *Plate tracery: see* Fig. 20(*a*). Early form of tracery where decoratively shaped openings are cut through the solid stone infilling in a window head. *Bar tracery:* a form introduced into England *c.*1250. Intersecting ribwork made up of slender shafts, continuing the lines of the mullions of windows up to a decorative mesh in the head of the window. *Geometrical tracery: see* Fig. 20(*b*). Tracery characteristic of *c.* 1250–1310 consisting chiefly of circles or foiled circles. *Y-tracery: see* Fig. 20(*c*). Tracery consisting of a mullion which branches into two forming a Y shape; typical of *c.* 1300. *Intersecting tracery: see* Fig. 20(*d*). Tracery in which each mullion of a window branches out into two curved bars in such a way that every one of them is drawn with the same radius from a different centre. The result is that every light of the window is a lancet and every two, three, four, etc., lights together form a pointed arch. This treatment also is typical of *c.* 1300. *Reticulated tracery: see* Fig. 20(*e*). Tracery typical of the early C14 consisting entirely of circles drawn at top and bottom into ogee shapes so that a net-like appearance results. *Panel tracery: see* Fig. 20(*f*) and (*g*). Perp tracery, which is formed of upright straight-sided panels above lights of a window.

TRANSEPT: transverse portion of a cross-shaped church.

TRANSOM: horizontal bar across the openings of a window.

TRANSVERSE ARCH: *see* Vault.

TRIBUNE: *see* Gallery.

TRICIPUT, SIGNUM TRICIPUT: sign of the Trinity expressed by three faces belonging to one head.

TRIFORIUM: arcaded wall passage or blank arcading facing the nave at the height of the aisle roof and below the clerestory (q.v.) windows. (*See* Gallery.)

TRIGLYPHS: blocks with vertical

grooves separating the metopes (q.v.) in the Doric frieze (Fig. 12).

TROPHY: sculptured group of arms or armour, used as a memorial of victory.

TRUMEAU: stone mullion (q.v.) supporting the tympanum (q.v.) of a wide doorway.

TUMULUS: *see* Barrow.

TURRET: very small tower, round or polygonal in plan.

TUSCAN: *see* Order.

TYMPANUM: space between the lintel of a doorway and the arch above it.

UNDERCROFT: vaulted room, sometimes underground, below a church or chapel.

UNIVALLATE: of a hill-fort: defended by a single bank and ditch.

UPPER PALAEOLITHIC: *see* Palaeolithic.

VAULT: *Barrel-vault: see* Tunnel-vault. *Cross-vault: see* Groin-vault. *Domical vault:* square or polygonal dome rising direct on a square or polygonal bay, the curved surfaces separated by groins (q.v.). *Fan-vault:* late medieval vault where all ribs springing from one springer are of the same length, the same distance from the next, and the same curvature. *Groin-vault* or *Cross-vault:* vault of two tunnel-vaults of identical shape intersecting each other at r. angles. Chiefly Norman and Renaissance. *Lierne:* tertiary rib, that is, rib which does not spring either from one of the main springers or from the central

boss. Introduced in the C14, continues to the C16. *Quadripartite vault:* one wherein one bay of vaulting is divided into four parts. *Rib-vault:* vault with diagonal ribs projecting along the groins. *Ridge-rib:* rib along the longitudinal or transverse ridge of a vault. Introduced in the early C13. *Sexpartite vault:* one wherein one bay of quadripartite vaulting is divided into two parts transversely so that each bay of vaulting has six parts. *Tierceron:* secondary rib, that is, rib which issues from one of the main springers or the central boss and leads to a place on a ridge-rib. Introduced in the early C13. *Transverse arch:* arch separating one bay of a vault from the next. *Tunnel-vault* or *Barrel-vault:* vault of semicircular or pointed section. Chiefly Norman and Renaissance. (*See* Fig. 21.)

VAULTING SHAFT: vertical member leading to the springer of a vault.

VENETIAN WINDOW: window with three openings, the central one arched and wider than the outside ones. Current in England chiefly in the C17–18.

VERANDA: open gallery or balcony with a roof on light, usually metal, supports.

VESICA: oval with pointed head and foot.

VESTIBULE: anteroom or entrance hall.

VILLA: (1) according to Gwilt (1842) 'a country house for the residence of opulent persons'; (2) Romano-British country houses cum farms, to which the description given in (1)

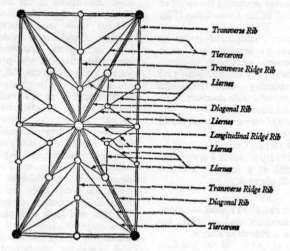

Fig. 21

more or less applies. They developed with the growth of urbanization. The basic type is the simple corridor pattern with rooms opening off a single passage; the next stage is the addition of wings. The courtyard villa fills a square plan with subsidiary buildings and an enclosure wall with a gate facing the main corridor block.

VITRIFIED: made similar to glass.

VITRUVIAN OPENING: A door or window which diminishes towards the top, as advocated by Vitruvius, bk. IV, chapter VI.

VOLUTE: spiral scroll, one of the component parts of an Ionic column (see Order).

VOUSSOIR: wedge-shaped stone used in arch construction.

WAGON ROOF: roof in which by closely set rafters with

arched braces the appearance of the inside of a canvas tilt over a wagon is achieved. Wagon roofs can be panelled or plastered (ceiled) or left uncovered.

WAINSCOT: timber lining to walls.

WALL PLATE: see Roof.

WATERLEAF: leaf shape used in later C12 capitals. The waterleaf is a broad, unribbed, tapering leaf curving up towards the angle of the abacus and turned in at the top (Fig. 22).

Fig. 22

WEALDEN HOUSE: timber-framed house with the hall in the centre and wings projecting only slightly and only on the jutting upper floor. The roof, however, runs through without a break between wings and hall, and the eaves of the hall part are therefore exceptionally deep. They are supported by diagonal, usually curved, braces starting from the short inner sides of the overhanging wings and rising parallel with the front wall of the hall towards the centre of the eaves.

WEATHERBOARDING: overlapping horizontal boards, covering a timber-framed wall.

WEATHERING: sloped horizontal surface on sills, buttresses, etc., to throw off water.

WEEPERS: small figures placed in niches along the sides of some medieval tombs (also called Mourners).

WHEEL WINDOW: *see* Rose Window.

INDEX OF PLATES

INDEX OF ARTISTS

INDEX OF PLACES

BEDFORDSHIRE

INDEX OF PLACES

THE COUNTY OF HUNTINGDON AND PETERBOROUGH

ADDENDA
(SEPTEMBER 1967)

p. 79 [Dunstable.] The new SHOPPING CENTRE by *Willoughby Fletcher & Associates* lies S of the Civic Centre. It is T-shaped with a short arm to High Street North, and the long arm parallel with that street and with access from Church Street and Vernon Place. In the centre, where the arms meet, an abstract Vertical Feature by *Robin Don* and also an 85 ft long abstract concrete relief by *William Mitchell*. Whose happiness do such things induce or increase?

p. 103 [Houghton Regis.] The new SHOPPING PRECINCT is by *Willoughby Fletcher & Associates*. It is L-shaped and lies immediately SE of a new LIBRARY, YOUTH HALL, etc., being built by the County Architect's Department. External staircase to maisonettes above the shops.

p. 173 [Wrest.] Mr Peter Curnow tells me that there is documentary evidence for *Edward Stevens* being the architect of the Bath House and *Batty Langley* of the Bowling Green House. He also draws my attention to the interesting fact that the figure of Architecture over the doorcase in the staircase hall of the house has books by Le Pautre, Mansart, and Blondel.

p. 275 [Kimbolton.] Mr Clifton-Taylor rightly complained that nothing was said about the minor service street running behind the High Street and the narrow lanes connecting the two.

p. 277 [Kimbolton Castle.] Mr Philip Burkett kindly helped me further to clarify this statement. The wall in question is now an inner wall, because Vanbrugh pushed the N wall of the S range out to the S, i.e. into the courtyard.

p. 277 [Kimbolton Castle.] The fireplace was found behind the panelling, and its frieze has, in relief, a black-letter inscription which is a quotation from the Cranmer Bible. That gives a *terminus post quem*. I owe this information also to Mr Burkett.

p. 329 [Peterborough.] WESTWOOD INDUSTRIAL ESTATE. Distribution Centre for Freemans Ltd, a mail-order firm, by *Scott, Brownrigg & Turner*. Begun in 1967. Mainly on one floor, 850,000 sq. ft.